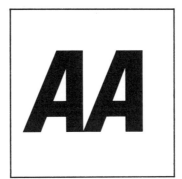

BOOK OF THE CAR

Published by Drive Publications Limited for the Automobile Association

AA BOOK OF THE CAR

was edited and designed by Drive Publications Limited, Berkeley Square House, London, W1X 5PD for the Automobile Association, Fanum House, Basingstoke, Hants., RG21 2EA

Third edition Copyright © 1976
Reprinted with amendments 1979
Drive Publications Limited

Printed in Italy

AA BOOK OF THE CAR

Technical Editor **M. A. I. Jacobson, DipAM(Sheff), CEng, FIMechE, MSAE(USA), MIProdE, FIMI**

Technical Adviser **Maurice Platt, MEng, FIMechE, MSAE(USA)**

Contributors

A. Baker, BSc(Eng), CEng, FIMechE, ACGI
Donald Bastow, BSc(Eng), CEng, FIMechE, MSAE(USA), MSIA(France),
D. F. Blake
M. A. Burtonshaw, FCII, DMS
J. B. Davey
Dr John Ebbetts
Clement Fennell, MRCVS
Patrick Forman, BA, LLB
Nicholas J. Frewing, DesRCA, MSIA
John Gaselee
D. R. Greig, OBE
Bill Hartley
Harry Heywood
D. J. Houston, BSc, CEng, MIMechE
B. E. Hunt
D. Hurtley, BSc
Dr Keith E. Jolles

Michael Kemp
Patrick Macnaghten
Peter Merritt
John Miles
Donald F. Norfolk, DO, MRO
R. D. Owen, CEng, MIMechE, MIRTE, FIAgrE
Jim Pestridge
Cyril Posthumous
Paulette Pratt
Ralph R. Reynolds
F. W. E. Saunders
M. F. Saunders, FCII
Dr J. H. Simpson
A. W. Sims, T Eng, MIRTE, AMBIM, AI ARB
Dr Tony Smith
J. A. Stubbs, MSE, AMIMI
Charles Surridge, AIRTE
Eric Tobitt
Stanley Unger, FRSH
Martyn Watkins

Artists, designers and photographers:

Lloyd Barnett, MSIA
Norman Brand
Derek Butler, Vogue Studio
Terry Collins, FSIA
John Curtis
John Davis
David J. Day, MDesRCA
De Denne Associates
Richard Draper
George Green, S. P. Hamill Ltd
Anthony Greenwood
Grosvenor Graphics
Brian Hatton
Hawke Studios
Graham Henderson
Nigel Holmes
Roger Hudson
Eric Ilett
Albert Jackson, MDesRCA
Jewell Associates
Launcelot Jones, MSIA
Norman Lacey, MISTC

Ken Lewis
Ley Dower & Associates
Linden Artists
Richard Marshall-Hardy
Neal Martin
Morgan & Swan Ltd
M.P.H. (Designers) Ltd
Roland Pearson
Graham Percy
David Playne
Les Smith
S. A. Thornton Ltd
Venner Artists
Brian Watson
Barry Weller, Vogue Studio
John Wood

The publishers wish to thank the following firms and organisations for their assistance in the preparation of this book:

AC Cars Ltd
Airfix Plastics Ltd
Alfa Romeo (GB) Ltd
Allparts (Croydon) Ltd
Autocar
The Automotive Products Group
Avon Rubber Co Ltd
Bell Products Limited
BMW Concessionaires GB Ltd
Borg-Warner Ltd
Britax (London) Ltd
British Leyland Motor Corporation Ltd
British Leyland (Austin Morris) Ltd
British Red Cross Society
British School of Motoring
Britool Ltd
Brown Brothers Ltd
Champion Sparking Plug Co Ltd
Chrysler International SA
Citroën Cars Ltd

Coventry Radiator & Presswork Co Ltd
Daimler Benz AG
Department of Transportation and Environmental Planning, University of Birmingham
Disabled Drivers' Association
L. F. Dove (Milne & Russell) Ltd
B. Draper & Son Ltd
The Dunlop Company Ltd
Ferodo Ltd
Fiat (England) Ltd
Firestone Tyre & Rubber Co Ltd
Ford Motor Company Ltd
General Motors Ltd
Girling Limited
Goodyear Tyre & Rubber Co (GB) Ltd
Gordon Tools Ltd
Holts Products Ltd
Jaguar Cars Ltd
Jensen Motors Ltd
K.L. Automotive Products

Lex Garages Ltd
Lockheed Hydraulic Brake Co Ltd
Lucas Electrical Limited (Parts and Service Division)
Mercedes-Benz (Great Britain) Ltd
Michelin Tyre Company Limited
Mobelec Limited
Mobile Electrics (Croydon) Ltd
Mobil Oil Co Ltd
Montagu Motor Museum
Motor
George Osborne Ltd
P.D.P. Group Ltd, Croydon
People's Dispensary for Sick Animals
Polco Products Limited
Radiomobile Ltd
Radio Times Hulton Picture Library
Raydyot Ltd
Reliant Motor Co Ltd
Renault Ltd
Road Research Laboratory

Rolls-Royce Ltd
Romac Industries Ltd
Rootes Motors Ltd
Royal Society for the Prevention of Accidents
Royal Society for the Prevention of Cruelty to Animals
The Rover Co Ltd
Shell Petroleum
Smiths Industries Ltd
Standard-Triumph International Ltd
Surrey Steel Components Ltd
Triplex Safety Glass Co Ltd
Tudor Accessories Ltd
University Motors Ltd
Vauxhall Motors Ltd
Vehicle Builders & Repairers Association
Volkswagen Motors Ltd
Volvo Concessionnaires
Waso Ltd
C. P. Witter Ltd

CONTENTS

ACCESSORIES FOR THE CAR

What to choose and how to fit it; conversions to improve the car's performance

THE COST OF MOTORING

How to buy and sell a car and get the most from your motoring budget

FITNESS TO DRIVE

The importance of being healthy and alert at the wheel

BETTER DRIVING

Ways of improving your driving technique and dealing with emergencies

Gottlieb Daimler (left) in the first four-wheeled car. It had a 1½ h.p. vertical engine

1895 Panhard-Levassor was the world's first saloon car

Ford built more than 15 million Model Ts from 1908 to 1927

The car: from dream to necessity

NO ONE actually invented the car. It evolved from the horse-drawn carriage, its near-relative the steam carriage and perhaps the 19th-century tricycle, but as the years went by it gradually lost its likeness to any of its progenitors.

Engine progress
The saga of the car really began as recently as 1860, the year in which Jean Etienne Lenoir, a Belgian inventor, built the first practicable gas engine, from which all other internal-combustion engines have developed. In that first engine, however, the mixture of coal gas and air was not compressed before ignition, so it was inefficient.

The next milestone was in 1876 when Count Nikolus Otto, a German engineer, first successfully applied the four-stroke principle that had been proposed by the Frenchman Beau da Rochas. The four-stroke cycle enabled the charge to be compressed, which gave significantly better performance. At about the same time gasoline – a distillate of petroleum later to be known also as petrol – came into use instead of coal gas.

During the 1880s most of the progress was made in Germany – by Gottlieb Daimler and Carl Benz. Daimler, working with Wilhelm Maybach, produced his first engine in 1883, and it created a sensation by running at more than four times the speed of Otto's engines – 900 rpm! Benz, on the other hand, started with the objective of making his own self-propelled vehicle, and in 1885 he installed his first engine in the back of a tricycle. Within a year or so, both were building cars for sale.

Then came the French engineers Réné Panhard and Emile Levassor who started in 1890 by building Daimler engines under licence in France. Their first car had the engine mounted centrally, but the next, in 1891, set the standard for generations to come by having it at the front, shielded from the worst of the dust and mud thrown up from poor roads.

Levassor made a fundamental contribution by seeing the car as a piece of machinery in its own right, not as a carriage without horses nor a motorised tricycle. His place in history is assured by his many practical advances – for example, replacing belt-drive by a clutch and multi-ratio gears, a form of transmission that is still used today.

Discouragement in Britain
By the turn of the century, in the search for more engine performance, designers were beginning to increase the number of cylinders. Experimental in-line 6-cylinder engines began to appear in 1902, and Napier in Britain actually went into production with such a layout the following year. But motoring in Britain had been

hamstrung by legislation. The Locomotives Act 1865, framed for steam-driven traction engines, applied an overall speed limit of 4 mph in open country and 2 mph in towns and villages. Cars had to be preceded by a man carrying a red flag to warn the drivers of horse-drawn vehicles.

Although the flag was abolished in 1878, the man was still required by law until 1896. Then, on Emancipation Day, as it was called, the speed limit was raised to 12 mph and the first London-to-Brighton run was held.

In spite of these discouragements, one British engineer, Frederick Lanchester, had developed by 1897 an epicyclic gearbox, had replaced the usual chain-drive by a shaft to a worm-drive rear axle, had introduced a fully balanced twin-cylinder engine with contra-rotating crankshafts and had patented a high-pressure lubrication system.

During the early 1900s the French were still making the running. Count Albert de Dion, a rich enthusiast, teamed up with George Bouton to form the de Dion Bouton company; de Dion contributed the rear drive and suspension system that still bears his name, while Bouton made engines that ran more than twice as fast as Daimler's. Bouton also pioneered an ignition system with a contact-breaker arrangement.

Another Frenchman, Louis Renault,

came into prominence at that time. He popularised shaft drive, with universal joints to allow for suspension movement, and in building a car with a closed body, he was 15 years ahead of the general trend.

Progress on many fronts
Car racing on the roads, often between Europe's major cities, was automobilism's shop window. And it really did help to advance the ordinary car; engine and chassis design, brakes, tyres, suspension, lights and fuel all improved as a result of the lessons learned in racing.

During the first few years of the 20th century, the whole configuration of the car began to change from the short and high to the longer and lower. A contributory factor was the reduction in wheel sizes that followed the adoption of the pneumatic tyre.

Although the inflatable tyre had been invented as far back as 1845, John Boyd Dunlop did not take out his famous patents until 1888, and seven years elapsed before such tyres were first fitted to a car – by Edouard Michelin for the 1895 Paris-Bordeaux race.

Brakes, too, were greatly improved. The first cars had carriage or bicycle brakes with very inefficient friction materials – wood, leather, metal or even camel-hair blocks! Lanchester patented a disc brake in 1902 that was 50 years ahead

Oil lamps did little more than mark a car's presence. This lamp also had an alternative electric bulb

1910 Dunhill mask protected lady motorists from dust

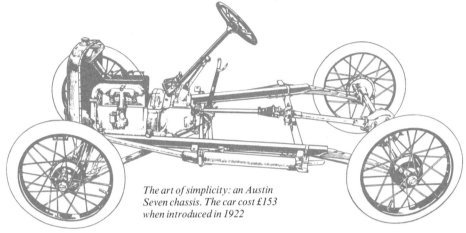

The art of simplicity: an Austin Seven chassis. The car cost £153 when introduced in 1922

Germany's KDF, launched by Hitler in 1938, became today's VW

of its time. However, in 1903, Mercedes, as the German Daimler cars were now called, featured internal-expanding drum brakes – another milestone.

Five years later, Herbert Frood (from whose name Ferodo is derived) made the first real breakthrough in friction materials: he introduced impregnation with resins. Even today, asbestos remains the principal ingredient of brake and clutch friction material.

Lighting also advanced during the golden years before the First World War. Dim oil lamps that were a legacy from coaching days had given way to acetylene which, although sometimes smelly and temperamental, produced enough bright white light to make night driving less hazardous. Electric lighting came in 1911 when Cadillac in the USA first offered it as standard.

Rolls-Royce and Ford
Of all motoring's immortals two of the greatest, at opposite ends of the price scale, are undoubtedly Rolls-Royce and Ford. Henry Royce, a perfectionist engineer, so impressed the Hon. C. S. Rolls (then an importer of foreign cars) with the quality of his first car that the two formed a partnership and in 1906 introduced the legendary Silver Ghost, one of the finest and quietest vehicles ever built. It was in production for 19 years and founded the

RR reputation as the world's best car.

But 1908 saw the real turning-point in the history of the car: in the USA the first Model T Ford – the original Tin Lizzie – rolled off the world's first moving car-assembly line to bring motoring within the reach of the ordinary man. It, too, was in production for 19 years, but in that period over 15 million were built!

Ford's genius lay not merely in his mass-production techniques but in his ability to combine simplicity (and therefore cheapness) with the use of high-grade materials. One of his most widely followed production simplifications was to cast cylinder heads separately from their blocks.

Until 1911 car engines had been started by hand – a laborious and sometimes dangerous process that certainly discouraged a lot of women from driving. Then, thanks to the ingenuity of Charles F. Kettering, one of America's leading vehicle engineers, Cadillac introduced the electric starter. An engine could literally be started by a child.

The 1914-18 war and after
Transportation and mobility were essential factors of warfare, so the First World War accelerated the car's development. Moreover, car-makers who changed temporarily to produce aircraft engines as part of the war effort learned valuable lessons in design, production and materials.

After the war, more people wanted cars, and more could afford them. William Morris in Britain and André Citroën in France headed the European move into production-line assembly. Then in 1922 Herbert Austin produced his immortal Austin Seven – a 'baby car' for the masses – family motoring at minimal cost had become a reality.

By this time, four-wheel mechanical brakes were coming into general use, but in the USA an expatriate Scotsman, Malcolm Loughead, was developing the more efficient hydraulic system that was eventually to take over. His brakes were called Lockheed, perhaps because of pronunciation difficulties with the correct spelling.

Another present-day feature that stemmed from the early 1920s was independent front suspension, adopted in 1922 by Vincenzo Lancia in Italy.

The 1920s were noteworthy also for the ascendancy of the sports car – Bentley, Sunbeam, Vauxhall, Alfa Romeo, Bugatti and Mercedes. At the other end of the scale, the Austin Seven's success spawned a number of small-car rivals – for example, Singer, Standard and Triumph.

The depression and after
The slump of the early 1930s closed several British car-building firms. By 1938 there were only 20, of which six accounted for 90

per cent of production. For those in the popular-price bracket, mass-production became essential for survival while technical progress had to be minimal because it cost money. In some respects design actually retrogressed, as in the tendency to shorten the wheelbase (to save material) and so to move the engine forward and the rear seat back over the axle.

Some worthwhile innovations were made however. Synchromesh, introduced by Cadillac in 1928 to help gear-changing, was widely adopted in Europe. An even easier system, the Wilson preselector gearbox (introduced by Armstrong Siddeley in 1928) became available on British cars and led to automatic transmission which began to appear in America towards the end of the 1930s.

During the 1930s the Americans developed big 'lazy' engines, often V8s, whereas Europe's higher running costs forced concentration on smaller, more efficient power units. Europe's most significant year was probably 1938, when Adolf Hitler introduced Dr Ferdinand Porsch's 'Strength through Joy' car, later to become the Volkswagen 'beetle' – Europe's biggest post-war seller.

Engine power increases in the 1930s were achieved mainly by raising compression ratios, possible because petrol had improved. Until then, compression ratios had been limited by the onset of an

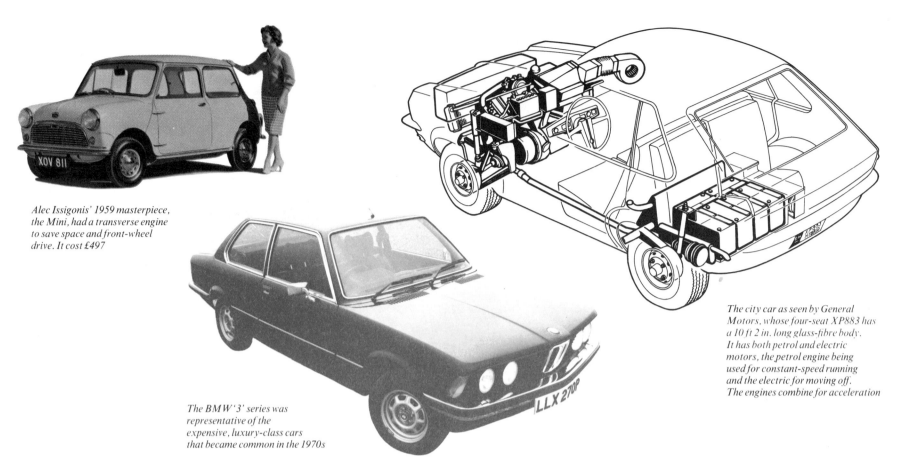

Alec Issigonis' 1959 masterpiece, the Mini, had a transverse engine to save space and front-wheel drive. It cost £497

The BMW '3' series was representative of the expensive, luxury-class cars that became common in the 1970s

The city car as seen by General Motors, whose four-seat XP883 has a 10 ft 2 in. long glass-fibre body. It has both petrol and electric motors, the petrol engine being used for constant-speed running and the electric for moving off. The engines combine for acceleration

unpleasant combustion condition called detonation or knock. However, research in the late 1920s showed that this limitation could be overcome by the addition to the petrol of small quantities of tetraethyl-lead, and 'leaded' fuels came on to the market shortly afterwards. Now, of course, for environmental reasons, lead content is being reduced again.

The post-war era
When the first new models began to appear after the Second World War, much had changed. The separate chassis frame and body was replaced by a single unitary or integral structure which saved material and facilitated production, but repairs became more costly, and because retooling was expensive, model changes or 'facelifts' became costly. The techniques found less favour in the USA than in Europe.

Independent front suspension, which had been beginning to get a foothold prewar, was generally adopted, and the elimination of the traditional beam axle allowed the engine to be moved forward, so the passenger compartment did likewise. The rear-seat occupants therefore gained in comfort by being brought ahead of the axle, and luggage capacity was increased also. Roof heights came down since the rear seats could be lowered on coming forward, and interior comfort was improved by the arrival of hypoid-bevel final-drive units which enabled the propeller shaft (and hence the floor or central tunnel) to be lowered also.

In 1959 the whole concept of the post-war small car changed with the introduction by the British Motor Corporation (an amalgamation of Austin with Morris, Wolseley, Riley and MG) of Sir Alec Issigonis' remarkable Mini – then called the Morris Mini-Minor.

In industrial terms, the biggest post-war development was the rapid rise of Japan's motor industry. During the early 1960s it was only just beginning to sell its rather dull products overseas, yet 10 years later it was challenging the European makers on their own ground and in their traditional foreign markets. Now Japan is the world's second largest vehicle producer.

Technical progress
Very substantial progress has been made since 1945 in tyres, brakes, suspension and handling, heating and ventilating, engine design, safety and exhaust emission.

The tyre revolution began in 1948 when Michelin made their commercial introduction of the radial-ply tyre, providing longer life and better roadholding than the conventional cross-ply type. Since then the radial has become almost standard on European and Japanese cars, and it is gaining wide acceptance in the USA. Tyres, moreover, have been broadening for some years – increasing the amount of rubber on the road – and rubber compounds with much improved grip have been developed.

Better braking has resulted mainly from the advent of the disc brake in the early 1950s, but even today most mass-produced cars have discs only on the front wheels with drum brakes at the rear. One reason is that an efficient handbrake is easier to arrange with a drum than a disc.

Many models now have independent suspension at the rear as well as the front. Rack-and-pinion steering, popularised mainly by the VW, Morris Minor and Mini, is now found also on medium and large cars because it is more precise and mechanically more efficient than other systems. Wider tyres mean heavier low-speed steering—hence the increasing use of hydraulic power assistance.

But the greatest progress has been in engines. More is now known about the combustion process and valve-gear design, weight has been saved by using aluminium instead of iron for cylinder heads and blocks, carburettors and ignition equipment have been improved, better bearings, piston rings and valve steels have become available. There has been a general trend towards bigger cylinder bores and shorter piston strokes, allowing higher engine speeds and bigger valves, and so greater power. Operating economy has become more important because of dwindling fuel reserves.

Two new types of rotary power units, the gas turbine and the Wankel, have appeared. The turbine, developed in the aircraft industry, has yet to be fitted to a production car for technical and economic reasons, but the Wankel was taken up by the German NSU company in the early 1960s. Its smoothness, compactness and low weight have been offset by higher cost and fuel consumption.

Safety considerations
On safety, the main objectives have been to reduce the likelihood of a crash and to minimise the injuries inflicted when one cannot be avoided. Handling, braking and vision have improved, seatbelts, stronger passenger compartments with crushable ends to absorb impact energy, reinforced doors with anti-burst locks, better safety glass, smoothed-out interiors and energy-absorbing steering columns and bumpers have been developed.

As for the future, it is unlikely that man, having known the convenience of the private car, will tolerate life without it, even when the world's petroleum reserves are exhausted. The next major development therefore is likely to be the exploitation of other sources of energy, nuclear or natural and self-replenishing.

CHOOSING THE TOOLS

Good tools last a lifetime and, if used correctly, simplify even the most difficult jobs on a car. This section helps to identify the tools you need and explains how to use them. It also shows how to turn your garage—whether single or double—into an efficient workshop.

CONTENTS

Tools/kits for the car and the garage

Choosing the right tools

BUILDING UP a kit of tools to service a car and deal with roadside emergencies does not involve a big initial outlay. A basic kit can cost a few pounds. With this as the starting point, the best way to build up a comprehensive kit is to buy extra tools as they are needed.

A vast selection of tools displayed above a workbench makes an impressive sight, but some of the tools will be of little value if they are used only rarely.

The quality of tools varies considerably and buying some of the cheaper ones can, in time, prove to be an expensive economy.

Buy the best tools you can afford—British and German makes are the most reliable. Those marked 'foreign made', although inexpensive, may be made badly from inferior metals.

A cheap spanner is a typical example. The jaws will eventually spread under pressure and mutilate a nut—rounding off the corners until it is impossible to shift and a nut-splitter may be needed. Apart from wasting time and causing damage, a badly fitting spanner can mean bruised knuckles.

When a job is finished, clean and dry off the tools and give them a thin smear of oil to prevent rusting. Properly used and cared for, they will last a lifetime. Mechanics in dealers' workshops use a number of special tools, designed to simplify difficult jobs. Many of these tools are not on sale to the general public and may be needed only on rare occasions.

If it is not possible to improvise with other tools, it may be worth going to a firm that operates a hire service for specialist equipment. This can include paint spray apparatus and hydraulic jacks.

The most important aid that any home mechanic should have is the workshop manual for his car. It gives vital information on operations such as the correct sequence of engine stripping and reassembling, the exact clearances and adjustments of various components, and the torque loading of nuts and bolts. Workshop manuals can be bought, usually from the car manufacturer or dealer.

Car and garage toolkits

In addition to the tools supplied with a new car—usually only a jack, a wheelbrace and perhaps a box spanner—a home mechanic should have two separate kits: one to carry in the car to cope with breakdowns, and another to keep in the garage for routine servicing and repairs.

Tools to carry in the car

Set of 7 or 8 open-ended spanners
Spark-plug box spanner and tommy-bar
Plug-gapping tool
Set of feeler gauges
Circuit tester
BA spanner for distributor terminal nut, or complete set of BA spanners
Magneto file for contact-breaker points
Engineers' screwdrivers—large and medium
Electricians' screwdriver—small
Cross-headed screwdrivers—small and medium

Combination pliers
Roll of insulating tape
Two jumper leads
Adjustable wrenches—medium and small
Hammer, ball pein
Tyre valve key
Tyre pressure gauge
Tyre depth gauge
Tyre pump
Drivers' handbook
Fire extinguisher

Tools for the garage

Set of ring spanners
Set of sockets (including plug socket) and their lever
Brake-adjusting spanner
Chubby screwdrivers—straight and cross-headed
Side-cutting, round and snipe-nosed pliers
Electricians' combination pliers
Calipers and metal rule
Hammers—hard and soft-faced
Universal drain-plug remover
Torque wrench
Lock-on wrench
Set of Allen keys
Wire brushes
Distilled water dispenser
Hydrometer
Battery trickle charger

Hydraulic jack and axle stands
Electric drill or hand-drill
Set of twist drills $\frac{1}{64}-\frac{1}{4}$ in.
Oil syringe and grease gun
Files and cold chisel
Creeper and car ramps
Receptacle for waste oil and funnel
Paraffin washing bath—plastic bowl
Workshop manual
Fire extinguisher

SPECIAL TOOLS
These may be purchased if sufficient use can be made of them to warrant their cost
Valve-spring compressor
Nut-splitter
Hub-puller
Stud-extractor

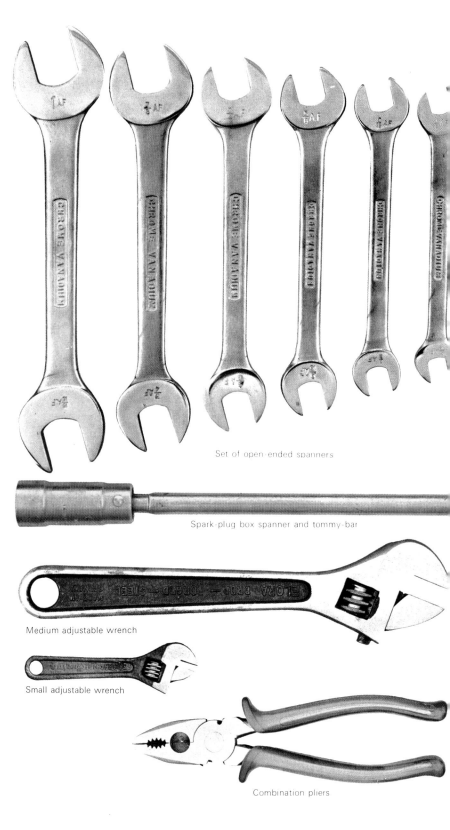

Set of open-ended spanners

Spark-plug box spanner and tommy-bar

Medium adjustable wrench

Small adjustable wrench

Combination pliers

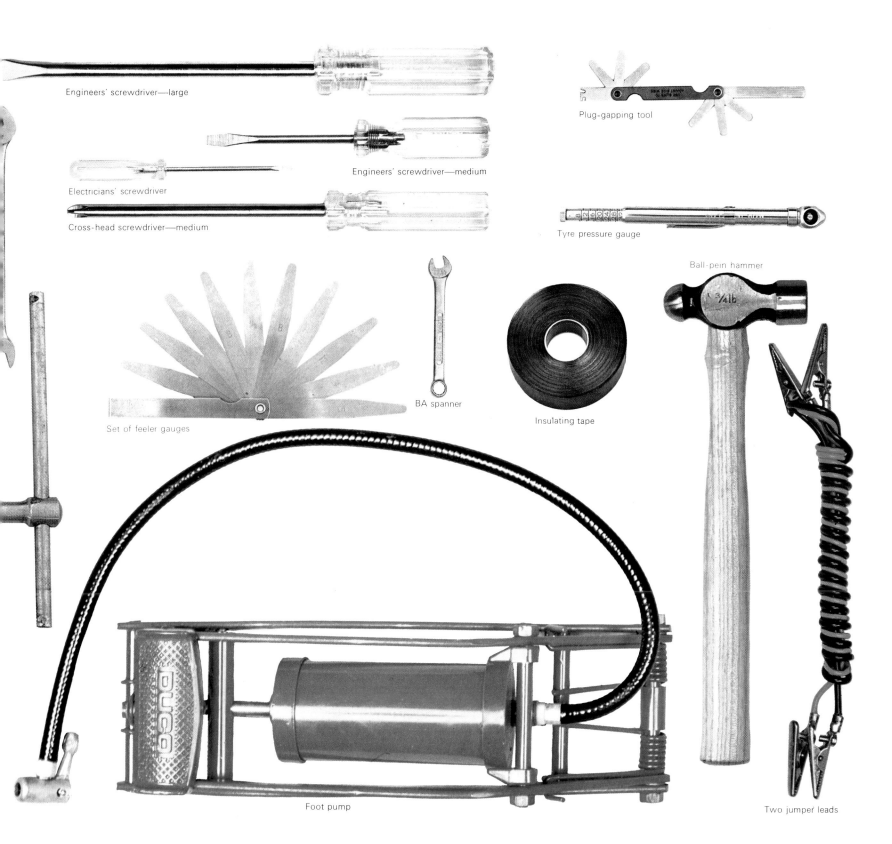

Engineers' screwdriver—large

Engineers' screwdriver—medium

Electricians' screwdriver

Cross-head screwdriver—medium

Plug-gapping tool

Tyre pressure gauge

Set of feeler gauges

BA spanner

Insulating tape

Ball-pein hammer

Foot pump

Two jumper leads

Tools/nuts, bolts and spanners

Thread sizes of nuts and bolts

THE NUTS and bolts on modern British cars have American (also called Unified) threads for bolts of $\frac{1}{4}$ in. dia. upwards.

The size of the hexagon bolt-head, or the nut, is determined by the diameter of the bolt thread itself, the sizes of which increase in $\frac{1}{16}$ in. steps.

The spanners to fit them are called AF (across flats) as the size of the nut or bolt-head is the distance between the opposing flat sides.

Cars made before 1951 had nuts and bolts of one of two standard threads—British Standard Fine (BSF) and British Standard Whitworth (BSW).

BSF and BSW identified nut and bolt

sizes in different ways. For example, a bolt taking a $\frac{7}{16}$ in. BSF spanner would take a $\frac{3}{8}$ in. Whitworth spanner. But since 1951—although spanners are still marked with both sizes—Whitworth & BSF have identified bolt sizes in the same way.

Smaller threads on British cars, particularly in the electrical equipment, are usually British Association (BA) threads. The biggest, 0BA, fits a bolt of 0·236 in. dia., and a 6BA one of 0·110 in.

Continental cars have metric threads, which will eventually be used exclusively in Britain. Although some components are already metricated, the changeover is a very gradual process.

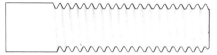

British Standard Fine (BSF) bolts have good locking quality and core strength due to the shallow pitch between the threads

British Association (BA) have a limited range of diameters—smaller than BSW or BSF—and are used for electrical work

Metric bolts have different threads and pitches from most other bolts and, except for some BA sizes, are not interchangeable

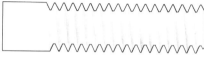

British Standard Whitworth (BSW or Whit) have fewer but deeper threads than BSF and are better for soft metals and cast iron

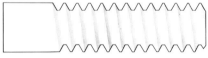

Unified Coarse (UNC) and Unified Fine (UNF) are not unlike BSW and have a hexagonal bolt for American Fine (AF) spanners

The size marked on the spanner for BSF, BSW and BA bolts is determined by the diameter of the bolt itself. For UNC and UNF bolts, the AF spanner size is the distance between the opposing flat sides

Some BA bolts from British cars. Only seven sizes are usually used, ranging from 0·236 in. (0BA) to 0·110 in. (6BA). They are referred to by a number from 0–6, followed by the letters BA

AF bolt sizes commonly found on British cars. The spanners used to turn these bolts or the nuts on them are known as AF spanners

Spanners

Open-ended spanners

A set of open-ended spanners can be used for the majority of nuts and bolts on a car, even though they may not be the best tools for the job.

Each spanner has two jaws—one at each end of a shank. Starting with the smallest spanner in the set, one of the jaws is usually one size larger than the other, and is repeated as the smaller jaw of the next spanner in the set.

For instance, the smallest spanner might have a $\frac{5}{16}$ in. jaw at one end of the shank and a $\frac{3}{8}$ in. jaw at the other. The next spanner in the set will have $\frac{3}{8}$ and $\frac{7}{16}$ in. jaws; the one after that $\frac{7}{16}$ and $\frac{1}{2}$ in.; and so on.

The sizes are duplicated in this way because sometimes two spanners are needed for a job—for example, one to hold a bolt-head and the other to manipulate the nut.

On the average car, the spanners most used in the AF range are the $\frac{7}{16}$ and $\frac{1}{2}$ in. and the $\frac{9}{16}$ and $\frac{5}{8}$ in. For those home mechanics who wish to keep their initial outlay low, these two spanners will make a good beginning, instead of buying the full set of five at once.

The length of a spanner is usually related to the size of the nut or bolt it will be used on, so avoid using extra leverage, or a hammer, when tightening a nut or bolt.

The jaws of a spanner are usually set at an angle of 15° to the shank, so that when the spanner is turned over the shank is in a different position. This enables the spanner to be used effectively where it is obstructed from turning through the full 60° needed to turn a six-sided nut through one-sixth of a circle. If a nut cannot be turned by this amount, the spanner will not be able to grip it for the next turn.

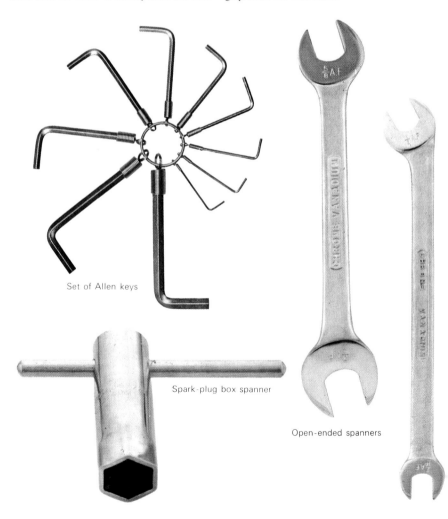

Set of Allen keys

Spark-plug box spanner

Open-ended spanners

In a variation of this design, some spanners have one jaw in line with the shank of the tool, and the other angled. These are designed for adjusting tappets.

Ring spanners
Ring spanners are stronger and lighter than open-ended spanners, and can turn a nut in a very restricted space because their holes are twelve-sided. They cannot slip and cause damage since they surround the nut completely.

Ring spanners have holes of different sizes at each end of the shank and these sizes are duplicated in successive spanners of a set in the same way as with open-ended spanners. Normally the ring portions make a slight swan-neck with the shank for ease of working.

The disadvantage of ring spanners is that most cannot be used on pipe unions,
or where there is no access over the top of a nut. Some specialist ones are available with a gap in the ring, which makes them a hybrid open-ended ring, designed to be used on pipe unions only. If used for anything else they tend to splay out.

For extensive maintenance work on a car, a set of ring spanners is essential. Use a ring spanner in preference to an open-ended spanner whenever possible.

Ignition spanners
On most cars only one BA spanner is needed—normally a 4BA—for the terminal nut on the distributor.

Box spanners
Box spanners are tubular and turned by a 'tommy-bar' passed through holes in the side. They turn a nut from above and there must be a clearance all round it.
Box spanners can reach into confined spaces and, because they bear on all six sides of a nut, do not damage it or slip off.

Spark-plug box spanner
If a spark-plug box spanner is not supplied with a car, choose one with a rubber collar inset. It must fit securely over the plug body without touching the insulator, and be long enough for the tommy-bar to clear components near the cylinder head. At the same time it should not be so long that it cannot be used on the rear plug—often the most difficult to get at.

Socket spanners
These consist of a set of sockets with a common extension and tommy-bar. More expensive sets have a speed brace, ratchet handles and jointed extensions. They are used like box spanners, but their use is
limited by the depth of the socket. A socket to fit the spark-plugs is worth having for use with a torque wrench. A spark-plug can then be tightened to the correct setting, which is much more efficient than the rule-of-thumb 'finger-tight and then half a turn' sometimes adopted when using a box spanner.

Combination spanner
Combination spanners have one open end and a ring of the same size at the other.

Allen keys
These are used on screws and bolts which have hexagonal-shaped socket indentations in their heads; the principal advantage of this type is that the bolt can be used in confined spaces. If Allen keys are needed, attach a set to a key ring, since they are small and easily lost.

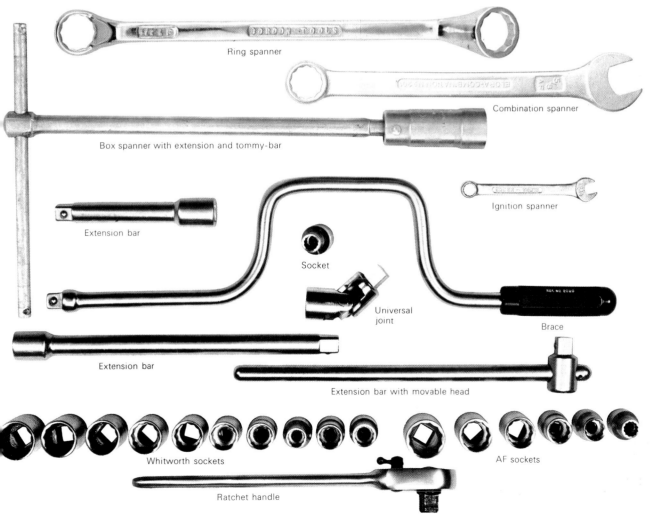

Ring spanner

Combination spanner

Box spanner with extension and tommy-bar

Extension bar

Ignition spanner

Socket

Extension bar

Universal joint

Brace

Extension bar with movable head

Whitworth sockets

AF sockets

Ratchet handle

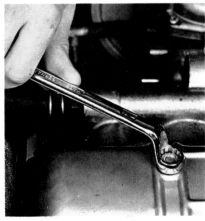

The twelve-sided interior of a ring spanner completely surrounds a nut and is ideal where extra tightness is required

Handling a spark-plug that is hot can be difficult. Use a plug socket, an extension bar and a ratchet handle

Tools/wrenches and screwdrivers

Adjustable wrenches

ADJUSTABLE WRENCHES will fit a large number of nut sizes, but they should be used only when the correct tool is not available.

They are difficult to fit accurately on a nut without rounding-off the edges, and can be strained; also, if a large adjustable is used on a small nut, the bolt can easily be broken or the thread damaged. Adjustables should be used so that the major load is carried by the fixed jaw.

The only two adjustable wrenches needed by a home mechanic are a medium-sized one (10 in.) for general work and a small one (6 in.) for electrical fittings.

Lock-on wrench

Although it has no specific job, a lock-on wrench is a useful supplementary tool because it can be used to grip a nut or bolt-head to leave a mechanic's hands free. The jaws have serrated teeth and will mark soft metals if used for turning.

Drain plugs and brakes

Other kinds of wrenches are available. Those for removing the drain plugs on the sump, gearbox and back axle, can be bought with male or female heads or with a combination of both.

There are wrenches for adjusting brakes, either with a fixed end or a swivel end for easier access to the adjuster studs.

Medium adjustable wrench

Small adjustable wrench

Brake-adjusting wrench

Brake-adjusting wrench

Combined male/female drain-plug wrench

Male drain-plug wrench

Lock-on wrench

Torque wrench

ALL the major nuts and bolts on a car have a 'torque-setting' determined by the car's manufacturer. The setting—listed in the workshop manual—indicates the exact amount of effort that should be used to tighten up the nut or bolt. This figure is important, since a nut or bolt which is tightened incorrectly may crack and fail, or work loose. The only tool that can be used for such accurate tightening is a torque wrench, which is used with a socket set.

There are two main types of torque wrench: one has a pointer which moves along a graduated scale to show how much effort is being exerted; and the other, which is much more expensive, can be pre-set by an adjustable mechanism.

A torque wrench can be bought as a separate item or with a set of sockets to fit a wide range of bolts.

Sets range from five sockets, with an L-bar to turn them, to more sophisticated collections containing dozens of sockets, extension bars of various lengths and a universal joint so that they can be turned through an angle. The extension bars may be fitted between the socket and the wrench according to the amount of space available.

Torque wrenches are expensive and it is sometimes possible to hire them from specialist shops.

A torque wrench being used to tighten the cylinder-head nuts. The turning effort can be read on a graduated scale near the handle

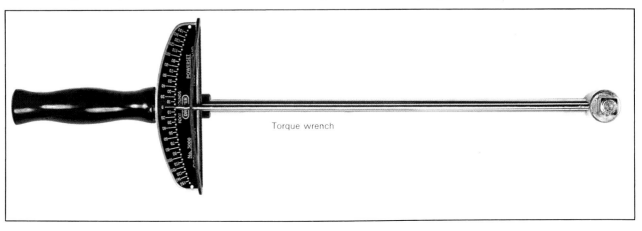

Torque wrench

Obstruction tools

BECAUSE engine compartments on modern cars are becoming more cramped, nuts and bolts are often difficult to get at.

Some ingeniously shaped tools are available which will get round most obstructions. There are, for instance, ring spanners with crescent-shaped shanks; open-ended spanners with their jaws at right angles to the shank; and screwdrivers, both straight and cross-headed, in the shape of a shallow Z with a blade at each end.

Most tool shops stock various tools for overcoming problems of inaccessibility. Sometimes, however, an old tool can be adapted very easily.

An open-ended spanner can be cut in two to make it shorter, or the head can be ground down to make it thinner, to fit into a restricted space. A box spanner can be cut off near the head and shortened, to tackle nuts that cannot be reached by a spanner of normal length.

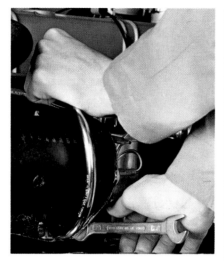

An obstruction spanner being used to hold the head of a fixing bolt on the generator while the spanner turns the nut

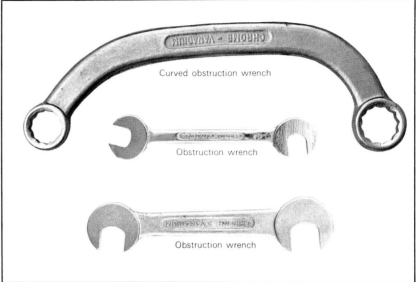

Curved obstruction wrench

Obstruction wrench

Obstruction wrench

Screwdrivers

IT IS an advantage to have several different-sized screwdrivers, since the blade should fit the slot in a screw-head exactly. Too small a blade may chew up the head of a screw; too large a blade may damage the surrounding metalwork.

Long screwdrivers are for heavy mechanical work, especially for shifting screws that are difficult to move; extra force can be exerted with a long screwdriver, provided the blade is kept square in the slot.

Pozi-driv screwdrivers are for the 'cross-headed' screws which are used on most modern cars to secure the trim and small components. The correct-sized screwdriver must be used with these screws or the crossed slots will be damaged.

Chubby screwdrivers, for straight or cross-headed screws, have short handles and are useful for getting into confined spaces. They can sometimes be bought with a tommy-bar in the handle, to give extra leverage.

Electricians' screwdrivers have rubber or plastic handles, insulating them for all electrical work. A screwdriver with a plastic handle that is cracked should be discarded.

Offset or right-angled screwdrivers for straight or cross-headed screws are handy for removing screws that are awkward to get at. A right-angled screwdriver has a blade at each end, so that it can be reversed in a limited space.

Keep screwdriver tips ground square and tapering evenly to the edge.

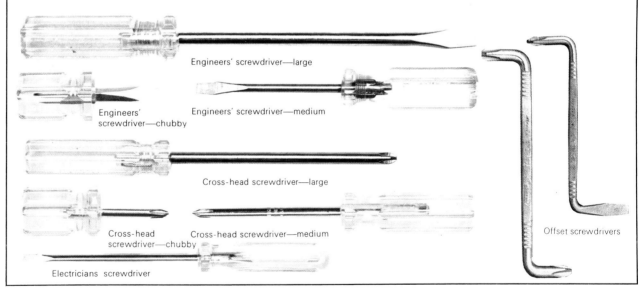

Engineers' screwdriver—large

Engineers' screwdriver—chubby

Engineers' screwdriver—medium

Cross-head screwdriver—large

Cross-head screwdriver—chubby

Cross-head screwdriver—medium

Electricians screwdriver

Offset screwdrivers

Using an offset screwdriver to get to an awkwardly positioned screw-head

Cross-head screwdriver being used to undo screws securing the top of a carburettor

Make sure that the tip of a screwdriver fits exactly into the slot in the screw-head

Tools/hammers, pliers and hacksaws

Hammers

A HAMMER can do more harm than good if used incorrectly; for instance, never use one to apply extra force to a spanner when tightening nuts or use a forged-steel head hammer on soft metals.

Choose a medium-weight hammer—such as a ball pein—with a hickory shaft. The shaft should completely fill the eye of the head and have two metal wedges visible. A forged-steel head is better than a cast one: cast steel is likely to shatter.

The materials used for soft-headed hammers are plastic, rubber, nylon and hide. Use this type of hammer wherever a hard hammer might cause bruising or damage to a surface.

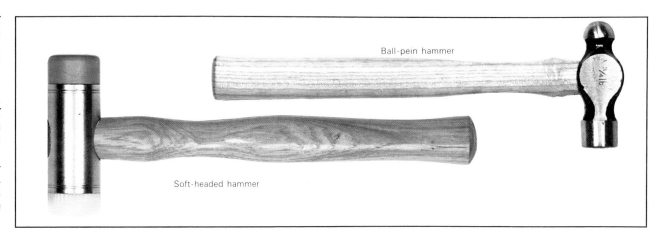

Ball-pein hammer

Soft-headed hammer

Pliers

PLIERS should never be used as a substitute for a spanner—they have serrated jaws and will damage the corners of a nut and make it difficult to remove.

Combination pliers—with or without insulated handles—have one round and one flat gripping area and two sets of cutters. The cutters cannot be used to cut spring wire or stainless steel.

For stripping wire and cutting cables, use side-cutting pliers.

Snipe-nosed and round-nosed pliers are mainly for handling small components and bending or forming metal.

Purpose-made pliers can be bought to remove internal or external circlips. These are often sold as circlip removers.

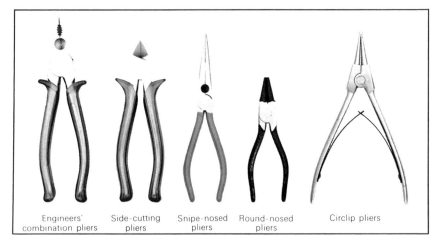

Engineers' combination pliers   Side-cutting pliers   Snipe-nosed pliers   Round-nosed pliers   Circlip pliers

A pair of side-cutting pliers being used to remove an old split-pin—in this case from a nut retaining a wheel-bearing assembly

Hacksaws

A HACKSAW is a tool for cutting metal. The frame of the saw is adjustable, and holds 10 or 12 in. long detachable blades, held in place by a wing nut. To tension the blade correctly, take up the slack on the wing nut and give it three more complete turns. The blade teeth must point away from the handle. Blades are fine or coarse according to the number of teeth they have to the inch. A coarse blade, for cutting softer metals, has a minimum of 18 teeth to the inch; a fine blade, for cutting harder metals, has a maximum of 32.

Junior hacksaws, with 6 in. long fine-toothed blades, are useful for small jobs where a full-sized one would be clumsy. Avoid excessive pressure when using a hacksaw, cut only on the forward stroke, and keep the blade straight in the cut.

Hacksaw blades cannot be resharpened.

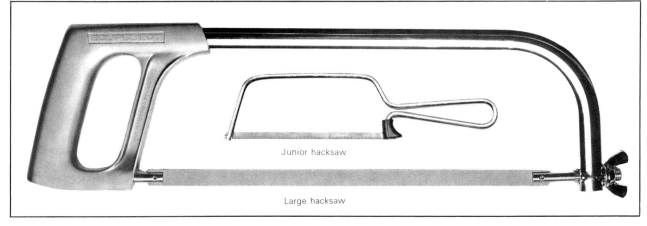

Junior hacksaw

Large hacksaw

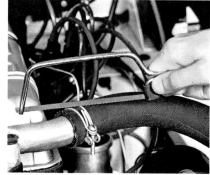

A junior hacksaw can be useful for getting into awkward corners where the large hacksaw would be too difficult to use

Files and drills

Cold chisels and files

COLD CHISELS are available in a number of shapes and sizes. A $\frac{1}{2}$ in. or a 1 in. diameter flat cold chisel—used with a hammer—is particularly useful for shifting corroded nuts and bolts.

Files are general-purpose tools, often used in conjunction with hacksaws and chisels. They can be flat, half-round, round, square or triangular; and with one of each it is possible to deal with most of the angles, curves, grooves and holes encountered in a car.

Files are graded according to the number of teeth they have to the inch, and the grades are rough, bastard, second-cut, smooth and dead smooth. The greater the number of teeth the smoother the cut.

A points file may be used for cleaning the contact-breaker points in the distributor if an oil-stone is not available.

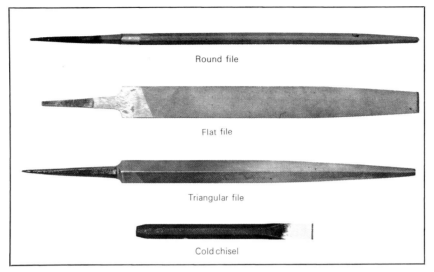

Round file

Flat file

Triangular file

Cold chisel

Cutting off a damaged rivet head with a cold chisel. Whenever possible hold the chisel at an angle of 30° to the work

Drills and accessories

A DRILL—preferably electric—with a range of accessories will save time on such jobs as grinding, cleaning off carbon deposits in the combustion chamber and making holes in the bodywork for cables to pass through.

Useful accessories are a set of twist drills ranging from $\frac{1}{16}$ in. to $\frac{1}{4}$ in., wire brushes, abrasive discs and a polishing pad. A rubber disc will provide a backing for the abrasive discs and the polishing pad.

Each disc is attached to the drill by a spindle which passes through the centre.

Mark out the centre of a hole to be drilled in metal with a centre-punch and hammer; this will prevent the tip of the drill from slipping. For large holes, first drill a pilot hole with a smaller drill.

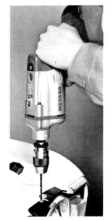 

Using a power drill (left) to drill out a rivet in the headlight trim and (right) to polish paintwork that has been made good. The polishing pad is made of lambswool

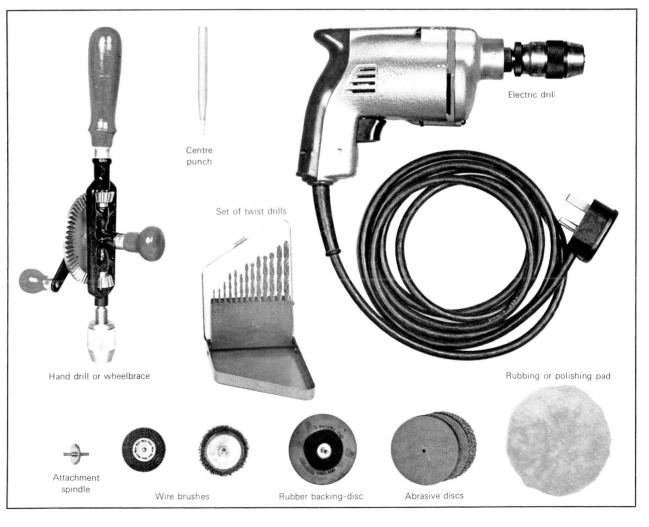

Centre punch

Hand drill or wheelbrace

Set of twist drills

Electric drill

Rubbing or polishing pad

Attachment spindle

Wire brushes

Rubber backing-disc

Abrasive discs

Tools/measuring and electrical equipment

Measuring tools

FOR TAKING MEASUREMENTS that do not need to be accurate to more than $\frac{1}{32}$ in. or 1 mm., a 30 cm. steel rule is adequate. It can also be useful as a straight-edge for scribing out metalwork or checking the amount of distortion in a cylinder head.

For more accurate measurements use a micrometer, or a vernier caliper which will measure accurately down to one-thousandth of an inch. A 1 in. micrometer is limited to a maximum range of 1 in.

The vernier caliper is for taking internal, external and depth measurements up to 6 in. and is sufficient for most do-it-yourself jobs on a car.

Spring calipers
A pair of outside spring calipers is useful for transferring measurements between the vernier caliper or metal rule and the part of the engine on which work is to be done.

Feeler gauges
A set of feeler gauges is necessary for measuring the gaps in spark-plugs, contact-breaker points and valve clearances.

30 cm steel rule

Vernier caliper

Outside micrometer

Outside spring calipers

Feeler gauge

Metric conversion

ALTHOUGH metric measurements are now widely used in the car industry, many components and tools still in use are graduated in inches.

For the home mechanic possessing a micrometer and a vernier caliper marked in inches only, the table below converts thousandths of an inch to millimetres—from 0·001 to 1 in.

For example 0·045 in. equals 1·143 mm, which is 1·016 mm (0·040 in.) added to 0·127 mm (0·005 in.).

in.	mm	in.	mm
0·001	0·025	0·060	1·524
0·002	0·051	0·070	1·778
0·003	0·076	0·080	2·032
0·004	0·102	0·090	2·286
0·005	0·127	0·100	2·540
0·006	0·152	0·200	5·080
0·007	0·178	0·300	7·620
0·008	0·203	0·400	10·160
0·009	0·229	0·500	12·700
0·010	0·254	0·600	15·240
0·020	0·508	0·700	17·780
0·030	0·762	0·800	20·320
0·040	1·016	0·900	22·860
0·050	1·270	1·000	25·400

Electrical equipment

Circuit-tester
Electrical faults usually head the list of causes of breakdown, so carry a circuit-tester as an aid to quick diagnosis of electrical or low-tension circuit defects. Buy one with a pointed probe—rather than one with a screwdriver blade—that can be pushed through a cable's insulation and will only make a pin-hole.

Soldering iron
A good soldering iron, preferably electric so as to maintain a constant heat level, is worth having for the maintenance of electrical equipment.

Points file
This is used for cleaning the contact points in the distributor and the spark-plug electrodes. A feeler gauge is sometimes attached to the handle of the file.

Strobe lamp
A stroboscopic timing lamp is used for checking the ignition timing of an engine.

If a mark on any rapidly rotating wheel is seen by the light of a lamp that flashes once for every rotation of the wheel, the mark will appear stationary. The timing lamp works on this principle.

On most cars there is a Top Dead Centre (TDC) mark on the crankshaft pulley at the front of the engine. Fixed to the timing-gear casing is a metal pointer.

Disconnect the HT lead to No. 1 plug and clip it to one of the lamp leads. Clip the other lamp lead to No. 1 plug—still in the cylinder head.

As the engine ticks over, the strobe lamp lights each time No. 1 plug sparks. When it is shone on the engine pulley, the pointer and correct timing mark should line up if the timing is accurate. If they do not, minor adjustments can be made to the timing at the distributor.

Using a strobe lamp to check the ignition timing of an engine. The lamp indicates the relative positions of the timing marks

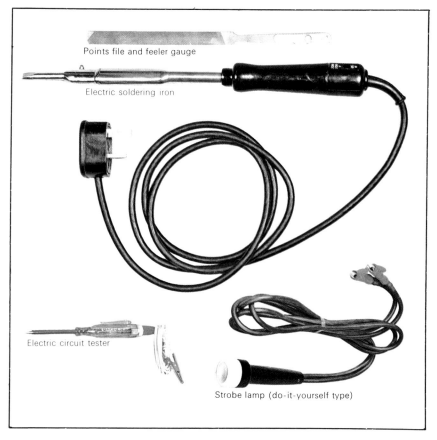

Points file and feeler gauge

Electric soldering iron

Electric circuit tester

Strobe lamp (do-it-yourself type)

Care of the battery

IF A BATTERY is stored for a long time, it will discharge through internal leakage. A battery charger will keep the battery in peak condition, especially during the winter. It also has a further use: a fully charged battery will produce only about two-thirds its power when cold, but half an hour on a trickle charge will warm it up, so that it can punch out full starting power.

A distilled-water filler avoids over-filling—and subsequent corrosion of the terminals—by cutting off the flow as soon as the correct level is reached.

Use a hydrometer to make a monthly check on each of the battery cells. This shows the specific gravity of the dilute sulphuric acid in the battery. Some hydro-meters show 'Full Charge', 'Half Charge' and 'Flat'; others have a graduated scale. With the latter a full charge will read between 1·270 and 1·290, a half charge will read 1·190–1·210 and a discharged battery 1·110–1·130.

Jumper leads, 6–8 ft lengths of cable with crocodile clips soldered to the ends, can be used to bypass a defective circuit.

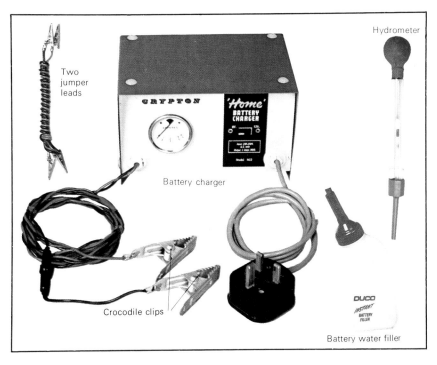

Two jumper leads

Hydrometer

Battery charger

Crocodile clips

Battery water filler

Make sure the positive and negative clips on the battery charger are connected to the corresponding terminals on the battery

The end of the filler has a device in it to regulate the flow of water

Valve-spring compressor and grinding equipment

BEFORE a valve can be removed from the engine, the valve spring must be compressed and the split collars which retain the spring cap must be withdrawn.

The tool for this job is a valve-spring compressor. There are various types available but all work on similar principles. Some have a cam-and-lever action; others have a G-clamp screw.

Workshop manuals usually specify which is the best spring compressor to use and illustrate the way to use it. An overhead valve is fairly easy to remove, since the cylinder head can be detached from the engine and worked on at a bench.

Side valves may be less accessible, unless the engine is out of the car, and the cylinder head will have to be detached before they can be removed from the cylinder block.

The valve-grinding tool consists of a wooden stem with a rubber sucker pad at each end. The suckers are used to grip the valve when grinding. The grinding paste is sold in duo-tins which have coarse paste for rough grinding in one end and fine paste for polishing in the other.

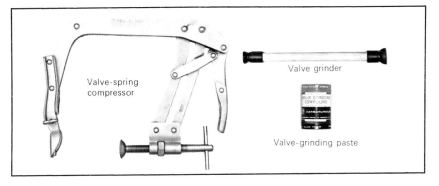

Valve-spring compressor

Valve grinder

Valve-grinding paste

Nut and stud-removers

NUTS AND STUDS sometimes become so badly corroded or damaged that they can be removed only with purpose-made tools.

A nut-splitter works like a nut-cracker but has a hydraulically operated cutting edge capable of exerting considerable pressure.

A stud-extractor will withdraw a broken stud or bolt. Drill a hole in the broken end for about three-quarters of the stud's diameter and most of its depth. Insert the appropriate extractor and, using a wrench, turn it anti-clockwise to bring out the stud.

A stud-remover fits over the stud and a knurled wheel provides grip when the tool is used with a socket set.

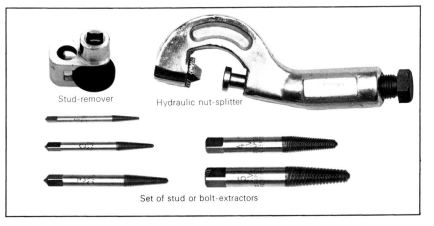

Stud-remover

Hydraulic nut-splitter

Set of stud or bolt-extractors

A nut-splitter in use. Its cutting edge is forced into the nut by the pressure head

Tools/major overhaul and routine servicing

Garage hoist

FOR THE AMBITIOUS home mechanic who is prepared to tackle a complete engine overhaul, which involves removing an engine from the car, a hoist is essential. Hoists are expensive to buy, but it is usually possible to hire one. Makeshift methods can be difficult as well as dangerous. The hoist below has four pulleys in each block and gives an 8:1 mechanical advantage—that is, it will lift 8 lb. for every 1 lb. applied. It has a safety locking device to hold a load at any height, and is fitted with 72 ft of nylon cord which will lift an engine to a height of 9 ft.

Make sure that the hoist is fitted to a beam capable of supporting an engine.

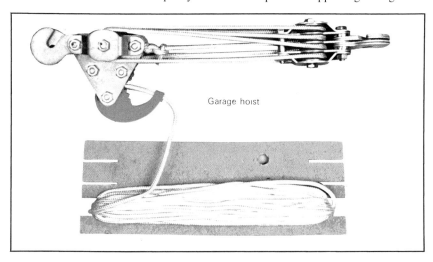

Garage hoist

Hub-puller

HUB-PULLERS can be bought from accessory shops or garages. A few cars require special hub-pullers but the tool illustrated is a loose-legged type, suitable for most jobs. The two outer legs are fixed to two of the studs that hold the wheel in place. As the centre portion of the puller is turned, it pushes against the end of the half-shaft and the tool pulls the hub out.

A sharp blow from behind with a soft-headed hammer will usually clear the hub from the axle.

Using a loose-legged hub-puller. It is fixed to the studs that normally hold the wheel in place

Tools for tyres

A TYRE-PRESSURE GAUGE is worth carrying in the glove compartment, since gauges on garage air-hoses are often inaccurate and tyres inflated incorrectly can be dangerous and illegal. Also keep a foot pump, a tyre-tread depth-gauge and a valve tool available. The foot pump and valve tool can often get you out of roadside trouble; the tread depth-gauge will help you to keep within the law.

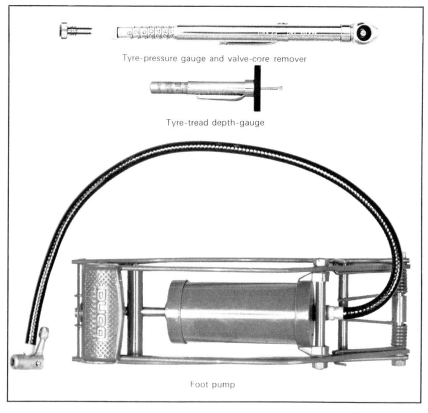

Tyre-pressure gauge and valve-core remover

Tyre-tread depth-gauge

Foot pump

Carry a pocket tyre-pressure gauge: garage pressure gauges are often inaccurate

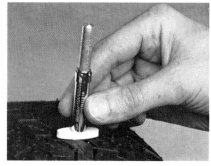

Use a tyre-tread depth-gauge to check that the tread is not below the legal limit of 1 mm

Wire brushes

A COUPLE of wire brushes—a heavy duty one with four rows of bristles and a metal scraper attached to its nose, and a smaller one—can be invaluable labour-savers.

The brush illustrated can be used for cleaning off corrosion from the underside of a car and removing dirt and grit from the area around grease nipples. The smaller brush is better for cleaning electrical connections, such as battery terminals, down to the bare metal, and for other similar jobs.

If the wire bristles become clogged with grease, clean them in petrol.

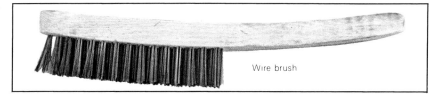

Wire brush

Working under the car

RAISING A CAR off the ground by about 6 in.—to provide extra working space underneath—can be an advantage for jobs like greasing linkages or replacing the exhaust pipe. Avoid makeshift methods: a car supported by a jack or bricks alone can be a killer.

Use a sturdy pair of ramps—preferably steel—and wedge the wheels that remain on the ground. Apply the handbrake when jacking the front wheels—except if the handbrake operates on the front instead of the rear wheels. In that case, use steel or wooden chocks to hold the wheels.

Never use two jacks—they are not stable enough. Axle stands, or stout wooden blocks, should be used to support the car's weight when the wheels and hubs are to be removed during maintenance jobs. A wandering-lead light, which can be clipped to the chassis or angled up from the floor, is essential when working on a car. Buy one with a shade to prevent dazzle, and be careful of the lead when using a power tool. Take care, too, that the lead does not lie in oil, water or—even more important—in petrol.

Moving about under the car is simplified by lying on a 'creeper'—a metal, plastic or wooden tray on castors. The next best thing is a sheet of hardboard, smooth side up; it makes movement easier and cleaner.

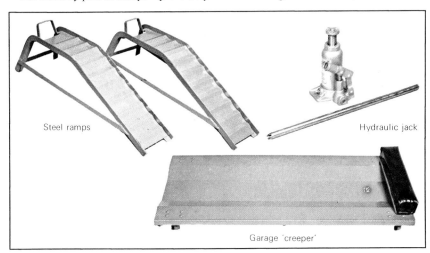

Steel ramps

Hydraulic jack

Garage 'creeper'

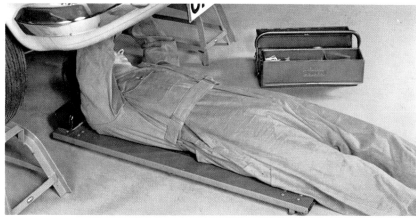

A metal 'creeper'—a tray on castors—simplifies moving about when working under the car. An upholstered pad is fixed to the tray as a head-rest

Lubricating equipment

CHANGING the engine oil is usually a straightforward job. An essential piece of equipment is a drain pan to hold the contents of the sump and filter bowl. Special plastic drainers are available but an old plastic washing-up bowl can be used. When the engine has been refilled with fresh oil, the old lubricant can be poured back into the empty can through a funnel. It is illegal to dispose of oil in a public sewer—consult your local garage who may dispose of it for you.

Some plastic basins are flexible enough to squeeze the rim into the shape of a pourer, so that the oil does not spill or splash.

On a car that has a filter bowl with a renewable element, one of the trickiest operations is replacing the sealing ring. This is in the annular groove on the housing, often out of sight. A darning needle, with its eye stuck in a cork as a handle, is useful for winkling out old sealing rings.

Grease guns
On cars that have grease nipples for chassis lubrication, use a side-lever grease gun; it develops high pressure.

Some guns can be refilled with cartridge containers, avoiding the messy job of filling from a grease or oil tin.

Gearboxes and back axles with side filler holes are difficult to top up, but this can be made a clean and simple job by using an oil syringe with a flexible delivery hose. Alternatively, the oil for the gearbox and back axle can be bought in a dispenser with a tube on the neck.

Drain-plug removers
Some drain and filler plugs on the gearbox and differential have recessed square or hexagonal sockets, or oddly shaped heads. Universal tools, for removing and tightening drain plugs, are worth having since they prevent damage to the plugs.

Using a syringe for topping up the gearbox oil through the filler plug

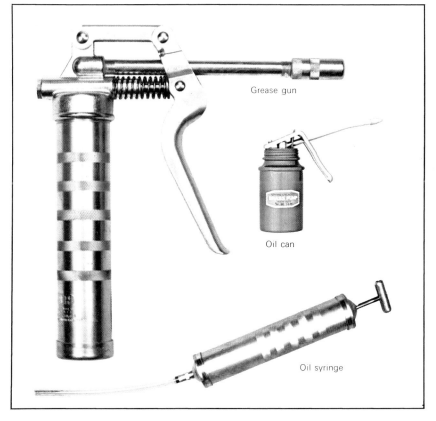

Grease gun

Oil can

Oil syringe

Equipping a garage as a workshop

THE LIMITED SIZE of the average private garage means that once a car is housed, the only place usually left for the workbench is against a wall at the end of the garage.

The workbench is the focal point of the motorist's workshop—a surface on which to repair components or to lay down tools during work on the car. It is essential that the bench is well lit—preferably by natural light through a window, but by carefully positioned artificial light if there are no windows.

Workbench and mechanic's vice
A good workbench should be sturdy and easy to use. Two designs which fulfil these requirements are illustrated on pp. 24, 25 and 26, with details of their construction.

A cheaper alternative is to use a solid door, at least $1\frac{1}{2}$–2 in. thick, covered on one side with $\frac{3}{8}$ in. plywood. Doors of this kind, measuring 6 ft 6 in. long and about 30–36 in. wide, can often be bought at a demolition site. The framework to support a door can be made from softwood, although Dexion, a system of metal brackets and girders which can be bolted together, is easy to erect and stronger.

The most necessary piece of workbench equipment is a vice; and the best height for the bench is one which brings the top of the vice level with the elbow of the person using it. If the garage floor is concrete, a wooden duckboard will make for warmer feet in winter, and the thickness of the duckboard should be allowed for when planning the height of a bench.

Buy the best vice you can afford, making sure that it has jaws at least 4 in. wide.

Vices have two kinds of base fittings, fixed or swivelled. A swivel-based vice is more expensive, but it can cope with awkward shapes and sizes of material.

Soft jaws—pads of hard fibre—can be fitted to the jaws of some vices so that an object can be gripped firmly without damage. The pads are in a range of sizes and are mounted on steel slip-on cases.

Lighting and socket outlets
Fluorescent lighting is ideal for the garage, but when used above a workbench it should be arranged so that light cannot shine directly into the user's eyes. This can be arranged by fixing a strip light to the underside of a shelf above the bench, with a strip of plywood 75–100 mm. (3–4 in.) wide pinned to the front edge of the shelf.

Many garages have their light fittings placed centrally in the ceiling or roof; these should be moved by an extension lead to the end of the garage, where they will not put the car's engine compartment in shadow when the bonnet or boot is opened.

A wandering-lead light is essential for work done under the car, or to provide concentrated areas of light in the engine compartment. A useful alternative is a hinged desk lamp which can be angled into almost any position.

Provide 13 amp. switched socket outlets near the bench for electrical appliances—the power drill, soldering iron, battery charger and heaters. Check that all sockets are earthed; that cables have the capacity to deal with the equipment used; and that each appliance is fitted with a fused plug. An extension lead is invaluable for vacuum-cleaning the interior of the car, or for using power tools when the car is out of the garage.

Ventilation and heating
Unless a garage is adequately ventilated, usually by airbricks in the walls, condensation will corrode the inside of the car and damage bodywork and carpets.

In winter, an undersump heater which is similar to a small paraffin heater will reduce condensation and keep the engine oil warm enough to make starting easier.

Another form of heater, which is fitted inside the car's cooling system and works like an immersion heater, can be plugged into the mains at night. This heater warms the water in the radiator and so simplifies starting in cold weather.

Inspection pit
An inspection pit is ideal for working under a car, but is expensive to build and needs to be properly drained and well lit. It should be just wide enough to provide a comfortable working space and at least 600 mm. (2 ft) longer than the longest car likely to use it. This length is essential to provide a quick means of escape, for petrol dropping from the carburettor or a manifold can ignite touching a hot lamp.

Wooden ramps
A good pair of ramps, as an alternative to an inspection pit, can be made from a 1200 mm. (4 ft) length of substantial timber, say 225–250 mm (9–10 in.) wide and 125–150 mm. (5–6 in.) deep. Timber of this size will need to be cut with a handsaw; this can be done cheaply at most timber yards. To prevent the wheels of a car slipping when climbing the ramps, nail 50 × 12 mm. (2 × $\frac{1}{2}$ in.) battens across the sloping faces at equal distances apart.

Ramps of this length are suitable for most cars. If longer ramps are used, it is difficult to crawl between them from the side of a car and they are heavier to move into position.

Treat the ramps with a preservative.

Storage of tools
In a damp garage, tools are best kept in an airtight metal box. They should be cleaned off after use and wiped with an oily rag to protect them from corrosion.

With a dry, well-ventilated garage, it is more convenient to leave those tools which are used regularly on a board within easy reach of the bench, or on tool racks fixed to the wall. This makes it easy to check that tools are in their place and not left under the car or on the radiator. A forgotten spanner that falls on to the fan can

A single garage, 5·2 x 2·7 m. (17 x 9 ft), is easily converted into a small but well-planned workshop by the addition of a free-standing bench, some shelves and tool racks

cause considerable damage to the engine. Designs for simple tool racks are on p. 26.

Shelf space is always valuable in a garage. The Spur shelving used in the small garage illustrated has two 1525 mm. (5 ft) long uprights plugged to the wall, with 125 mm. (5 in.) metal brackets supporting softwood shelves.

A small metal cabinet with a series of plastic drawers is useful for storing screws, nuts and washers. Metal cabinets are made in various sizes and patterns. The one on the bench in the larger garage is 300 mm. (12 in.) long 160 mm. (6¼ in.) high and 145 mm. (5¾ in.) from front to back.

A roll of tissue on a wall bracket near the bench is useful for mopping up spilt fluids and cleaning excess grease off components. A kitchen roll and wall bracket can be bought from most stores.

Fire precautions

If petrol is kept in a private garage, its storage must comply with the regulations laid down by the Home Office. No more than 5 litres (2 gallons) may be kept; they must be kept in a metal container, secure against leakage and breakage, and be marked Petrol.

A licence to keep additional quantities of petrol can be obtained on application to the local authority. There are no restrictions governing the storage of paraffin or the bottle gas used for blowlamps.

It is worth keeping a fire extinguisher, besides the one you may have in the car, and a bucket of sand near the door.

Keep the floor of the garage free of oil or grease stains. If grease patches develop, use a de-greasing fluid to emulsify the grease. Wash away with water.

A double garage, 7 x 5 ·2 m. (23 x 17 ft), equipped as an efficient workshop. The interior is dry, well ventilated and provided with a good spread of lighting around the bench area. Up-and-over doors allow more natural light and white painted walls act as reflectors. A nylon hoist, for lifting the engine, is suspended from the steel beam

Design for a large workbench

THE TOP of this workbench is 610 mm. (24 in.) wide, 2450 mm. (8 ft) long and 878 mm. (34½ in.) above the floor. It is fitted with a Record No. 4 mechanic's vice (190 mm.) 7½ in. long.

To alter the height of the bench, add or subtract the required difference to or from parts 3, 5, 6, 7 and 17.

To alter the length of the bench, add or subtract the required difference to or from parts 1, 2, 13, 14, 17, 18, 27 and 28. If alterations in length are limited to these, the dimensions of the centre cupboard and the drawers need not be changed.

A sheet-steel top to protect the woodwork projects 100 mm. (4 in.) to give space for fixing the vice and cramping.

The backboard is mounted on 50 × 25 mm. (2 × 1 in.) battens plugged to the wall. Above the backboard there is a 225 × 25 mm. (9 × 1 in.) softwood shelf with a 50 × 25 mm. (2 × 1 in.) softwood strip pinned to its front edge.

Construction

Cut the top rails (1), the bottom rails (2) and the legs (3) to length. Cut joints on the legs as in fig. 2.

Hold the inner faces of the top rails together and mark the position of the cross rails (4). The centre-line of the middle cross rail is 32 mm. (1¼ in.) to the left of the centre-line of the front rail. The centre-line of the next two cross rails is 345 mm. (13⅝ in.) from the centre of the front rail. The centre-line of the cross rails at each end is 135 mm. (5⅜ in.) from the ends of the top rails.

Cut the cross rails to length and cut 6 mm. (¼ in.) deep housings across the top rails to receive them. Glue the cross rails in the housings, securing each joint with two 100 mm. (4 in.) cut nails. Glue and screw the bottom rails to each pair of legs.

Fit the legs to the assembled top frame, drive the front joints home and check they are tight. Drill a 12 mm. (½ in.) hole through each leg joint. Pass 90 mm. (3½ in.) bolts through the front legs and 125 mm. (5 in.) bolts through the back legs.

Check that the frame is square, attach washers and nuts to the bolts and tighten.

Cut the end panel (5) to size and screw it to the end of the framework.

Cut the two division panels (6) to size and cut out the corners to fit.

Cut the lippings (7) to length. Cut a

The worktop is finished with sheet steel to withstand hard wear, and the backboard is fitted with socket outlets for power tools

10 mm. (⅜ in.) deep × 18 mm. (¾ in.) wide rebate along each lipping, and cut away the top 96 mm. (3⅞ in.) to receive the top rail, as in fig. 3.

Mark out the grooves for the drawer shelves (8) on the inner faces of the division panels by drawing lines across the panels 180 mm. (7⅛ in.), 198 mm. (7⅞ in.), 344 mm. (13⅝ in.) and 362 mm. (14⅜ in.) from the top edge. Cut housings 7 mm. (⁵⁄₁₆ in.) deep. If the chipboard is slightly less than 18 mm. (¾ in.) thick, reduce width of the housings

Slide the panels in and screw them to the outer faces of the cross rails. Glue and pin the lippings to the front edge of the division panels, flush with the top edge.

When the glue is dry, plane or sand the joints smooth. Cut drawer shelves to size.

Cut a 18 mm. (¾ in.) wide × 7 mm.

(⁵⁄₁₆ in.) deep groove centrally across the upper face of the top shelf. Glue the lippings (9) to the front edges of both shelves, 7 mm. (⁵⁄₁₆ in.) in from each end.

Slide the upper drawer shelf into position from the back of the bench.

Cut the drawer divider (10) to size and remove the top corners as for the division panels. Glue lipping (11) to the front edge of the drawer divider, 7 mm. (⁵⁄₁₆ in.) up from the bottom and projecting 9 mm. (⅜ in.) above the cut-out at the top corner.

Spring the drawer divider in position and screw it to the central cross rail. Fix upper drawer shelf to the drawer divider with three equally spaced screws. Slide the lower shelf into its grooves from the back.

Screw 150 × 50 × 25 mm. (6 × 2 × 1 in.) softwood blocks to each side of the

division panels, their edges level with the tops of the bottom rails, to give support to the cupboard floors. Fix blocks to the inner face of end panel and wall opposite.

Measure the distance between the division panels, cut the centre cupboard floor (12) to size, and drop it into position. It oversails the bottom rail by 18 mm. (¾ in.). Screw it into position.

Cut side cupboard floors (13) to size and screw into position, flush with the bottom rail. Cut shelves (14) to size. Cut shelf battens (15) to length and screw them to the division panels. Cut battens (16) and house into legs.

Screw the shelves in position. Cut the doors (17) to size and hang them so that they overlap the front top rail by 9 mm. (⅜ in.). Use T-hinges, which are easy to fit. Screw the catches to the underside of the top rail and fix the handles to line up with

PARTS LIST

No.	Name	Qty.	Long	Wide	Thick	Material
1	Top rails	2	2432 mm.(95¼")	46 mm.(1¾")	96 mm.(3¾")	softwood
2	Bottom rails	2	2432 mm.(95¼")	96 mm.(3¾")	22 mm.(¾")	softwood
3	Legs	4	839 mm.(32⅞")	71 mm.(2¾")	71 mm.(2¾")	softwood
4	Cross rails	5	361 mm.(14¼")	96 mm.(3¾")	46 mm.(1¾")	softwood
5	End panel	1	839 mm.(32⅞")	518 mm.(20¾")	18 mm.(¾")	chipboard
6	Division panels	2	839 mm.(32⅞")	500 mm.(20")	18 mm.(¾")	chipboard
7	Lippings for 6	2	743 mm.(29⅛")	28 mm.(1¹⁄₁₆")	28 mm.(1¹⁄₁₆")	softwood
8	Drawer shelves	2	750 mm.(29⅝")	500 mm.(20")	18 mm.(¾")	chipboard
9	Lippings for 8	2	736 mm.(29")	22 mm.(¾")	22 mm.(¾")	softwood
10	Drawer divider	1	500 mm.(20")	187 mm.(7⁷⁄₁₆")	18 mm.(¾")	chipboard
11	Lipping for 10	1	96 mm.(3¾")	22 mm.(¾")	22 mm.(¾")	softwood
12	Centre cupboard floor	1	736 mm.(29")	518 mm.(20¾")	18 mm.(¾")	chipboard
13	Side cupboard floors	2	830 mm.(32¾")	500 mm.(20")	18 mm.(¾")	chipboard
14	Shelves	2	830 mm.(32¾")	475 mm.(19")	18 mm.(¾")	chipboard
15	Shelf battens—middle	2	475 mm.(19")	46 mm.(1¾")	22 mm.(¾")	softwood
16	Shelf battens—end	2	385 mm.(15¼")	46 mm.(1¾")	22 mm.(¾")	softwood
17	Doors	4	656 mm.(25¾")	374 mm.(14½")	18 mm.(¾")	chipboard
18	Wooden top (two layers)	2	2450 mm.(96")	585 mm.(23½")	18 mm.(¾")	chipboard
19	Small drawer fronts	2	359 mm.(14⅛")	96 mm.(3¾")	22 mm.(¾")	softwood
20	Small drawer backs	2	341 mm.(13⅜")	71 mm.(2¾")	15 mm.(⅝")	softwood
21	Small drawer sides	4	490 mm.(19½")	84 mm.(3⅜")	15 mm.(⅝")	softwood
22	Small drawer bottoms	2	490 mm.(19½")	341 mm.(13⅜")	3 mm.(⅛")	plywood
23	Large drawer front	1	736 mm.(29")	146 mm.(5¾")	22 mm.(¾")	softwood
24	Large drawer back	1	721 mm.(28⅜")	121 mm.(4¾")	15 mm.(⅝")	softwood
25	Large drawer sides	2	490 mm.(19½")	146 mm.(5¾")	15 mm.(⅝")	softwood
26	Large drawer bottom	1	721 mm.(28⅜")	490 mm.(19½")	6 mm.(¼")	plywood
27	Steel top	1	2450 mm.(96")	585 mm.(23½")	10g	mild steel
28	Front lipping	1	2450 mm.(96")	46 mm.(1¾")	15 mm.(⅝")	softwood

Hardware One Record No. 4 mechanic's vice; three 75 × 12 mm. (3 × ½") dia. hexagonal bolts with nuts and washers; four 90 × 12 mm. (3½" × ½") dia. coach bolts with nuts and washers
Note Dimensions are finished sizes. Measurements in brackets are imperial sizes

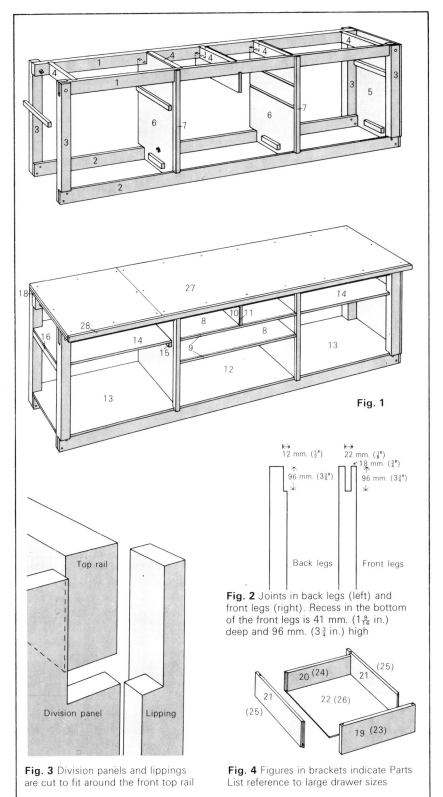

Fig. 1

```
12 mm. (½")      22 mm. (⅞")
                 18 mm. (¾")
96 mm. (3¾")     96 mm. (3¾")

Back legs        Front legs
```

Fig. 2 Joints in back legs (left) and front legs (right). Recess in the bottom of the front legs is 41 mm. (1⁹⁄₁₆ in.) deep and 96 mm. (3¾ in.) high

Fig. 3 Division panels and lippings are cut to fit around the front top rail

Fig. 4 Figures in brackets indicate Parts List reference to large drawer sizes

the centre-line of the long drawer.

Cut the wooden top (18) to size, lay it in position on the framework and screw through the two layers using 2½ in. No. 10 countersunk screws.

Lay the steel top (27) on the wooden top, butt-jointing separate pieces together if necessary.

Drill and countersink clearance holes for 1¼ in. countersunk screws and screw the steel top and wooden top together.

Cut front lipping (28) to size; screw it to the wooden top, flush with the steel top.

Position the vice, drill the fixing-bolt holes and bolt in position. The rear jaw should slightly oversail the front lipping.

Drawers

Cut and plane both the small and the large drawer parts (19–26) to size.

Cut all joints as in fig. 4. The drawer backs are set 50 mm. (2 in.) in from the ends of the sides. Cut grooves 9 mm. (⅜ in.) deep in the drawer fronts and sides, to receive the drawer bottoms. These are 4 mm. (⅛ in.) wide in small drawers, 6 mm. (¼ in.) wide in the large drawer, and 9 mm. (⅜ in.) up from the bottom.

The small drawer fronts are 9 mm. (⅜ in.) higher than the sides, to act as stops. The front and sides of the large drawer are equal in height. Glue two small blocks to the lower drawer shelf, 18 mm. (¾ in.) in from the front edge, to act as drawer stops.

Assemble the drawers dry to test the fit of the joints, glue and pin them together, check that they are square and allow to dry. Cut the drawer bottoms to slide into the grooves and lightly grease running surfaces with candle wax. Radius drawer-front edges. Fit handles.

Design for a small workbench

THE BENCH TOP is 610 mm. (24 in.) wide, 1220 mm. (4 ft) long and 920 mm. ($36\frac{1}{4}$ in.) above the floor; it is fitted with a Record No. 1 mechanic's vice at an elbow height of 1066 mm. (42 in.).

If the user's elbow height is not about 1066 mm. (42 in.), adjust the bench height accordingly by altering the length of the bench legs.

Timber connectors—available from most builders' merchants—can be used as an alternative to the housed joints in fig. 1, provided the 75 and 145 mm. (3 and 5 in.) coach bolts are increased to 100 and 150 mm. (4 and 6 in.) and rails (3) are shortened by 12 mm. ($\frac{1}{2}$ in.).

Construction

Cut legs (1), side rails (2) and front and back rails (3) to size.

Cut housings in the legs to receive side, front and back rails: 12 mm. ($\frac{1}{2}$ in.) deep on narrow edge, 6 mm. ($\frac{1}{4}$ in.) deep on wide edge, and 150 mm. (6 in.) from the bottom of each leg.

Dry-fit side rails and legs together, to make two side frames. Place the side frames back and check that they are square and flush with each other.

Cramp the joints of each side frame together and drill 9 mm. ($\frac{3}{8}$ in.) dia. holes for 125 mm. (5 in.) coach bolts, as in fig. 1. Insert the bolts and tighten the nuts and washers sufficiently to grip the joint.

Dry-fit and cramp the side frames to the front and back rails and drill 9 mm. ($\frac{3}{8}$ in.) dia. holes through the joints, as in fig. 1. Insert 75 mm. (3 in.) coach bolts and tighten nuts and washers sufficiently to grip the joints.

Check for square and tighten all nuts.

Cut the bench top (5) to size.

Cramp the bench top to the framework, fix the position of the vice and drill the fixing-bolt holes. If the bolts foul the rail underneath, cut away the top edge of it. The rear jaw of the vice should slightly oversail the front of the bench.

Drill and countersink clearance holes for $2\frac{1}{2}$ in. countersunk screws, and screw the bench top to the front and side rails.

Cut the shelf (4) to size and cut out the corners to fit around the legs.

Drill and countersink clearance holes for $1\frac{1}{2}$ in. countersunk screws in the shelf, and fix it to the upper edges of the lower rails. Bolt the vice in position.

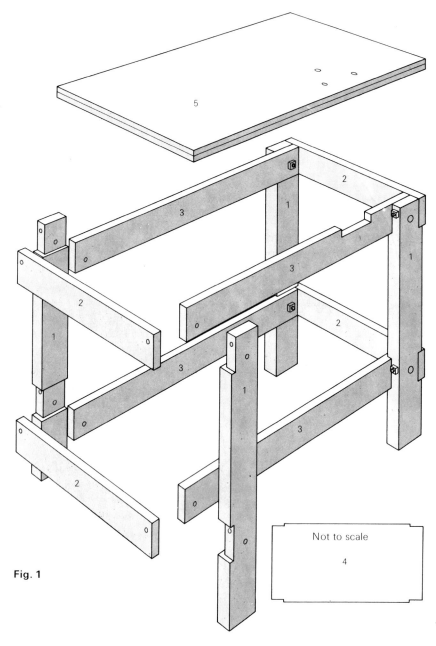

Not to scale

4

Fig. 1

PARTS LIST

No.	Name	Qty.	Long	Wide	Thick	Material
1	Legs	4	884 mm. ($34\frac{3}{4}$")	96 mm. ($3\frac{3}{4}$")	46 mm. ($1\frac{3}{4}$")	softwood
2	Side rails	4	605 mm. ($23\frac{3}{4}$")	96 mm. ($3\frac{3}{4}$")	28 mm. ($1\frac{1}{16}$")	softwood
3	Front and back rails	4	1160 mm. ($45\frac{3}{4}$")	96 mm. ($3\frac{3}{4}$")	28 mm. ($1\frac{1}{16}$")	softwood
4	Shelf	1	1220 mm. (48")	530 mm. (21")	18 mm. ($\frac{3}{4}$")	chipboard
5	Bench top (two layers)	2	1220 mm. (48")	610 mm. (24")	18 mm. ($\frac{3}{4}$")	chipboard

Hardware One Record No. 1 mechanic's vice; eight 75×9 mm. ($3 \times \frac{3}{8}$") dia. coach bolts, nuts and washers: eight 125×9 mm. ($5 \times \frac{3}{8}$") dia. coach bolts, nuts and washers; 12 $2\frac{1}{2}$" No. 12 steel countersunk screws; ten $1\frac{1}{2}$" No. 10 steel countersunk screws
Note Dimensions are finished sizes. Measurements in brackets are imperial sizes

Simple wood-joints and coach bolts make a rigid fixing for the leg-frame construction

Tool racks

Simple but effective tool racks can be made from short pieces of softwood fixed behind the workbench.

A rack suitable for a set of five ring spanners can be made using a $220 \times 95 \times 28$ mm. ($8\frac{3}{4} \times 3\frac{3}{4} \times 1\frac{1}{8}$ in.) softwood batten. Cut five equally spaced slots 18 mm. ($\frac{3}{4}$ in.) deep to suit the different thicknesses of the spanners, as in fig. 2. To hold the spanners horizontally, cut the slots at an angle of 15° and fix the rack to the wall or backboard so that the slots slope down from front to back.

The basic design can be used to make racks for a variety of other tools.

For awkwardly shaped tools such as hacksaws, grease-guns and calipers, let short lengths of 9–12 mm. ($\frac{3}{8}$–$\frac{1}{2}$ in.) dowelling into the wall or backboard.

Paint the racks black, or finish them with two coats of clear polyurethane.

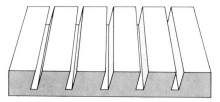

Fig. 2 A home-made rack for ring spanners

HOW A CAR WORKS

*Understand how a car works and you will
appreciate the design and skill that have
produced it. You can also identify its faults or,
where necessary, explain to a garage what
may be wrong. This section is a step-by-step
explanation of the mechanics of a car,
describing the construction and function of
each basic component.*

CONTENTS

Mechanics of the car

Seven steps to understanding how it works

THE MASS of tubes, pipes, wires and components scrambled together under the bonnet of a car can present a bewildering picture.

The average family saloon is assembled from over 13,000 different parts—1500 of them synchronised to move together—many of them working to within tolerances of 0·0005 in. or less. Nearly 60 different materials go into a car's construction—varying from steel to straw-board, from nickel to nylon.

The understanding of a car's mechanics can be simplified by splitting it up into seven groups; for despite the enormous range of differences in styling, performance and cost, modern cars follow the same principles.

Whatever the make of car, this section of the book explains the principles of its operation and provides an understanding of any faults which may arise.

The economical life of the average car is 8 years or 80,000 miles of motoring. Well cared for, the same car could go on for a few more years.

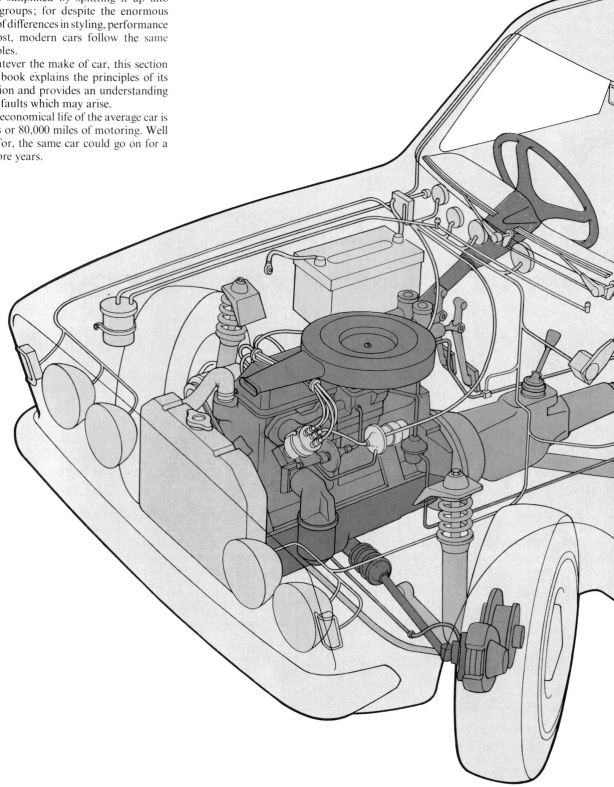

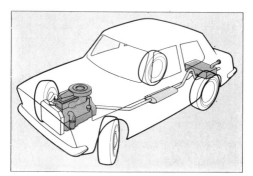

Engine Temperatures of over 700°C (1300°F) are produced inside the engine. Only a quarter of this heat is converted into power: the remainder is dissipated to the cooling and exhaust systems. An engine has 120–150 moving parts that need to be separated by oil to operate efficiently

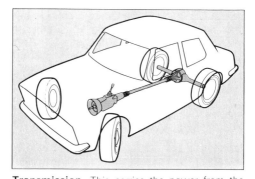

Transmission This carries the power from the engine to the wheels. It includes the gearbox, which provides the means of selecting the appropriate speed to turn a corner or climb a hill, and the clutch to disengage the gears. A motorist driving through the outskirts of a large city and making a journey of 50 miles might have to change gear more than 500 times

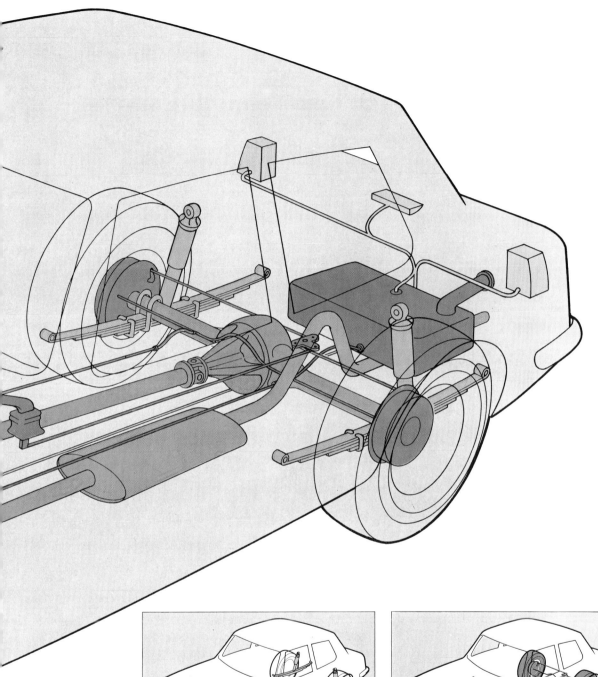

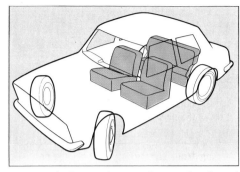

Bodywork Few modern cars have a chassis, and it is the bodywork that holds the car together. The average car uses about 400 sq. ft of sheet metal, varying in thickness between 0·015 and 0·035 in. The bodywork must be able to withstand immense stresses while the car is in motion and absorb collision-impact energy by controlled collapse

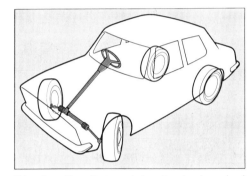

Steering The effort needed on the steering wheel to turn an average-sized car round in a tight circle varies from 10 to 20 lb. Power-assisted steering can reduce this effort to mere ounces. But without the sophistication of modern steering equipment, the weight of the average car ($\frac{3}{4}$ ton) would make it too difficult for a driver to manipulate

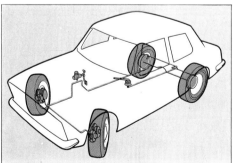

Suspension Modern suspension systems of springs, torsion bars and dampers, moving at 1000–1200 times a minute, help to cushion occupants against the irregularities in the road surface and make driving conditions acceptable

Wheels, tyres and brakes After travelling 60,000 miles, an average of six years' motoring, each wheel has turned 95 million times. In stopping a car from 60 mph, brakes generate enough heat to boil 2 pints of water

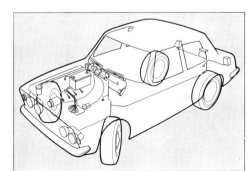

Electrics A 12 volt battery provides the primary source of power to start the engine. The coil boosts this to 30,000 volts. The system also includes the starter motor, lights, heater, windscreen wipers and other devices

Looking inside the engine

How the engine produces power

THE ENGINE is the powerhouse of the car. It converts the heat produced by burning fuel into mechanical energy to turn the wheels. The fuel, normally a mixture of petrol and air, is burnt in closed cylinders inside the engine—hence the term 'internal combustion'.

Petrol and air are mixed in the carburettor and drawn into a combustion chamber at the top of each cylinder. Pistons, inside the cylinders, compress the mixture, which is then ignited by a spark-plug. As the mixture burns it expands, forcing the piston down on its power stroke.

The up-and-down movement of the pistons is transformed into rotary movement to drive the crankshaft, which in turn transmits power to the wheels through the clutch, gearbox and final drive. Connecting rods link the pistons to the crankshaft.

A camshaft, driven by the crankshaft, controls inlet and exhaust valves at the top of each cylinder.

Initial impetus to set the engine in motion comes from the starter motor. This is connected to a starter ring which is fitted around the edge of the flywheel—a heavy disc bolted to the end of the crankshaft.

The starter motor, which is geared to the flywheel, is operated electrically and turns the flywheel and crankshaft, which starts the pistons and connecting rods moving up and down.

The flywheel smooths out the power impulses of the pistons and gives a relatively smooth rotation of the crankshaft.

Because of the heat produced by an internal combustion engine, the metal parts would seize without a cooling system.

In most cars, water is circulated through channels in the engine called a water-jacket. The hot water then passes through a radiator where the heat is dispersed to the atmosphere. This dispersal of heat is speeded by a fan, which draws cooling air through the radiator.

Other cars, mostly those with engines at the rear, are cooled by air which circulates over fins cast in the cylinder head. These fins increase the contact area with the atmosphere.

To prevent wear and overheating, the engine has a lubrication system. Oil, kept in a sump underneath the cylinder block, is pumped around the engine.

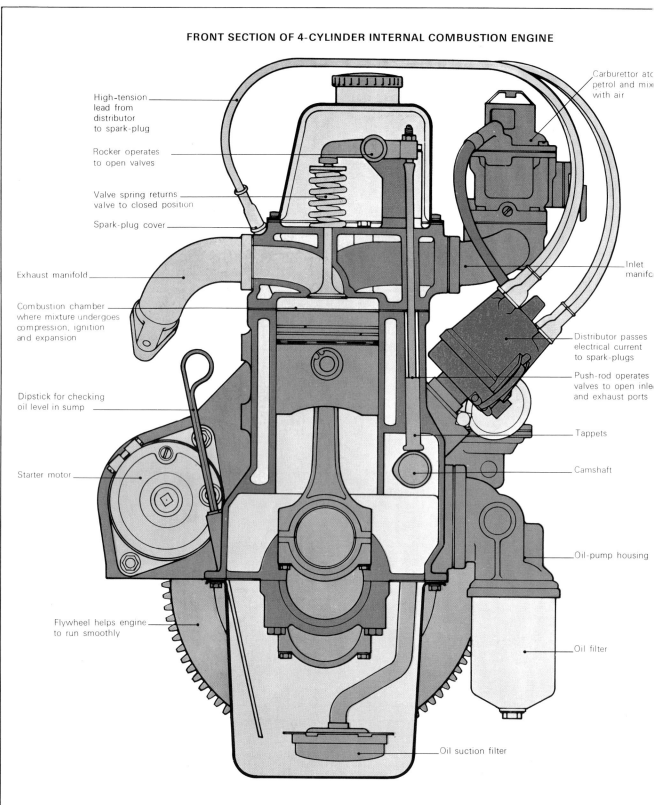

FRONT SECTION OF 4-CYLINDER INTERNAL COMBUSTION ENGINE

High-tension lead from distributor to spark-plug

Rocker operates to open valves

Valve spring returns valve to closed position

Spark-plug cover

Exhaust manifold

Combustion chamber where mixture undergoes compression, ignition and expansion

Dipstick for checking oil level in sump

Starter motor

Flywheel helps engine to run smoothly

Carburettor atc petrol and mix with air

Inlet manifo

Distributor passes electrical current to spark-plugs

Push-rod operates valves to open inle and exhaust ports

Tappets

Camshaft

Oil-pump housing

Oil filter

Oil suction filter

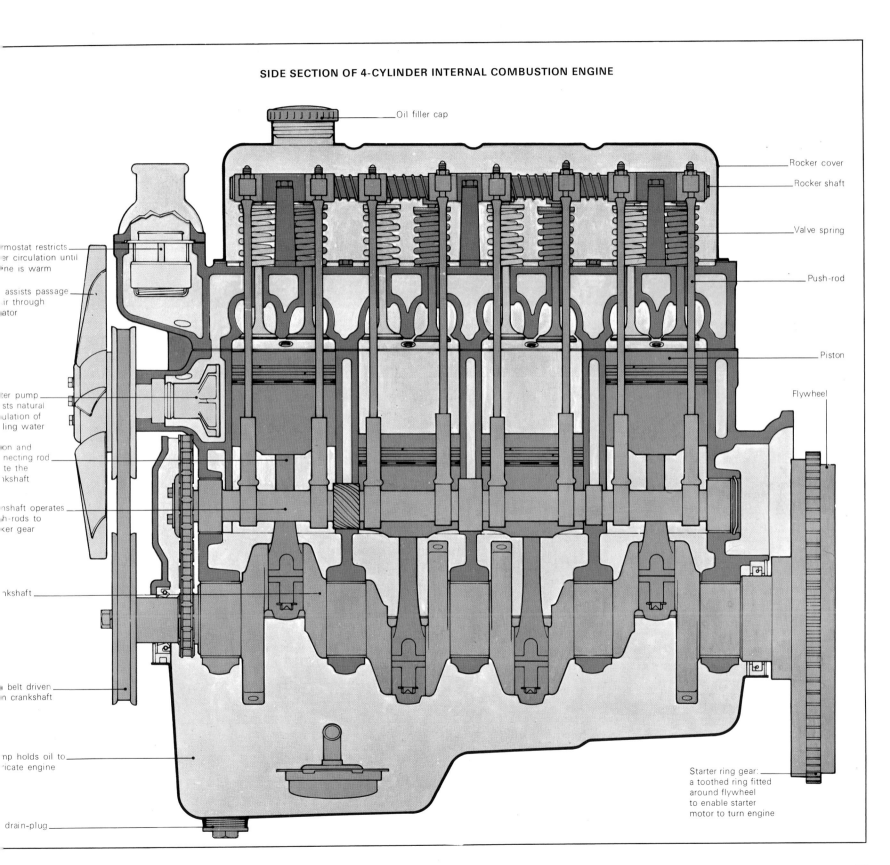

SIDE SECTION OF 4-CYLINDER INTERNAL COMBUSTION ENGINE

Oil filler cap

Rocker cover

Rocker shaft

Valve spring

Push-rod

Piston

Flywheel

...rmostat restricts
...er circulation until
...ne is warm

...assists passage
...ir through
...ator

...ter pump
...sts natural
...ulation of
...ling water

...on and
...necting rod
...te the
...nkshaft

...nshaft operates
...h-rods to
...ker gear

...nkshaft

...belt driven
...n crankshaft

...mp holds oil to
...ricate engine

...drain-plug

Starter ring gear:
a toothed ring fitted
around flywheel
to enable starter
motor to turn engine

Four views of a typical engine

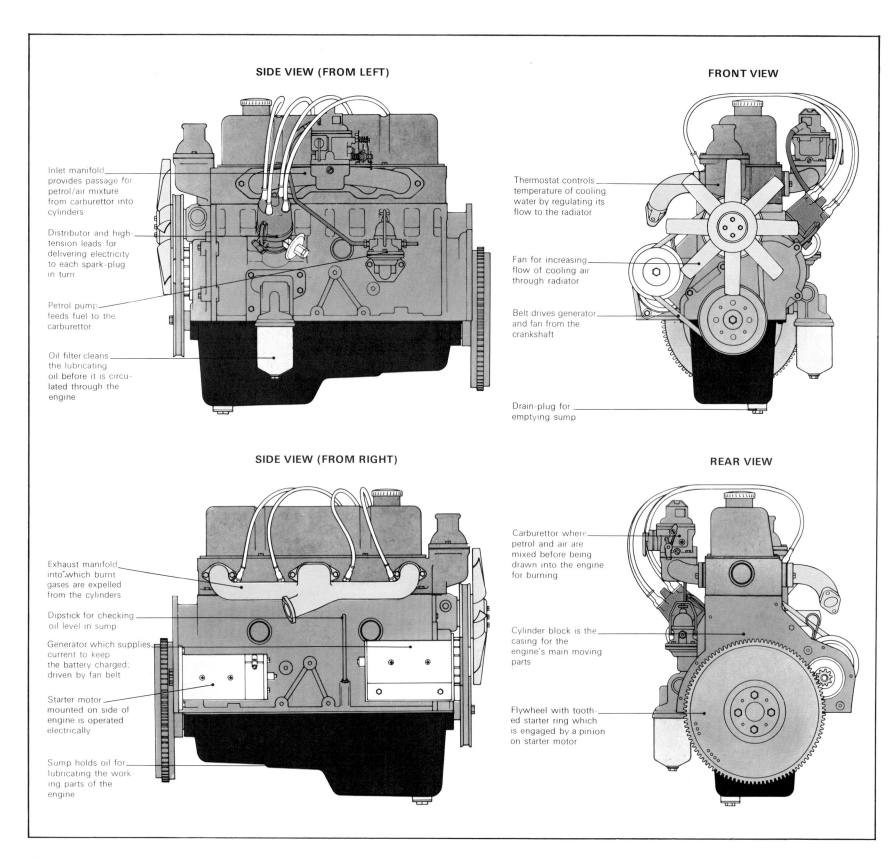

SIDE VIEW (FROM LEFT)

Inlet manifold provides passage for petrol/air mixture from carburettor into cylinders

Distributor and high-tension leads for delivering electricity to each spark-plug in turn

Petrol pump feeds fuel to the carburettor

Oil filter cleans the lubricating oil before it is circulated through the engine

FRONT VIEW

Thermostat controls temperature of cooling water by regulating its flow to the radiator

Fan for increasing flow of cooling air through radiator

Belt drives generator and fan from the crankshaft

Drain-plug for emptying sump

SIDE VIEW (FROM RIGHT)

Exhaust manifold into which burnt gases are expelled from the cylinders

Dipstick for checking oil level in sump

Generator which supplies current to keep the battery charged; driven by fan belt

Starter motor mounted on side of engine is operated electrically

Sump holds oil for lubricating the working parts of the engine

REAR VIEW

Carburettor where petrol and air are mixed before being drawn into the engine for burning

Cylinder block is the casing for the engine's main moving parts

Flywheel with tooth-ed starter ring which is engaged by a pinion on starter motor

Separating the main parts

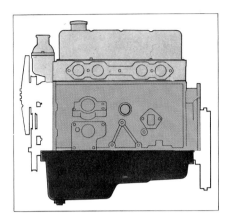

THE ENGINE must be a rigid structure in order to withstand the heavy loads applied to the crankshaft bearings and other internal parts.

It is made of two basic parts bolted together: the upper is the cylinder head, the lower is the cylinder block, which contains the crankshaft assembly. Both the head and the block are usually made of cast iron, but aluminium is an alternative material for lightness and good heat dissipation.

Practically all modern engines have their valves incorporated in the cylinder head and are known as overhead-valve (OHV) engines.

In the cylinder head are a combustion chamber, two valve ports and two valves, for each cylinder.

The engine draws in the petrol/air mixture through one set of valves (the inlets) and expels burnt gases through the other (the exhausts). On top of the cylinder head is the valve-operating gear.

The cylinder block is usually in one piece with the crankcase. It contains the cylinders and carries the crankshaft, to which are attached the connecting rods and pistons. It may also contain the camshaft by which the valves are opened and closed.

Alternatively, the camshaft may be carried on the cylinder head, in which case the engine is known as an overhead-camshaft (OHC) unit.

Both the cylinder head and the block contain passages, known as the water jackets, through which water circulates to cool the engine.

The sump, which is the reservoir for the engine lubricating oil, is made of sheet steel, cast aluminium or magnesium, and is bolted to the bottom of the crankcase.

A cover, usually of similar material to the sump, is fitted over the valve gear to exclude dust and retain oil.

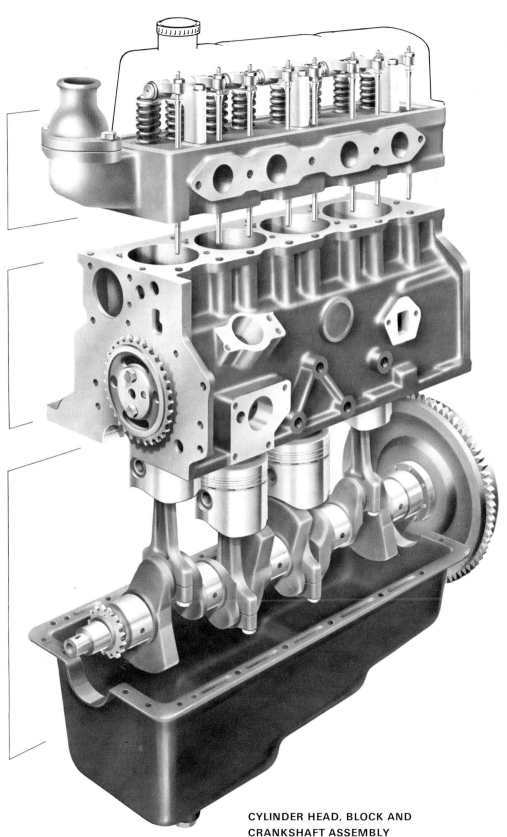

Cylinder head This carries the valves, the rocker gear for opening them and springs for closing them. The head also contains the inlet and exhaust ports and, usually, the combustion chambers

Cylinder block The largest part of the engine; it has bores for the pistons, passages for water to cool the cylinders, oilways for the lubrication system and tunnels for push-rods if these are used to operate the rocker gear

Crankshaft assembly Pistons moving up and down in the cylinders are linked to the rotating crankshaft by connecting rods. The crankshaft is carried in main bearings at the base of the cylinder block. At one end of the crankshaft is the flywheel, which smooths out the power impulses of the individual cylinders

CYLINDER HEAD, BLOCK AND CRANKSHAFT ASSEMBLY

Engine/how heat becomes driving power

Fuel burning

HEAT-ENERGY produced by the combustion of petrol and air is converted into mechanical power by the pistons, connecting rods and crankshaft of an engine. The engine's efficiency depends on how much of this energy becomes useful power.

The more petrol/air mixture that can be drawn into a cylinder, and the more it can be compressed, the higher will be the specific output of the engine.

A comparison of the volumes of gas in the cylinder before and after compression takes place is expressed as the compression ratio. The average family car has a compression ratio of about 9:1, which means gas in the cylinder is compressed to one-ninth of its original volume.

The compressed mixture, when ignited by a spark, should burn rapidly but progressively and smoothly across the top of the piston. It should not detonate.

If the compression ratio is too high for the grade of petrol being used, the burning will not be progressive. Some of the mixture furthest away from the spark-plug will explode violently, or detonate. This is known as knocking or pinking (see p. 64).

Apart from the loss of power, this detonation can cause overheating and if allowed to continue will damage the engine.

Loss of efficiency and overheating can also occur in an engine from pre-ignition—ignition before the timed sparking occurs at the spark-plug. This can arise from defective or incorrect spark-plugs, or it can be caused by deposits in the combustion chamber which have grown hot and glow continuously. Pre-ignition, like knocking, can cause extensive damage, as well as reduce engine power.

The action cycle in most car engines is the 4-stroke or Otto cycle, with the power stroke of the piston occurring once every four strokes. During one revolution of the crankshaft, the piston descends on its induction stroke and rises on its compression stroke. During the next revolution of the shaft, the piston is forced down on its power stroke, then rises on its exhaust stroke to expel burnt gases.

Since the inlet and exhaust valves must open only once in each cycle, the camshaft operating them is driven at half the speed of the crankshaft, which makes two revolutions during the 4-stroke cycle.

A few makes of cars are fitted with 2-stroke engines, in which combustion takes place on each downward stroke of the piston, or once in each revolution of the crankshaft. This cycle is basically simpler, but less efficient, than the 4-stroke cycle.

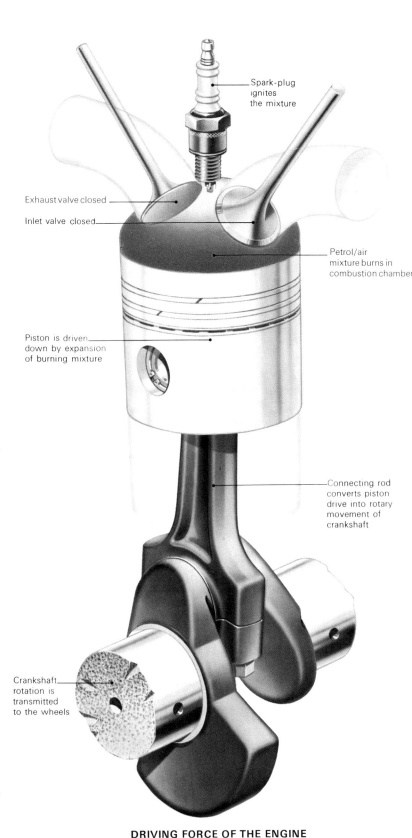

Spark-plug ignites the mixture

Exhaust valve closed

Inlet valve closed

Petrol/air mixture burns in combustion chamber

Piston is driven down by expansion of burning mixture

Connecting rod converts piston drive into rotary movement of crankshaft

Crankshaft rotation is transmitted to the wheels

DRIVING FORCE OF THE ENGINE

The 4-stroke cycle

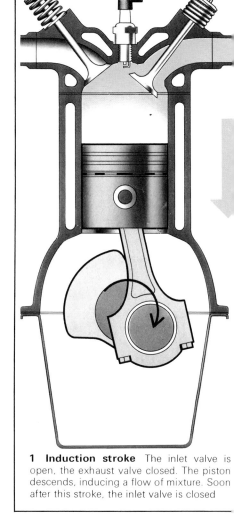

1 Induction stroke The inlet valve is open, the exhaust valve closed. The piston descends, inducing a flow of mixture. Soon after this stroke, the inlet valve is closed

Compression ratio This is the ratio between gas in the cylinder before and after compression. If the gas is reduced to one-ninth of its volume, the compression ratio is 9:1

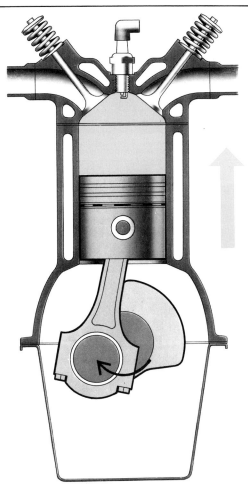

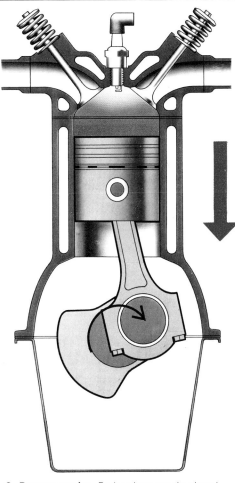

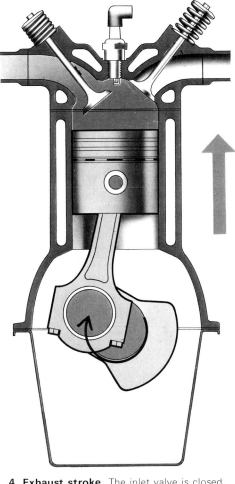

2 Compression stroke Both inlet and exhaust valves are closed. The rising piston compresses the mixture in the combustion chamber and compression heat vaporises the mixture

3 Power stroke Both valves remain closed. The compressed gas is ignited by a spark from the spark-plug. Expansion of burning gas drives the piston down. Exhaust valve opens

4 Exhaust stroke The inlet valve is closed, and exhaust valve open. The piston rises to expel burnt gases, inlet valve opens, exhaust valve closes. Then the cycle restarts

Valve overlap speeds the flow of gases

IT MIGHT be expected that valves would open and close when the piston is at the top or bottom of its stroke. But in practice there is an overlap in the timing of the valves.

The exhaust valve opens before the piston reaches the bottom of its stroke and closes after it reaches the top; the inlet valve opens before the top and closes after it reaches the bottom.

During the overlap period, both valves are open together, and the momentum of gases flowing in and out of the cylinder helps to fill the cylinder with petrol/air mixture and complete the release of exhaust gases.

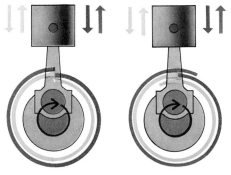

Arrows indicate strokes of piston and related coloured lines shows period valves are open. Theoretical timing (left) permits no overlap

Firing order of the cylinders

The webs on the crankshaft are arranged to give the best balance as well as to ensure that firing strokes occur regularly. In a 4-cylinder engine, if the firing order were to be 1, 2, 3, 4, the crankshaft and engine mountings would be subjected to considerable stress and vibration. This stress is minimised by a firing order of 1, 2, 4, 3 or 1, 3, 4, 2

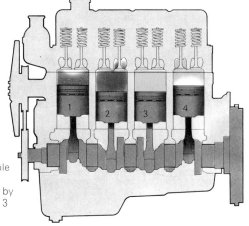

Engine/pistons and connecting rods

The driving force

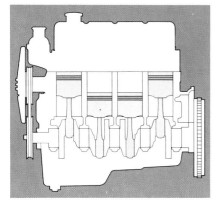

PISTONS, powered by the expansion of burning petrol/air mixture in the combustion chambers, provide the driving force of the engine.

In a medium-sized car, when the engine is running at maximum speed, each piston may be sliding up and down inside its cylinder as many as 100 times a second. Because of this rapid succession of stops and starts, the pistons must be strong yet light in weight. In most modern cars they are made of an aluminium alloy.

Heat generated by the combustion of the fuel causes expansion both in the pistons themselves and in the cylinders, which are of cast iron.

Piston rings seal the gap between the piston and the cylinder bore. Compression rings, usually two, prevent gases escaping past the piston into the crankcase; and a 'scraper' ring removes excess oil from the cylinder wall and returns it to the sump.

Power is transmitted from the pistons to the crankshaft—and at the same time converted to rotary motion—by the connecting rods and crankshaft. The connecting rods are usually steel forgings.

The top end of each connecting rod, called the small-end, is fitted inside the piston to the gudgeon pin, which allows the rod to pivot as it moves up and down with the piston. The gudgeon pin, also known as the wrist pin, is usually hollow to save weight and is often located in the piston by two spring clips called circlips.

The bottom end of the connecting rod, called the big-end, is bolted to the crankshaft and follows a circular orbit, while the small-end follows the up-and-down movement of the piston.

A big-end may be split horizontally or obliquely. An oblique split, by reducing the width of the rod at its widest point, allows a larger connecting rod to be withdrawn upwards through the cylinder bore.

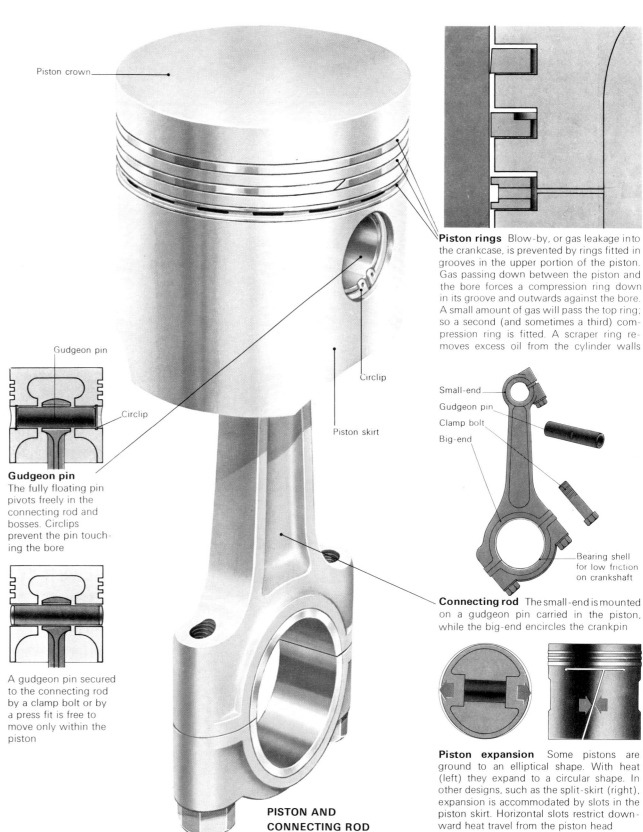

Gudgeon pin
The fully floating pin pivots freely in the connecting rod and bosses. Circlips prevent the pin touching the bore

A gudgeon pin secured to the connecting rod by a clamp bolt or by a press fit is free to move only within the piston

PISTON AND CONNECTING ROD

Piston rings Blow-by, or gas leakage into the crankcase, is prevented by rings fitted in grooves in the upper portion of the piston. Gas passing down between the piston and the bore forces a compression ring down in its groove and outwards against the bore. A small amount of gas will pass the top ring; so a second (and sometimes a third) compression ring is fitted. A scraper ring removes excess oil from the cylinder walls

Connecting rod The small-end is mounted on a gudgeon pin carried in the piston, while the big-end encircles the crankpin

Piston expansion Some pistons are ground to an elliptical shape. With heat (left) they expand to a circular shape. In other designs, such as the split-skirt (right), expansion is accommodated by slots in the piston skirt. Horizontal slots restrict downward heat travel from the piston head

Engine/crankshaft

Transmitting the power

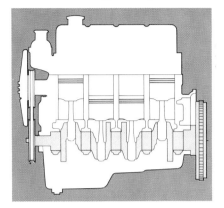

THE CRANKSHAFT, revolving in most cars at up to 6000 times a minute, transmits engine power to the gearbox, and so to the wheels. It is cast or forged in a single piece, and in places is machined to an accuracy of less than a thousandth of an inch.

The main parts of the shaft are the journals, which rotate in, and are supported by, the main bearings; the crankpins, which rotate in the big-end bearings of the connecting rods linking them with the pistons; and the webs, or cranks, which join the journals to the crankpins and are shaped so that they serve as balance weights for smoother running.

The flywheel, a heavy and carefully balanced disc fitted at the gearbox end of the crankshaft, helps smooth running by maintaining a steady rate of turning.

With the downward thrusts of the pistons giving repeated sudden thrusts to the crankshaft as the flywheel maintains its momentum, the shaft is subject to slight twisting and untwisting, known as torsional vibration. A damper—a metal disc incorporating a ring of rubber—is fitted to the front end of the crankshaft to help control torsional vibration.

The firing order of the cylinders is also important in making the crankshaft rotate smoothly. Counting the cylinder nearest the fan as No. 1, the firing order in a 4-cylinder engine is usually 1, 3, 4, 2 or 1, 2, 4, 3, so as to give reasonably even turning of the crankshaft.

On their firing strokes, the pistons push the crankshaft down; and on their other three strokes they are forced up or pulled down by the continuing rotation of the crankshaft. The crankpins are set at different angles to the shaft so as to give a uniform spacing of the firing impulses.

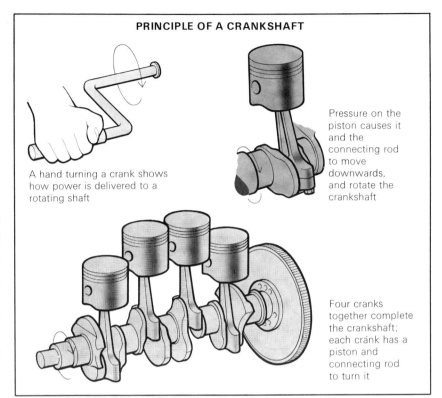

PRINCIPLE OF A CRANKSHAFT

A hand turning a crank shows how power is delivered to a rotating shaft

Pressure on the piston causes it and the connecting rod to move downwards, and rotate the crankshaft

Four cranks together complete the crankshaft; each crank has a piston and connecting rod to turn it

ARRANGEMENT OF THE CRANKS

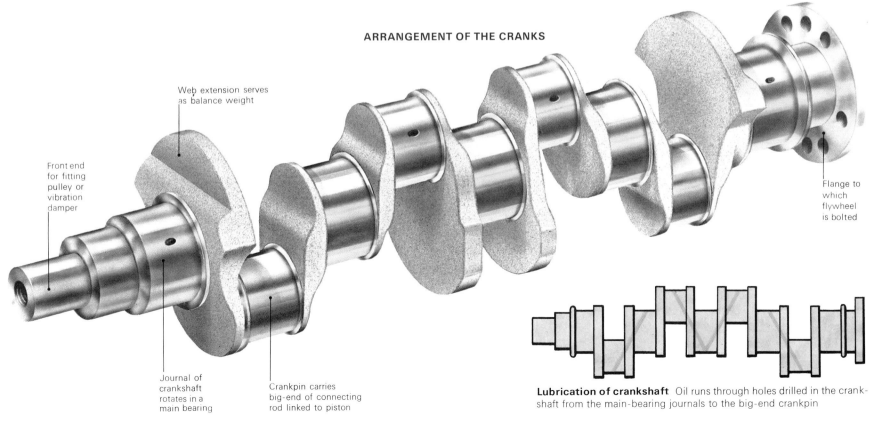

Web extension serves as balance weight

Front end for fitting pulley or vibration damper

Flange to which flywheel is bolted

Journal of crankshaft rotates in a main bearing

Crankpin carries big-end of connecting rod linked to piston

Lubrication of crankshaft Oil runs through holes drilled in the crankshaft from the main-bearing journals to the big-end crankpin

Engine/cylinder block

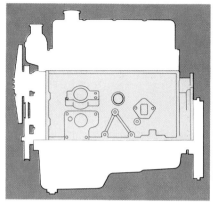

THE CYLINDER BLOCK, the main shell of the engine, is usually combined with the crankcase in one casting.

Most blocks are made of cast iron because it is fairly strong, cheap and easy to machine for mass-production. The block's strength can be improved by alloying cast iron with other metals.

Some cylinder blocks are made of light alloys, which makes them lighter and better for conducting heat; but they are more costly.

They are also too soft to provide a working surface for the cylinder bores, and separate cast-iron liners or sleeves must be inserted into the bores.

The water jacket—passages through which water circulates to cool the cylinders—is usually cast as an integral part of the cylinder block. It is linked with the corresponding water jacket of the cylinder head through openings at the top.

A block can be cracked by water expanding as it freezes in the jacket. Sometimes the expansion will dislodge the core plugs which seal holes required in the process of casting the cylinder block; but core plugs cannot be relied on to act as 'safety valves' in this way.

Cylinders can be arranged in one row (in-line), in two rows set at an angle (V engine) or set sideways in two rows, on either side of the crankshaft (flat or horizontally opposed). Most 4 and 6-cylinder engines are in-line.

The greater the number of cylinders in an engine, the smoother will be the running, particularly at low engine speeds. In some larger cars, with six or eight cylinders, the V-6 or V-8 layout is used.

Horizontally opposed cylinders are used in only a few engine designs, frequently those with engines at the rear, where space is limited. However, one air-cooled range is produced in very large numbers.

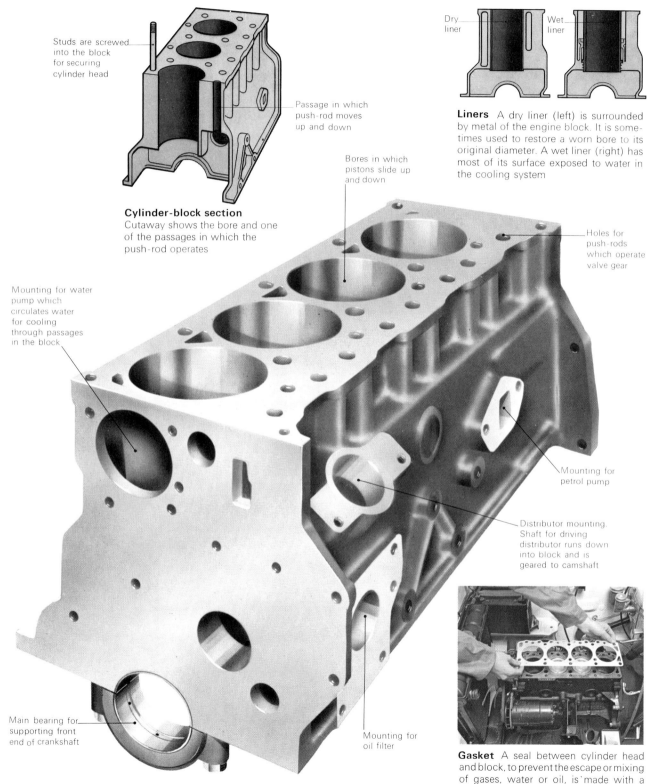

Studs are screwed into the block for securing cylinder head

Passage in which push-rod moves up and down

Cylinder-block section
Cutaway shows the bore and one of the passages in which the push-rod operates

Bores in which pistons slide up and down

Liners A dry liner (left) is surrounded by metal of the engine block. It is sometimes used to restore a worn bore to its original diameter. A wet liner (right) has most of its surface exposed to water in the cooling system

Dry liner   Wet liner

Holes for push-rods which operate valve gear

Mounting for water pump which circulates water for cooling through passages in the block

Mounting for petrol pump

Distributor mounting. Shaft for driving distributor runs down into block and is geared to camshaft

Main bearing for supporting front end of crankshaft

Mounting for oil filter

CYLINDER BLOCK OF 4-CYLINDER IN-LINE ENGINE

Gasket A seal between cylinder head and block, to prevent the escape or mixing of gases, water or oil, is made with a gasket—often asbestos with a thin steel or copper covering

Cylinder head and valves

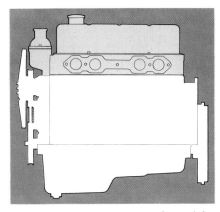

THE MATERIAL most commonly used for the cylinder head of an overhead-valve engine is cast iron. An alternative used in many engines is aluminium alloy.

Aluminium alloy, although more expensive, is used on high-performance engines, because it weighs less and is a better conductor of heat. But an aluminium cylinder head needs inserts to strengthen the valve seats and guides, and may present difficulties in making an effective joint with a cast-iron cylinder block, as the two metals expand at different rates.

The lower face of the cylinder head is machined flat to mate with the upper face of the cylinder block. A gasket usually seals the two surfaces, but a few designs rely on a perfect face-to-face gas seal, with small rubber seals to prevent any seepage of water from the cooling system.

Any distortion of the faces of the head and block can lead to gasket failure which will result in gas or water leakage or oil contamination. Distortion can be caused by running an engine with insufficient water in the cooling system.

Because of the high temperatures they can reach, the combustion chambers and exhaust ports must be adequately cooled.

While the inlet manifold can be of aluminium, the exhaust manifold must be of a heat-resistant material such as cast iron or steel.

Cooling the valves

Inlet valves are usually larger than exhaust valves, as the gas flow into the cylinder is slower than the flow of exhaust gas which escapes under pressure.

The exhaust valve may become red hot when the engine is driven hard, so it has to be made of heat-resistant metal. It gets rid of excess heat through its seating when it is closed, and through the guide in which its stem slides.

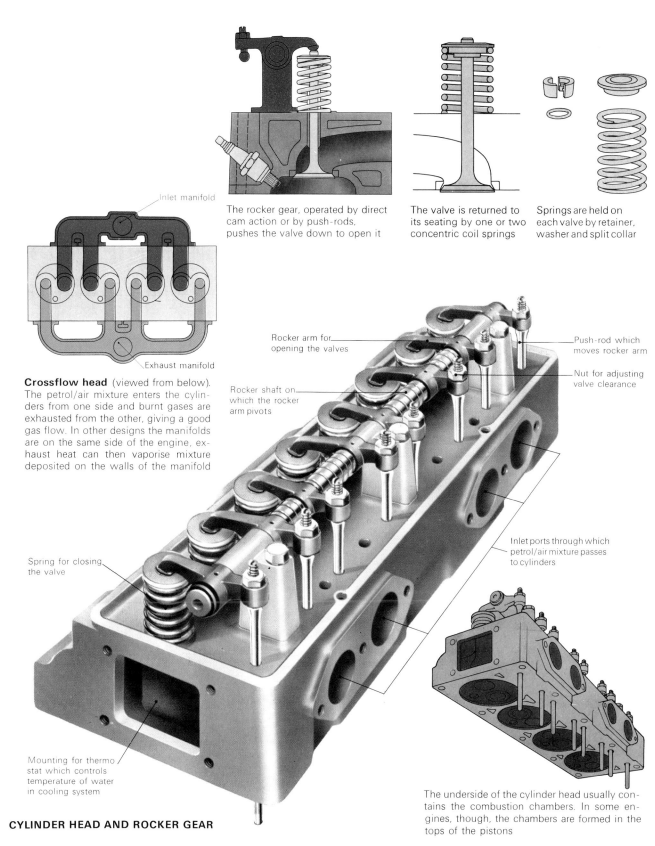

The rocker gear, operated by direct cam action or by push-rods, pushes the valve down to open it

The valve is returned to its seating by one or two concentric coil springs

Springs are held on each valve by retainer, washer and split collar

Inlet manifold

Exhaust manifold

Crossflow head (viewed from below). The petrol/air mixture enters the cylinders from one side and burnt gases are exhausted from the other, giving a good gas flow. In other designs the manifolds are on the same side of the engine, exhaust heat can then vaporise mixture deposited on the walls of the manifold

Rocker arm for opening the valves

Rocker shaft on which the rocker arm pivots

Push-rod which moves rocker arm

Nut for adjusting valve clearance

Inlet ports through which petrol/air mixture passes to cylinders

Spring for closing the valve

Mounting for thermostat which controls temperature of water in cooling system

CYLINDER HEAD AND ROCKER GEAR

The underside of the cylinder head usually contains the combustion chambers. In some engines, though, the chambers are formed in the tops of the pistons

Engine/how the valves open and close

Camshaft with push-rods

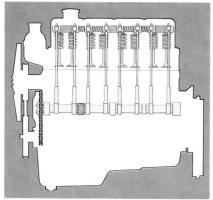

THE VALVE-OPERATING GEAR is designed so that it opens and closes each valve at the right point in the 4-stroke cycle, gives an adequate opening period to allow free gas flow, and operates quietly and reliably over a wide range of engine speeds.

There are several ways of meeting these requirements. Still widely used is the system with push-rods and rockers operated by a camshaft placed inside the cylinder block. The camshaft is driven by a chain (or set of gears) from the adjacent crankshaft, at half engine speed.

As the camshaft rotates, each cam in turn lifts a tappet and push-rod, causing the corresponding rocker to pivot and push the valve down. The valve is closed by a spring when further rotation of the cam allows the tappet to descend. Some engines have two springs for each valve.

For efficient operation, the valves must return fully to their seats. To ensure this, a gap known as tappet clearance is allowed between the closed valve and its rocker. This allows the valve gear to expand when it is hot.

Tappet clearances vary considerably on different makes of engine, but it is important that they should be adjusted to the precise dimension recommended. Too great a clearance results in noise, too small in premature failure.

As the ignition system must provide a spark at each spark-plug at the right time in relation to the valve operation, the distributor, which supplies high-voltage current to the plugs, is usually gear-driven from the camshaft or by the crankshaft.

The camshaft is carried on three or five bearings mounted in the block. The cams are spaced around the camshaft at intervals to match the firing order (see p. 35). The profiles and timing of the cams have a major effect on the power output and fuel economy of the engine.

Camshaft This shaft is of either forged steel or cast iron, machined and hardened to give maximum resistance to wear of the flanks of the cams. The cams are spaced at intervals to match the firing order

Operating the valves A cam operates an overhead valve through a tappet, push-rod and rocker arm. As the tappet and push-rod are lifted, the rocker pivots and depresses the valve. Further rotation of the cam allows the tappet and push-rod to descend, allowing the valve to be closed by a spring

Alternative rocker gear Pressed-steel rocker arms on ball mountings are used on some engines

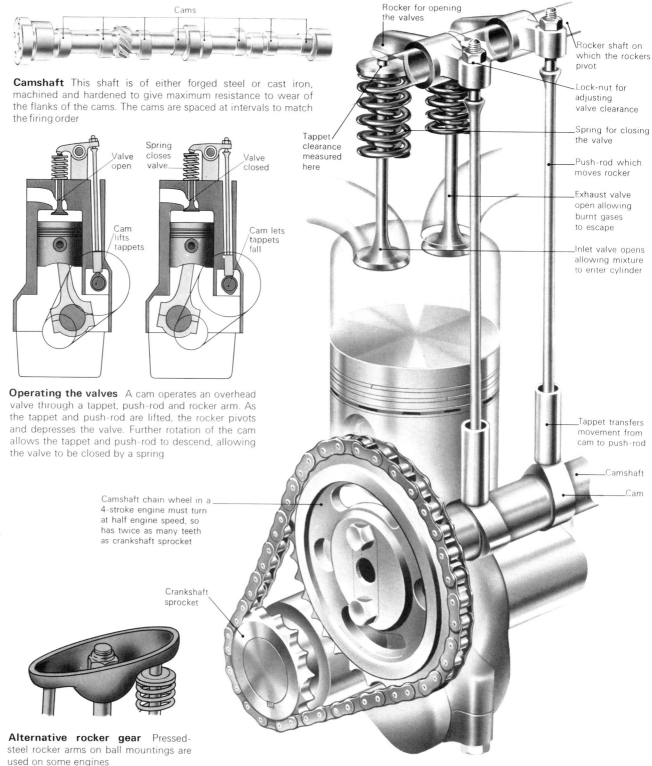

Cams

Rocker for opening the valves

Rocker shaft on which the rockers pivot

Lock-nut for adjusting valve clearance

Spring for closing the valve

Push-rod which moves rocker

Exhaust valve open allowing burnt gases to escape

Inlet valve opens allowing mixture to enter cylinder

Tappet transfers movement from cam to push-rod

Camshaft

Cam

Camshaft chain wheel in a 4-stroke engine must turn at half engine speed, so has twice as many teeth as crankshaft sprocket

Crankshaft sprocket

Tappet clearance measured here

Valve open

Spring closes valve

Valve closed

Cam lifts tappets

Cam lets tappets fall

TYPICAL VALVE GEAR USING PUSH-RODS

Single and double overhead camshafts

DESIGNERS strive to reduce the number of parts and weight of the valve-operating gear to obtain quiet operation at high speed and longer engine life. To do this, single or double overhead camshafts are used; they are located on the cylinder head.

The valves can be operated more directly from an overhead camshaft (that is, with fewer intervening parts) than from a camshaft placed in the crankcase.

A simple form of drive from the crankshaft to an overhead camshaft is by chain. But a long chain drive will tend to whip unless fitted with a tensioning device.

The type of tensioner used on most chain drives is a long and slightly curved steel strip or rubber-faced spring. This is bowed against the chain by a coil spring.

Another type consists of a synthetic rubber pad attached to a small spring-loaded piston operated by oil pressure.

A third type incorporates a ratchet and an idler sprocket on a spring-loaded slide.

Some racing-car engines use gear drives from the crankshaft to the camshaft, but these are inclined to be noisy.

Some of the latest overhead camshaft drives to be developed use a toothed rubber belt outside the engine casing.

These belts need no lubrication and are made of oil-resistant rubber moulded on to non-stretch cord. To prevent slip, the teeth are shaped to fit accurately into the teeth of the pulleys on the crankshaft and the camshaft.

Overhead camshaft designs have used rockers or fingers next to the camshaft to operate the valves, but the trend today is to eliminate rockers and place the valves directly under the cams.

To resist side thrust by the cam, an inverted bucket-shaped tappet is inserted between the cam and the valve stem. This tappet slides in a guide which is big enough to surround the valve-spring assembly.

Some designs of overhead camshaft use hydraulic tappets, which are self-adjusting and operate with no clearance. Hence there is no tappet noise.

Hydraulic tappets are not fitted to mass-produced cars in Britain, but they are fitted by some specialist firms and by certain continental manufacturers. They are in common use in push-rod engines fitted to American cars.

A hydraulic tappet is made in two parts (one sliding within the other), and oil, supplied under pressure, causes the tappet to lengthen and take up clearance when the engine is running.

Bucket tappets To protect the valve against side thrusts from the rotating cam of an overhead camshaft, a bucket tappet is placed between them. Clearance is adjusted by the insertion of shims (spacers), or by a key through a hole in the tappet side

Belt drive In some engines a belt instead of a chain drives the camshaft. Teeth on the inside are shaped to fit into the teeth of the pulleys on the camshaft and crankshaft

Single overhead camshaft The chain drive from the crankshaft can be direct or by two chains running over intermediate sprockets, depending on the length of the drive. The valves are operated either by cams and tappets (direct) or by cams and levers (finger-operated)

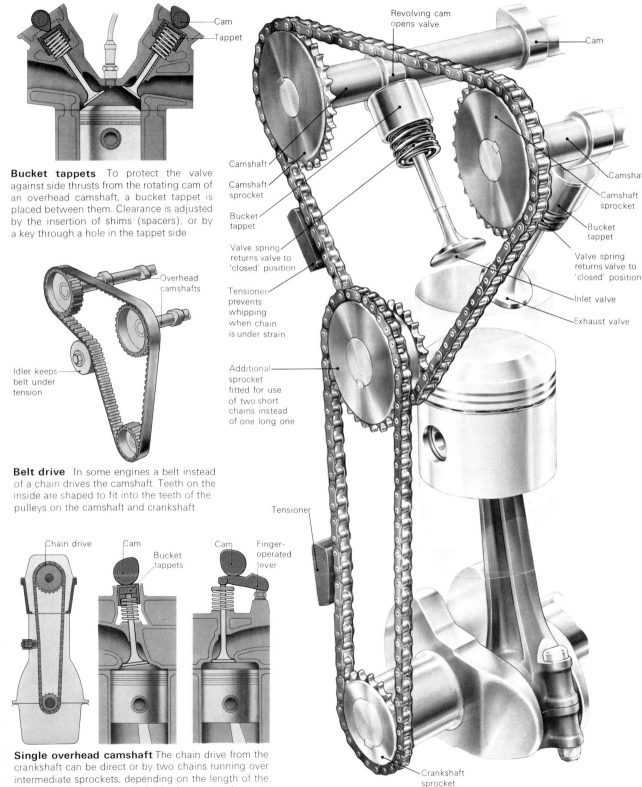

CHAIN DRIVE TO OVERHEAD CAMSHAFTS

Engine/variations in layout

THE SIMPLEST FORM of 4-stroke engine has a single cylinder, but this is not acceptable in a car because of the uneven torque (turning effort) which results from only one power stroke at every second revolution of the crankshaft, and because of the vibration that would be set up.

Uneven torque can be improved by the stored energy of a heavy flywheel, but this is insufficient in a 4-stroke engine to give smooth running at low speeds. There is no simple way of counterbalancing the up-and-down movement of the single piston.

To give reasonable smoothness, the minimum number of cylinders is two, providing one power stroke for each crankshaft revolution. This greatly improves the balance, compared with that of a single-cylinder engine, but the torque remains noticeably irregular at low speeds.

All British cars have at least four cylinders, and they provide one power stroke for each half revolution of the crankshaft. The cylinders can be arranged in-line, in V fashion, or horizontally opposed—that is, set sideways in two lines on either side of the crankshaft.

Torque and balance

An in-line 4-cylinder engine has evenly spaced power strokes and so gives reasonably smooth torque. It tends to produce some vibration, but this is largely suppressed by the rubber mountings on which the engine is fitted.

The torque of the compact V-4 can be as good as that of an in-line 4-cylinder, but this layout is fundamentally not as well balanced, whatever the angle between the banks of cylinders.

Hence the V-4 suffers from vibration which can be kept to an acceptable level only by incorporating an extra shaft which is counter-weighted to cancel out vibration of the crankshaft assembly.

The horizontally opposed 4-cylinder is more compact and better balanced than the in-line. These advantages are offset in some makes of car by the difficulty of access for working on the engine. Six cylinders give the best balance of in-line engines used in modern cars.

The V-6 is theoretically less smooth than the in-line, but both have an even torque delivery. So has the horizontally opposed 'six', which runs very smoothly but is costly to build.

Of the 8-cylinder variants, the V-8 is mainly used in modern cars. It is a compact, well-balanced engine with even torque. Some earlier cars had 'straight eights' (eight cylinders in-line), but their long crankshafts were prone to torsional vibration at high speeds.

THE 6-CYLINDER IN-LINE

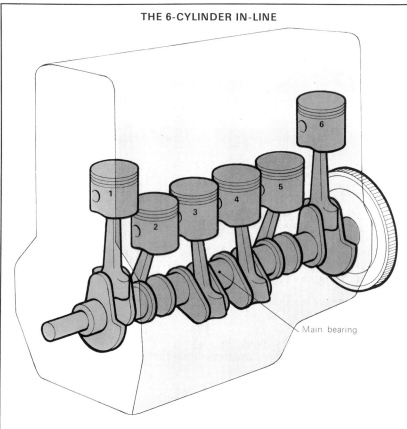

Main bearing

The 6-cylinder in-line engine, although longer and a little heavier than an in-line 'four', has two major advantages: its torque delivery is significantly smoother, because successive power strokes overlap; and its better mechanical balance means that vibration is negligible. Such engines have four or seven main bearings. The larger number of main bearings provides the crankshaft with better support against bending

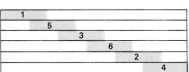

Power strokes (above, blue shading) overlap for smooth turning of crankshaft (diagrammatic end view, right)

PISTONS HORIZONTALLY OPPOSED

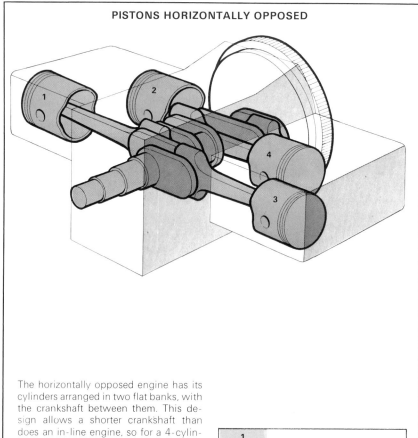

The horizontally opposed engine has its cylinders arranged in two flat banks, with the crankshaft between them. This design allows a shorter crankshaft than does an in-line engine, so for a 4-cylinder engine three main bearings are sufficient. Its size and shape make it better suited to installation at the rear than at the front. Any 4-stroke horizontally opposed or 'flat' engine has even firing impulses. In 4-cylinder or 6-cylinder forms the arrangement provides excellent mechanical balance; movement of a component in one direction is balanced by movement of a similar component in the opposite direction

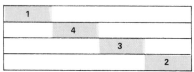

Crankshaft layout of flat 'four' (right) is usually similar to in-line 'four'. Firing and power strokes are shown above (blue)

THREE VARIATIONS OF V-ENGINES

The main advantages of the V-engine are that it can be made shorter than the in-line design, and that the short crankshaft is more rigid. This allows the engine to run smoothly at higher speeds. The V-8 engine needs only four crank-pins, provided they are placed at 90° intervals and are long enough to take two big-end bearings side by side. The shaft needs a main bearing between each pair of 'twinned' big-end bearings. V-6 engines are not as smooth as the V-8, which is extremely well balanced and provides four equally spaced power impulses in each crankshaft revolution

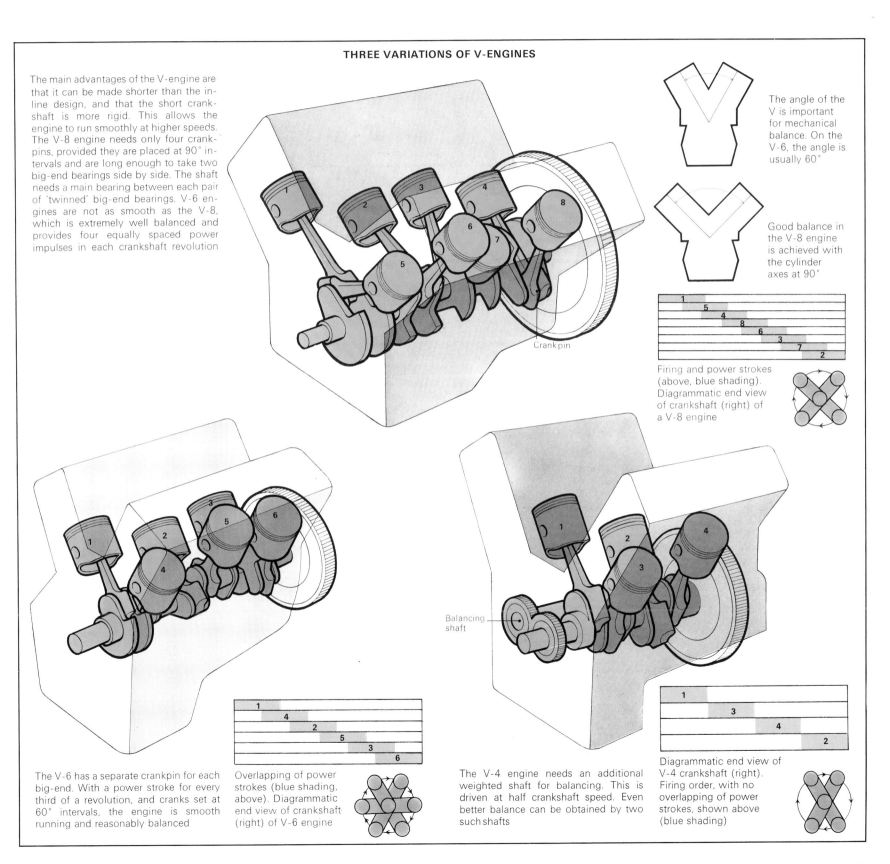

The angle of the V is important for mechanical balance. On the V-6, the angle is usually 60°

Good balance in the V-8 engine is achieved with the cylinder axes at 90°

Firing and power strokes (above, blue shading). Diagrammatic end view of crankshaft (right) of a V-8 engine

Crankpin

The V-6 has a separate crankpin for each big-end. With a power stroke for every third of a revolution, and cranks set at 60° intervals, the engine is smooth running and reasonably balanced

Overlapping of power strokes (blue shading, above). Diagrammatic end view of crankshaft (right) of V-6 engine

Balancing shaft

The V-4 engine needs an additional weighted shaft for balancing. This is driven at half crankshaft speed. Even better balance can be obtained by two such shafts

Diagrammatic end view of V-4 crankshaft (right). Firing order, with no overlapping of power strokes, shown above (blue shading)

Engine/where the fuel burns

The different shapes of combustion chambers

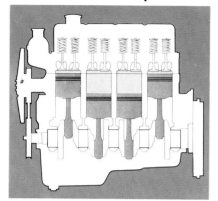

THE PERFORMANCE of an internal combustion engine depends to a large extent on the shape of the combustion chambers.

An efficient combustion chamber must be compact, so that the surface area of the walls through which heat can be lost to the cooling system is minimal.

It is generally accepted that the most efficient form of combustion chamber would be a sphere with the point of ignition at its centre. This would give even burning in all directions and the least heat loss through the walls. But such a design is impracticable for a car engine; the best compromise is a hemisphere. Combustion

chamber shapes currently used in car engines can be divided into four main categories: hemispherical, bath-tub, wedge and chamber-in-piston, all with overhead valves (OHV). Two other types, now largely superseded, are the side-valve (or 'L' head), and the 'F' head.

The hemispherical head is used mainly in high-performance engines as it is expensive to produce. Most modern cars use one of the four main shapes, all of which can be designed for operation on engines with high compression ratios.

The hemispherical chamber is usually the most efficient, mainly because of its

compactness. Of the others, the chamber-in-piston layout has manufacturing advantages, in terms of consistency of chamber size and shape.

The cheapest layout is the side-valve, used in many earlier designs. However, the chamber shape restricts the compression ratio to little more than 6:1, which is too low for good power output or petrol economy. The 'F' head uses a combination of side valves and overhead valves; it has exhaust valves in the cylinder block and inlet valves in the cylinder head. This design also restricts the compression ratio, without being cheap to produce.

Hemispherical head—the classic combustion-chamber shape

ONE OF THE most efficient, practical shapes of combustion chamber is the classic hemispherical form, in which the piston top forms the base of a hemisphere, with the valves inclined at 90° to each other, and the spark-plug centrally between them. This design, classic in its symmetry, gives short flame travel from the spark-plug to the piston head, and therefore good burning.

It is used on high-performance engines, though nowadays the angle between the valves is usually less than the classic 90°.

The hemispherical layout requires the use of one or two overhead camshafts—or one side camshaft associated with complicated rocker and push-rod gear—to operate the two rows of valves.

Its shape assists the crossflow of gases, which enter the cylinder from one side of the engine and are exhausted from the other. This gives room for large and free-flowing inlet tracts, arranged so that the mixture enters the chamber easily and with a swirling motion.

The good gas flow resulting from the unobstructed opening of its large valves gives the hemispherical head a high volumetric efficiency. This means it can 'breathe deeply', drawing in a large volume of gas for the space available, although this space is never completely filled.

With efficient combustion, the hemispherical head gives a high power output.

However, the modern tendency towards larger cylinder bores and shorter piston strokes enables valves on an ordinary in-line engine, without hemispherical combustion chambers, to be big enough for most normal requirements. Such valves do not need special camshafts or rocker arrangements, making the engine less costly to produce.

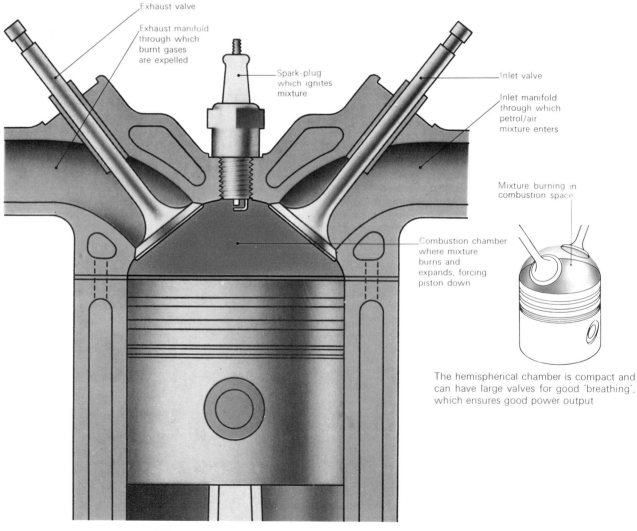

Exhaust valve

Exhaust manifold through which burnt gases are expelled

Spark-plug which ignites mixture

Inlet valve

Inlet manifold through which petrol/air mixture enters

Mixture burning in combustion space

Combustion chamber where mixture burns and expands, forcing piston down

The hemispherical chamber is compact and can have large valves for good 'breathing', which ensures good power output

THE HEMISPHERICAL CHAMBER

Bath-tub and wedge

TWO combustion-chamber shapes which are widely used to give a short flame path with overhead valves are the inverted bath-tub and the wedge.

The bath-tub consists of an oval-shaped chamber with inlet and exhaust valves placed vertically in the top and the spark-plug inclined at the side. The wedge-shaped combustion chamber has the valves in its sloping roof and the spark-plug inclined in the deeper side.

Both combustion chambers allow the use of a single side camshaft, with push-rods to the rockers which operate the valves; and the valves are all in-line. Alternatively, the valves can in these chambers be operated by a single overhead camshaft.

Chamber-in-piston

ONE modern design has a combustion space formed in the head of the piston, leaving the cylinder head flat. This is known as the chamber-in-piston, bowl-in-piston or flat-head type and is suited to high compression ratios.

It is used chiefly with an over-square engine—where the diameter of the piston is greater than the length of its stroke.

When the piston reaches the top of the compression stroke, its rim causes a certain amount of 'squish', or squirting of gas from the circumference of the piston into the bowl. This promotes good combustion with freedom from pinking. The combustion chamber is literally bowl-shaped and, being in the piston, remains hot and so helps vaporisation.

BATH-TUB CHAMBER

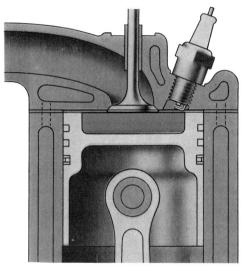

The bath-tub chamber gives a short flame path from a side spark-plug. The long, oval shape controls excessive turbulence and there is a small amount of 'squish' between piston crown and cylinder-head face, to minimise pinking

In this design the combustion space is in the head of the piston. In some cases small 'cut-outs' in the top edge of the piston ensure sufficient valve clearance. This layout 'breathes' well (that is, draws in a large volume of mixture)

WEDGE-SHAPED CHAMBER

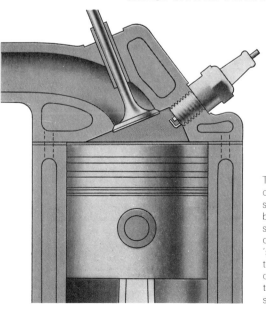

The wedge-shaped chamber has advantages similar to those of the bath-tub chamber, with a short flame path, controlled turbulence and 'squish'. As the flame travels into the thin end of the wedge, its lowered temperature tends to suppress pinking

Side valve

THE combustion chambers of a side-valve engine lack one of the basic requirements for efficient combustion—compactness. But the valve gear is comparatively simple and is cheap to produce.

Valves are alongside the cylinder, and the combustion chamber is formed above them in the cylinder head. The roof of the chamber slopes downwards over the cylinder, finishing with a small clearance above it. This forms a 'squish' area, causing mixture to be squirted at the spark-plug.

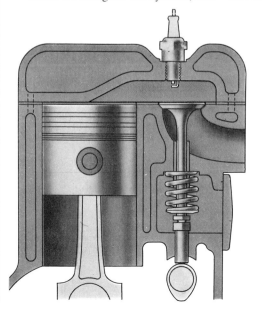

The most effective design of side-valve chamber provides a narrow space between the piston and the cylinder head to reduce any tendency to detonation of the burning petrol/air mixture. Even with this improved layout, the maximum compression ratio is still lower than is attainable with OHV engines

Engine/bearings for smooth running

BEARINGS are used to minimise friction and to support all the rotating parts of a car's mechanism—parts which are either rotating shafts or wheels on fixed shafts.

They fall into two main types: plain bearings, in which the moving part rotates in a shell or liner, with adjacent surfaces usually separated by a film of oil or grease; and rolling bearings, in which the load is borne by balls or rollers.

Shell bearings

If a plain bearing is in halves for ease of assembly, it is known as a shell bearing. This is the type used on the journals for the crankshaft main bearings, and in the big-ends of the connecting rods.

Each shell bearing consists of a strong steel backing to which thin layers of softer metal alloy are bonded.

The main bearings of the crankshaft are housed in the crankcase, and the big-end bearings in the big-ends themselves. Contact between the shell bearing and its housing is necessary to support the shell and to allow heat created by friction to be conducted from the shell, so preventing overheating and engine failure. The bearing material may be one of several metal alloys —white metal, copper–lead or tin aluminium, for instance.

At one time white metal (also called Babbitt metal) was widely used, but nowadays it is used only for the more lightly loaded bearings. White metal, an alloy of tin and lead, has the advantage of being soft, so that any trapped dirt will sink into the bearing rather than scratch the shaft. But this alloy has a low melting point, and quickly loses its strength as temperatures rise. Modern engines use a multi-layer steel-backed bearing shell, combining strength with good heat conductivity and low wear.

Thrust is imposed on the end of the crankshaft by pressure from the clutch, and in some cases by reaction from gears driving auxiliary components. If uncontrolled, this thrust would cause slight endways movements of the crankshaft, resulting in greater wear and engine noise. To resist end thrust, one of the main bearings is flanked by thrust washers—thin steel segments faced with bearing material. If a shaft begins to move under end thrust, one of its thrust faces comes up against a thrust washer and the shaft is held in position.

Oil, fed under pressure from a pump through passages in the crankcase, enters the main bearings through a hole running through each shell. The hole leads to a grooved channel running round the inside face of the shell, and the oil is distributed from this groove.

Some of the oil enters passages drilled in the crankshaft and leading to the big-end bearings, which the oil reaches under pressure, aided by centrifugal force.

The size of the clearance between the shaft and the bearings, never more than 0·005 in., controls the oil flow and, to a large extent, the amount of oil flung up to the pistons and bores.

The oil hole feeding a bearing is located near the point of minimum loading—the point at which working pressure on the bearing is lowest—so that oil is fed in where the clearance between bearing and shaft is widest. It is directed round the bearings by the rotation of the shaft to form an 'oil wedge' with its thin end forced into the point of maximum loading. The self-generated pressure in the oil wedge is far higher than the oil-pump pressure in the supply pipes; it prevents rubbing contact between the metal surfaces even when bearing loads are very high.

Cylindrical bush bearings

Plain bearings which consist of a complete cylinder with no split are termed cylindrical bush bearings. They form the bearings in, for example, the rockers and the small-ends of the connecting rods.

The simplest bush is made of the same metal or alloy throughout, usually bronze. It is pressed into its housing with its oil hole lining up with the oil-feed hole from the housing.

If the supply of lubricant is limited, a bush bearing can embody a plastic material such as 'PTFE'—the material used for coating non-stick saucepans.

Occasionally a porous metal bush is used. This is made from a powdered metal, formed under heat and pressure so that the particles fuse together into a material which will absorb and carry oil.

Rolling bearings

Ball bearings and roller bearings give the lowest friction of all types of bearings, but are also the most expensive. They are used in the auxiliary components of car engines, such as the water pump and dynamo, and in some racing-car engines and overhead-camshaft drives.

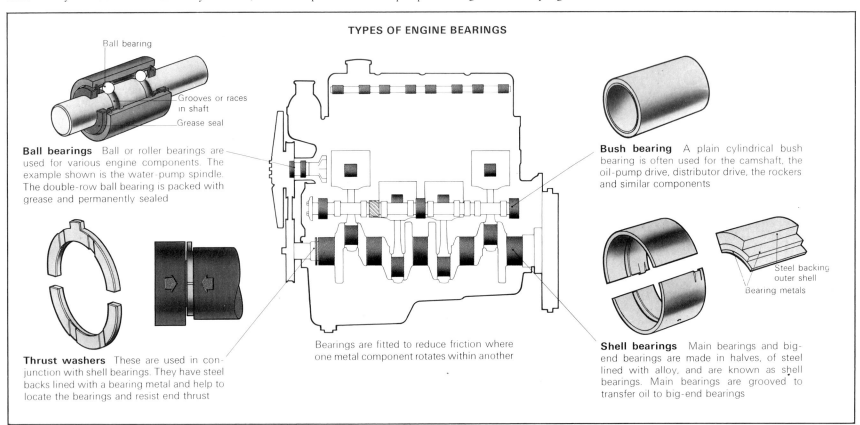

TYPES OF ENGINE BEARINGS

Ball bearing

Grooves or races in shaft

Grease seal

Ball bearings Ball or roller bearings are used for various engine components. The example shown is the water-pump spindle. The double-row ball bearing is packed with grease and permanently sealed

Thrust washers These are used in conjunction with shell bearings. They have steel backs lined with a bearing metal and help to locate the bearings and resist end thrust

Bearings are fitted to reduce friction where one metal component rotates within another

Bush bearing A plain cylindrical bush bearing is often used for the camshaft, the oil-pump drive, distributor drive, the rockers and similar components

Steel backing
outer shell
Bearing metals

Shell bearings Main bearings and big-end bearings are made in halves, of steel lined with alloy, and are known as shell bearings. Main bearings are grooved to transfer oil to big-end bearings

The diesel engine

IN A PETROL ENGINE a mixture of petrol and air is ignited by an electric spark from the spark-plug; but a diesel has no spark-plugs. Another essential difference is that it uses a different type of fuel—gas oil.

Ignition in a diesel engine is caused by compression, which raises the temperature of air in the combustion chamber above the flash-point, or self-ignition temperature, of the fuel.

Diesel fuel, less easily evaporated than petrol, is not drawn in with air as a mixture, but is sprayed under high pressure from an injector into the combustion chamber, where it ignites on contact with the hot, compressed air. Each injector is supplied with fuel in metered quantities and at a high pressure by an engine-driven pump. The accelerator controls the amount of fuel delivered by the pump, and hence the power delivered by the engine.

The diesel's advantages lie in its greater efficiency (resulting in lower fuel costs), longer life and lower maintenance costs.

Its disadvantages include a high initial cost, greater weight, a somewhat rougher idling, some smell, a higher noise level and slower acceleration.

In a medium-sized car, gas is compressed to about one-ninth of its original volume, giving a compression ratio of 9:1; in a diesel engine it may be as high as 22:1, to increase the temperature of air to the flash-point temperature of the diesel fuel.

A diesel engine has a much smaller combustion chamber than a petrol engine, and its higher compression ratio results in greater efficiency, because more potential heat-energy is converted into power and less heat is wasted.

To ensure that the correct amount of fuel is injected at the right moment, each cylinder on a diesel engine is fitted with an injector. A pump, driven at half crankshaft speed, forces fuel into the combustion cylinders in their firing order.

In the diesel 4-stroke cycle, pure air is drawn into the cylinder on the suction stroke; fuel is injected and starts to burn towards the end of the rising compression stroke; pressure from expanding gases forces the piston down on its power stroke; and burnt gases escape as the piston rises on its exhaust stroke.

In some diesel engines, a heater plug is fitted to help starting in low temperatures. This does not produce a spark but glows continuously until air temperature in the engine cylinders is high enough to ensure self-ignition of the fuel sprayed into the combustion chamber.

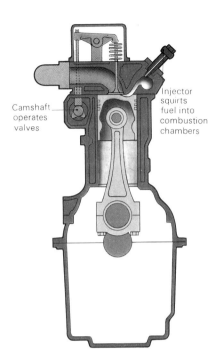

Camshaft operates valves

Injector squirts fuel into combustion chambers

A typical diesel engine Each cylinder has its own injector at the end of a fuel feed from a high-pressure pump

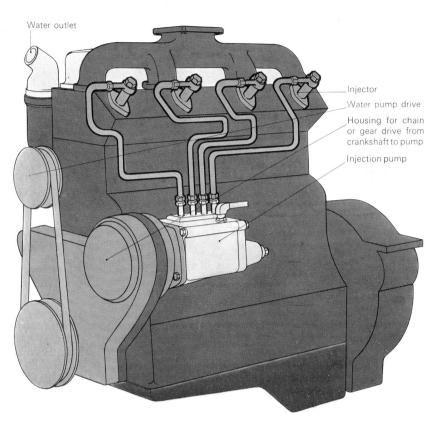

Water outlet

Injector
Water pump drive
Housing for chain or gear drive from crankshaft to pump
Injection pump

The combustion chamber
This can be formed by a depression in the piston crown or by a separate chamber in the cylinder head. Both promote a swirling motion in the compressed air

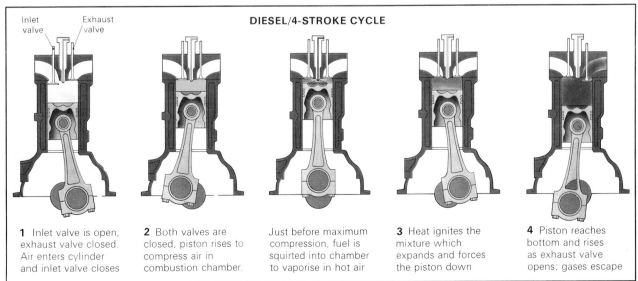

DIESEL/4-STROKE CYCLE

Inlet valve   Exhaust valve

1 Inlet valve is open, exhaust valve closed. Air enters cylinder and inlet valve closes

2 Both valves are closed, piston rises to compress air in combustion chamber.

Just before maximum compression, fuel is squirted into chamber to vaporise in hot air

3 Heat ignites the mixture which expands and forces the piston down

4 Piston reaches bottom and rises as exhaust valve opens; gases escape

47

Engine/the rotary design

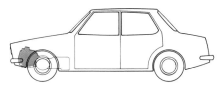

ROTARY ENGINES produced for cars today are all of the Wankel type, named after their German inventor. Although only in production since 1964, the Wankel engine may one day challenge the supremacy of the conventional piston engine.

The great advantage of the rotary engine is that nothing goes up and down, only round and round. It is lighter, more compact and has fewer moving parts than a piston engine.

The Wankel has a fixed casing, with the internal shape of a wide-waisted figure-of-eight, and a near-triangular rotor. For higher power, the engine can have two or more rotors phased together. The output shaft turns at three times the rotor speed.

The rotor revolves eccentrically within the casing in such a way that the three rotor tips are continually in contact with the internal surface. Planetary gearing (see p. 94) connects the rotor to an output shaft which is equivalent to the crankshaft of a piston engine.

Between the three sides of the rotor and the inside of the casing are three working spaces, or chambers, each of which alternately expands and contracts in size as the rotor 'orbits'.

The casing is provided with a spark-plug (or sometimes two) an inlet port and an exhaust port which are uncovered, in sequence, as the rotor revolves.

As a result, a 4-phase operating cycle occurs in each chamber during each orbit of the rotor, corresponding to the 4-stroke cycle of a piston engine—namely induction, compression, power and exhaust. As there are three chambers between the sides of the triangular rotor and the casing, it follows that there are three power 'strokes' for each rotor revolution.

Sealing the gases

Efficient gas seals have to be provided at the three tips of the rotor and at the sides. The development of effective and durable seals has been a major problem.

Although most Wankel engines have a carburettor, some have been operated with fuel injection.

The Wankel is essentially a water-cooled engine with oil-cooling for the rotor. There are air-cooled Wankel engines, but they are not fitted to cars.

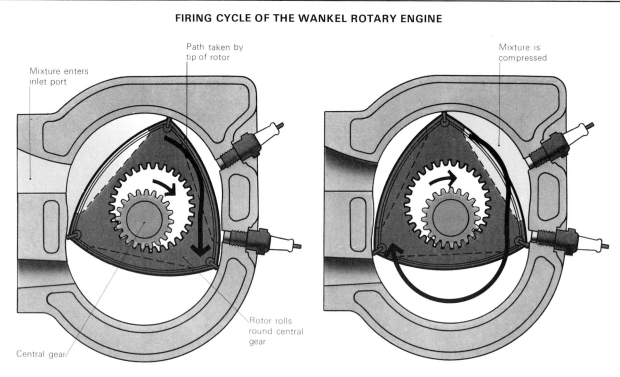

FIRING CYCLE OF THE WANKEL ROTARY ENGINE

1 Induction As a tip of the rotor passes the inlet port, the petrol/air mixture enters the following chamber, which is increasing in size because of the rotor's eccentric orbit

2 Compression As the rotor continues to revolve, the chamber containing the mixture decreases in size and the mixture is compressed

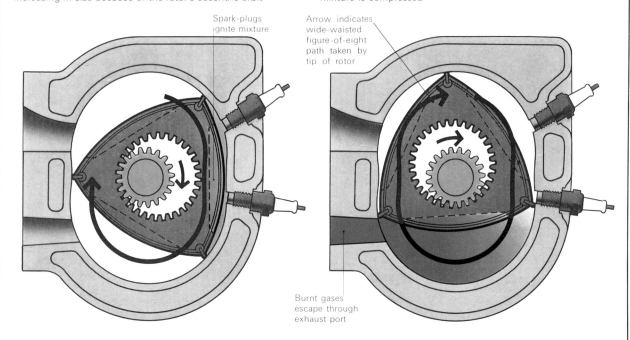

3 Power Ignition causes the mixture to burn and expand, imparting energy to the rotor for its power 'stroke' as the size of the chamber increases

4 Exhaust The leading lobe passes the exhaust port and leaves it open for gases to escape. The cycle goes on in all three chambers simultaneously

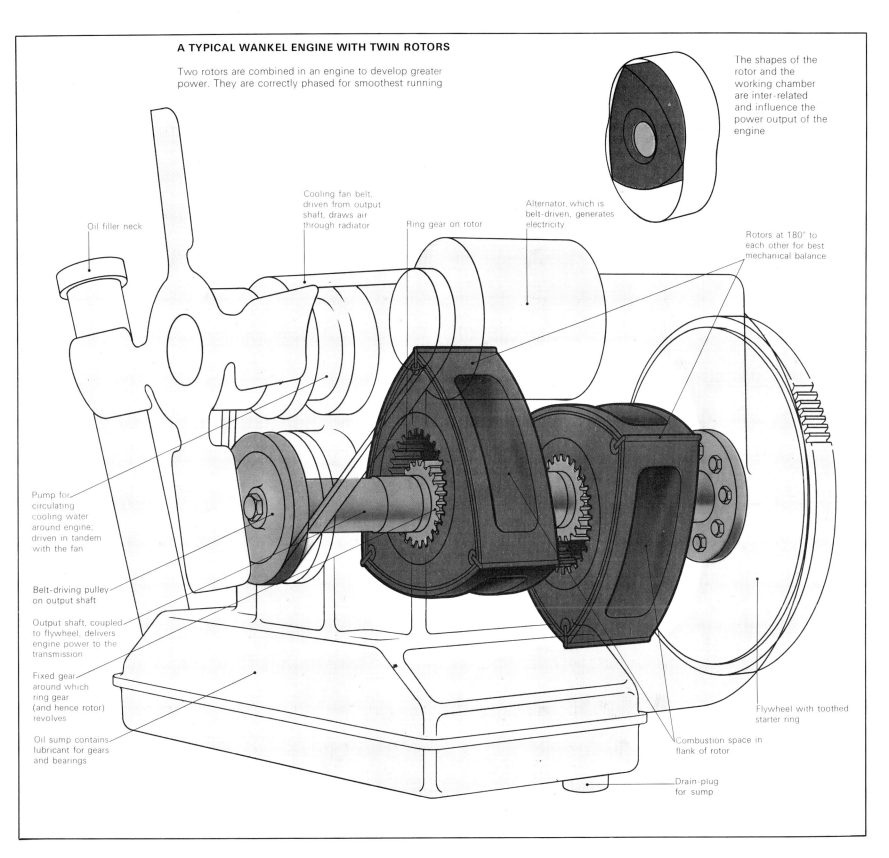

A TYPICAL WANKEL ENGINE WITH TWIN ROTORS

Two rotors are combined in an engine to develop greater power. They are correctly phased for smoothest running

The shapes of the rotor and the working chamber are inter-related and influence the power output of the engine

Oil filler neck

Cooling fan belt, driven from output shaft, draws air through radiator

Ring gear on rotor

Alternator, which is belt-driven, generates electricity

Rotors at 180° to each other for best mechanical balance

Pump for circulating cooling water around engine; driven in tandem with the fan

Belt-driving pulley on output shaft

Output shaft, coupled to flywheel, delivers engine power to the transmission

Fixed gear around which ring gear (and hence rotor) revolves

Oil sump contains lubricant for gears and bearings

Flywheel with toothed starter ring

Combustion space in flank of rotor

Drain-plug for sump

49

Fuel system/how the carburettor works

What the fuel system does

CARBURATION plays an essential part in allowing a car engine to start easily, accelerate without hesitation, cruise economically, give full power and be free from stalling in traffic.

Its job, briefly, is to mix the right amount of petrol with the right amount of air, so that the mixture will burn in the cylinders, and to deliver the correct amount of vaporised mixture to each cylinder.

The complete process of carburation extends from the time the petrol is mixed with air to the time the mixture starts to burn in the cylinders. So the carburettors, inlet manifold, inlet valves and even the combustion chambers and pistons are all involved in carburation.

Petrol for the carburettor is supplied by the fuel system which consists of a remotely mounted fuel tank, a fuel pump to force petrol up to the float chamber and several filters to prevent the entry of dirt.

Air/fuel ratio

With most petrols, a mixture of about 15 parts of air—by weight—to one of petrol (called the chemically correct ratio) will ensure complete combustion of the fuel.

But this mixture strength, or air/fuel ratio, does not produce maximum power; nor does it in general give maximum economy. Starting in cold weather may require a mixture consisting of 1 part air to 1 part petrol. But a much weaker mixture—of, say, 16 parts of air to 1 part of petrol—is needed to give cruising economy.

The mixture requirements, in general, are: rich for starting; less rich for slow running and idling; weak for economical cruising; and richer again for acceleration and high speeds.

Substances formed when petrol and air are burnt together include carbon monoxide, carbon dioxide, hydrocarbons and oxides of nitrogen. The proportion of these in the exhaust gases depends on the richness of the mixture.

Control by law

In the USA, Canada, Europe, Japan and Australia, the level of emission of these substances, some of them poisonous, is strictly controlled by law. This has increased the need for precise control of carburation, combustion and ignition and has stimulated greater research into carburation, combustion, electronic ignition and maintenance-free fuel-injection systems.

Where the petrol and air are mixed

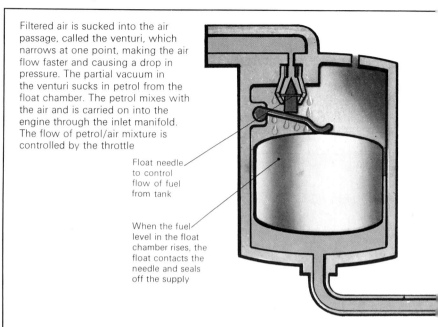

Filtered air is sucked into the air passage, called the venturi, which narrows at one point, making the air flow faster and causing a drop in pressure. The partial vacuum in the venturi sucks in petrol from the float chamber. The petrol mixes with the air and is carried on into the engine through the inlet manifold. The flow of petrol/air mixture is controlled by the throttle

Float needle to control flow of fuel from tank

When the fuel level in the float chamber rises, the float contacts the needle and seals off the supply

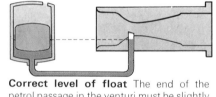

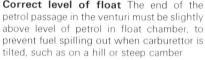

Correct level of float The end of the petrol passage in the venturi must be slightly above level of petrol in float chamber, to prevent fuel spilling out when carburettor is tilted, such as on a hill or steep camber

Pressure on petrol The float chamber contains a small vent hole in the lid, and atmospheric pressure on fuel in the float chamber forces fuel into the venturi where there is a partial vacuum

The principle of carburation

AIR IS DRAWN into the combustion chambers of an engine because of the partial vacuum created when the pistons move down the cylinders on the induction stroke. The air passes through the carburettor, and the amount drawn in is controlled by a pivoted flap, called the throttle valve, which is opened and closed by the accelerator.

The quantity of air drawn in depends on the engine speed as well as on the position of the throttle valve. It is the function of the carburettor to ensure that the correct amount of petrol is drawn into the airstream, so that the right mixture will be delivered to the combustion chambers.

Petrol, piped from a reservoir in the carburettor, joins the airstream in a narrow-throated passage known as the venturi, or choke. This works on the principle that as the speed of an airstream increases, its pressure drops. When air flows through the narrow part of the venturi, its speed increases, and it is in the region of low air pressure that petrol is sucked into the airstream from a jet.

The air flow will be at a maximum when the engine is running at full speed, with the throttle valve wide open; and the greater the air velocity through the venturi, the greater the flow of petrol from the pipe.

In practice, a carburettor as simple as this would not be satisfactory, because petrol and air do not have the same flow characteristics. As air flows faster, it becomes less dense, but petrol remains at the same density whatever its rate of flow. Since air and petrol must be mixed by

FROM TANK TO CARBURETTOR

Carburettor where petrol and air are mixed

Pump to force fuel up into float chamber

Pipeline link between tank and carburettor system

Petrol tank, tucked away at rear of car, remote from engine and passengers

Petrol flows from the tank along a pipeline to the float chamber. As the chamber is higher than the fuel level in the tank, a pump is needed to force the fuel up into the float chamber, which is usually embodied in the carburettor

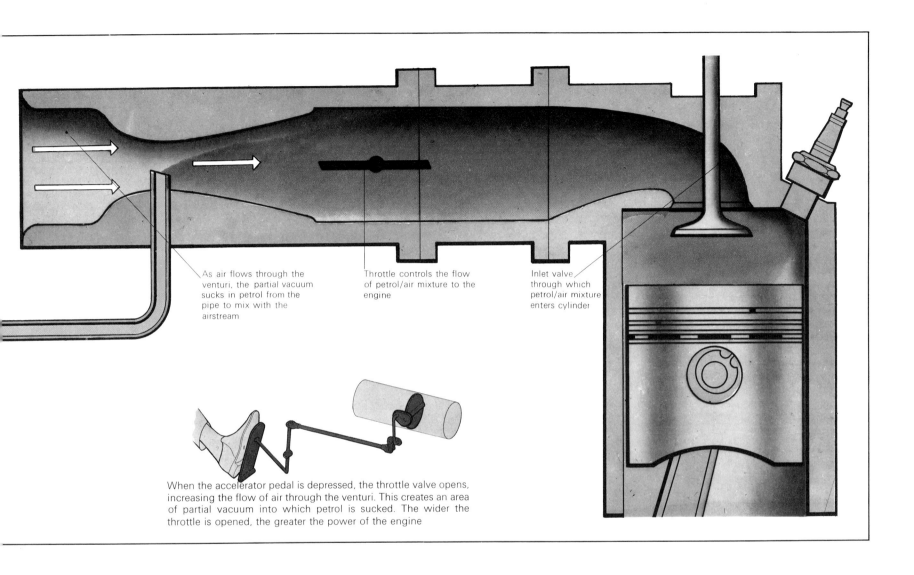

As air flows through the venturi, the partial vacuum sucks in petrol from the pipe to mix with the airstream

Throttle controls the flow of petrol/air mixture to the engine

Inlet valve through which petrol/air mixture enters cylinder

When the accelerator pedal is depressed, the throttle valve opens, increasing the flow of air through the venturi. This creates an area of partial vacuum into which petrol is sucked. The wider the throttle is opened, the greater the power of the engine

weight (roughly in the proportion of 15:1) for efficient combustion, the mixture would become progressively richer as the air flow increased and its density dropped. Eventually, the mixture would become too rich to burn in the cylinders.

There are two ways of overcoming this problem. In a fixed-jet carburettor (see p. 52) some air is mixed with the petrol before it leaves the jet, through an arrangement of emulsion tubes or correction jets. In a variable-jet carburettor (see p. 54) the amount of petrol leaving the jet and the size of the venturi throat are varied to maintain the correct proportions of petrol and air.

Petrol in the reservoir, or float chamber, is maintained at a constant level by means of a float-operated valve. The end of the

petrol pipe in the venturi has to be above the petrol level in the float chamber to prevent fuel spilling out if the car is tilted —on a hill or steeply cambered road, for instance. This means that before the petrol can mix with the airstream it has to be lifted a small distance—in practice, about $\frac{1}{4}$ in. The suction produced by the partial vacuum is sufficient to lift the petrol to the top of the jet and to draw it into the venturi in the form of droplets.

As well as drawing in petrol and air, the carburation system must vaporise the petrol, mix it thoroughly with the air and then distribute the mixture uniformly to the cylinders. Petrol is already in the form of droplets when it enters the venturi: with a fixed jet it has been emulsified by pre-mixing with air; with a variable jet the

droplets have been broken up by the speed of the airstream.

When the spray of petrol and air passes the throttle valve, it enters an area of partial vacuum created by the piston suction, so that the petrol droplets start to evaporate. The rate of evaporation depends on the degree of vacuum in the inlet manifold, and this is governed by the engine speed and the position of the throttle valve.

At high speed, when the throttle is fully open, the vacuum can be so low that most of the petrol is still in liquid form and is carried along in the air, or flows along the walls of the manifold. At cruising speed, when the throttle is partially closed, the vacuum increases and most of the petrol will then be in vapour form.

In engines with one carburettor to each

cylinder, the fact that the mixture is part liquid is of little consequence; it will still reach the combustion chamber, where it will be vaporised by heat. But when one carburettor supplies a number of cylinders, even distribution is of primary importance; and this is difficult to achieve if the mixture is 'wet'.

The addition of heat to the inlet manifold by means of an exhaust-heated or water-heated 'hot spot' promotes further vaporisation of the petrol (see p. 56), and so ensures an even distribution of mixture.

Except in a cold engine, this vaporisation is completed when the mixture enters the cylinders and comes into contact with the hot exhaust valve and the cylinder walls, and with any exhaust gas remaining from the previous combustion cycle.

Fuel system/fixed-jet carburettor

THE FIXED-JET (or fixed-choke) carburettor incorporates various jets and an accelerator pump to alter the mixture's strength according to engine needs.

As the airstream through a carburettor's venturi speeds up, the air becomes 'thinner' and without some compensating device the mixture would become progressively richer until it was too rich to burn.

The fixed-jet carburettor solves this problem by air correction—mixing some air with petrol before the petrol is drawn into the venturi. On most carburettors, air correction is by means of a perforated tube which emulsifies the mixture. The main jet supplies petrol to a spraying well which contains the perforated tube, closed at the top by a calibrated air-correction jet. As the engine speed rises and the petrol level in the well falls, an increasing amount of air is drawn through the series of holes in the tube, automatically weakening the mixture.

The alternative method is to put in a compensating jet in addition to the main jet. As the fuel level drops in a well alongside the float chamber, air is drawn into the compensating jet so that a mixture of air and petrol, instead of petrol alone, reaches the main discharge point. The weakness of the mixture from the compensating jet cancels out the increasing richness of the mixture supplied by the main jet.

The size of the main jet is usually designed to give the relatively weak mixtures necessary for economic cruising.

To give the richer mixtures needed for full throttle, the fixed-jet carburettor has an additional jet feeding the main discharge well. This supplements the main jet which can be kept small for economy.

Labels (left cutaway diagram): Venturi · Choke flap or strangler · Emulsifying tube · Idling jet · Feed pipe from accelerator pump · Fuel supply cut-off · Accelerator pump · Main jet · Accelerator pump linkage · Throttle butterfly · Volume-control screw

EMULSION TUBE

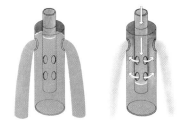

The emulsion tube consists in fact of two tubes, one inside the other. Petrol is drawn into these tubes before it is discharged into the main airstream at the venturi. As the engine speeds up, air from an air-correction jet enters the innermost tube, which has a number of holes drilled in it at different levels, and automatically weakens the mixture

A TYPICAL FIXED-JET CARBURETTOR

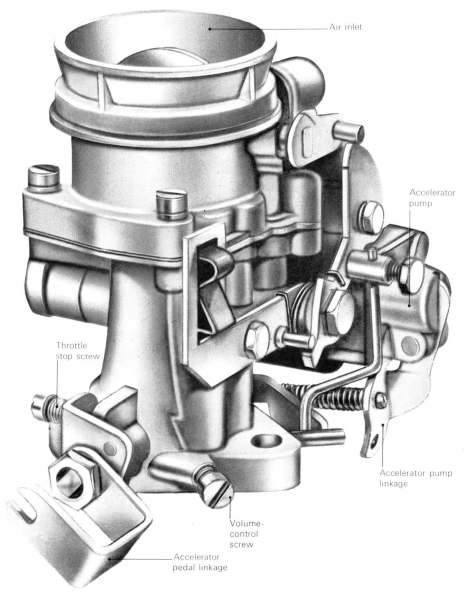

Labels: Air inlet · Accelerator pump · Accelerator pump linkage · Throttle stop screw · Volume-control screw · Accelerator pedal linkage

Varying the mixture for different speeds

PULLING OUT the choke on the dashboard closes a spring-loaded butterfly valve, called a strangler or choke flap, and opens the throttle valve slightly. This restricts the air flow and increases suction from the main jet into the venturi, so giving the richer mixture needed for starting. When the engine fires and speeds up, the additional air drawn in forces the strangler flap to open partially, and ensures a weakening of the mixture, to prevent crankcase oil dilution and cylinder bore wear. It also minimises air pollution.

When the engine is hot, the movement of the pistons on starting causes a partial vacuum in the inlet manifold. Since the throttle is closed, this partial vacuum becomes effective at the 'idle' discharge hole, and draws fuel from the float chamber via the main jet through the idling system of the carburettor.

Air is drawn into this fuel through the pilot air-bleed, to emulsify the mixture. As the fuel flows through the idle circuit, the fuel level drops in the main emulsion well, uncovers some of the emulsion holes and allows air to enter and mix with the fuel.

Opening the throttle by pressing the accelerator pedal adds to the air flow through the air-correction jet, and the increased partial vacuum at the venturi causes the emulsified petrol/air mixture to rise in the well and discharge into the main airstream, passing through the venturi.

Simultaneously, the partial vacuum at the idle discharge decreases and the flow of fuel at this point ceases.

To avoid any undue weakening of the mixture, which would cause flat spots, during this transition stage, it is usual to provide one or more 'progression' holes in the idle circuit.

To give the additional fuel needed for acceleration and sudden throttle openings, an accelerator pump is provided. This consists of a well, filled with fuel and fitted with a spring-loaded plunger or diaphragm, linked to the throttle. When the throttle is opened, the fuel in the well is discharged by the plunger through a separate passage into the venturi.

On some carburettors the plunger stroke can be adjusted to provide increased fuel delivery for winter conditions, or less for summer motoring.

Present-day engines and motoring conditions have resulted in a wide variety of fixed-jet carburettors with a complex arrangement of fuel passages, jets and discharge holes.

Their great advantage is the absence of moving parts; all the metering of fuel and air is controlled by fixed jets and venturi throats of fixed size which are factory-set.

OPERATIONAL STAGES OF A FIXED-JET CARBURETTOR

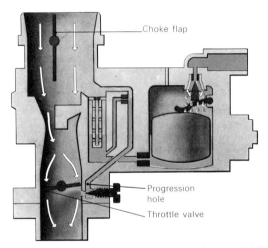

Idling Petrol and air are supplied to the manifold through a separate circuit with a progression hole

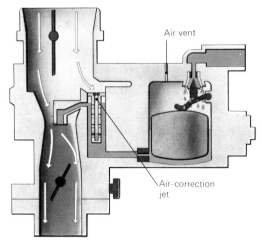

Approaching full throttle Fuel is drawn from the main discharge system and fed into the venturi

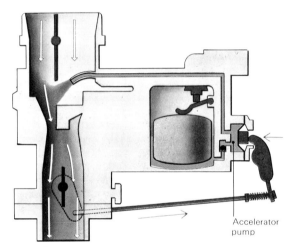

Acceleration The extra fuel required is supplied by the accelerator pump, which also delivers into the venturi

Choke increases mixture strength for cold starting

A RICH MIXTURE with an air/fuel ratio of between 1:1 and 3:1 is needed to start the engine in cold weather. This is provided by closing a choke flap or strangler, operated automatically or by a choke control.

Because the carburation system is cold, and because the air speed through the venturi is low, due to the slow cranking speed of the engine, only part of the petrol will be able to vaporise.

When the engine fires, the inlet manifold starts to heat up and the mixture can then be weakened to between 4:1 and 6:1. This weakening is essential to avoid dilution of oil, and undue wear of the cylinder bores caused by liquid fuel running down the cylinder walls. At idling the mixture strength is usually about 9:1, but 15:1 is enough once the engine is warm.

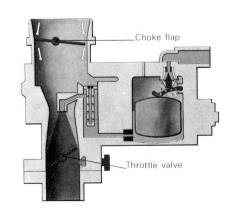

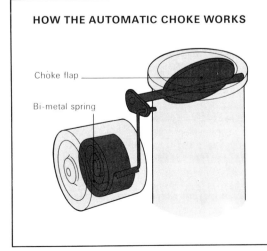

HOW THE AUTOMATIC CHOKE WORKS

Some carburettors have an automatic choke to increase mixture strength during a cold start. Pressing the accelerator moves the choke into position. The choke flap, which is open during normal running, is held closed by a bi-metal spring. When the spring is heated—by hot air from the exhaust, or directly from the water in the cooling system—it expands and pushes the flap open

Fuel system/variable-jet carburettor

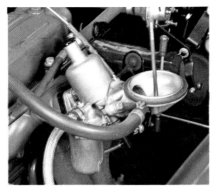

THE VARIABLE-JET or constant-depression carburettor, like the fixed-jet type, has a constant-level fuel supply, a throttle valve and a venturi. The main difference is that the size of the venturi throat can be varied to maintain an almost constant partial vacuum at the fuel-discharge jet.

A sliding piston controls the area of the venturi throat, and the position of the piston is determined by the degree of throttle opening. If the throttle is almost closed, as when the engine is idling, the flow of air through the venturi drops. The weight of the piston and its spring causes the piston to fall, leaving only a small gap for the passage of air.

When the throttle is opened by depressing the accelerator pedal, the swifter passage of air through the venturi increases the partial vacuum above the piston. This causes the piston to rise, and further increases the flow of air into the engine.

The flow of fuel is controlled by a tapered needle attached to the piston and passing into the fuel jet. As the piston rises, the needle rises too, allowing more petrol to be drawn from the jet. The position of the jet and shape of the needle ensure the correct proportion of petrol and air.

Enrichment of the mixture when accelerating is provided by a damper, which slows the rate of rise of the piston when the throttle is opened. This increases the partial vacuum at the fuel jet and so provides a temporary enrichment.

Since the air pressure in the venturi remains reasonably constant at any given engine speed, there is no need to provide a separate fuel circuit for idling, as in the fixed-jet carburettor. The fuel is fed into the airstream at the point of maximum velocity, ensuring efficient atomisation (breaking up into droplets) of the fuel.

The idling-mixture strength can be altered by an adjusting nut, which controls the jet position, and the idling speed is controlled by a throttle-stop screw.

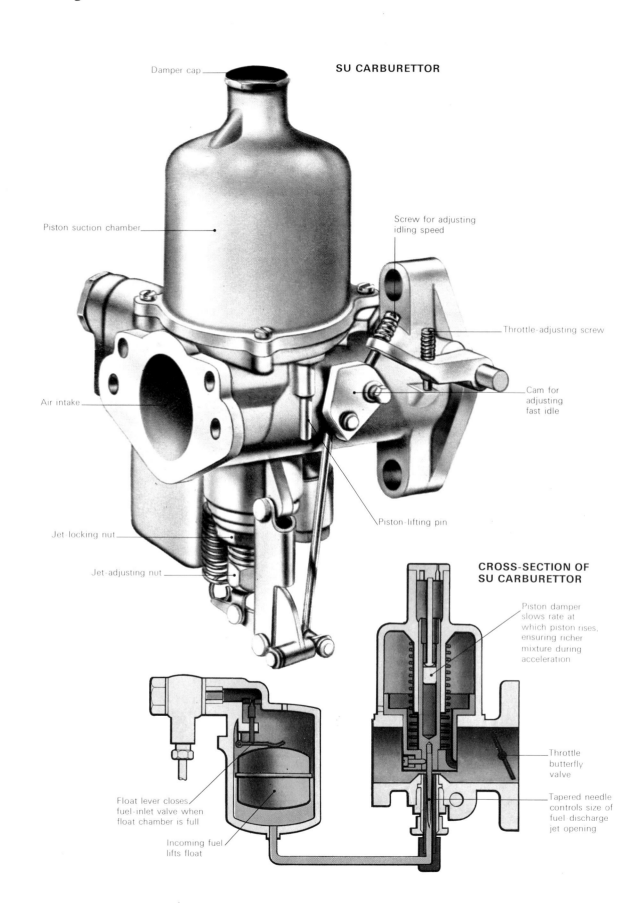

SU CARBURETTOR

Damper cap

Piston suction chamber

Air intake

Jet-locking nut

Jet-adjusting nut

Screw for adjusting idling speed

Throttle-adjusting screw

Cam for adjusting fast idle

Piston-lifting pin

CROSS-SECTION OF SU CARBURETTOR

Piston damper slows rate at which piston rises, ensuring richer mixture during acceleration

Throttle butterfly valve

Tapered needle controls size of fuel-discharge jet opening

Float lever closes fuel-inlet valve when float chamber is full

Incoming fuel lifts float

The H-type SU carburettor in action

A WIDE VARIETY of variable-jet carburettors are manufactured by SU. They differ only in the method of jet assembly and in the means of feeding the fuel from the float chamber to the jet. The H-type is fairly widely used and is produced in a range of throttle body sizes.

The piston is a close fit in the suction chamber, to prevent excessive air leaks.

The main air passage is connected to the suction chamber by a passage in the piston, so that air can be drawn from the chamber.

The float chamber in an SU is separated from the rest of the carburettor and is attached to it by a single bolt, either rigidly or with a flexible rubber mounting.

Fuel is fed to the jet through a short flexible pipe. The position of the jet can be altered by sliding it in a long bearing pressed into the carburettor body. Adjustments are made by means of a nut or a remote screw and linkage.

For cold starting, pulling out the choke control on a car's instrument panel lowers the jet assembly about $\frac{3}{8}$ in. This ensures a larger fuel discharge area and gives the required rich mixture; it also opens the throttle slightly.

The latest types of SU carburettors give the correct mixture strength to satisfy all operating conditions and still meet air-pollution regulations.

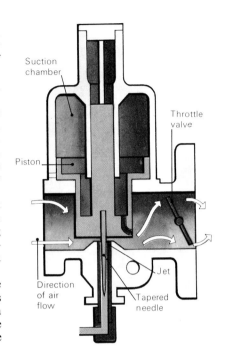

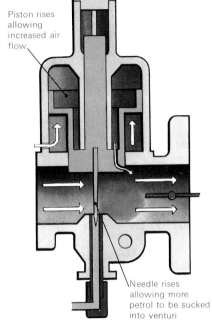

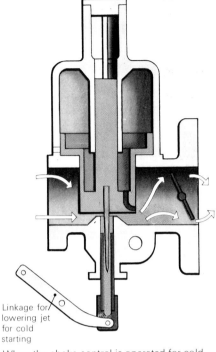

The closed throttle gives little engine suction; the piston drops to its lowest position, leaving only a small gap for the flow of air

On full throttle, engine suction lifts the piston, which widens the passage to give an increased flow of air to the engine

When the choke control is operated for cold starting, it lowers the jet assembly; increased fuel-flow gives a richer mixture

The Stromberg CDS carburettor

THOUGH IT WORKS on the same constant-pressure principle as the SU carburettor, the Stromberg CDS differs in several design features. Instead of having a closely fitting piston, the suction chamber is sealed with a flexible diaphragm.

The float chamber surrounds the jet and is fitted with two floats, one on each side of the jet, mounted on a common spindle. The double floats make this design less sensitive to flooding when the car is tilted. The main jet is spring-loaded against an adjustment screw; and the jet assembly is retained by a housing, and is sealed by 'O' rings. As with SU carburettors, alternative needles and piston springs are available for engine tuning.

The mixture for cold starting is provided through a disc valve operated by the choke control. Rotation of the disc, which draws fuel from the float chamber, aligns a series of holes drilled in the disc with a fuel passage into the carburettor body. Operation of the disc is linked by means of a 'fast idle' cam to the throttle which is opened a predetermined amount.

To prevent over-rich mixtures at idle when temperatures are high, a further valve may be fitted. This is controlled by a bi-metal spring, which reacts to the air temperature, and allows extra air to enter the carburettor, between the venturi and the throttle. An automatic starter valve, which replaces the disc valve, an idle air regulator and a deceleration valve, which quickly reduces fuel flow, are among refinements to meet air-pollution control standards.

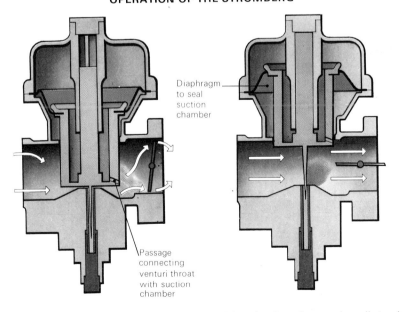

Idling engine has little flow of air and small flow of fuel past the jet

Full throttle raises piston and needle to give greater flow of air and fuel intake

55

Fuel system/inlet manifold

Inlet manifolds

THERE ARE two jobs the inlet manifold has to do: assist vaporisation of the petrol/air mixture from the carburettor, and distribute that mixture as evenly as possible to each cylinder.

An even distribution would be straightforward if all the mixture were vaporised in the carburettor. But this is not possible under all engine conditions, and some petrol is still in liquid form when it reaches the inlet manifold.

In an engine with a carburettor to each cylinder, this is of little consequence, because all the fuel reaches the correct cylinder. But where the carburettor has to feed more than one cylinder, additional vaporisation is needed to improve the distribution.

Extra vaporisation is usually administered by means of an exhaust 'hot spot' or by hot water circulating in a jacket surrounding the air intake. Both systems make use of waste combustion heat.

In this way, as soon as the engine is started, heat is supplied to the area where fuel droplets are likely to form.

Excessive heating at this point could lead to loss of power by reduction of the air density. To prevent this, some exhaust hot spots are fitted with a thermostatically controlled flap valve which shuts at high exhaust temperatures.

If the design of an engine makes it difficult to incorporate an exhaust hot spot, the inlet manifold can be heated by a 'water jacket' fed from the cooling system.

This jacket provides a more constant temperature over a greater area, but may not become effective as quickly as the exhaust hot spot after a cold start.

The shape and cross-section area of the manifold must help to prevent the formation of fuel droplets without restricting the flow of air. These conflicting requirements result in a variety of inlet-manifold shapes and sizes.

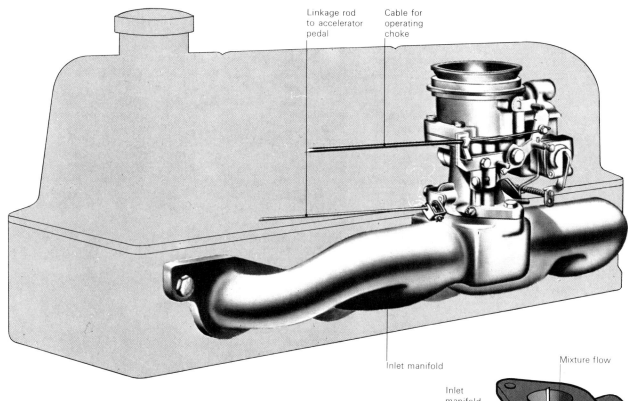

TYPICAL INLET MANIFOLD ON 4-CYLINDER ENGINE

Linkage rod to accelerator pedal

Cable for operating choke

Inlet manifold

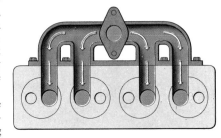

Distributing the mixture The inlet manifold helps to vaporise the petrol/air mixture and distribute it evenly to the cylinders

Assisting vaporisation The exhaust manifold may be mounted immediately below the inlet manifold for exhaust heat to help vaporise the mixture. Some exhaust manifolds have a thermostatically controlled valve operated by a bi-metal spring, which shuts at high temperatures

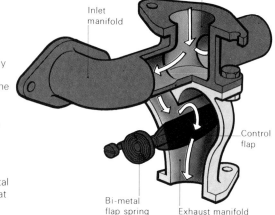

Mixture flow

Inlet manifold

Control flap

Bi-metal flap spring

Exhaust manifold

Twin carburettors and forked manifolds

IN THE PAST, most family cars had only a single carburettor. But today a number are fitted with twin or even triple carburettors which result in higher performance. In America, and to some extent on the Continent, multi-choke carburettors with more than one barrel are more common. When two single carburettors are used on a 4-cylinder engine, they are normally fitted to short, forked manifolds, each feeding two cylinders. The same arrangement is used on 6-cylinder engines fitted with three car-burettors. If two twin-barrel (better known as twin-choke) carburettors are used, each carburettor barrel feeds only one cylinder on a 4-cylinder engine.

Flexible carburettor mountings are often used on high-performance cars to prevent fuel frothing or flooding because of engine vibration.

With all multi-carburettor installations, it is necessary to link the separate manifolds with a balance pipe to prevent uneven mixture distribution.

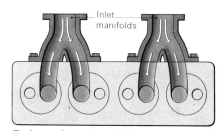

Inlet manifolds

Twin carburettors When two are used on a 4-cylinder engine they are sometimes fitted to short forked manifolds

Multiple carburettors

Twin-barrel carburettors

THE TWIN-BARREL CARBURETTOR, more often referred to as a twin-choke unit, has two main air passages or barrels, each with its own venturi and petrol-metering system, but having a common float chamber. Their throttles are usually on the same spindle and operate simultaneously.

One of the most experienced manufacturers of twin-barrel carburettors is the Italian Weber company. Several of their carburettors have a secondary venturi tube in the barrel, positioned slightly in front of the main venturi. Fuel is fed to the throat of the secondary venturi which discharges at the throat of the main venturi. This adds to the air velocity, increasing the partial vacuum, which in turn increases the flow of fuel.

The main fuel mixture is fed through a jet and emulsion tube. The accelerator pump consists of a spring-loaded piston which discharges a metered amount of fuel. Its piston-operating rod is controlled by a lever on the throttle spindle.

Compound carburettors

THE COMPOUND CARBURETTOR has two or more fixed-choke barrels which feed a common manifold. The throttles are so coupled that the carburettor will operate on only one barrel until the air requirement reaches a certain level. The second throttle valve then opens to provide higher power.

This arrangement allows the primary venturi area to be made small enough to give smooth running at low speeds.

On Solex and Weber carburettors, the throttle is opened against a spring, using a diaphragm which is sensitive to the air pressure in the manifold.

On others, the secondary throttles are joined to the primary ones by a linkage and start to open only when the primary throttle reaches a pre-determined position.

Most American compound carburettors also include an auxiliary air valve in the secondary barrel. This remains closed when the accelerator is fully depressed at low speeds. At high speeds, increased air flow opens the auxiliary valve.

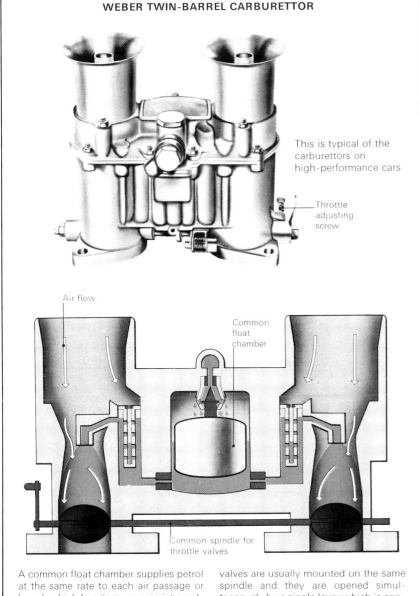

WEBER TWIN-BARREL CARBURETTOR

This is typical of the carburettors on high-performance cars

Throttle adjusting screw

Air flow

Common float chamber

Common spindle for throttle valves

A common float chamber supplies petrol at the same rate to each air passage or barrel, which has its own main jet emulsion tube and idle circuit. Both throttle valves are usually mounted on the same spindle and they are opened simultaneously by a single lever which is connected to the accelerator pedal

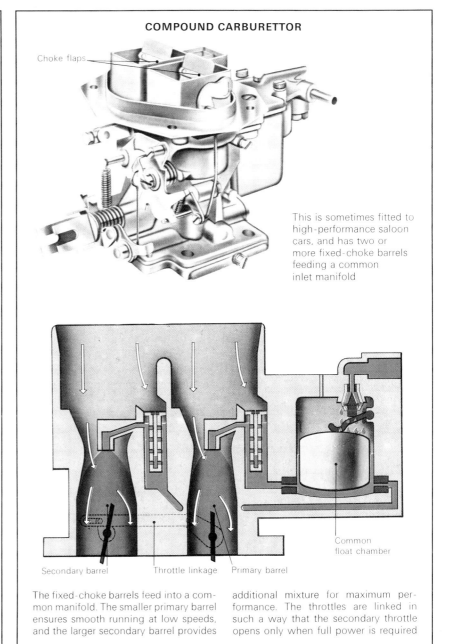

COMPOUND CARBURETTOR

Choke flaps

This is sometimes fitted to high-performance saloon cars, and has two or more fixed-choke barrels feeding a common inlet manifold

Common float chamber

Secondary barrel   Throttle linkage   Primary barrel

The fixed-choke barrels feed into a common manifold. The smaller primary barrel ensures smooth running at low speeds, and the larger secondary barrel provides additional mixture for maximum performance. The throttles are linked in such a way that the secondary throttle opens only when full power is required

Fuel system/petrol supply

Petrol tanks

FUEL TANKS today are positioned well away from the engine, at the rear of a front-engined car or at the front of a rear-engined model.

This reduces the risk of fire, and allows the tank to be at a lower level than if it were in the engine compartment. Some full petrol tanks can weigh as much as 180 lb., and the lower this weight is, the less it will affect the car's handling and stability.

Modern tanks are fitted with baffles, or compartment walls, to restrict the surging of fuel when the car is cornering.

To conform to a variety of safety regulations, the petrol tank and its fuel-line attachments are now constructed in such a manner that there is little danger of their splitting open or spilling fuel, even in the case of a serious rear-end collision.

Moulded plastic tanks, which have the advantage of being completely rust-proof, but have disadvantages, are fitted to a few cars in the U.S.A.

Capacities of petrol tanks vary from 4 to 25 gal., depending on the vehicle's size and its engine capacity, but most cars can run for a minimum of 200 miles on a full tank. Some cars have a reserve petrol supply, others have a low-fuel warning light.

The filler pipe on a tank must be wide enough to take the full rate of flow from filling-station pumps and allow air in the tank to escape during filling.

It is essential to ensure that as the fuel level in the tank sinks, the evacuated space is filled with air from the outside to ensure that the air pressure inside and outside are balanced. If there is a lower pressure inside, the larger air pressure exerted on the outside panels would collapse the fuel tank.

Petrol filters

When a car's tank is filled, dirt and moisture can enter with the petrol. Several filters are incorporated in the fuel supply system to prevent this material accumulating in the carburettor, blocking fuel passages and affecting engine performance.

A fairly coarse filter in the tank itself prevents larger dirt particles and water droplets entering the fuel supply lines.

As temperature rises, petrol expands and gives off fumes. The free venting of these to the atmosphere is no longer permitted in an ever-increasing number of countries. Yet it is impractical to seal the fuel system, including the fuel tank, hermetically. A cylindrical filter, containing a charge of active carbon, can act as a 'scrubber', allowing the air to escape but trapping the hydrocarbon vapours.

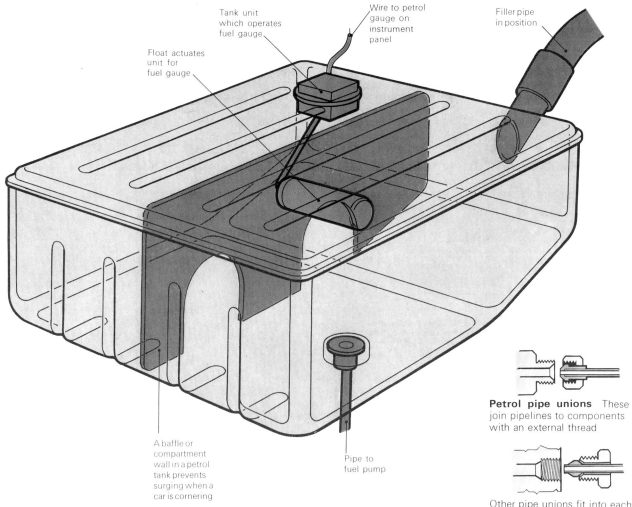

PETROL TANK

Tank unit which operates fuel gauge

Wire to petrol gauge on instrument panel

Filler pipe in position

Float actuates unit for fuel gauge

A baffle or compartment wall in a petrol tank prevents surging when a car is cornering

Pipe to fuel pump

Petrol pipe unions These join pipelines to components with an external thread

Other pipe unions fit into each other with an internal thread

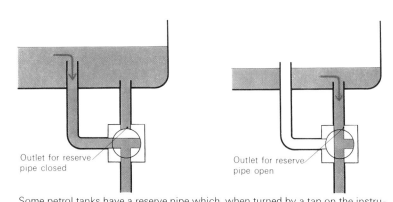

PROVIDING A RESERVE SUPPLY

Outlet for reserve pipe closed

Outlet for reserve pipe open

Some petrol tanks have a reserve pipe which, when turned by a tap on the instrument panel or in the boot, allows petrol to be drawn from a lower level

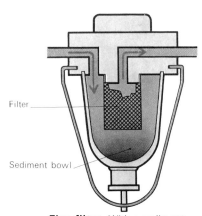

Filter

Sediment bowl

Fine filter With a sediment bowl that can be removed for emptying

Pumping petrol to the carburettor

A PETROL PUMP is necessary in the fuel system, since the carburettor, through which petrol flows, is usually higher than the tank and some distance from it. The pump sucks up petrol by creating a partial vacuum, then pushes it under light pressure towards the carburettor.

There are two types of pump: a mechanical one, which must be in the engine compartment because it is driven by the engine itself; and an electric pump, which is generally fitted close to the tank, away from the engine and its heat.

A mechanical pump consists of a chamber divided by a diaphragm. The top portion contains a filter and a sediment bowl, and has two spring-loaded valves to control the flow of petrol.

The lower portion contains a spring which regulates the pressure of the petrol supply and an operating link and rocker arm driven from the camshaft. The diaphragm is alternately pulled down by the link and pushed up by the spring. When the carburettor is full and its needle valve closed, no petrol can flow and the diaphragm remains in its lower position. This allows the rocker arm to oscillate without moving the diaphragm. Mechanical pumps are extremely reliable, but they operate only when the engine is turning. Although insulated, they are subject to heat from the engine which can cause vapour lock in the fuel system.

Electric pumps work on the same principle as mechanical pumps, except that the diaphragm in the pump is operated by a solenoid (electro-magnet) instead of by the camshaft.

When the solenoid is energised through a pair of contact points, the diaphragm is pulled against its spring and draws petrol from the tank. The contacts then open and the spring pushes the diaphragm and pumps petrol to the carburettor. When the float chamber is full the contact points remain open.

Electric pumps are not affected by engine heat, since they are usually located close to the petrol tank. They start to operate as soon as the ignition circuit is switched on.

This is indicated by a characteristic ticking sound which is rapid at first, as the float chamber fills, but gradually slows to a rate of one tick every few seconds.

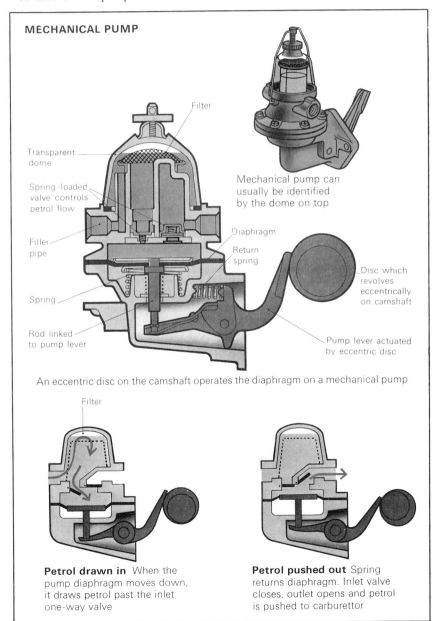

MECHANICAL PUMP

Filter

Mechanical pump can usually be identified by the dome on top

Transparent dome

Spring-loaded valve controls petrol flow

Filler pipe

Diaphragm

Return spring

Spring

Disc which revolves eccentrically on camshaft

Rod linked to pump lever

Pump lever actuated by eccentric disc

An eccentric disc on the camshaft operates the diaphragm on a mechanical pump

Filter

Petrol drawn in When the pump diaphragm moves down, it draws petrol past the inlet one-way valve

Petrol pushed out Spring returns diaphragm. Inlet valve closes, outlet opens and petrol is pushed to carburettor

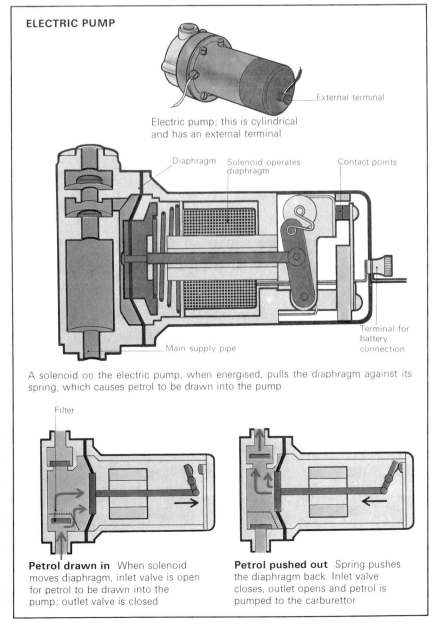

ELECTRIC PUMP

External terminal

Electric pump; this is cylindrical and has an external terminal

Diaphragm

Solenoid operates diaphragm

Contact points

Terminal for battery connection

Main supply pipe

A solenoid on the electric pump, when energised, pulls the diaphragm against its spring, which causes petrol to be drawn into the pump

Filter

Petrol drawn in When solenoid moves diaphragm, inlet valve is open for petrol to be drawn into the pump; outlet valve is closed

Petrol pushed out Spring pushes the diaphragm back. Inlet valve closes, outlet opens and petrol is pumped to the carburettor

Fuel system/air cleaners

Filtering dust from the air

ALL MODERN CARS are fitted with an air cleaner on the carburettor intake. Its most important function is to prevent dust and other particles from getting into the carburettor and engine cylinders.

A normal car engine uses about 100–200 cu. ft of air a minute, and a filter is essential to prevent particles of dust or dirt blocking air jets and causing wear to pistons and cylinder bores.

Filters offer a resistance to air flow and will affect carburettor performance as they become blocked with dirt. They should be replaced or cleaned at regular intervals—say every 12,000 miles.

The air cleaner also acts as a silencer. The filter itself muffles the hissing noise from the carburettor air intake; and the casing and air-intake tube are designed to damp out the resonance of pressure fluctuations in the inlet manifold.

Most engines are fitted with a closed crankcase breathing system, which prevents the engine crankcase fumes reaching the atmosphere. Some systems vent the crankcase to the air cleaner through a tube which connects the rocker cover to the air-cleaner casing. Others vent directly to the inlet manifold.

Emission control
As part of an advanced emission-control system, some air cleaners incorporate temperature-control devices—to supply the engine with air at a constant temperature. Many have a two-position air-intake tube, one (for winter operation) to receive the air warmed by the heat radiated from the exhaust manifold, and the other pointing away from the exhaust to receive a cooler charge for summer conditions.

The cleaners in common use today have either a paper element, which can be discarded and replaced when no longer serviceable, or an oil bath and filter.

The latest designs have plastic units which are light, corrosion-free and less resonant than pressed-steel units.

PAPER-ELEMENT FILTER

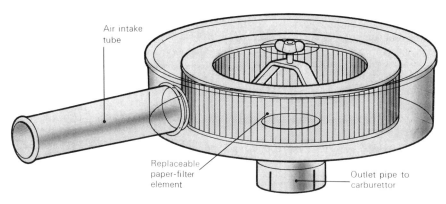

Air intake tube

Replaceable paper-filter element

Outlet pipe to carburettor

There are several types of air cleaners, and their shapes and sizes are generally dictated by engine-compartment space and air flow. A good air cleaner reduces air-intake noise considerably. The paper-element cleaner is the most commonly used. The ring-shaped filter element (below) is made of resin-treated fibrous paper concertinaed to offer a larger surface area to the air passing through it

OIL-BATH FILTER

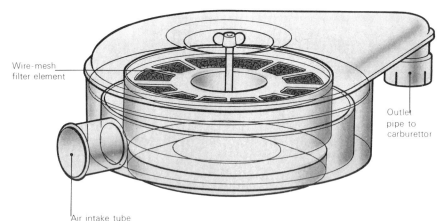

Wire-mesh filter element

Outlet pipe to carburettor

Air intake tube

The oil-bath cleaner is widely used in countries where the air is laden with large quantities of dust. Air entering the centre of the cleaner picks up some of the oil as it passes over the oil bath, which traps the heavier dust particles. As the air is drawn through the wire-mesh filter (below), oil and dust are trapped by the close mesh, leaving clean air to continue on to the carburettor

METAL-MESH FILTER

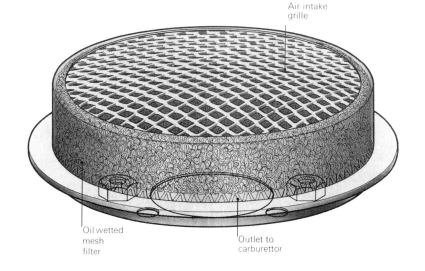

Air intake grille

Oil wetted mesh filter

Outlet to carburettor

The simplest type of air cleaner, the metal-mesh, consists of a coarse metal mesh wetted with oil before being fitted to trap the dust. It is virtually everlasting if the mesh is removed for cleaning and re-oiling at regular intervals. The mesh filter is fitted in a variety of differently shaped casings, some of which have a chamber, similar to that in an exhaust silencer, to reduce noise

Reducing exhaust fumes

International attempts to overcome the problem of atmospheric pollution

THE AIR we breathe is made up of numerous gases. The predominant ones are nitrogen (78 per cent) and oxygen (21 per cent); and the remainder are mainly carbon dioxide, argon and sulphur dioxide, with traces of oxides of nitrogen and ozones. There are nowadays also carbon monoxide and hydrocarbon fumes.

The atmosphere in and around heavily industrialised areas is affected by oil-fired power stations, factories, petro-chemical plants and the spread of oil-fired central heating. But it is the automobile that has become one of the biggest polluters, for the petrol engine emits unburnt and partially burnt fuel plus minute quantities of oxides of nitrogen that are formed in the combustion chambers at very high temperatures. In conditions of strong sunlight and little natural air movement, these hydrocarbon compounds and oxides become the ozone constituents of photochemical smog, a phenomenon that is particularly un-acceptable in places as Los Angeles, San Diego and Tokyo.

Carbon monoxide content

In Western Europe and Britain, the carbon monoxide content of the pollution emitted by cars has always been more significant than smog. The result is that although all industrialised nations have since 1966 been exercising increasingly strict control over vehicle exhaust gases, quite different anti-pollution systems and devices have been developed to meet the specific needs and conditions in different parts of the world.

Most countries have adopted bolt-on afterburning devices which unfortunately result in poorer performance, driveability and fuel consumption. They are moreover expensive and difficult to install. Western Europe, on the other hand, follows the ECE 15 regulations which concentrate on improved combustion inside the engine and are cheaper and more efficient. They cannot, however, achieve the ultra-clean emissions that are demanded in north America and Japan.

Some features are common to all antipollution packages. Positive Crank Case Ventilation (PCV) ensures that hydrocarbon fumes that have been generated within the engine cannot reach the atmosphere. They are instead recon-sumed by the engine via the air intake.

Similarly fumes from the petrol tank are vented through an active carbon filter pack which has been designed to scrub off their volatile hydrocarbon content.

Two thirds of all pollutants are emitted through a car's exhaust system, and it is that emission that has attracted attention in recent years. The new breed of emission-control carburettors and petrol-injection systems, for example, all have features that ensure the combustion process in the engine is as ideal as it can practically made to operate. But prolonged idling, accelera-tion, deceleration and engine warm-up, as well as hot and cold starts offer partic-ularly difficult conditions.

Certainly the systems now used on European cars meet all current and impending legislation, but where the demand for even stricter emission-control the car designers have to sacrifice engine flexibility, performance, fuel consumption and power for all auxilary bolt-on devices consume power.

Compromise solutions

All solutions are in fact a technical and economic compromise. The six most favoured solutions are:

1 Improved combustion in the engine—achieved by better carburation and im-proved manifolding to ensure even mixture distribution, better ignition and timing, better combustion chambers, and better camshaft design.
2 The Man-Air-Ox system—an engine-driven air pump, exhaust recirculation and valves prevent overrich running when the driver suddenly eases off the throttle.

3 Thermal Reactor—instead of an exhaust manifold, the car has a thermal reactor which introduces extra fuel when required to burn up any remaining hydro-carbons or carbon monoxide. The system also requires exhaust gas recirculation and possibly an engine-driven air pump.
4 Oxidising catalyst—partially burnt gases are oxidised in a precious-metal or ceramic-matrix catalyst without the addition of any extra fuel. This system is an improvement on the thermal reactor concept, but the catalysts have a limited life and their effectiveness deteriorates progressively with mileage. They can operate only with totally lead-free petrol and rely on perfect spark plug condition.
5 Twin catalysts—one catalyst can deal with the complete burning of all hydro-carbons and carbon monoxide, but a twin system is needed to meet the most stringent Nox (nitrogen oxides) regula-tions. The first catalyst reduced the oxides into nitrogen, carbon dioxide and steam. To achieve that, the engine must run rich with excess fuel, and that extra fuel needs to be mixed with a controlled amount of air before it enters the second catalyst for oxidation or completion of burning.
6 Selective catalyst—a single catalyst with a sensor unit ahead of its inlet to register the presence of free oxygen, controls electronically the admission of fuel and air into the intake manifold to ensure that the mixture strength is as near as possible to the one which the catalyst can deal effectively to reduce hydrocarbons, carbon monoxide, and the oxides of nitrogen to the desired limits. Although its effectiveness deteriorates with age, it is a significant improvement over the other after burning systems (2, 3, 4 and 5).

With the introduction of anti-pollution legislation and better engineering, great strides have been made in most countries. Taking the model years 1966–1968 as a starting point, the reduction of air pollution achievable on 1977–1978 models (conforming to different national and regional air pollution standards) were:

COUNTRY	EMISSION CONTROL SYSTEM	PRACTICAL REDUCTION OF EMISSION ON 1977–78 MODEL CARS		
		Hydrocarbons (HC)	Carbon Monoxide (CO)	Oxides of Nitrogen (NOX)
Western Europe (ECE 15)	(1)	65%–70%	65%–75%	35%–50%
Sweden/Australia	(2) (3) or (4)	75%–80%	75%–80%	50%–65%
US (except California)	(4)	90%–95%	87%–90%	75%–80%
California	(5) or (6)	about 95%	90%–95%	92%–95%
Japan	(5) or (6)	about 95%	about 95%	about 95%

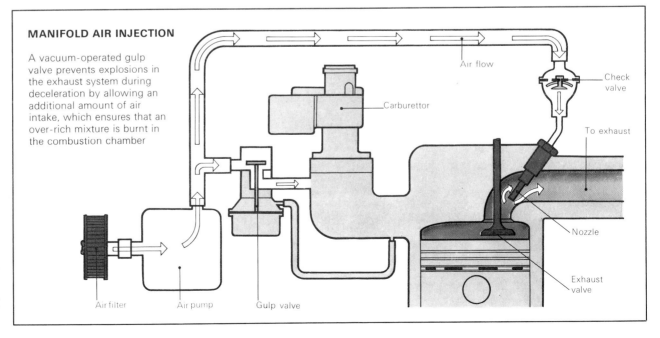

MANIFOLD AIR INJECTION

A vacuum-operated gulp valve prevents explosions in the exhaust system during deceleration by allowing an additional amount of air intake, which ensures that an over-rich mixture is burnt in the combustion chamber

Air flow

Check valve

Carburettor

To exhaust

Nozzle

Exhaust valve

Air filter

Air pump

Gulp valve

Fuel system/petrol injection

TO MEET TODAY's demanding requirements a continuous petrol-injection system has been evolved in which the metering of fuel injected is directly related to the amount of air drawn into the cylinders, and is continuously modulated by the air flow through the air-flow sensor. It is a more reliable, more accurate and more flexible system and it operates at a lower pressure than the original mechanical fuel-injection systems of Lucas, Bosch and Kugelfischer.

In all the latter systems, the metering and injection was carried out under hydraulic pressure, broadly following the diesel injection-pump principle. The limitations of these systems was the lack of instant response to closing the throttle and their mechanical complexity.

To obtain perfect combustion under all the many and rapidly varying operational conditions, the amount of fuel admitted to the cylinders must follow within very close limits the total amount of air drawn in at any one given moment. This gives a basically lean mixture of air and fuel.

For cold-starting, the mixture is enriched by an extra amount of fuel injected by a cold-start valve. A finely atomised spray of neat petrol is injected into the air-intake manifold for as long as the valve is open.

The main metering of petrol to be delivered to each injector is carried out by the fuel-distributor valve, a stepped, cylindrical control plunger which moves up and down in a barrel that has a number of very fine uniform-width slots, one for each cylinder. The greater the air flow, the higher the plunger rises, and a proportionally larger amount of petrol is admitted to the injectors—which are mounted in the cylinder head upstream of the air inlet valve.

The system is so designed that it compensates for any differences in the opening pressure-setting of the injectors, thereby ensuring that measured and equal amounts of petrol are delivered to each cylinder as the inlet valve opens to admit a fresh charge of air-and-fuel mixture.

A fuel accumulator smoothes out the pump pulses and also ensures that when the engine is switched off, pressure is retained in the system for a ready restart—important for hot starts.

Mechanical system

THE LUCAS MECHANICAL SYSTEM uses a shuttle device to control the supply of petrol, instead of the plunger-pump employed on most mechanical systems.

An electrically driven pump, mounted near the fuel tank, draws the fuel through a paper-element filter and delivers it at a pressure of 100 psi to the control unit or metering distributor. Pressure is kept constant by a relief valve which returns excess fuel to the tank. Delivery of the fuel is timed by an engine-driven cylinder or rotor, revolving inside the metering distributor, which has a fuel inlet and outlets.

The cylinder has radial holes, or ports, leading to its bore, which contains a shuttle that is free to move between two stops, one fixed and one adjustable. As the rotor turns at half engine speed, its ports align with the fuel inlet and allow fuel pressure to force the shuttle to and fro between its stops, delivering fuel to each injector in turn. The adjustable stop is positioned by a cam controlled by engine manifold pressure, thus varying the maximum shuttle travel and the quantity of fuel delivered.

From the metering distributor, the accurately timed and carefully metered quantities of fuel are delivered to each of the injectors in turn. The injector valves are held closed by springs until they are opened by the fuel pressure. They deliver a highly atomised spray of fuel on to the back of the inlet valves.

A manual control to enrich the fuel supply for cold starting is provided on the instrument panel. It operates in a similar way to the normal choke control, and alters the amount of shuttle movement in the metering distributor.

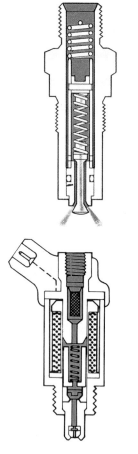

LUCAS MECHANICAL PETROL INJECTION

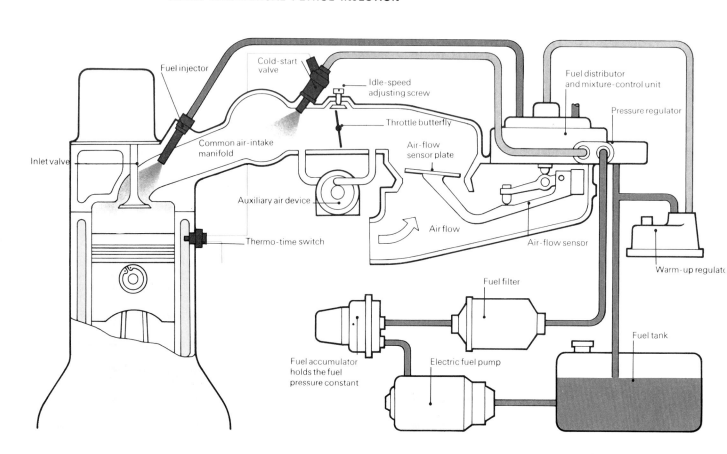

Fuel injector
Cold-start valve
Idle-speed adjusting screw
Fuel distributor and mixture-control unit
Pressure regulator
Throttle butterfly
Inlet valve
Common air-intake manifold
Air-flow sensor plate
Auxiliary air device
Air flow
Thermo-time switch
Air-flow sensor
Warm-up regulator
Fuel filter
Fuel accumulator holds the fuel pressure constant
Electric fuel pump
Fuel tank

Electronic system

THE MAIN difference between electronic and mechanical injection is that in an electronic system the admission of fuel and air is governed by a complex electronic control unit, not by a mechanical or pneumatic input. Electronic circuits govern both the timing and duration of admission.

These advantages are well illustrated in one of the most common electronic systems, the Bosch, which operates at lower fuel pressures (25–30 psi) than mechanical systems. It has an electrically driven pump which draws more fuel from the tank than is needed for injection; the excess fuel returns to the tank through a pressure regulator, reducing the possibility of vapour lock.

The injectors are held closed by springs and opened by solenoids (electromagnets). The amount of fuel injected depends on how long the solenoid holds the injector open. This in turn depends on the signal the solenoid receives from an electronic control unit, or computer.

This computer is linked to a number of sensing devices which measure various engine conditions, such as air pressure in the manifold, air and water temperatures, rate of acceleration and throttle position. The sensors enable the computer to determine instantly the signal strength for the injectors. To simplify the electronic system, pairs of injectors usually squirt simultaneously just before the inlet valves open. This cuts down the number of devices needed to trigger the injectors.

BOSCH ELECTRONIC PETROL INJECTION

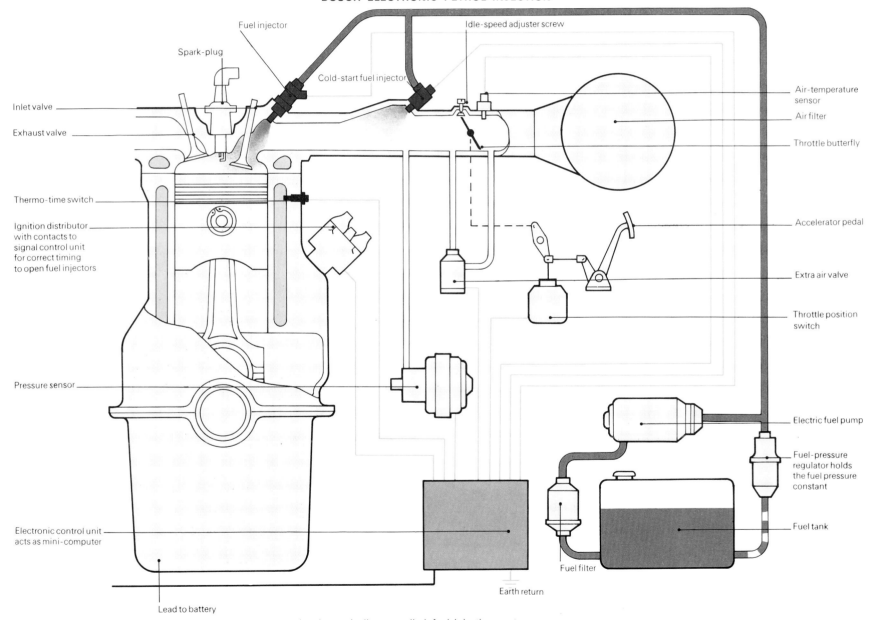

In electronically controlled fuel-injection systems, sensors measure changes in conditions in the engine and pass impulses to the control unit which governs the petrol/air mixture supply to each of the combustion chambers

Petrol/what it has to do

Additives raise the octane number

PETROL has to contain a combination of properties to be suitable for use in a car engine. It has to be volatile (that is, it must vaporise easily) to give trouble-free starting in cold weather and quick warm-up with little use of the choke. But it must not be so volatile that it vaporises too readily, causing a condition known as vapour lock, or is uneconomical in use.

Petrol must also be resistant to detonation (evidenced by a noise known as knocking or pinking). It should be clean, and free from any tendency to leave deposits.

Knocking occurs when a car is using a grade of petrol that is too low in octane number for the compression ratio of the engine. Continuous knocking will overheat the piston and eventually burn a hole in it.

If the octane number of the petrol is not high enough, the mixture detonates (explodes uncontrollably) instead of burning smoothly across the combustion space. The detonation can be heard at low speeds outside the engine as a metallic knock.

Almost any fault that increases temperature within the engine above the normal working temperature will result in an increased octane number requirement.

All petrols contain a range of petrol-soluble additives to resist oxidation, vapour locking, gum formation and corrosion. The amount of lead per gallon (which improves the octane rating) is strictly controlled—although its harmfulness to humans in small quantities has not been proved. On the other hand, even minute quantities can make certain anti-pollution systems ineffective. For that reason, lead-free petrols of 90–92 octane rating have been introduced in the USA.

Mixture strength

The correct ratio of air and petrol for good combustion is approximately 15 parts of air to 1 part of petrol by weight. This allows complete combustion with minimum waste; but it may be weakened to 16:1 for economical, steady-speed cruising, and may need to be enriched to about 12:1 for maximum power, as when accelerating, and 1:1 for starting in very cold weather.

A mixture that is either too rich, because the proportion of petrol is greater than it should be, or is too weak, may fail to ignite. If the engine stalls through over-richness (from excessive use of the choke, for example) the cylinders should be cleared by depressing the accelerator and operating the starter until the engine fires.

Condensation of moisture occurs inside all fuel tanks, especially in those exposed to low temperatures at night after the car has been in warm sunshine during the day. The least condensation occurs in underground storage tanks.

When a car is parked at night, it is usually warm. As it cools, air—which contains moisture—is drawn into the petrol tank. Condensation occurs and water droplets, which are heavier than petrol, fall to the bottom of the tank and promote rust.

It is good practice in any case to fill up the tank before the petrol level becomes low, so that any water or dirt in the bottom of the tank remains undisturbed and is not drawn into the system.

If petrol is stored in the garage at home, it must be kept in a Home Office approved container. It is illegal to store more than 2 gallons (see p. 23). Petrol should be drained from the pump and carburettor before a car is left in store for a long time, to prevent the formation of gum deposits which may clog the fuel system.

NORMAL COMBUSTION

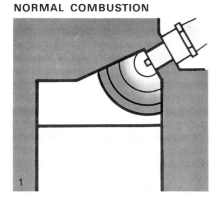

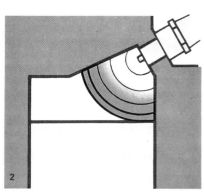

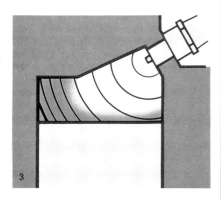

With petrol of the correct octane, the spark at the spark-plug starts the burning (fig. 1) and the flame spreads progressively through the compressed petrol/air mixture (figs. 2 and 3) causing it to expand rapidly and so giving an even thrust to the piston

KNOCKING

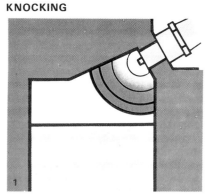

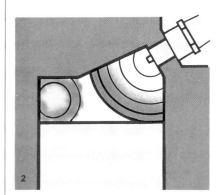

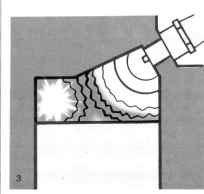

A violent explosion takes place (fig. 3) when unsuitable petrol causes high temperatures which detonate some of the mixture (fig. 2) before it can be reached by the flame front. Continuous knocking will eventually burn a hole in the piston

PRE-IGNITION

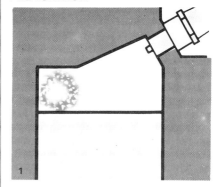

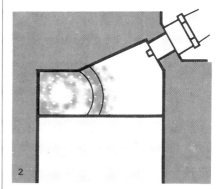

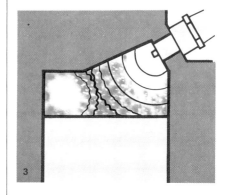

Glowing deposits of carbon on the piston head or in the combustion chamber (fig. 1) ignite the petrol/air mixture before sparking occurs, and this results (fig. 3) in a form of knocking. Pre-ignition can also be caused by faulty ignition timing

Octane numbers and star rating

A PETROL'S OCTANE NUMBER is determined by matching the petrol against a mixture of two petroleum fluids in a laboratory test engine. One, iso-octane, has a high resistance to knocking. The other, normal-heptane, has a low resistance.

A petrol is said to have a 90 octane number if it has the same anti-knock ability in the laboratory test engine as 90 parts of octane mixed with 10 parts of heptane.

The compression ratio of the test engine is adjustable while running, so that a 'just knocking' condition can be produced in any petrol.

The octane number given to petrols sold at garages in Britain comes under a British Standard 'star rating' system. Two-star petrol has a minimum octane number of 90, three-star 94, four-star 97 and five-star petrol at least 100 octane. The British Standard also sets limits to the volatility,

lead content and other features which control deposit formation, odour and the storage life of petrol.

Petrol is a very complex mixture of hydrocarbons, and the octane number is only one of a number of characteristics that affect its behaviour in engines. These characteristics change during storage to varying degrees, and it is therefore a wise precaution to use busy filling stations which have a rapid turnover. The octane requirement of an engine will also vary with time and mileage, due to the gradual build-up of carbon in the combustion chambers, and other factors.

The best course is to follow the octane recommendation of the car manufacturer. There is no advantage in using a petrol with a higher number than required, although there is no disadvantage, apart from the extra cost.

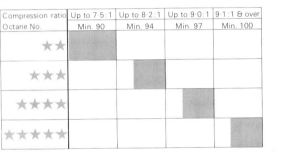

Compression ratio	Up to 7·5:1	Up to 8·2:1	Up to 9·0:1	9·1:1 & over
Octane No.	Min. 90	Min. 94	Min. 97	Min. 100
★★				
★★★				
★★★★				
★★★★★				

Octane rating The number of stars on a petrol pump indicates the petrol's knocking resistance, or octane rating

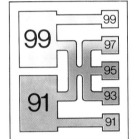

Blending pump gives choice of octane numbers

Vapour lock and icing

THE FUEL SUPPLY can be restricted in warm weather by vapour lock. Vapour bubbles form in the fuel system between the tank and the carburettor, and prevent the pump delivering petrol to the carburettor. This trouble develops when the fuel system is too hot.

Sometimes engine heat can cause petrol in the carburettor bowl to boil when the engine has stopped. This causes an excessively rich mixture in the induction pipe or manifold and makes starting difficult until the engine has cooled.

To avoid these troubles, petrol companies alter the volatility to suit summer and winter temperature changes.

Carburettor icing occurs in cold, damp weather when moisture in the air supply freezes inside the carburettor.

Frost on the outside of the carburettor does no harm, but on the inside it restricts, and sometimes closes, the air passages. The engine loses power and stalls when idling. Although additives in the petrol help to minimise the chances of this happening, icing may still occur in very damp weather. It can be cured by switching off the engine, waiting a few minutes until engine heat has had time to melt the ice, and then restarting.

The compounds of lead which are added to improve petrol's anti-knock qualities could by themselves cause deposits on the valve seats. Other additives help to prevent this happening.

Fuel consumption

DRIVING METHODS have a considerable effect on fuel consumption; variations can occur even in similar runs made on consecutive days, because of differences in speed and traffic conditions.

A car travelling on a motorway might cover 40 miles on a gallon of petrol at 50 mph, but only 25 miles to the gallon at 70 mph. In stop-start traffic, it might cover as little as 20 miles to the gallon.

The first mile, run with a cold engine, uses much more fuel than a mile run when the engine is warm, so it is important to get the engine warm quickly. In most cases, this is best done by driving the car away immediately after the engine has started and not allowing it to idle, and by using the choke as little as possible. This procedure also minimises engine wear.

Some car designs require that the engine should be run at a fast idle (about 1000 rpm) without choke for a couple of minutes after a cold start. Manufacturers make recommendations accordingly.

Measuring fuel consumption accurately is not easy, but a fair idea can be obtained by filling the petrol tank to the neck before a long journey. After the run, refill the tank to the same level. Dividing the number of replaced gallons into the miles covered will indicate consumption.

A conclusion should never be based on the result of a single observation—cumulative records over several runs give a more accurate picture.

How petrol is refined and processed to suit car engines

PETROL is one of the many products derived from petroleum—more commonly known as crude oil. The crude oil is distilled in a refinery in a tall metal container known as a fractionating tower.

The oil is heated in a furnace to a temperature that will ensure that all the products to be extracted are vaporised. As the vapour rises in the column, it condenses into liquid at different levels.

Petrol obtained from the fractionating tower is low in octane number. It has to be processed to obtain a suitable octane number and treated to remove, or at least counteract, corrosive or gum-forming elements. Then it is blended into various grades and treated with additives to increase its resistance to detonation, and to control carburettor icing.

Petrol, especially some of the higher grades, is also produced as a by-product of other chemical processes, but the source of most petrols is crude oil.

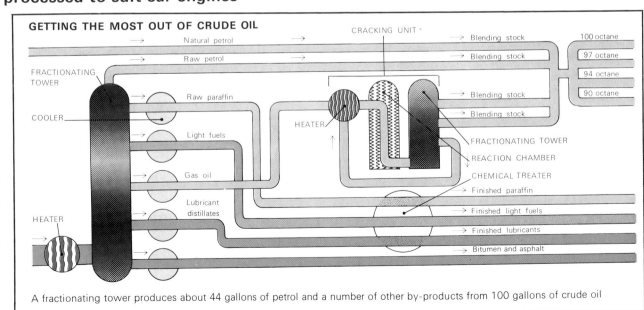

A fractionating tower produces about 44 gallons of petrol and a number of other by-products from 100 gallons of crude oil

Ignition system

How sparks are produced

A PETROL ENGINE provides power to propel the car by burning a mixture of petrol and air in its cylinders. The ignition system provides the electric sparks that ignite the mixture.

Each cylinder has a spark-plug with two metal points called electrodes, which project into the combustion chamber. When electricity is fed to the spark-plug at a high enough voltage, current jumps across the gap between the electrodes as a spark.

Spark-ignition systems are basically the same on all modern cars. Those using electronic ignition may differ in detail.

The rest of the ignition system supplies electricity to the spark-plugs at a high enough voltage and at exactly the right moment in each cylinder.

Electricity will not easily jump the gap between the spark-plug's electrodes. The further apart the electrodes are, the higher is the voltage needed to make a spark. But as the spark must be 'fat' enough for effective burning of the petrol/air mixture, and as the width of the gap between the electrodes governs the size of the spark, the gap is usually set to about 0·025 in.

The voltage fed to the spark-plugs must be high—approximately 14,000 volts. To allow for some loss of voltage in the system, up to 30,000 volts may need to be generated. A normal car battery delivers only 6 or 12 volts; this voltage is boosted thousands of times by the coil. Once this increased voltage has been produced, it has to be delivered to each spark-plug at the correct moment in the 4-stroke cycle.

The distributor feeds electricity to each of the cylinders in turn, depending on the firing order. One part of it, the contact-breaker, also works with the coil in generating the necessary high voltage.

A condenser wired to the contact-breaker prevents excessive 'arcing' (sparking) across the points.

The battery

ELECTRICITY is supplied by the battery to the ignition system, the starter motor, the lights, indicators and the rest of a car's electrical equipment.

The battery is made up of a number of cells, each of just over 2 volts, connected by metal bars. Car batteries have either three cells, giving a total of 6 volts, or six cells, giving 12 volts.

Each cell consists of two sets of plates (the electrodes) in a solution of dilute sulphuric acid (the electrolyte). One electrode is made of lead dioxide and the other of spongy lead.

When the cell is functioning, the acid reacts with the plates, converting chemical energy into electrical energy. A positive charge is built up on the lead peroxide electrode and a negative charge on the other electrode.

Electric current, measured in amperes (amp.), flows from one pole of the battery through the car circuit, back to the battery and then through the electrolyte.

As the chemical reaction goes on, lead sulphate forms on the surface of both electrodes, and the sulphuric acid turns to water. When the surfaces of both plates have turned completely to lead sulphate, the battery is flat. Recharging the cell with an electric current restores the electrodes to their original condition and regenerates the sulphuric acid.

A battery eventually goes dead and cannot be recharged for a number of reasons: the plates become encrusted with sulphate, so that a charge cannot get through to them; they may disintegrate; a leakage between the cells may cause a short circuit.

The heaviest demand is made on a battery when the car is being started. Once the engine is running, the generator provides a flow of current to the battery to recharge it and keep it charged.

In most modern cars the negative terminal of the battery is earthed by connection to the chassis or bodywork.

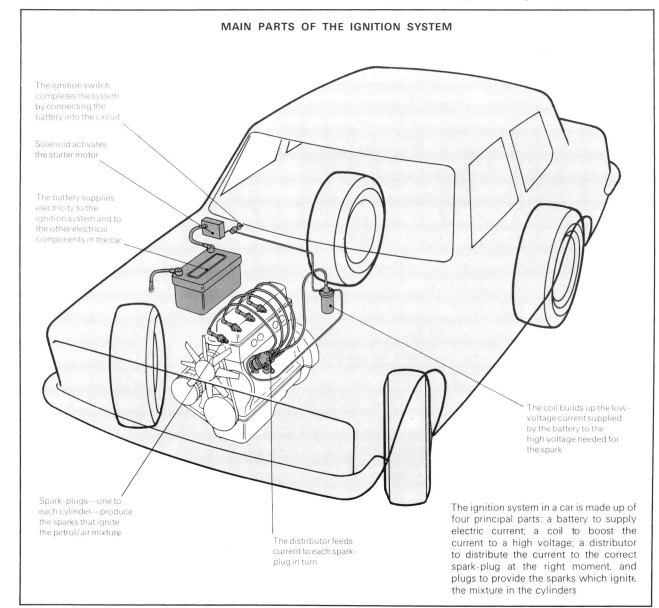

MAIN PARTS OF THE IGNITION SYSTEM

The ignition switch completes the system by connecting the battery into the circuit

Solenoid activates the starter motor

The battery supplies electricity to the ignition system and to the other electrical components in the car

Spark-plugs—one to each cylinder—produce the sparks that ignite the petrol/air mixture

The distributor feeds current to each spark-plug in turn

The coil builds up the low-voltage current supplied by the battery to the high voltage needed for the spark

The ignition system in a car is made up of four principal parts: a battery to supply electric current; a coil to boost the current to a high voltage; a distributor to distribute the current to the correct spark-plug at the right moment, and plugs to provide the sparks which ignite the mixture in the cylinders

WHAT THE BATTERY HAS TO DO

The battery is an essential reservoir for storing power to start the car and to operate the lights when the engine is not running. Its capacity is measured in amp. hours. A 56 amp. hour battery should be able to deliver a current of 1 amp. for 56 hours, or 2 amp. for 28 hours, and so on. The heaviest demand on a battery is when the car is being started. It can take an initial 300 to 400 amp. to rotate the engine from standstill, whereas a single parking light may need only $\frac{1}{2}$ amp.

THE SINGLE CELL

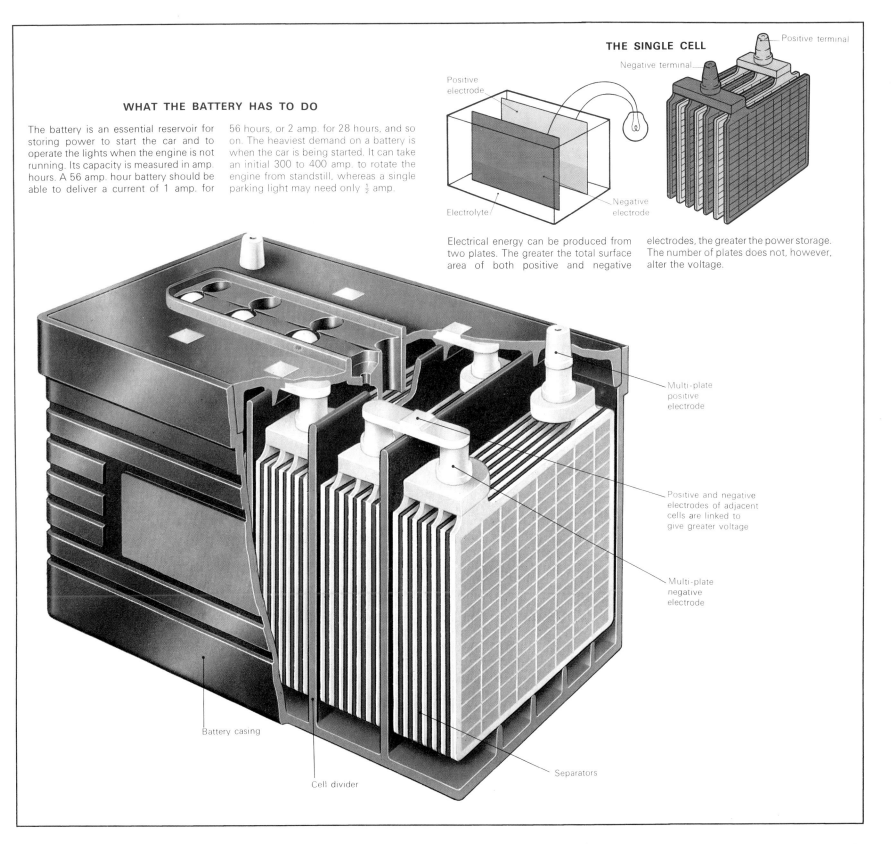

Positive terminal

Negative terminal

Positive electrode

Electrolyte

Negative electrode

Electrical energy can be produced from two plates. The greater the total surface area of both positive and negative electrodes, the greater the power storage. The number of plates does not, however, alter the voltage.

Multi-plate positive electrode

Positive and negative electrodes of adjacent cells are linked to give greater voltage

Multi-plate negative electrode

Battery casing

Cell divider

Separators

Ignition system/the coil

A CAR BATTERY produces either 6 or 12 volts, but a voltage thousands of times higher is needed to produce the sparks which ignite the petrol/air mixture.

It is the coil which boosts the low-voltage current from the battery, transforming it into high voltage for the spark-plugs. The coil in an average car can produce as much as 30,000 volts to provide the high voltage for the spark-plugs.

It works on the principle that when electricity flows in a coil of wire, a magnetic field is produced; and conversely, when a magnetic field breaks down, elec-tricity is generated in any coil of wire within the field's lines of force.

The original voltage will be boosted if there are two windings of wire, one with many more turns than the other.

The coil's two windings surround a soft iron core, which concentrates the magnetic field. One, the primary winding, consists of a few hundred turns of fairly thick wire. This is the low-voltage part, and takes electricity from the battery. The other, the secondary winding, is made up of thousands of turns of fine wire (perhaps a mile in all). This is the high-voltage part, feed-ing current to the spark-plugs. When the ignition key is turned, electricity from the battery flows to one terminal on the ignition coil, through the primary winding, and from the winding's other terminal to the contact-breaker points in the distributor (see p. 70).

If the contact-breaker points are closed, current will flow through them, turning the primary winding and iron core into an electro-magnet and so building up a magnetic field. The current then completes its circuit through the body of the car and back to the battery.

THE COIL AND DISTRIBUTOR

Low-voltage current from the battery builds up a magnetic field and the rapid collapse of this field induces in the coil a high-voltage current which is passed on to the distributor

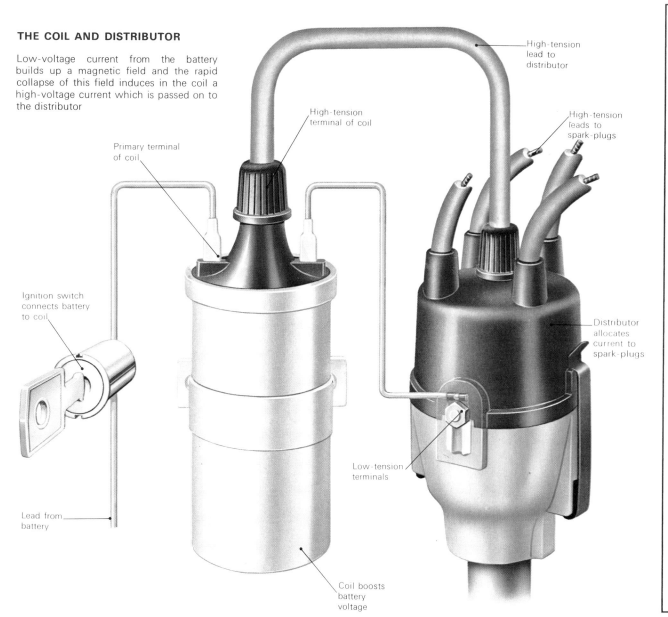

High-tension lead to distributor

High-tension terminal of coil

High-tension leads to spark-plugs

Primary terminal of coil

Ignition switch connects battery to coil

Distributor allocates current to spark-plugs

Low-tension terminals

Lead from battery

Coil boosts battery voltage

HOW THE COIL WORKS

The closed contact-breaker allows current to flow through the primary winding of the coil. When the breaker points open, the circuit is momentarily interrupted to generate high-voltage current in the secondary winding, which is fed through the distributor to the spark-plugs

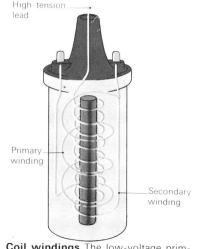

High-tension lead

Primary winding

Secondary winding

Coil windings The low-voltage primary winding has only a few hundred turns of wire; secondary has thousands

When the contact-breaker points open, current ceases to flow in the primary winding of the coil and the magnetic field collapses—through the thousands of turns of wire in the secondary winding.

This generates a very high voltage in the secondary winding. The greater the number of turns it has, the stronger the magnetic field; and the faster its collapse, the higher the voltage produced.

High-tension (HT) current from the secondary winding is passed to the spark-plugs through the distributor, and back to the coil through the car body.

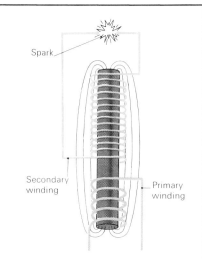

Spark

Secondary winding

Primary winding

Principle of the coil Low-voltage current sets up a magnetic field around a core to induce a voltage high enough for the spark required

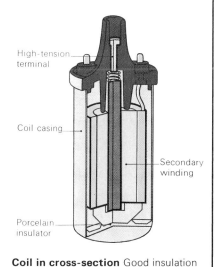

High-tension terminal

Coil casing

Secondary winding

Porcelain insulator

Coil in cross-section Good insulation is needed for the high voltage

Low-tension (12v.) system

High-tension system

Earth

Plug leads not receiving current

THE COMPLETE SYSTEM

In a coil ignition system, low-voltage current flows from the battery through the primary circuit to the condenser and contact-breaker. The circuit is completed, with the current returning through the engine and car body High-tension current generated in the coil flows through the distributor to the spark-plugs

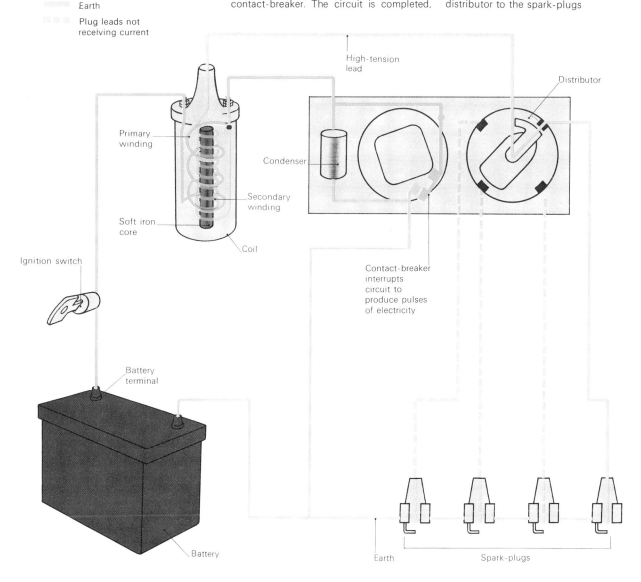

High-tension lead

Distributor

Primary winding

Condenser

Secondary winding

Soft iron core

Coil

Ignition switch

Contact-breaker interrupts circuit to produce pulses of electricity

Battery terminal

Battery

Earth

Spark-plugs

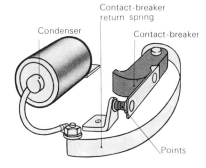

Condenser

Contact-breaker return spring

Contact-breaker

Points

CONDENSER WITH CONTACT-BREAKER

When the magnetic field collapses, a voltage is induced in the primary winding which is high enough to cause an arc across the opening contact-breaker points. As this would soon cause burning and pitting, a condenser (more correctly called a capacitor) is added to suppress arcing. It is housed in the distributor and is connected across the contact-breaker points.

Current cannot pass through a condenser because it consists of two metallic parts separated by insulation; but it acts as a reservoir for the electrical energy which would otherwise cause arcing when the points are separated.

This energy flows back on the rebound through the primary winding of the coil, speeding the collapse of the magnetic field and so increasing the voltage in the secondary winding

Ignition system/distributor

THE DISTRIBUTOR is the moving mechanical link between the electrical components of the ignition system and the engine.

It switches on and off the current to the coil's primary winding by means of a contact-breaker, and distributes the coil's high-voltage output to the spark-plugs in the required firing order by means of a rotor arm.

The rotor arm is attached to the distributor shaft, and as it rotates it connects the centre terminal of the cap, which is wired to the coil, to the spark-plug leads, one after the other.

The outer terminals in the distributor cap are connected by separate leads to the spark-plugs.

Since the firing order of the cylinders governs the sequence in which current is transmitted to the spark-plugs, it is essential that any disconnected plug leads should be reconnected to their correct spark-plugs.

The distributor shaft is usually driven by the camshaft through gearing that rotates the two shafts at the same speed. In this way, current is fed to the spark-plugs at the correct moment in relation to the 4-stroke cycle. With some engines the distributor shaft is driven directly from the crankshaft, gearing reducing it to half engine speed.

Ignition advance

Whatever the engine speed, combustion takes a similar amount of time. When the engine is idling ignition occurs just before the piston reaches the top of its compression stroke, which allows time for expansion to drive the piston down.

As the engine speed increases, there is less time between the up and down strokes, so the firing must be advanced to give time for combustion and expansion. This is done by a centrifugal advance timing mechanism, which can be supplemented by a vacuum advance unit.

MAIN PARTS OF THE DISTRIBUTOR

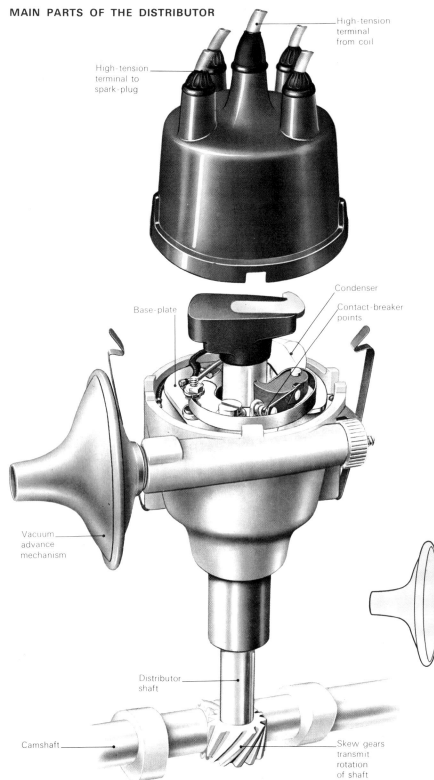

High-voltage current is supplied to each of the spark-plugs in their order of firing

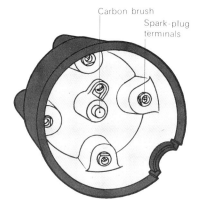

Distributor cap A lead from the coil to the distributor cap carries current to a central stud or spring-loaded carbon brush always in contact with the rotor arm. Terminals round the brush, one for each cylinder, are connected to the spark-plugs

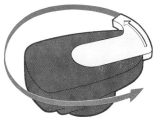

Rotor arm When the arm rotates, current flows through its metal electrode from the central brush and sparks across a gap to each of the spark-plug terminals in turn

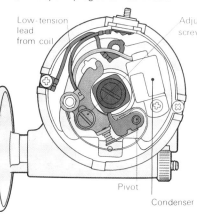

Distributor body The body contains the low-voltage section of the distributor including the contact points—the devices which time the ignition. The contact-breaker has one moving point operated by a cam on the distributor shaft. The other point of the breaker is fixed to the base-plate of the distributor body and remains stationary except for adjustments to the contact-breaker gap. The condenser, which protects the contact-breaker points from excessive arcing, is also mounted on the base-plate

How the contact-breaker interrupts the current flow

THE CONTACT-BREAKER is operated by a cam which forms part of the distributor shaft. There are as many lobes on the cam as there are cylinders in the engine.

As the shaft rotates, the cam operates an arm that forces the contact-breaker points apart. A spring closes them when the cam moves round. In this way the points continually make and break the low-voltage circuit.

Arcing (sparking) between the points is reduced by a condenser which is connected across the points. When the contact-breaker points open, the low-voltage current flowing from the battery through the primary winding of the coil switches off and the magnetic field collapses.

This induces a high-voltage current in the secondary winding of the coil; and this current flows through a cable to the distributor cap and along the rotor arm electrode to one of the cap's outer metal electrodes. From there, a cable provides a path for the current to flow to a spark-plug.

There is no contact between the rotor arm and the terminals. The gap between them and the arm is not large enough to hinder seriously the high-voltage impulses from the coil. It serves as a spark intensifier.

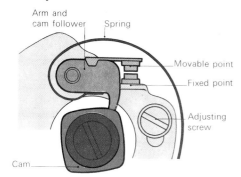

Contact-breaker has two points, one fixed, the other movable and operated through an arm by a cam on the rotating shaft

As the cam turns, the spring forces down the arm, and the points close, so that current once more flows between them

THE ROTOR ARM IN ACTION

High-voltage current from the coil flows into the rotor arm and is passed to the spark-plug terminals in rotation

Automatic ignition advance for higher engine speeds

AUTOMATIC ignition advance ensures that under every operating condition, ignition takes place at the best instant to give clean combustion, fuel economy and power.

The precise timing of the spark significantly affects the level of free hydrocarbons and carbon monoxide emitted in the engine exhaust. For a typical emission-controlled vehicle, the amount of spark advance at 2500 engine rpm may be 40° before top dead centre for cruising, 25° for full-load pulling uphill and 15° for going downhill with a closed throttle. For idling or overrun braking with a closed throttle over the engine speed range of 600 to 1200 rpm, the ignition point may be timed to occur 10° after TDC.

The overrun closed throttle and idling correction is usually achieved by a dual-diaphragm vacuum-advance mechanism. In addition to the standard vacuum-advance unit, there is a retard unit to counteract the suction of the advance mechanism only when the engine is at idle or the throttle is closed during overrun engine braking. It is vacuum-operated, but derives its suction power from a bleed pipe on the other side of the throttle valve.

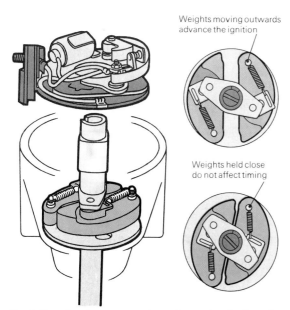

Centrifugal advance consists of a pair of pivoted weights held close to the distributor shaft by springs. Centrifugal force throws the weights outwards as the engine speed increases; they are linked to the cam so that the farther they move out the earlier the points open

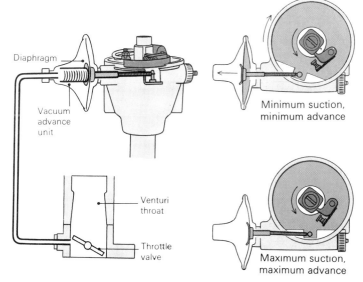

Vacuum advance is operated by a partial vacuum in the inlet manifold. When the throttle is only partly open, suction pulls on a diaphragm. This advances the spark timing by moving the contact-breaker points in relation to the cam. With the throttle fully open, there is reduced pull on the diaphragm and less vacuum advance

Ignition system/spark-plugs

How a spark-plug works

SPARK-PLUGS produce the electric sparks which ignite the petrol/air mixture in an engine's cylinders. The remainder of the ignition system produces the correctly timed high-voltage pulses of electricity that make the sparks.

A spark-plug consists of a metal electrode passing through the centre of a ceramic insulator. Surrounding the lower portion of the insulator is a metal casing that is screwed into the cylinder head. Welded to the bottom of the casing, and so 'earthed' to the car through the cylinder head, is another electrode. It is separated from the tip of the centre electrode by a small gap.

High-tension (HT) current from the distributor flows down the centre electrode and jumps this gap in the form of a spark.

For good engine performance, the spark must be big enough to ignite the fuel mixture efficiently. This means the gap must be fairly wide; but the wider it is, the higher the voltage needed to produce a spark. Most plugs on modern cars have a recommended gap of 0·020 to 0·040 in. The clearance must be checked regularly, as the electrodes will be slowly eroded and may become coated with deposits.

Combustion deposits on the spark-plug insulator nose divert some of the ignition energy to earth, for they constitute a lower resistance to the flow of electrons than the spark-plug gap. Electrons always take the easiest path. Condensation, dirt and oily deposits on the distributor cap, high-tension cables and spark-plug rob the spark of a great deal of its ignition energy. And a crack in the insulator, or a film of oil or water, will cause leakage of electricity and a weak spark or failure to spark.

A gasket ensures a gas-tight seal between the spark-plug and the cylinder head. Alternatively, some plugs have a conical seating portion which enters a conical recess in the cylinder head and so provides a seal without a gasket.

SECTIONAL VIEW THROUGH TYPICAL SPARK-PLUG

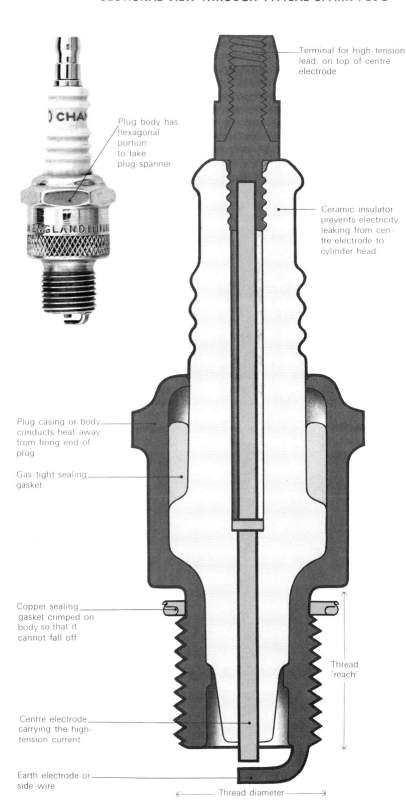

Terminal for high-tension lead, on top of centre electrode

Plug body has hexagonal portion to take plug spanner

Ceramic insulator prevents electricity leaking from centre electrode to cylinder head

Plug casing or body conducts heat away from firing end of plug

Gas-tight sealing gasket

Copper sealing gasket crimped on body so that it cannot fall off

Thread 'reach'

Centre electrode carrying the high-tension current

Earth electrode or side-wire

Thread diameter

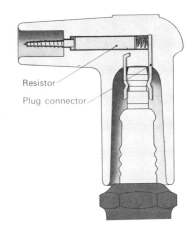

Resistor

Plug connector

Suppressors When a spark is formed, it acts as a miniature radio transmitter and causes interference to nearby radio and television reception. All cars are required by law to be fitted with suppressors (resistors), which limit interference. Earlier practice was to embody the suppressor in the high-tension lead or connector (above). However, on many modern cars there is no problem; the leads themselves form the suppressors, being made of a graphite-impregnated material

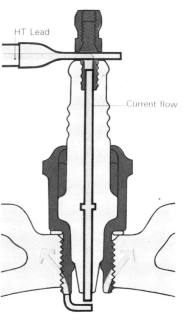

HT Lead

Current flow

Current Flow path is from the distributor, along the high-tension lead, through the terminal at the top of the plug and down the centre electrode. At the bottom, electricity jumps the gap—in the form of a spark—to the earth electrode, which is connected to the engine block

Why spark-plugs vary in different engines

SPARK-PLUGS vary in their design to suit the loading and speed range of an engine, its combustion-chamber design, varying mixture strengths, compression ratios and operating temperatures.

Hot and cold plugs

Plugs are classified according to their heat range—that is, their ability to transfer heat from the firing tip of the centre electrode and dissipate it to the engine's cooling system (see p. 74).

A 'cold' plug has a short insulator and hence a shorter distance for heat to travel. This plug transfers heat quickly and so is used for highly tuned engines and continuous high-speed running. In a cooler-running engine, it would become fouled up.

A 'hot' plug has a longer insulator and takes longer to transfer heat from the firing tip, so operating at a higher temperature to compensate for the cooler running of the engine. A hot plug is unsuitable for a highly tuned engine, since it would overheat and cause pre-ignition.

Spark-plugs are made in various heat ranges from 'cold' to 'hot', to ensure dependable performance in any engine.

Long and short-reach plugs

The length of the threaded portion of a spark-plug varies according to the thickness of the cylinder head above the combustion chamber. The length of the thread is known as the 'reach' of a plug. A long-reach plug should never be fitted in a short-reach head because the protruding end may damage a valve or piston. A short-reach plug in a long-reach head will expose cylinder-head threads to combustion, and make it difficult to fit a plug of the correct length later.

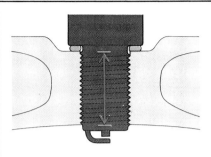

Long-reach plug Used where the cylinder-head section is very deep. In a thinner head, such a plug would project too far into the combustion chamber

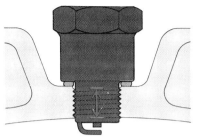

Short-reach plug Used where the cylinder-head section is thin. In a deeper head, this plug's electrodes would be too far recessed for efficient ignition

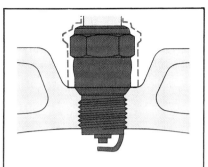

Tapered-shoulder plug Used instead of a plug with a gasket. The conical shoulder is tightened into a recess to provide a gas-tight seal

Side-gap plug Often used in highly tuned engines

Three-gap plug Has three earthed electrodes (one obscured in drawing) to give longer plug life

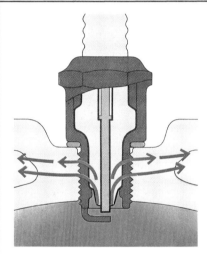

Cold plug Has a short insulator and therefore a short heat-flow path. Used on high-performance engines to prevent pre-ignition through overheating

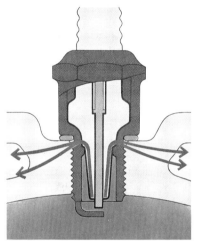

Hot plug Has a long insulator and therefore a long heat-flow path; used for low-performance engines. A hot plug also burns off any deposits

The advantages of electronic ignition

THE MORE CYLINDERS and the higher the engine rpm range, the greater the need for an electronic ignition system.

In a conventional system, the ignition energy and voltage available at the spark-plug to fire the mixture of petrol and air in the cylinder are limited by the electrical and mechanical switching capability of the contact-breaker points. Such systems can reliably produce only about 24,000 sparks a minute.

Problems overcome

Arcing and poor gap-setting at the points, unsatisfactory low-speed performance, high-speed cam bounce and the inevitable gradual deterioration of contact-breaker performance are all overcome in electronic systems.

The main advantages are:
1. They enable more precise ignition control and so can tolerate a leaner fuel/air mixture strength giving some slight fuel saving.
2. They are almost maintenance-free for 30,000–40,000 miles and they prolong spark-plug life by about 50 per cent—because they provide strong sparks and are less affected by moisture and dirt on the high-tension cable or by spark-plug deposits.
3. They are essential to keep an engine accurately tuned in compliance with strict exhaust emission regulations.

Two basic types

There are two basic types—inductive and capacity discharge. In both systems the make-and-break mechanism of the conventional system is replaced by an optical or magnetic trigger which is quicker and more precise. This helps to generate the high-voltage output from the coil or capacity-discharge device and overcomes poor starting, occasional misfire and other malfunctioning associated with such severe operating conditions as dampness, cold winter motoring, stop-start and slow-speed city driving.

The inductive system is usually adequate for 4-cylinder engines, but for high-speed 6-, 8- or 12-cylinder machines, there may be some advantages in the more complex, costlier capacity discharge system—because it can develop a very strong spark and it has a higher potential spark rate than even the best inductive electronic systems.

As the need for more precise sparking increases, more and more new cars will be equipped with electronic ignition as standard. Meanwhile even used cars can have their ignition system adapted (see p. 272).

Engine/cooling system

Water circulation

LESS THAN a quarter of the heat energy developed in a spark-ignition engine is converted into useful work.

The remainder of the heat has to be disposed of without causing any engine part to become so hot that it ceases to work. At full throttle, about 36 per cent passes out of the exhaust system, some 7 per cent is lost to internal friction and heating the lubricating oil, and a further 33 per cent is dissipated in the cooling system.

There are two types of cooling system: direct and indirect. In the direct system, air is blown over fins on the outside of the cylinders and cylinder heads. In the indirect system a coolant, usually water, flows through passages inside the engine.

The essential parts of a modern water-cooling system are:

A jacket surrounding the hot regions—the cylinder bores, combustion spaces and exhaust ports. Some inlet manifolds have a jacket which helps fuel vaporisation.

A radiator, in which hot water returning from the engine is cooled by air.

A pump to drive water round the system.

A fan to draw air through the radiator. Note, however, that in some conditions a standard fan would result in overcooling. For that reason, fans can sometimes be de-coupled from the water pump—or the pump itself may be thermostatically controlled.

Hoses at the top and bottom of the radiator, connecting it to the engine to make a circulatory system.

A thermostat at the water outlet from the engine, to restrict the circulation of cooling water until the engine reaches an efficient working temperature.

A pressure cap on the radiator to raise the boiling point of the water, and so suppress the formation of steam pockets near the combustion spaces. Such pockets could lead to hot-spots, distortion of the cylinder block or head, and piston seizure.

The best working temperature for an engine, no matter what its speed, is one which heats the coolant at a point near the thermostat housing to about 80–85°C (176–185°F). But engines can overheat—for instance when there is not sufficient water in the radiator, or on long climbs.

With a typical pressure-cap setting of 7 lb. per sq. in. (psi), the water will not boil until it reaches 112°C (233°F) at sea level. Its boiling point drops by about 1·1°C (2°F) for every 1000 ft the car climbs.

Fitting a cap which gives higher pressure will not necessarily increase engine efficiency. It could cause damage.

HOW WATER IS USED FOR COOLING AND HEATING

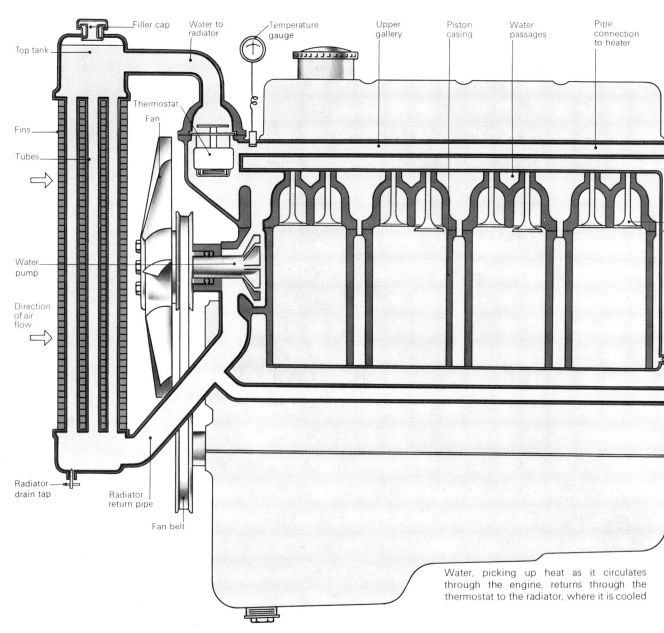

Water, picking up heat as it circulates through the engine, returns through the thermostat to the radiator, where it is cooled

HOW AIR FLOW IS USED TO COOL THE RADIATOR

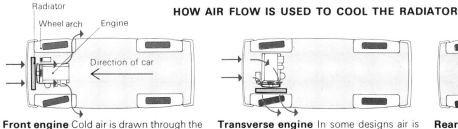

Front engine Cold air is drawn through the grille and on to the radiator by the fan

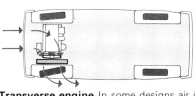

Transverse engine In some designs air is blown through a side-mounted radiator

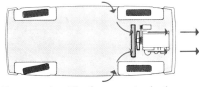

Rear engine The fan operates in the same way as a fan on a front engine

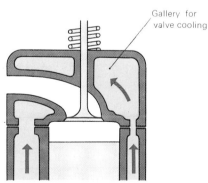

Booster fan
Heater control

Heater
radiator

Heater
control

Heaters Most British cars are fitted with a heater working off the water-circulating system. Since the diversion of warm water to the heater can delay the engine reaching its best working temperature, the heater should not be used until the engine has had time to warm up

Return supply from heater

Block drain tap

Gallery for valve cooling

Valve cooling Valves are cooled mainly by the transfer of heat from the valve head to the valve seat which, in turn, is cooled by water in the cooling system. Since exhaust valves operate at temperatures as high as 700°C (1300°F), a copious flow of water is necessary in the jacket around the valves and ports, to prevent the formation of steam pockets and development of hot-spots

Thermosyphon cooling

BASICALLY, an engine water-cooling system works on the principle that as water is heated it expands and rises, and as it cools it contracts and falls.

Before 1940, most cooling systems relied entirely on this 'thermosyphon' principle and had no pump to speed the circulation of water. Hot water from the engine rose through a large pipe and into the top of the radiator. As it cooled, it became more dense and fell to the bottom of the radiator, then returned to the engine.

This form of natural circulation was slow, resulting in less rapid heat-exchange throughout the cooling system. As it depended on gravity to assist the circulation, earlier cars had tall radiators, and thus taller bonnets than those of later designs.

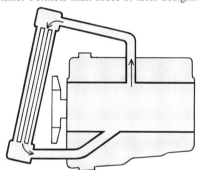

Natural flow needed a tall radiator

The thermosyphon system alone would be insufficient for present-day cars with their more compact engine design and greater output.

All modern water-cooled engines incorporate a water pump to maintain circulation through the water jacket, and so discourage the formation of hot-spots.

Corrosion

HOT WATER circulating in contact with different metals will set up corrosion and form deposits if the water contains no corrosion inhibitor.

Minute particles of iron rust or corroded aluminium will settle on the ledges in the cooling system; and lime deposits, from hard water, will form over the hot areas. Rust or aluminium deposits can be removed by flushing the radiator and the engine and heater separately, after removal of the hoses and thermostat.

Lime deposits can be dissolved by proprietary preparations. Ensure that the solvent used is the correct one for the engine —an alkaline preparation, for instance, can corrode aluminium.

Thermostat shuts off flow

THE JOB of the thermostat is to shut off cold water from the radiator when the engine is cold. There are two main types: bellows (now little used) and wax element. The bellows type consisted of a circular concertina of thin metal containing a volatile fluid. As the fluid was heated by the water it expanded the bellows, causing the thermostat valve to open.

The wax element type has a rubber diaphragm surrounded by wax and containing a pencil-shaped rod. The wax is sealed in a brass container in contact with the water. When the wax is cold, the valve is closed and water cannot flow between the radiator and the engine. When the wax is hot, it melts and expands, forcing the container downwards and so opening the valve. A spring pushes the rod back when the wax cools.

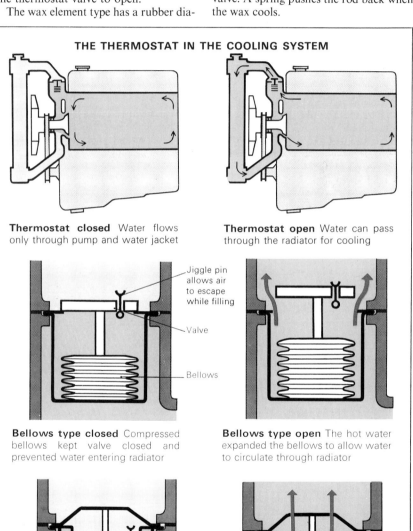

THE THERMOSTAT IN THE COOLING SYSTEM

Thermostat closed Water flows only through pump and water jacket

Thermostat open Water can pass through the radiator for cooling

Jiggle pin allows air to escape while filling

Valve

Bellows

Bellows type closed Compressed bellows kept valve closed and prevented water entering radiator

Bellows type open The hot water expanded the bellows to allow water to circulate through radiator

Piston

Rubber diaphragm

Wax pellet

Wax element closed The valve-opening rod does not operate until hot water expands the wax

Wax element open In expanding, the wax opens the valve, allowing water to flow into the radiator

Engine/radiator and water pump

Where heat is lost

THE FUNCTION of the radiator is to dissipate heat from the hot water circulating in the cooling system. It consists of a header or top tank and a bottom tank, with a core, usually of thin-walled metal tubes, between them.

Hot water enters the header tank through the thermostat from the water jacket, and flows downwards through the core, where it gives up its heat. The tubes are fitted with fins to provide a greater contact area for the cooling air.

The cooled water passes into the bottom tank and is then returned to the engine through the water pump.

In many radiators a space is left between the surface of the water and the top of the header tank for expansion of water. Any surplus water (or steam) escapes through the overflow to the ground.

In later designs, the overflow is taken to an extra expansion tank away from the radiator. As the water cools, it is drawn back into the header tank.

This is known as a sealed system. Since no water is allowed to escape, the system is usually filled at the factory with a mixture of water and antifreeze. As long as the cooling system remains leakproof, no further attention, other than the occasional inspection, is called for.

Antifreeze

In cold weather, freezing water can cause a burst in the radiator of a car which has been left standing. It is equally possible for a radiator to freeze and burst when a car is being driven—even though the water in the engine may be boiling. This is because the thermostat prevents hot water from the engine circulating through the radiator until the engine reaches a set temperature. If a car is driven through cold air, water in the radiator can freeze before the thermostat valve has opened.

Freezing of the radiator can be avoided by adding a chemical, usually an ethylene glycol compound, to the water to lower its freezing point. Good-quality solutions sold as antifreeze have a sodium-based inhibitor added, to prevent corrosion.

Generally a 25 per cent content of antifreeze in the radiator water will give protection against the degree of frost likely to occur in Britain; but a $33\frac{1}{3}$ per cent solution is specified by some manufacturers.

As antifreeze gives protection against corrosion, it is advisable to leave it in the system all the year round. In most instances it can be left in for two years.

HOW WATER COOLS IN THE RADIATOR

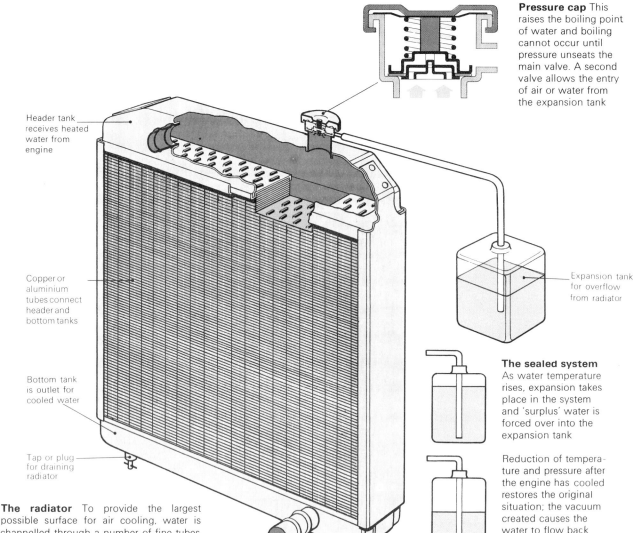

Pressure cap This raises the boiling point of water and boiling cannot occur until pressure unseats the main valve. A second valve allows the entry of air or water from the expansion tank

Header tank receives heated water from engine

Copper or aluminium tubes connect header and bottom tanks

Bottom tank is outlet for cooled water

Tap or plug for draining radiator

Expansion tank for overflow from radiator

The sealed system As water temperature rises, expansion takes place in the system and 'surplus' water is forced over into the expansion tank

Reduction of temperature and pressure after the engine has cooled restores the original situation; the vacuum created causes the water to flow back into the radiator

The radiator To provide the largest possible surface for air cooling, water is channelled through a number of fine tubes or passages, which have fins to increase heat transfer

RADIATOR CORE DESIGNS

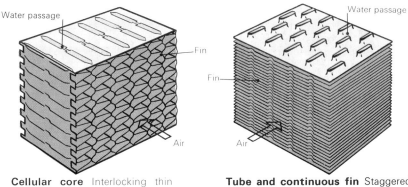

Water passage

Fin

Air

Cellular core Interlocking thin components form vertical passages

Water passage

Fin

Air

Tube and continuous fin Staggered spacings provide longer air passages

Water passage

Fin

Air

Tube and fin Fins have indentations to give increased turbulence to air flow

Speeding the flow

IN MODERN ENGINES, the water pump is mounted on the front of the cylinder block and is driven by the fan belt. It delivers cool water from the bottom of the radiator into the engine's water jacket. Water heated by the engine then flows through the cylinder head and through the thermostat back into the top of the radiator.

A small flow to the car's heater, and in some makes to the induction manifold, is returned to the radiator without passing through the thermostat.

The impeller of the pump is a rotating disc carrying vanes, which fling the water outwards against the pump's casing by centrifugal force and impel it forwards into the water jacket. A seal prevents water from escaping along the impeller shaft.

When the thermostat restricts circulation of the coolant through the radiator, the impeller still revolves, circulating water round the engine only, through the by-pass pipe.

Any squeak from the water-pump seal is usually only temporary. It should not be treated, as some garages advise, by mixing soluble oil (also known as cutting oil) with the radiator water. Minerals in the soluble oil will quickly rot the rubber hoses in the cooling system.

Air-cooled engines

AIR-COOLING without proper ducting and fan-assisted circulation cannot overcome the difficulty of cooling all cylinders evenly, particularly with in-line engines.

The cylinders at the rear of the engine would get little cooling effect from the flow of air through the grille at the front of the car.

To overcome this, air-cooled engines use a fan to force a cooling airstream over the cylinders. Thermostatic control adjusts the air flow to suit temperature conditions.

Fins on the cylinders and cylinder heads increase the surface exposed to the air. Since certain areas of the cylinders and heads, such as the exhaust ports of the combustion chambers, develop more heat that must be dissipated, the fins are usually bigger in those areas than elsewhere on the engine.

Heat always flows from a large mass of material to the thinnest section exposed to a cooler medium. Fins are therefore tapered, to promote the dissipation of heat.

An air-cooled engine is much noisier than a water-cooled engine, in which the water jacket damps down a great deal of the engine noise.

WATER-PUMP ASSEMBLY

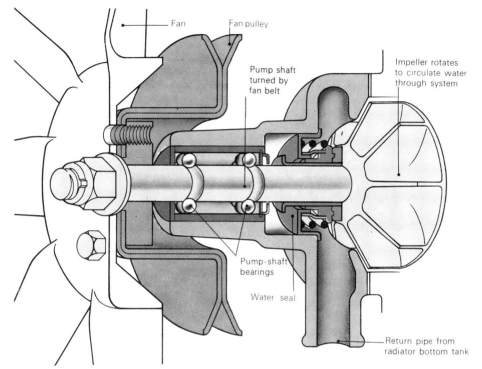

Fan · Fan pulley · Pump shaft turned by fan belt · Impeller rotates to circulate water through system · Pump-shaft bearings · Water seal · Return pipe from radiator bottom tank

WATER FLOW

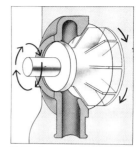

With thermostat closed, impeller recirculates water only in the engine

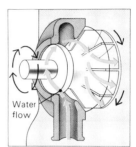

Water flow

When thermostat is open, water circulates through engine and radiator

AIR-COOLING THROUGH FINS

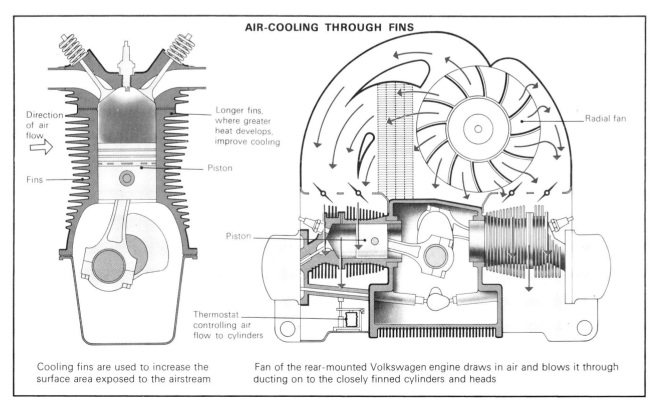

Direction of air flow · Fins · Longer fins, where greater heat develops, improve cooling · Piston · Piston · Thermostat controlling air flow to cylinders · Radial fan

Cooling fins are used to increase the surface area exposed to the airstream

Fan of the rear-mounted Volkswagen engine draws in air and blows it through ducting on to the closely finned cylinders and heads

Lubrication system

Why the engine needs oil

THE OIL in an engine does more than simply cut down friction and wear by lubricating the pistons, bearings and other moving parts. It also helps to seal hot high-pressure gases; takes heat away from hot areas and disperses it to the air in the sump; reduces corrosion; and absorbs some of the harmful waste products of combustion.

Oil is carried in the sump, at the bottom of the engine, and forced by a pump through a filter to the main bearings. The pump will normally deliver several gallons of oil a minute, at a pressure controlled by a relief valve.

From the main bearings, the oil passes through feed-holes or grooves into drilled passages in the crankshaft and on to the big-end bearings of the connecting rods. In some engines the oil is taken to the gudgeon pins through passages drilled in the connecting rods.

The cylinder walls and gudgeon-pin bearings are lubricated by oil fling—oil escaping from the ends of the bearings and dispersed by the rotating crankshaft. The excess is taken off the cylinders by scraper rings on the pistons and then drops back to the sump.

A bleed, or tributary, from the main supply passage feeds each camshaft bearing; and in many overhead-valve engines there is another bleed leading to the rocker-shaft bearings. The oil then drains back from the cylinder head to the sump, where excess heat is dispersed to the surrounding air. Another bleed supplies the timing chain or gears on the camshaft drive, and in some cases supplies the chain tensioner.

Oil wedge

No shaft makes a perfectly tight fit in its bearing—otherwise it would be unable to turn. There is a minute clearance between the two surfaces (about 0·003 in. in a big-end bearing with a diameter of 2 in.) and a film of oil is fed to the bearing at the point where this clearance is greatest. The rotation of the shaft draws oil round to the point of maximum loading, where the clearance is smallest, forcing it into an 'oil wedge' between shaft and bearing and allowing high loads to be taken safely.

Engine wear

An insufficient flow of lubricant will lead to rapid wear or seizure of the engine's moving parts, by allowing metal to grind against metal. It will also cause engine failure by destroying the surfaces of the piston rings and allowing high-temperature gases to blow past the pistons.

SEPARATING MOVING PARTS

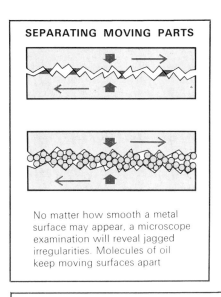

No matter how smooth a metal surface may appear, a microscope examination will reveal jagged irregularities. Molecules of oil keep moving surfaces apart

WEDGING ACTION OF OIL

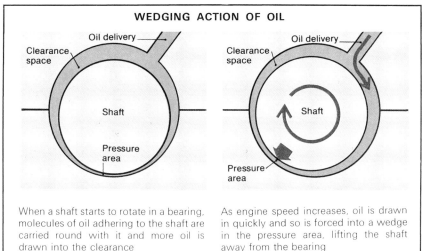

When a shaft starts to rotate in a bearing, molecules of oil adhering to the shaft are carried round with it and more oil is drawn into the clearance

As engine speed increases, oil is drawn in quickly and so is forced into a wedge in the pressure area, lifting the shaft away from the bearing

---

LUBRICATION OF THE CYLINDER WALLS

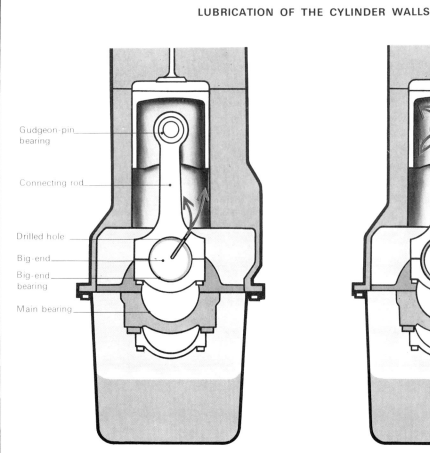
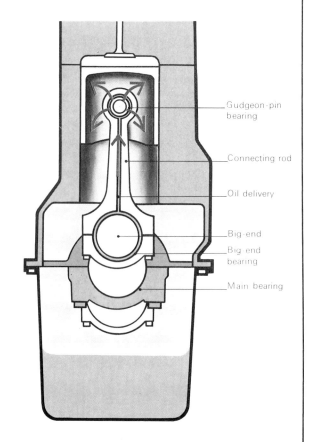

Oil fling—oil thrown out by the rotating bearings—is used to lubricate cylinder walls. From the main bearing, oil is fed through a passage in the crankshaft to the big-end bearing

When the gudgeon pin is pressure-lubricated through a passage in the connecting rod, the oil is expelled in a series of squirts to the inside of the piston

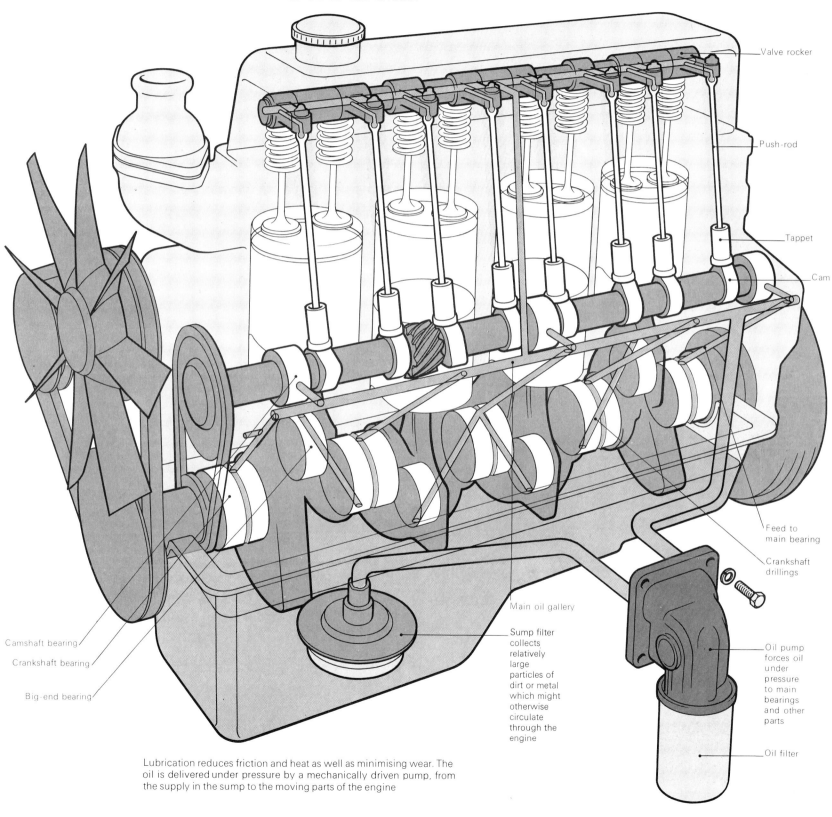

THE CIRCULATION OF OIL IN THE ENGINE

Valve rocker

Push-rod

Tappet

Cam

Feed to main bearing

Crankshaft drillings

Main oil gallery

Oil pump forces oil under pressure to main bearings and other parts

Sump filter collects relatively large particles of dirt or metal which might otherwise circulate through the engine

Oil filter

Camshaft bearing

Crankshaft bearing

Big-end bearing

Lubrication reduces friction and heat as well as minimising wear. The oil is delivered under pressure by a mechanically driven pump, from the supply in the sump to the moving parts of the engine

Lubrication/pumps and filters

Oil pumps

TWO KINDS of oil pump are in general use —the gear and the rotor type. Each is usually driven from the camshaft or the crankshaft. The gear type has a pair of meshing gears. As the gears rotate the spaces between the teeth are filled with oil from the sump. When the teeth come together, or mesh, the oil is forced out under pressure. The rotor pump consists of an inner and an outer rotor in one cylinder, with oil filling the gap between them. As in the gear-type pump, oil is first drawn in from the sump then delivered under pressure to the engine.

When the oil is cold, the pressure re-quired to push it through the small clear-ances in the bearings could be high enough to damage the pump. A pressure-relief valve inside the pump opens under excess pressure and 'leaks' some of the oil back to the sump.

Breathers

Crankcase ventilators, also known as breathers, provide an escape for blow-by gases that get past the pistons into the crankcase. If they were released into the atmosphere, they would pollute the air. Modern systems, therefore, ensure that they are vented back into the air intake.

Oil filters

IN MOST ENGINES, oil enters the pump through a strainer—a gauze screen which excludes large particles of dirt.

A full-flow pressure filter is normally fitted outside the crankcase. As this filter can become blocked with sludge, it is fitted with a by-pass valve which opens when the pressure across the filter exceeds a set amount, usually about 10–20 psi. This valve also opens when the oil is cold and therefore too thick to flow through the filter. The filter can be made of various materials capable of holding back fine particles, but with a surface area large enough to allow sufficient oil to pass.

Centrifugal filters

This less-common type of filter works on the principle that solid matter is usually heavier than oil. A circular container re-volves at high speed, and the solid particles are flung to the outside and retained in the bowl, while oil passes through a central escape route.

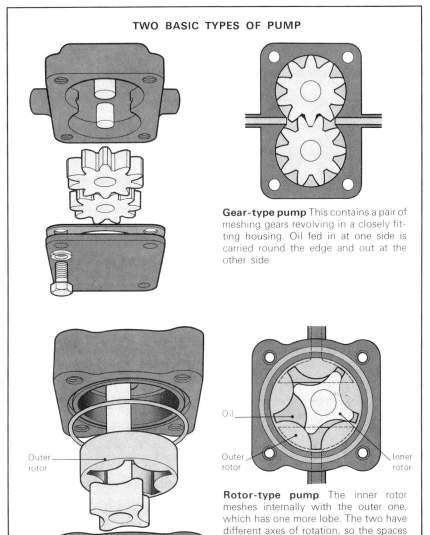

TWO BASIC TYPES OF PUMP

Gear-type pump This contains a pair of meshing gears revolving in a closely fitting housing. Oil fed in at one side is carried round the edge and out at the other side

Outer rotor

Oil

Outer rotor

Inner rotor

Rotor-type pump The inner rotor meshes internally with the outer one, which has one more lobe. The two have different axes of rotation, so the spaces vary in size, causing oil to be drawn in and forced out

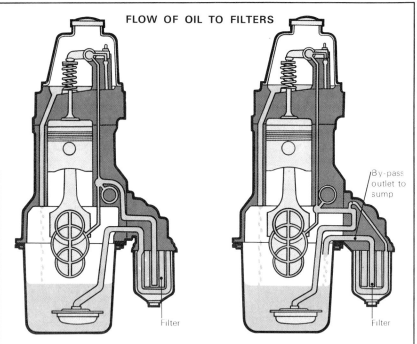

FLOW OF OIL TO FILTERS

By-pass outlet to sump

Filter

Filter

Full-flow system. All oil is pumped through the filter into the engine block

By-pass system. Only a small amount of the oil is filtered at any one time

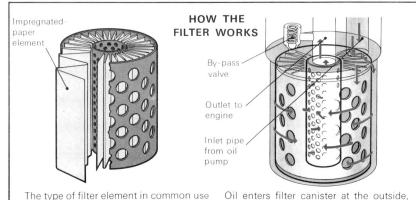

HOW THE FILTER WORKS

Impregnated-paper element

By-pass valve

Outlet to engine

Inlet pipe from oil pump

The type of filter element in common use today is made of resin-impregnated paper. It cannot be cleaned but should be periodically renewed

Oil enters filter canister at the outside, passes through the perforated cover, then through the actual element to the central outlet tube and so to the engine

Lubricants

Choosing the right oil

THERE ARE three kinds of oils—mineral, synthetic and vegetable (invariably castor oil in car engines). Engine manufacturers today recommend the use of mineral-based oils only. Castor oil, once used in many racing cars, has been superseded by mineral oil. Synthetic oil, used in aviation, is not yet economic.

A refined mineral stock oil looks like engine oil but would be solid at −35°C (−31°F), thick at winter temperatures, as thin as paraffin at piston temperatures, and would start to burn above 230°C (446°F). An engine run on it would soon foul with sludge and carbon.

All premium grades contain a balanced amount of various additives. Some provide protection against oxidation and froth—oil's principal deterioration factors. Some give a protective thin film for boundary lubrication where components rub together under high loading, and where surfaces are too irregular to allow a complete film of oil to separate them at all times. Others prevent the formation of hard lacquers which would shorten engine-component life.

Viscosity

To separate the moving parts of an engine and seal off hot, high-pressure gases, oil must have the right viscosity—fluidity or 'thickness'. If it is too thick, it will seal but will not allow the moving parts to slide easily, and so will produce drag, increasing fuel consumption.

If the oil is too thin, the film that should separate the moving surfaces will break down, permitting contact and wear; and the oil will not lubricate the piston rings and cylinder bores adequately.

The viscosity required in an oil varies according to the use of the car and the outside temperatures; the same viscosity would not be ideal for both the U.K. and the Arctic.

Temperatures in the engine vary widely. The engine must be able to start below freezing point; yet an ideal sump temperature when running is about 82°C (180°F), because this evaporates moisture formed by the process of combustion. The temperature in the main and big-end bearings will be about 11°C (20°F) above the sump temperature, but the piston-ring temperature may reach 232°C (450°F) when the car is at full throttle.

All oils get thinner as they are heated, but some thin out more rapidly than others. The rate at which they thin out is known as the viscosity index; the less the

viscosity changes with the temperature, the higher the viscosity index number.

An oil's viscosity is identified by its SAE number, named after America's Society of Automotive Engineers, which devised viscosity standards. The numbers SAE 20, 30, 40 and 50 indicate that an oil falls within certain viscosity limits at 99°C (210°F). The numbers SAE 5W, 10W, and 20W show that the viscosity falls within certain limits at −18°C (0°F). The lower the number, the thinner the oil.

A multigrade oil is a lubricant that has the qualities of a high viscosity index. It may, for instance, have an SAE rating of 10W/30, or 20W/50.

The advantage of a multigrade oil is that it provides easy winter starting, because it is thin when cold, yet retains its lubricating qualities at high temperatures.

Corrosion reduction

Another of the oil's main functions is to reduce the corrosion that is caused by

acids formed during combustion.

At running temperatures these acids remain as gases and are carried out in the exhaust. But at low temperatures they condense and cause internal corrosion.

If the oil is made slightly alkaline, it can neutralise these acids. This action is assisted by the use of a thin oil which circulates quickly when cold—when there is the greatest concentration of combustion acids in the engine.

Detergents and dispersants

Some partially burnt materials find their way past the piston rings into the sump. These blow-by products include acids and sooty, tarry materials. They have to be absorbed by the oil, which holds them in suspension. If not absorbed, the blow-by products will form deposits in the piston-ring grooves, on the filters and in the oil-ways, obstructing oil circulation and causing seized piston rings.

An oil with dispersant and detergent

additives will hold these materials in suspension, provided they are so small as to be practically molecular.

Gear oils

Many manufacturers specify the same oil for engine and gearbox. Where a hypoid gear is used for the final drive, a different oil is essential to ensure a quiet and long life under the severe conditions of relative sliding of the gear teeth over one another. These oils contain e.p., or extreme pressure, additives, which act when contact pressures and temperatures are too high for a straight mineral oil.

Automatic transmission oils

These have to meet very exacting requirements to ensure that the actions of torque converter, clutches and brake bands are smooth and jerk-free. The working temperature of the very thin oil is generally quite high, so very special blends of mineral oils and additives are needed.

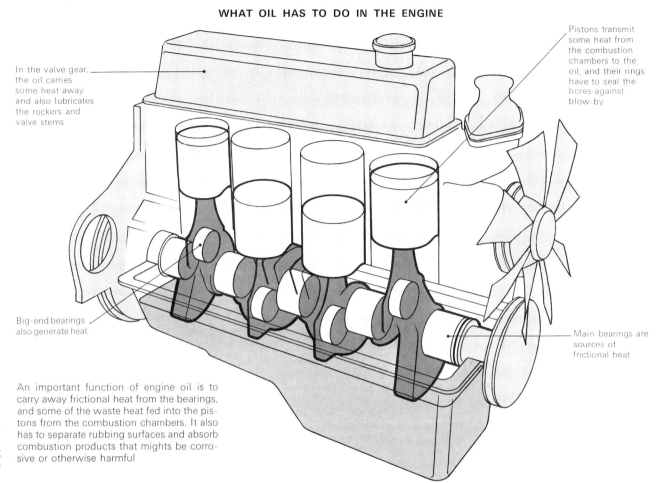

WHAT OIL HAS TO DO IN THE ENGINE

In the valve gear, the oil carries some heat away and also lubricates the rockers and valve stems

Pistons transmit some heat from the combustion chambers to the oil, and their rings have to seal the bores against blow-by

Big-end bearings also generate heat

Main bearings are sources of frictional heat

An important function of engine oil is to carry away frictional heat from the bearings, and some of the waste heat fed into the pistons from the combustion chambers. It also has to separate rubbing surfaces and absorb combustion products that mights be corrosive or otherwise harmful

Engine/exhaust system

A CAR exhaust system has two main functions. Firstly, it takes hot, waste gases from the engine to a point where they can be released into the atmosphere without danger to the occupants of the car. Secondly, it reduces the noise made when used gases are expelled by the engine. This is done by a silencer.

The gases produced in an engine expand with great force and are released into the exhaust system under pressure. Each time the gases pass into the exhaust manifold, a shock wave is set up. With shock waves occurring at the rate of several thousand a minute, the noise from cars would be socially unacceptable if it were not moderated.

After travelling a short distance down the exhaust pipe, the shock waves, which are initially supersonic, slow down to below the speed of sound.

By the time exhaust gases leave the silencer, they have expanded sufficiently for their pressure to drop to about that of the outside air, and most of the noise has been curbed.

If exhaust gases are not cleared effectively, the incoming flow of petrol/air mixture into the combustion chamber will be impeded, and the mixture will be contaminated by the residual burnt gases. This will reduce the efficiency of the engine.

Exhaust manifolds are designed to avoid interference between the pulses of exhaust gas that leave each cylinder in turn. The object is to allow the gases to flow to the exhaust pipe as freely as possible.

Some back pressure is unavoidable in the exhaust system, due to the restrictive effect of the manifold, piping and silencer. The designer allows for this; his objective is to quieten the exhaust with minimum restriction to the flow of gases.

Silencers

A silencer breaks up or absorbs the sound waves, reducing them to a noise level that is socially acceptable and meets the law's requirements.

The gas flow is usually slowed down by baffles, or metal plates, inside the silencer; these break up and impede the action of the sound waves.

A variation of this design is the perforated, 'straight-through' silencer, in which gases pass through holes into a sound-absorbing material. The perforations do not impede gas flow as much as baffles do.

Silencers and exhaust systems are usually made of mild-steel tubing and sheet steel. Constant exposure to road grit, salt, slush and mud reduce the life of the average system to little more than one or two winters. Aluminium paint on the outside is no protection, but the use of aluminised or stainless steel can give an exhaust system a much longer life.

Silencers and exhaust systems rust from the inside as well as from the outside. Every gallon of petrol burnt produces a gallon of water along with lead salts and acids, which pass as gas or vapour into the exhaust system.

If the silencer or pipe is cold, as in the first start of the day, these corrosive elements will condense on the interior surfaces of the exhaust system.

They act as weak acids, eventually eating through the metal. Every time a car starts from cold, a minute amount of internal corrosion takes place. This is why a car used only for short trips needs more frequent exhaust replacements than one used regularly for long journeys.

Fume dangers

Exhaust gases include carbon monoxide, which has no smell but in sufficient concentration is poisonous, and carbon dioxide, which can cause suffocation. A gas leak near the hot exhaust manifold can be a fire hazard, too. Never ignore an exhaust leak; it could be lethal.

A loose exhaust pipe rattling against the underside of the car indicates a broken bracket or the failure of a flexible mounting. These should be replaced as soon as possible. Undue flexing of the pipe will strain the joints at the manifold or at the silencer; neglect can be costly.

Smoking exhausts

Engine faults can often be detected by listening to the exhaust. If the exhaust note is irregular, check for ignition defects, incorrect carburettor settings or 'blowing' at the manifold gasket, exhaust pipe or silencer.

Sooty exhaust gas and a soft, sooty lining of the tail pipe indicate that too rich a mixture is being used.

Blue smoke from the exhaust, particularly when accelerating after coasting down a hill in gear, indicates that oil is getting into the combustion chambers past piston rings or worn valve guides.

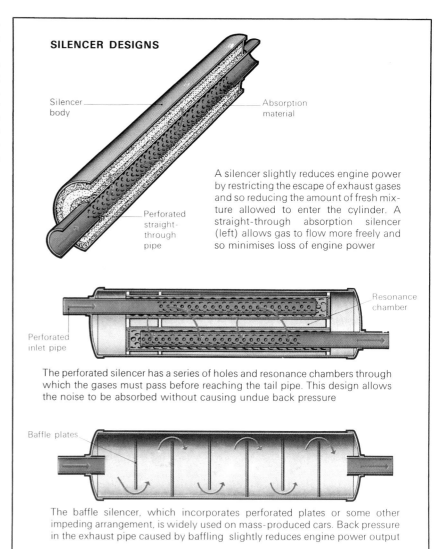

SILENCER DESIGNS

Silencer body · Absorption material · Perforated straight-through pipe

A silencer slightly reduces engine power by restricting the escape of exhaust gases and so reducing the amount of fresh mixture allowed to enter the cylinder. A straight-through absorption silencer (left) allows gas to flow more freely and so minimises loss of engine power

Resonance chamber · Perforated inlet pipe

The perforated silencer has a series of holes and resonance chambers through which the gases must pass before reaching the tail pipe. This design allows the noise to be absorbed without causing undue back pressure

Baffle plates

The baffle silencer, which incorporates perforated plates or some other impeding arrangement, is widely used on mass-produced cars. Back pressure in the exhaust pipe caused by baffling slightly reduces engine power output

DANGER FROM EXHAUST FUMES

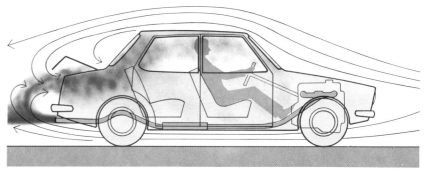

When an average-sized car is travelling with an open boot, exhaust fumes can swirl into the boot and may seep into the car, possibly overcoming the driver. Keep the boot, or the tail-gate of an estate car, closed when driving. If this is not possible, open the side windows to ensure a flow of fresh air through the car

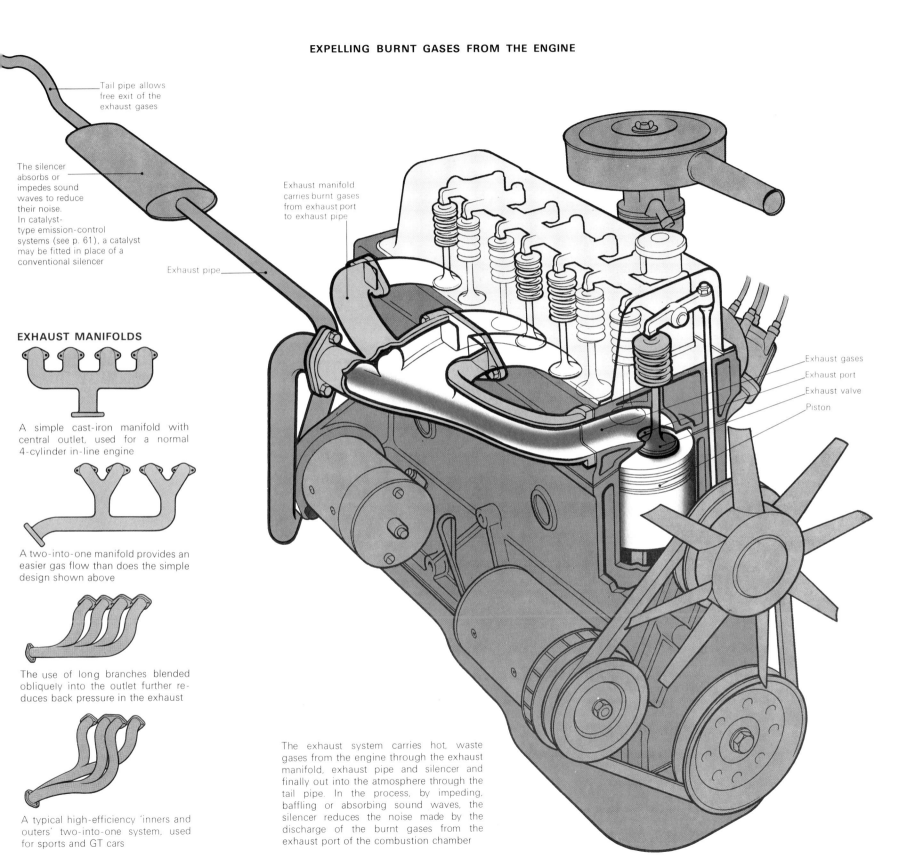

Tail pipe allows free exit of the exhaust gases

The silencer absorbs or impedes sound waves to reduce their noise. In catalyst-type emission-control systems (see p. 61), a catalyst may be fitted in place of a conventional silencer

Exhaust pipe

Exhaust manifold carries burnt gases from exhaust port to exhaust pipe

Exhaust gases

Exhaust port

Exhaust valve

Piston

EXHAUST MANIFOLDS

A simple cast-iron manifold with central outlet, used for a normal 4-cylinder in-line engine

A two-into-one manifold provides an easier gas flow than does the simple design shown above

The use of long branches blended obliquely into the outlet further reduces back pressure in the exhaust

A typical high-efficiency 'inners and outers' two-into-one system, used for sports and GT cars

The exhaust system carries hot, waste gases from the engine through the exhaust manifold, exhaust pipe and silencer and finally out into the atmosphere through the tail pipe. In the process, by impeding, baffling or absorbing sound waves, the silencer reduces the noise made by the discharge of the burnt gases from the exhaust port of the combustion chamber

Transmission

How the engine turns the wheels

THE TRANSMISSION channels power from the engine to the road wheels. In a conventional car, with a front-mounted engine, transmission starts at the flywheel and continues through the clutch, gearbox, propeller shaft and final drive to the rear wheels.

Cars with front engines and front drive, or rear engines and rear drive, do not need a propeller shaft; power is transmitted through short drive-shafts.

The clutch, set between the flywheel and the gearbox, allows the engine power to be disconnected from the transmission to free it from torque (turning effort) when gears are engaged or changed.

The purpose of the gearbox

Greater torque is required from the engine when the car is starting to move or climbing a hill than when it is running at a constant speed along a level road.

A gearbox is needed to enable the engine to cope with the wide variations in the power and torque required to drive the car under such different conditions. In effect, the faster the crankshaft revolves in relation to the road wheels, the greater is the force available to drive the car; but the speed of the car is proportionately reduced. Several gears are used, giving a wide range of speed ratios between the engine and the wheels.

The final drive, or rear-axle assembly, includes a differential gear which enables the road wheels to rotate at different speeds. When a car turns a corner, the outer wheel has to travel further than the inner wheel. The wheels that are not under power rotate at the speeds demanded of them without any mechanical assistance.

Power finally reaches the wheels from the final drive through a half-shaft on each side of the differential.

Automatic transmission

Most cars have a pedal-operated clutch and a gear lever for changing gear by hand. But repeated operation of the clutch can be tiring. Manual gear-changing, even by the most skilled driver, causes wear to the clutch and gearbox mechanism.

The alternatives are semi-automatic or fully automatic transmission. With semi-automatic transmission the driver has only to select the gears; the clutch operates automatically. In fully automatic transmission, gears are selected and changed by a control mechanism which responds to car speed and the use made of the accelerator.

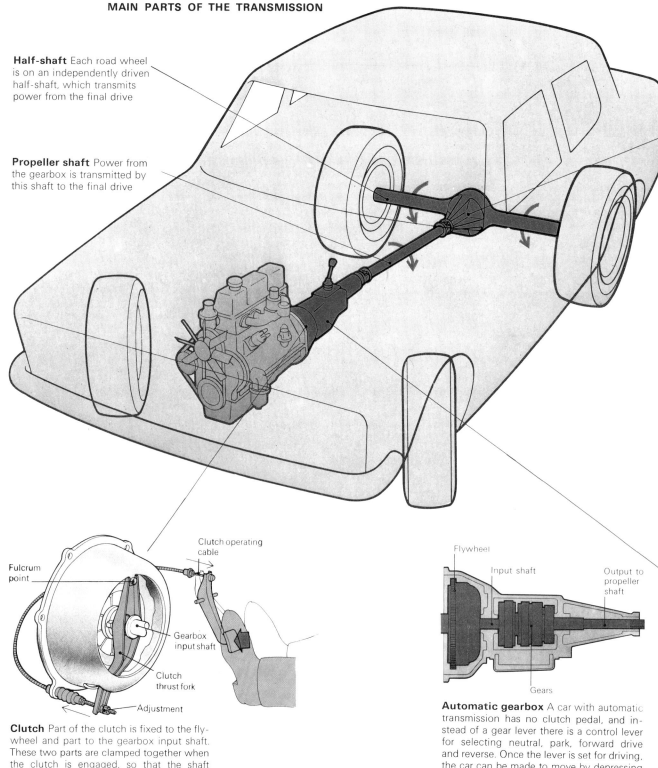

MAIN PARTS OF THE TRANSMISSION

Half-shaft Each road wheel is on an independently driven half-shaft, which transmits power from the final drive

Propeller shaft Power from the gearbox is transmitted by this shaft to the final drive

Clutch operating cable

Fulcrum point

Gearbox input shaft

Clutch thrust fork

Adjustment

Clutch Part of the clutch is fixed to the flywheel and part to the gearbox input shaft. These two parts are clamped together when the clutch is engaged, so that the shaft rotates with the flywheel. When the clutch is disengaged, power from the engine is not transmitted to the road wheels

Flywheel

Input shaft

Output to propeller shaft

Gears

Automatic gearbox A car with automatic transmission has no clutch pedal, and instead of a gear lever there is a control lever for selecting neutral, park, forward drive and reverse. Once the lever is set for driving, the car can be made to move by depressing the accelerator; as the engine speed increases, a hydraulic device starts to transmit power to move the car

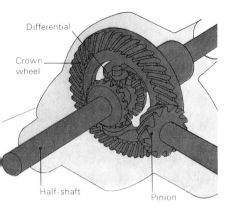

Differential
Crown wheel
Half-shaft
Pinion

Final drive The propeller shaft speed is reduced to a suitable speed for coupling to the road wheels in the final drive. This is done by a reduction gear called the crown wheel and pinion. The crown wheel rotates at right angles to the smaller pinion so that the drive line is turned through 90° from the propeller shaft to the half-shafts on each side of the final drive. Associated with the crown wheel is the differential, a set of gears which allow the half-shafts to revolve at different speeds when the car rounds a bend

Universal joints The rear axle is sprung so that it moves vertically when the car travels over uneven ground. This means the angle of the propeller shaft, and the distance between the gearbox and the final drive are constantly changing. Flexibility at each end of the shaft is provided by the universal joints, one of which has a sliding coupling to allow the shaft to adjust its length

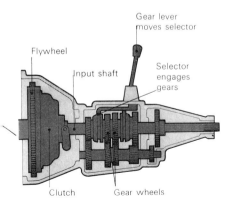

Gear lever moves selector
Flywheel
Input shaft
Selector engages gears
Clutch
Gear wheels

Manual gearbox Moving the gear lever engages the pair of gear wheels giving the most suitable ratio between engine speed and road-wheel speed. There are usually three or four forward gears besides neutral and reverse. Neutral disconnects the gearbox from the clutch so that a driver can run the engine with the clutch engaged when the car is stationary

Transmissions without propeller shafts

THERE ARE several ways of arranging the transmission in addition to the conventional method of a front engine driving the rear wheels. These alternatives eliminate the need for a propeller shaft by using an engine which forms a unit together with the gearbox and the final drive.

Such a unit can be fitted along or across the chassis to drive either the front or the back wheels. When the engine is mounted across the chassis there is no need to turn the drive line through 90°, as all the shafts are parallel to the axes of the road wheels.

The final drive is in or attached to the gearbox, which is fixed to the chassis. This means that on an uneven surface the road wheels move up and down in relation to the final drive. To accommodate this vertical movement, the half-shafts have universal joints next to the differential.

All front-drive cars and some rear-drive cars also have universal joints at the road-wheel ends of the half-shafts. These additional universal joints are essential in front-drive cars to permit swivelling movement of the road wheels when they are steered.

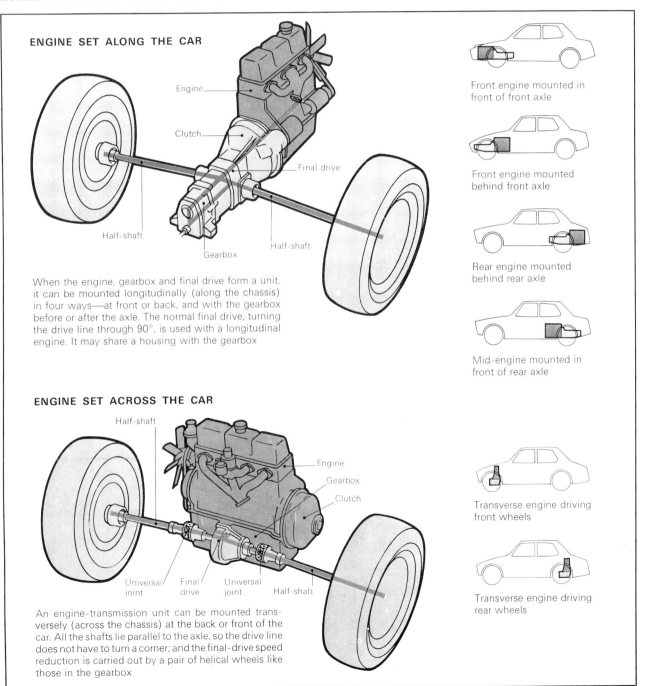

ENGINE SET ALONG THE CAR

Engine
Clutch
Final drive
Half-shaft
Gearbox
Half-shaft

When the engine, gearbox and final drive form a unit, it can be mounted longitudinally (along the chassis) in four ways—at front or back, and with the gearbox before or after the axle. The normal final drive, turning the drive line through 90°, is used with a longitudinal engine. It may share a housing with the gearbox

ENGINE SET ACROSS THE CAR

Half-shaft
Engine
Gearbox
Clutch
Universal joint
Final drive
Universal joint
Half-shaft

An engine-transmission unit can be mounted transversely (across the chassis) at the back or front of the car. All the shafts lie parallel to the axle, so the drive line does not have to turn a corner; and the final-drive speed reduction is carried out by a pair of helical wheels like those in the gearbox

Front engine mounted in front of front axle

Front engine mounted behind front axle

Rear engine mounted behind rear axle

Mid-engine mounted in front of rear axle

Transverse engine driving front wheels

Transverse engine driving rear wheels

Transmission/the clutch

What the clutch has to do

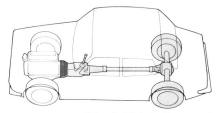

THE PURPOSE of the clutch is to disconnect the engine from the road wheels when a car is changing gear or being started from rest. This allows a new gear to be engaged smoothly before transmission is re-engaged; or, on starting, it allows the engine to pick up sufficient speed to drive the car.

Disengaging the clutch separates three parts of the clutch assembly—the flywheel, the driven plate (also known as the centre plate or clutch plate) and the pressure plate. The flywheel is bolted to the end of the crankshaft and rotates with it; the driven plate is splined to the gearbox input shaft so that they rotate together; and the pressure plate clamps the driven plate to the flywheel.

When this pressure is released, by depressing the clutch pedal, the crankshaft and gearbox input shaft rotate independently; when the driver takes his foot off the pedal, they rotate as one.

Both sides of the driven plate, a thin disc of high-tensile steel, are faced with a friction material known as the lining. When the driven plate is clamped to the flywheel by the pressure plate, the clamping load must be great enough to prevent any slipping at the maximum torque delivered by the engine to the flywheel.

The terms coil-spring clutch, diaphragm clutch and centrifugal clutch refer to different methods of applying a load to the friction linings.

In a coil-spring clutch, the pressure plate is backed by a number of coil springs and housed with them in a pressed-steel cover bolted to the flywheel. The springs push against this cover.

Neither the driven plate nor the pressure plate is connected rigidly to the flywheel; both can move either towards it or away from it.

When the driver depresses the clutch pedal, a thrust pad, riding on a carbon or ball thrust-bearing to reduce wear, is forced towards the flywheel. Levers, pivoted so that they engage with the thrust pad at one end and the pressure plate at the other, pull the pressure plate back against its springs. This releases pressure on the driven plate, disconnecting the gearbox from the engine.

PARTS OF A COIL-SPRING CLUTCH

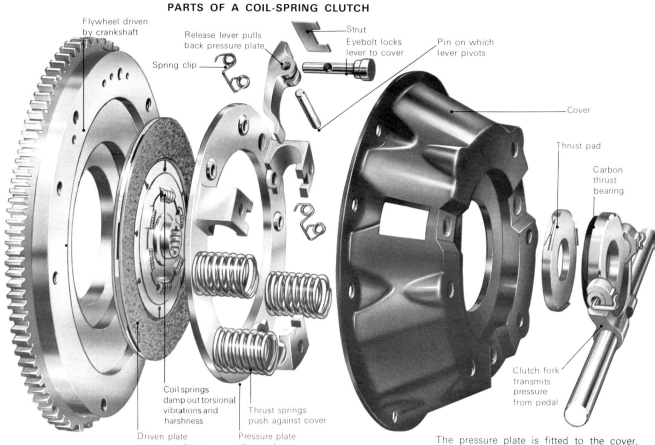

Flywheel driven by crankshaft

Release lever pulls back pressure plate

Spring clip

Strut

Eyebolt locks lever to cover

Pin on which lever pivots

Cover

Thrust pad

Carbon thrust bearing

Clutch fork transmits pressure from pedal

Coil springs damp out torsional vibrations and harshness

Driven plate passes on drive to gearbox

Thrust springs push against cover

Pressure plate clamps driven plate to flywheel

The pressure plate is fitted to the cover, which in turn is bolted to the flywheel, so that all three revolve together. The thrust springs, pushing against the cover, clamp the driven plate between the pressure plate and the flywheel and it revolves with them

PRINCIPLE OF A CLUTCH

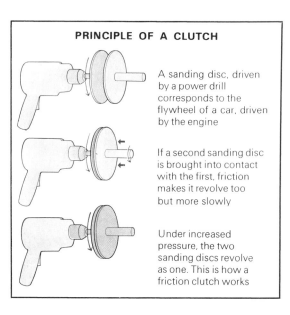

A sanding disc, driven by a power drill corresponds to the flywheel of a car, driven by the engine

If a second sanding disc is brought into contact with the first, friction makes it revolve too but more slowly

Under increased pressure, the two sanding discs revolve as one. This is how a friction clutch works

THRUST PAD IN OPERATION

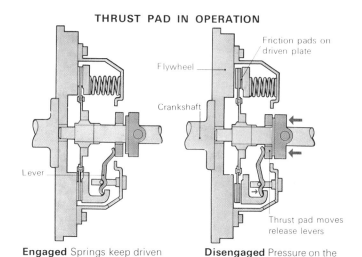

Friction pads on driven plate

Flywheel

Crankshaft

Lever

Thrust pad moves release levers

Engaged Springs keep driven plate clamped between pressure plate and flywheel. Only one spring and lever are shown

Disengaged Pressure on the pedal, transmitted through the thrust pad, forces the levers to pull the pressure plate back

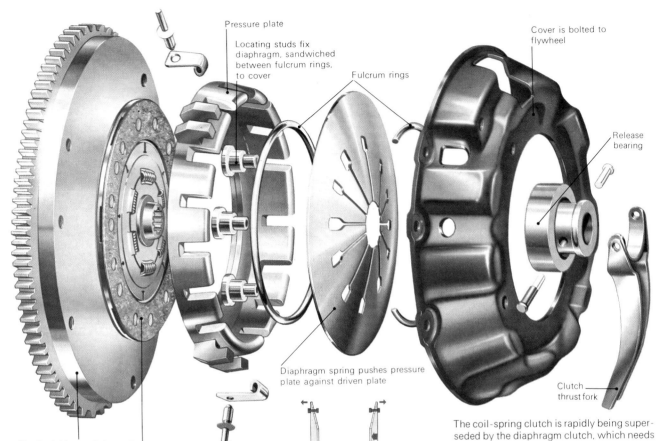

Pressure plate

Locating studs fix diaphragm, sandwiched between fulcrum rings, to cover

Fulcrum rings

Cover is bolted to flywheel

Release bearing

Diaphragm spring pushes pressure plate against driven plate

Clutch thrust fork

Flywheel driven by crankshaft

Driven plate

Conical diaphragm spring can be flexed to reverse direction of thrust

The coil-spring clutch is rapidly being super-seded by the diaphragm clutch, which needs less pedal effort. It contains a conical spring, with slots radiating from the centre, and is almost flattened, so that in trying to regain its conical shape it exerts an even pressure round its outer edge. This presses against the pressure plate. The thrust pad, acting against the diaphragm, flexes it the other way and frees the pressure plate

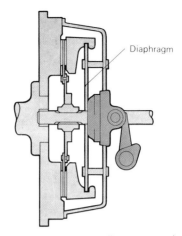

Engaged The flattened diaphragm spring pushes against the pressure plate

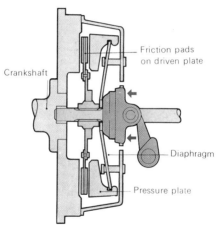

Diaphragm

Friction pads on driven plate

Crankshaft

Diaphragm

Pressure plate

Disengaged Thrust pad flexes the spring and so frees the pressure plate

Centrifugal clutch

A FEW CARS are equipped with centrifugal or centrifugally assisted clutches. These resemble the coil-spring clutch, but weights are fitted to the release levers.

As the clutch assembly rotates with the engine, these weights are flung outwards by centrifugal force and cause the levers to press more strongly against the pressure plate. The faster the engine runs, the greater is the force exerted.

This centrifugal clutch system can be used either in place of springs or as a supplement to spring loading.

Nowadays, centrifugal clutches are used only with some of the simpler automatic or semi-automatic transmissions, notably the CVT system of the Volvo 66.

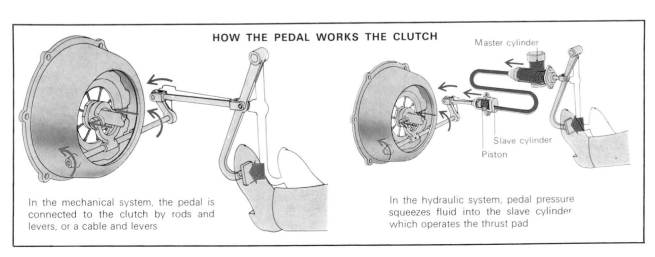

HOW THE PEDAL WORKS THE CLUTCH

Master cylinder

Slave cylinder

Piston

In the mechanical system, the pedal is connected to the clutch by rods and levers, or a cable and levers

In the hydraulic system, pedal pressure squeezes fluid into the slave cylinder which operates the thrust pad

Transmission/manual gearboxes

Why a car has a gearbox

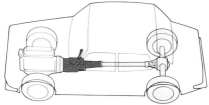

THE TOP SPEED of a car depends upon the maximum power of its engine, and this is developed near the engine's maximum speed. A typical car engine may run at 4000 rpm for a top speed of 70 mph.

But road wheels of average size turn at only about 1000 rpm to cover 70 miles in an hour, so they cannot be connected directly to the engine. There must be a system which allows the road wheels to make one revolution for every four of the engine. This is done by a reduction gear in the final drive (see p. 100).

The relationship between the rotation speeds of the engine and the wheels is the axle ratio; 4:1 is common. As long as the car is driven at a steady speed on the level, this gearing will suffice; but when the car meets a hill its speed will drop and the engine will falter and stall.

A slow-running engine cannot provide enough torque for climbing hills or starting from rest.

Selecting a lower gear enables the engine to run faster in relation to the road wheels and also multiplies the torque.

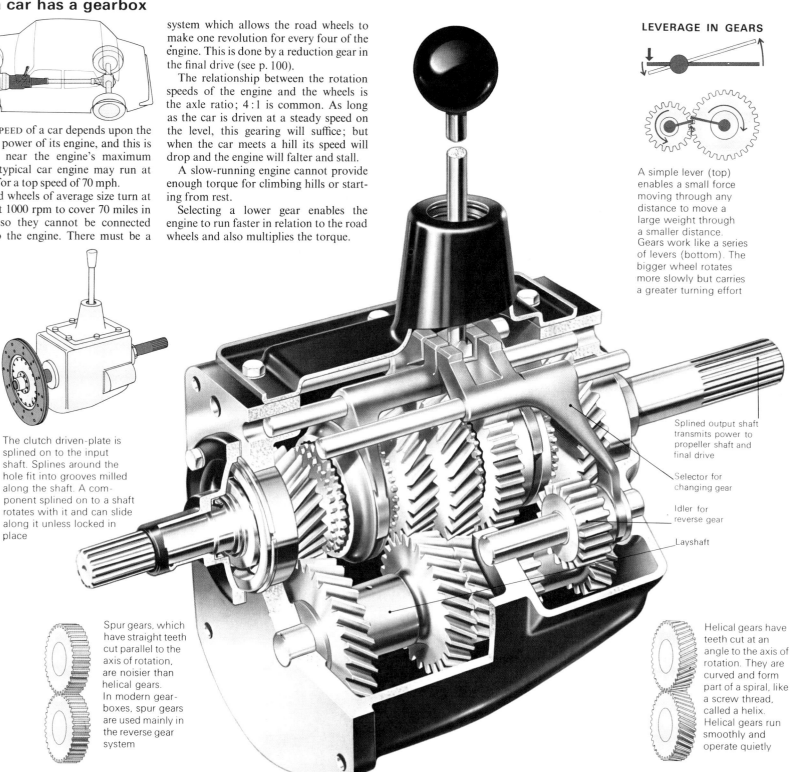

LEVERAGE IN GEARS

A simple lever (top) enables a small force moving through any distance to move a large weight through a smaller distance. Gears work like a series of levers (bottom). The bigger wheel rotates more slowly but carries a greater turning effort

Splined output shaft transmits power to propeller shaft and final drive

Selector for changing gear

Idler for reverse gear

Layshaft

The clutch driven-plate is splined on to the input shaft. Splines around the hole fit into grooves milled along the shaft. A component splined on to a shaft rotates with it and can slide along it unless locked in place

Spur gears, which have straight teeth cut parallel to the axis of rotation, are noisier than helical gears. In modern gearboxes, spur gears are used mainly in the reverse gear system

Helical gears have teeth cut at an angle to the axis of rotation. They are curved and form part of a spiral, like a screw thread, called a helix. Helical gears run smoothly and operate quietly

A TYPICAL FOUR-SPEED GEARBOX

How gear ratios are determined

THE LOWEST GEAR in the gearbox must multiply the engine torque sufficiently to start the fully laden car moving up a steep hill.

A small car needs a bottom gear of 3·5:1. Other typical gearbox ratios in a small car with a four-speed gearbox are 2:1 in second, 1·4:1 in third and 1:1 in top. All these are multiplied by the axle ratio, so that, if the axle ratio is 4:1, the corresponding ratios between the engine speed and the road-wheel speed are 14:1, 8:1, 5·6:1 and 4:1.

The same car with a bigger engine de-veloping more torque would not need such a low bottom gear, so the gearbox ratios might be adjusted to 2·8:1, 1·8:1, 1·3:1 and 1:1. Closer spacing of gear ratios makes gear changing smoother and quicker.

Alternatively, a bigger engine might be designed to provide easier performance, so that the driver need not change gear so often. This could be provided by a three-speed gearbox. Bottom gear would still have to be 2·8:1 to retain the same climb-ing ability, but second gear would be about 1·5:1, making a convenient step between bottom and top gears.

NEUTRAL

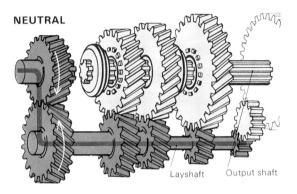

All the gear wheels except the three needed for reverse are constantly in mesh. Wheels on the output shaft revolve around it and those on the layshaft are fixed. In neutral, no power is transmitted

FIRST GEAR

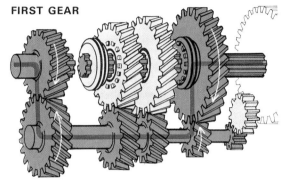

When a gear is engaged, the appropriate wheel is locked to the output shaft and power is transmitted. In first gear, the widest ratio is used to provide the greatest torque output, for low-speed driving and hill climbing

SECOND GEAR

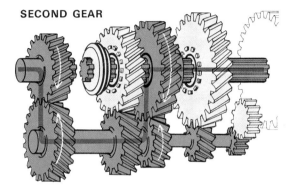

In second gear, a narrower ratio gives a smaller increase in turning effort

THIRD GEAR

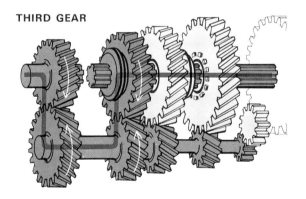

Third gear uses a still narrower ratio, and top gear (centre) is obtained by coupling the input shaft directly to the output shaft so that power is transmitted through the gearbox without the help of the meshing wheels

FOURTH GEAR

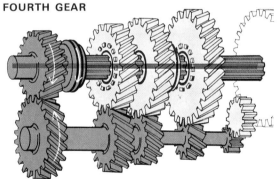

Direct-top gearboxes are usually fitted to cars which have the engine in front and the driving wheels at the back. The direct drive in top gear provides negligible loss of power through friction, but about 3 per cent is lost in other ratios

REVERSE

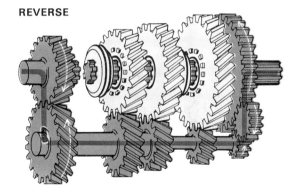

In reverse gear a third wheel, the idler, has the effect of reversing the normal direction of the output shaft

Indirect gearing

CARS with the engine and the driving wheels at the same end usually have the final drive located between the engine and the gearbox, to save space. The power is led into the gearbox by a shaft which passes over the final drive, and led out to the final drive by a lower, parallel shaft.

The meshing gear wheels needed for the various ratios are mounted on these two shafts, and only one pair is involved in any particular ratio. This system is called an all-indirect gearbox.

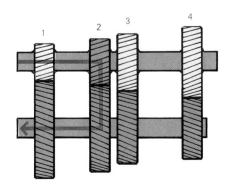

Second gear in an all-indirect gear-box Only two gear wheels are involved in transmitting power from the input shaft at the top to the output shaft beneath. The upper gear is smaller than the lower gear, giving a speed reduction

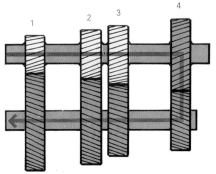

Top gear in an all-indirect gearbox The two gears which transmit the power from the input shaft at the top to the output shaft beneath differ in size from the gears used for second gear, and the output shaft runs faster

Transmission/changing gear

What happens when gears are engaged

THE GEAR WHEELS in a constant-mesh gearbox cannot all be fixed to their shafts, or no movement would be possible; so there has to be a system which permits all the gear wheels except those required for a particular ratio to run freely. Usually all the gear wheels on one shaft are fixed to it and the wheels on the other shafts can revolve around their shaft until a ratio is selected. Then one of the free-running wheels is locked to the shaft, and that pair of wheels can transmit power.

The locking of the gear wheels to a shaft is done by collars, which are splined to the shaft. This method of fixing means that the collar must revolve with the shaft but it can slide along to lock on to the gear wheels on either side, or remain between them, allowing both to spin freely.

Around each collar is a groove engaged by a two-pronged fork which is fixed to a sliding rod mounted in the gearbox housing. One, two or three of these selector rods are linked to the gear lever. Moving the gear lever causes a selector rod to slide to or fro. As it slides, the collar gripped by the selector fork is slid along the shaft to engage with, or move away from, a gear.

SELECTOR RODS IN A TYPICAL 4-SPEED GEARBOX

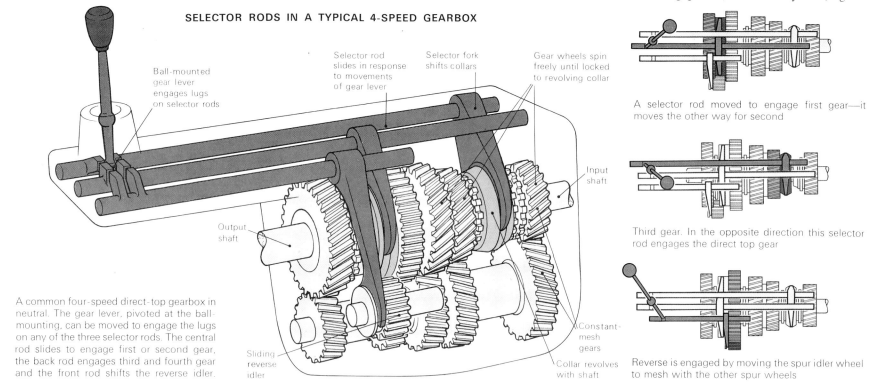

Ball-mounted gear lever engages lugs on selector rods

Selector rod slides in response to movements of gear lever

Selector fork shifts collars

Gear wheels spin freely until locked to revolving collar

Input shaft

Output shaft

Constant-mesh gears

Collar revolves with shaft

Sliding reverse idler

A common four-speed direct-top gearbox in neutral. The gear lever, pivoted at the ball-mounting, can be moved to engage the lugs on any of the three selector rods. The central rod slides to engage first or second gear, the back rod engages third and fourth gear and the front rod shifts the reverse idler.

A selector rod moved to engage first gear—it moves the other way for second

Third gear. In the opposite direction this selector rod engages the direct top gear

Reverse is engaged by moving the spur idler wheel to mesh with the other spur wheels

Dog clutch helps to mesh gears

COLLARS are locked on to constant-mesh gear wheels by a mechanism called a dog clutch. The face of the collar carries a ring of projections, called dogs, which look rather like gear teeth.

There is a corresponding set of dogs on one face of the gear wheel next to the collar. When the collar is slid along the splined shaft to engage a gear, the two sets of dogs mesh and the wheel revolves with the collar.

A collar usually has a dog clutch on each face, so that when slid one way it engages one gear and when slid in the opposite direction it engages another gear.

At an intermediate point the collar is not engaged with either gear wheel, and both can run freely without power being transmitted. In a direct-top gearbox a dog clutch is also used to link the input shaft and the output shaft to provide direct drive to the wheels in top gear.

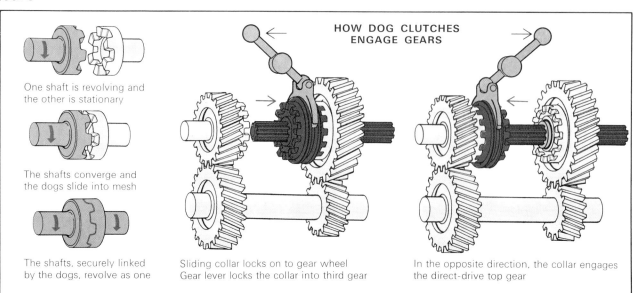

HOW DOG CLUTCHES ENGAGE GEARS

One shaft is revolving and the other is stationary

The shafts converge and the dogs slide into mesh

The shafts, securely linked by the dogs, revolve as one

Sliding collar locks on to gear wheel Gear lever locks the collar into third gear

In the opposite direction, the collar engages the direct-drive top gear

Synchromesh for smooth gear changes

IN THE simplest type of constant-mesh gearbox, which is now obsolete, gears could be engaged simply by snatching the gear lever from one position to the next as fast as possible. This was noisy and jerky.

To do the job more quietly and smoothly, the two sets of dogs had to be allowed to reach the same speed, so that they would slide together without clashing. This synchronisation was achieved in changing up by pausing slightly in neutral. The pause allowed friction and oil drag to slow down the free-running input component to the speed of the output one—the gear connected to the road wheels through the remainder of the transmission.

In changing down, the gears were synchronised by double de-clutching—engaging the clutch with the gearbox in neutral and revving the engine to speed up the input component, then disengaging the clutch again and engaging the appropriate gear.

Drivers today are relieved from the need for double de-clutching by a synchronising device built into the sliding collars in the gearbox. This synchromesh device is usually fitted to all forward gears, but in some cars it is not provided in bottom gear.

Synchromesh works like a friction clutch. As the collar is pushed towards the gear wheel with which it is to mesh, a conical ring on the gear wheel in front of the dogs comes into contact with the surface of a matching conical hole in the collar. The friction between the conical surfaces brings the free-running gear wheel up or down to the speed of the input shaft.

The collar continues to move along and the two sets of dogs slide smoothly into mesh. However, if the gear lever is moved too fast on some cars, the gears will clash.

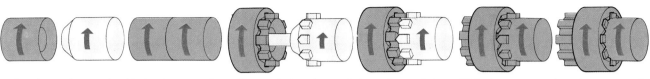

Synchromesh uses the friction between the mating conical surfaces of two components to modify the speed of one of them

The conical surfaces of the collar and the free-running gear wheel come into contact, and friction slows or speeds up the wheel

With the parts rotating at same speed, the spring-loaded outer ring of the collar is pushed forward and dogs mesh

A TYPICAL SYNCHROMESH SYSTEM

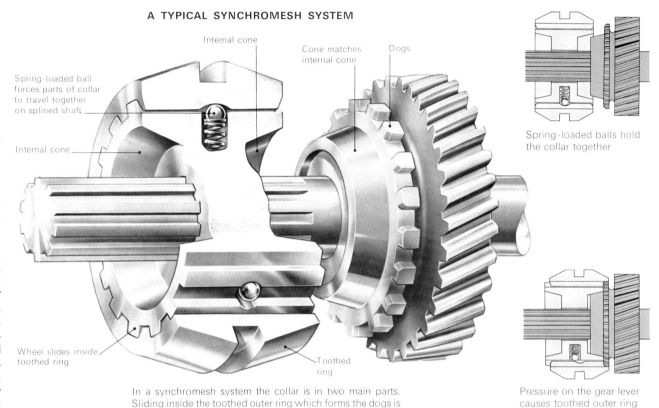

Internal cone

Cone matches internal cone

Dogs

Spring-loaded ball forces parts of collar to travel together on splined shaft

Internal cone

Wheel slides inside toothed ring

Toothed ring

Spring-loaded balls hold the collar together

Pressure on the gear lever causes toothed outer ring to slide into engagement

In a synchromesh system the collar is in two main parts. Sliding inside the toothed outer ring which forms the dogs is a wheel with internal cones to match the gear-wheel cones

Baulking system prevents engagement until gears are synchronised

MODERN synchromesh mechanisms incorporate a baulking system which obstructs the movement of the collar and will not allow the dogs to engage until perfect synchronisation has been achieved.

If the revolving parts do not turn at the same speed, perhaps because the clutch is not properly disengaged, the gear lever will resist the driver's efforts to push it into position.

There are at least three different kinds of baulking systems in general use today, but all produce the same effect. One common type uses a baulk ring to keep the two sets of dogs apart until they are revolving at the same speed.

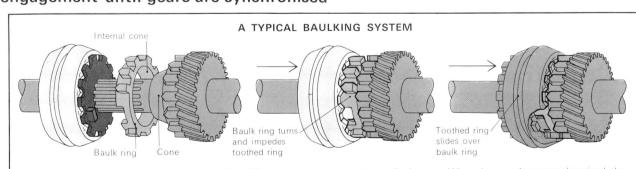

A TYPICAL BAULKING SYSTEM

Internal cone

Baulk ring   Cone

Baulk ring turns and impedes toothed ring

Toothed ring slides over baulk ring

Collar and gear wheel separated to show baulk ring, which contains internal cone — normally loosely fixed between wheel and collar

When the cones meet, the baulk ring shifts slightly and its dogs prevent the toothed ring from moving forward

When the speeds are synchronised, the baulk ring shifts back and the toothed ring is free to move into mesh

Transmission/fluid coupling

Passing on power through fluid

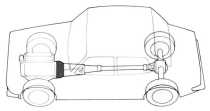

THE FUNCTION of a fluid drive is to act as an automatic clutch between the engine and gearbox. It allows the engine to idle when the car is stationary, but takes up the drive smoothly and progressively when the driver speeds up the engine by depressing the accelerator pedal.

There are two main rotating parts: an impeller driven by the engine, and a turbine which drives the gearbox. Each is bowl-shaped and contains a number of partitions called vanes.

The two bowls are placed face to face in a casing filled with oil, and they are separated by a small clearance so that there is never any rubbing contact between them.

The fluid flywheel

The basic form of fluid drive, known as a fluid flywheel, or fluid coupling, is used in place of a friction clutch in cars with pre-selector gearboxes. It consists essentially of an impeller and turbine with oil continuously circulated between the two whenever the engine is running. The impeller is driven by the engine, and the turbine drives the gearbox input shaft.

When the engine is idling, oil is flung from the impeller by centrifugal force. Directed forward by the vanes, it enters the turbine, which remains stationary because the force of the oil is not yet sufficient to turn it.

When the driver depresses the accelerator the speed of the impeller increases and the turning effort derived from the fast-moving oil becomes great enough to overcome the resistance of the turbine, which begins to rotate, so setting the car in motion.

After giving up energy to the turbine, the oil re-enters the impeller and is circulated back to the turbine again.

If the speed of the engine continues to increase, the difference between the rotational speeds of the impeller and the turbine gradually diminishes until the 'slip' between them is reduced to as little as 2 per cent. The limitation of a fluid flywheel is that the torque, or turning effort, which is applied to the turbine can never be greater than that delivered by the impeller.

THE FLUID FLYWHEEL

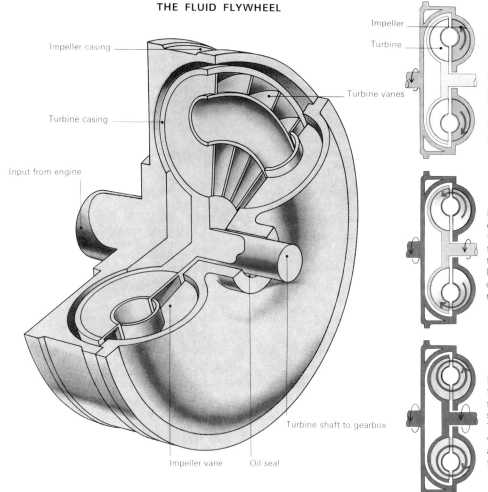

Impeller casing

Turbine casing

Input from engine

Turbine vanes

Turbine shaft to gearbox

Impeller vane   Oil seal

Idling The driving part of the fluid flywheel (the impeller) is attached to the engine and faces the driven half (the turbine), from which it is separated by a small clearance. At idling speed there is insufficient centrifugal force for the oil to turn the turbine and so move the car

Impeller
Turbine

Low to medium revs As the engine speeds up, centrifugal force pushes the oil into the turbine and some turning effort is transmitted. But there is still a large degree of 'slip' in the unit; the output shaft is therefore rotating more slowly than the input shaft

Medium to high revs Once the engine reaches a pre-set speed, the force of the oil is sufficient to transmit full power. This gives in effect a direct drive with the output shaft rotating at about 98 per cent of the speed of the input shaft

FLUID FLYWHEEL AND TORQUE CONVERTER: THE BASIC DIFFERENCE

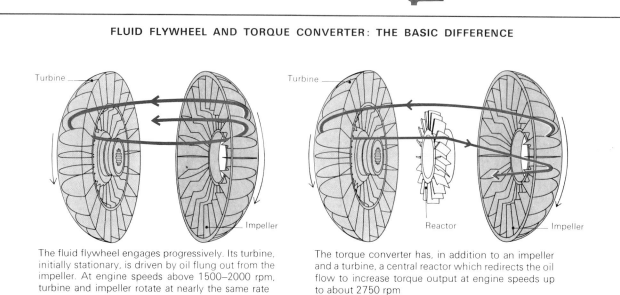

Turbine   Impeller

Turbine   Reactor   Impeller

The fluid flywheel engages progressively. Its turbine, initially stationary, is driven by oil flung out from the impeller. At engine speeds above 1500–2000 rpm, turbine and impeller rotate at nearly the same rate

The torque converter has, in addition to an impeller and a turbine, a central reactor which redirects the oil flow to increase torque output at engine speeds up to about 2750 rpm

Torque converter

MOST CARS with automatic transmission use a form of fluid drive known as a torque converter. As the name implies, it converts the torque, or turning effort, of the engine into the higher torque needed by the car at low road speeds.

An increase in torque has the same effect as changing to a lower gear; so a torque converter is also a gear reducer, acting like an extra set of gears before the engine's drive reaches the gearbox.

Like the fluid flywheel, the torque converter has an engine-driven impeller and a turbine which is connected to the gearbox input shaft. It is able to deliver a higher torque than the engine produces because it also has, between the impeller and the turbine, a small, vaned wheel known as the reactor, or stator. A one-way clutch locks the reactor to the gearbox casing at low engine speeds.

In a fluid flywheel, oil returning from the turbine tends to curb the speed of the impeller. But in a torque converter, the vanes of the locked reactor direct the oil along a more favourable path back to the centre of the impeller, enabling it to give extra thrust to the turbine blades.

At pull-away speeds, the torque converter can double the turning effort produced by the engine and applied to the gearbox.

As the engine picks up speed, this 2:1 increase in turning effort is reduced until, at cruising speed, there is no torque increase at all. The reactor is then spun round by the oil at the same rate as the turbine. The torque converter now acts like a fluid flywheel, with the reactor 'free-wheeling' and having no torque-increasing effect. Neither a fluid coupling nor a torque converter can be 'declutched' by the driver. Consequently, they are generally used in conjunction with various types of epicyclic transmission (see p. 94), which allow gear changes to be made without disconnecting the engine.

An alternative, used on a few models, is to provide a friction clutch in addition to a torque converter. This enables a synchro-mesh gearbox to be used, as the friction clutch disconnects the engine when gears are being changed.

THE TORQUE CONVERTER

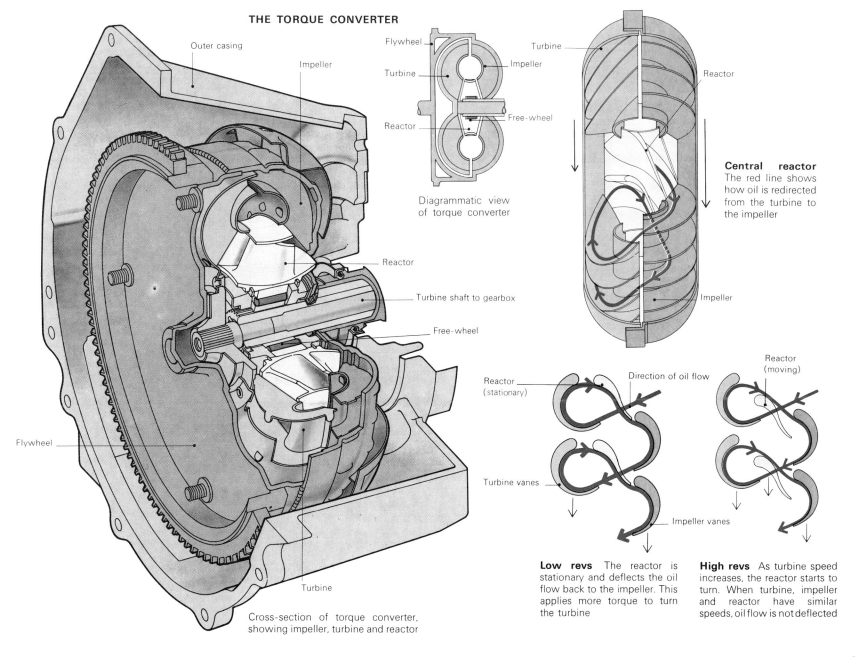

Diagrammatic view of torque converter

Central reactor The red line shows how oil is redirected from the turbine to the impeller

Cross-section of torque converter, showing impeller, turbine and reactor

Low revs The reactor is stationary and deflects the oil flow back to the impeller. This applies more torque to turn the turbine

High revs As turbine speed increases, the reactor starts to turn. When turbine, impeller and reactor have similar speeds, oil flow is not deflected

Transmission/automatic gearbox

Changing gear without a clutch pedal

THE BASIS for most automatic gearboxes is a set of gears called a planetary or epicyclic gear train. This consists of a sun wheel, planet gears rotating round it, a planet carrier, and an outer ring gear which is known as an annulus.

The sun wheel is mounted centrally. In the simple epicyclic gear, a pair of planets revolve on spindles supported by the U-shaped planet carrier, which is mounted on a shaft on the same axis as the sun wheel. As the carrier rotates, the planet gears turn on their spindles and orbit the sun wheel, with which they mesh. The planet gears also mesh with teeth on the inside of the annulus, which can rotate

around the sun and planet gears, also on the same axis. By holding stationary any one of these parts, the others can be rotated to provide different speed relationships according to the respective sizes of the gears.

If the sun wheel is locked and the planet carrier revolves, the planets will roll around the sun wheel and drive the annulus in the same direction as their carrier, but at a different speed.

If the planets are locked, or if the sun wheel is locked to the annulus, the gear train will revolve as one unit, with the planet shaft, sun-wheel shaft and annulus rotating at the same speed.

If the planet carrier is locked and the sun wheel rotates, the planets will drive the annulus in the opposite direction.

If the annulus is locked and the planet carrier revolves, the planets will roll inside the annulus and drive the sun wheel in the same direction at a different speed.

In order to obtain the required number of gear combinations, an automatic gearbox has two, three or four sets of planets 'compounded' together. Some parts of each are connected together permanently; others are connected temporarily or stopped by a system of brake bands and clutches selected by hydraulic shift valves which are located in the bottom of the gearbox. Oil, under pressure to operate the

brake bands and clutches, is provided by a pump which draws its supply from the gearbox lubricating oil. Sometimes two pumps are used, driven from the input and output ends of the gearbox.

The gear selector controls the shift valves directly, unless automatic forward drive is selected. Then the operation of the valves is governed by throttle opening and road speed. With a wide throttle opening, the oil pressure is reduced and the gears tend to stay in a lower gear.

When the car reaches a pre-set speed, a governor allows the pump pressure to take over from the throttle control and a change to a higher gear is made.

SIMPLE EPICYCLIC GEAR IN OPERATION

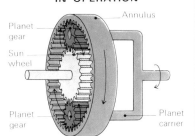

With the sun wheel locked, planets turn around it, with carrier and annulus turning in the same direction at different speeds

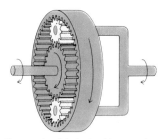

If sun wheel is locked to annulus, planets cannot rotate, so carrier turns whole unit together

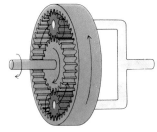

When planet carrier is locked, sun wheel turns planets which drive annulus in the opposite direction

HOW EPICYCLIC GEAR TRAINS PROVIDE THE RATIOS

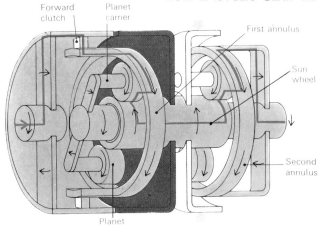

First gear Forward drive clutch is engaged, so engine drive (red line) causes first annulus to turn. This causes planet gears to drive common sun wheel the opposite way. Second planet carrier is held by brake band (light grey), so planets drive second annulus and output shaft, producing two reductions in engine speed

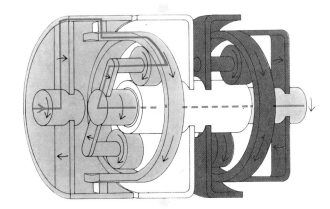

Second gear Forward drive clutch is engaged, so engine drives first annulus. Common sun wheel is braked, so annulus drives planet gears around it, which drives carrier in same direction. Carrier shaft is also output shaft, so one reduction is used. Second planet gears and their carrier (dark grey) then free-wheel

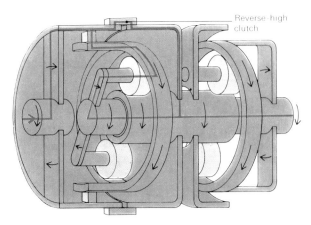

Top gear Forward drive clutch is engaged, so engine drives first annulus. Reverse-high clutch is also engaged, which locks sun wheel to annulus so that both turn at same speed. Planet gears (light grey) therefore cannot turn, so carrier also turns at same engine speed. Output shaft thus turns at engine speed (direct drive)

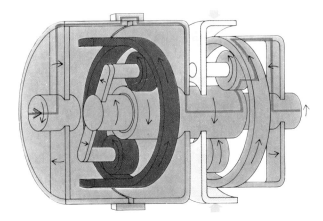

Reverse gear Forward drive clutch is disengaged, so first annulus free-wheels. Reverse clutch is engaged, so engine drives common sun wheel. Second planet carrier is braked, so sun wheel causes planet gears to drive second annulus in the opposite direction to give a single reduction reverse drive

MULTI-PLATE CLUTCH IN ACTION

Drive from engine is connected to and disconnected from parts in epicyclic train by means of multi-plate friction clutches running in oil. These are operated by oil pressure from master shift valves

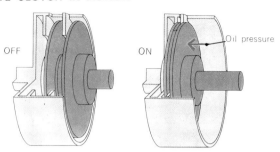

OFF   ON   Oil pressure

BRAKE BANDS

When necessary, parts of the epicyclic train are stopped by a hydraulically operated band with a lining

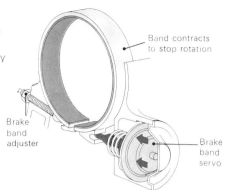

Band contracts to stop rotation

Brake band adjuster

Brake band servo

INSIDE AN AUTOMATIC GEARBOX

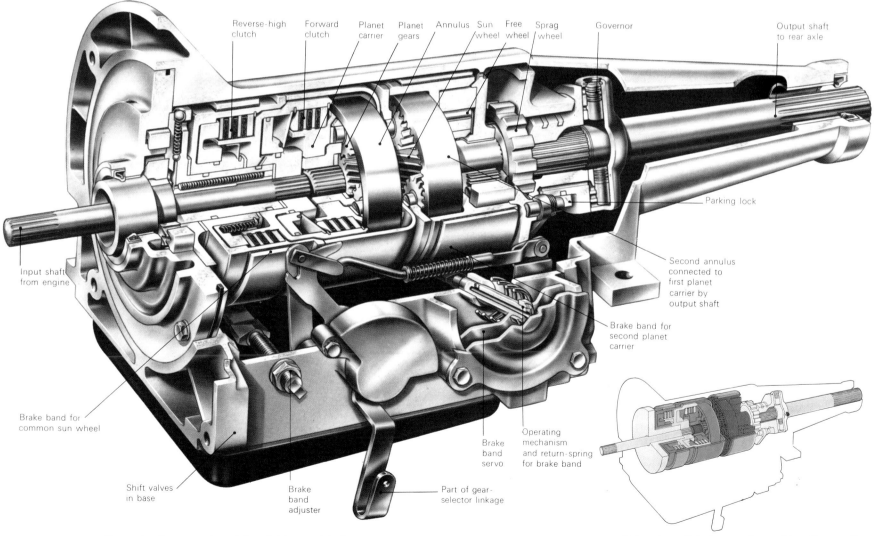

Reverse-high clutch
Forward clutch
Planet carrier
Planet gears
Annulus
Sun wheel
Free wheel
Sprag wheel
Governor
Output shaft to rear axle

Parking lock

Second annulus connected to first planet carrier by output shaft

Brake band for second planet carrier

Operating mechanism and return-spring for brake band

Brake band servo

Part of gear-selector linkage

Brake band adjuster

Shift valves in base

Brake band for common sun wheel

Input shaft from engine

Two epicyclic gear sets and the clutches and brake bands are fitted compactly together in a typical automatic gearbox. Drawing on right shows relative positions of the major sections

Colour key: Pale brown: input drive. Brown: first epicyclic set and clutches. Dark grey: second set. Green: brake bands. Mid grey: output shaft. Light grey: casing, parking lock, governor

Transmission/automatic gear controls

Selecting the gears in different designs

AN AUTOMATIC transmission selects and changes gear to suit different speeds and road conditions, without the driver having to do this by hand.

In its simplest form, all that is necessary to drive a car with automatic gear control is to select forward or reverse gear and accelerate. There are only two pedals—one for accelerating, the other for braking.

The different designs of automatic transmission offer a variety of 'gear holds' and inhibitors, and their selection is controlled by a lever.

All systems have the control-lever positions N for neutral, and most have P for park (which incorporates a locking device). For reasons of safety, the engine can be started only when the lever is in one of these two positions. R indicates reverse, D is the forward drive position, and L is used to hold low gear. Accidental selection of park and reverse is prevented by a device such as a mechanical stop.

The simplest sequence is PRNDL. By placing the lever in position D, fully automatic up-and-down changes are obtained, using all forward gears. The occurrence of the changes depends upon a governor responsive to speed, but is also affected by the position of the accelerator pedal.

Full throttle gives maximum use of each gear up to the highest safe engine speed; alternatively, by accelerating at part throttle the driver can cause upward changes to occur (first to second, and second to top) at considerably lower speeds. There is also a kick-down switch (brought into action by pressing the accelerator down firmly), which immediately initiates a change to a lower gear, provided that the speed permits this. For example, a kick-down change from top to second is usually obtainable at, say, 55 mph, but may be inhibited by the automatic control when travelling at a higher speed.

In some of the widely used Borg Warner three-speed automatic transmissions, the sequence of gear-selector lever positions is PRND21. By placing the lever in position 2, the driver obtains automatic changes (up and down) between first and second gears, but top gear is excluded. If the lever is placed in position 1, the driver restricts the box to first gear. The purpose of this arrangement is to enable maximum engine braking to be obtained on steep descents. A similar sequence is followed in a General Motors automatic transmission used by Vauxhall and Opel, but the letters I and L (intermediate and low) are used instead of the numerals 2 and 1.

The automatic transmission supplied by Automotive Products to some of the British Leyland range gives the driver the option of selecting each of four forward gears as and when he wishes, or allowing changes of gear to occur automatically.

In an automatic transmission, the gears are selected by hydraulic pressure from one or two oil pumps.

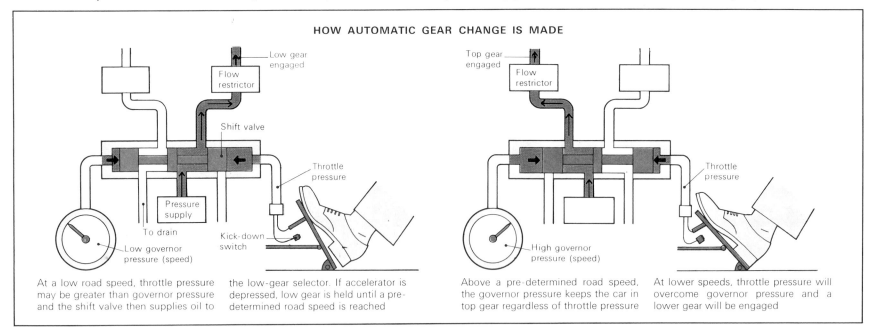

HOW AUTOMATIC GEAR CHANGE IS MADE

Low gear engaged · Flow restrictor · Shift valve · Throttle pressure · Pressure supply · To drain · Kick-down switch · Low governor pressure (speed)

At a low road speed, throttle pressure may be greater than governor pressure and the shift valve then supplies oil to the low-gear selector. If accelerator is depressed, low gear is held until a pre-determined road speed is reached

Top gear engaged · Flow restrictor · Throttle pressure · High governor pressure (speed)

Above a pre-determined road speed, the governor pressure keeps the car in top gear regardless of throttle pressure

At lower speeds, throttle pressure will overcome governor pressure and a lower gear will be engaged

TWO TYPES OF AUTOMATIC GEAR CONTROL

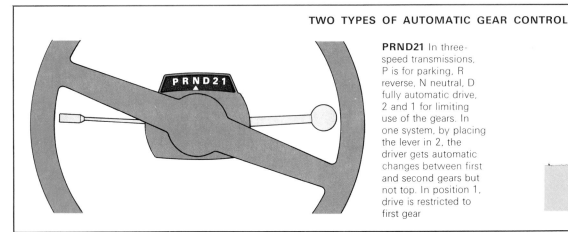

PRND21 In three-speed transmissions, P is for parking, R reverse, N neutral, D fully automatic drive, 2 and 1 for limiting use of the gears. In one system, by placing the lever in 2, the driver gets automatic changes between first and second gears but not top. In position 1, drive is restricted to first gear

D4321NR In the sequence for the selector lever in Automotive Products' transmission, D gives fully automatic gear selection, while 4321 and R are selected manually. This gives the driver the option of allowing changes to take place automatically or selecting gear changes by hand

The Volvo (Daf) belt-drive transmission

VOLVO's small-car range (originally Dafs) has a belt-driven system called CVT (continuously variable transmission), which provides fully automatic and stepless variations of gear ratio to suit all conditions.

When starting from rest, the drive is taken up automatically by a centrifugal clutch which in turn drives two pulleys through a reduction gearbox. The pulley diameters are varied according to their speed and throttle position. On the larger cars, two toothed V-belts run to two rear pulleys, which are pressed together by springs. The lower-powered cars have single belts.

If the accelerator is suddenly depressed, the gearing is reduced, to give better acceleration; but as speed increases, the centrifugal weights contract the pulleys, to return to a higher gear effect.

BELT-DRIVEN AUTOMATIC GEAR CHANGE

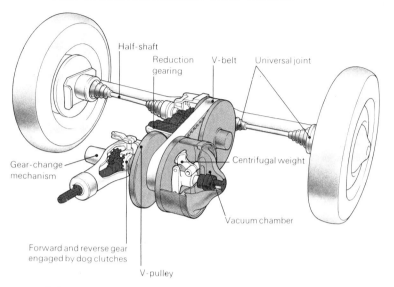

Half-shaft
Reduction gearing
V-belt
Universal joint
Gear-change mechanism
Centrifugal weight
Vacuum chamber
Forward and reverse gear engaged by dog clutches
V-pulley

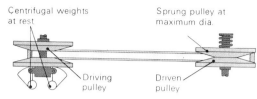

Centrifugal weights at rest
Sprung pulley at maximum dia.
Driving pulley
Driven pulley

Low speed Centrifugal weights do not alter the driving-pulley diameter and the driven pulley remains at maximum diameter for lowest possible gear ratio

Centrifugal weights fully extended
Sprung pulley at minimum dia

High speed Centrifugal weights increase effective diameter of driving pulley, and driven pulley has to expand against its spring to give a high gearing

Economical cruising with overdrive

OVERDRIVE is a unit fitted behind the gear-box to provide an extra gear (higher than top) which allows economical cruising at a reduced engine speed, without reduction of the road speed.

In some cars the overdrive is also effective when third gear is in use (or even with second gear), and so adds to the driver's choice of gear ratios.

Most overdrives have an epicyclic gear arrangement (see p. 94) that includes a hydraulically operated cone clutch. When the overdrive is not in operation, the clutch, which is attached to the central sun wheel, is locked by spring pressure to the annulus connected to the output shaft. The planet carrier connected to the gearbox shaft turns the whole unit to give a direct drive.

When the driver selects overdrive, the clutch locks to the outer casing and stops the sun wheel turning. The planet carrier is then driven around the sun wheel and in turn drives the annulus at a slightly higher speed than itself. The effect is that the output shaft turns faster than the input shaft.

Overdrives are controlled electrically or hydraulically by a dashboard or steering-column switch. Changes can be made without using the clutch, but some designs require momentarily lifting the accelerator when changing into overdrive, and depressing it to operate a kick-down switch when changing back to direct drive.

Most overdrives cut out automatically below a pre-determined road speed.

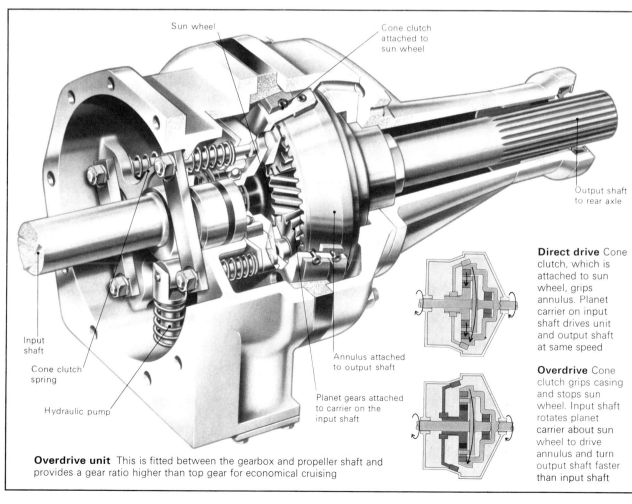

Sun wheel
Cone clutch attached to sun wheel
Output shaft to rear axle
Input shaft
Cone clutch spring
Hydraulic pump
Annulus attached to output shaft
Planet gears attached to carrier on the input shaft

Overdrive unit This is fitted between the gearbox and propeller shaft and provides a gear ratio higher than top gear for economical cruising

Direct drive Cone clutch, which is attached to sun wheel, grips annulus. Planet carrier on input shaft drives unit and output shaft at same speed

Overdrive Cone clutch grips casing and stops sun wheel. Input shaft rotates planet carrier about sun wheel to drive annulus and turn output shaft faster than input shaft

Transmission/propeller shafts

How the propeller shaft swings and 'stretches' as the car rides over bumps

IN MOST CARS, power is transmitted from the gearbox to the final drive by the propeller shaft. This shaft is a metal tube, strong enough to transmit the full power of the engine multiplied by the gearing.

The front end of the propeller shaft is connected to the gearbox, which is bolted to the chassis or body of the car. The other end is connected to the final drive in the rear-axle assembly.

When the car runs on an uneven surface, the rear-axle assembly rises and falls as the springs flex, so the rotating propeller shaft must be able to change its angle correspondingly. This swinging is made possible by universal joints which are fitted at each end of the propeller shaft.

Axle movement on the springs continuously alters the distance between the gearbox and final-drive couplings, so the effective length of the propeller shaft must be able to vary correspondingly.

This is allowed for by a sliding connection; usually the universal-joint coupling is splined on to the gearbox output shaft so that it can slide in and out.

Front-drive cars and rear-engined rear-drive cars do not have propeller shafts; in these cars, power is transmitted from the final drive in the engine gearbox unit to the road wheels. The half-shafts have universal joints, to allow for spring and steering movements, and splined connections to the final drive for changes in length.

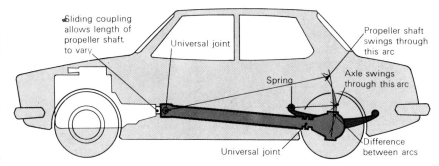

Allowing for movement As the axle rises and falls with the flexing of the springs, universal joints at each end of the propeller shaft allow its angle to change. The axle swings through an arc determined by the rear springs. The propeller shaft moves through a different arc and its effective length has to vary, to compensate for the difference. A sliding coupling at one end of the shaft makes this possible

COMPONENTS OF A TYPICAL PROPELLER SHAFT

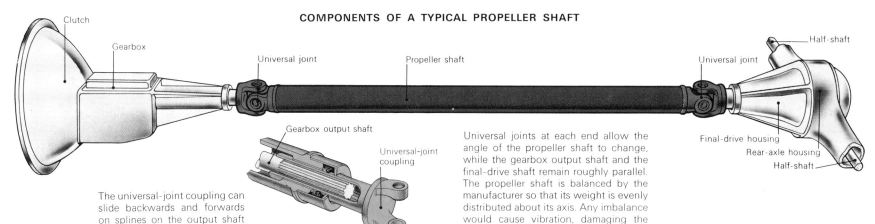

The universal-joint coupling can slide backwards and forwards on splines on the output shaft as both rotate

Universal joints at each end allow the angle of the propeller shaft to change, while the gearbox output shaft and the final-drive shaft remain roughly parallel. The propeller shaft is balanced by the manufacturer so that its weight is evenly distributed about its axis. Any imbalance would cause vibration, damaging the gearbox and final-drive bearings

Passing on the drive through a universal joint

THE MOST COMMON universal joint on modern cars is the Hooke type. It consists of two yokes pivoted on a central cross-piece, or 'spider', formed by two pins intersecting at right angles.

The yokes, one on an input shaft and the other on an output shaft, are connected to the spider so that they are at right angles to each other. This kind of joint allows the shafts to rotate together, even when their axes do not form a straight line.

Friction between the yokes and the spider is reduced by bearing-caps containing needle-roller bearings. These caps fit over the arms of the spider and are held in the yokes by circlips sprung into grooves.

In the latest versions of this type of universal joint, the bearing-caps are packed with grease by the manufacturer and do not need periodic lubrication.

When the shafts connected by a Hooke-type universal joint are rotating at an angle, the speed of the output shaft fluc-tuates. The greater the angle between the shafts, the greater the fluctuation in speed.

In a front-engined rear-drive car, the fluctuation is not significant, because the propeller shaft is so long that the universal joints bend at angles so slight that the output speed does not vary greatly.

In addition, the input and output shafts are roughly parallel, and the fluctuations in the joints at each end of the propeller shaft cancel themselves out.

Front-drive cars and rear-engined rear-drive cars do not have propeller shafts, but they still need universal joints to allow for springing movements. On these cars the half-shafts which transmit power to the road wheels have universal joints fitted beside the final drive. Front-drive cars also have constant–velocity universal joints fitted at the road-wheel ends of the half-shafts to permit steering movements, as well as up and down movements caused by the suspension.

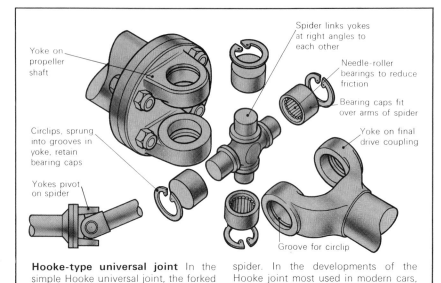

Hooke-type universal joint In the simple Hooke universal joint, the forked ends of the shafts pivot directly on the spider. In the developments of the Hooke joint most used in modern cars, needle-roller bearings reduce friction

Cushioning the shocks on front or rear drive

WHEN a front-engined rear-drive car starts from rest, the shock to the transmission is cushioned by the long propeller shaft, which twists slightly and then untwists. On front-drive cars and rear-engined rear-drive cars, the half-shafts which transmit power are too short to twist; the shock is cushioned by the universal joints on each side of the final drive.

There are two types of universal joint. In one type a rubber-sleeved spider is clamped to the yokes. The compressed rubber provides the cushioning effect and its flexibility permits angular movement.

The second type uses a hexagonal rubber 'doughnut' to absorb transmission shock and provide articulation. This is fixed to triangular flanges on the ends of the input and output shafts by bolts passing through metal sleeves bonded into the rubber. The flanges are bolted to the rubber, but not fixed directly to each other.

In some cases, the elasticity of the doughnut permits small variations in the effective length of the half-shaft, and a splined sliding joint is unnecessary.

The universal joints which permit steering movement in front-drive cars have to cope with angles of 30° or more between the input and output shafts. Speed fluctuations in Hooke-type joints at such angles would cause jerky drive, so constant-velocity joints are used. These allow the output shaft to rotate constantly at the same speed as the input shaft.

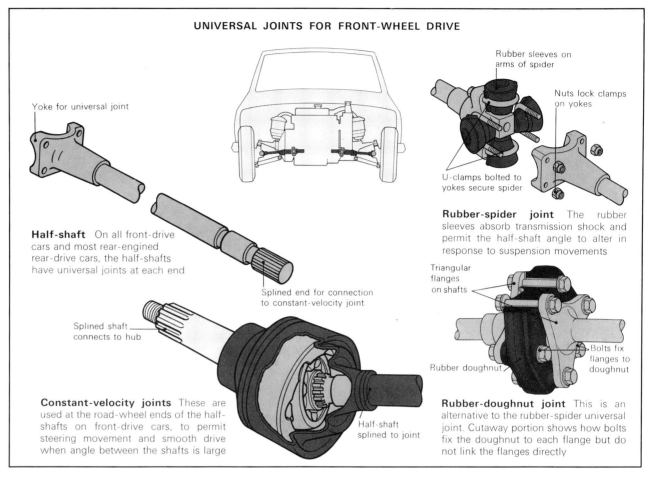

UNIVERSAL JOINTS FOR FRONT-WHEEL DRIVE

Yoke for universal joint

Rubber sleeves on arms of spider

Nuts lock clamps on yokes

U-clamps bolted to yokes secure spider

Half-shaft On all front-drive cars and most rear-engined rear-drive cars, the half-shafts have universal joints at each end

Splined end for connection to constant-velocity joint

Rubber-spider joint The rubber sleeves absorb transmission shock and permit the half-shaft angle to alter in response to suspension movements

Triangular flanges on shafts

Splined shaft connects to hub

Bolts fix flanges to doughnut

Rubber doughnut

Constant-velocity joints These are used at the road-wheel ends of the half-shafts on front-drive cars, to permit steering movement and smooth drive when angle between the shafts is large

Half-shaft splined to joint

Rubber-doughnut joint This is an alternative to the rubber-spider universal joint. Cutaway portion shows how bolts fix the doughnut to each flange but do not link the flanges directly

Birfield constant-velocity joint

ONE OF THE most successful designs of constant-velocity joint is the Birfield joint, which gives equal input and output shaft speeds, without fluctuation, over a wide range of angles.

One shaft has a hollow sphere on one end, in which six grooves are machined in line with the shaft axis. The other shaft is splined into a sphere, which has similar grooves and lies inside the hollow sphere.

Between these two components is a steel ring cage carrying six steel balls, which engage both sets of grooves. The drive is transmitted from one shaft to the other through the balls.

When the shafts move out of line through steering or suspension movement, the balls move in the grooves. With this type of joint, the input and output shafts rotate at the same speed, whatever the angle between them, and the drive remains constant without the speed variations of a simple universal joint.

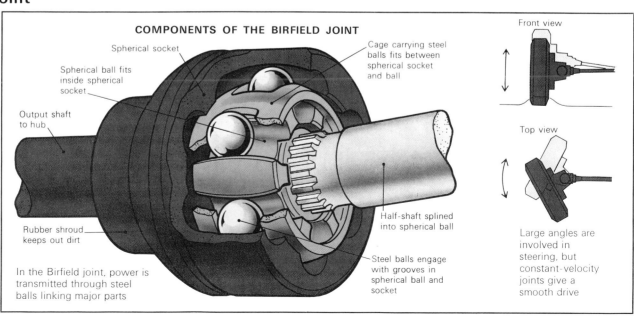

COMPONENTS OF THE BIRFIELD JOINT

Spherical socket

Cage carrying steel balls fits between spherical socket and ball

Spherical ball fits inside spherical socket

Output shaft to hub

Front view

Top view

Rubber shroud keeps out dirt

Half-shaft splined into spherical ball

Steel balls engage with grooves in spherical ball and socket

In the Birfield joint, power is transmitted through steel balls linking major parts

Large angles are involved in steering, but constant-velocity joints give a smooth drive

Transmission/final drives

Passing on power to the wheels

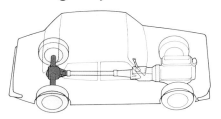

ON THE LAST stage of its journey to the road wheels, power from the engine passes through the final drive.

This assembly has three jobs to do: it gears down the speed of the propeller shaft to the speed required by the road wheels; it allows the inner wheel on the powered axle to turn more slowly than the outer wheel when a car rounds a bend; and, ex-cept when the engine is mounted across the car, it turns the drive through a right angle to drive the wheels.

The flywheel of a medium-sized car runs at speeds up to 6000 rpm, and that of a sports car at up to 7500 rpm. Such speeds have to be reduced greatly before power is transmitted to the road wheels, which even at 70 mph turn at only 750–1150 rpm, according to their size.

In top gear, the speed-reduction ratio provided by the final drive ranges between about 6·5:1 and 3:1—that is, taking the 3:1 ratio, the propeller shaft revolves three times for every single revolution of the wheels. With conventional cars, this reduction takes place entirely in the back-axle assembly. In cars with all-indirect gearboxes, part of the reduction is done in the gearbox. Cars with 4-wheel drive have a reduction for both axles.

The reduction is achieved by an assem-bly called the crown wheel and pinion. A pinion on the propeller shaft drives a larger gear, the crown wheel, which is mounted in the centre of the axle housing.

Speed reduction depends on the num-bers of teeth used in the crown wheel and pinion. If, for instance, the pinion has 10 teeth and the crown wheel 40, the propel-ler shaft turns four times to turn the crown wheel and the road wheels once. This gives a 4:1 speed reduction.

Rotating with the crown wheel is the differential, a gear system which allows for differences in speed between the powered wheels when rounding a bend. The crown wheel and pinion also turn the drive line through 90°. This is possible because they are bevel gears, meshing with their axes at right angles to each other.

There are three types of bevel gears—straight, spiral and hypoid-spiral. Straight bevel gears have teeth cut in line with the axes of the shafts, and spiral bevel gears have curved teeth. Hypoid-spiral bevel gears also have curved teeth, but the axes of the wheels are not in the same plane. This means that the centre of the pinion can be set below the centre of the crown wheel, giving a lower propeller shaft. Con-sequently, the tunnel in the floor which houses the propeller shaft can be made lower, or can even be eliminated.

MAIN PARTS OF A FINAL DRIVE

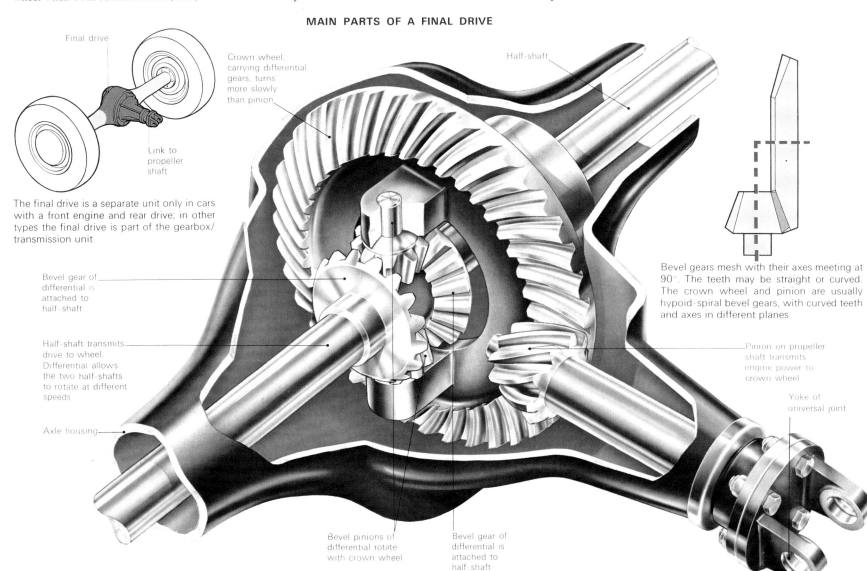

The final drive is a separate unit only in cars with a front engine and rear drive; in other types the final drive is part of the gearbox/transmission unit

Bevel gears mesh with their axes meeting at 90°. The teeth may be straight or curved. The crown wheel and pinion are usually hypoid-spiral bevel gears, with curved teeth and axes in different planes

Crown wheel, carrying differential gears, turns more slowly than pinion

Half-shaft

Bevel gear of differential is attached to half-shaft

Half-shaft transmits drive to wheel. Differential allows the two half-shafts to rotate at different speeds

Axle housing

Bevel pinions of differential rotate with crown wheel

Bevel gear of differential is attached to half-shaft

Pinion on propeller shaft transmits engine power to crown wheel

Yoke of universal joint

Final drive

Link to propeller shaft

How the differential allows wheel speeds to differ

WHEN THE CAR rounds a bend, the inner wheels trace a shorter path than the outer ones. If both driving wheels were fixed rigidly to one axle driven by the crown wheel, they would have to run at the same speed, causing the inner wheel to skid.

This is avoided by dividing the axle into two half-shafts. Each half-shaft is driven independently by the differential, so that when the inner wheel slows, the outer wheel speeds up, and the crown wheel turns at the average speed of the wheels. If the inner wheel turns at 50 rpm and the outer wheel at 100, the crown wheel will run at 75.

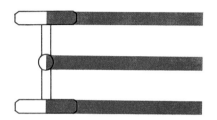

Travelling straight ahead Both wheels cover the same distance at the same speed

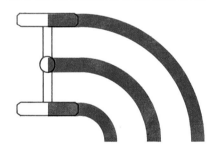

Rounding a bend The inner wheel covers less ground than the outer one. The differential lets them run at different speeds; the crown wheel runs at their average speed

DIFFERENTIAL IN ACTION

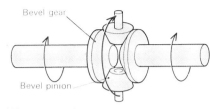

When the shafts rotate in unison, the bevel pinions orbit with the bevel gears, but do not turn on their own axes

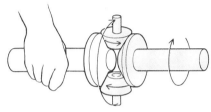

When one shaft is stopped, the other can continue to rotate because, as it does so, its bevel gear makes the bevel pinions turn on their axes. This allows the pinions to orbit around the stationary gear

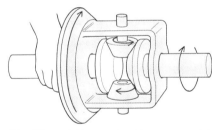

The differential is contained by a cage which is fixed to the crown wheel. The half-shafts pass through this assembly

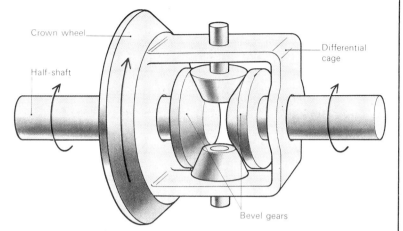

On the straight The cage rotates with the crown wheel; the bevel pinions, orbiting but not spinning, turn the bevel gears and with them the half-shafts

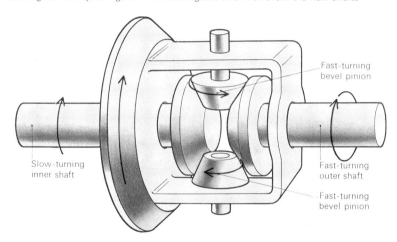

Taking a bend When the inner bevel gear turns more slowly than the crown wheel, the outer gear, driven by the bevel pinions, turns correspondingly faster

Limited-slip differentials to counter wheel-spin

THE DISADVANTAGE of a differential is that it will allow a wheel which cannot grip a slippery surface to spin at twice the speed of the crown wheel, leaving the opposite wheel motionless.

This is because the differential always applies equal torque (turning effort) to each road wheel. If one wheel is spinning, doing no work, the other wheel will not do any work either.

This problem is overcome in some high-powered cars by a limited-slip differential, using self-locking or frictional mechanisms.

In one common type of limited-slip differential, clutch cones are fitted between the differential bevel gears and the cage in which they are housed. Springs between the gears press the conical surfaces into contact, creating a frictional resistance to any difference between the speeds of the gear and the cage.

The resistance is not enough to stop the differential action when the car is following a curved path; but it builds up when the driving torque applied to the differential is increased—when using full throttle in a low gear, for example.

Driving torque tends to force the differential bevel gears apart, so adding to the load on the cones and increasing their resistance to speed differences between the half-shafts. This prevents wheel-spin.

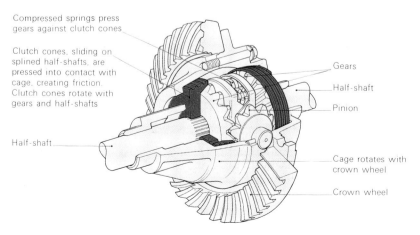

Transmission/axles

Housings for beam axles

MOST AVERAGE-SIZED front-engine cars with rear-wheel drive are fitted with a rigid rear axle or beam axle. The half-shafts and final-drive assembly, which includes the differential, are enclosed by a rigid housing which contains bearings to support the rotating parts.

Usually, it is only the more expensive rear-drive models, or those with front-wheel drive and therefore no differential at the rear, which have independent suspension on the back wheels.

There are two main types of axle housing. In one, the banjo axle, the axle is a single unit and the final drive assembly is carried in a separate casing which is bolted to the axle housing. In the other, a central housing contains the final drive and is fitted with a tube at each side.

Support for the half-shafts

Axles are classified according to the way in which the half-shafts and wheel hubs are supported. In all types, the inner ends of the half-shafts are connected to the gears of the differential.

In the semi-floating axle each half-shaft is supported at its inner end by a bearing which also carries the final drive unit. At the outer end there is a bearing between the shaft and the inside of the axle housing. The half-shaft has to withstand bending loads imposed by the weight of the car, as well as transmit torque.

The three-quarter floating axle also has a bearing inside the axle housing which carries the final-drive unit, but the outer bearing is placed between the wheel hub and the axle housing, to support the weight of the car. The half-shaft is subjected to a bending load only during cornering.

In a fully floating axle, there are two bearings between each hub and the axle housing, and these carry both the weight of the car and the cornering forces. This design is rarely used for cars.

In front-drive cars and in independently sprung rear-drive cars, each hub is supported by two bearings.

Coping with twisting forces

When power is transmitted to the rear axle by an open propeller shaft, torque reaction twists the axle on its springs. This can be prevented by enclosing the propeller shaft in a torque tube, which forms a rigid extension of the axle housing. The torque tube is bolted to the axle housing and is connected to the gearbox at its front end by a large spherical bearing so that it resists the torque reaction.

COPING WITH TWISTING FORCES

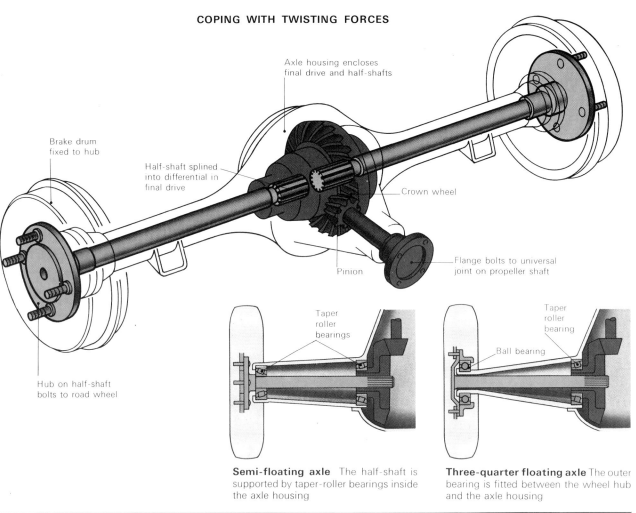

Axle housing encloses final drive and half-shafts

Brake drum fixed to hub

Half-shaft splined into differential in final drive

Crown wheel

Hub on half-shaft bolts to road wheel

Pinion

Flange bolts to universal joint on propeller shaft

Taper roller bearings

Taper roller bearing

Ball bearing

Semi-floating axle The half-shaft is supported by taper-roller bearings inside the axle housing

Three-quarter floating axle The outer bearing is fitted between the wheel hub and the axle housing

TORQUE-TUBE HOUSING FOR THE PROPELLER SHAFT

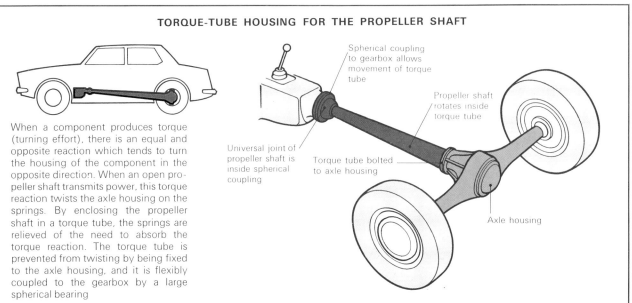

When a component produces torque (turning effort), there is an equal and opposite reaction which tends to turn the housing of the component in the opposite direction. When an open propeller shaft transmits power, this torque reaction twists the axle housing on the springs. By enclosing the propeller shaft in a torque tube, the springs are relieved of the need to absorb the torque reaction. The torque tube is prevented from twisting by being fixed to the axle housing, and it is flexibly coupled to the gearbox by a large spherical bearing

Spherical coupling to gearbox allows movement of torque tube

Propeller shaft rotates inside torque tube

Universal joint of propeller shaft is inside spherical coupling

Torque tube bolted to axle housing

Axle housing

Direct drive to front or rear wheels

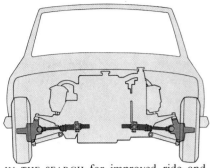

IN THE SEARCH for improved ride and handling, designers have adopted independent front suspension and, on some cars, independent suspension is also used at the rear instead of a beam axle.

There are several basic layouts of final drive where suspension is independent, according to whether the front or rear wheels are involved and whether the engine is longitudinal (along the car) or transverse (across the car).

If the engine is installed along the line of the car, it is usual to sandwich the final drive between it and the gearbox for compactness. The normal type of hypoid-bevel unit is used, but in a common housing with the gearbox.

With a transverse engine, the final drive is parallel to the crankshaft and helical gears can be used instead of bevel gears. The gearbox can be placed either at the end of the engine or beneath it where space is limited.

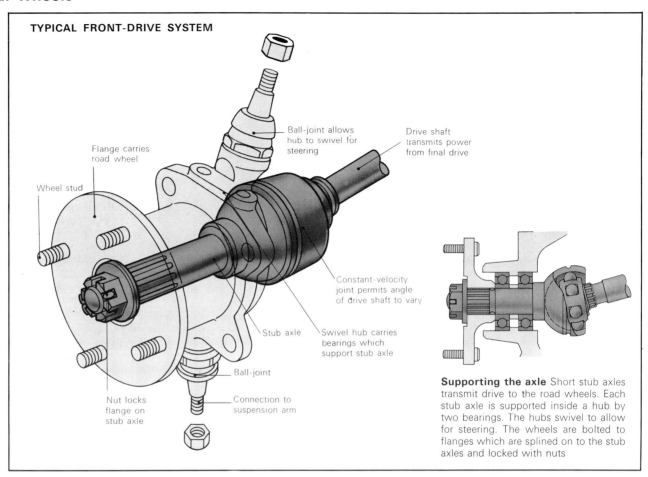

TYPICAL FRONT-DRIVE SYSTEM

Flange carries road wheel

Ball-joint allows hub to swivel for steering

Drive shaft transmits power from final drive

Wheel stud

Constant-velocity joint permits angle of drive shaft to vary

Stub axle

Swivel hub carries bearings which support stub axle

Ball-joint

Nut locks flange on stub axle

Connection to suspension arm

Supporting the axle Short stub axles transmit drive to the road wheels. Each stub axle is supported inside a hub by two bearings. The hubs swivel to allow for steering. The wheels are bolted to flanges which are splined on to the stub axles and locked with nuts

Four-wheel drive for more grip

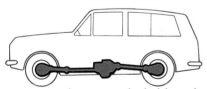

MOST CARS have two-wheel drive—the engine drives either the back or the front wheels. When snow, ice or mud makes the road slippery, the driven wheels may not get enough grip and one or both of them may spin, even though the final drive incorporates a 'limited-slip' differential.

If all four wheels are driven, the tyres can grip better on slippery ground, because the whole weight of the car is being utilised for traction.

Four-wheel drive is common on cross-country vehicles, such as the Land Rover, and on military vehicles. They normally operate with rear-wheel drive on made-up roads on which four-wheel drive is not suited to prolonged running. Front-wheel

drive is engaged when needed by using an extra gear lever. The change to four-wheel drive involves a lower gear ratio.

This compromise is not acceptable for a powerful four-wheel-drive passenger car capable of high speeds; when four-wheel drive is to be in continuous operation, complications arise since allowance has to be made for the differing revolution speeds of the wheels on bends without risk of 'winding up' the transmission system.

One British-made car, the Range Rover, is fitted with four-wheel drive which is always operative.

Its transmission system makes allowance for differences in speed between the front and rear wheels due to the distances travelled on turns and to minor differences in tyre diameter, arising from wear of the treads. This speed variation is permitted by a master differential, which can be locked for operation in extreme conditions to maintain drive.

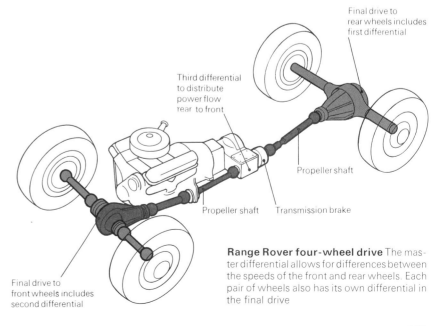

Final drive to rear wheels includes first differential

Third differential to distribute power flow rear to front

Propeller shaft

Propeller shaft

Transmission brake

Final drive to front wheels includes second differential

Range Rover four-wheel drive The master differential allows for differences between the speeds of the front and rear wheels. Each pair of wheels also has its own differential in the final drive

Brakes/how they work

Operation of drum and disc brakes

A BRAKE works by causing friction between a non-rotating part of the car and a disc or drum which turns with a road wheel. Friction produces the force needed to slow the car, and converts the energy of the moving vehicle into heat which disperses into the air around the brakes.

For many years the rotating part of a brake consisted of a drum with which two alternative kinds of friction mechanism could be used: an external band which contracted around the drum, or internal 'shoes' which expanded against the inner surface of the drum. A heat-resistant lining containing asbestos was secured to the band or the shoes.

Internal expanding drum brakes are still used on many cars, sometimes on all four wheels and sometimes on the rear wheels only.

The footbrake actuates all four brakes simultaneously as long as the pedal is depressed. The hand or emergency brake operates on one set of wheels (usually the rear) only. This mechanical brake has a ratchet that enables it to be left on for parking the car.

Manufacturers design drum brakes so that rain, snow, ice or grit cannot get inside and decrease braking efficiency, for moisture greatly reduces the friction between the linings and the drum. But the shield which protects the drum cannot cope with immersion in water, so after passing through a flood or a ford, a driver should partially apply his brakes so that friction and heat will dry them.

To dissipate quickly the considerable amount of heat generated when braking a fast-moving, heavy car, large brake drums would be required. Disc brakes do the job more efficiently, for the cooling air can get to the rubbing surfaces, which may be red hot, more readily. Excessive brake heating tends to distort cast-iron brake drums and adversely affect any rubber that is close to the heat—for example, brake hoses and tyres. Temporary loss of effectiveness during prolonged braking, such as on a long descent, is called brake-fade.

A disc brake works like the caliper brake on a bicycle. The caliper has a pair of brake blocks which straddle the bicycle wheel and grip the rim.

A car's disc brake also has a pair of friction pads, but instead of acting directly on the wheel they straddle a metal disc which turns with the wheel. When the driver applies the brake, the pads press against the disc and slow the wheel.

The shoes of a drum brake can be designed to provide a self-applying or 'self-wrapping' effect which reduces the pedal effort needed. Disc brakes lack this advantage and consequently require 'servo assistance' (in all but the lightest cars) to supplement the physical effort applied by the driver (see p. 114).

(see p. 114).

BASIC BRAKE TYPES

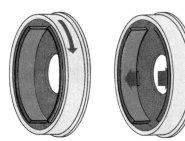

Drum brake Two curved brake shoes, each with a lining, press against the inside of a drum. Many cars use this system of internal expanding brakes on all four wheels

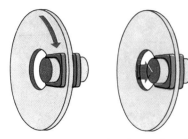

Disc brake A pair of pads are forced by hydraulic pressure against each side of a rotating metal disc, which is attached to the wheel. When the disc is slowed down or halted, the wheel slows or halts too

A TYPICAL BRAKING SYSTEM

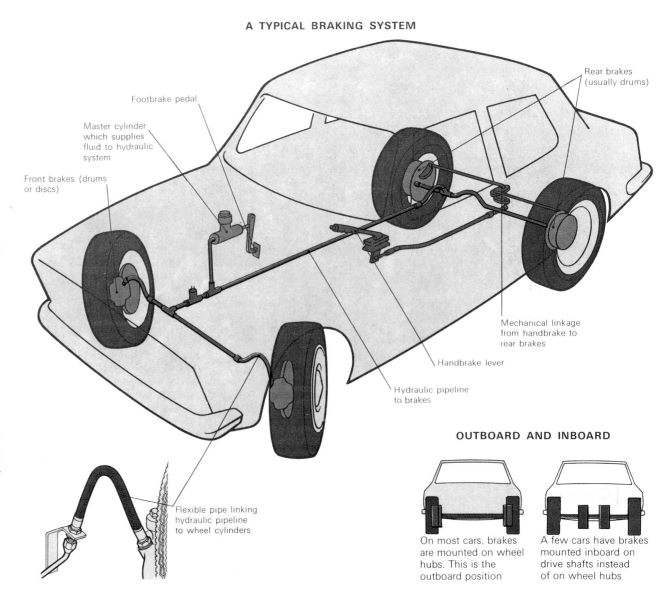

Footbrake pedal

Master cylinder which supplies fluid to hydraulic system

Front brakes (drums or discs)

Rear brakes (usually drums)

Mechanical linkage from handbrake to rear brakes

Handbrake lever

Hydraulic pipeline to brakes

Flexible pipe linking hydraulic pipeline to wheel cylinders

OUTBOARD AND INBOARD

On most cars, brakes are mounted on wheel hubs. This is the outboard position

A few cars have brakes mounted inboard on drive shafts instead of on wheel hubs

Braking distances with 60 per cent and 80 per cent efficient brakes

THE TIME a driver takes to stop depends on the time it takes him to react, 0·4–0·7 seconds, as well as the time it takes the brakes to halt the car. During this reaction time, the car travels for what is called the 'thinking distance'.

The chart shows the average thinking and braking distances for medium-sized cars with 60 per cent efficient brakes and 80 per cent efficient brakes, travelling at speeds of 30, 50 and 70 mph on a dry road.

The efficiency of properly adjusted brakes, in good condition, should be at least 80 per cent, but in order to obtain the equivalent stopping distances the tyres must provide an adequate grip on the road. If the surface is slippery the stopping distances that can actually be obtained are much greater than those shown on the chart. Locking the wheels extends the braking distance and can lead to loss of directional control.

To give best braking results, without loss of directional control and regardless of road-surface grip condition, anti-lock braking systems are being developed.

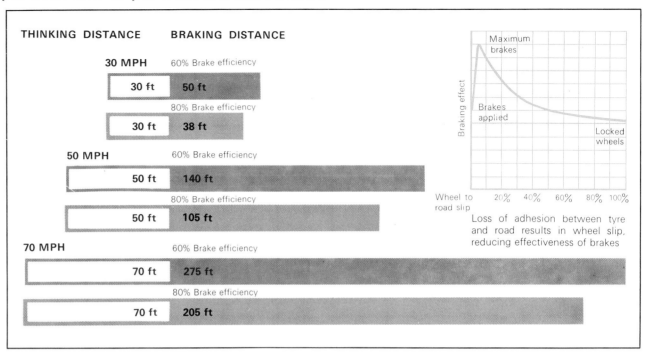

Loss of adhesion between tyre and road results in wheel slip, reducing effectiveness of brakes

Weight transference

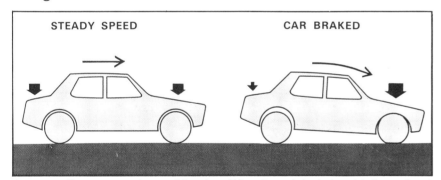

A car travelling at a steady speed has its weight distributed fairly evenly

When the car is braked, weight is transferred forwards, pushing down on the front wheels

IDEALLY, the braking effort should be distributed between the front and rear wheels in proportion to the weight that they carry. This will vary according to the design of the car (whether it is front engined or rear engined, for example), the number of passengers and the amount of luggage. But the effect of applying the brakes is to throw some of the weight forward; this 'transfer' adds to the load on the front wheels and, similarly, reduces the load on the rear wheels. Most of the braking is done by the front brakes.

When the brakes are applied hard there is a greater transfer of weight and the rear wheels tend to lock, which often causes the tail of the car to slide sideways. If the front wheels become locked first, the car will usually slide in a straight line, but steering control will be lost. Locking the wheels by heavy braking is much more likely on slippery roads, so caution is needed on a treacherous surface.

The designer proportions the braking effect between front and rear wheels to match the weight distribution under average conditions. In many cars the system makes allowance for weight transfer by setting a limit to the maximum braking effort that can be applied to the rear wheels. Beyond this limit, extra pedal pressure acts on the front brakes only.

Brake-fade

EXCESSIVE heating of the brakes can result in fade. Heat causes temporary changes in the friction properties of the material used for brake pads and linings, and the brakes become less efficient as they get hotter. Normal efficiency generally returns when they cool again.

Brake pads and linings also wear away faster at higher temperatures.

Brake fade can also be caused by vapour formation in hydraulic fluid that has not been replaced at the intervals recommended by the makers.

Tyres and braking

FOR good braking, tyres should grip the road well; badly worn tyres have little grip and reduce braking effectiveness.

The condition of the road surface may also reduce the friction between the road and the tyres. Water, ice, oil, loose gravel and wet leaves, as well as the general polishing caused by streams of traffic, all reduce tyre-to-road friction. Severe braking may lock the wheels and cause the car to skid. A locked wheel has less adhesion between the tyres and the road than a rolling wheel.

Slowing down and stopping the car

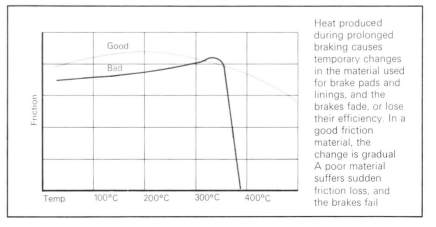

Heat produced during prolonged braking causes temporary changes in the material used for brake pads and linings, and the brakes fade, or lose their efficiency. In a good friction material, the change is gradual. A poor material suffers sudden friction loss, and the brakes fail

Brakes/hydraulic operation

Easier braking for the driver

HYDRAULIC SYSTEMS rely on the fact that liquids are virtually incompressible. Pressure applied anywhere in a fluid is transmitted equally throughout it. A piston-and-cylinder arrangement, operated by a pedal, can be used to generate pressure at one end of a hydraulic line in a car's braking system. This fluid pressure can then move another piston at the other end of the system, to apply a brake.

If the second piston has a larger area than the first, the force it exerts will be proportionally greater than that applied to the first piston; but the distance moved by the second piston will be correspondingly less. If, for instance, the second piston has three times the area, it will exert three times the force through one-third of the distance.

In most cars the majority of the braking effort is undertaken by the front wheels, because the car's weight is thrown forward when the brakes are applied. For this reason larger hydraulic pistons are used for the front brakes.

The footbrake on all modern cars operates the brakes hydraulically. Mechanical linkage by rods or cables, or both, is reserved for the handbrake system, which is normally used only after the driver has stopped the car.

A hydraulic braking system has several advantages over mechanically operated brakes. It is silent, flexible and self-lubricating, and ensures that braking forces to both sides of the car are automatically equalised.

The brake pedal connects by a short push-rod with a master cylinder. When the driver depresses the pedal, the push-rod moves a piston in the cylinder, pushing on the hydraulic fluid and forcing it along pipes to the wheel cylinders which operate the brakes. A check valve at the output end of the master cylinder ensures that a slight pressure remains in the brake line even when the brakes are off, so that air is excluded.

When the pedal is released, the master cylinder becomes connected to a reservoir from which fluid can flow by gravity. This makes good any small losses of fluid, and also provides for expansion and contraction due to temperature variation. It is important to check the level of fluid in the reservoir from time to time.

Some cars have separate hydraulic circuits for front and rear brakes, each circuit having its own master cylinder (see p. 115). Should the pressure fail in one circuit, the other will not necessarily fail.

MULTIPLYING THE PEDAL'S FORCE

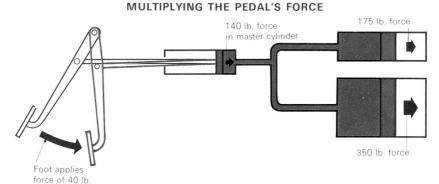

140 lb. force in master cylinder

175 lb. force

350 lb. force

Foot applies force of 40 lb.

Brake-pedal force applied by the driver is multiplied by leverage at the master piston, then passed on by hydraulic fluid to the wheel pistons, where it is multiplied again because they are larger in diameter than the master piston. In this diagram, which exaggerates size for the sake of simplicity, the pedal travels $3\frac{1}{2}$ times further than the master piston; and the wheel pistons, $1\frac{1}{4}$ and $2\frac{1}{2}$ times bigger than the master piston, apply correspondingly more force, but with less movement

THE HYDRAULIC SYSTEM

Pressing the brake pedal forces hydraulic fluid from the master cylinder through pipelines to the wheel cylinders

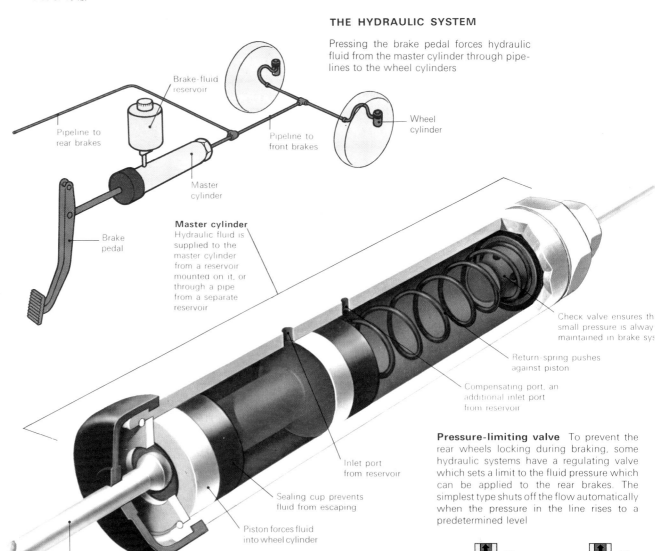

Brake-fluid reservoir

Pipeline to rear brakes

Pipeline to front brakes

Wheel cylinder

Master cylinder

Brake pedal

Master cylinder Hydraulic fluid is supplied to the master cylinder from a reservoir mounted on it, or through a pipe from a separate reservoir

Check valve ensures th small pressure is alway maintained in brake sys

Return-spring pushes against piston

Compensating port, an additional inlet port from reservoir

Inlet port from reservoir

Sealing cup prevents fluid from escaping

Piston forces fluid into wheel cylinder

Dust seal

Push-rod, leading from brake pedal

Pressure-limiting valve To prevent the rear wheels locking during braking, some hydraulic systems have a regulating valve which sets a limit to the fluid pressure which can be applied to the rear brakes. The simplest type shuts off the flow automatically when the pressure in the line rises to a predetermined level

Closed It shuts off fluid to the brakes

Open The valve allows fluid to flow through

Hydraulic brake fluid

THE HYDRAULIC FLUID used in brakes is a synthetic liquid which is stable at high temperatures and harmless to natural rubber which can be deformed by contact with oil, petrol, paraffin or grease. These substances must be kept out of hydraulic systems using natural-rubber seals.

With age and use brake fluid absorbs moisture, mostly through the flexible hoses. A 2–3 per cent water content lowers the brake fluid's boiling point from 200–220°C to about 140°C, thereby causing very spongy brake-pedal response (for the fluid becomes compressible). For that reason fluid should be changed at periods recommended.

The car manufacturer's handbook always specifies which fluid should be used in the braking system; it is important to avoid substitutes.

Wheel cylinder In a double-acting wheel cylinder, pressure forces a pair of pistons outwards to apply brakes

Spring holds seals against pistons
Brake-seal
Piston
Dust-seal
Shoe return-spring
Brake shoe

ALTERNATIVE WHEEL CYLINDERS

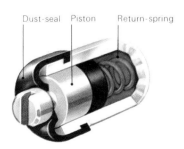

Dust-seal   Piston   Return-spring

Single-acting wheel cylinder This type has only one piston; the cylinder itself moves taking the place of a second piston

Dust-seal

Fluid chamber

Piston

Disc-brake cylinder Two cylinders like this operate pistons which apply friction pads to each side of the disc

How the cylinders work together

PRESSURE to work hydraulic brakes is generated in the master cylinder. A push-rod, moved by the brake pedal, forces the piston forward. Fluid then flows through the check valve along the pipeline to the brakes. There the pressure moves the pistons of the wheel cylinders. Because pressure from the master cylinder is transmitted equally throughout the hydraulic system, braking pressure on all wheels is equal and simultaneous as long as the fluid remains incompressible.

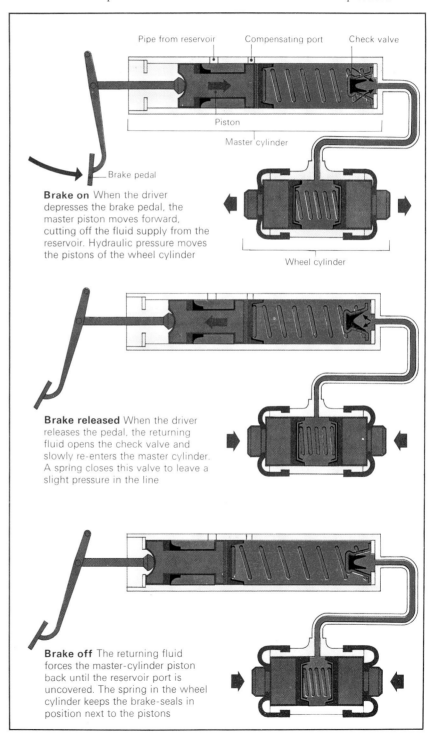

Pipe from reservoir   Compensating port   Check valve

Piston

Master cylinder

Brake pedal

Brake on When the driver depresses the brake pedal, the master piston moves forward, cutting off the fluid supply from the reservoir. Hydraulic pressure moves the pistons of the wheel cylinder

Wheel cylinder

Brake released When the driver releases the pedal, the returning fluid opens the check valve and slowly re-enters the master cylinder. A spring closes this valve to leave a slight pressure in the line

Brake off The returning fluid forces the master-cylinder piston back until the reservoir port is uncovered. The spring in the wheel cylinder keeps the brake-seals in position next to the pistons

Brakes/the operation of drum brakes

Shoes press against drums to slow the wheels

A DRUM BRAKE consists of a cast-iron drum containing a pair of semicircular brake shoes. The drum is attached to a wheel and revolves with it, so that when the drum is slowed and halted, the wheel slows and stops too. Friction to slow the drum is applied from inside by the shoes, which do not rotate but are mounted on a stationary metal back-plate. Each shoe consists of a curved length of steel or light-alloy casting faced with a hard-wearing lining.

In most drum brakes, the shoes are forced against the rotating drum by a pivoting arrangement; one end of each shoe hinges on a pivot point and the other end can be moved by a cam, or by hydraulic fluid forced into the wheel cylinder from the brake's master cylinder (see p. 106).

In one hydraulic system, the wheel cylinder is rigidly fixed to the back-plate and contains two pistons which operate the shoes individually. An alternative plan is to use a single piston in a cylinder which can slide on the back-plate. When the brakes are applied, fluid pressure acts equally on the piston and on the closed end of the cylinder, pushing them apart. They in turn force the shoes apart, so that the linings rub against the drum.

Return springs, stretched between the shoes, ensure that when the brake pedal is released the shoes are retracted until the linings are clear of the drum.

When two shoes are hinged on the same pivot point, the braking system has one

BRAKES OFF

When the drum brake is in the off position, there is a gap between the shoes and the rotating drum

BRAKES ON

When the brake is applied, the shoes are forced against the rotating drum, slowing and eventually halting it

WORKING PARTS OF A DRUM BRAKE

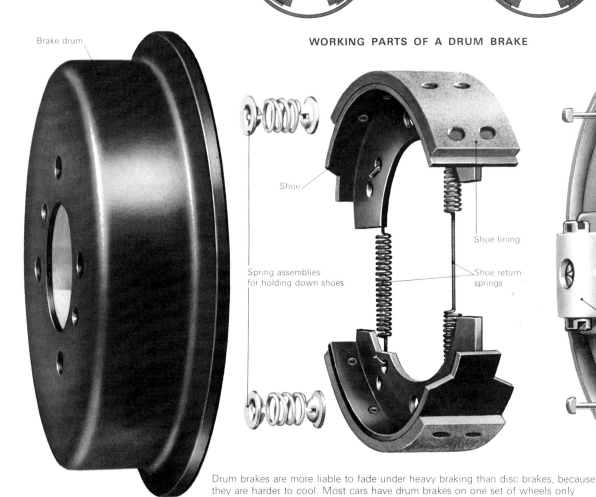

Brake drum

Shoe

Shoe lining

Spring assemblies for holding down shoes

Shoe return-springs

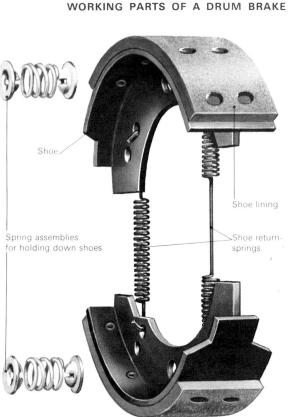

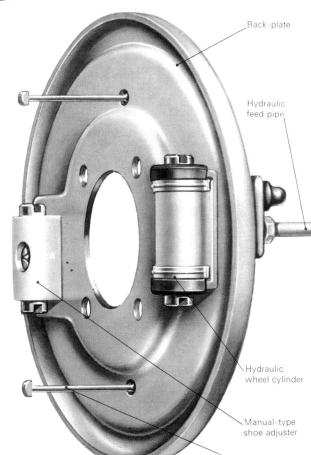

Back-plate

Hydraulic feed pipe

Hydraulic wheel cylinder

Manual-type shoe adjuster

Shoe hold-down assembly bolt

Drum brakes are more liable to fade under heavy braking than disc brakes, because they are harder to cool. Most cars have drum brakes on one set of wheels only

leading shoe and one trailing shoe. An alternative arrangement is to hinge the shoes separately, at opposite points on the back-plate. Both then act as leading shoes when the car is running forwards.

A leading shoe tends to be forced into closer contact by the frictional drag of the rotating drum—a 'self-applying' action which increases the braking force on the wheel. A trailing shoe tends to be pushed away from the drum, and so does considerably less work than a leading shoe.

DRUM BRAKE IN POSITION

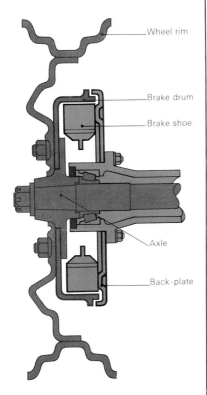

The back-plate, carrying the shoes, is fixed to a stationary part of the axle, while the drum is fixed to the wheel

Different types of drum braking

A TWO-LEADING-SHOE arrangement gives an augmented response to pedal effort because of its self-applying action. This system is usually used on the front wheels, where extra weight is transferred during braking and where there is less likelihood of the wheels locking and skidding.

The two-leading-shoe system is not suitable for rear brakes which, applied by hand, may have to hold the car against running backwards on a slope; in reverse, leading shoes become trailing shoes.

A leading-trailing shoe brake is a cheaper and better alternative for the rear wheels, since it is equally effective whether the car is going forwards or backwards.

In another arrangement, called a duo-servo brake, the leading shoe is hinged to the trailing shoe. When the leading shoe is forced against the drum by hydraulic pressure, the frictional drag is transferred to the trailing shoe, which is pushed into contact with the drum.

Brake linings
Brake linings are riveted to the shoes (or bonded to them with an adhesive) after which the working surface is ground to precise limits. Two types of linings are manufactured: woven and moulded.

Both contain similar materials, always including asbestos, but the manufacturing process is different. Moulded linings are the more widely used.

It is important when replacing linings to use *only* the type recommended by the manufacturers. The safest plan is to use replacement shoes which can be obtained (with linings already fitted) in part exchange for shoes with worn linings. In handling brake shoes, take care to avoid contaminating the linings with oil. Brake

LEADING AND TRAILING SHOES

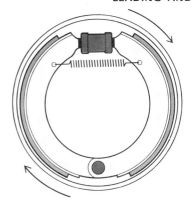 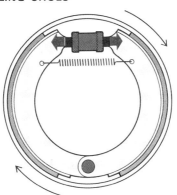

Leading-trailing shoes in 'off' position Both brake shoes hinge on same pivot

Same brake 'on' Leading shoe (right) exerts more force than trailing shoe (left)

TWIN LEADING SHOES

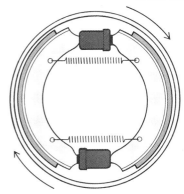

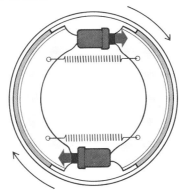

Two-leading-shoe brake Shoes pivot against the drum from opposite points

Same brake 'on' Both shoes are leading, so they exert equal force

linings should not be allowed to wear so that rivet-to-drum contact occurs: this would score the drum and substantially reduce braking power, because there is less friction with metal-to-metal contact than with metal-to-lining contact. A badly scored drum needs re-machining, and it is usually better to replace it.

Self-adjusting drum brakes

CARS FITTED with front disc brakes, which need no adjustment, often have self-adjusting rear drum brakes, so that in the 'brakes off' position the shoes always travel through the same distance to contact the drum. In one system a screw-and-ratchet wheel is the adjuster; a pawl, or pivoted lever attached to the handbrake operating lever, engages with the ratchet. As the handbrake is applied, the shoes move outwards and the pawl rides up the back of a ratchet tooth.

If the shoes are sufficiently worn, the pawl will engage the next tooth. When the handbrake is released, the pawl returns, turning the adjuster.

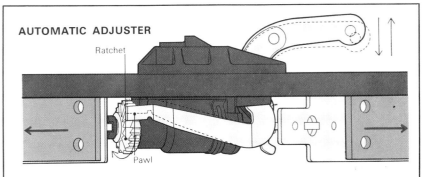

AUTOMATIC ADJUSTER
Ratchet
Pawl

A self-adjusting rear-brake layout, showing the pawl and the ratchet-adjusting wheel. If the handbrake lever can move far enough, the pawl will engage the next tooth

Brakes/the advantage of discs

Pinching action of pads slows the car

A DISC BRAKE consists of a solid cast-iron disc which rotates with the car wheel. Part of the disc is surrounded by a caliper which contains cylinders and pistons, pipe connections to the hydraulic system, and friction pads which press against the disc to halt or slow down the car.

Dust and moisture are prevented from entering the cylinders, or piston housings, by rubber sealing rings.

As only part of the disc is covered by the caliper, the disc is more easily cooled by air than is possible with a drum brake, and water is quickly spun off. A back-plate —sometimes called a splash shield— protects the inner face of the disc not covered by the caliper.

When the brake pedal is applied, hydraulic pressure forces the pistons out from their cylinders to press the pads against the smooth faces of the disc.

The disc expands slightly with the heat, but instead of moving away from the pads—as a drum moves away from the linings—the disc moves nearer to them.

Shim plates—thin sheets of metal which have sprung ends—help to keep the pads firmly in position, which reduces squeal.

The pads can be seen through an opening in the caliper and are easily changed when worn. Each pad is held in place by two retaining-pins, which pass through holes in the caliper, the metal backing plates on the pads and the shim plates. The pins are secured by spring clips.

The friction pads on disc brakes are made from an extremely tough compound of materials bonded to a steel backing plate. The backing plates take the torque reaction on the caliper during braking. The pads are usually segmental in shape, but can be square, rectangular or oval.

Some cars use friction pads which have a metal contact inside them. When they wear down to replacement level, the contact completes a circuit and lights a warning lamp on the instrument panel.

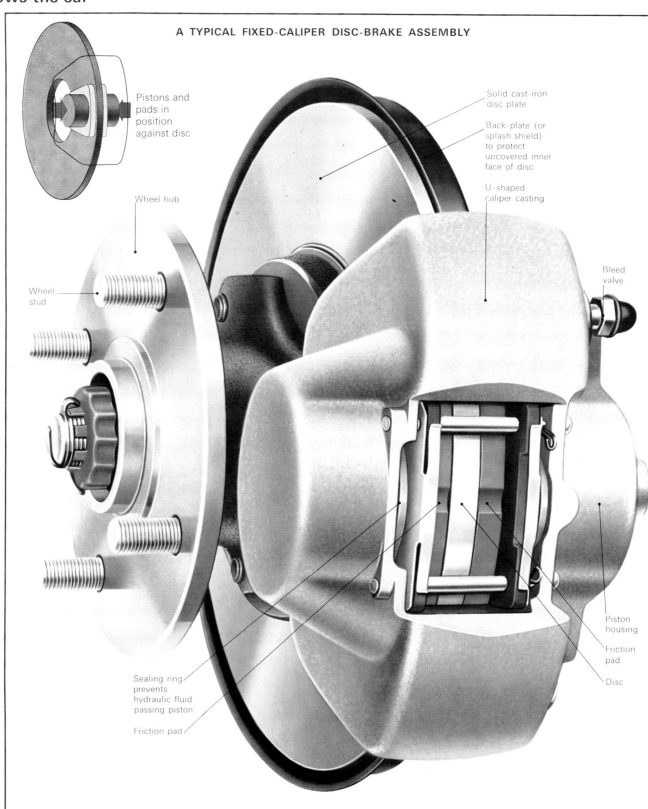

A TYPICAL FIXED-CALIPER DISC-BRAKE ASSEMBLY

Pistons and pads in position against disc

Wheel hub

Wheel stud

Solid cast-iron disc plate

Back-plate (or splash shield) to protect uncovered inner face of disc

U-shaped caliper casting

Bleed valve

Piston housing

Friction pad

Disc

Sealing ring prevents hydraulic fluid passing piston

Friction pad

MAIN PARTS OF A DISC BRAKE

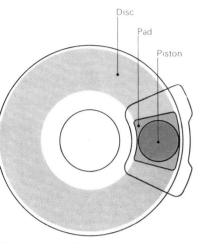

Disc
Pad
Piston

Disc and pad Because only a small part of the area of the disc is covered by the caliper, the disc is easily cooled by air, and water is quickly spun off

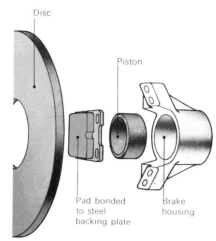

Disc
Piston
Pad bonded to steel backing plate
Brake housing

Main components The caliper casting is made in halves—each containing a cylindrical housing, a piston and a pad—which are bolted together

A DISC BRAKE IN ACTION

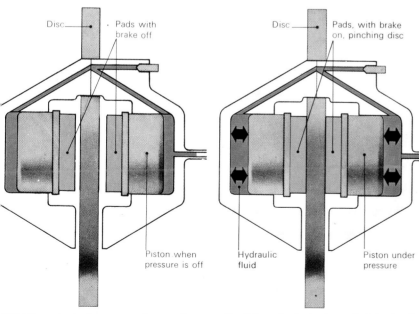

Disc
Pads with brake off

Disc
Pads, with brake on, pinching disc

Piston when pressure is off

Hydraulic fluid

Piston under pressure

Off When the brakes are not in use, the pressure on the friction pads is released. They keep slight contact with the disc, but not enough to cause wear

On When the brake is applied, hydraulic pressure forces the pistons to press the friction pads against the faces of the disc and slow it down

The 4-piston caliper

THE MOST common form of disc brake has two single-piston cylinders. The hydraulic fluid which operates them is fed directly to one cylinder and linked to the other by a bridge pipe. In other designs, fluid is fed to both cylinders through a passage in the caliper casting.

The pistons in a disc-brake caliper are made of steel and are plated on their outer cylindrical surface with a hard coating, to resist wear and corrosion.

To limit the amount of heat transmitted from the disc through to the fluid, the pistons are machined in the form of a cup—the open end making contact with the backing plate of the friction pads.

The arrangement of the pistons in the caliper varies according to the type of braking performance required or the design of the car in which they are used.

The 4-piston caliper is the most efficient arrangement, because with two small pistons on each side of the disc—opposite each other and exerting the same pressure —larger pads can be used, giving a greater effective braking area.

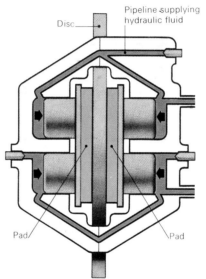

Disc
Pipeline supplying hydraulic fluid
Pad
Pad

The 4-piston caliper Two pistons on each side of the disc exert greater braking pressure. The upper pistons work independently of the lower, providing a 'fail safe' system.

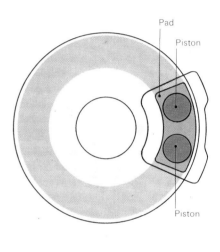

Pad
Piston
Piston

Side view showing two of the pistons on a pad. Some cars with limited wheel space have three pistons—two on one side and one larger one on the other

Vented disc keeps pads cool

AT LEAST two main types of disc brakes are used on British cars: Girling and Lockheed. They use the same principle of gripping the edge of a disc, but have minor differences of design.

Disc brakes are less susceptible to the effects of heat than drum brakes, because on most cars the discs are adequately ventilated by air flowing over them.

But for high-performance and racing cars where considerably higher temperatures are generated, discs need extra ventilation to keep them cool.

To increase the surface area of a disc and simplify cooling, it is cast in the form of two thin metal plates—rather than one thick one—linked by metal ribbing.

The ribs are arranged to allow air to flow readily through the disc and rapidly cool the plates.

Metal ribbing

By casting the disc in the form of two thin sheets of metal—linked internally by ribbing —instead of one thicker one, the disc can be cooled more quickly by air which can flow through the disc in all directions

Brakes/disc variations

Designs that reduce weight

A DISC BRAKE consists basically of a rotating disc, a U-shaped bracket called a caliper, and two friction pads. The caliper is fixed to a non-rotating part of the car; and the friction pads, carried by the caliper, are placed one each side of the disc.

In a widely used arrangement, each of the two pads is operated by a separate hydraulic piston and cylinder. When the driver depresses the brake pedal, fluid pressure forces the pads towards one another so that they clamp the disc between them and slow it down.

Simpler and lighter types of disc brake have been developed in which a U-shaped or ring-shaped caliper is either mounted on a pivot, so that it is free to swing, or is allowed to slide to a limited extent. In such designs, only one of the friction pads is directly operated by a hydraulic piston; the other pad is applied by movement of the caliper itself. When fluid pressure is applied to operate the single piston of a swinging-caliper brake, it sets up an equal and opposing pressure on the closed end of the cylinder.

This moves the entire caliper in the opposite direction to that in which the piston is moving, so that the disc is clamped between the two pads.

In a 'fist'-type disc brake, the hydraulic fluid forces the piston, with the brake pad attached to it, against one face of the rotating disc. The piston moves in the cylindrical part of the 'fist'.

The sliding-caliper disc brake is operated by two pistons working in a single cylinder.

When fluid under pressure acts between them, it forces them apart. One piston applies a friction pad to the disc by direct action, and the other piston forces the caliper in the opposite direction, and so applies the companion pad.

Swinging-caliper brakes

Swinging-caliper disc brake This contains a single direct-acting hydraulic piston which operates one friction pad; fluid pressure on the cylinder causes the caliper to operate the other pad

'Fist'-type disc brake Designed for compactness and robustness, the 'fist'-type brake has special V-slots in the fixed housing to prevent jamming of the mechanism

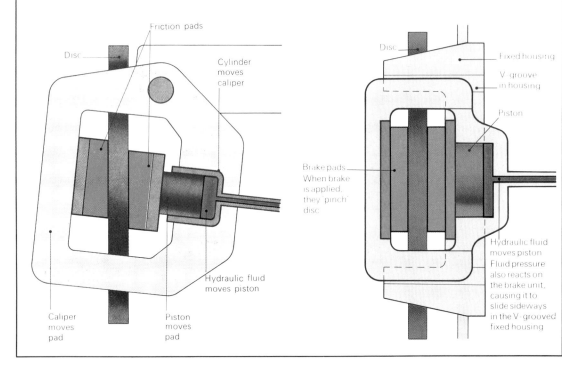

Sliding-caliper brake

Sliding-caliper brake This also has only one hydraulic cylinder, which contains two pistons. One piston acts directly on a friction pad; the other moves the caliper and applies the second pad

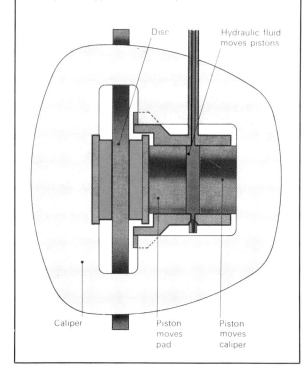

Different systems of parking-brake operation

The brake for parking ... and emergencies

THE HANDBRAKE is normally used only after the driver has stopped the car by using the footbrake. Its other use is as an emergency brake, to stop the car if the footbrake system should fail.

The law requires that a mechanically operated brake should be left on when the car is parked. On most cars this is achieved by a hand-operated brake, but because the average person can exert more effort by pushing his foot than by pulling a handle, most North American and some heavier European cars have foot-operated parking brakes.

Both types hold the car by a pawl engaging with a ratchet and thereby locking the mechanical brakes on. Release of the ratchet frees the brakes. To neglect the adjustment is dangerous.

The hand or parking brake operates on a pair of brakes, frequently the rear brakes. When drum-type rear brakes are used, the same shoes can be used for both hand and foot control.

The handbrake lever may pull on a single cable, which is connected to a pivoted T-piece to transmit the pull equally to both brakes, or there may be two cables from the handbrake lever, one to each brake.

When disc brakes are used on the rear wheels, there are sometimes two pairs of pads straddling the disc, with one pair operated hydraulically from the pedal and the other pair cam-operated by the handbrake cables.

In yet another arrangement, small drum brakes, operated by the hand lever, are embodied in the rear disc brakes.

Some disc-brake systems are so arranged that the same pair of discs is used for both footbrake and handbrake operation. When the footbrake is depressed the power is transmitted hydraulically to the working piston; for parking, a mechanical linkage operated by the handbrake provides the locking force.

Where brakes have been used extensively during a journey, for instance on a long downgrade, the working surfaces get hot, and the discs or drums change dimensionally by a small amount. Certain precautions are therefore needed when parking on an incline. As the working surfaces of a disc or drum brake cool down, so the preload applied by the handbrake mechanism diminishes. In the conventional drum arrangement, the self-wrapping action compensates for any slackening. But the disc arrangement calls for an additional effort by the driver.

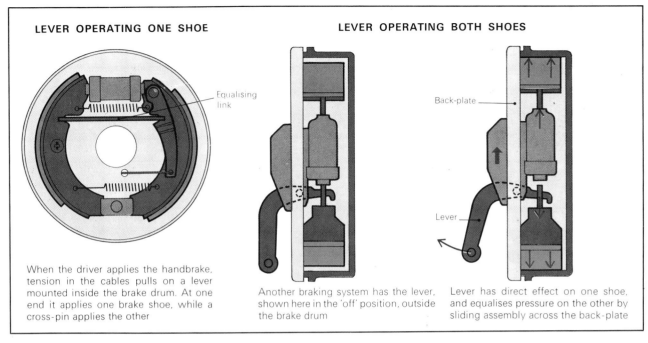

LEVER OPERATING ONE SHOE

Equalising link

When the driver applies the handbrake, tension in the cables pulls on a lever mounted inside the brake drum. At one end it applies one brake shoe, while a cross-pin applies the other

LEVER OPERATING BOTH SHOES

Back-plate

Lever

Another braking system has the lever, shown here in the 'off' position, outside the brake drum

Lever has direct effect on one shoe, and equalises pressure on the other by sliding assembly across the back-plate

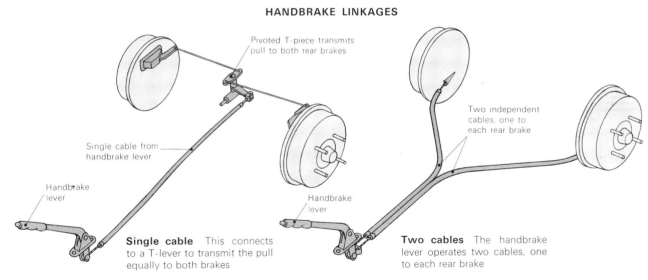

HANDBRAKE LINKAGES

Pivoted T-piece transmits pull to both rear brakes

Single cable from handbrake lever

Handbrake lever

Single cable This connects to a T-lever to transmit the pull equally to both brakes

Two independent cables, one to each rear brake

Handbrake lever

Two cables The handbrake lever operates two cables, one to each rear brake

Engaging and releasing the handbrake

THE HANDBRAKE lever has a spring-loaded ratchet arrangement which allows the driver to set the brake with the required amount of tension between fully off and fully on. The lever is usually placed to the left of the driver, but it is sometimes on the right, between the seat and the door. An alternative is the 'umbrella-handle' control, placed beneath the instrument panel, with its release mechanism built into the handle grip.

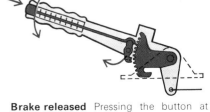

Brake released Pressing the button at the end of the lever trips a pawl to allow free movement of the lever

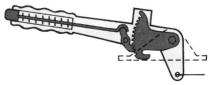

Brake set Engagement of the spring-loaded pawl in the teeth of the rachet retains the lever in any desired position.

Brakes/servo-assisted systems

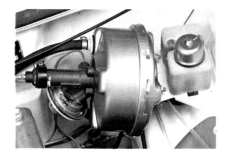

A SERVO MECHANISM fitted to the braking system reduces the physical effort the driver has to use on the brake pedal.

The servo cylinder contains a piston or a diaphragm. When air is exhausted from one end of the cylinder and atmospheric pressure is admitted to the other end, the difference in the pressures on the two sides of the piston (or diaphragm) can be used to help the driver to apply the brakes. The amount of servo assistance increases with the physical force used on the pedal.

Most servo-mechanisms are of the vacuum assistance type, in which the boost is provided by the engine-manifold partial vacuum. But as more demanding air-pollution-control systems become more common, manifold depression will be less readily available. For that reason, hydraulic power boosters are likely to be fitted. They take their power from an engine-driven hydraulic pump, which may also give power assistance to the steering.

The main difference is that a hydraulic boost comes into operation as soon as the driver depresses the brake pedal; most vacuum servos do not boost the driver's effort immediately.

TYPICAL DIAPHRAGM-TYPE VACUUM SERVO

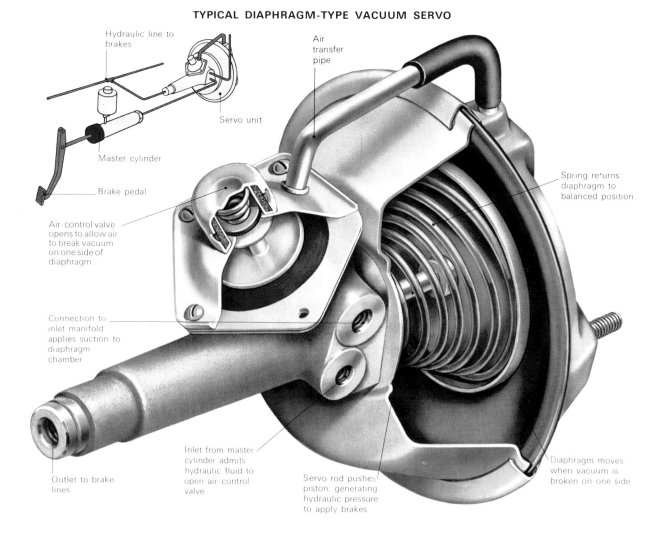

Hydraulic line to brakes

Air transfer pipe

Servo unit

Master cylinder

Brake pedal

Air-control valve opens to allow air to break vacuum on one side of diaphragm

Connection to inlet manifold applies suction to diaphragm chamber

Outlet to brake lines

Inlet from master cylinder admits hydraulic fluid to open air-control valve

Servo rod pushes piston, generating hydraulic pressure to apply brakes

Spring returns diaphragm to balanced position

Diaphragm moves when vacuum is broken on one side

VACUUM SERVO UNIT IN ACTION

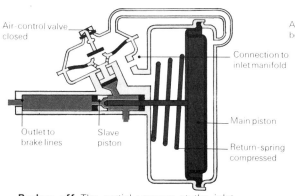

Air-control valve closed

Connection to inlet manifold

Outlet to brake lines

Slave piston

Main piston

Return-spring compressed

Brakes off The partial vacuum at the inlet manifold sucks air from both sides of the main piston, which is then held in place by its return-spring. The air-control valve remains closed, maintaining low pressure

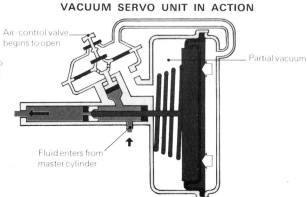

Air-control valve begins to open

Partial vacuum

Fluid enters from master cylinder

Slight pressure Hydraulic fluid lifts the air-control valve, letting in air which applies atmospheric pressure to one side of the main piston. This applies a force to a supplementary hydraulic piston, the slave piston

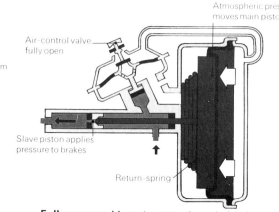

Air-control valve fully open

Atmospheric pressure moves main piston

Slave piston applies pressure to brakes

Return-spring

Full pressure More air passes through the air-control valve, greatly increasing the air pressure behind the main piston, which moves fully across, pushing the slave piston and applying maximum pressure to the brakes

'Fail safe' braking systems

THE WEAKNESS of any hydraulic circuit is that leakage at any point puts the whole system out of action.

A dual-braking system, which has two independent hydraulic circuits overcomes this problem. There are several types. One has a master cylinder with one piston which operates the front brakes only and a second piston for the rear brakes. If one fails, the car still has brakes.

In the more complex split system (below, centre), each front disc brake has a pair of pads with individual cylinders and pistons linked by separate circuits to a dual master piston. Each master piston also operates one of the rear brakes. If one circuit fails, the car still has two effective front brakes and one rear brake.

In an alternative arrangement (below, left), one master piston and circuit operates all four brakes and the other piston and circuit operates the front brakes only.

Another system uses the diagonal-split principle, with one front wheel and a rear wheel in the diagonally opposite corner making up a separate circuit. This is commonly used with cars having a negative offset (negative scrub radius) wheel geometry.

TANDEM DUAL MASTER CYLINDER

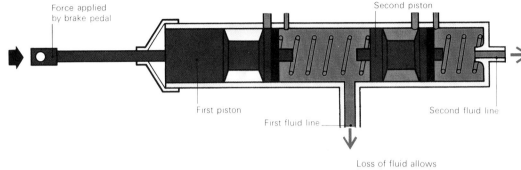

Force applied by brake pedal

Second piston

First piston

First fluid line

Second fluid line

In normal operation, the first master piston generates pressure in one hydraulic line and applies fluid pressure to the second piston, which generates pressure in the other line. Each half of the dual master cylinder has its own reservoir and hydraulic fluid supply

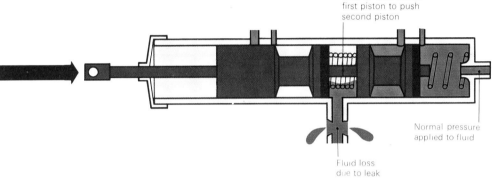

Loss of fluid allows first piston to push second piston

Normal pressure applied to fluid

Fluid loss due to leak

If there is a leak in the first fluid line, the first piston meets no resistance and travels forward until it comes up against the second piston. This piston then generates pressure in the second hydraulic line. The driver feels the greater pedal travel, but the brakes still operate

THREE TYPES OF DUAL-BRAKING SYSTEMS

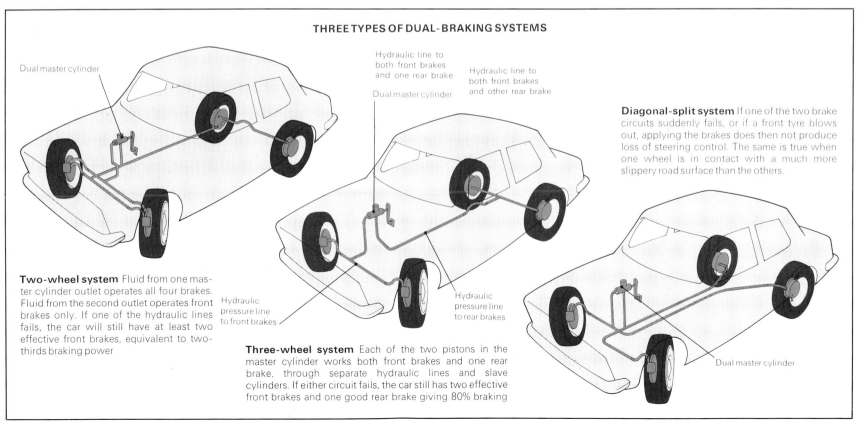

Dual master cylinder

Hydraulic line to both front brakes and one rear brake

Hydraulic line to both front brakes and other rear brake

Dual master cylinder

Hydraulic pressure line to front brakes

Hydraulic pressure line to rear brakes

Dual master cylinder

Diagonal-split system If one of the two brake circuits suddenly fails, or if a front tyre blows out, applying the brakes does then not produce loss of steering control. The same is true when one wheel is in contact with a much more slippery road surface than the others.

Two-wheel system Fluid from one master cylinder outlet operates all four brakes. Fluid from the second outlet operates front brakes only. If one of the hydraulic lines fails, the car will still have at least two effective front brakes, equivalent to two-thirds braking power

Three-wheel system Each of the two pistons in the master cylinder works both front brakes and one rear brake, through separate hydraulic lines and slave cylinders. If either circuit fails, the car still has two effective front brakes and one good rear brake giving 80% braking

Wheels/basic requirements

Variations in the three main designs

IT IS NOT enough for a wheel to be round: it must also be strong, light, well-balanced, resilient to some forces, stiff against others, and not too expensive for a mass market.

The three types of wheel in use today—pressed-steel discs, wheels with steel-wire spokes, and light-alloy castings—meet all these requirements, though the last two are more expensive to produce.

The need for lightness, combined with strength and low cost of manufacture, has governed wheel design since the earliest days of motoring; and the first big break-through towards achieving these aims came early this century with the all-metal wheel, which could be mass produced, and the pneumatic tyre.

Stiffness is necessary in a wheel in order for it to respond accurately to the demands made on it in steering; but the wheel must not be brittle. Resilience is necessary too, so that the wheel will absorb the hard knocks it inevitably takes.

The wheel has to have what is called a well-base rim to enable the tyre to be fitted or removed; if the bead (or edge) of the tyre is pushed down into the well at one point, the diametrically opposite part can be eased over the flange of the rim without serious difficulty.

Width of the wheel rim is an important factor in the handling characteristics of a car. A rim that is too narrow in relation to the tyre width, for example, will allow the tyre to distort excessively sideways under fast cornering. On the other hand, unduly wide rims on an ordinary car tend to give rather a harsh ride because the sidewalls have not enough curvature to make them flex over road irregularities.

Steel disc wheels

Most cars today are fitted with pressed-steel disc wheels. They are light, strong, stiff and resistant to accidental damage. They are also easy to produce in large numbers at low cost.

It was once a disadvantage of this design that the disc had to be liberally perforated to allow for the passage of cooling air to the brakes; and piercing holes in the disc could weaken it.

By using a slightly more expensive technique, modern designers can turn the disadvantage into an advantage. The holes are swaged—that is, their edges are turned smoothly inwards—and this may actually increase the strength of the wheel. Swaging of this kind is now a standard technique on production cars.

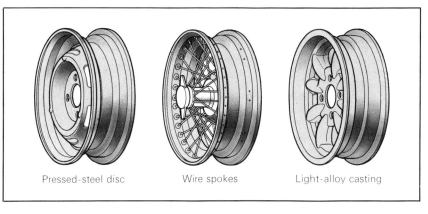

Pressed-steel disc   Wire spokes   Light-alloy casting

VENTILATED DISC WHEEL

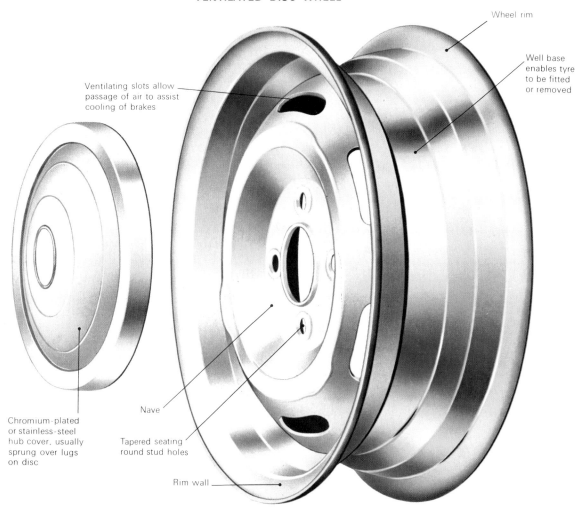

Wheel rim

Well base enables tyre to be fitted or removed

Ventilating slots allow passage of air to assist cooling of brakes

Chromium-plated or stainless-steel hub cover, usually sprung over lugs on disc

Nave

Tapered seating round stud holes

Rim wall

The pressed-steel disc wheel is the type most widely used on cars today. Central mounting to a flange on the hub is usually by studs and nuts

How the wheel is secured to the axle

THE MOST common type of wheel mounting consists of either four or five threaded studs equally spaced in a circle around the hub flange. These studs pass through holes in the wheel, which is secured by nuts screwed on to the studs.

The holes through which the studs pass are not simply pierced through the disc. The area around each hole is pressed out to form a tapered seating which allows the hub to centre the wheel correctly. Each nut has a corresponding taper.

Some manufacturers provide nuts with both ends tapered: others make nuts which are tapered only at one end and flat-faced at the other.

Wheel nuts should be fitted so that the tapered face engages with the tapered seating in the wheel; otherwise the nuts will not centralise the wheel on the hub and the wheel will be likely to work loose.

It is dangerous to reverse a wheel so that it is mounted back to front. The nave area is designed to engage with the hub or brake drum over a considerable area, and it is friction between these faces that transmits the drive.

Never leave nuts only finger-tight after replacing a wheel. They should be tight enough to ensure that the two faces are held firmly together.

One recent wheel-mounting design has the wheel positioned by the hub itself, which engages with a precisely-machined hole in the centre of the nave. Studs secure rather than locate the wheel.

Centre-lock disc wheels on splined hubs are fitted to some sports cars. The centre lock, or 'knock-off' nut, was evolved many years ago to enable racing-car wheels to be changed quickly by knocking off the nut with a soft-headed hammer. The wheel is positioned by matching tapered faces within the wheel centre and on its hub, the splines enabling driving or braking forces to be transmitted from one to the other.

In some versions, the single securing nut is shaped for tightening and loosening with a soft-headed hammer: others require the use of a special spanner.

Centre-lock mountings have an additional advantage now that radial-ply tyres are in general use: radials are intolerant of inaccuracies of wheel centring, and the precise location of the centre-lock wheel helps to minimise tyre vibration.

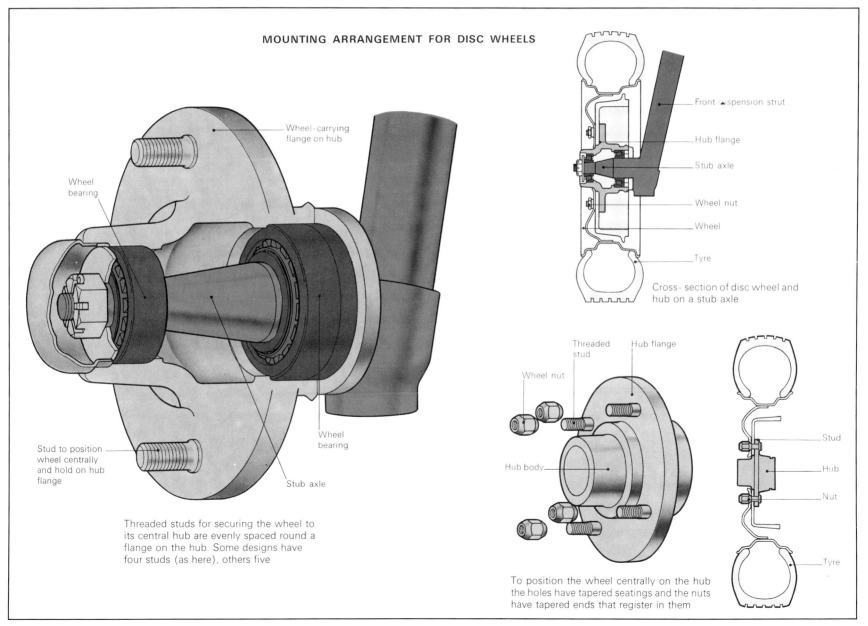

MOUNTING ARRANGEMENT FOR DISC WHEELS

Wheel-carrying flange on hub

Wheel bearing

Stud to position wheel centrally and hold on hub flange

Wheel bearing

Stub axle

Threaded studs for securing the wheel to its central hub are evenly spaced round a flange on the hub. Some designs have four studs (as here), others five

Front suspension strut

Hub flange

Stub axle

Wheel nut

Wheel

Tyre

Cross-section of disc wheel and hub on a stub axle

Threaded stud

Hub flange

Wheel nut

Hub body

Stud

Hub

Nut

Tyre

To position the wheel centrally on the hub the holes have tapered seatings and the nuts have tapered ends that register in them

Wheels/wire-spoke and alloy types

Spokes criss-cross to give wire wheel strength

THE EARLIEST type of wheel still in production is the wire-spoke variety, a light but very strong wheel now used mostly for sports and racing cars.

All loads on the wheel are transmitted from the rim to the hub, by spokes made of steel, which are much stronger in tension than in compression.

Spokes individually have little resistance to bending stresses, so they have to be laced in a complex pattern, criss-crossing in three planes. This ensures that all the complex loads fed into a wheel are resolved into tensile loads (that is, pulling rather than pressing or bending loads), evenly distributed among an adequate number of spokes.

Assembling a wire-spoke wheel is a skilful operation. Each spoke is hooked at one end into the hub and its other end is pushed through a hole in the wheel rim, where a tapered nut (the nipple) is screwed down to pull the spoke tight. If any spokes are too loose or too tight, the relatively flimsy rim will distort.

The pierced rim of a wire wheel makes it impossible to fit tubeless tyres, as they need airtight rims.

Wire wheels are expensive because of their complicated construction. This expense was justified in the days when the alternatives available were not so strong or light; but, strictly from an engineering point of view, there is little justification for wire wheels today.

A wire wheel is fitted in the same way as a centre-lock disc wheel. The wheel hub and axle shaft are both splined; when the wheel is slid on to the stub shaft, the splines engage, so that when the shaft revolves it turns the wheel.

The wheel is secured to the shaft by a large wing nut which can be tightened or loosened by a soft-headed hammer.

WIRE-SPOKE WHEELS

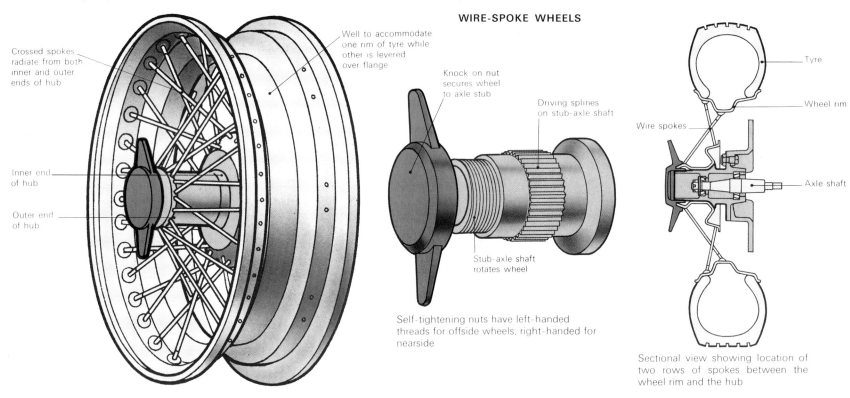

Crossed spokes radiate from both inner and outer ends of hub

Inner end of hub

Outer end of hub

Well to accommodate one rim of tyre while other is levered over flange

Knock on nut secures wheel to axle stub

Driving splines on stub-axle shaft

Stub-axle shaft rotates wheel

Self-tightening nuts have left-handed threads for offside wheels, right-handed for nearside

Tyre

Wheel rim

Wire spokes

Axle shaft

Sectional view showing location of two rows of spokes between the wheel rim and the hub

Coping with stresses from different directions

THE CAR WHEEL is subjected to extreme loads and stresses even in normal road use.

It has to withstand the car's weight and forces of acceleration, braking and cornering; and it often has to cope with several of these stresses at once. Cornering, for instance, can be combined with acceleration or braking, which subjects the wheel to different stresses at the same time.

For steering control the wheels must be of rigid construction. There is no difficulty in obtaining the necessary stiffness with a cast light-alloy wheel, because the short 'spokes' can be cast in the form of substantial radial ribs.

With a pressed-steel wheel, the 'spoke' portion is usually of near-conical shape for extra lateral (side-to-side) stiffness.

In the traditional wire wheel, where the spokes are the only connection between the hub and the rim, this essential side-to-side stiffness is achieved by using a relatively wide hub with two or three sets of spokes arranged at different angles. The spokes are arranged in pairs, inclined so that, with the hub, they form a series of rigid triangles for resisting side-to-side forces when the car is cornering.

Backward and forward weight transfer, when the car is braking or accelerating, is absorbed by the steel spokes acting alternately in tension. Properly designed disc or alloy wheels cope readily with these forces.

Spokes arranged to transmit the engine's drive

Spokes arranged to take braking stresses

Spokes arranged to take the weight of the car

Spokes take side-to-side stress when cornering

Section showing triangular arrangement of spokes

The cast light-alloy wheel

CAST LIGHT-ALLOY wheels have been used on many racing cars since 1953 and on road cars since 1962, although some Bugatti designs used them as long ago as the 1920's.

At present the number of production cars fitted with these wheels as standard is relatively small, but it is increasing.

Because of their light weight compared with steel, aluminium and magnesium alloys permit the use of thicker sections, which promote stiffness and distribute stresses over a wider area.

The wider rim possible with light-alloy wheels is the main reason for their use on some sports cars. They allow wider tyres to be fitted, so improving road-holding, especially on corners.

Light alloys are also good conductors of heat, and therefore disperse the heat generated by brakes and tyres more quickly than steel does. Some precautions are necessary with light-alloy wheels. They react badly to salt spray and must be checked regularly for signs of corrosion.

There is also a danger of electrolytic corrosion, which may occur when steel comes into contact with a light alloy. To prevent this, the holes through which retaining or locating studs pass should be greased; and if balance weights are used, avoid those which are held in place by steel clips or screws.

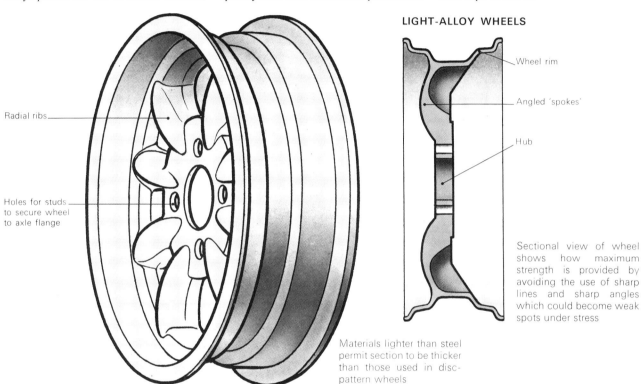

Radial ribs

Holes for studs to secure wheel to axle flange

Materials lighter than steel permit section to be thicker than those used in disc-pattern wheels

LIGHT-ALLOY WHEELS

Wheel rim

Angled 'spokes'

Hub

Sectional view of wheel shows how maximum strength is provided by avoiding the use of sharp lines and sharp angles which could become weak spots under stress

Wheel spacers

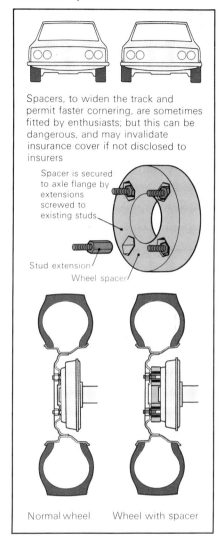

Spacers, to widen the track and permit faster cornering, are sometimes fitted by enthusiasts; but this can be dangerous, and may invalidate insurance cover if not disclosed to insurers

Spacer is secured to axle flange by extensions screwed to existing studs

Stud extension

Wheel spacer

Normal wheel   Wheel with spacer

Wheel balancing

A WHEEL that is not properly balanced may set up alarming vibrations which can affect steering control even at moderate speeds.

Wheels, tyres and tubes are usually checked for balance within certain limits before they leave the factory; but the balance of a wheel can be upset by damage, and that of a tyre by wear, especially on a car driven continuously at high speeds. The whole unit, therefore, should be checked every few thousand miles.

There are two types of balancing: static and dynamic.

Static balancing can be done, as its name implies, with the wheel almost stationary. Small lead weights are clipped to the wheel rim to counterbalance any local heaviness of rim and tyre at the opposite point on the wheel. The weights required rarely exceed 2–3 oz., and consist of slugs of lead increasing in $\frac{1}{4}$ oz. units.

A wheel that is in static balance can still need dynamic balancing.

The effect of a wheel being dynamically out of balance is as if it had a concentration of weight at one point on the edge of its rim so that, as the wheel spins, it wobbles rapidly from side to side. The wider the rim the greater the chances of this imbalance being troublesome.

It can be checked only on special garage equipment which most large garages have.

A new tyre or wheel should always be balanced before being fitted and needs rebalancing after 500 miles or if the wheel is moved to another position.

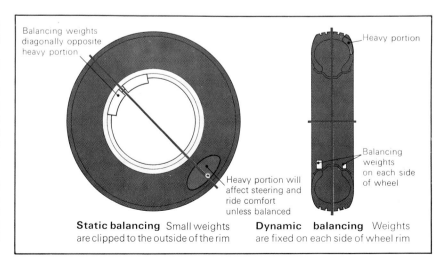

Balancing weights diagonally opposite heavy portion

Heavy portion will affect steering and ride comfort unless balanced

Heavy portion

Balancing weights on each side of wheel

Static balancing Small weights are clipped to the outside of the rim

Dynamic balancing Weights are fixed on each side of wheel rim

Tyres/what they have to do

Stresses imposed on a tyre

A MODERN CAR tyre is an inflatable rubber ring fitted round the road wheel. It is built up on a strong inner carcass, with metal hoops embedded in the tyre where it fits the rim. It has flexible sidewalls to absorb loads, and a tread pattern to grip the road under varying conditions.

There are three main types of tyre—named after the three main methods of carcass construction—cross-ply, radial-ply and bias-belted (see pp. 122–3).

Tyres, besides improving ride comfort by carrying the vehicle on a cushion of air, have to cope with considerable forces generated in accelerating, braking and cornering. The technical problems involved are considerable, but great advances have been made in tyre design in recent years.

The real problem is that no one tyre can be good for all conditions. It must be strong enough to resist damage, yet flexible enough to cushion impacts. It must respond accurately to steering, without deflection by ridges in the road. It must provide good grip for traction, accelerating, cornering and braking. It must do all these things in all weathers and on all surfaces, wet or dry, without overheating.

From the motorists' point of view, it must give a comfortable ride, run quietly, have long life and above all be cheap. Therefore, any tyre must be a compromise.

Some cars handle better on a particular type of tyre, and a recent trend is for car suspensions to be designed with an individual make and model of tyre in mind.

Treads vary to cope with different surfaces. For example, the chunky-treaded all-weather tyre is ideal for snow and mud, but unsuitable for high-speed driving because the thick tread generates excessive heat which can cause tyre failure.

The performance of a tyre depends not only on its design and the materials used, but also on its inflated pressure. Car and tyre manufacturers recommend pressures for the front and rear tyres which should be adhered to. If the pressure is too low or too high, the tyre may perform poorly, overheat and wear out rapidly; the handling of the car will also suffer. The recommended pressure will give proper road-holding, cool running, low rolling resistance and therefore better fuel consumption, and long life.

MAIN PARTS OF A TYRE AND WHEEL

Main drainage grooves to get rid of bulk of water

Sipes or knife-cuts which mop up remaining water

Secondary drainage grooves

Sidewall must flex to absorb loads

Wheel rim

Hub cover

Rim

Tyre bead

Valve

Sidewall

Tread

Tyre section This shows the tread with main drainage grooves and bead seated on wheel rim

Differences between tubed and tubeless tyres

TUBED and tubeless tyres are made in similar ways. The difference between them is that the tubed tyre has a separate rubber innertube to hold the air, whereas the tubeless tyre holds the air itself.

A tubeless tyre is made airtight by a soft rubber lining to the casing; this lining also forms a seal between the tyre bead and the wheel rim. The tubeless tyre has a number of advantages over the tubed: it is easier to fit; when punctured it deflates slowly, because the soft lining has a self-sealing effect; and a temporary puncture repair can be made without removing the wheel, by stopping the hole with a special rubber plug. Because of these advantages, most British cars are now fitted with tubeless tyres.

Tubed tyres are still necessary for wire wheels, because of the difficulty of making an air seal at the spoke ends.

Materials in a tyre

FOR MANY YEARS all car tyres were made entirely of natural rubber; now most tyre manufacturers use a variety of synthetic rubbers.

These, used in various blends, produce a wide variety of tyres for different cars, conditions and purposes. Natural rubber is used in some blends and also remains the best material for impregnating and coating the carcass fabrics.

The synthetic most widely used in tyres is styrene butadiene rubber—SBR for short. It has much less bounce than natural rubber, which means a softer ride, and when used in tyre treads SBR maintains closer contact with the road, providing a good grip, especially in wet weather. It also has excellent resistance to abrasion.

Another synthetic used in tyres is poly-butadiene—PB for short. This is hard-wearing and less sensitive to temperature than other synthetics, but too much of it in a blend makes tyres scream in the dry and slip in the wet. PB is usually mixed in small quantities with SBR, with natural rubber or with both. Another favoured material is polyisoprene (IR).

Other synthetics are used in small quantities. But whatever the blend, it must have other additives, including oil, carbon black and sulphur. Oil improves road-holding—at the expense of rapid tyre wear. Carbon black adds abrasion resistance, and sulphur acts as a vulcanising agent.

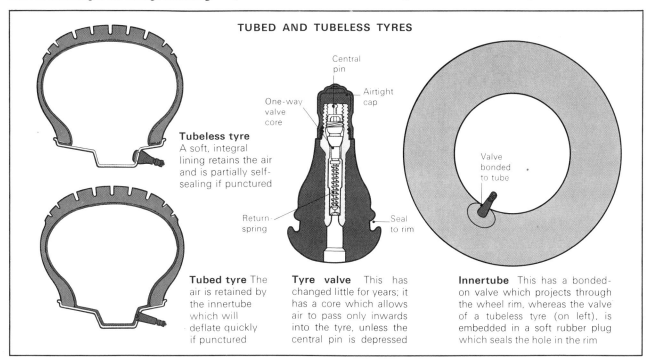

TUBED AND TUBELESS TYRES

Tubeless tyre A soft, integral lining retains the air and is partially self-sealing if punctured

Tubed tyre The air is retained by the innertube which will deflate quickly if punctured

Tyre valve This has changed little for years; it has a core which allows air to pass only inwards into the tyre, unless the central pin is depressed

Central pin — Airtight cap — One-way valve core — Return spring — Seal to rim

Innertube This has a bonded-on valve which projects through the wheel rim, whereas the valve of a tubeless tyre (on left), is embedded in a soft rubber plug which seals the hole in the rim

Valve bonded to tube

The shapes of tyres

THE TREND in modern tyres is to make them wider and shallower, reducing the height from tread to rim while increasing the width across the tyre's section.

The relation between height and width is known as the aspect ratio. This is usually expressed as a percentage. A tyre which is 4 in. from tread to rim and 5 in. wide has an aspect ratio of 80 per cent.

Because the pneumatic tyre evolved from a simple circular-section tube in which height and width were equal, the aspect ratio remained 100 per cent for many years. Then it was discovered that a tyre behaved better when fitted to a wider rim, which increased the tyre's width.

The next step was to make the tyres themselves wider without increasing their height. These wider tyres put more tread on the road and gave better high-speed performance, better cornering, better load-carrying capacity and longer life than the old symmetrical type. Today, production-car tyres are being made still wider and shallower. The latest radial-ply tyres for road cars have an aspect ratio of 70 per cent. On racing cars, with their extra-wide wheels, the ratio can be much lower.

THE TREND TOWARDS WIDER TYRES

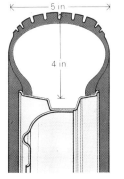

Modern tyre with 80 per cent aspect ratio

Modern tyre mounted on average-width wheel

Racing tyre mounted on ultra-wide wheel

Older tyre on narrow wheel with 100 per cent aspect ratio

Trend is to a wider tyre on wider wheel with 70 per cent aspect ratio

Ratios below 60 per cent are possible for road use, but ultra-wide tyres would be difficult to accommodate

Tyres/types and their construction

Cross-ply tyres

THE CROSS-PLY is the oldest type of tyre and has a casing made up of two or more plies, or layers, of fabric.

It was so named because originally the threads, or cords, ran across the tyre at right angles to the direction of rotation.

This design gave a comfortable ride but had side-effects on the steering. It was found that placing the cords parallel to the direction of rotation greatly improved the directional stability; but it also reduced the comfort.

The plies were therefore imposed at an angle so that their cords ran across each other diagonally, allowing the layers to retain their strength while being stretched in different directions.

For many years cords were placed at an angle of 45 degrees; but this has now been reduced to 40 degrees, and even less in some specially designed high-speed tyres.

In addition to a tyre's inner lining various strips and fillers are incorporated to strengthen the casing.

A tyre's strength and load-carrying ability were at one time indicated by its number of plies: a four-ply tyre indicated that the casing was built up from four layers of inner lining material and could carry a specific load with safety.

Modern materials and man-made fibres, such as polyester and glass fibre, embedded in the rubber, are much stronger than the cotton fibres originally used; and the ply rating can no longer be related to the number of plies.

Ply-ratings are still used, but only to indicate the strength and load-carrying capacity; a four-ply rating may well be given to a tyre which has only two plies.

Radial-ply tyres

MORE AND MORE manufacturers are fitting radial-ply tyres, and there is little doubt that most cars will eventually have them.

The construction of a radial-ply tyre reduces cornering wear and considerably increases the overall life of the tyre; but this is at the expense of slightly harder rides at lower speeds.

Radial-ply tyres are made in two parts: the layers, or plies, and a belt of cords.

The cords in the plies run from bead to bead across the crown at right angles, not diagonally as in the cross-ply tyre. This gives great pliability and comfort, but little or no directional stability. Stability comes from a belt of cords, known as a breaker, running around the circumference of the tyre beneath the tread. Breaker cords are usually spun from a man-made fibre or fine steel wire and are flexible, but do not lose their tautness. So the breaker firmly restricts lateral stretching.

Many new types of tyres are reaching commercial exploitation—using, for example, a combination of steel and polyester or steel and nylon cording to give extra strength. All these involve manufacturing problems, for it is difficult to ensure that the bonding of cording materials and rubber compounds remains trouble-free throughout the arduous life of the tyre.

To help keep a tyre's stiffness against sideways forces, a breaker is made of at least two layers of cord which are slightly diagonal to the circumference. The angle between the cords varies from 18 to 22 degrees. The number of layers depends on the material used, the lateral stiffness needed and the likely load.

CONSTRUCTION OF A CROSS-PLY TYRE

Tread pattern

Drainage channels and sipes

Tread pattern and shoulder buttress

Casing plies—diagonal cords

Rubbing strip

Bead wires and bead wrapping

Inner liner

CONSTRUCTION OF A RADIAL-PLY TYRE

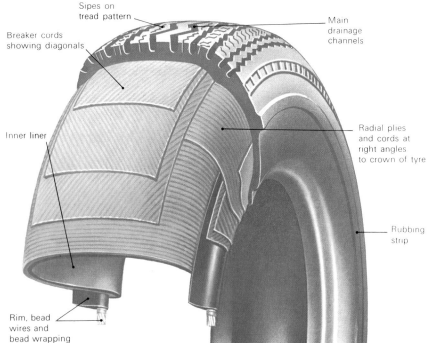

Sipes on tread pattern

Main drainage channels

Breaker cords showing diagonals

Inner liner

Radial plies and cords at right angles to crown of tyre

Rubbing strip

Rim, bead wires and bead wrapping

Shoulder

Cross-ply tyre Profile of tread

Hollow contour Sectional diagram of tyre before inflation (left) and after, showing wide road contact from broad tread

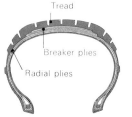

Tread

Breaker plies

Radial plies

Radial-ply tyre Profile of tread

Safety tyres

If steel cords are used in a breaker, there are usually only two; but as many as four, five or six cords may be used if they are made of rayon or other fibre. Where four are used, they are doubled over and sometimes interleaved, to increase their lateral stability. Steel makes a stronger cord and does not stretch under inflation pressure.

Nylon, first used for breakers in aircraft tyres, is stronger, more elastic and more flexible than rayon and keeps the tyre cooler. It is used in car tyres for high speeds or heavy loads, but only in combination with other materials.

When cold, nylon cords tend to lose their flexibility. If nylon cords alone were used, the section of the tyre resting on the road would change its shape and give a bumpy ride until the casing had warmed up enough to recover its flexibility.

THE DUNLOP DENOVO tyre can be run safely and without damage after being punctured for up to 100 miles at speeds as high as 40 mph. Even when punctured it allows steering and braking control of the vehicle. With the use of a temporary repair kit, the usuable distance can be extended to 600 miles before a permanent repair becomes necessary.

Tyre and wheel are both of a special design. The tyre is basically a profile tubeless radial, containing canisters filled with a special fluid.

As an ordinary tyre deflates, the air-tight seal between rim and tyre is broken and the internal walls of side walls and tread rub on each other and the rim. This rubbing rapidly generates heat and thereby destroys the tyre carcass. The design of Denovo tyre and rim is such that

the air-tight seal is not broken even with sudden *total* deflation. Deflation, moreover, causes the canisters to puncture and release their fluid.

The fluid has several functions: it acts as a lubricant, separating the rubber surfaces, and it cools them; because of the heat generated, it produces a vapour pressure which partially re-inflates the tyre; and it seals small punctures.

A cheaper alternative that can be used with standard tyres and wheels is the RoSafe system. A well-filler (which can be a split steel ring to *bridge* the wheel well or foam plastic inserts to *fill* it) is fitted to prevent one of the tyre beads from sinking into the well. When that happens during a normal deflation, the tyre becomes mangled and steering control is lost. The RoSafe system allows a safe halt.

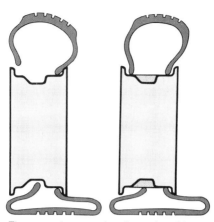

The car can be steered and brought safely to a halt when well fillers are fitted to ordinary tyres. The tyres have no long-distance mobility they are often damaged beyond repair

CONSTRUCTION OF A SAFETY TYRE

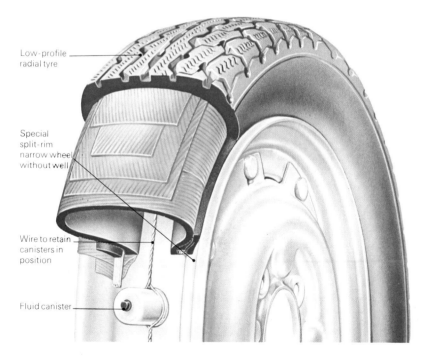

Low-profile radial tyre

Special split-rim narrow wheel without well

Wire to retain canisters in position

Fluid canister

Normal position

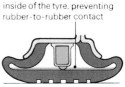

Fluid acts as lubricant on the inside of the tyre, preventing rubber-to-rubber contact

Tyre fully deflated

Partial re-inflation

HOW TYRES BEHAVE

THE RADIAL-PLY TYRE looks more bulbous than the cross-ply and generally has a broader-looking tread. The difference between them in their behaviour on the road is governed by the difference in their carcass constructions.

The radial-ply has a stiffness and resistance in its tread area, so that in motion the tread in the contact patch (the section that touches the road surface) retains virtually all of its grip.

On the cross-ply, the contact patch becomes pinched and compressed.

The radial-ply tyre corners more tightly than the cross-ply because it has a lower slip angle. This is the difference between the path in which the wheel is

pointed on a corner and the path it actually follows.

The cross-ply steers better at low speeds and is easier for parking.

The deflection of a tyre—the extent to which the carcass is deformed radially under the vertical load which it carries—provides a cushioning effect. The higher the deflection, the greater the cushioning.

A radial-ply has a higher deflection than a cross-ply and gives a more comfortable ride at 40 mph and over. But below 40 mph, the comparative stiffness of the radial hoop reflects road irregularities. It is sometimes less comfortable riding on radial-ply tyres than on cross-ply tyres.

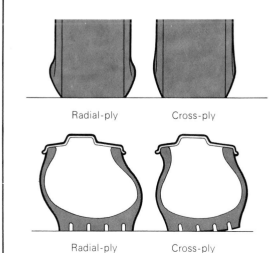

Radial-ply   Cross-ply

Correctly inflated, the radial-ply tyre bulges much more than the cross-ply just above the contact patch

Radial-ply   Cross-ply

Distortion in cornering is dispersed throughout the radial-ply, which is more supple and elastic than the cross-ply

Tyres/importance of tread patterns

Getting the right grip for safety and economy

TREADS are designed to help tyres grip the road and to enable the car to move with maximum comfort, speed, safety and economy in any kind of weather.

Tyre treads are made of natural or synthetic rubber bonded directly on to the casing, or on to the breaker strip (the belt of cords running around the circumference of radial tyres to stiffen them).

A wide variety of patterns are moulded into the tread to drain away water and cope with various other factors dictated by the road surface and the type of vehicle being used.

On a dry road the best grip is afforded by a fairly smooth tyre, as this provides the greatest possible contact patch, that part of the tyre in direct touch with the road at any moment. But on a wet road a smooth tyre has hardly any grip, and the least trace of water acts as a lubricant. If there is a lot of water on the road, it will form a wedge in front of and underneath a smooth tyre, causing a form of skidding known as aquaplaning. The tyre, lifted off the road and riding on the water, stops turning and steering control is lost.

If there is a thin film of water on the road, the tread pattern breaks through it and grips the hard road surface.

With larger amounts of water, the tread pattern does three things. It first pushes the water aside or pumps it through zigzag grooves and channels in the tread which run parallel to the wheel. In this way the water is driven to the back of the contact patch, where it spins off behind the tyre.

Secondly, the film of water left is mopped up by sipes—slits like tiny knife-cuts in the tread which act like a sponge.

Thirdly, the tread pattern grips the remainder of the now-dry contact area.

As speed increases, contact time decreases and the first two parts of the process take up more of the contact patch, leaving less for a dry grip.

At 60 mph on a wet road, the tread pattern on an average-sized tyre needs to move more than one gallon of water out of the way every second—two gallons in heavy rain—to dry enough surface to provide a grip.

Even with a moderate amount of tread pattern, a tyre's grip on a wet road decreases appreciably as the speed increases, and it will still aquaplane if there is plenty of water about.

A bold and rugged tread gives a reasonable grip in winter, because the tread can quickly channel away snow, slush, mud or loose stones.

Dispersing bulk of water through tread channels

This high-speed photograph shows the contact patch, the area of the tyre in direct touch with the road at any one moment, when a tyre goes through water. It was taken beneath plate glass on a test track and shows first the bulk of water being pushed away to the sides of the tyre, or being pumped through its main channels. Then the remaining film of water is mopped up through sipes in the tread, finally leaving a tiny strip of dry surface for the tyre to grip

A smooth tyre has no tread to disperse the water on a wet road, so water builds up in front and the tyre aquaplanes —slides on the surface of the water out of control

THE 'FOOTPRINT' OF A TYRE

'Knife-cuts', or sipes

High-speed tyre The exceptionally wide and deep centre channel rapidly takes up water from the contact area, transverse patterns disperse the water to the side of the tyre, and thin slots in the tread squeeze out the remaining water to leave a comparatively dry contact area—roughly the size of the sole of a man's shoe

Variations in tread

TREAD PATTERNS differ to suit different purposes. A tyre that is to be used for long periods in wintry conditions needs a tread with a deep bite to get a grip, and with channels deep enough to get rid of snow, slush or mud.

Other tyres may be needed for use in generally wet weather, when the most important requirement is a tread that ensures rapid drainage. A tyre with a heavy rugged tread intended for rough roads would quickly wear out if used on dry roads at high speed.

Below are three tread patterns, each designed for a different job. On the left is a high-speed nylon cross-ply tyre with through drainage in the main channels and many sipes to give a good grip in wet weather.

The centre tyre is a radial-ply with the outer shoulder built up to withstand heavier wear at high speed and to give the tyre a longer life.

The winter tyre (right) has hardened steel studs embedded in the tread to give a grip on ice and snow.

TREAD PATTERNS

Symmetrical tread
The pattern of the tread is the same from the centre to each shoulder

Asymmetrical tread
This tread pattern is deeper on the outer shoulder than the inner

Studded tyre
Hardened steel studs give a good grip on icy surfaces

Buttressed shoulder

Deep coarse tread

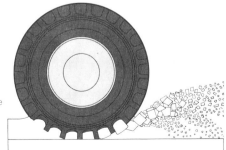

Winter tyre This has been specially designed for use on loose surfaces such as those found in wintry conditions. Some can be fitted with hardened steel studs for a better grip on ice. Wide and deep grooves on the shoulder of the tread help to channel away loose upper surfaces of mud, snow, slush and stones for the tyre to get a grip on the firmer surface beneath. These tyres wear out rapidly if used on dry roads

Danger of wrongly mixing tyres

CUTTING COSTS on tyres is false economy and is not worth the risk on the road.

Changing to a different type of tyre may alter the handling of a car and make the suspension too soft or too hard for comfort. Drivers should get expert advice before changing to tyres different from those recommended.

It is considered safe to use cross-ply tyres on the front and radial-ply on the rear; it is illegal to have radial-ply at the front and cross-ply at the rear, and to mix cross-ply with radial-ply on the same axle.

This is because they behave differently during cornering. Radial-ply tyres have a lower slip angle than cross-ply (see p. 155) and follow more accurately the intended cornering line of the car. With cross-ply fitted to the rear and radial to the front, the driver may lose control on a corner. It is also illegal to use a cross-ply tyre on the rear axle with a bias-belted tyre on the front axle.

Because radial tyres with steel breakers and those with textile breakers are affected differently during cornering, they should not be mixed on the same axle. Tyres with textile breakers may be used on front wheels and those with steel breakers on rear wheels. But in general it is better to use the same type all round.

Opinions differ but the only completely satisfactory answer is never to mix tyres. Not only should all four tyres and the spare be of the same type, whether radial or cross-ply, but they should also, for maximum safety, be of the same make, size and tread pattern.

MIXING OF TYRES (Tyre type must be same on same axle)		
Front (Treat bias belt as cross-ply except where mentioned)	**Rear** (Treat bias belt as cross-ply except where mentioned)	**Is it safe to fit them?** (Subject to local speed limits)
Cross-ply	Cross-ply	Yes
Bias belt	Cross-ply	No
Cross-ply	Radial, textile or steel	Yes Except on fast sports cars
Cross-ply	Winter tread, cross-ply	Yes Recommended limit 75 mph*
Radial, textile or steel	Cross-ply	No
Radial, textile	Radial, textile	Yes
Radial, steel	Radial, steel	Yes
Radial, textile	Radial, steel	Yes
Radial, steel	Radial, textile	Not recommended
Radial, textile or steel	Winter tread, cross-ply	No
Radial, textile or steel	Winter tread, radial	Yes
Winter tread, cross-ply	Cross-ply	Yes Recommended limit 75 mph*
Winter tread, cross-ply	Radial, textile or steel	Yes Recommended limit 75 mph*
Winter tread, radial	Cross-ply	No
Winter tread, radial	Radial, textile or steel	Yes Recommended limit 85 mph*

*Deduct 10 mph when travelling long distances on continental roads

Tyres and speed

CODE LETTERS are moulded on tyres to show the maximum speeds at which they can be used. The letter R or the word Radial signifies that the tyre is radial.

Radial tyres marked SR are suitable for speeds up to 113 mph (180 km/h), those marked HR for up to 130 mph (210 km/h), and those marked VR for more than 130 mph.

Markings and speeds for cross-plies:

Rim dia.	Size mark only	Speed mark S	H	V
10 in.	Up to 75 mph 120 km/h	Up to 95 mph 150 km/h	Up to 110 mph 175 km/h	
12 in.	Up to 85 mph 135 km/h	Up to 100 mph 160 km/h	Up to 115 mph 185 km/h	
13 in. and over	Up to 95 mph 150 km/h	Up to 110 mph 175 km/h	Up to 125 mph 200 km/h	Over 125 mph 200 km/h

Remoulds and retreads

REMOULDS and retreads can be used up to 70 mph (112 km/h) on 10 in. dia. wheels and up to 75 mph (120 km/h) on wheels over 10 in. dia. But they are not suitable for prolonged high-speed driving.

On a remould, the rubber is completely renewed from bead to bead. On a retread, however, only the tread of the tyre is renewed.

Remoulds should be used according to their speed rating. If a tyre is downgraded during the remoulding process, the remoulder must erase the original speed rating and specify a revised safe rating.

Remoulds are as good only as the residual life of their casing. Their quality depends largely on the skill and integrity of the remoulder. Buy only those carrying the BSI AU 144A or BSI AU 144B designation.

Suspension/basic principles

Reason for suspension

IF ROAD ENGINEERS could build perfect roads, there would be no need for cars to have a complex suspension system to cushion the occupants.

Unfortunately, a perfect road does not exist. Nor does an ideal suspension system that will cope equally well with all types of road surface and driving.

A good suspension system must have springiness and damping. Springiness is an elastic resistance to a load; damping is the ability to absorb some of the energy of a spring after it has been compressed. If this energy is not absorbed, a spring will seriously overshoot its original position and continue to bounce up and down until eventually its oscillations die out.

Damping converts work energy into heat energy. To reduce noise and add further softness, springs are mounted on rubber; and a car's suspension system incorporates a final cushioning in seating the occupants' bodies, as a last-stage protection against vibration.

The size of the wheels is an important factor for smooth travelling. A large wheel will ride over most road irregularities. A wheel big enough to iron out the effects of all road irregularities would be impracticable; but a wheel should not be so small that it will roll into every hollow, as this would result in a very bumpy ride.

No suspension Every irregularity in the road surface will be transmitted to the occupants of the car

No dampers The car will bounce up and down continuously unless the oscillations of the springs are controlled by dampers

Good suspension Wheels move up and down easily, but springing and damping isolate the occupants from these movements

Types of springs and their uses

IN FULFILLING their primary functions of cushioning the body and occupants of a car from road shocks, the springs act as reservoirs of energy.

Steel springs store this energy by being bent, as in the case of leaf springs, or by being twisted, as in the case of coil springs or the rod in a torsion-bar spring. The energy is released by the spring resuming its normal state.

Leaf springs are generally referred to as semi-elliptic, although today they curve so little that they are almost flat.

Usually the two ends are attached to the car frame or structure by bolts supported in rubber bushes, and the middle of the spring is clamped to the axle. If the spring is fitted across the body, the middle is located on the frame and the ends on the wheel carriers.

The best energy-storing shape for a given weight of spring is circular; and a coil spring stores the energy produced by up-and-down movement in the most efficient way.

Where coil springs are used, the end coils usually sit square, for stability, upon the surfaces through which the load is applied, and act as the lever for the twist to be applied to the rest of the spring.

A torsion bar, which has one end anchored to the car structure and the other to a component subjected to loading, stores energy when it is twisted. The twist is applied at this end by a lever.

The torsion bar is often used as an anti-roll device. A steel bar is mounted in rubber bushes across the vehicle, with its ends bent round to act as levers, which in turn are connected to the suspension.

When the wheels go up and down as a pair, the anti-roll bar merely rotates in its

A TYPICAL SUSPENSION SYSTEM

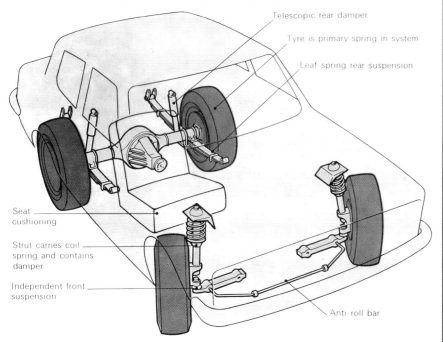

Telescopic rear damper

Tyre is primary spring in system

Leaf-spring rear suspension

Seat cushioning

Strut carries coil spring and contains damper

Independent front suspension

Anti-roll bar

THE LEAF SPRING

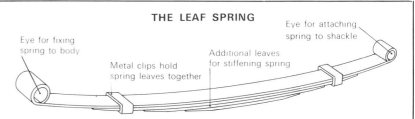

Eye for fixing spring to body

Eye for attaching spring to shackle

Metal clips hold spring leaves together

Additional leaves for stiffening spring

Leaf spring This is strengthened near the middle, where the bending effect is the greatest, either by a thickening of the leaves or by the use of additional leaves. The ends form eyes to house rubber bushes and mounting bolts

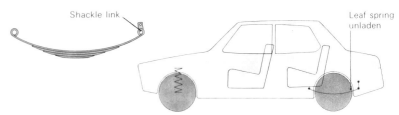

Shackle link

Leaf spring unladen

No load When a car with leaf springs at the rear is unladen, the springs have an upward curvature. One end, usually the rear, is attached to the body through a shackle link, which allows for length variations as the spring operates

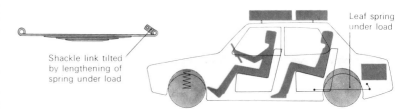

Shackle link tilted by lengthening of spring under load

Leaf spring under load

Full load In this condition, the leaves of the spring are almost flat, or may even have some downward curvature. The leaf springs on many cars have to position the axle and resist the twisting applied by acceleration and braking

126

bearings without effect on the suspension. But when only one wheel rises or falls, or the body rolls on a bend, the torsion bar twists, reacting against the movement.

Rubber is used in various ways for car springing. It is most effective when used in a combination of shear (side-to-side movement of successive layers) and compression.

An important example is the Moulton Hydrolastic system; in it, the main suspension medium is still rubber springiness, but fluid is used to transmit the movement of the wheels from front to rear, or vice versa.

In compressed-air or gas springs, up-and-down movements of the wheel operate a diaphragm against compressed air or gas. As soon as the wheel has passed over an irregularity in the road surface, the compressed air pressure returns the system to its original position.

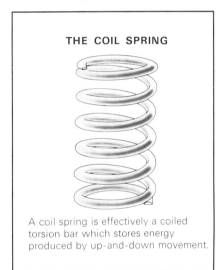

THE COIL SPRING

A coil spring is effectively a coiled torsion bar which stores energy produced by up-and-down movement.

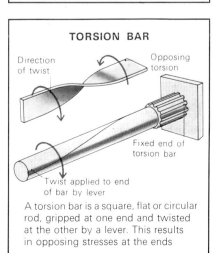

TORSION BAR

Direction of twist

Opposing torsion

Fixed end of torsion bar

Twist applied to end of bar by lever

A torsion bar is a square, flat or circular rod, gripped at one end and twisted at the other by a lever. This results in opposing stresses at the ends

Advantages of hydraulic dampers

DAMPERS, often incorrectly referred to as 'shock absorbers', damp out vibrations so that springs do not continuously bounce up and down.

The secret of good suspension is that there should be no resonance (build-up of oscillations) in the various parts of the suspension system—which includes the tyres and seats, as well as the springs. Each spring has its own frequency of vibration, and so has each damper. It is the difference between these frequencies, along with the amount of damping, that curbs resonance and gives a comfortable ride.

Earlier damper designs worked on the resistance of a friction joint; but these have been superseded by hydraulic dampers, in which movement of a piston causes oil to be displaced through small holes which resist the flow of the fluid.

The most widely used damper today is telescopic—in essence, a cylinder containing a piston on a rod. The closed end of the cylinder is attached to the wheel-carrying linkage or axle, and the outer end of the rod, which passes through a sealing gland on the cylinder, is connected to the car body.

Relief valves and leak passages provide controlled flow of the oil each way through the piston. The space above the piston is smaller than that below it, for it contains the piston rod; and this space cannot accept all the oil displaced by the piston as it travels towards the lower end of the cylinder. A valve controls the escape of the surplus oil into a reservoir or 'recuperating chamber' which surrounds the cylinder.

As the damper extends, the piston does not displace enough oil from the top section of the cylinder to fill the lower, which is topped up from the reservoir through a replenishment valve.

The reservoir is usually kept under pressure by sealing the damper.

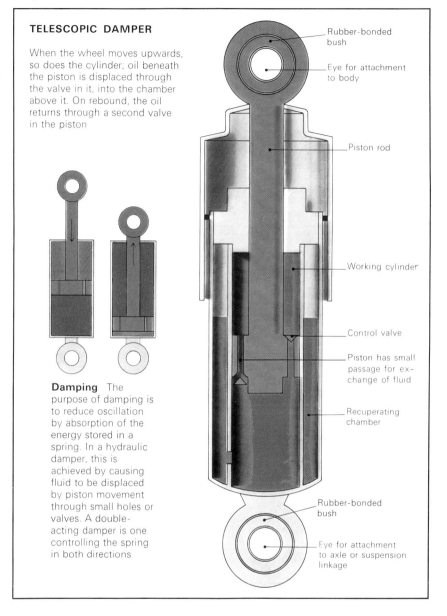

TELESCOPIC DAMPER

When the wheel moves upwards, so does the cylinder; oil beneath the piston is displaced through the valve in it, into the chamber above it. On rebound, the oil returns through a second valve in the piston

- Rubber-bonded bush
- Eye for attachment to body
- Piston rod
- Working cylinder
- Control valve
- Piston has small passage for exchange of fluid
- Recuperating chamber
- Rubber-bonded bush
- Eye for attachment to axle or suspension linkage

Damping The purpose of damping is to reduce oscillation by absorption of the energy stored in a spring. In a hydraulic damper, this is achieved by causing fluid to be displaced by piston movement through small holes or valves. A double-acting damper is one controlling the spring in both directions

Principles of rocking-lever dampers

SOME VEHICLES still have double-piston rocking-lever dampers, in which movement of the road wheel is transmitted to a lever which turns a rocker shaft.

The rocker shaft is attached, within an oil-filled casing, to a rocking lever which engages with twin pistons.

Any up or down movement of the wheel operates the rocking lever which moves the pistons. As these travel towards one end of their casing, the oil is displaced through a valve and travels to the other end, damping the bounce of the spring.

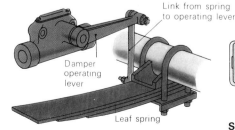

Link from spring to operating lever

Damper operating lever

Leaf spring

Lever damper Movement of the wheel is transmitted through a lever to operate twin pistons in an oil-filled casing

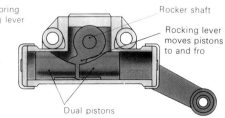

Rocker shaft

Rocking lever moves pistons to and fro

Dual pistons

Section through lever damper As the rocking lever moves the pistons, oil is displaced from one end of the casing to the other, through a restrictor valve

Suspension/systems for the front wheels

Wheels move up and down independently

ONE-PIECE FRONT AXLES, supporting the body on leaf springs, were superseded years ago on cars by independent suspension for each front wheel. This provides better steering and is a great improvement on the old beam-axle arrangement in terms of a comfortable ride.

In an independent front-suspension system, each front wheel is connected to the car's body by its own linkage and

springing, so that its movement does not affect that of the other wheel. However, the two separate suspensions may be joined by an anti-roll bar which is hinged across the chassis, bent, and joined to the lower wishbone on each side to resist body roll when cornering.

A vital feature of front suspension is that the wheels have to be steered as well as moving up and down. When a car corners

or goes over bumps, it is subjected through the wheels to a variety of forces.

The suspension must not allow these forces to deflect the car from the course chosen by the driver. Nor must they cause the wheels to wobble, move any significant distance backwards, forwards or sideways, or alter their angle of tilt to any serious degree. Any such effects would interfere with the handling of the car.

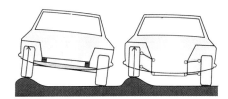

Independent front suspension This helps to keep the body of the car riding level on bumpy roads

Action of double wishbones

ONE COMMON FORM of independent front suspension is the double-wishbone system. In this, two wishbone links, so called because of their shape, are hinged at their broad ends to the body or sub-frame of the car, and at their narrow ends to the swivel members which have stub axles to carry the wheels. Between each wishbone assembly and the car structure are a spring and a hydraulic damper to intercept road shocks.

As well as positioning the wheels and transmitting loads to the spring, the wishbones must also resist acceleration, braking and cornering forces.

Since the first two of these forces act along the car, a simple sideways link would yield to them. It follows that a form of triangle is necessary to give a broad base, which is why links of triangulated or wishbone shape are used.

The geometry of the wishbone layout— the lengths, positions and angles of the links—governs the path of the wheels when the car rides over bumps; this path in turn affects steering, road-holding and tyre wear.

If the upper and lower wishbones are parallel and of equal length, the wheels will not tilt as they move up and down over bumps. However, the track (distance between the wheels, across the car) does change somewhat, with bad effect on tyre life. On corners, the wheels lean outwards with the body, which reduces their cornering ability.

In most modern designs, the wishbones are neither of equal length nor parallel, the upper one being the shorter. Hence the wheel no longer remains upright as it moves up or down over bumps, but leans slightly inwards.

This gives better cornering characteristics than the other layout: when the body rolls outwards, the outside wheel—which carries the greater load and therefore exerts the higher cornering power of the two—remains more or less at right angles to the road surface.

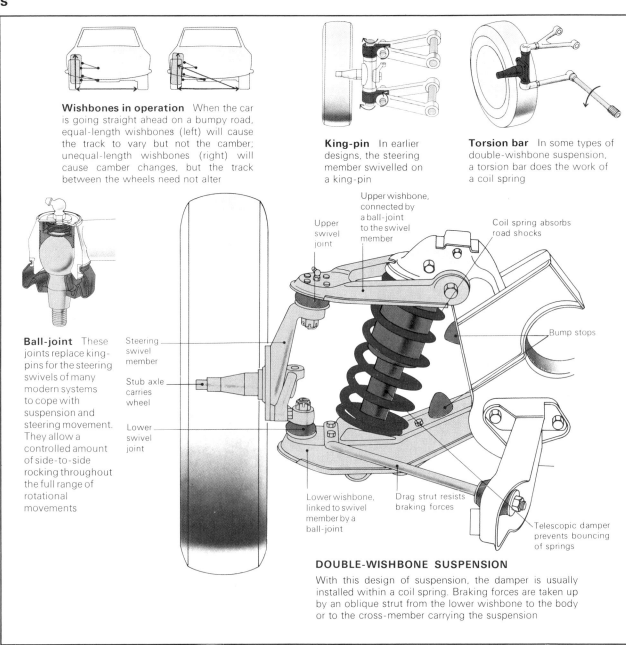

Wishbones in operation When the car is going straight ahead on a bumpy road, equal-length wishbones (left) will cause the track to vary but not the camber; unequal-length wishbones (right) will cause camber changes, but the track between the wheels need not alter

King-pin In earlier designs, the steering member swivelled on a king-pin

Torsion bar In some types of double-wishbone suspension, a torsion bar does the work of a coil spring

Ball-joint These joints replace king-pins for the steering swivels of many modern systems to cope with suspension and steering movement. They allow a controlled amount of side-to-side rocking throughout the full range of rotational movements

Upper swivel joint

Upper wishbone, connected by a ball-joint to the swivel member

Coil spring absorbs road shocks

Steering swivel member

Stub axle carries wheel

Lower swivel joint

Bump stops

Lower wishbone, linked to swivel member by a ball-joint

Drag strut resists braking forces

Telescopic damper prevents bouncing of springs

DOUBLE-WISHBONE SUSPENSION

With this design of suspension, the damper is usually installed within a coil spring. Braking forces are taken up by an oblique strut from the lower wishbone to the body or to the cross-member carrying the suspension

MacPherson strut assembly

INSTEAD of using double wishbones, some suspension systems have a telescopic strut, anchored at its top to the body structure (usually high up in the wing) by a flexible mounting. It has a transverse-link arrangement to locate the lower end.

The lower links have to locate the wheel in such a position that neither suspension movement nor braking force deflects the wheel unduly from its true position. This can be achieved by a wishbone with its wide base towards the centre-line of the car or a single strut and an anti-roll bar.

These are attached to the body structure via rubber-bonded bushes to reduce transmitted noise and give a degree of compliance or limited relative movement.

To absorb road shocks, a coil spring surrounds the upper part of the strut, which contains a hydraulic damper.

This system is mechanically simple, it helps the wheels to follow road irregularities and it does not cause the camber (angle of wheel tilt) to vary much.

But the body has to be strong where the strut is attached.

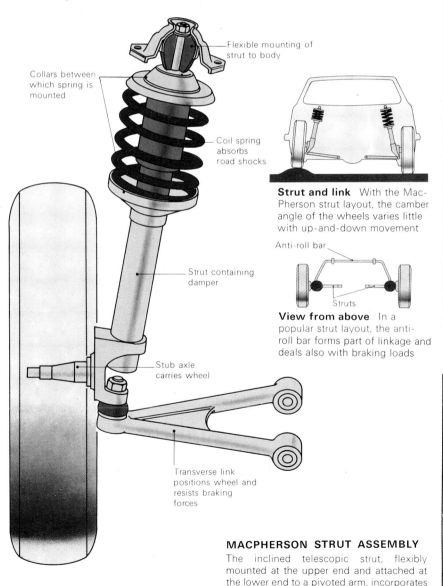

- Flexible mounting of strut to body
- Collars between which spring is mounted
- Coil spring absorbs road shocks
- Strut containing damper
- Stub axle carries wheel
- Transverse link positions wheel and resists braking forces

Strut and link With the Mac-Pherson strut layout, the camber angle of the wheels varies little with up-and-down movement

Anti-roll bar

Struts

View from above In a popular strut layout, the anti-roll bar forms part of linkage and deals also with braking loads

MACPHERSON STRUT ASSEMBLY
The inclined telescopic strut, flexibly mounted at the upper end and attached at the lower end to a pivoted arm, incorporates a damper to prevent the spring bouncing. The wheel path is often controlled by a triangular link between the bottom of the strut and the body

Variations in front-suspension design

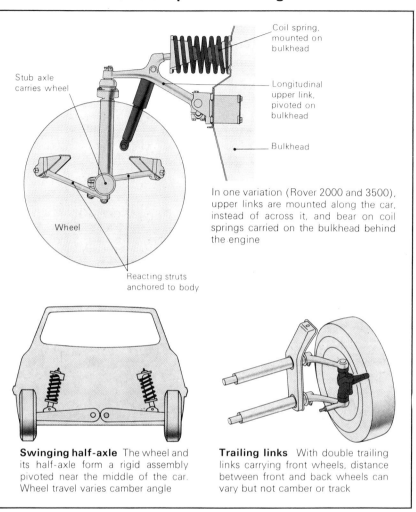

- Coil spring, mounted on bulkhead
- Stub axle carries wheel
- Longitudinal upper link, pivoted on bulkhead
- Bulkhead
- Wheel
- Reacting struts anchored to body

In one variation (Rover 2000 and 3500), upper links are mounted along the car, instead of across it, and bear on coil springs carried on the bulkhead behind the engine

Swinging half-axle The wheel and its half-axle form a rigid assembly pivoted near the middle of the car. Wheel travel varies camber angle

Trailing links With double trailing links carrying front wheels, distance between front and back wheels can vary but not camber or track

Anti-roll bar

Sideways roll of the car occurs in cornering, due to centrifugal force transferring weight to the outside springs. Roll can be reduced by fitting an anti-roll bar between the wheels so that any cornering roll is resisted by the 'winding-up' of the bar

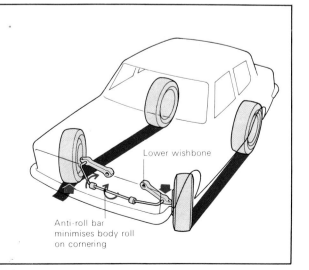

- Lower wishbone
- Anti-roll bar minimises body roll on cornering

Suspension/systems for the rear wheels

The problems of extra weight

IN MOST CARS, the rear suspension has to carry the greater part of the extra weight of passengers and luggage. If the suspension springs are stiff enough only for the car with driver, they will be too soft for the car when it is fully laden. Conversely, springs that are right for the laden car will be too stiff with only the driver to carry.

The same difficulty occurs with the settings of dampers, which prevent the springs from bouncing.

Designers solve this problem in a variety of ways. The rear suspension may include driving axles with leaf springs; driving axles with other types of springs and positioning devices; and variations of independent suspension, using leaf or coil springs, torsion bars, rubber, Hydrolastic elements or compressed gases.

The driving axles combine the right-angle drive, differential, axle shafts and wheel-hub mountings in one rigid unit.

This unit, known as a live axle, is connected to the propeller shaft, and is attached to the vehicle structure in such a way that it can move up and down on its springs and can cope with the loads and the torque, or turning forces, imposed on it.

The rear suspension should be designed also to position the axle in a way that minimises the bouncing and associated vibrations to which it is liable, particularly when moving off, braking and cornering.

Dampers, which suppress bouncing of the springs, are mostly hydraulic, and the telescopic type is favoured in preference to the piston type widely used earlier.

The simplest design that combines springing and positioning, or locating, of the rear axle is known as the Hotchkiss drive. In this, a pair of leaf springs are set as far apart on the axle as possible.

The axle may be carried exactly in the middle of the springs, but many axles are set forward from the middle to give a downward tilt as the axle rises when riding over bumps. This reduces the amount by which the rear end of the propeller shaft lifts on a bump and, in turn, minimises the height of the propeller-shaft tunnel and the amount it intrudes into the car.

To reduce variations in axle tilt under different driving conditions, some rear suspensions have fore-and-aft torque-control links (that is, links controlling forward-and-backward twisting movement), to supplement the leaf springs.

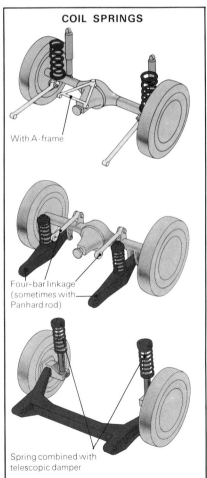

LEAF SPRINGS

With radius rods

With Panhard rod

COIL SPRINGS

With A-frame

Four-bar linkage (sometimes with Panhard rod)

Spring combined with telescopic damper

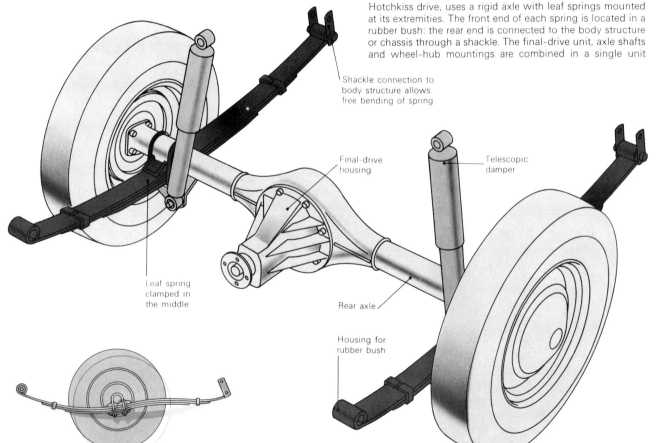

HOTCHKISS DRIVE

One of the more common forms of rear suspension, the Hotchkiss drive, uses a rigid axle with leaf springs mounted at its extremities. The front end of each spring is located in a rubber bush: the rear end is connected to the body structure or chassis through a shackle. The final-drive unit, axle shafts and wheel-hub mountings are combined in a single unit

Shackle connection to body structure allows free bending of spring

Final-drive housing

Telescopic damper

Leaf spring clamped in the middle

Rear axle

Housing for rubber bush

One of the disadvantages of the leaf spring is that it tends to distort (as here) when the axle tries to turn during acceleration or braking

Independent rear suspension

SOME TYPES of independent suspension applied to the rear of the car are similar to those used at the front.

Swinging half axle In its original form, this system has two axle tubes pivoted to a central drive casing carried by the car structure. A universal joint is centred on each pivot. Suspension is usually by a leaf

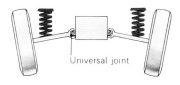

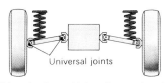

Additional universal joints (bottom) reduce wheel-camber changes when cornering

spring lying across the car, bolted to the frame or axle casing in the middle and shackled at its ends to the axle tubes.

A variation of the system is the low-pivot version used by Mercedes-Benz.

MacPherson strut This is similar in most respects to the MacPherson strut used in the front suspension.

Trailing arm Each rear wheel is supported by an arm hinged to the car structure. The hinge is at right angles to the centre-line of the car, so that the wheel rises and falls over bumps without any change of camber or alignment.

Semi-trailing arm In this widely used system, the centre-line of the hinge on which the arm swings is set at a considerable angle to the centre-line of the car. This enables the designer to give the wheel a pre-determined degree of variation in both camber and alignment as the wheel rises and falls over bumps in the road.

Double wishbone This differs from the double wishbone used on front suspension in one respect: the wheels have to be held straight instead of being left free to swivel, and often one wishbone link has its broad base nearer the wheel, supplemented by a tie-rod to take fore-and-aft loads.

This construction meets the fundamental need of keeping the inner and outer ends of one link parallel and providing them with sufficient length to perform their guiding function. In one design, a drive shaft of fixed length is used in conjunction with a fore-and-aft tie as the equivalent of a wishbone member.

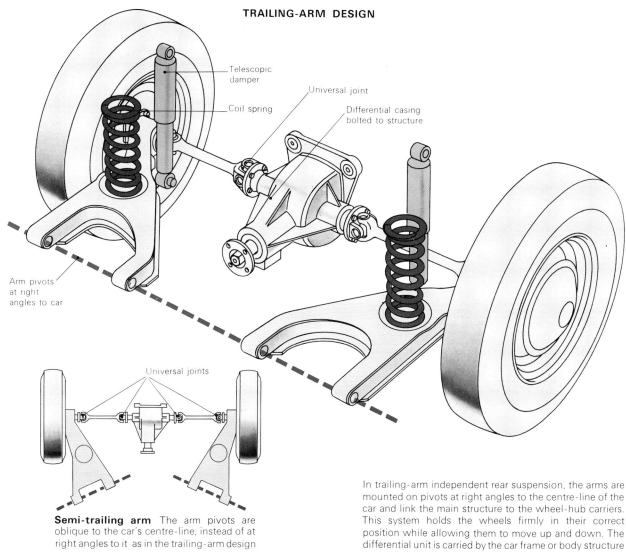

TRAILING-ARM DESIGN

Telescopic damper
Universal joint
Coil spring
Differential casing bolted to structure

Arm pivots at right angles to car

Universal joints

Semi-trailing arm The arm pivots are oblique to the car's centre-line, instead of at right angles to it as in the trailing-arm design

In trailing-arm independent rear suspension, the arms are mounted on pivots at right angles to the centre-line of the car and link the main structure to the wheel-hub carriers. This system holds the wheels firmly in their correct position while allowing them to move up and down. The differential unit is carried by the car frame or body structure

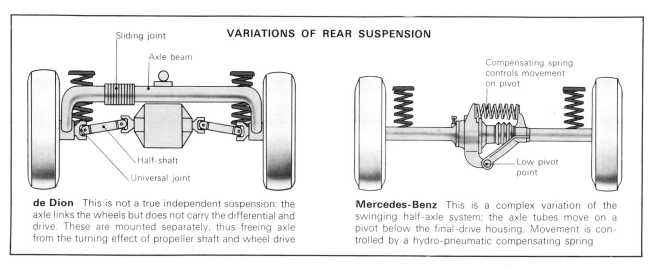

VARIATIONS OF REAR SUSPENSION

Sliding joint
Axle beam
Half-shaft
Universal joint

Compensating spring controls movement on pivot
Low pivot point

de Dion This is not a true independent suspension: the axle links the wheels but does not carry the differential and drive. These are mounted separately, thus freeing axle from the turning effect of propeller shaft and wheel drive

Mercedes-Benz This is a complex variation of the swinging half-axle system; the axle tubes move on a pivot below the final-drive housing. Movement is controlled by a hydro-pneumatic compensating spring

Suspension/linked systems

Connecting front and rear spring units

WHEN THE FRONT and rear suspension units are inter-connected, the result is known as a linked suspension system.

The primary advantage of connecting front and rear springing in this way is that it greatly reduces any tendency of the car to pitching (rocking in a fore-and-aft direction). Outstanding examples of linked suspension are the Hydrolastic and Hydragas suspensions used on British Leyland models and the spring-linkage system used on smaller Citroën models.

The main difference between the British and French systems is that the simple Citroën one works mechanically; others, including those on larger Citroën cars, have a hydraulic system linking back and front on each side.

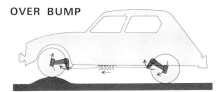

OVER BUMP

The mechanically linked suspension used by Citroën has the front and rear wheels on each side of the car connected by a coil

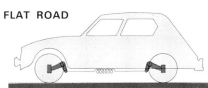

FLAT ROAD

spring. When a bump pushes the front wheel upwards, the spring is extended, pulling the rear wheel down and keeping the car level

Hydrolastic system

IN THE HYDROLASTIC system, each wheel has a 'displacer' which fulfils the functions of spring and damper. The displacer is mounted on the car body and inside it, at one end, is a bonded-on conical rubber spring.

Closing the other end of the displacer is a flexible diaphragm, in the middle of which is a piston connected to the wheel-suspension linkage. The chamber between spring and diaphragm is divided by a metal separator plate containing a rubber two-way valve. A pipe connects the front and rear chambers on each side of the car; chambers and pipes are filled with fluid.

When the front wheel rises over a bump, the diaphragm moves inwards, forcing fluid through holes in the separator plate past the two-way valve, the resistance of which provides the damping effect.

The diaphragm movement reduces the chamber volume and increases pressure, displacing some fluid along the connecting pipe. This causes the diaphragm of the other displacer to be pushed outwards, extending the rear suspension.

Any lifting of the front end of the car over the bump is thus matched by a rise of the rear end. When in turn the rear wheel meets the bump, the process is reversed, the front suspension being extended to keep the car level.

Linking front and rear suspension units
Hydrolastic suspension units serve the purpose of both springs and dampers on a range of British Leyland cars, including Minis, Maxis, 1100s, 1300s and 1800s. Hydragas is fitted on the Allegro and Princess range

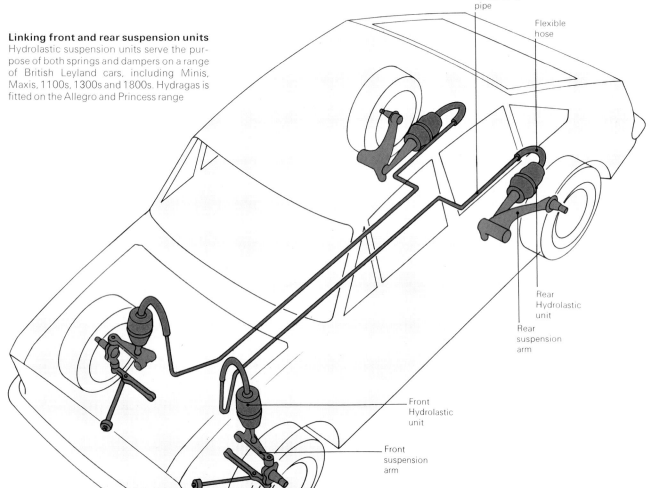

Connecting pipe

Flexible hose

Rear Hydrolastic unit

Rear suspension arm

Front Hydrolastic unit

Front suspension arm

HOW THE SYSTEM WORKS

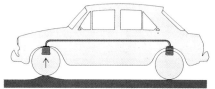

When a front wheel hits a bump, it causes fluid to be displaced to the rear suspension unit, which therefore extends, raising rear

Once the bump is passed, the fluid returns from the rear unit (right) to the front, restoring the original situation

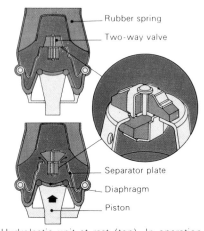

Rubber spring

Two-way valve

Separator plate

Diaphragm

Piston

Hydrolastic unit at rest (top). In operation (bottom), fluid is forced through a two-way valve and compresses the rubber spring

Hydro-pneumatic suspension

Gas compression provides springing effect

ON THEIR medium-size and larger cars, Citroën and British Leyland (and others) use hydro-pneumatic suspension, a design that combines a hydraulic system with pneumatic springing to achieve self-levelling.

Each wheel has its own independent suspension unit. In each unit, a fixed quantity of nitrogen is contained under pressure in the upper half of a metal sphere above a fluid-resistant diaphragm.

The lower half of the sphere is connected to a hydraulic cylinder. Sliding inside this cylinder is a piston with a push-rod joined to a suspension arm by a pivot pin.

When a wheel moves up to ride over a bump in the road, this movement is passed on by the suspension arm to the piston. Movement of the piston exerts pressure on the special fluid, and this in turn compresses the gas, which acts as a spring. Downward movement of the wheel causes the piston to travel downwards also, reducing pressure on the gas.

Height adjustment is achieved by the flow of fluid into or out of the cylinder. The fluid is kept under pressure in a reservoir supplied by a pump, and its flow is controlled by a slide valve.

If the load on the car is increased, the body at first sinks in relation to the wheels and suspension arms. Each arm then operates a linkage that opens the slide-valve connection to the reservoir, and fluid enters the cylinder to push the body up. The linkage returns to neutral when the body regains its original height.

The reverse happens if the load on the car is decreased. The body rises, the valve linkage opens the return pipe to the reservoir, and excess fluid flows back.

A damper is fitted at the top of the cylinder. It consists of a valve restricting the flow of fluid into and out of the sphere.

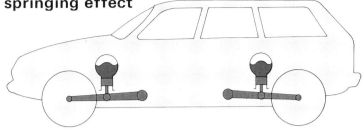

Each wheel is linked independently to the chassis by a suspension arm attached to a piston. When the wheel rises, the piston moves up, pushing against fluid which compresses gas held behind a flexible diaphragm in a sphere. When the wheel falls, the pressure is relaxed and the gas expands to act as a spring over bumps

HYDRO-PNEUMATIC UNIT

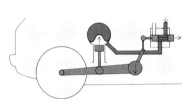

When the load increases, the car body sinks, operating a linkage from the suspension arm which moves a slide valve, allowing fluid into the cylinder

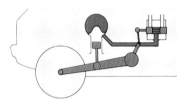

Increasing pressure of fluid in the cylinder raises the car body, reversing the movement until the valve reaches neutral and the car regains its original level

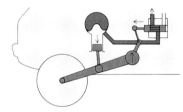

When the load decreases, the car body rises, causing the slide valve to open the return pipe, along which surplus fluid flows from the cylinder. As fluid leaves the cylinder, the car body settles down on its suspension

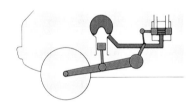

The fluid continues to flow to the hydraulic reservoir until the car returns to its original level, when once again the slide valve has returned to neutral. It remains in this position until the car height changes again

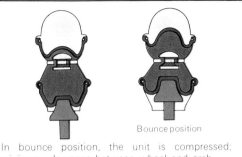

Bounce position

In bounce position, the unit is compressed; minimum clearance between wheel and arch

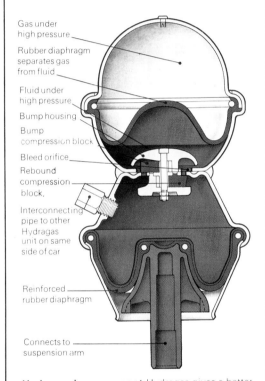

Gas under high pressure

Rubber diaphragm separates gas from fluid

Fluid under high pressure

Bump housing

Bump compression block

Bleed orifice

Rebound compression block

Interconnecting pipe to other Hydragas unit on same side of car

Reinforced rubber diaphragm

Connects to suspension arm

Hydragas improvement Hydragas gives a better ride than the Hydrolastic system

Self-levelling suspension

SELF-LEVELLING suspension systems prevent a car from 'squatting down' on its suspension when it has a full load of passengers and luggage. They are used on some cars with limited suspension travel, and automatically compensate for changes in load by modifying the springing characteristics of the car so that it always remains approximately the same height off the road.

This ensures that, even when the car is fully laden, the full upward travel of the suspension system is available for absorbing bumps. It also means that the head-lights are kept in proper focusing alignment, whatever the distribution of load. A weakness of conventional suspension systems is the way in which the addition of rear-seat passengers, or luggage in a rear boot, makes the car 'sit down' at the back and so tilts the headlight beams upwards.

Any form of self-levelling is operated by one or more load-sensing devices which measure the vertical distance between, say, the floor and a point on a suspension arm. The greater the load, the smaller this distance tends to become. An initial variation in the distance operates a valve which controls the height-adjusting system. Usually, height adjustment takes place at both ends of the car, but it can be at the rear end only.

Air suspension

Control of the riding height of a car is simple with air suspension, a system which is at present standard on few cars.

It could become more widely adopted in the future, because of the ease with which the springing characteristics can be suited to individual vehicles. Air suspension is simple in principle. Collapsible, pressurised air containers take the place of conventional springs; the upward movement of the wheel reduces the volume of the air spring, raising its pressure, so that it tries to extend itself again.

If the air spring is inflated more, it can carry a heavier load before contracting to a given height.

A height-control valve connects the air spring to a high-pressure air reservoir when the load is increased; and pressure is released through the valve to the atmosphere when the load is reduced. The pressure source is usually engine-driven.

Steering/how the driver controls the car

What the mechanism has to do

ALL CARS are steered by turning the front wheels in the required direction and allowing the rear wheels to follow.

There would be several disadvantages in trying to steer a car by its rear wheels, the main one being that the car would be directionally unstable.

On a bicycle, the steering is controlled directly by the handle-bars. But in a car, the driver would not be strong enough to control the front wheels if they were connected directly to the steering wheel. So the steering must include a gearbox, and sometimes power assistance, to multiply the driver's effort.

Major requirements in any steering mechanism are that it should be precise and easy to handle, and that the front wheels should have a tendency to return to the straight-ahead position after a turn.

The steering must not 'kick back' from road shocks, although there must be some degree of reaction, or 'feed-back', from the road to the driver.

The steering column, which encloses and supports the steering shaft, often carries controls, such as the windscreen wiper and washer, horn and light switches.

A combined headlamp-flasher and dip-switch unit is frequently fitted just below the steering wheel, with a direction indicator switch opposite it; or the two functions may be controlled by a single lever.

Some cars still have the gear-selector lever on the steering column. Some European models have the lever just below the instrument panel. Many have an adjustable steering column, so that the wheel can be moved to suit the driver.

Considerable research has been carried out in recent years to safeguard the driver against injuries inflicted by the steering wheel (or column) when the car is in a front-end collision.

The steering column can be designed to collapse on impact. For example, in the AC Delco design, the tubular column is made of an 'expanded-metal' grid so that, although strong in twist, it collapses and absorbs energy if compressed lengthwise. A telescopic joint is provided in the steering shaft.

Another design divides the steering shaft into sections which are connected by joints, but not placed in line.

The steering wheel is 'dished' and provided with a large boss and wide spokes in order to spread the load of impact over the driver's chest. The wheel or boss can also be designed to collapse when under a pre-determined load.

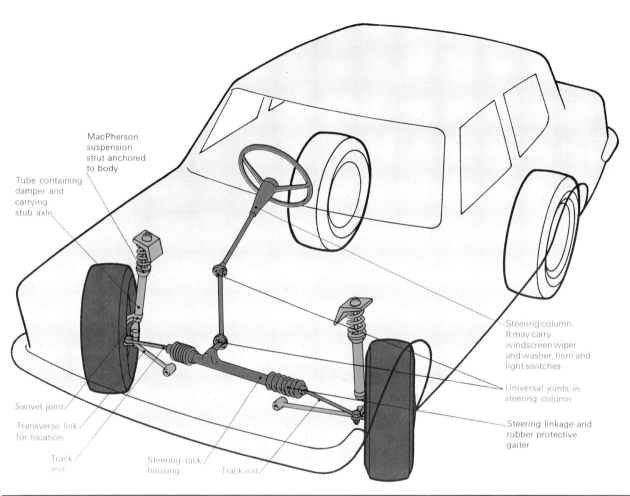

A TYPICAL STEERING ARRANGEMENT

MacPherson suspension strut anchored to body

Tube containing damper and carrying stub axle

Swivel joint

Transverse link for location

Track rod

Steering rack housing

Track rod

Steering column. It may carry windscreen wiper and washer, horn and light switches

Universal joints in steering column

Steering linkage and rubber protective gaiter

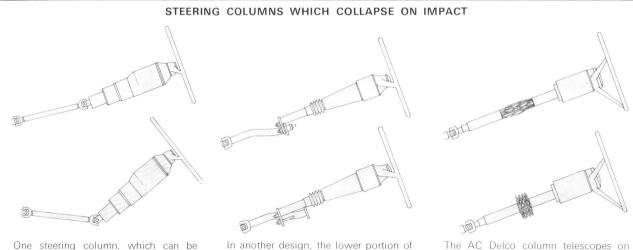

STEERING COLUMNS WHICH COLLAPSE ON IMPACT

One steering column, which can be angled to suit the driver's needs, collapses at a universal joint on impact

In another design, the lower portion of the column rides up the upper portion to absorb impact energy

The AC Delco column telescopes on impact and the mesh section compresses to cushion the driver

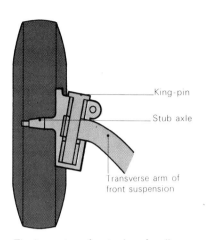

The beam-type front axles of earlier cars had king-pins on which the stub-axle carriers swivelled for steering the wheels

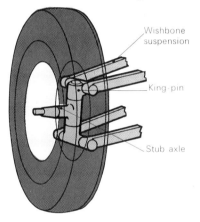

Some of the first independent suspension systems still had a king-pin between the wishbones to carry the swivel member

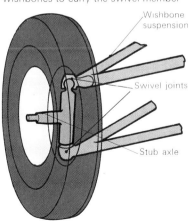

On many cars the king-pin swivel system has been replaced by a pair of ball-joints with the swivel member between

Different steering systems

A CAR is steered through a steering gearbox and a linkage—a system of rods and levers —designed to give the driver directional control with minimal effort.

The steering wheel itself is attached to a shaft which is enclosed in a supporting tube known as the steering column.

The shaft is connected to a steering gearbox, which converts the turning motion of the steering wheel into a to-and-fro movement of the steering linkage and provides the driver with the extra leverage he needs to steer the road wheels without excessive effort.

Various types of steering boxes used over the years include those known as the cam and peg, worm and nut, and recirculating ball; but most cars today use a rack-and-pinion system.

With this design, a toothed rack is moved by a small pinion at the lower end of the steering shaft. When the steering wheel is turned, the rack moves from side to side and causes the stub axles—the two short shafts on which the front wheels are mounted—to swivel.

On earlier designs, the steering box carried a short lever known as a drop-arm, which operated the rest of the linkage.

On old cars fitted with a beam front axle, and on some types of independent front suspension, the stub axles swivel on a spindle called a king-pin. On cars with modern types of independent front suspension, the stub axles swivel on two widely separated hemispherical bearings.

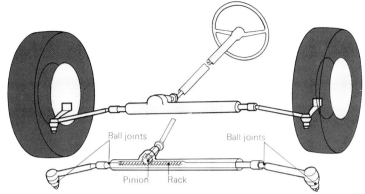

Rack and pinion In this simplest form of steering gear, a pinion rotated by the shaft moves a rack connected to the wheels through ball-joints which allow rise and fall

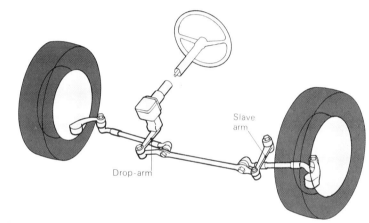

Steering box The steering wheel operates a cam and peg or worm and nut gear which moves a drop-arm connected to the wheels through links and a slave arm

Steering gearbox reduces effort needed by driver

THE AMOUNT of reduction of effort—or leverage—to be provided by the steering box depends on the weight, type and use of the car.

A light sports car requires little reduction, as the driver needs quick control to correct skids or 'drifts'; but a heavy car, with 'fat' tyres, requires a big reduction and/or some form of power assistance to make low-speed turns.

The steering box and the linkage also pass back to the steering wheel the reaction of the wheels to the road surface.

This reaction gives immediate warning to the driver of changing conditions, but designers have different ideas as to how much reaction there should be.

Some mechanisms are efficient in transmitting the driver's effort to the road wheels but are less effective in feeding back information about irregularities in the road surface to the driver.

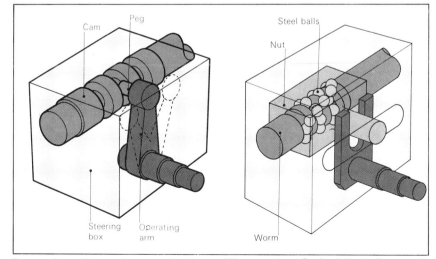

Cam and peg A tapered peg moving along a modified form of worm gear on the end of the steering shaft moves the operating arm

Worm and nut Recirculating balls are used to reduce friction between a rotating worm and a nut moving along it

Steering/arrangement of the front wheels

Ackermann principle of correct steering

IN 1818, long before the advent of the car, the German inventor Rudolf Ackermann patented a device based on the principle of geometrically correct steering. He stated the principle that when a vehicle travels in a curved path, its wheels should describe circles round the same centre. A wheel which follows a markedly different path will slide to some extent; and this will cause tyre wear.

The application of Ackermann's principle makes it possible to arrange for imaginary lines through the axes of all the wheels, front and back, to pass through, or very near, the same point—the centre of the curve on which the car is travelling. This is achieved by turning the inner front wheel through a greater angle than the outer front wheel.

However, modern car designers no longer need to follow the Ackermann principle strictly, because of improvements in suspension and tyres. When a car rounds a bend at speed the deflection of the tyres on the road surface creates a sideways force which assists steering. This must be allowed for to achieve predictable and safe cornering at speed.

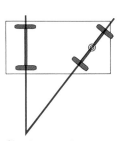

Simplest steering mechanism—front axle turning on central pivot. Wheels turn round same centre

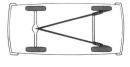
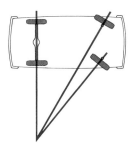

Ackermann-based steering uses independent stub axles (top) to keep wheels circling same centre (below)

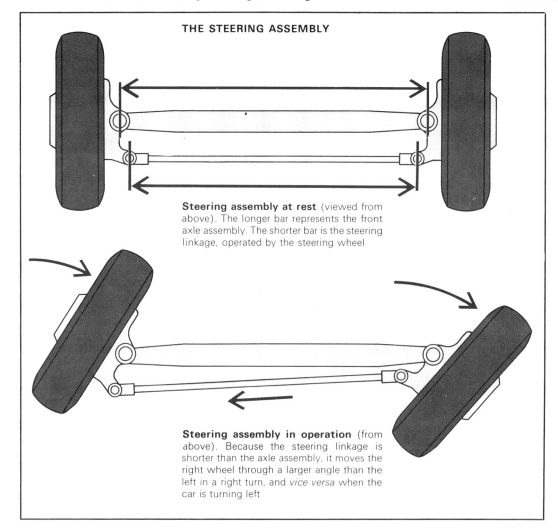

THE STEERING ASSEMBLY

Steering assembly at rest (viewed from above). The longer bar represents the front axle assembly. The shorter bar is the steering linkage, operated by the steering wheel

Steering assembly in operation (from above). Because the steering linkage is shorter than the axle assembly, it moves the right wheel through a larger angle than the left in a right turn, and *vice versa* when the car is turning left

STEERING LINKAGES

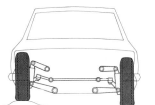

Car with independent front suspension has multi-jointed steering linkage

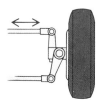

Transverse linkage to steering gearbox, viewed from above. For clarity the link is shown ahead of the stub axle; usually it is behind the axle

In this arrangement the link to the steering gearbox runs parallel to the wheel

Toe-in and toe-out

ALTHOUGH in theory the front wheels should be parallel when pointing straight ahead, the best practical results are usually obtained by setting them slightly out of parallel. This gives the steadiest steering and least tyre wear. On most cars, when the steering is centralised, the front wheels point inwards by a fraction of an inch at the front. This is known as toe-in. It can be regarded as a compensation for the fact that no steering and suspension can be perfect and no steering linkage is free from a certain amount of 'give'. Some cars—usually those with front-wheel drive—have the wheels pointing slightly outwards. This is known as toe-out. A means of adjusting the amount of toe-in or toe-out is always provided.

Wheel alignment is the term used to describe the amount of toe-in or toe-out, and rarely exceeds $\frac{3}{16}$ in. Incorrect alignment of the rear wheels, due to wear or accident damage, can also affect steering in cars with independent rear suspension.

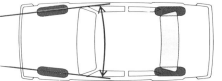

Toe-in Front wheels are set to run slightly towards one another. On rear-wheel-drive cars, this offsets the wheels' tendency to move outwards. Diagram exaggerates the adjustment, which rarely exceeds $\frac{3}{16}$ in.

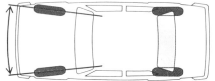

Toe-out Front wheels are set to run slightly outwards to offset a tendency for them to move inwards, as found in some front-wheel-drive cars. The adjustment is similar to that for toe-in—rarely more than $\frac{3}{16}$ in.

Steering ratio

THE STEERING RATIO is the ratio between the rotation of the steering wheel and the angle of movement imparted to the steering arms—those parts of the steering linkage connected directly to the stub axles and which move the wheels.

If, for instance, a full turn (360 degrees) of the steering wheel moves the steering arms through 30 degrees, the steering ratio is 12:1 (360:30).

Most popular lightweight saloon cars have a steering ratio of about 15:1. To move the front wheels from lock to lock (about 60 degrees) takes two-and-a-half turns of the steering wheel. But a heavy car may need four or five turns—a steering ratio of at least 24:1.

All cars are fitted with positive lock stops, to limit the steering movement of the wheels and so ensure that the tyres do not rub against any part of the car. The stops may be at the wheel pivots or on the steering gearbox.

The minimum turning circle of a car is either the diameter of the circle traced by the extreme outer corner of the car or, more usually, the diameter of the circle traced by the outer front wheel.

Camber angle

THE FRONT WHEELS of most cars, when seen from the front, lean slightly—either inwards or outwards. The tilt of the wheel is called the camber, and the amount that it tilts is called the camber angle.

The camber is usually 'positive', with the wheels leaning slightly outwards, so that they are further apart at the top than at the bottom. Wheels which are closer together at the top than at the bottom have a 'negative' camber.

The object is that, when viewed from the front, the centre of the tyre's area of contact with the road is brought close to the point where an imaginary extension of the steering pivot's axis cuts the ground. This is called centre-point steering.

Camber is a condition forced on the car designer because he cannot relieve stress on the steering linkage by placing the pivot directly over the wheel, as on a bicycle. The best the designer can do is to use a 'dished' (saucer-shaped) wheel and slope either the wheel or the steering pivot, or both.

With many independent suspension systems the camber changes from positive to negative as a wheel rises or falls.

It has been found that a small amount of offset, which reduces steering effort when parking and eliminates feedback judder from the road wheels to the steering wheel at high speeds is a desirable feature and is incorporated on practically all modern cars.

The effect of this offset is that each wheel tries to turn outwards. But, provided each wheel has the same amount of offset, this tendency will be cancelled out by reaction through the steering linkage connecting the two wheels.

On many cars the imaginary line connecting the steering swivel joints meets the ground inside the centre-line of the tyre-to-road contact area. This distance is referred to as offset or scrub radius. The advantage of an outboard scrub radius, particularly on light front-wheel-drive cars, is that it makes steering easier and safer in severe braking conditions.

For instance, if one of the front tyres hits a slippery patch of road, or if only one of the tyres suddenly deflates, then the reaction forces tend to keep the car on a straight course rather than slew it due to the imbalance.

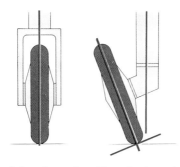

Principle of camber The wheel on the left is vertical to the ground and has no camber. The other wheel is tilted out from the vertical, but still meets the road near the axis of its steering pivot

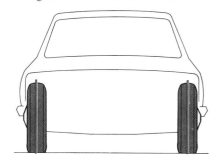

No camber The wheels are vertical to the road and have no camber. Wheels without camber make for heavier steering. The vertical loads which the steering pivots are subjected to are increased

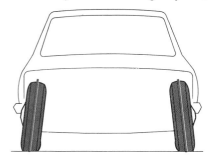

Negative camber The wheels are closer together at the top than they are at the bottom. With independent suspension, a wheel can tilt from negative camber to its opposite, positive camber, and *vice versa*

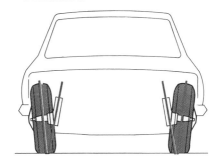

Positive camber The wheels are set further apart at the top than at the bottom. This reduces wear on the steering linkage and gives lighter steering, provided the camber is kept equal on both wheels

Castor angle

A CAR should have an inbuilt tendency to travel straight and to return to the straight-ahead position after a turn.

This tendency, which makes a car stable in motion and makes the steering wheel spin back after a corner, is controlled by many factors, including the suspension and resilience of tyres. One of the most important direction-controlling factors is castor angle.

The effect of this is most simply seen on the castor used on furniture. On a tea trolley, for example, the castor wheels, trailing behind their pivots, swing round to follow the direction in which the trolley is pushed, so that it travels in a straight line unless it is deliberately steered. In a car, the castor angle has exactly the same effect of making a wheel trail behind its steering pivot. The central point of contact of the wheel on the road is behind that of an imaginary line extending the steering-pivot axis to the road.

The castor angle is the angle between the line extending the steering-pivot axis and a vertical line through the centre of the wheel. As with camber angle, it needs checking after accident damage.

An excessive amount of castor angle or trail, coupled with very freely moving joints in the steering linkage, could lead to violent front-wheel wobble.

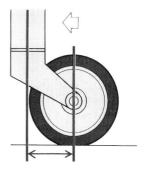

Tea-trolley castor The wheel lines up behind the axis of its steering pivot, giving it an inbuilt tendency to return to the straight after taking a corner

Car-wheel castor The steering-pivot axis meets the ground at a point ahead of the tyre's mid-point of contact, so that the wheel lines up behind its pivot

Steering/power-assisted systems

The benefits of power assistance

MANY LARGER CARS are fitted with power-assisted steering as standard equipment. It reduces the effort needed to turn the steering wheel and it makes manoeuvring at low speed—when parking in a confined space, for instance—much easier than with conventional steering.

Power assistance may also contribute to safety. With conventional steering, some steering wheels may be wrenched out of a driver's grip if a tyre bursts or if the car hits a large bump. Power-assisted steering reduces the steering wheel 'kicking back' and can help the driver to correct a sudden swerve.

Most systems use hydraulic fluid or a light oil, supplied under pressure by an engine-driven pump from a separate hydraulic tank. If the system fails, the car can still be steered manually. When the steering is 'at rest'—that is, not being moved in either direction—the fluid passes through two equal-sized ports, giving equal pressure to both sides of a piston in a ram connected to the linkage.

Movement of the steering wheel first takes up a small amount of slack, which is used to open one port and close the other.

The fluid then applies pressure to one side of the piston, which moves the steering linkage in the required direction. Ideally, the amount of fluid pressure applied to the piston should depend on the force applied to the steering wheel by the driver; but because of design limitations, many systems have a time lag and respond to steering-wheel movement rather than effort.

The main components of the system are the pump which supplies the fluid, driven either by an extension on the generator or by a V-belt, sensing valves operated by movement of the steering wheel or by deflection of the road wheels, the ram and piston assembly, and connecting pipes.

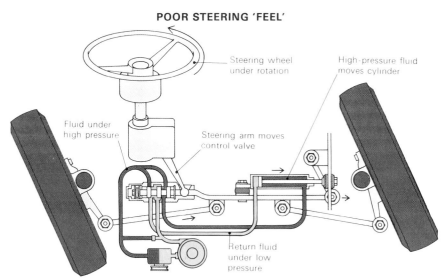

POOR STEERING 'FEEL'

The kind of power assistance common on larger vehicles lacks steering 'feel' and precision because it has to have many joints and linkages

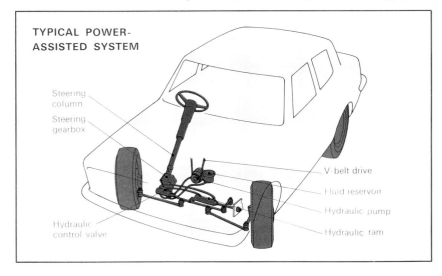

TYPICAL POWER-ASSISTED SYSTEM

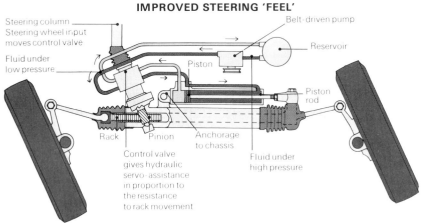

IMPROVED STEERING 'FEEL'

Power assistance combined with rack-and-pinion or quill-shaft drive and pinion is proportionate to road-wheel resistance and so gives good steering 'feel'

The Adwest power-assisted system

IN THE Adwest power-assisted rack-and-pinion steering system, the hydraulic assisting pressure is controlled and directed by a rotary valve.

Rotation of the steering column turns this control valve, directing the hydraulic pressure to one side or the other of a piston mounted on the rack member itself.

This hydraulic pressure then moves the rack member to the left or right, augmenting the effort applied by the driver to the steering wheel.

A torsion bar connecting the steering column to the valve ensures that the assistance provided varies with the resistance of the tyres to steering.

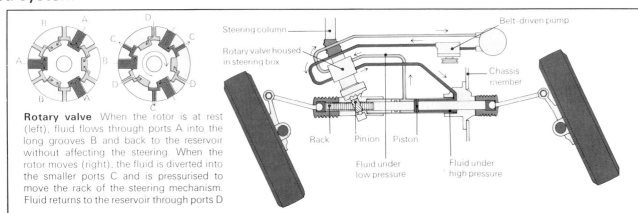

Rotary valve When the rotor is at rest (left), fluid flows through ports A into the long grooves B and back to the reservoir without affecting the steering. When the rotor moves (right), the fluid is diverted into the smaller ports C and is pressurised to move the rack of the steering mechanism. Fluid returns to the reservoir through ports D

Cornering

Effects of oversteering and understeering

ADHESION between the tyres and the road makes it possible to steer a car around curves; it is persuaded to leave a straight path by the lateral (sideways) forces applied to it by the rolling tyres.

Because a tyre is flexible and springy, the direction in which it rolls on a curve diverges to some extent from the direction in which the wheel is pointed. This divergence is called the slip angle, although it would be more accurately described as creep, or drift.

At low speeds and on gentle curves, the slip angles are small; sharp, fast cornering results in much larger slip angles up to a breakaway point when the tyre slides sideways in a skid. Slip angles also depend upon tyre design, inflation pressure, the load carried by the tyre, wheel camber and other factors, such as road surface conditions.

A car is said to understeer when the slip angles of the front tyres are greater than those of the rear tyres; the car tries to run wide on a bend in the road and the driver has to correct this by extra movement of the steering wheel.

An oversteering car is one in which the slip angles at the rear are greater than those at the front; the car responds eagerly to the steering and will require less initial steering-wheel movement. Neutral steer means equal front and rear slip angles.

Most cars are designed to give moderate understeer in normal driving conditions; but their behaviour will often change to neutral steer and then to oversteer if cornering speeds are progressively increased. A sharp transition to oversteer can be dangerous.

Front-wheel-drive cars (and high-performance rear-drive cars) are also sensitive to the way that the driver uses the accelerator, because this affects slip angles.

Although understeer and oversteer are most easily explained in relation to cornering, their influence on a car's behaviour when holding a straight course is equally important. A car that is being driven along a straight road is often subjected to sideways forces—for example, a gust of wind or a change in road camber. The response of an understeering car is stable—that is, self-correcting—but an oversteering car is unstable and requires continual correction by the driver.

The higher the speed, the less time there is for correction by steering, so that beyond a certain speed (depending upon the road conditions and the skill of the driver), all directional control may be lost.

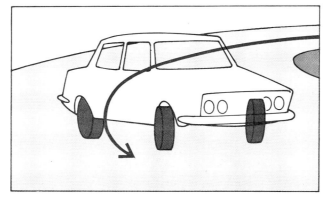

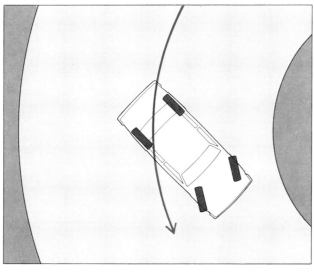

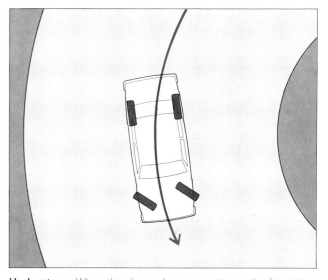

Oversteer Centrifugal force tends to move the car sideways when cornering. If the rear-tyre slip angles are greater than those of the front tyres, the car will turn more sharply than the driver intends. The tail will move outwards and the car may become difficult to control. Angular position of car and wheels are deliberately exaggerated

Understeer When the slip angles are greater on the front tyres than on the rear, understeer will cause the car to turn less sharply than intended, the car will 'run wide' on a curve. A moderate amount of understeer is an advantage, as it gives the car good directional stability, particularly at high speed on long straight runs

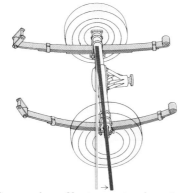

Suspension effects on steering Semi-elliptic spring suspension can affect steering when cornering. The axle is slewed by centrifugal force, causing the outside spring to flatten, and the inside spring curves more deeply because of sideways weight transfer

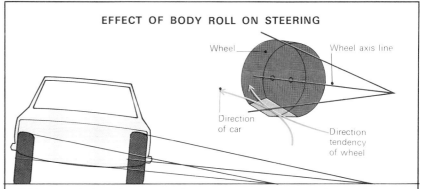

EFFECT OF BODY ROLL ON STEERING

With some independent suspensions, body roll on sharp corners affects the camber of the wheels so that they 'lean with the car'. The wheels then tend to roll in circles, each with its centre where an extension of the axis meets the ground, just as a cone lying on a flat surface will circle about its apex. This has an understeering effect, as the wheels roll away from the corner

Electrics/the complete system

Wires colour-coded for identification

The modern car has about 200 ft of wire joining its electrical components. All the wiring, with the exception of earth straps, battery leads and high-tension ignition leads, is colour-coded. The coding is standardised in most British cars to allow quick recognition of the different circuits when any repairs are necessary. The battery acts as a reservoir to supply current to the system when the engine is not running; when it is running above tick-over, the generator supplies all the car's needs and recharges the battery. Only a few parts of the electrical system are needed to keep the car's engine running: the remainder operate the lights, windscreen wipers and other accessories. Some of these are required by law, such as the horn, but many others are fitted as standard. Older cars have a

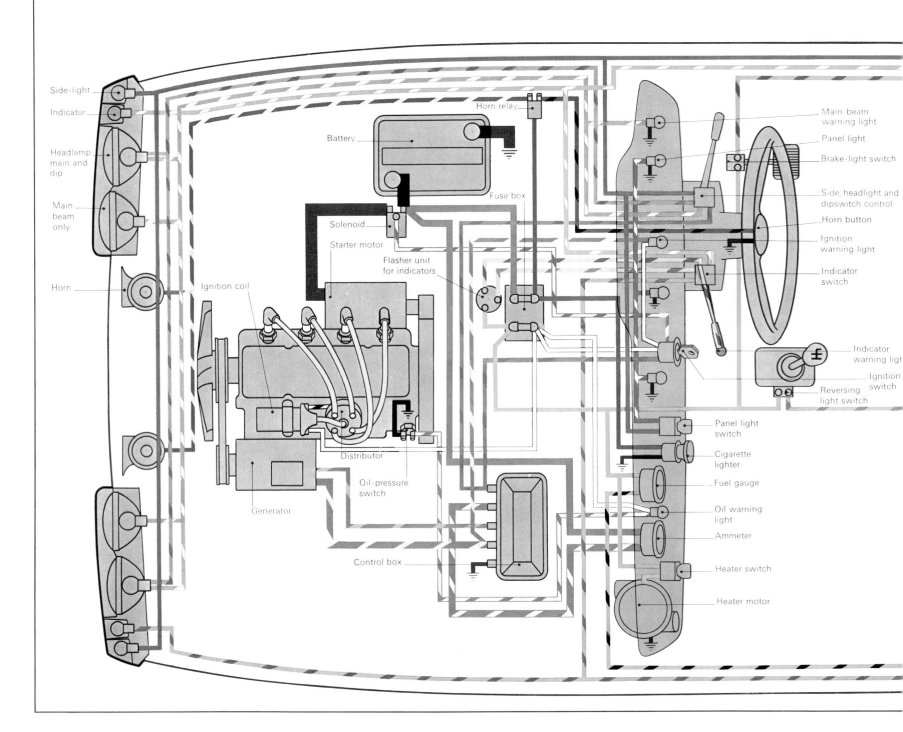

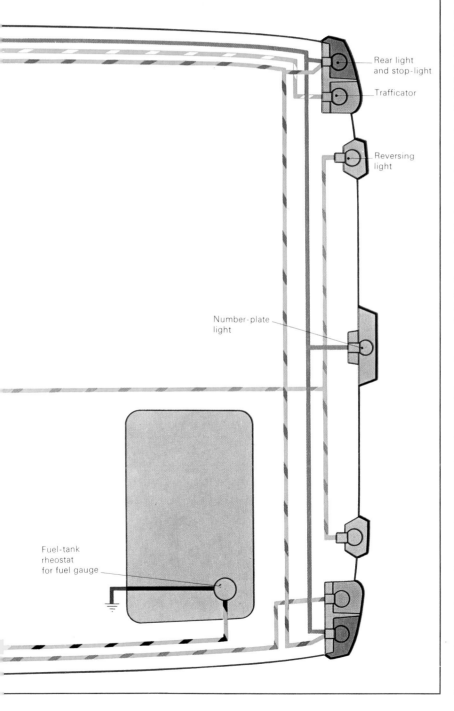

separate starter button, but on modern cars the wiring runs to the ignition switch. In the wiring diagram below, the windscreen wiper motor has been deliberately left out. This is because there are several different types of motor in use—single speed, two-speed and intermittent—and the wiring varies according to the type. The live wire supplying the wiper motor, however, is always green

Rear light and stop-light

Trafficator

Reversing light

Number-plate light

Fuel-tank rheostat for fuel gauge

How different circuits are wired

CURRENT for a car's electrical system is supplied by the battery when the engine is not running, and by the generator. The generator is often a dynamo on older models; but on most modern cars, an alternator is fitted, as it more easily supplies the current needed for the ever-increasing number of electrical accessories.

All the current is at the voltage of the battery (usually 12 volts) or the generator (approx. $15\frac{1}{2}$ volts), except the current to the spark-plugs, which is boosted by the ignition system to as much as 30,000 volts as required.

One of the main functions of the electrical system is to provide ignition, in the form of a spark, to the compressed petrol/air mixture in the cylinders. Another is to start the engine with the starter motor.

A car's electrical system is divided into circuits, all with different basic functions and different controls. They are: the ignition circuit; the starter circuit; the charging circuit; the lighting circuit; and accessories circuits, which are sometimes controlled by the ignition switch, and in most cases are protected by a fuse. A blown fuse, more often than not, is a symptom of

trouble elsewhere than in the fuse itself, such as the overloading of a circuit, assuming the correct fuse is fitted.

The electrical components in a car are connected through switches to one side of the battery. The other side of the battery is connected to the car body or chassis. In this way the circuit to any component is completed through the body of the car, which becomes one 'wire' of the circuit, the earth return.

This method of earthing not only saves the cost of about 100 ft of copper wire, but also reduces the possibility of disconnections and simplifies fault finding and the fitting of extras.

Different thicknesses of wire are used to enable the required current to pass without causing overheating of the wire. The connection between the starter motor and the battery, for instance, is extremely thick in comparison with the other wiring because it has to carry a much higher current—up to 300 to 400 amp.

Circuit diagrams in car handbooks and workshop manuals are not always easy to follow, although the symbols used are standard in most of them.

Diagrams bear little or no relationship to the actual positions of wiring or components in the car and, for reasons of space, are considerably abbreviated. But such diagrams show all accessories fitted as standard equipment.

Cable colours are usually indicated by letters, and a coding table is then given to permit easy identification.

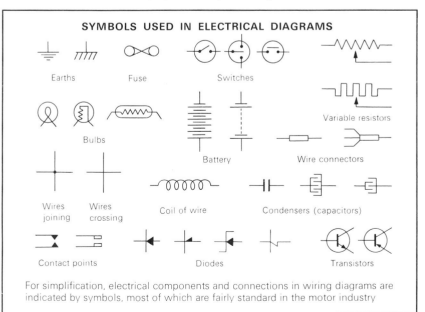

SYMBOLS USED IN ELECTRICAL DIAGRAMS

Earths   Fuse   Switches   Variable resistors

Bulbs   Battery   Wire connectors

Wires joining   Wires crossing   Coil of wire   Condensers (capacitors)

Contact points   Diodes   Transistors

For simplification, electrical components and connections in wiring diagrams are indicated by symbols, most of which are fairly standard in the motor industry

Electrics/starter motor

Current from the battery rotates the engine

THE JOB of the starter motor is to turn the engine until it fires and can continue to run under its own power.

Most petrol engines have to be rotated at least 50 rpm to start them. This needs considerable electric power, particularly in winter when the engine is cold and the oil is thick. Anyone who has started a car with a cranking handle will know how much effort is needed to turn the engine.

The starter motor imposes the biggest drain of any electrical component on the car battery. The instant it operates, it can draw as much as 300 to 400 amp. In just three seconds it can drain as much current from the battery as would last a parking light for a full hour. Because of this high current, the starter motor needs a heavy-duty switch and is connected to the battery by a thick, heavy cable.

At the same time as it works the starter motor, the battery must supply current to the ignition system to generate the sparks. This demand on it can lead to difficulty in starting if the battery is failing. The starter motor may drain so much current from a battery in poor condition that the ignition system cannot work at peak efficiency, and so fails to generate a high enough voltage to cross the spark-plug points.

The starter motor turns the engine's crankshaft through a pair of gear wheels. One, the pinion, is mounted on the starter-motor shaft. It engages with the other, a toothed ring fitted around the edge of the flywheel, which rotates the crankshaft.

The gear ratio between these two is generally about 10:1—that is, the turning effort of the starter motor is multiplied ten times. The starter motor's pinion must disengage from the flywheel gear when the engine fires, or the engine would drive the motor. The most common mechanism for this purpose is the Bendix drive.

CROSS-SECTION OF STARTER MOTOR

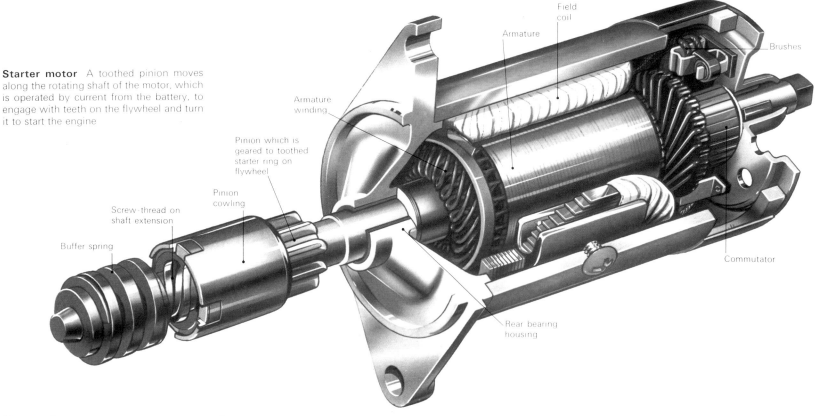

Starter motor A toothed pinion moves along the rotating shaft of the motor, which is operated by current from the battery, to engage with teeth on the flywheel and turn it to start the engine

Field coil

Armature

Brushes

Armature winding

Pinion which is geared to toothed starter ring on flywheel

Pinion cowling

Screw-thread on shaft extension

Buffer spring

Commutator

Rear bearing housing

How the starter motor works

THE STARTER MOTOR operates on the same principle as any other electric motor—it makes use of movement between magnets. If two magnets are held close together, the two like poles (two north or two south poles) push each other apart, and the unlike poles (a north and a south) attract each other.

An electric motor contains electro-magnets—coils of wire wound on soft iron cores. Electricity flowing through each coil magnetises the core, setting up a magnetic field which has north and south poles. A starter motor has a fixed set of coils, generally four, spaced round the inside of the motor body. These are the field coils. Free to rotate inside them is the armature, which consists of a series of coils, each joined to a pair of the insulated copper segments that make up the armature's commutator. When current flows through an armature coil, this coil also behaves as a magnet.

Current is fed by stationary brushes (which make contact with the commutator) to an armature coil. Attraction and repulsion between the magnetic fields of the field coils and the armature coil cause the armature to rotate.

As soon as the commutator begins to rotate, the brushes make contact with the next pair of copper segments, which are connected to another armature coil. This results in further rotation. The action is repeated in sequence as each pair of commutator segments makes contact with the brushes. In this way, the armature continues to spin as the brushes feed current to each armature coil.

The starter motor needs no control unit; the same connection to it supplies both the armature and the field windings and is wired in such a way that it draws from the battery as much current as it requires to turn the engine, and no more.

THE STARTER SIMPLIFIED

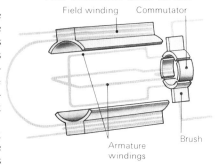

Field winding   Commutator

Armature windings

Brush

Current fed to the armature coil by the brushes and commutator will cause it to rotate between two stationary magnets

Bendix starter drive

ONCE the engine is running, the starter-motor pinion must be disengaged from the flywheel which it has set in motion. This is achieved by having a pinion which fits loosely on a threaded shaft and is free to move along the thread.

When the shaft starts to rotate, the inertia of the pinion (its resistance to being moved) makes it rotate more slowly than the shaft. As a result, the pinion travels along the threaded shaft and engages with the teeth on the flywheel. Once engaged, it rotates the flywheel which, since it is bolted to the crankshaft, turns the engine.

When the engine starts to run under its own power, the flywheel gear starts to drive the pinion instead of being driven by it. Once the driven speed of the pinion exceeds that of the starter-motor shaft, the pinion screws itself back along the shaft, out of engagement. It is flung out of mesh as soon as the engine fires.

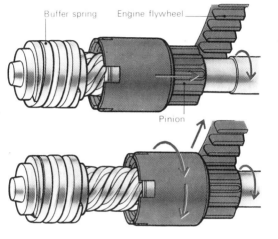

Bendix drive Shaft begins to turn; pinion turns more slowly and is screwed forward to engage with the flywheel

Pinion at end of screw-thread engages with flywheel so that starter-motor shaft, pinion and flywheel rotate together

When engine fires, flywheel drives pinion faster than shaft, screwing it back along thread and out of engagement

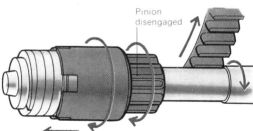

Pre-engaged starter drive

SOME MAKES of car use a mechanical lever, linked to the starter pedal or switch, to engage the pinion with the flywheel before the starter motor begins to turn. A small overrun clutch between the motor shaft and the pinion disconnects the pinion from the starter motor when the engine starts.

This prevents the engine driving the starter-motor armature at a very high speed and so damaging it.

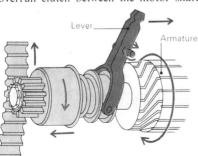

Pre-engaged starter An overrun clutch allows pinion to turn with flywheel

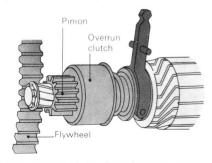

Lever releases pinion from flywheel when the starter switch is released

Starter switch

SINCE the starter motor uses high current, the switch that operates it must also be able to pass high current. To do this it needs heavy-duty contacts.

On old cars, the heavy-duty switch was generally mounted on the starter motor and worked by a cable pulled by the driver. On most modern cars, the switch is worked by a relay or solenoid, in which a strong electromagnet pulls the heavy-duty contacts together. The starter solenoid, which needs only a low current, is in turn operated by a smaller switch mounted near the driver or incorporated with the ignition switch.

The electrical leads from the battery to the solenoid and from the solenoid to the starter motor must be thick and heavy and securely fastened to carry the high current involved. On the other hand, the lead to the driver's switch, which passes only low current, can be thin and light.

THE SOLENOID SWITCH

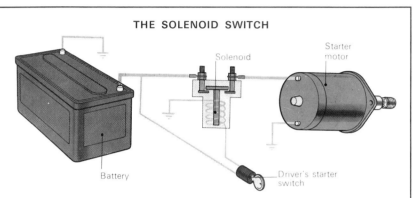

The solenoid is a relay device that enables heavy current from the battery to the starter motor to be controlled safely by the driver, using a light-duty switch

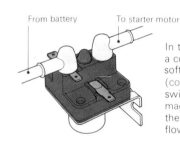

In the solenoid switch (left and below), a coil of many turns of wire encloses a soft iron plunger. When electricity (controlled by the driver's starter switch) flows through the coil, its magnetism moves the plunger, closing the contacts and allowing current to flow from the battery to the starter motor

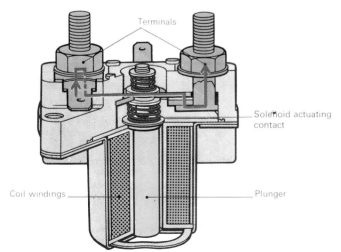

Sectional view of solenoid, showing coil windings, plunger and cable terminals

Electrics/generators

Producing current for the electrical system

ALL CARS are fitted with a generator, without which the electrical demands of a modern car could drain a fully charged battery in just over an hour.

The generator may be either a dynamo, which produces direct current (DC), or an alternator, which produces alternating current (AC).

An alternator can produce more current than a dynamo of the same size, and charge the battery when the engine is idling. This gives it an advantage in heavy traffic and permits the use of extra accessories. But a battery is charged by DC current only, so an alternator needs a rectifier to convert AC into DC current.

Both the dynamo and the alternator generate current through the movement of an armature. The generator windings in a dynamo are inside the armature and move with it; those of the alternator are outside the armature, and are stationary.

Because of the difficulty in passing current from the armature, with its complicated windings, and of cooling the moving armature, a dynamo's maximum output is limited to about 30 amp. and its maximum speed to about 6000 rpm.

For engines whose maximum speed is 6000 rpm, the dynamo is made to turn at the same speed as the engine.

But a generator rotating at below 1200 rpm will not produce sufficient current to charge the battery; so when an engine is idling, at say 600 rpm, the battery will not be charged by a dynamo.

An alternator presents no major cooling problem because its generating windings are stationary. It can be designed to produce more than 45 amp. and, since the armature is less complicated, it can turn at over 12,000 rpm. When an engine is idling at 600 rpm, the alternator, driven by a pulley that is smaller than the engine's pulley, turns at 1200 rpm—fast enough to charge the battery.

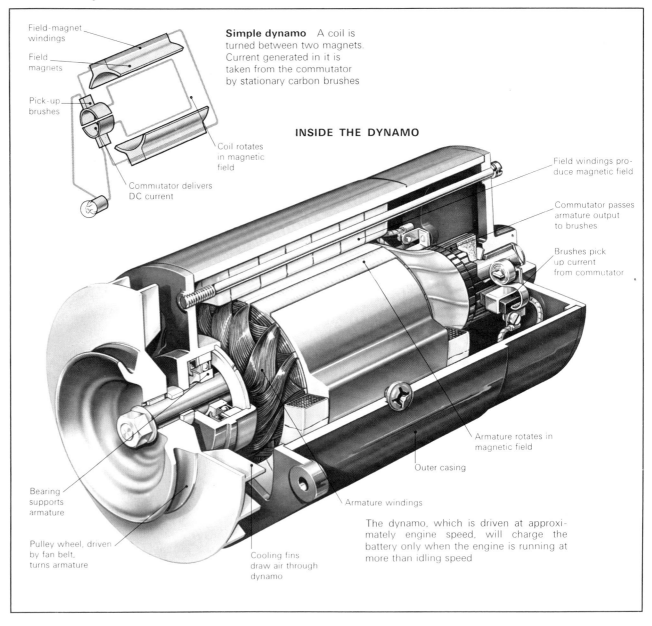

Simple dynamo A coil is turned between two magnets. Current generated in it is taken from the commutator by stationary carbon brushes

Field-magnet windings

Field magnets

Pick-up brushes

Coil rotates in magnetic field

Commutator delivers DC current

INSIDE THE DYNAMO

Field windings produce magnetic field

Commutator passes armature output to brushes

Brushes pick up current from commutator

Armature rotates in magnetic field

Outer casing

Armature windings

Bearing supports armature

Pulley wheel, driven by fan belt, turns armature

Cooling fins draw air through dynamo

The dynamo, which is driven at approximately engine speed, will charge the battery only when the engine is running at more than idling speed

How the dynamo generates current

THE DYNAMO consists of a round outer casing with two stationary electromagnets, known as field magnets, opposite each other inside it. Between the magnets is an armature, generally containing 28 separate coils of wire. The ends of each coil are joined to copper segments that make up the commutator. The armature is mounted on bearings and is driven by the fan belt. In contact with the commutator are two stationary carbon brushes.

When current is passed through the stationary field windings, a magnetic field is created.

As the armature revolves in the magnetic field, a current is generated in the armature windings. This current leaves each winding through the commutator and the carbon brushes in contact with it. One brush always receives negative current, the other positive, so that the output is DC.

The amount of current generated depends on the speed at which the armature is turning and on the strength of the field

magnets. The magnetic field will vary according to the amount of current the field magnets receive.

When the dynamo is charging a low battery, or when the headlights and other high-current consuming components are in use, it can take more than half of one horsepower to turn the armature at the necessary speed. A slack fan belt will slip, this will stop the dynamo from producing sufficient current, and the battery will gradually discharge.

How the alternator works

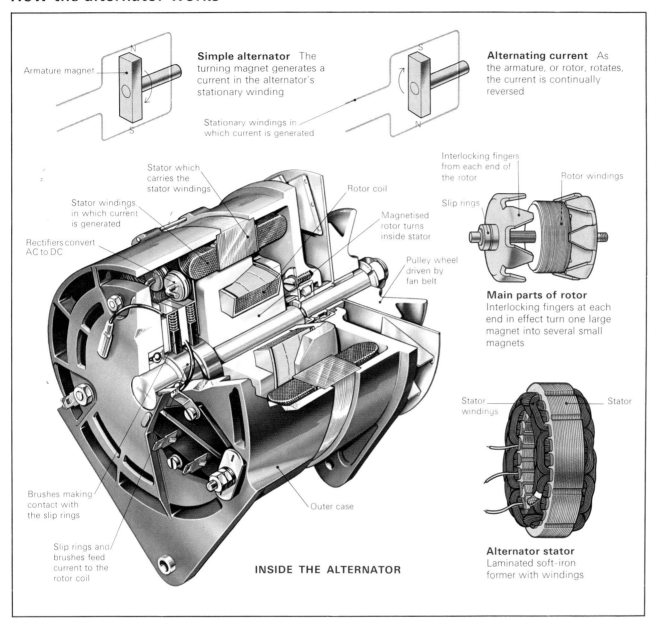

Simple alternator The turning magnet generates a current in the alternator's stationary winding

Armature magnet

Stationary windings in which current is generated

Alternating current As the armature, or rotor, rotates, the current is continually reversed

Stator which carries the stator windings

Stator windings in which current is generated

Rectifiers convert AC to DC

Rotor coil

Magnetised rotor turns inside stator

Pulley wheel driven by fan belt

Brushes making contact with the slip rings

Slip rings and brushes feed current to the rotor coil

Outer case

INSIDE THE ALTERNATOR

Interlocking fingers from each end of the rotor

Rotor windings

Slip rings

Main parts of rotor
Interlocking fingers at each end in effect turn one large magnet into several small magnets

Stator windings

Stator

Alternator stator
Laminated soft-iron former with windings

THE ALTERNATOR has its generating windings on the inside of a stationary soft-iron ring—the stator. The armature, more properly called a rotor, is mounted on bearings inside the stator, and is driven by the fan belt.

The armature contains only one winding, or coil, with each end connected to a separate slip ring. Current is fed to the slip rings through two small stationary carbon brushes; and when current flows through the armature coil it turns into a magnet—one end becoming the north pole, the other the south pole.

Current is generated in the stator winding when a magnet passes each stator coil; and the more magnets passing each coil in a given time, the higher the current generated. The armature, though a single magnet, behaves like a set of magnets; for its ends are formed into metal fingers, each of which becomes a magnet. These fingers interlock but do not touch.

Unlike the dynamo, an alternator has no commutator to ensure that its output is DC. As a succession of north and south poles passes each stator winding, they generate alternately positive and negative current in the winding.

This AC current is changed into the DC current needed to charge a battery by one-way electronic valves known as diodes, or rectifiers, which are built into the alternator. Some pass only negative and others pass only positive current, so that the final output to the terminals is DC.

Before the advent of the semi-conductor diode, or transistor, rectifiers were very large and difficult to cool. This meant that alternators could be used only on large commercial vehicles.

An alternator limits its own current output. The rectifiers, which will not pass current in reverse, do the job of the cut-out. For this reason the alternator needs only voltage regulation and the control box, fully transistorised, is often fitted in the alternator casing.

Control unit regulates output

BECAUSE the dynamo's output increases with engine speed, it has to be regulated by a control unit. The unit limits the output to about $15\frac{1}{2}$ volts, so that the battery is not over-charged or electrical components damaged.

The control unit also limits the current, to prevent damage to the generator itself; and, by means of a cut-out switch, it stops the battery discharging itself back through the dynamo. An alternator limits its own current output.

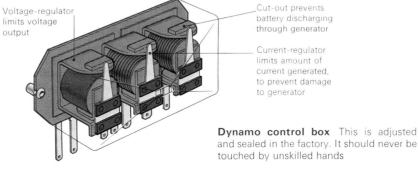

Voltage-regulator limits voltage output

Cut-out prevents battery discharging through generator

Current-regulator limits amount of current generated, to prevent damage to generator

Dynamo control box This is adjusted and sealed in the factory. It should never be touched by unskilled hands

Electrics/headlamps

Reflectors and bulbs

ALL CARS have at least two headlamps working together. The headlamp system provides two types of light beam: a main beam to give maximum light well ahead of the car, and a dipped beam which is shorter and lower so that it will not dazzle oncoming drivers, and can be used in fog.

Separate filaments in a single bulb in each headlamp provide the main and dipped beams. In a four-headlamp system, the extra lamps are usually main beam only and are extinguished when the dip-switch is operated.

All headlamps have a method of controlling or shaping the light beam. The light source is generally a tungsten filament, either in a bulb or inside a sealed-beam headlamp unit. The beam is shaped by a reflector and prisms in the front glass lens.

With twin filaments, that of the main beam is generally located at the focus point of the reflector, to give a straight-ahead parallel beam. The dipped-beam filament is either located off-centre, or shielded so that it uses only half the reflector, to give a downward-sloping, broader beam.

Headlamp units are fitted in the car in such a way that, by screwing spring-loaded mountings in or out, the light beam can be moved for accurate setting.

SEALED-BEAM UNIT

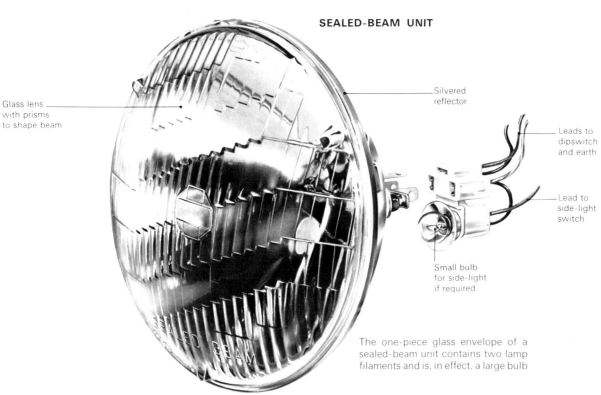

Glass lens with prisms to shape beam

Silvered reflector

Leads to dipswitch and earth

Lead to side-light switch

Small bulb for side-light if required

The one-piece glass envelope of a sealed-beam unit contains two lamp filaments and is, in effect, a large bulb

Dipped-beam filament

Main-beam filament

Bulb contact

Cut-away in flange for exact location

The cut-away in the flange of a pre-focus bulb ensures that it is correctly located and focused

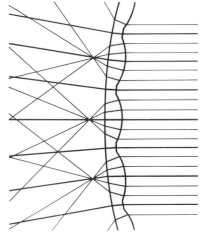

Glass lens Prisms are formed in the glass to give the beam the required shape

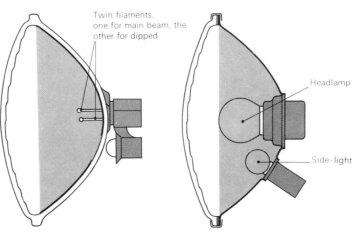

Twin filaments, one for main beam, the other for dipped

Headlamp

Side-light

Sealed headlamp Lens, reflector and twin filaments are combined in a single unit

Ordinary headlamp Lens, reflector and plug-in bulb(s) are fitted as separate units

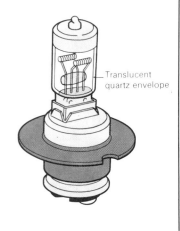

Translucent quartz envelope

Quartz-halogen bulbs These are obtainable for fitting into pre-focused units in place of ordinary bulbs. They give a brighter, more powerful light than tungsten-filament bulbs

The bulb that is a complete lamp

UNTIL a few years ago, most headlamps consisted of a bulb mounted in a metal reflector behind a glass lens. With time and use, the bulbs blackened and the reflectors became tarnished.

The modern headlamp consists of an all-glass sealed unit containing two filaments, but without a bulb. The back of the unit is silvered to form a reflector, and the front glass is moulded in the shape of a lens. In effect, the unit is a large bulb which is sealed for life against the entry of dirt or damp.

In a two-headlamp system most sealed-beam units have a 60 watt filament for the main beam and a 45 watt filament for the dipped beam. More powerful units are available. Generally, a sealed-beam lamp can be fitted without wiring changes to replace the older removable-bulb lamp.

Quartz-halogen bulbs

QUARTZ-HALOGEN BULBS, sometimes called tungsten-halogen, which have a greater light output than ordinary tungsten-filament bulbs, were originally made with only one filament, and a solenoid was required to move the bulb or reflector to dip the beam. For this reason quartz-halogen bulbs were usually found in spot lamps or in fog lamps. Today's twin-filament halogen headlamp bulbs are interchangeable with ordinary bulbs. These are now available as sealed-beam units.

Quartz-halogen bulbs do not suffer from blackening as ordinary bulbs do. The outer envelope is made of quartz, not glass, and filled with halogen gas. It should not be handled with bare fingers, because salt (a content of body perspiration) can stain the quartz; if this happens, the bulb should be wiped carefully with methylated spirit.

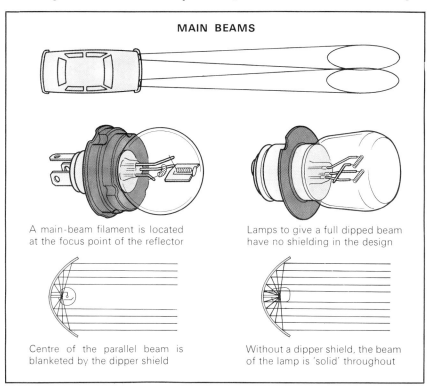

MAIN BEAMS

A main-beam filament is located at the focus point of the reflector

Lamps to give a full dipped beam have no shielding in the design

Centre of the parallel beam is blanketed by the dipper shield

Without a dipper shield, the beam of the lamp is 'solid' throughout

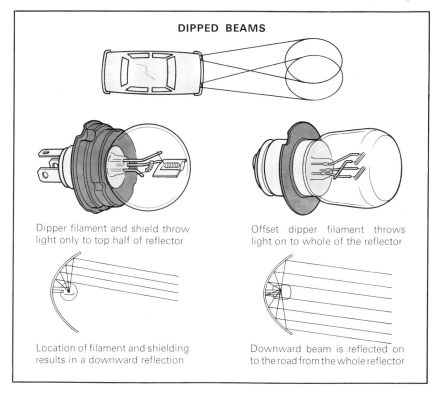

DIPPED BEAMS

Dipper filament and shield throw light only to top half of reflector

Offset dipper filament throws light on to whole of the reflector

Location of filament and shielding results in a downward reflection

Downward beam is reflected on to the road from the whole reflector

Beam patterns for fog and fast driving

FOG LAMPS, which are useful in fog, sea mist, low cloud and even snow, can be fitted as accessories (see p. 286).

So can high-intensity spot-lamps, which have all their available light concentrated into a narrow beam to give maximum penetration and range—essential requirements for fast driving on unlit roads.

Fog lamps are designed to produce a wide beam with a sharp cut-off at the top. This enables the driver to see the nearside kerb and the cats' eyes at the centre of the road. It also helps him to keep his sense of direction, as it is easy to become disorientated in fog if only one part of the road can be seen.

For best visibility, the brightest part of the beam should be high up A lamp with a large diameter and a deep reflector will give a brighter beam. Wherever they are mounted, fog lamps should be aimed so that the top of the beam reaches the road about 30 ft ahead of the car.

Some fog lamps produce a yellow-tinted light which can help reduce glare. This colouring is a matter of driver preference, and unless a sealed-beam unit has been fitted, the bulb can easily be changed.

A yellow transparent paint can be bought and used on the lens to produce the same effect. But there is no basis for the belief that a yellow beam gives better visibility than a white one—except, possibly, in light mist.

A spot-lamp, which will give a concentrated beam, can be aimed well to the left and just above the top of the dipped headlamp beam (see Lighting law, p. 330).

As it is illegal to use a single spot-lamp except when the headlights are on, a single spot-lamp is usually wired into the dipped-beam circuit. The spot-lamp can be turned off by a separate switch.

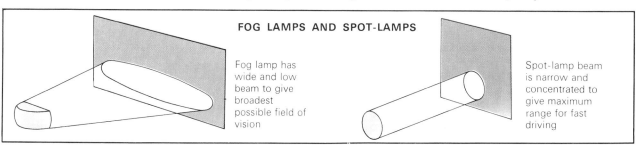

FOG LAMPS AND SPOT-LAMPS

Fog lamp has wide and low beam to give broadest possible field of vision

Spot-lamp beam is narrow and concentrated to give maximum range for fast driving

Electrics/secondary units

Side and rear lights

MOST CARS ARE REQUIRED by law to have headlamps, side-lights, rear lights, stop-lights, rear reflectors, flashing trafficators and a lamp to illuminate the rear number plate.

Side-lights are incorporated in the headlamp housing on a few cars. But most have them either separate or mounted in the same housings as the flashing turn-indicators, with separate filaments for the side-light and the indicator in each bulb.

Similarly, the rear and stop-lights can be entirely separate, but usually they are incorporated into a single bulb containing two filaments.

One filament has a low wattage (6) for the rear lamp and a higher wattage (usually 21) for the stop-light. Both rear and stop-lights can be mounted in the same housing as the rear flashing turn-indicators.

Rear lamps are enclosed by red lenses, so that even when they are switched off they give a red reflection from an approaching car's headlights.

Turn-indicators have amber lenses at front and rear and should flash between 60 and 120 times a minute to comply with legal requirements.

On most cars the side, rear and number-plate lights are all controlled by a single switch. This is wired independently of the ignition switch, so that these lights can be switched on when the car is parked in the road at night.

Side, rear and turn-indicator light bulbs have a single bayonet fitting. Twin-filament rear stop-light bulbs always have bayonet fitting caps with their pins offset so that they cannot be fitted the wrong way.

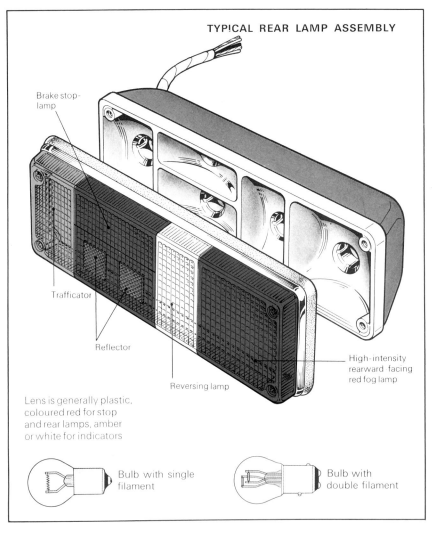

TYPICAL REAR LAMP ASSEMBLY

Brake stop-lamp

Trafficator

Reflector

Reversing lamp

High-intensity rearward facing red fog lamp

Lens is generally plastic, coloured red for stop and rear lamps, amber or white for indicators

Bulb with single filament

Bulb with double filament

Flashing indicators

ALL MODERN cars have flashing turn-indicator lights at the front and rear. Some also have small repeater flashers on each side of the car. Other repeater lights inside the car act as a reminder to the driver that the indicators are switched on.

The device which causes the lights to flash is called the flasher unit. When the switch is operated, current from the battery passes through a circuit which includes a taut resistance wire.

The current heats the resistance wire, causing it to expand, and this allows a set of contacts to close.

Current then ceases to be limited by the resistance wire, and passes through the indicator bulbs to light them.

As soon as the bulbs light, the resistance wire begins to cool and contract. This opens the points again and switches off the lights. This cycle continues at between 60

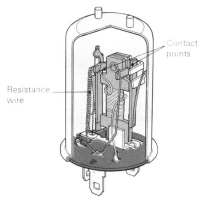

Contact points

Resistance wire

Flasher unit Resistance wire controls contact points by expansion and contraction

Electric and air horns

MOST SMALL production cars have a simple diaphragm-type horn. Others have a wind-tone horn, usually fitted in pairs to larger models. Air horns can be fitted as an extra.

The diaphragm and wind-tone horns work in a similar way. An electric current passes through a pair of contact points, making and collapsing a magnetic field, which causes a diaphragm to vibrate.

Different noises are produced in the diaphragm-type horn by variation in the size of the diaphragm, and in the wind-tone type by varying the shape of the horn. Air under pressure is supplied to the air horn by an electric pump; this causes a diaphragm to vibrate at high frequency

It is illegal to fit horns in such a way that they emit a 'two tone' note, such as those used by ambulances.

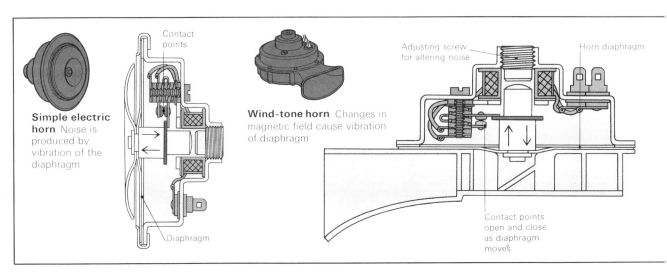

Contact points

Simple electric horn Noise is produced by vibration of the diaphragm

Diaphragm

Wind-tone horn Changes in magnetic field cause vibration of diaphragm

Adjusting screw for altering noise

Horn diaphragm

Contact points open and close as diaphragm moves

Windscreen wipers

and 120 times a minute until the switch is cancelled, either automatically, as in most cars, or by the driver.

The indicator switch on most cars is fitted on the steering column and has a self-cancelling device worked by the steering. This device consists of a small peg fitted into the steering shaft.

When the indicator switch is operated, a small flexible lever is moved into the path of the peg.

The lever is able to flex and pass over the peg when the steering wheel is moved in the direction indicated; but when the steering is turned back to the straight-ahead position, the peg moves the lever, switching off the indicator.

The flasher unit can be so wired that, from a separate switch, all four lights flash simultaneously as a hazard warning that the car has broken down.

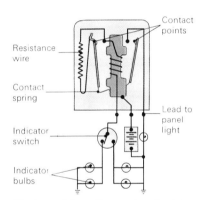

Flasher wiring Contraction of resistance wire causes contact points to open

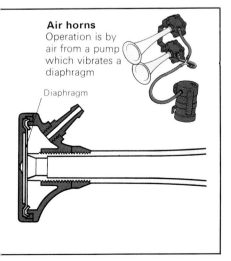

Air horns
Operation is by air from a pump which vibrates a diaphragm

Diaphragm

WIPER MOTOR WITH FLEXIBLE DRIVE

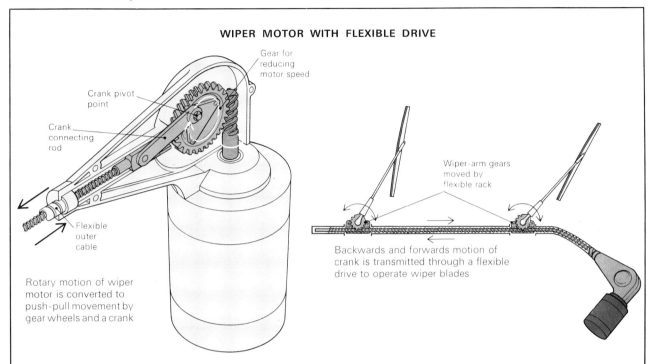

Gear for reducing motor speed

Crank pivot point

Crank connecting rod

Flexible outer cable

Rotary motion of wiper motor is converted to push-pull movement by gear wheels and a crank

Wiper-arm gears moved by flexible rack

Backwards and forwards motion of crank is transmitted through a flexible drive to operate wiper blades

Windscreen wipers are worked by a small electric motor. It turns a crank unit which converts the rotary movement of the motor into the push-pull movement required to operate the wiper blades. The size of the crank and in some designs the mechanical drive influences the sweep of the blades. As well as the wiper switch on the instrument panel, there is a switch attached to the crank unit. When the driver switches off the wipers, they continue to operate until they reach the park position. It is this two-switch arrangement which parks the blades.

Some wiper motors also have a thermostatic unit, so that if the wipers are stuck in any position because of ice or snow, the motor will not burn out in attempting to move them. Two-speed motors provide a second, higher speed of wiping for storm conditions

WIPER MOTOR WITH DIRECT-ACTING LINKAGE

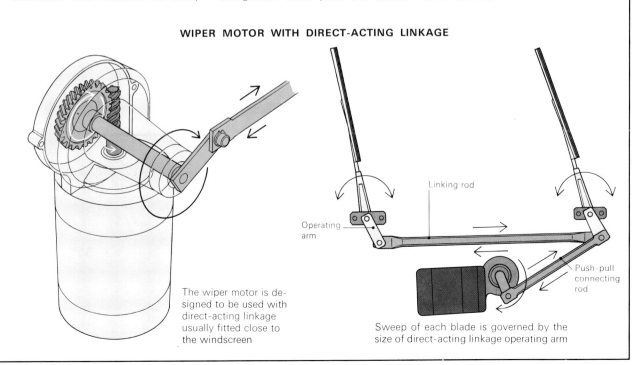

The wiper motor is designed to be used with direct-acting linkage usually fitted close to the windscreen

Linking rod

Operating arm

Push-pull connecting rod

Sweep of each blade is governed by the size of direct-acting linkage operating arm

Electrics/instruments

Dials and lights to help the driver

ONLY ONE of the instruments on a car's instrument panel is required by law: the speedometer. The remainder are there solely for the convenience of the driver.

Most panels have a fuel gauge, a water-temperature gauge and various coloured warning lights. Larger, more expensive cars, and those driven by enthusiasts, have a number of additional instruments to tell the driver more about the efficiency of the engine.

Speedometer
The usual speedometer has a round dial, clearly marked with numbers in tens. Road speed is indicated by a pointer needle.

Another type has a coloured band operated by a revolving drum and moving along a horizontal scale. Some designs of this type have different colours in the band so that the driver, without reading his exact speed, can more quickly tell whether he is below 30 mph, between 30 and 60 mph, or above 60 mph.

Mileage recorder
The speedometer usually incorporates an odometer, a mileage recorder which shows the distance covered. It is geared to the speedometer drive and its reading is shown in an inset in the speedometer dial. Some speedometers give two odometer readings, one showing the total mileage and the other the current journey mileage.

Tachometer
A tachometer, also referred to as a revolution counter, is fitted to many cars, especially sports, fast touring and racing cars. It is operated either electronically or mechanically and shows the speed at which the engine crankshaft is rotating in revolutions (revs) per minute.

The dial is usually marked in units of ten and the reading must be multiplied by 100 to give the rpm.

Water-temperature gauge
The temperature gauge and the fuel gauge commonly found in the modern car work on similar principles. They have different dials, but both usually incorporate a bi-metal strip and a needle.

When current flows through a coil wound around it, the strip is heated and bends because its metals expand at different rates. As the strip bends, the needle linked to it moves over the scale. The amount of current, and so the temperature of the strip, is governed by a sensor unit.

In the temperature gauge the sensor unit

is a thermosistor, an electrical resistance that is sensitive to heat, set into the water jacket. The hotter the water gets, the more current it allows to pass through.

Fuel gauge
The sensor unit for the fuel gauge is a rheostat, or variable resistance, mounted on the petrol tank. A float which rises or falls with the fuel level moves a lever across the variable resistance, changing the amount of current passing through the gauge. The higher the fuel level, the lower is the resistance, the greater the current and the higher the reading. The time the heat takes to affect the bi-metal strip is the factor governing the comparatively slow swing of the needle to its reading when the ignition is first switched on.

Oil-pressure gauge
The oil-pressure gauge shows the pressure of oil in the engine's lubrication system.

A reading noticeably lower than normal may indicate wear in the main bearings or big-end bearings; wear implies wider clearances, which result in lower pressure.

Erratic variations in the reading, or a fall from normal when cornering, indicate that the level in the sump is so low that oil is surging away from the point where it is picked up by the oil pump.

Ammeter
On some cars the ignition warning light is supplemented by an ammeter, to show the rate at which the battery is being charged or discharged.

When the electrical system is working perfectly and the battery is in a reasonable state of charge, the ammeter should show a fairly high reading for the first few minutes while the current used by the starter motor is being replaced in the battery. The reading will then drop back to indicate a low trickle charge.

Battery-condition indicator
Whereas the ammeter measures the rate of flow of electrical current, the battery-condition indicator registers the voltage or electrical charge of the battery. The indicator is wired so that when the ignition is switched on, it records the voltage between the two battery terminals, and hence gives an indication whether there is enough stored energy to allow prolonged parking with lights and a subsequent restart. If after a few miles' motoring the battery indicator still shows a low state of charge, have the battery checked:

THE INSTRUMENT PANEL
The principal instruments—those which must be checked most frequently—are directly in front of the driver, so that his gaze is diverted from the road for the shortest possible time. The law requires a speedometer to be accurate to within 10 per cent at more than 10 mph.

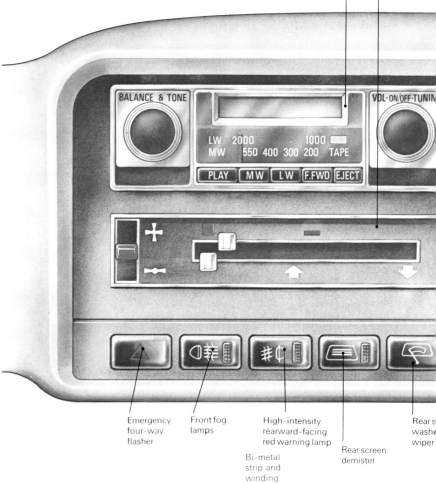

Stereo cassette tape player with MW/LW ra

Heater and demister contro

Emergency four-way flasher

Front fog lamps

High-intensity rearward-facing red warning lamp

Rear screen demister

Rear s washe wiper

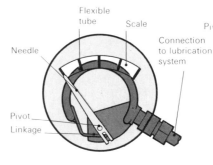

Oil-pressure gauge A flexible tube coiled inside the gauge is connected to the oil lubrication system by a pipe. As oil pressure builds up, the tube tends to uncoil. In doing so, it moves the needle linked to it around the dial, to register the oil pressure

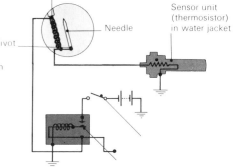

Temperature gauge As the temperature of the coolant changes, a sensor in the water jacket varies the current flowing through a coil heating a bi-metal strip and so moves the dial needle linked to it. A stabiliser ensures constant electrical supply

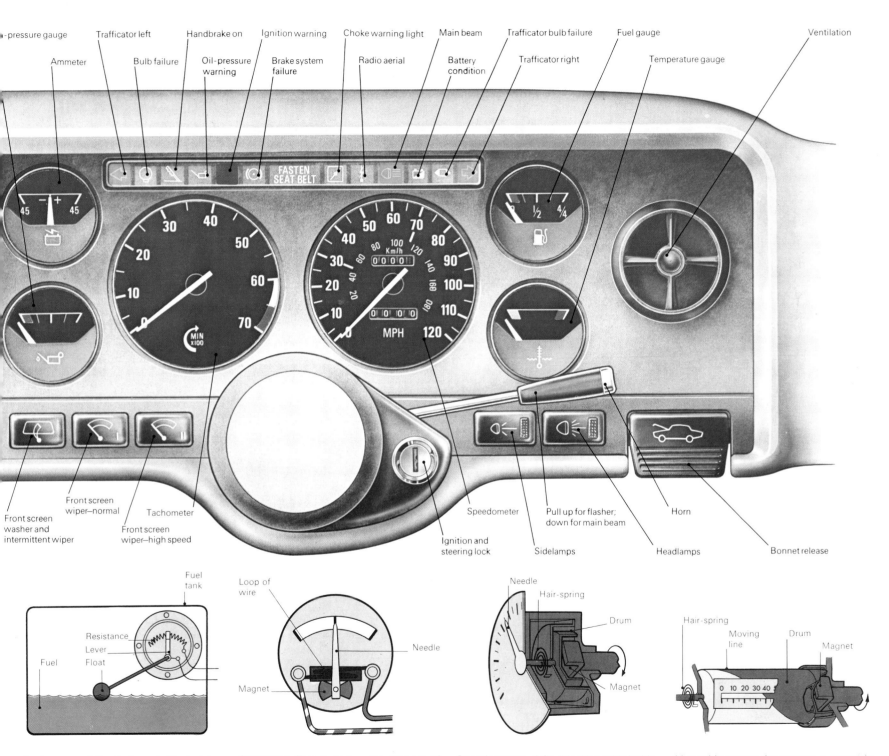

Fuel gauge A float in the petrol tank, rising and falling with the fuel level, moves a lever across a variable resistance. The current passing through the resistance is converted into a reading on the dial of the fuel gauge to indicate the amount of fuel left in the tank

Ammeter This indicates the amount of current flowing to or from the battery. The current passes through a loop, setting up a magnetic force which, dependent on the direction of flow, attracts or repels a magnet to which the ammeter needle is attached

Speedometer A flexible drive cable inside a flexible metal tube connects a front wheel or the gearbox output shaft to the speedo-meter. The drive cable rotates a magnet in a metal drum, and the speed of rotation is converted to indicate the road speed. As the drive cable rotates the magnet, a magnetic force tries to rotate the drum. This is resisted to some extent by a hair-spring; but the faster the rotation, the further the line moves. Some speedometers have a moving line instead of a swinging needle

Bodywork/basic requirements

Functions of the car body

AT ITS SIMPLEST, a car is a beam supported at each end by the wheels. So it has to be strong enough not to sag in the middle—a property called beam stiffness.

A car must also have torsional stiffness: the ability to resist the twisting stresses imposed by any irregular road surface.

Structural strength is also necessary to cope with particular loads, such as the weight of the engine, thrust of the springs and minor impacts. To have a strong structure without too much weight means using the material as efficiently as possible. But strength is not everything: in addition to providing space for the occupants and their luggage, the bodywork must also protect them in an accident.

Too rigid a body will absorb little of the impact energy in a collision, so more will be transmitted to the occupants. On the other hand, a body that is too weak might collapse on to them. For seat-belted occupants, the ideal is an impenetrable, rigid box, with weaker ends, that will absorb impact energy by progressive crumpling and stop the vehicle less suddenly.

The requirements of good performance will also affect the designer's final decision on the shape of his car. The car's movement is opposed by the air it is travelling through, as well as by the rolling resistance of the tyres. This air drag, as it is called, increases proportionately to the square of the speed; for example, if speed is doubled, drag is quadrupled; if speed is trebled, drag is nine times as great.

The effect of drag can be minimised by using a truly aerodynamically shaped body; but that is impracticable because of

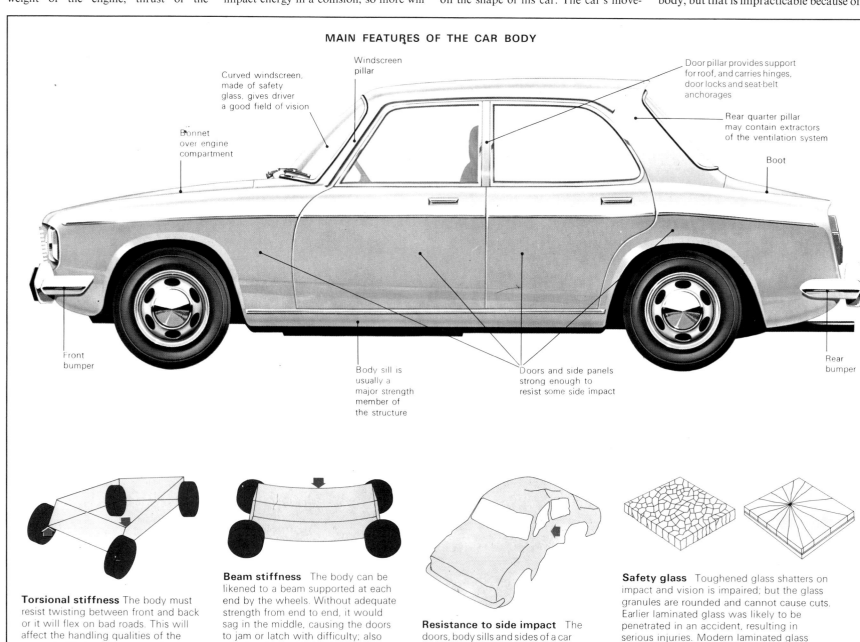

MAIN FEATURES OF THE CAR BODY

Windscreen pillar

Curved windscreen, made of safety glass, gives driver a good field of vision

Door pillar provides support for roof, and carries hinges, door locks and seat-belt anchorages

Bonnet over engine compartment

Rear quarter pillar may contain extractors of the ventilation system

Boot

Front bumper

Rear bumper

Body sill is usually a major strength member of the structure

Doors and side panels strong enough to resist some side impact

Torsional stiffness The body must resist twisting between front and back or it will flex on bad roads. This will affect the handling qualities of the car and will give rise to squeaks and rattles

Beam stiffness The body can be likened to a beam supported at each end by the wheels. Without adequate strength from end to end, it would sag in the middle, causing the doors to jam or latch with difficulty; also a body with low beam stiffness is unlikely to be torsionally stiff either

Resistance to side impact The doors, body sills and sides of a car should be strong enough to resist side impact in an accident

Safety glass Toughened glass shatters on impact and vision is impaired; but the glass granules are rounded and cannot cause cuts. Earlier laminated glass was likely to be penetrated in an accident, resulting in serious injuries. Modern laminated glass resists heavy impacts without shattering. When it fractures, vision remains good

the limited passenger space that can be provided in any given length.

A compromise has had to be found between this shape and the earlier bodies, with upright windscreens and external lamps, which caused a high drag. Height has gradually been reduced, windscreens sloped and lamps built in.

Sometimes, however, such changes have gone too far for occupant comfort. On some cars design considerations have resulted in cramped seating.

The body has to keep bad weather from the occupants, and must also resist the elements itself. If the body is of steel, the designer has to avoid not only embodying traps for rust-producing moisture, but also using certain other metals in contact with the steel, since corrosion would result through electro-chemical action.

Variations in design

THE BASIC car body shape is the saloon, with two or four doors and a luggage compartment at the front or rear.

The estate car or station wagon, with its rear door and big loading space, is an increasingly favoured layout. Some manufacturers have successfully combined the best features of saloon and estate car in the versatile 'five-door' body.

The 'convertible', or drop-head coupé, has a folding roof, but when closed is often draughtier, noisier and less roomy than the equivalent saloon.

The true open sports car is almost a thing of the past; apart from a small number of models, it has been replaced by the 'Gran Turismo' (GT) car. Some GTs are merely more powerful versions of saloon cars; others have been designed specifically for luxurious, high-speed touring.

WIND RESISTANCE AND DESIGN

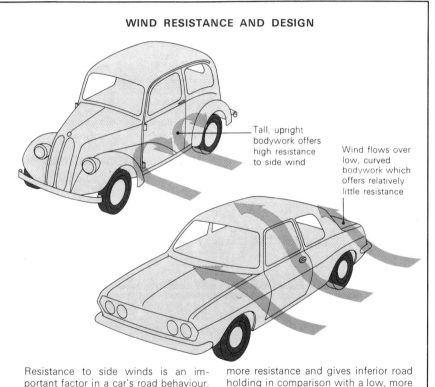

Tall, upright bodywork offers high resistance to side wind

Wind flows over low, curved bodywork which offers relatively little resistance

Resistance to side winds is an important factor in a car's road behaviour. A relatively flat high-sided design offers more resistance and gives inferior road holding in comparison with a low, more rounded body style

ATTACHMENT OF MECHANICAL PARTS TO BODY STRUCTURE

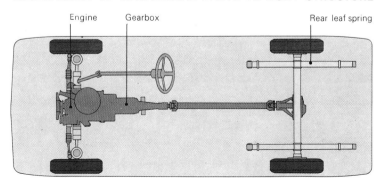

Engine   Gearbox   Rear leaf spring

To minimise vibration and noise, various types of rubber mountings are used to attach major mechanical assemblies to the body structure. The assemblies that are flexibly mounted include the engine, gearbox and suspensions

PASSENGER SPACE AND OVERALL LENGTH

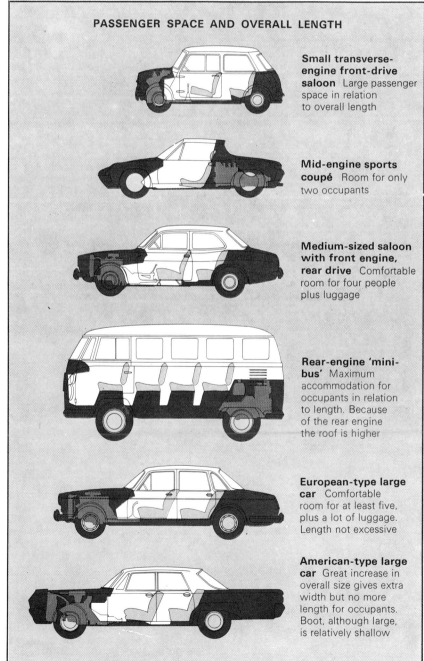

Small transverse-engine front-drive saloon Large passenger space in relation to overall length

Mid-engine sports coupé Room for only two occupants

Medium-sized saloon with front engine, rear drive Comfortable room for four people plus luggage

Rear-engine 'mini-bus' Maximum accommodation for occupants in relation to length. Because of the rear engine the roof is higher

European-type large car Comfortable room for at least five, plus a lot of luggage. Length not excessive

American-type large car Great increase in overall size gives extra width but no more length for occupants. Boot, although large, is relatively shallow

Bodywork/different methods of construction

Advantages and disadvantages of combining the chassis with the car body

A CAR can be constructed either of a separate chassis frame and body shell bolted together, or of a combination of chassis and shell in a single self-supporting assembly.

The most common construction in Europe and Japan is the combined body and chassis—usually called a unitary structure. Its main advantage over the separate chassis design is that, because parts of the panelling contribute to the strength, the structure can be lighter.

Unitary construction has three variations—fully unitary, endo-skeletal (or semi-unitary), and unitary with subframes. The fully unitary type is a completely self-supporting chassis-body structure, consisting of sheet-steel pressings which are welded together, and is well suited to the small and medium-sized car. Resistance to bending (bending stiffness) is derived partly from box-section sills along the outside edges of the floor unit, between the front and rear wheels.

With front-engined rear-wheel-drive cars, extra strength is obtained from the central transmission tunnel that is formed in the floor. In some designs, other stiffeners are incorporated under the floor. The roof of a saloon model adds to the stiffness, as it is connected to the floor by the door pillars and body panels. The bulkheads, reinforced structures at front and back of the passenger section, provide the main resistance to twisting, though some resistance comes, too, from the 'boxing-in' effect of the wings and roof, connected by the windscreen and quarter pillars.

A fully unitary structure has its disadvantages—particularly in production costs. It requires considerable outlay by the makers on highly sophisticated press-tools, and to justify this expense there must be a reasonably long production run.

Because the panelling is part of the car's structure, the repair of accident damage can be very expensive. A whole section of the bodywork may have to be cut out and replaced by a section much larger than the damaged area.

There is also the risk that a major impact may cause some distortion of the structure beyond the limits of obvious external damage to the panelling.

A minor disadvantage of this construction is that, in a normal saloon, the rear-end is much stiffer with a high sill to the boot than with a low one, so that luggage often has to be lifted quite high during loading and unloading.

THE 'ONE PIECE' CAR

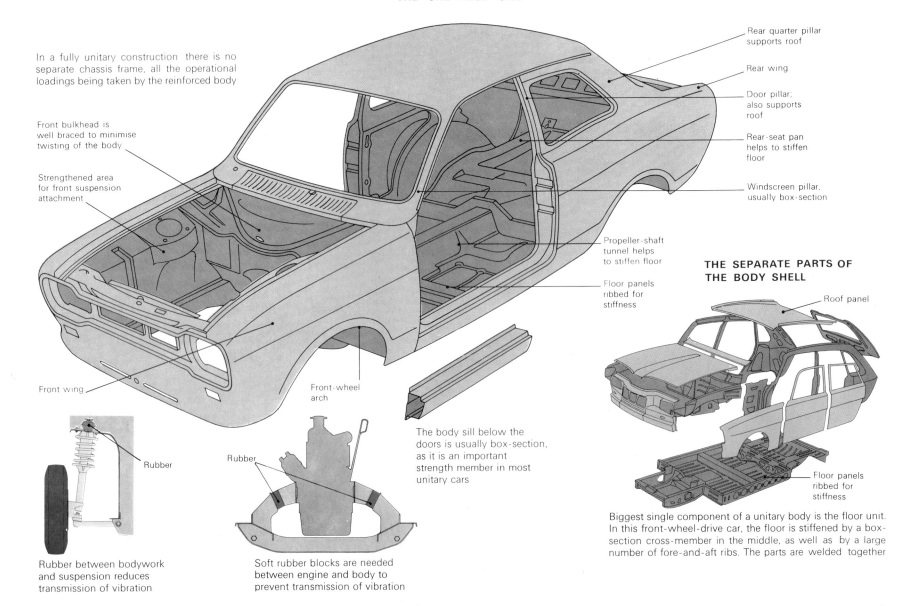

In a fully unitary construction there is no separate chassis frame, all the operational loadings being taken by the reinforced body

Front bulkhead is well braced to minimise twisting of the body

Strengthened area for front suspension attachment

Front wing

Rubber

Rubber between bodywork and suspension reduces transmission of vibration

Rubber

Soft rubber blocks are needed between engine and body to prevent transmission of vibration

Front-wheel arch

The body sill below the doors is usually box-section, as it is an important strength member in most unitary cars

Rear quarter pillar supports roof

Rear wing

Door pillar; also supports roof

Rear-seat pan helps to stiffen floor

Windscreen pillar, usually box-section

Propeller-shaft tunnel helps to stiffen floor

Floor panels ribbed for stiffness

THE SEPARATE PARTS OF THE BODY SHELL

Roof panel

Floor panels ribbed for stiffness

Biggest single component of a unitary body is the floor unit. In this front-wheel-drive car, the floor is stiffened by a box-section cross-member in the middle, as well as by a large number of fore-and-aft ribs. The parts are welded together

Starting from a 'skeleton'

THE VARIATION known as endo-skeletal construction was pioneered several years ago in the Rover 2000 and has since been adopted for other makes of cars.

It is based on a fully unitary skeleton structure, comprising the floor, bulkheads, engine and suspension mounts, and side and roof frames, to give the necessary basic strength.

To this skeleton are then bolted the unstressed metal or moulded panels of the body exterior—the wings, the roof and the lower frontal panel. Before these components are bolted on, but after the suspension and wheels have been fitted, the car can be pushed about—or even driven—without risk of damage.

Because the panels do not add to the strength of the structure, cars built in this way are a little heavier than the fully unitary design. But as the body panels are detachable, they can be replaced more easily and cheaply if damaged.

This structure also allows the manufacturer to make minor changes to the car's external shape with little difficulty. It would be possible, for example, to alter the shape of a wing or roof pressing without affecting the main structure.

Advantages of sub-frames

A TREND among some of the major European car makers has been to use sub-frames to carry one or more of the main mechanical units—the engine, final drive and suspension. These sub-frames are attached to a somewhat simplified unitary body structure.

Although this kind of car is rather heavier than the fully unitary one, it has definite advantages.

Because the mountings between body and sub-frames are flexible, there is no direct feedback path for noise or vibration, giving the car's occupants a quieter and smoother ride.

The mechanical parts are more accessible, too, which can save time on maintenance and so reduce cost if a repair is being carried out by a garage.

This construction, which can work equally well on all sizes of car, simplifies production, as mechanical units can be separately built up on their sub-frames. But styling changes are no easier than with the fully unitary layout.

Some makers fit only one sub-frame, for the engine and front suspension, while others have them at the rear also, for the rear suspension and the final drive.

DETACHABLE PANELS FOR CHEAPER REPAIRS

Roof panel

Basic skeleton of unitary construction incorporates floor and bulkheads

Rear-wheel arch connects body side to floor

Rear wing

The main feature of the endo-skeletal design is a unitary 'skeleton' which, on its wheels, forms a self-contained, mobile unit; the outside panels are bolted on

Lower frontal panel

Front-wing unit

SUB-FRAMES MAKE MAINTENANCE EASIER

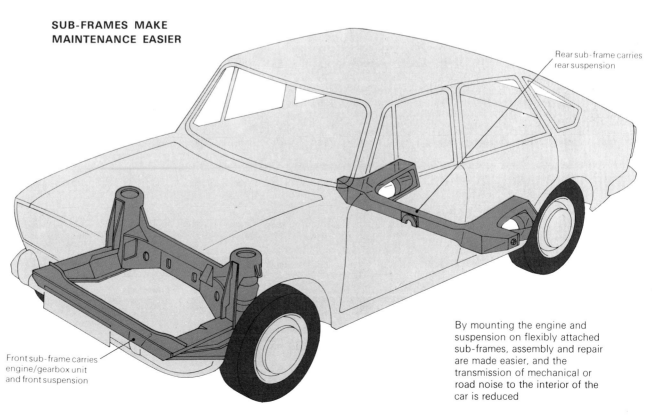

Rear sub-frame carries rear suspension

Front sub-frame carries engine/gearbox unit and front suspension

By mounting the engine and suspension on flexibly attached sub-frames, assembly and repair are made easier, and the transmission of mechanical or road noise to the interior of the car is reduced

Bodywork/chassis construction

Framework for the car

THE CHASSIS, a strong steel frame which supports the body and engine, is still in general use on American cars, though it is no longer a feature of most quantity-produced British and European models. Exceptions are some small sports cars. Most specialist manufacturers also use separate chassis frames, particularly when using a moulded plastic body shell.

This classic design for a chassis, dating from the 1930's, consists of channel-section side members combined with X-shape bracing amidships to provide torsional rigidity. Nowadays, box sections are commonly used for the side members and X-bracings, to give much greater stiffness.

A version of the X-frame, based on a deep 'backbone' girder, is favoured by at least one sports-car manufacturer, Lotus. In complete contrast is the flat, reinforced-floor chassis layout used by Volkswagen on the Beetle and its derivatives.

Most American chassis frames are of the perimeter type to permit a low floor line. This design is basically an open rectangle of box-section members, with the end members built up to contribute to the rather poor torsional stiffness.

A few manufacturers use large-diameter steel tubes, instead of channel or box members, for the frame; others have built 'space frames', welding a large number of small-section tubes to produce a light but rigid three-dimensional structure.

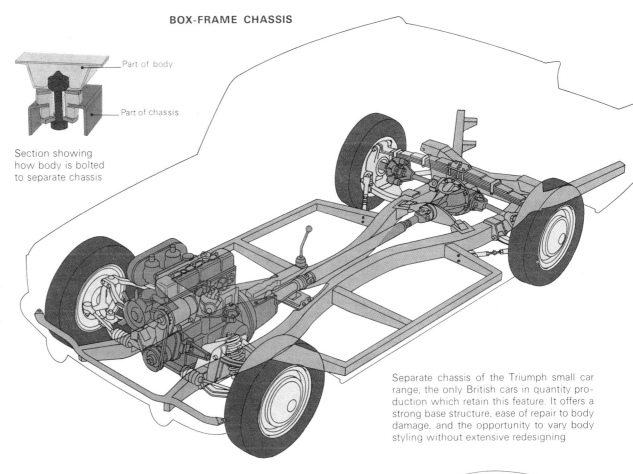

BOX-FRAME CHASSIS

Part of body

Part of chassis

Section showing how body is bolted to separate chassis

Separate chassis of the Triumph small car range, the only British cars in quantity production which retain this feature. It offers a strong base structure, ease of repair to body damage, and the opportunity to vary body styling without extensive redesigning

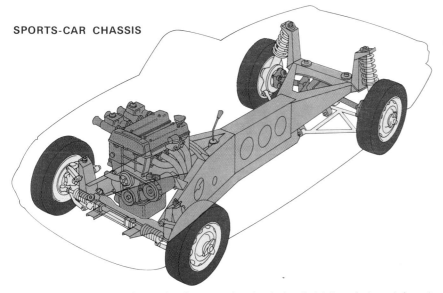

SPORTS-CAR CHASSIS

Modern version of the X-frame chassis produced by Lotus for one of their sports cars. The strong 'backbone' girder compensates for the lack of rigidity of the reinforced plastic body and has integral brackets to carry the suspension

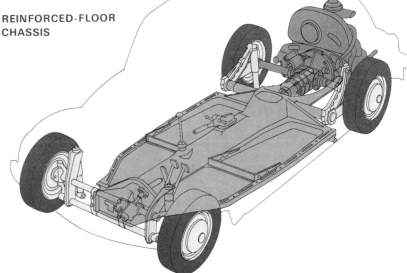

REINFORCED-FLOOR CHASSIS

Platform-type chassis is used for the Volkswagen. A floor pressing incorporates all the members necessary for longitudinal and torsional rigidity. As with the separate frame, this design allows restyling without change of the base structure

Bodywork materials

STEEL is still the cheapest and the most efficient material for mass-produced separate bodies. The parts are stamped out by machine presses from varying thicknesses of sheet steel.

Aluminium, though more expensive than steel, is often used by smaller manufacturers because it is more easily shaped by hand or can be formed on comparatively simple machines. It is also lighter than steel and does not rust. The disadvantage is that it is usually less stiff.

Moulded plastic bodies are becoming more common. Most popular are the glass-reinforced plastics (GRP). The plastic used is normally polyester resin, or occasionally the more expensive epoxy resin. These are known as thermosetting materials—that is, heat hardens them and they do not soften on reheating.

Thermo-plastics tend to soften at high temperatures and are less rigid than GRP though easier to mould. Most promising is ABS (acrylonitrile-butadiene-styrene) which is tough and reasonably stiff. It is used for boot lids, grilles and front ends, and might one day be used for major body parts. ABS bumpers can withstand minor collisions.

Carbon fibre gives plastics a better strength/weight ratio than steel. It could have potential in car-body construction once its very high cost can be cut.

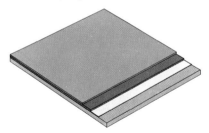

Metal car body Protective coating is built up with anti-corrosion compound, usually phosphate, primer, undercoats and topcoat of paint

Glass-reinforced plastic This section shows glass fibres distributed through a laminate of polyester resin for strengthening

Built-in safety

A CAR STRUCTURE must not be so rigid that the full shock of a collision is felt by the occupants, nor so weak that it collapses on them without absorbing much energy.

The safest type of car body is one which provides a strong and rigid box for the driver and passengers, sandwiched between ends that can absorb impact energy by collapsing progressively in a crash.

Unitary construction is best for this purpose, because the body can be designed to have the necessary strong and weak sections. Space frames also have a high safety rating, because their many tubes absorb impact energy. But the rigid conventional chassis tends to pass on much of the shock to the occupants.

Some plastic bodies are more resistant than metal ones to minor bumps; an ABS shell may snap back to shape after a collision. But plastic does not crumple on impact, as metal does, and this increases the risk of injury. Glass-reinforced plastic bodies may shatter on impact in severe collisions and there is a greater risk of the material catching fire than there is with steel panels.

Rust is a real hazard in unitary-built steel cars—especially when it occurs in stress-bearing parts of the body. Many accidents have occurred when badly rusted parts have failed at speed. Manufacturers are constantly developing improved methods to limit rusting. These include avoiding moisture traps, better painting and using pre-coated steel.

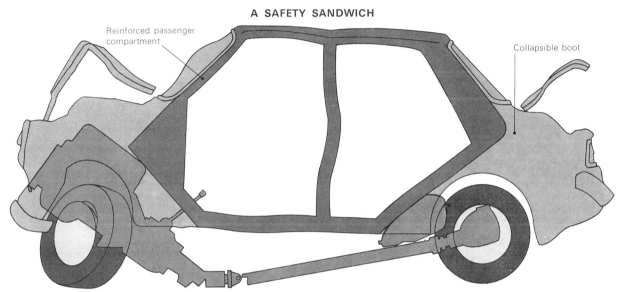

A SAFETY SANDWICH

Reinforced passenger compartment

Collapsible boot

A car of unitary construction consists of a strong and rigid box, enclosing the driver and passengers, sandwiched between front and rear ends which collapse progressively in the event of a collision. In crumpling, the front and rear ends absorb energy and lessen the impact felt by the central section. Although measured only in tenths of a second, the collapse gives the seat belts a chance to hold back the occupants and prevent serious injury; if the occupants are not wearing belts, they will be thrown forwards with a force that is virtually unaffected by how the structure crumples

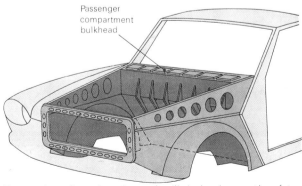

Passenger compartment bulkhead

Progressive collapse in an impact is a likely development in safety design. Impact energy is thereby dissipated so that the shock to occupants (wearing seat belts) is less severe. The pressings offer least resistance to impact at the front, the resistance gradually increasing to the bulkhead which forms part of the rigid occupant safety compartment

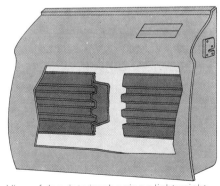

View of door interior showing a lightweight reinforcing box-section girder used in a few cars to provide protection in side impacts. The girder, shown in section, extends the full width of the door. Hollow tubes may also be used as such stiffeners

Bodywork/interior safety and comfort

Requirements in structure and fittings

TWO KINDS of safety should be built into a car. One, 'primary safety', involves designing a vehicle which is least likely to be involved in an accident. The other, 'secondary safety', ensures that, if the car does crash, the risk of injury to its occupants is minimised.

Planning primary safety for the interior entails giving the driver good vision and making him comfortable, so that he will not tire easily. Vision depends partly on minimising the 'blind spots' caused by body pillars and quarters, partly on keeping the windscreen exterior clear in rain or fog, and partly on good ventilation, which prevents the glass misting-up on the inside in bad weather. Control of ventilation

also benefits the driver's efficiency, since cold or stuffiness are both tiring.

Comfort for a driver, and for passengers, begins with the seats. These should support the back to give a good posture (see p. 338), and to hold the occupants to some extent against cornering forces.

Once seated, the driver should be able to see the various instruments on the fascia panel and reach the various controls without stretching or other distraction. (Ways of improving seating comfort are detailed on p. 339.)

Designers have been turning their attention increasingly to secondary safety during the last few years, and car interiors are becoming much less likely to inflict

injury. This is largely because of legislation introduced in America, Britain, Europe and Japan.

These safety standards call for padding on all areas likely to be struck in a crash. Steering columns must not move far backwards in a frontal collision and must be shock-absorbent; switches and controls must not project dangerously from the fascia; and locks must prevent doors bursting open in an impact. Interior mirrors must be so constructed that they cannot injure the occupants.

Cars sold in America and some other countries also need head restraints to prevent neck injury in a rear collision, though a headrest on the driver's seat can

badly obstruct vision while reversing. Glass for windscreens and windows has been much improved. The latest laminated safety glass resists penetration better and so is less likely to cause injury.

Seat belts (required by law in Britain for the driver and front-seat passenger in all cars first registered after December 31, 1964) make a significant contribution to safety, reducing the risk of serious injury by at least half. In many countries the law demands that seat belts should be worn; they became compulsory because many motorists did not use them. Among alternatives now being tested are 'restraint bags' which inflate automatically in a violent impact.

FEATURES WHICH HELP TO MAKE A CAR SAFER

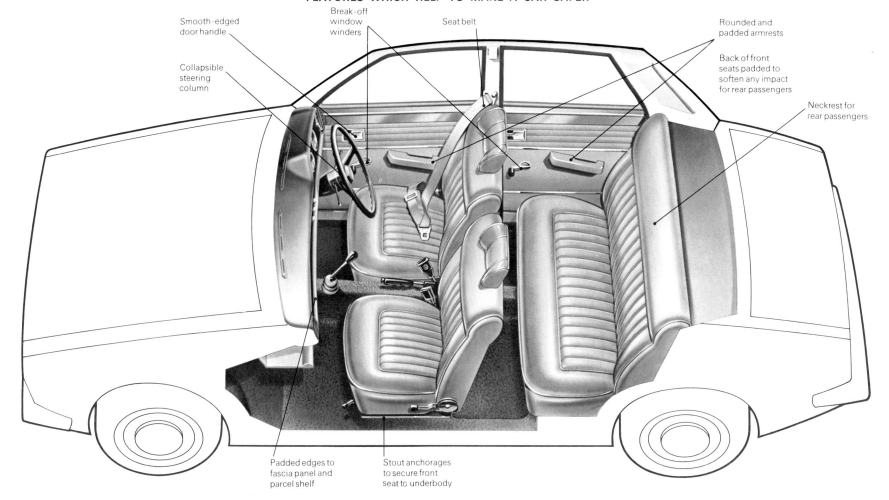

Smooth-edged door handle

Break-off window winders

Seat belt

Rounded and padded armrests

Collapsible steering column

Back of front seats padded to soften any impact for rear passengers

Neckrest for rear passengers

Padded edges to fascia panel and parcel shelf

Stout anchorages to secure front seat to underbody

To help minimise the danger of injury to the occupants in an accident, the interior of a car should be as free as possible of sharp projections on the sides and roof and on the fascia panel. Some controls and switches on earlier models stood out like spikes and so were dangerous. Any projection in the form of a ledge, edge or shelving should be covered with absorbent padding to soften the blow if the car's occupants are thrown against it, as happens during violent braking. Window winders should break off on impact

Keeping the air fresh inside the car

WHILE CAR HEATERS are becoming easier to adjust to the desired temperature, the biggest advance has come with 'through-flow' ventilation. There are fixed air inlets usually under the windscreen and adjustable ones on the fascia. The flow goes over the windows to demist them, and is drawn out through vents at the rear of the car.

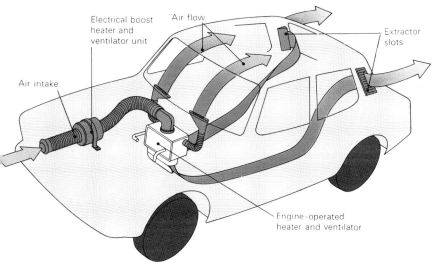

Through-flow The latest 'through-flow' ventilation and heating systems provide fresh air and warmth, as well as minimising misting-up of the windows

Safety points for the driver

SOME OF THE better modern front seats embody an adjustable lumbar support in the backrest. Where the seat must hinge forward to give access to the rear compartment, a catch is usually fitted on recent models to secure it in a collision. Fascias and parcel shelves are now well padded to minimise injury, and some inside mirrors are designed to break from their mountings on impact, instead of shattering.

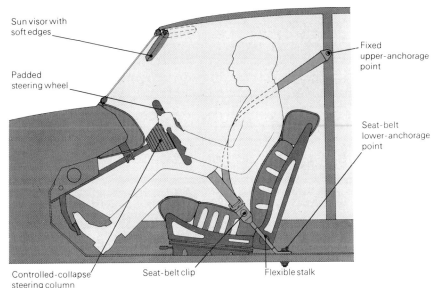

Comfort The seat-belt anchorage, which incorporates the retaining clip, should be so located that the belt can be put on and taken off quickly, using only one hand. The belt must fit comfortably and must not slip off or cut into the wearer. A settled, restful position reduces strain and fatigue—a considerable safety factor

Door locks

IN ADDITION to the usual internally and externally operated door locks, many cars have locks which prevent children opening the doors from the inside. These locks are operated by setting a catch on the jamb of the door. In a serious crash, anyone who is not wearing a seat belt and is thrown out of the car through a door which bursts open is twice as likely to be killed as a person who is not thrown out. An improved lock that maintains its grip is a significant safety measure. Some cars have locks that can be pneumatically or electronically operated from a central control.

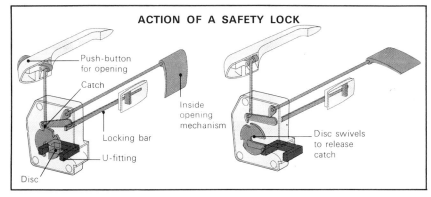

ACTION OF A SAFETY LOCK

Door closed A slotted disc rotates and fastens into a U-fitting when the door closes. It is secured by a catch and locking bar

Door open To unlock the door, the bar is moved to raise the catch: the disc then rotates, free from the U-fitting

Window-winding mechanism

HANDLES of window winders and doors should be designed so as not to be injury hazards in an accident. The winding mechanism should lift the glass squarely. Many mechanisms, which may also be operated electrically, consist of a winder, geared to a quadrant to which the lifting arm is attached.

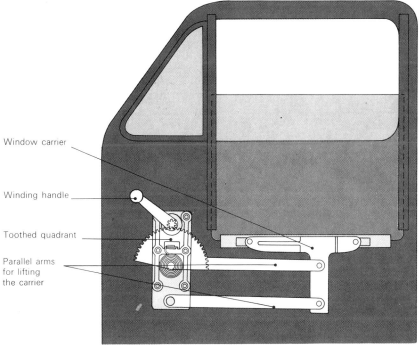

Winding mechanism Turning the winding handle rotates the two parallel links which move the window carrier up and down squarely and smoothly

Bodywork/windscreen wipers and washers

The importance of clear vision

ONE OF THE BEST contributions to road safety a car manufacturer can make is to give the driver clear vision in all directions, with as little obstruction as possible. Two factors determine the quality of vision from a car: the basic design of the vehicle, and the efficiency of its accessories.

The safety-conscious designer ensures that the driver can sit high enough to have a good view of the road; that the windscreen is not so shallow as to impede vision on hilly roads; that screen, door and quarter-light pillars are thin enough not to cause dangerous blind spots; and that, if possible, the driver can see all four corners of the car, for parking and driving in dense traffic.

Rain or road dirt on the windscreen reduces forward vision. To cope with this, windscreen wipers and washers are required by law to be fitted to all cars.

Wipers vary in their effectiveness, usually on account of the pattern swept by the blades. This in turn depends on the position of the arm pivots. With the customary two-arm installation, it is impossible to provide a layout that clears both sides of the screen equally well, so designers concentrate the largest wiped area in front of the driver. If a manufacturer is producing right and left-hand-drive models of a car, he should provide alternative pivot points for the wiper arms; some do not, because of the cost. As cars have become lower and their windscreens more sloping, more road dirt finds its way on to the glass. So screen washers became essential to remove dirt.

The simplest screen washer is operated by a small hand-pump mounted on the fascia. Others are operated by an electric pump or by inlet-manifold suction.

Rear vision is provided by a mirror, or mirrors. The law requires that a car should have at least one rear-view mirror.

WIPER PATTERNS

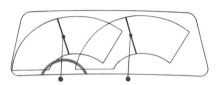

Orthodox wiper pattern for right-hand-drive car, seen from front. Wiper-arm pivots are offset from centre to driver's side, ensuring a clean area immediately in front of the driver and leaving unwiped the areas where clear vision is less essential

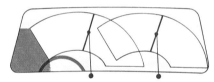

The orthodox pattern should be reversed, and the pivots repositioned, for a left-hand-drive car. If, on a right-hand-drive car. the orthodox pattern is fitted for a left-hand drive, it will leave a large and important area of the windscreen unwiped in front of the driver, as shown above

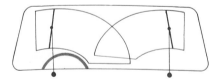

This pattern uses widely spaced pivots to try to provide a single layout that is suitable for installation in both left and right-hand-drive cars. A disadvantage of this design is that its opposed arms leave big unwiped areas at the sides, and a central blind spot

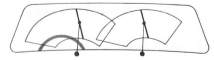

A windscreen which is low in relation to its width is difficult to clean properly with only two wipers. With the proportions shown, longer blades might help, but a better solution would probably be to fit a system using three wipers

WINDSCREEN WASHER IN OPERATION

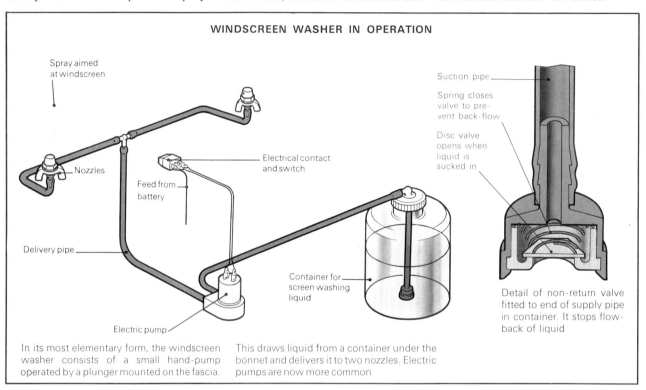

Spray aimed at windscreen

Nozzles

Electrical contact and switch

Feed from battery

Delivery pipe

Container for screen washing liquid

Electric pump

Suction pipe

Spring closes valve to prevent back-flow

Disc valve opens when liquid is sucked in

Detail of non-return valve fitted to end of supply pipe in container. It stops flow-back of liquid

In its most elementary form, the windscreen washer consists of a small hand-pump operated by a plunger mounted on the fascia. This draws liquid from a container under the bonnet and delivers it to two nozzles. Electric pumps are now more common

WINDSCREEN WIPER AND BLADE

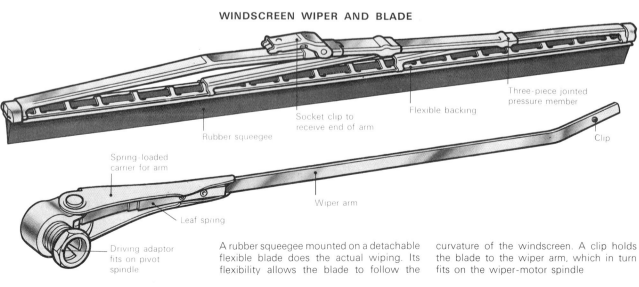

Three-piece jointed pressure member

Flexible backing

Socket clip to receive end of arm

Clip

Rubber squeegee

Spring-loaded carrier for arm

Leaf spring

Wiper arm

Driving adaptor fits on pivot spindle

A rubber squeegee mounted on a detachable flexible blade does the actual wiping. Its flexibility allows the blade to follow the curvature of the windscreen. A clip holds the blade to the wiper arm, which in turn fits on the wiper-motor spindle

FAULT FINDING AND MAINTENANCE

Regular maintenance and servicing backed by the knowledge of how a car works and a measure of common sense help to ensure a long car life. The vehicle's 5000 or so parts, many of them working to a tolerance of only 0·001 in. (0·0254 mm.), do not take kindly to unskilled adjustment; yet, given the right guidance and using the right tools, there are a surprising number of jobs any owner can tackle with confidence. They are described in the pages which follow; and to help the owner decide what repairs are needed, this section starts with an 18 page fault-finding chart.

CONTENTS

Fault finding at a glance

When checking, always begin with the faults at the top of the list. These are the most likely to be the cause of the trouble, and their remedies are usually the simplest. The symbol ● indicates that the job is within the scope of a home mechanic. The symbol ■ indicates that the work is beyond the scope of all but the most experienced mechanics, and you should consult a garage. The ▲ sign indicates that on emission-control carburettors, the work must be done by a specialist.

Symptom	Fault	Remedy
Engine starting conditions		
Starter will not turn engine (headlamps dim)	Battery low in charge, often causing the solenoid to chatter	Charge battery ● (p. 195) and check charging system ■
	Defective battery	Replace battery ●
	Corroded battery cables or loose connections	Clean battery connections or replace battery cables. Tighten battery and starter-motor connections ● (p. 195)
	Starter jammed	Free starter ● (p. 230)
	Water in cylinders or seized engine	Remove spark-plugs to check (p. 202). Seek help ■
(Headlamps bright)	Defective starter solenoid	Replace ● (p. 230)
	Defective starter engagement, confirmed by starter-motor whine	Clean Bendix unit ● (p. 231)
	Defective starter	Repair or replace ● (p. 231)
	Defective starter switch	Replace ■
	On automatic cars	Select park or neutral ●
Engine turns slowly but will not start	Battery low in charge	Charge battery ● (p. 195) and check charging system ■
	Defective battery	Replace battery ●
	Corroded battery cables or loose connections	Clean battery connections or replace battery cables. Tighten battery and starter-motor connections ● (p. 195)
	Bad engine-to-chassis earth strap	Clean or replace ● (p. 228)
	Defective starter	Repair or replace ● (p. 231)
	Incorrect viscosity of engine oil in crankcase (if multigrade oil is not being used)	Drain crankcase and refill with proper-viscosity engine oil (p. 81). Change oil filter if necessary ● (p. 228)
Engine turns normally but will not fire	Ignition fault	Check for spark at plug lead ● (p. 194)
	Where no spark is observed at plug lead	Check output from coil to confirm high or low-tension fault. If there is a spark from the coil, check HT leads, distributor cap and rotor arm, particularly for cracks, tracking or dampness. Where no spark is observed from coil output, check ignition-coil connections and contact-breaker points for short circuits or disconnection ● (p. 194)
	Where spark is observed at plug lead	Remove air cleaner at carburettor and check choke operation. If necessary, assist with gentle finger pressure—a drop of oil on the butterfly spindle may help. Loosen petrol-pipe union at carburettor. Turn engine by starter for a mechanical pump, or switch on ignition for electric pump. Check if petrol is being delivered ● (p. 193)
	If fuel is reaching carburettor	Look into carburettor mouth. Operate throttle and observe whether damp or dry. If dry, clean jets and needle valve (p. 193). If damp, remove spark-plugs, dry, clean and check gaps ● (p. 202)

	Symptom	Fault	Remedy
Engine starting conditions	Engine turns normally but will not fire *(contd)*	No fuel to carburettor	Remove petrol-tank cap and check for fuel (fuel gauge may be inaccurate) ●
		If car is fitted with electric fuel pump	Check pump has a good earth and give pump a sharp tap. If it starts pumping, which will be heard, replace pump ● (p. 191). If not, seek advice, as fuel lines may be blocked ■
		Where a mechanical pump is fitted	Check if there is a tap in the fuel line at the inlet to the pump. Make sure that any tap is switched on. Remove pump-top cover, clean pump filter and make sure the cover, when refitted, is airtight. Check flexible pipe to pump for air leaks ● (p. 192). If the fault is not found, seek advice ■
	Engine backfires violently, kicks back or bangs through carburettor	Ignition timing faulty	Check and reset ignition timing ● (p. 200)
		Damp distributor cap and leads	Dry thoroughly and check firing order ● (p. 196)
	Engine fires, but fails to keep running	Ignition or fuel fault	Refer to order of checks for 'Engine turns normally but will not fire' (p. 162), with special emphasis on choke, plug condition and continuous HT spark at plug lead ●
Engine performance	Engine stalls when idling (engine cold)	Choke throttle-stop requires adjustment	Adjust ● (pp. 190 and 193)
		Choke not operating correctly	Remove air cleaner. Check choke operation ● (p. 193)
	Engine stalls when idling (engine hot)	Engine idle speed too low	Adjust idle speed if possible ● (p. 190)
		Engine idle fuel mixture improperly adjusted	Adjust idle fuel mixture if possible ● (pp. 189 and 190) ▲
		Pilot air jet blocked	Clean ● (p. 187)
		Choke stuck in operation	Check choke operation at carburettor ● (p. 193)
		Contact-breaker points incorrectly set or worn	Clean and adjust or replace breaker points ● (p. 198)
		Carburettor flooding	Adjust fuel level or float setting to specification. Clean needle valve ● (p. 193)
		Intake vacuum leak	Check manifold, carburettor mounting, any connections to manifold and vacuum advance. Also check butterfly spindle and bosses; if worn, seek advice ■
	Engine has rough idle	Idle mixture and throttle-stop screw out of adjustment	Adjust idle-speed fuel mixture and idle speed to specifications ● (pp. 188 and 190) ▲
		Contact-breaker points incorrectly set or worn	Clean and adjust (or replace) breaker points ● (p. 198)
		Fouled or improperly gapped spark-plugs	Clean and adjust plug gaps or replace plugs ● (p. 202)
		Incorrect ignition timing	Adjust ● (p. 200)
		Intake vacuum leak	Check manifold, carburettor mounting, any connections to manifold and vacuum advance ● (pp. 187 and 197)
	Engine stalls on acceleration	Carburettor accelerator pump inoperative or not functioning properly	Check fuel supply into float chamber (p. 187) ● before repairing accelerator pump ■
		Choke not functioning properly or improperly adjusted	Check choke operation at carburettor ● (p. 193)
		Insufficient fuel supply to carburettor	Clean needle valve and jets. Check float level ● (p. 193)

Fault finding

Symptom	Fault	Remedy
Engine performance (contd)		
Engine stalls on acceleration *(contd)*	Short in distributor caused by automatic-advance operation	Check internal distributor wires for short ● (p. 197)
	Air-cleaner element dirty	Clean or replace filter element. Observe recommended maintenance schedule ● (p. 186)
	Variable-choke carburettor (SU or Stromberg) has a seized piston	Polish piston and cylinder with dry or petrol-damp rag. Check that correct oil is used in dash-pot and top up to the required level ● (p. 189)
	Cars with 2-stroke engines—blocked exhaust	Clean or change silencers ● (p. 261)
Engine has poor acceleration	Incorrect ignition timing	Adjust ● (p. 200)
	Intake vacuum leak	Tighten or replace faulty gaskets ● (p. 185)
	Insufficient fuel supply	Clean needle valve and jets. Check fuel ● (pp. 192 and 193)
	Accelerator linkage out of adjustment	Check that full throttle in the car is also full throttle at the carburettor. Adjust as necessary ■
	Valve clearances incorrect	Adjust clearances ● (p. 181)
	Insufficient engine compression	Regrind valves or replace cylinder-head gasket ● (p. 184)
	Incorrect distributor automatic advance	Replace worn or damaged parts. Adjust engine timing to specifications ● (p. 200). Remove restriction or carry out repair, or tighten connections in vacuum line ● (p. 197)
Engine misses or surges	Spark-plug breakdown. Ignition circuit defective	Clean, test or replace ● (p. 202). Check spark, contact-breaker, LT and HT wiring. Ensure all parts of ignition system are clean and dry (p. 194). Check timing ● (p. 200)
	Damaged HT leads where suppressed lead or suppressor is fitted	Check if lead is broken. If so, the lead should be changed ● (p. 194)
	Intake vacuum leaks	Tighten all parts associated with inlet manifold, including vacuum advance ● (pp. 185 and 197)
	Insufficient fuel, or water in fuel	Clean as necessary ● (pp. 187, 191 and 192)
	Carburettor flooding	Clean needle valve. Check float level ● (pp. 187 and 193)
	Exhaust system restricted	Repair exhaust system ● (p. 260)
Engine has less power	Ignition timing incorrect	Adjust ● (p. 200)
	Distributor automatic advance incorrect	Repair and adjust as necessary ● (p. 197)
	Intake vacuum leaks	Tighten all parts associated with inlet manifold ● (p. 185)
	Valve clearances incorrect	Adjust clearances ● (p. 181)
	Engine compression low	Check compression ■
	Fuel starvation	Check supply, carburettor jets and needle valve ● (p. 193)
	Throttle linkage out of adjustment	Check full throttle at pedal is full throttle at carburettor ■
Engine stops when vehicle is brought to a halt. Otherwise performs normally	Throttle-setting screw needs adjustment	Adjust to increase idling speed ● (pp. 188 and 190)
	Pilot air jet blocked	Clean ● (p. 187)
	Inlet manifold vacuum leaks	Check all parts associated with inlet manifold, including vacuum advance ● (pp. 185 and 187)

	Symptom	Fault	Remedy
Engine performance (contd)	Engine 'runs on' when switched off	Engine overheating	Check static timing, cooling system, carburettor adjustment, fan-belt tension and thermostat ● (pp. 186, 200 and 204–6)
		Spark-plug overheating	Check that correct grade of plug is fitted ● (p. 202)
		'Hot spots' inside combustion chamber	Decarbonise ● (p. 182)
		Valve clearances incorrect	Check and adjust clearances ● (p. 181)
		Vacuum leak	Tighten all parts associated with inlet manifold ● (p. 185)
	Engine 'pinks'	Wrong fuel	Fill with correct grade ●
		Ignition timing too far advanced	Retime static advance ● (p. 200)
		Centrifugal automatic advance faulty	Check bob-weight springs ● (p. 197)
		Engine overheating	Check cooling system ● (pp. 204–7)
		Spark-plug overheating	Check that correct grade of plug is fitted ● (p. 202)
		Excessive deposits in combustion chamber	Decarbonise ● (p. 182)
	Water drips from exhaust tail-pipe—after cold start	No fault: normal in cold weather	No action
	Water drips from exhaust tail-pipe—at normal temperature	Cylinder-head gasket blown	Replace ● (p. 185)
		Cracked or warped cylinder head	Machine the head face ■
	Engine misses at high speed	Dirty or loose electrical connections in ignition system	Check all connections, especially those at the distributor and coil. Clean, tighten and check condition of leads, especially carbon-cored plug leads. Check that rivets holding connectors to the coil are tight ● (pp. 194 and 196)
		Contact-breaker points dirty or burnt—or gap wrongly set	Check and correct the condition of the points and reset clearances if necessary ● (p. 199)
		Spark-plugs faulty	Clean, adjust or replace ● (p. 202)
		Dirt in carburettor	Clean ● (p. 186)
		Valve clearances incorrect	Check and reset clearances ● (p. 181)
		Air cleaner dirty	Clean or replace as necessary ● (p. 186)
	Engine coughs and splutters continuously	Water or dirt in petrol feed system	Clean carburettor, filter and possibly whole system ● (p. 186)
		Low fuel level in carburettor	Adjust float level ■
	Engine coughs and splutters irregularly, often backfiring	Fuel starvation	Electric pump: clean points and connections, ensuring good earth and that air can enter the fuel tank (check tank breather). If unsuccessful, replace pump ● (p. 191). Mechanical pump: clean out pump and filters. Check for air leaks in fuel-tank side of the pump ● (p. 192)

● indicates that the job is within the scope of a home mechanic
■ indicates that the work is beyond the scope of all but the most experienced mechanics, and you should consult a garage

Fault finding

	Symptom	Fault	Remedy
Engine performance (contd)	Engine coughs and splutters irregularly, often backfiring *(contd)*	Water in petrol	Clean carburettor and possibly whole fuel system ● (p. 186)
	Engine falters, picks up and finally stops; possible backfiring	Lack of petrol	Fill tank or check fuel system ● (p. 192)
	Engine falters and stops when hot, but restarts	Vaporisation in fuel pipeline	Allow time for pump and pipeline to cool before attempting to restart ●
	Engine does not appear to reach normal operating temperature	Thermostat defective or of incorrect heat range	Fit new thermostat of specified heat range ● (p. 205)
		Defective temperature sensing unit	Replace ● (p. 205)
		Faulty temperature gauge	Replace temperature gauge or bulb ■
Cooling system	Engine overheats	Lack of coolant	Check for leaks and lack of coolant, but allow half an hour to cool before filling up ●
		Loose fan belt	Adjust belt tension to specification. Replace defective belt(s) ● (p. 206)
		Cooling-system hoses defective	Replace defective hoses ● (p. 204)
		Defective or wrong radiator pressure cap	Check that the radiator cap's rubber seal is in good condition and that the cap is of specified pressure rating. If not, fit one of the correct type ●
		Cooling system clogged	Flush the cooling system ● (p. 204)
		Thermostat defective	Replace defective thermostat with one of specified heat range ● (p. 205)
		Ignition timing incorrect	Adjust to specification ● (p. 200)
		Water pump faulty or leaking	Fit new or reconditioned water pump ● (p. 207)
		Defective pressure bottle pipe (where fitted)	Check pipe for breaks and loose union connections ●
		Air passages through radiator blocked, particularly on transverse engines	Clear passages by using grease dissolver and water. Do not scrape in any way ● (p. 236)
		Thermostatically controlled fans faulty	Seek expert help ■
		Distributor automatic advance incorrect	Remove restriction, or repair or tighten connections in vacuum line ● (p. 197). Replace worn or damaged parts. Adjust distributor advance to specifications ■
	Overheating and steaming soon after starting on cold morning	Coolant frozen	Stop the engine. Wait for radiator to be warmed by conducted heat. Use stronger antifreeze solution ●
	Loud screech when engine is started cold	Fan belt slipping because of frozen water pump	Stop the engine. Move the car to a warm place and allow the ice to thaw ●
		Fan belt loose	Adjust ● (p. 206)

	Symptom	Fault	Remedy
Cooling system (contd)	Loud screech when engine is started cold *(contd)*	Water-pump bearings require lubrication	If there is no external lubricating point, use a water additive recommended by manufacturer ●
		Generator bearings require lubrication	Add a drop or two of light oil ● (p. 232)
		Power-steering fault	Seek expert help ■
	Leaks from water pump	Worn seal	Fit new pump ● (p. 207)
	Continuous bubbling and overheating	Blown gasket or cracked cylinder head	Check for distortion or fit new gasket ● (p. 185)
	Radiator continually requires water	External leakage. (Rust stains usually show where.)	Check and replace hoses, core plugs and cylinder-head gasket as necessary ● (pp. 185 and 204)
		Leakage into engine	Check dipstick for unusually high level and drops of water in engine oil. In bad cases, the oil will become white in colour. Check for excessive steam in the exhaust emission ●
Car heating system	Car heater remains cool	Insufficient flow to heater	Check heater water-flow valve. Bleed the system ● (p. 205)
		Thermostat stuck in open position	Fit new thermostat ● (p. 205)
		Heater element partly blocked	Remove heater pipes where they join the engine. With the heater tap turned on, flush in both directions ● (p. 205)
	Car heater suddenly goes cold	Defective fan belt	Replace the fan belt ● (p. 206)
Battery	Low specific gravity readings, taken with hydrometer	Low state of charge	Check battery and charging system. Recharge battery ● and cure any faults in charging system or wiring ■ (p. 195)
		Loss of acid through leaks	Top leak can be sealed ■. If leak is at side, replace battery ●
		Loss of acid by overfilling	Take battery to specialist. Never add acid ■
		Defective battery	Fit new battery ●
	Low current capacity tested with heavy discharge tester	Low state of charge	Check specific gravity. Recharge ● (p.195)
		Defective cell	Plates can be replaced ■; but preferable to renew battery ●
	Although electrical system appears to be in good order, there is great difficulty in turning engine in cold weather	Battery too small for vehicle demands	Fit new battery of the correct, or greater, amp./hour rating. Seek expert advice ■
Fuel system	Engine uses too much petrol	Carburettor needs adjusting	Adjust carburettor ● (pp. 186–90)▲

● indicates that the job is within the scope of a home mechanic
■ indicates that the work is beyond the scope of all but the most experienced mechanics, and you should consult a garage
▲ indicates that on emission control carburettors, work must be done by a specialist

Fault finding

	Symptom	Fault	Remedy
Fuel system (contd)	Engine uses too much petrol *(contd)*	Air intake restricted	Replace air-cleaner element ● (p. 186)
		Choke stuck in operation	Check choke action ● (p. 193)
	Engine spits back or backfires when pulling	Fuel starvation or water in fuel	Clean carburettor jets and needle valve. Check fuel supply and fuel tank ● (p. 187) ▲
		Air leak in inlet manifold	Tighten all parts associated with inlet manifold ● (p. 185)
		Faulty ignition timing	Check timing ● (p. 200)
Lubrication	Engine needs frequent topping up with oil—blue smoke emitted from exhaust	Wear in cylinders, piston rings or valve guides	Seek expert advice, as it may be far cheaper and not particularly detrimental to tolerate condition until eventual engine change ■
	Engine needs frequent topping up with oil—exhaust normal	Oil leaks	Clean engine thoroughly. Run engine (hot) and look for leaks. Replace or tighten gaskets as necessary ● (p. 185)
		Engine breather blockage	Clean ■
		Excessive crankcase pressure	As this is caused by piston blow-by, seek advice ■. Repair may not be necessary.
Warning instruments	Oil warning-light does not go out	Lack of oil	Check oil level ●
		Oil warning-light faulty or pressure failure	Remove wire from oil warning-light switch on side of the engine. If the light stays on, there is a fault in the wiring ■. If it goes out, there is a fault in the oil-pressure switch or high-pressure system. Seek expert advice before restarting ■
		Engine oil-pressure system faulty	Take car to garage ■
	Oil warning-light comes on when cornering	Low oil level	Top up ●
	Oil warning-light goes out only when engine is speeded up	Inadequate oil pressure at low speeds	If correct grade of oil has been used, seek expert advice ■
	Oil-pressure gauge reading fails to rise when engine is started from cold	Not enough oil	Check level ●
		Fault in pressure system	Stop engine and consult expert ■
	Oil reading falls suddenly during normal driving	Low oil level	Check for leaks, repair and top up. Drive carefully and recheck ●
		Fault in pressure system	Stop engine. Do not restart. Seek expert advice ■
	Ignition warning-light stays on when engine runs at speeds above tick-over	Broken fan belt	Fit new belt ● (p. 206)
		No generator output	Check commutator and brushes. If melted solder can be seen on looking into end of generator, a replacement generator and control box are required ■
		No generator output (but generator appears to be working)	Check control-box earth ● (p. 227). All further tests should be made by a skilled vehicle electrician ■

	Symptom	Fault	Remedy
Warning instruments (contd)	Ignition warning-light stays on when engine runs at speeds above tick-over *(contd)*	No generator output (when alternator is fitted)	If there are no obvious disconnected leads, seek expert help. ■ Leads which have been disconnected must not be reconnected while the engine is running ●
Transmission	Car vibrates when driving or coasting	Wheels loose, buckled or out of balance. Wheel-balance problems will normally be identified by periods of vibration at certain speeds	Tighten wheel nuts ● (p. 219). If wheels are buckled, seek expert help ■
		Damaged or incorrectly fitted tyres	Fit new tyres ■
		Loose or worn universal joints. Propeller shaft or drive shaft may also be damaged	Replace immediately ■
		Fan blade broken	Fit new fan blade ● (p. 207)
		Front-wheel bearing failure	Fit new bearings ■
	Engine runs, but car does not move when in gear (if propeller shaft turns)	Broken half-shaft or half-shaft key	Seek assistance; car may require lift tow ■
		Rear axle failure	Seek assistance; car will require lift tow ■
	Engine runs but car does not move when in gear (if propeller shaft does not turn)	Clutch slipping or failed	Check for correct free-play ● (p. 210). If in doubt, allow $\frac{1}{8}$ in. at point of adjustment and seek advice ■
		Automatic gearbox faulty	Check automatic gearbox oil level in the way recommended in the car handbook. If correct, seek advice ■
	Difficulty in engaging gear	Tick-over too fast	Adjust ● (pp. 188 and 190)
		Clutch does not disengage fully	Check that there is not too much free-play; that when the pedal is depressed, the activating lever on the side of the clutch housing is moved by the linkage, cable or hydraulic action. If linkage or cable is broken, replace. If the hydraulic system is empty, fill the reservoir and bleed the system ● (p. 210)
		Pressure-plate out of adjustment, causing centre-plate drag	Replace clutch assembly ■
		Broken or damaged centre-plate	Replace clutch assembly ■
	Difficulty in engaging gear after vehicle has been stored	Centre-plate stuck to flywheel or seized on spigot-shaft splines	Jack up a driving wheel, start engine in gear, press clutch pedal and apply brake ● If not successful, clutch will have to be dismantled and freed ■
	Clutch slips	Faulty adjustment	Adjust to recommended clearances ● (p. 210)
		Oil or grease on linings	Replace clutch unit. Find oil source and repair ■
		Clutch worn out	If the clearance is correct, replace the clutch ■
	Clutch judders	Pressure-plate out of adjustment	Replace clutch unit ■
		Engine mountings broken or too soft	Renew mountings ■

● indicates that the job is within the scope of a home mechanic
■ indicates that the work is beyond the scope of all but the most experienced mechanics, and you should consult a garage
▲ indicates that on emission control carburettors, work must be done by a specialist

Fault finding

	Symptom	Fault	Remedy
Transmission (contd)	Clutch judders *(contd)*	Engine tie-rod (if fitted) out of adjustment	If broken, adjust or replace ■
	Clutch is noisy when pedal is fully released with engine running	Clutch linkage wrongly adjusted	Adjust free-play ● (p. 210)
	Clutch noisy when pedal is depressed	Clutch-release bearing worn or damaged	Replace bearing ■
		Flywheel-spigot bearing dry	If particularly annoying, lubricate or replace (which entails stripping the clutch) ■
	Noise (thud) when clutch is released— engine running and transmission in gear	Free-play in rear axle	Seek advice. This is often found in older cars, but is not necessarily serious or worth correcting
	Clutch pedal will not come all the way back	Fault in linkage	Adjust as necessary ● (p. 210)
	Gear lever rattles or makes buzzing noise	Gear-stick loose	Check and tighten ■
		Gear-stick damper loose or missing	Check, tighten or replace ■
		Gear-stick ball and socket over-lubricated	Remove, dry ball and socket, lubricate sparingly and replace ■
		Remote-control linkage worn	Fit new parts as necessary ■
	Gear-grinding noise during engagement (car not moving)	Engine idling too fast	Adjust as required ● (pp. 188 and 190)
	Grinding noise during gear changes	Synchromesh worn	Seek advice ■
		Worn gearbox bearings	Seek advice ■
		Clutch not operating correctly	Change clutch ■
	Gear slips out of engagement	Worn gearbox	Seek advice ■
		Worn engine/gearbox mountings, allowing engine movement to knock out of gear	Replace mountings, torque-reaction struts or rubbers ■
	Transmission noisy in forward gears	Lubricant level low	Top up ● (pp. 210–11)
		Transmission misaligned	Align and tighten bolts ■
		Transmission internal component(s) worn, broken or damaged	Repair or replace defective parts ■
	Transmission noisy in reverse	Reverse idler-gear or shaft worn or damaged	Replace defective part(s) ■
	Transmission sticks in gear	Lubricant level wrong	Fill according to car handbook ● (p. 209)

	Symptom	Fault	Remedy
Transmission (contd)	Transmission sticks in gear *(contd)*	Gear-selector linkage not operating properly	Free or replace parts as required ■
		Internal gearbox fault	Seek advice ■
	Little or no increase in vehicle speed when accelerator is pressed, although engine rpm increases	Clutch slipping	Adjust free-play. If it is correct, the clutch is worn out. To continue journey, do not induce slip ● (p. 210)
Braking system	Brakes judder	Loose mountings, worn or faulty drums or discs	Check and tighten back-plate, spring U-bolts, and worn swivel pins and bushes. Replace drums or discs as necessary ■
		Brake linings damaged	Renew brake linings ● (pp. 214–17)
	Vehicle pulls to one side	One tyre under-inflated	Check tyre pressures ● (p. 218)
		Unequal brake adjustment	Adjust all brakes ● (p. 212)
		Oil on linings on side opposite to the pull	Fit new oil seals ■
		Seized wheel-cylinder piston on side opposite to the pull	Free piston or replace complete cylinder ■
	Too much pedal travel before brakes operate	Brake shoes need adjusting or replacing	Adjust shoes. If worn, replace ● (pp. 212 and 214)
		Master-cylinder push-rod has excessive clearance	Adjust ■
	Vibration felt on pedal when pressure is applied	Cracked or warped brake drums. Discs out of true	Replace ● (pp. 214–17)
	Pedal feels 'spongy'	Brakes not properly bled—air in system	Bleed system ● (p. 213)
		New brake shoes not run in	Condition will improve with use
	Pedal can only be applied by 'pumping'	Air in system	Bleed and adjust brakes ● (pp. 212–13)
		Master-cylinder fault	Replace master cylinder or rubbers ■
		Slight leak in system	Trace and cure ■
	More effort than usual required to operate the brakes	Brake linings worn	Replace ● (p. 214)
		Seized wheel-cylinder units	Repair or replace ■
		Servo, where fitted, not working	Check manifold-to-servo vacuum supply. If satisfactory, put a hand on the servo; if operation cannot be felt when the brakes are applied and the engine is running, seek advice ■
		Wrong linings	Replace with manufacturer's exchange unit ● (pp. 214–15)
	Brakes drag or fail to release	Shoes adjusted too close to drum (binding)	Re-adjust ● (p. 212)
		Air hole in reservoir cap blocked	Use pin to clear cap hole ●
		Wheel-cylinder piston seized	Replace or free ■
		Handbrake cables seized	Clean, lubricate and check action ● (p. 212)
		Shoe-return springs weak or broken	Replace ● (p. 214)

● indicates that the job is within the scope of a home mechanic

■ indicates that the work is beyond the scope of all but the most experienced mechanics, and you should consult a garage

Fault finding

	Symptom	Fault	Remedy
Braking system (contd)	Brakes drag or fail to release *(contd)*	Adjustment of push-rod from pedal to master-cylinder	Re-adjust to give free play at pedal before rod contacts master-cylinder piston ∎
		Hydraulic cylinder cups swollen	Wrong fluid in system. Drain and replace all cups and fill with new fluid ∎
	Brakes grab	Shoes faulty	Inspect shoes and linings. If not worn to replacement level, chamfer leading edges to prevent grabbing. Fit new return springs ● (p. 214)
		Distorted or cracked drums or discs	Replace ● (pp. 214–17)
	Brakes overheating or smoking	Shoes binding	Re-adjust shoes ● (p. 212)
		Prolonged use of brakes during steep descent, fast driving or towing	Stop and allow to cool as often as possible ●
	Brakes suddenly fail	Broken brake pipe or leak	Consult garage ∎
Suspension	Car low at front	Tyre pressure wrong	Inflate to correct pressure ● (p. 218)
		Broken spring(s)	Replace broken spring(s) ∎
		Weak spring(s)	Replace the front springs if the front-wheel riding height is below specification ∎
		Weak or defective damper spring unit(s)	Replace ∎
		Hydraulic or compressed gas unit leak	Seek advice ∎
	Car low at rear	Tyre pressure wrong	Inflate to correct pressure ● (p. 218)
		Vehicle is overloaded at rear	Distribute weight evenly ●
		Broken spring(s)	Replace broken spring(s) ∎
		Weak spring(s)	Replace the rear springs if the rear-wheel riding height is below specification ∎
		Weak or defective damper spring unit(s)	Check and replace ∎
	Car low at one wheel	Tyre pressure wrong	Inflate to correct pressure ● (p. 218)
		Car unevenly loaded	Distribute weight evenly ●
		Broken spring	Replace spring ∎
		Weak spring	Replace spring ∎
		Worn or damaged suspension parts	Replace all suspension arms and bushes that are worn or damaged ∎
	Car tilts to one side	Hydragas or Hydralastic pressure wrong	Check pressure and increase as required ∎
		Chassis damaged or broken	Check alignment and repair ∎
		Weak or defective damper spring unit(s)	Check and replace ∎
	Hard or rough ride	Tyre pressure wrong	Check tyre pressure ● (p. 218)
		Vehicle overloaded or unevenly loaded	Distribute weight evenly ●

	Symptom	Fault	Remedy
Suspension (contd)	Hard or rough ride *(contd)*	Out-of-round tyre	Replace tyre ■
		Loose or defective damper unit(s)	Tighten or replace ■
		Broken spring	Replace spring ■
		Seized suspension parts	Lubricate or replace ● (p. 222)
	Car sways	Loose or defective damper unit(s)	Tighten or replace ■
		Broken spring	Replace spring ■
		Weak spring	Replace spring ■
		Loose or broken anti-roll bar	Seek help ■
		Roof-rack overloaded	Unload: use roof-rack for bulky but not heavy items ●
Steering	Car wanders	Tyre pressure wrong	Inflate to correct pressure ● (p. 218)
		Car overloaded or unevenly loaded	Distribute weight evenly ●
		Loose, worn or damaged steering linkage or connections	Replace parts where necessary ■
		Incorrect front-wheel alignment	Adjust wheel alignment to specification ■
		Loose steering box	Tighten box attachment or replace if housing is broken ■
		Broken spring	Replace spring ■
		Weak spring	Replace spring ■
		Incorrect front-wheel bearing adjustment	Adjust wheel bearings to specification ■
		Incorrect steering-box adjustment	Adjust to specification ■
	Steering hard to turn	Tyre pressure wrong	Inflate to correct pressure ● (p. 218)
		Not enough lubrication	Grease as recommended. Top up oil in steering box ● (p. 224)
		Steering-gear adjustment wrong	Adjust ■
		Front-wheel alignment wrong	Adjust wheel alignment to specification ■
		Damaged steering box	Overhaul or replace ■
	Play in steering	Loose, worn or damaged steering linkage or connections	Replace parts as necessary ■
		Loose steering-box mounting	Tighten box attachment or replace if housing is cracked ■
		Steering-box adjustment wrong	Adjust to specification ■
		Suspension ball-joints or king-pins worn	Replace as necessary ■
	Car pulls to one side	Tyre pressure wrong	Inflate to correct pressure ● (p. 218)
		Tyres on front wheels in different states of wear	Seek expert help ■
		Brakes binding	Adjust or repair as necessary ● (pp. 212–17)

● indicates that the job is within the scope of a home mechanic

■ indicates that the work is beyond the scope of all but the most experienced mechanics, and you should consult a garage

Fault finding

	Symptom	Fault	Remedy
Steering (contd)	Car pulls to one side (*contd*)	Broken spring	Replace spring ■
		Weak spring(s)	Replace spring(s) ■
		Front-wheel alignment wrong	Adjust wheel alignment ■
		Rear axle loose	Tighten rear suspension mountings and tie rods ■
Wheels and tyres	Tyre wear conditions	Front-wheel alignment wrong	Adjust alignment ■
		Wheels out of balance	Balance each wheel ■
		Buckled wheels	Renew ■
		Front-wheel bearing adjustment wrong	Adjust wheel bearings to specification ■
		Worn or damaged suspension components	Replace ■
		Loose, worn or damaged steering linkage or connections	Replace ■
	Tyres show excess wear on edges of tread	Tyres under-inflated	Inflate to correct pressure ● (p. 218)
		Front-wheel alignment wrong	Adjust alignment ■
	Tyres show excess wear in tread centre	Tyres over-inflated	Reduce tyre pressure to specification ● (p. 218)

Identifying engine noises

Engine noises often require explanation, if only for the motorist's peace of mind. Although some hints are given here, it is emphasised that they are only *hints*. The same fault in two different engines will not necessarily make the same sound. A simple way to hear engine noises, and often to pinpoint their source, is to use a long screwdriver as a stethoscope. But take care to avoid the engine fan and its driving belt if you have long hair, or are wearing a tie or loose clothing.

Symptom	Fault	Remedy
Light tapping	Tappets out of adjustment	Check and adjust tappets ● (p. 181)
Persistent light tap after tappet adjustment	Worn cams, tappets or rocker arms	Check and replace worn parts ■
Persistent light tap, varying with engine load and speed	Worn small-end bush, piston slap or broken piston ring	Seek expert assistance ■
Heavy knock varying with engine speed or engine load	Big-end bearings worn	Immediate workshop job to prevent further damage ■
Rattle or grind when clutch is operated	Clutch-release bearing worn	Remove gearbox and fit new clutch assembly ■
Squeal or whine	Worn seals on water pump, or slack fan-belt	Check pump body for leaks; check fan-belt ● (p. 206)
Hissing pop as throttle is opened	Exhaust leak at manifold flange, or damaged silencer	Tighten or replace as necessary ● (pp. 260–1)
Rattle noticeable during tick-over	Worn timing chain, or tensioner out of adjustment	Re-adjust tensioner or fit new chain ■
Hiss varying with engine speed	Air leak into inlet manifold	Check carburettor flange gasket ● (p. 187)

	Symptom	Fault	Remedy
Starter system	Starter motor does not turn and lights fail to operate	Battery flat	Recharge or replace ● (p. 195)
		Open circuit in line from battery	Clean and remake connections to the battery. If fault persists, check battery earth connection, and connection at starter solenoid terminal ● (pp. 195 and 230)
	Starter motor does not turn and lights go out	Poor connection at battery	Clean and remake connections to battery (as above) ● (p. 195)
	Starter motor does not turn and lights go very dim	Battery in too low a state of charge	Recharge or obtain replacement ● (p. 195)
		Starter-motor pinion jammed	Free the pinion ● (p. 230)
		Short-circuit in or at starter motor	Check that the lead to starter motor is not loose or touching a metal part. Otherwise, remove and repair or replace starter motor ● (pp. 230–1)
		Engine seized	Seek expert help ■
	Starter motor does not turn engine; lights go slightly dim	Pinion not engaging, although motor runs freely	Listen for sound of running motor to confirm diagnosis. Then remove motor, clean pinion and sleeve. Check for satisfactory operation and refit motor ● (p. 230)
	Starter motor does not turn; lights stay fully bright	Ignition key not operating circuit	Operate solenoid by hand, if possible ● (p. 230). If not, seek expert help ■
		Solenoid switch faulty or circuit open	Check and replace ● (p. 230)
		Open circuit in starter motor	Tap the starter motor sharply and turn the armature a little as if to free pinion. Check connections, also motor commutator and brushes. If none of this works, replace starter motor ● (pp. 230–1)
	Solenoid switch chatters	Battery flat	Charge or push start ● (p. 195)
	Engine starts but starter fails to disengage, making a loud noise	Faulty ignition/starter switch	Disconnect solenoid activating wire from solenoid; start by manual button or push start. Fit new switch as soon as possible ■
		Pinion jammed in mesh with flywheel gear teeth	Free the pinion. If the fault continues, remove the motor to inspect the pinion and the flywheel ring gear for damage. Replace if necessary ● (p. 230)
DC generator system	The vehicle generator is meant to supply the correct charging rate at all times—that is, a high rate of charge for a discharged battery and a low rate for a fully charged battery. If an ammeter is fitted, it is possible to monitor the charging rate. If there is no ammeter, the only visual indication of a fault is the failure of the light to go out above idling speed. This will mean that the charging system has failed		
	Charge rate zero or too low	Drive-belt slipping or broken	Adjust or replace ● (p. 206)
		Poor connections or faulty leads	Clean and tighten connections on dynamo and control box ● (p. 232)
		Electrolyte level in battery very low	Top up with distilled water ● (p. 195)

● indicates that the job is within the scope of a home mechanic
■ indicates that the work is beyond the scope of all but the most experienced mechanics, and you should consult a garage

Fault finding

	Symptom	Fault	Remedy
Dynamo	Not charging	Sticking brushes	Remove brushes. Renew if worn, or clean them and their guides and refit in original positions ● (p. 233)
		Weak springs	If colour suggests springs have been very hot or if they are obviously worn or damaged, replace them ● (p. 233)
		Dirty commutator	Clean surface with petrol-moistened rag ● (p. 233)
		Burnt commutator	Polish surface by rotating commutator against a piece of fine glasspaper (not emery) ● (p. 233). If more drastic treatment is necessary to remove pitting, have the dynamo overhauled by a vehicle electrical specialist or fit a complete exchange unit ■
		Internal wiring defects	Consult vehicle electrician or fit replacement dynamo ■
	Erratic charging	Faulty control box or bad earth, indicated by an extra bright ignition warning-light (above tick-over) or a fluctuating ammeter reading	Check that the control box has a good earth ● (p. 227). Replace or have control box adjusted by vehicle electrician ■
	Fluctuating charging rate	Control box defective	Have control box tested by vehicle electrician ■
	Noisy dynamo	Loose mounting bolts or pulley	Check and tighten ● (p. 232)
		Worn bearings	Replace bearings or complete dynamo ■
AC generator (alternator)	An alternator can be damaged easily: any charging fault, apart from fan-belt adjustment or loose connections, should be left to a vehicle electrician		
	Not charging	Loose or broken fan belt	Replace or adjust ● (p. 206)
		Loose connection	Check and tighten any loose or disconnected wires. The engine must not be running while connections are made or broken ● (p. 232)
Lighting system	All lamps fail to light	Poor connection at battery	Clean and remake ● (p. 195)
		Battery completely flat	Charge or replace ● (p. 195)
	All lamps fail when starter motor is operated or fail to light after starter has 'gone dead'	Arcing at poor battery-terminal connection has caused high resistance between terminal and cable clamp	Clean and remake battery connection(s) ● (p. 195)
	Lamps in series with main lighting switch fail	Switch defective	Using a lead with a clip at each end, short-circuit the input and output terminal of switch. If lamps light, switch is faulty and should be replaced. This test is not easy to make—if in doubt, seek expert help ■
		Feed-wire to switch disconnected or broken	Check and replace or reconnect ■
	Pair or set of lamps fail to light	Bad earth return	Make temporary earth with wire to test. Clean as necessary ● (p. 227)
		Faulty switch	Check and repair or replace ● (p. 226)
		Connector or a feed-wire common to both lights has become defective	Trace wiring and repair. Check push connectors ● (p. 228)
		Bulbs blown	Check and replace ● (p. 226)

	Symptom	Fault	Remedy
Lighting system (contd)	One lamp of a pair (or set) fails	Bulb blown	Check and replace ● (p. 226)
		Poor contact at bulbholder	Remove bulb, scrape contacts (in bulb cap and holder) to clean, then refit firmly ● (p. 226)
		Poor earth connection	Check. Clean point of connection and remake ● (p. 228)
		Broken feed wire to lamp or loose connector	Trace wiring and repair ● (p. 228)
	All side and rear lights fail, but flashers and stoplights work	Fuse (often a line fuse) broken	Check handbook for location of fuse, and replace ● (p. 226)
	An independent lamp (or accessory) fails	Fuse failed (if fitted)	Investigate cause and repair, then fit new fuse ● (p. 226)
		Same fault as when one lamp fails (above)	Remedies as above ● (pp. 226 and 228)
		Accessory fault	Repair or replace ● (p. 229)
		Faulty switch	Repair or replace ● (p. 229)
	Panel lamp fails to light	Faulty switch	Repair or replace ● (p. 229)
		Faults as for independent lamp failing	Remedies as above ● (pp. 226, 228 and 229)
	Interior lamp fails to operate ('on' or 'off') from door pillar switches	Bulb failed	Check and replace ● (p. 226)
		Poor contact with switch holder	Remove, scrape contacts and refit. This switch earths at its locating hole in the door jamb ● (p. 229)
		Defective wiring or connections	Check and repair ● (p. 228)
	All lights dim when car is stationary or at low speed	Fan belt loose	Tighten ● (p. 206)
		Battery in low state of charge	Charge or replace ● (p. 195)
	All lights dim even when car is running at moderate to high speeds	Fan belt loose	Check and tighten ● (p. 206)
		Generator output too low	Adjust control box ■
	Poor illumination from one or more lamps	Excessive blackening of bulbs	Replace ● (p. 226)
		Bad earth	Check and clean ● (p. 227)
		Reflector tarnished	Renew light unit(s) ● (p. 256)
		Defective wiring or connection	Check and repair ● (p. 229)
	Lights flicker or increase appreciably in brilliance when generator is charging the battery	Defective or flat battery	Replace or charge ● (p. 195)
		Fan belt loose	Tighten ● (p. 206)
		Excessive load on battery (i.e., too many accessories)	If possible, remove some of the load ●
		Bad earth	Check and clean control-box earth ● (p. 227)
		Faulty control box	Replace, or seek help from vehicle electrician ■

● indicates that the job is within the scope of a home mechanic
■ indicates that the work is beyond the scope of all but the most experienced mechanics, and you should consult a garage

Fault finding

	Symptom	Fault	Remedy
Lighting system (contd)	Bulbs blacken frequently or keep blowing	Excessive generator voltage (assuming correct-voltage bulb)	Control-box fault: seek help from vehicle electrician ■
Accessories	All accessories on the same fuse fail to operate	Fuse blown, or dirty fuse or holder	Clean fuse holder if fuse is serviceable. Switch everything off, including ignition switch, and fit replacement fuse. Switch on ignition and note if fuse blows again. If so, there is a 'short' in a circuit that receives power without the need of another switch. If fuse does not blow, switch on each accessory branch until the fuse blows, thus indicating the faulty branch. Inspect closely for defective accessory or wiring. Repair ● (p. 226). If in doubt, seek expert help ■
		Ignition switch defective	Check by by-passing switch, using a lead ■
		Circuit between power supply and fuse defective	Trace wire, check and repair ■
Direction indicators	Completely inoperative	Fuse blown, or dirty fuse or holder	As for when all accessories fail ● (p. 226) ■
		Faulty flasher unit	Check and replace ● (p. 229)
		Faulty wire between power supply, via fuse, to flasher unit; or faulty connections	Check and repair ■
		Faulty cable or connections between flasher unit and direction-indicator switch	Check and repair ■
	Warning lamp not flashing (flasher unit not clicking)	Set of indicator bulbs on one side of vehicle not working	Check bulbs and wiring connections. Rectify as necessary. Check indicator switch ● (p. 227)
		System completely inoperative	See checks under 'Completely inoperative' section above
	Warning lamp not flashing (flasher unit clicking)	Warning light or one indicator bulb not working	Check whether bulb is blown, wiring connections are defective, or if there is a bad earth. Repair as necessary ● (p. 227)
	Increased rate of flashing of indicator lamps and warning lamp	Fault in flasher unit or wrong type for vehicle	Check and replace if necessary ● (p. 229)
Heater blower	Repairs to most heater blowers are impractical: it is usually wiser to replace the unit. However, some minor jobs can be done		
	Blower unit inoperative	Fuse blown	Investigate and replace ● (p. 226)
		Loose connections or broken wires	Check (including earth) and repair ● (p. 227)
		Faulty switch	Check by short-circuiting switch, using a lead with a clip on each end. Fit replacement switch ● (p. 227)
		Electrical failure in motor	Fit new blower unit unless motor is accessible for servicing ■
Windscreen wipers	Failure to operate	Fuse blown	Investigate and replace ● (p. 226)
		Connections and wiring faulty	Check and repair ● (p. 228)
		Faulty switch	Check by by-passing, replace if necessary ● (p. 227)
		Mechanical drive seized	Seek expert help ■
		Faulty motor	Fit new motor, or dismantle and replace defective part (e.g., brushes, armature, etc.). In either case, follow manufacturer's instructions ●. If in doubt, seek expert help

Symptom	Fault	Remedy
Windscreen wipers (contd)		
Failure to operate *(contd)*	Thermostatic overload device has cut out	Re-attempt to operate motor after 10–15 minutes. If successful, but motor cuts out after a short period, there is an overload. Check as for mechanical drive. This check is best performed with windscreen wetted to reduce load ■
Motor operates too slowly	Excessive resistance in circuit or wiper-blade drive	Trace wiring and repair poor connections. Lubricate drive ■
	Worn brushes	Fit new brushes ■
Incorrect parking position for blades	Parking switch out of adjustment	Adjust parking switch (on wiper motor) ● (p. 229)
Electric horn	Most horns are not meant to be dismantled by the owner, but an adjusting screw may be provided to take up the wear of the moving parts	
Complete loss of sound	Fuse blown or holder dirty	Investigate and replace ● (p. 226)
	Flat battery	Charge or replace ● (p. 195)
	Faulty or loose connections	Check and correct ● (p. 229)
	Faulty relay	Refer to wiring diagram and short-out to confirm ■
	Horn out of adjustment	If possible, adjust to maker's instructions in handbook ● or seek expert help ■
	Internal failure of horn unit	Replace ●
	Bad earth at horn button	Check connections, and ensure the button contact makes a good earth when operated ● (p. 227)
Loss of volume or intermittent sound	Faulty or loose connections	Check and correct ● (p. 229)
	Horn out of adjustment or foreign matter between contact points	Adjust to maker's instructions or replace ●
	Internal failure of horn	Replace ●
	Something pressing on external diaphragm	Remove obstruction ●
SU electric fuel pump		
Pump not working	Power not reaching pump	Check fuse (if fitted), wiring and connections. Repair as necessary. Check connections between wire and connector at pump end if the pump is exposed to weather ● (p. 226)
	Contact points dirty	Clean the points with fine emery paper. The cover must be weather-sealed if fitted under the car ● (p. 191)
	Pump faulty	Replace ● (p. 191)
Pump noisy and working faster	No fuel	Check fuel in tank. If it is parked on severe camber and fuel level is low, push the car on to level ground ●
	Dirt under valve	Unscrew outlet union and withdraw valve cage. Clean and reassemble ● (p. 191)
	Air leak on suction side	Check all pipe unions for tightness ● (p. 191)
	Carburettor flooding	Check carburettor needle valve ● (p. 193)

● indicates that the job is within the scope of a home mechanic
■ indicates that the work is beyond the scope of all but the most experienced mechanics, and you should consult a garage

Engine/routine checks

REGULAR MAINTENANCE not only extends the life of the car; it cuts running costs too.

A motorist who intends to service a car himself should have a copy of the maker's handbook—or the more detailed workshop manual—the correct tools, and preferably a clean and well-lit workshop.

For the car owner who is not mechanically minded, garage attention has often been the only solution to his car problems. But there are many repair and maintenance jobs—all of those described in this section—which are well within the ability of most people.

Do not try to cut corners on car maintenance and servicing. It can be dangerous. All the jobs recommended on the following pages are safe; but the detailed instructions should always be followed.

Running in The working surfaces of a new car engine are extremely close-fitting and have to be 'bedded in' with care to avoid seizure or damage. When the engine is used, tiny metal particles are scraped away from the surfaces and are then picked up by the oil. To clear them, engine oil should be changed after 500 miles and again at 3000 miles. Always change the oil when the engine is hot because it will then flow out much more freely, carrying all the particles with it.

Engine speed must be kept down during the running-in stage. Instructions are given in the handbook. Avoid slogging—going uphill in too high a gear—or over-revving in low gear, but give the engine more and more work to do as the mileage increases.

Routine servicing Oil should be used and changed according to the handbook instructions. Magnetic drain-plugs for the sump, gearbox and final drive may be worth fitting to catch metal particles in the oil.

It is not enough to change the oil only at given mileage intervals. A car being used entirely for short journeys will probably not get hot enough to evaporate the condensation caused by starting the engine. This in time will dilute the oil, reduce its lubrication value and cause sludging. This is why the handbook instructs that oil should be changed after a certain time interval even if the mileage covered is below the recommended figure. The engine will almost certainly need fresh oil.

Starting from cold Use the choke for as short a time as possible, since the extra petrol entering the combustion chambers washes away the oil film between the pistons and cylinders, and between the valves and valve guides. This leads to metal rubbing against metal and promotes rapid wear. An upper-cylinder lubricant, contained in the higher grades of petrol, helps to minimise this wear. It is in the first few minutes' running, when the engine is still cold, that the greatest wear takes place. Avoid hard use—fierce acceleration—until the engine is warm.

Do-it-yourself Much of the servicing and maintenance required to cope with normal engine wear can be carried out by the motorist himself.

Regular inspection at the points shown in the diagram on this page will prevent leaks becoming serious. Tappet adjustment is relatively easy. But even decoking—no longer required at fixed mileages, but nevertheless advisable if the valves have to be renewed—is not beyond the ability of the amateur mechanic.

WHERE LEAKS OCCUR, WHAT KIND, AND WHAT TO DO

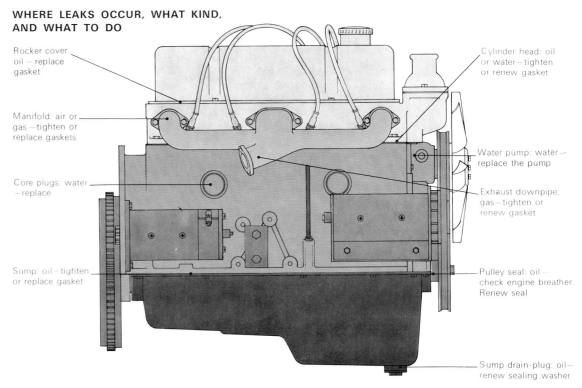

Rocker cover oil — replace gasket

Manifold: air or gas — tighten or replace gaskets

Core plugs: water — replace

Sump: oil — tighten or replace gasket

Cylinder head: oil or water — tighten or renew gasket

Water pump: water — replace the pump

Exhaust downpipe: gas — tighten or renew gasket

Pulley seal: oil — check engine breather. Renew seal

Sump drain-plug: oil — renew sealing washer

Removing the rocker cover

1 Remove the leads to the spark-plugs if necessary and number them with tags. Take off any breather pipes and, to give better access, remove the air filter. Unscrew the rocker-cover fastenings

2 Hold the rocker cover (which is quite light) at both ends, and lift it vertically from the cylinder head. Do not use force, and always make sure that there is a new gasket of the correct size available for reassembly

Adjusting the tappets and valve clearance

'ADJUSTING THE TAPPETS' is a misleading description, for it is in fact the valve clearance that is adjusted.

There has to be a clearance between the camshaft and its cam-followers (the tappets), to cope with expansion in a hot engine, making sure that the valves can close. Because it is not practicable to measure this clearance at the camshaft, adjustment is made at the rocker arm.

Most manufacturers give the valve-clearance figures for a cold engine. Some give figures for both hot and cold. Check in the handbook. On some makes, the clearance for the exhaust and inlet valves may be different. If in doubt as to which is which, use the inlet and exhaust manifolds as a guide or seek advice.

The clearance is measured by inserting a feeler gauge between the valve stem and the rocker arm. Before making any adjustment, ensure that the valve is fully closed. One way to do this on engines with siamesed ports—exhaust, inlet, inlet, exhaust, exhaust and so on—is to follow the rule of 9 for a 4-cylinder engine (or 13 for a 6-cylinder engine). For example, turn the engine until valve 2 is fully open, subtract 2 from 9 (or from 13 on a 6 cylinder), and valve 7 (or 11) will be fully closed. The valves can be numbered from either end of the engine. This system cannot be used on some V engines or inline engines if the valves are positioned alternately—inlet, exhaust, inlet, exhaust and so on.

On V-engines, follow the maker's recommended order. Adjusting the clearance on overhead camshaft engines is often a garage job; it can mean removing the camshaft.

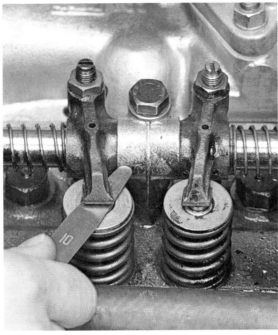

1 Make sure that the valve is fully closed—using the rule of 9 or 13 given on this page—by turning the engine over slowly by hand. Check the existing clearance gap with the correct size of feeler gauge

2 Loosen the lock-nut with a spanner and adjust the screw until the correct gap is obtained. Check with the feeler gauge. Hold the screw with the screwdriver, and tighten up the lock-nut with the spanner. Check finally

Removing the rocker gear

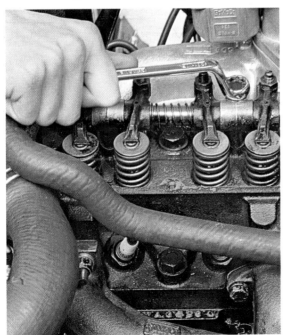

1 As a preliminary to removing the cylinder head, loosen the rocker-gear securing nuts evenly from the centre—in alternate order—about half a turn at a time. This prevents distortion when open valves close

2 The rocker shaft can now be removed. Be sure to place it on a clean, dry surface. To help with reassembly, it is advisable to lay the various engine components down in the order in which they are dismantled

3 With the shaft removed, the push-rods can be taken out. Shake them before removal so that the cam-followers are not dislodged with them. Pin them in a piece of paper to keep them in order

Engine/working on the cylinder head

Removing the cylinder head

1 Drain off the coolant at least to below the level of the cylinder head. Save the coolant if it contains antifreeze so it can be used again. Remove and inspect for damage any hoses and take out the spark-plugs

2 Remove the controls and pipes attached to the carburettor, and unbolt the exhaust downpipe from the manifold. Remove any connections (for example, the earth strap or temperature-gauge lead) fitted to the cylinder head

3 Loosen the retaining nuts securing the cylinder head in the order given in the handbook, half a turn at a time. Break the seal between head and block by turning the engine or by tapping the head with a soft mallet (not hammer)

Decarbonising the cylinder head

DEPOSITS OF CARBON in the engine combustion chambers and on the valves and their stems reduce the efficiency of the engine. The removal of this carbon, known as decarbonising or decoking, is normally carried out only when the head is removed to attend to a valve fault (which can be quickly diagnosed by compression testing). It is not usual, on modern cars, to have to decoke the pistons and valves unless some other work is necessary.

Required for the job are: a decoke gasket set; some grinding paste (coarse and fine); a valve-grinding tool and compressor; a socket set; hand spanners and a torque spanner; clean rag and paraffin.

Disconnect the battery earth terminal, for a live starter motor is potentially dangerous on a dismantled engine. Remove all fittings attached to the head, drain the cooling system and remove the spark-plugs, rocker shaft (see p. 39) and manifolds. Lift off the head. Take care on wet-linered engines (ones with removable cylinders) that the cylinders are not pushed out when the engine is turned. If this happens, garage help will be needed.

When cleaning the tops of the pistons, stuff clean rags into the other cylinders so that bits of carbon do not drop into them. Do not scratch the piston. Leave a ring of carbon about $\frac{3}{16}$ in. wide round the outer edge of each piston to ensure that there will be no temporary increase in oil consumption after a decoke.

When decoking the cylinder head, do not damage the flat surfaces, especially if it is a light alloy. When all the carbon is removed, brush the surface clean with paraffin.

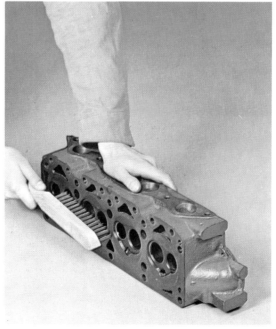

1 Gentle use of a wire brush, taking care not to score the metal, will move all but the most stubborn carbon deposits. These can be dislodged with a scraper or a piece of hardwood. Take special care with light-alloy cylinder heads

2 An electric drill, fitted with wire brushes, may help in speeding up the cleaning of the exhaust and inlet ports. Again, take care to avoid damage. Wash the surfaces thoroughly with paraffin after decarbonising

Removing the valves from the cylinder head

TO DISMANTLE the valves from the cylinder head, move the head to a clean bench or working surface where there is sufficient space to carry out the job. When removing small parts such as collets, store them carefully in a box.

Valve-spring compressors are obtainable in different sizes, and the dealer will advise which is suitable for a particular car. The compressor is similar in shape to a G-clamp and is used to compress the valve spring so that the split collets which retain the spring can be removed. Once the spring has been freed in this way, it and the valve can be removed from the cylinder head.

Check the height of valve springs against the manufacturers' standards (usually given in the workshop manual). If they are significantly less, fit new springs.

Before using a valve-spring compressor, loosen the cotters in the spring collar by tapping sharply downwards on the collar (not on the valve). If this is not done, it is possible that the compressor may be strained.

As valves are often easily bent by misuse, and even the slightest bend means they have to be replaced, great care is needed when handling or cleaning them, especially if any kind of machine tool is used for the job.

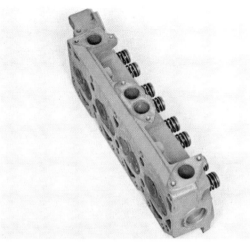

1 Remove and store the exhaust and inlet manifolds. Clean the cylinder head with paraffin before attempting to start any work on the valves. The head can quite easily be damaged if it is dropped, so handle it with care

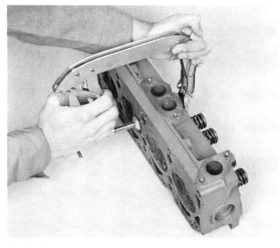

2 Fit the G-shaped compressor exactly over the valve-spring retaining collar and in the centre of the head of the valve. Make sure there is no sideways movement as the spring is compressed, and tighten the compressor tool

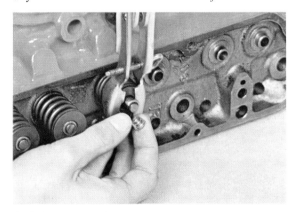

3 With the spring fully compressed, remove the two split collets which retain the spring collar on the stem. Make sure that the collets, which are small and tend to be easily lost, are carefully stored in a safe place

4 As the compressor is released, the valve spring expands to its fullest extent. The collar on the valve spring is loose and may come away with the compressor. It is easy to lose or overlook it. For safety's sake, store it with the collets

5 Remove the spring itself and inspect it for any defect. If it is to be refitted, place it carefully aside and make sure that the different valve assemblies are kept in their correct order, so they can be replaced in the same position

6 The valve-spring seat or guide is now exposed. In some cases, the guide contains an oil-sealing ring. It can be discarded, for there will be a replacement in the decoke set. But check how it is fitted; there is usually a right and wrong way

7 Before removing the valve from the cylinder head, wipe the exposed valve stem with a clean rag. When they have been removed, the valves can be pushed into a piece of card and numbered for future identification purposes

8 A valve and spring assembly: on the left, the valve and the two segments of the split collet; on the right, the spring collar, the spring and the oil seal. All components should be thoroughly cleaned before replacing

Engine/cylinder-head overhaul and reassembly

Grinding in the valves

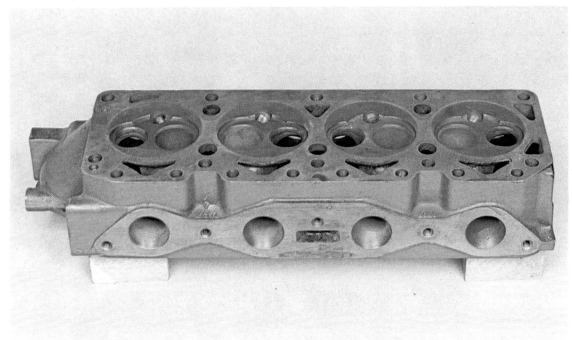

1 Support the cylinder head so that the valves can be fitted without their stems coming into contact with the bench. First check (from the handbook) that the valves have not been coated with another metal; if so, they cannot be reground. Their seats, however, can be ground, with a used uncoated valve. If the valves can be ground, inspect each seat. If they are cracked, pitted or burnt, a machine shop repair or replacement may be necessary

2 The tool used to grind the valve is a length of wood with a rubber pad at either one or both ends. The pad is pressed on to the face of the valve head and is held by suction, enabling the valve to be lifted and rotated as necessary

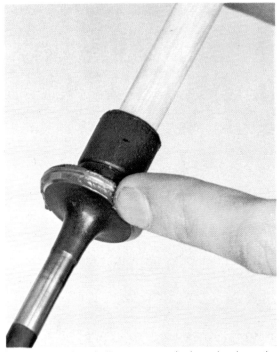

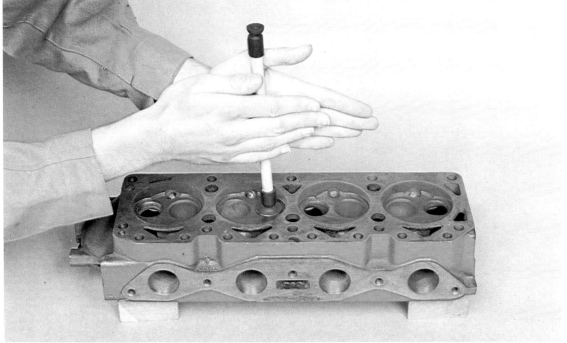

3 Always apply grinding paste sparingly and only to the contact edge of the valve head or its seating. Keep all the other parts free of paste, and make sure that none can enter the engine, where it can cause extensive damage

4 As the valve is rotated in both directions in its seating, the grinding paste cuts away any roughness or prominence on either surface. Continuous one-way rotation will produce scoring. Periodically, lift the valve off its seat and rotate it 90°, grind until both surfaces are clean and free of blemish. After grinding, clean all the surfaces thoroughly with paraffin to ensure that all the grinding paste is removed. Lightly lubricate stems and seats with engine oil

Replacing the cylinder head and gasket

AFTER THE VALVES are ground and the cylinder head is completely clean, replace the valve-spring assembly, making sure new valve-stem oil seals are fitted where necessary, in reverse order to dismantling. Ensure that the collets are located correctly in the valve-stem grooves.

Clean the engine-block face thoroughly and smear a little engine oil inside the cylinder bores. Check that the new cylinder-head gasket is correct for the engine by holding it against the old gasket. Place it on the cylinder block right side up. Many gaskets are marked 'top' or 'front' as a guide to ensure they are fitted correctly.

Place the cylinder head on the gasket and screw all the cylinder-head retaining nuts or bolts finger tight. On light-alloy cylinder heads, use a flat washer between the head and the nut, to prevent damage to the head.

Tightening sequence The tightening of the cylinder head is one of the most important parts of the reassembly operation. When the nuts are finger tight, they must be screwed down further—following exactly the sequence recommended by the manufacturer. If this is not detailed in the handbook, check with the manufacturer before starting the work. At the same time, find out the torque-setting figures for final tightening and do not exceed them.

Tighten in three stages. In the first two, gently pull the head down by screwing the nuts in the correct sequence with a socket and very short bar (which will prevent over-tightening). Carry out the final tightening with a torque spanner correctly set—again in the correct sequence.

Before fitting the rocker shaft, the push-rods should be replaced and carefully located in the cam-followers from which they were removed. When replacing the rocker gear, ensure that the adjusting end of the rocker arm is correctly placed in the cup on the push-rod.

The rocker shaft has to be carefully and evenly tightened to avoid undue strain and damage, since one or more of the valves are opened during tightening.

Final adjustment The tappets can now be adjusted. For light-alloy heads, this is the final adjustment.

Clean the manifold thoroughly. If the inlet manifold has dirt or metal particles in it, they will enter the engine. Use new gaskets for the reassembly and tighten evenly. Replace the hoses, throttle linkage and any other head attachments which may have been removed and fill with coolant. This is the stage, before starting the engine, at which to change the oil if necessary.

Start the engine and check that the oil is reaching the valve rockers. Keep the engine running—during this period it may be advisable to replace the rocker cover loosely to avoid oil splashes. When the engine is thoroughly warm, tighten the cylinder-head nuts with a torque spanner in the correct sequence. This does not apply to light-alloy heads, however, unless specifically recommended by the manufacturer.

Give the tappets a final adjustment and replace the rocker cover, using a new gasket.

Adjust the carburettor and ignition as required (see pp. 188, 190 and 201) and check for leaks.

Cast-iron cylinder heads and, where recommended, light-alloy heads should be retightened after 500 miles' running. If not, the cylinder-head gasket may blow, or water may leak into the engine.

1 Use a new cylinder-head gasket of the correct size and type, checking it against the old one. As a guide, it will normally be marked 'top' or 'front'. Make sure it is placed correctly on the clean face of the engine block

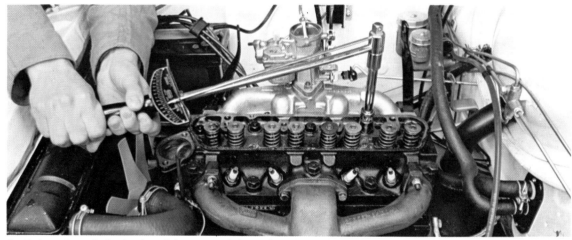

2 Tighten the cylinder-head retaining nuts or bolts in the order given in the car handbook. For final tightening, use a torque spanner, which must be set to the figures recommended by the vehicle manufacturers

3 During reassembly, use new gaskets throughout. Cleanliness at this stage is particularly important. Do not use excessive force when tightening the exhaust-downpipe or manifold studs. They are difficult to replace if broken

Carburettor/routine jobs

THE CARBURETTOR mixes fuel with air to provide a vapour which will burn and expand in the engine's cylinders, and so power the pistons. Its setting and operation must be correct to obtain the right balance between good performance and fuel economy.

Although there are many variations of carburettors, there are some basic design features common to all types. All have a reservoir (float chamber); a float and needle valve to control the amount of petrol in the carburettor; jets to regulate accurately the amount of petrol being mixed with air; a mixing chamber (the venturi); a choke to enrich the mixture when starting from cold; and a 'butterfly' throttle-control valve.

Dirty petrol The most common problem with carburettors is dirty petrol, which can leave deposits in the float chamber, and eventually block the jets. Even when the carburettor is regularly serviced, this kind of fault can occur if the car has run out of petrol or been filled from a can instead of a garage fuel pump. There is almost always dirt in the bottom of the petrol tank. It is easier to ensure that the bottom of the tank is never reached than to have to remove the tank to clean it.

Although it is unlikely to affect the carburettor itself, the air entering has to be filtered so that dirt cannot reach the moving parts of the engine and increase wear.

The maintenance of a carburettor, therefore, mainly means ensuring that it is clean. Both the air filter at the top and the petrol filter (if there is one fitted) can be removed for cleaning. If they are very dirty or damaged, they may have to be replaced. When removing the top of the carburettor, lift it off slowly and take care that any spring-loaded balls or distance pieces do not fall into the inlet manifold.

Most carburettor jets can be removed and cleaned. Do not try to poke them clear with a piece of wire. Only air pressure can clean them without widening or distorting the fine jet hole, so upsetting the petrol metering.

The float can be taken out and the needle valve inspected. It should not stick.

Leaking float If petrol is heard inside the float, when it is held close to the ear and shaken gently, the float has been leaking and the only practical solution is to replace it.

When the air cleaner is removed, there is a direct path open to the engine. Anything dropped accidentally into the carburettor will lie at first in the inlet manifold. If it is not removed, it can enter the engine, when it is started, and cause extremely expensive damage to the pistons.

On many cars the choke, which enriches the mixture during cold starting, is mechanical and is controlled from inside the car by the driver; but more and more cars are now being produced with a choke controlled automatically by the engine temperature. Chokes of this type require very fine setting, and it is advisable to leave this work to a specialist mechanic with the necessary equipment.

Carburettors are almost always made of a light metal alloy which, in comparison with other metals, is extremely soft. Because of this, the carburettor can be easily broken by rough handling. A common cause of damage is that screw threads are crossed when pipes are being rejoined.

Note especially that few, if any, adjustments are possible on emission-control carburettors.

Renewing a paper-element filter

1 Engines should receive filtered air. Many use a paper-element filter. This is reached by undoing the centre bolt and removing the top of the filter casing

2 The element can be removed and inspected. If it is very dirty, fit the manufacturer's recommended replacement. Take care not to drop anything in the carburettor mouth

Cleaning a wire-mesh filter

1 Another type of filter is the wire-mesh or gauze unit, which may be located in a 'pancake' filter housing attached to the mouth of the carburettor

2 Remove the mesh filter from its housing for cleaning. Wash it thoroughly in petrol to remove all accumulated dirt. Dip it in clean oil and drain before refitting

Carburettor/regular checks

1 Remove the top of the float chamber. This is secured by bolts which may be of differing lengths; note their positions, so that they can be replaced correctly

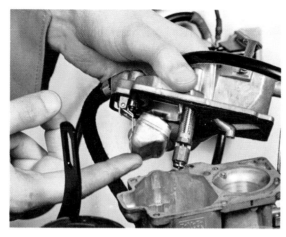

2 The fuel level is controlled by a needle valve. Check the valve's operation by lifting the float. The valve should close and shut off the fuel supply from the pump

3 Use a piece of clean cotton rag soaked in petrol to clear any sediment out of the float chamber. Remove any harder particles with a piece of hardwood

Main jet On some fixed-jet carburettors, the main jet is fitted into an extension of the float-chamber lid. It can be seen here just to the right of the float

Jet removal The main jet—illustrated on a twin-choke carburettor, where it is easier to see—is often found at the bottom of the float chamber. Avoid damaging it

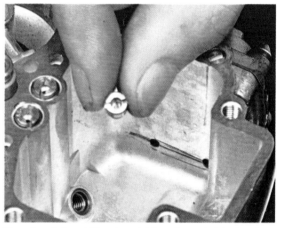

Cleaning jets Lift out and blow through jets to clean them. In severe cases, use a high-pressure air line. Never try probing dirt out of a jet with a piece of wire

Linkage(s) Lubrication of the linkage(s) is an important part of carburettor maintenance. Clean any dirt from the pivot points and then oil the linkage and cables

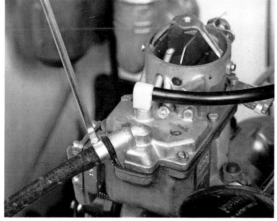

Connections Check all the fuel-line connections. Ensure that hose-clips, if used, are tight and that the fuel pipe is not perished or cracked. Replace them if necessary

Air leakage The gasket between the carburettor and manifold must be sound; an air leakage will affect performance. When fitting a new gasket, ensure all surfaces are clean

Carburettor/tuning a variable jet

Tuning procedure

1 Warm up the engine to its normal working temperature and switch off. Undo the throttle screw until it is just clear of its stop. Retighten it one-and-a-half turns

2 Screw up the jet-adjusting nut, which controls the height of the jet (below the carburettor) as far as possible. Ensure that the **main** jet below the nut moves up with it

3 Raise the piston. Release it and it should return freely on to the bridge. If the piston sticks, the jet into which the tapered needle on the piston fits will need centralising

4 To centralise, pull out jet and undo jet-adjusting nut. Remove spring and replace nut tightly. Loosen the jet lock-nut, hold the piston down firmly and retighten. Reassemble

5 With the engine running, raise the lifting pin $\frac{1}{32}$ in. The revs should rise sharply, then drop. If not, turn the nut a little. Test again and readjust until the setting is correct

6 Adjust the choke setting by pushing in the choke control until the main jet stops moving up. Adjust the throttle-control screw for a fast tick-over (about 1000 rpm)

Servicing the SU and Stromberg

THE TWO main makes of variable-jet carburettors are the SU and the Stromberg. Both operate on similar principles, but there are some differences in maintenance.

Before carrying out any work on them, bring the engine to a normal working temperature to ensure a realistic tick-over. On SUs, check the piston and make sure that it is returning correctly to its seating. If it is not, loosen the dashpot (suction-chamber) screws, reseat the dashpot and retighten the screws evenly, in rotation. If the piston is still not returning correctly, remove and clean it. If this fails, adjust and realign the main jet. Although this is theoretically a simple task, in practice it can be very difficult and it should not be attempted by the novice home mechanic without skilled help.

If the piston return is satisfactory, however, when the engine is running at tick-over, raise the piston lifting pin $\frac{1}{32}$ in. and release it. If the mixture setting is correct, the revs will rise slightly and then settle. If it is too rich, the revs will rise and stay there; so screw the adjuster nut upwards slightly to weaken the mixture. Repeat the test with the lifting pin. If the mixture is now too weak, the revs will drop. Lower the nut.

Top up the piston damper chamber, ensuring that only SAE 20 engine oil is used.

Stromberg carburettors are tuned similarly but, unlike the SU, have a diaphragm in the suction chamber. Check it for damage and replace it if necessary. As with the SU, it is difficult to realign the main jet and needle; garage assistance may be necessary. The final test is the same—to get the right response when the piston is raised.

Cleaning Mark one side of the dashpot so it can be replaced exactly. Remove the dashpot and damper piston. Clean them with petrol (not an abrasive) and replace

Topping up Fill the dashpot to $\frac{1}{2}$ in. above the piston tube inside, if the cap has a vent. If there is no vent, fill to $\frac{1}{2}$ in. below the tube. Use SAE 20 engine oil

Additional maintenance on some variable-jet carburettors

1 On Strombergs, remove the suction-chamber damper cap and the four screws holding the chamber itself. Lift off the cap carefully to gain access to the diaphragm

2 Remove the piston and the diaphragm. Remember that the needle can easily be damaged. Check the diaphragm for damage. Refit it, with the tab in its locating notch

3 There are two positions for the choke setting on Strombergs. For summer, press in the adjusting screw and turn it clockwise; for winter, press in, turn anti-clockwise and release

Carburettor/fixed-jet type

How to tune a fixed-jet

ADJUSTING a fixed-jet carburettor, unlike making adjustments to the variable-jet type, affects only the engine's slow-running and tick-over speeds. This is because of its jets. In a variable-jet type there is only one jet. Any mixture adjustment made to it at tick-over will affect its full range of operation. The fixed-jet carburettor, on the other hand, has its jet sizes determined by the manufacturer, and as a result is not affected to any great extent at higher speeds by a mixture adjustment made at tick-over, when the engine is idling.

First, make sure that the contact-breaker and spark-plugs are correctly set and clean. Make sure that the ignition timing is correct (see p. 201).

Engine idle speed Warm up the engine until it is at its normal running temperature and adjust the throttle-stop screw to obtain a slightly faster engine idle speed.

Next adjust the volume-control screw (sometimes called the mixture screw) in or out until the engine begins to 'hunt'—that is, when the engine sound becomes a rhythmic beat and the engine tends to stall. Immediately this point is reached, turn the volume screw in the opposite direction until the same effect is produced. Halfway between these two positions should be a reasonable setting. Note how many turns of the screw were required to move it from one stalling point to the other. At the middle setting, the engine should run smoothly.

Bring the engine back to normal idling speed by slightly adjusting the throttle-stop screw.

If necessary, the volume-control screw can now be slightly readjusted. It may be possible to improve the even running of the engine still further.

Avoiding undue force The volume-control screw should never be tightened home hard, as it has a tapered end which goes into a small hole. Both can easily become damaged if undue force is used on them.

If, when adjusting the mixture, an even-running engine cannot easily be achieved, remove the complete volume-adjusting screw and spring. If the tapered end shows signs of wear, replace it. Lightly turn the new screw as far as it will go, then slacken it one-and-a-half turns. Start the engine and again carry out the entire adjustment procedure as already outlined.

Smooth running It is in the idling that many faults—including incorrect tappet clearance, manifold leaks and poor valve condition—can show up. So if smooth running cannot be achieved after all the possible adjustments and checks have been made, it is advisable to seek expert diagnosis. It may then be possible to make the necessary repairs, once the fault is traced.

An over-rich mixture setting can be detected by looking at the exhaust for black smoke. On the other hand, if the mixture is too weak, the exhaust will sound 'splashy' and uneven. The colour of the inside of the exhaust pipe, like that of the spark-plugs, is a good guide to how correctly the mixture is set (see p. 202).

Compound twin-choke carburettors have only one adjusting screw and are tuned in the same way as the single-choke carburettor. But twin-choke carburettors which have a mixture-control screw for each choke, require more careful setting and are best left to the qualified mechanic.

1 The throttle-stop screw (which prevents the throttle from shutting completely) should be adjusted with a screwdriver to give a fairly fast idling speed

2 Turn the volume-control or mixture screw in or out until the best engine-running position is reached. Do not over-tighten or force the screw

3 After setting the volume-control screw to its best position, slightly readjust the throttle-stop screw until the engine has reached its normal tick-over speed

Compound twin-choke Set a compound twin-choke carburettor in the same way; but leave twin-choke carburettors with separate mixture screws to the specialist

Fuel pumps/electric and mechanical

Routine maintenance

THE ONLY do-it-yourself jobs on an electric petrol pump are to ensure that the contact points are in good condition and that the filter is not blocked.

To inspect the contact points, remove the lead at the terminal post on the pump cover. Undo the retaining nut and take off the cover. Remove the top contact—which also exposes the lower contact—and examine both. If they are burnt or badly pitted, cleaning them with fine emery cloth will serve as a 'get-you-home' measure; but the pump will soon have to be replaced.

On some types of pump, the filter can be reached by removing a hexagonal nut on the side of the pumping chamber. On others which use plastic pipe-connectors, the filter is under the inlet-pipe bowl, which has to be completely removed. This type pushes the petrol efficiently through the pipes, but its suction action is poor. For this reason it is normally located so that it has a gravity supply from the tank.

Insert a pencil or a similar-shaped object in the inlet pipe to stop fuel running out when it is disconnected. There will be some leakage, so naked lights are extremely dangerous. Clean and replace the filter, reassemble the pump cover and make sure that the washer is tightly fitted.

Maintenance work on a mechanical pump is even simpler. All it needs is to be kept clean and free from sediment trapped by the filter, and to have the gasket renewed if it is damaged.

To clean the filter, unscrew the retaining bolt on top of the pump and remove the domed cover and its gasket. A new gasket may be required. Remove the wire-mesh filter and clean it in petrol.

When refitting the filter, place it the same way up as it was originally. Replace the pump cover so that the gasket or washer forms a completely airtight seal. The cap screw must be tight, but it is easy to damage the pump by overtightening. When removing or reconnecting pipes, avoid crossing the thread or overtightening. Rough handling or excessive force can easily damage the pump.

Electric pumps

1 The electric fuel pump is fed by a single live lead. Make sure the ignition is switched off. Disconnect the cable. To clean the points, the pump may have to be removed entirely

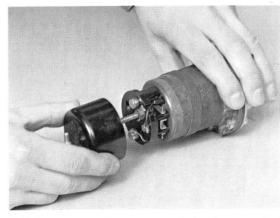

2 Before removing the cap on most electric pumps, first take off the weather-sealing strip. Unscrew the cap retaining nut and remove the cap

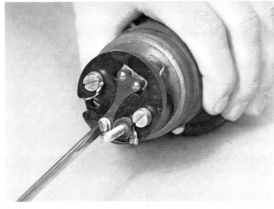

3 Loosen the screw and remove the top contact-breaker point. If the points are pitted or burnt, fit a new pump. Clean light blemishes with emery. Reassemble and reseal

Blocked filter Two plastic connectors may have to be removed to gain access to the filter at the pump inlet. Brush it lightly with petrol

Mechanical pumps

1 On a mechanical pump, unscrew the hexagonal nut and remove the filter cover (this can be made of glass and retained by a wire clip). Take care not to damage the washer between the cover and the pump body

2 Remove the fine-mesh filter from the pump and clean it by brushing lightly with petrol. Note, to help when re-assembling the pump, which side of the filter was facing upwards before it was removed

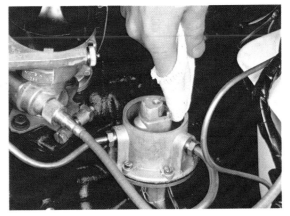

3 Clean the inside of the pump body with a lint-free rag, to remove any sediment. Reassemble the pump and, when tightening, make sure that there is no air leak at the gasket between the pump body and its cap

Fuel system/fault finding

How to check that fuel is reaching the carburettor

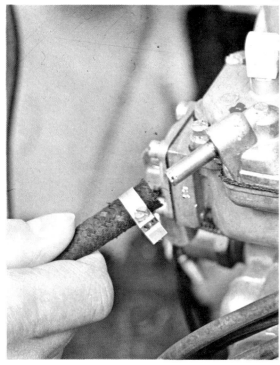

1 If a car is reluctant to start, it may be that fuel is failing to reach the carburettor. To check this possibility, disconnect the fuel inlet pipe to the carburettor

2 Place end of fuel pipe in a jar. Switch on ignition to operate electric pump. Use hand primer (if fitted) or the starter solenoid for mechanical pumps. Check fuel flow

3 If fuel comes through, the fault is in the carburettor. If no fuel is pumped out, tighten the pump cover and disconnect the pipe from the inlet side of the pump

4 Place a moistened finger over the inlet hole and again operate the pump. If no suction is felt, connect a tube to the pump inlet and blow through it to clear the valves

5 If there is suction, fix some flexible hose (the radiator overflow pipe can be removed and used) to the fuel-supply pipe from the tank, and blow through to clear any obstruction

6 When fitting a replacement mechanical pump, always use a new gasket of the correct type and locate the operating arm in the correct position on the cam

Tracing fuel faults

IF AN ENGINE will not start after several attempts, assuming that the starter motor is working normally, something may be wrong in the ignition or fuel system. For tracing fuel faults, there is a simple test routine.

First, ensure that there is petrol in the tank. Check that the fuel is getting to the carburettor. If it is not, the fault must be in the fuel feed system to the carburettor. Test the pump itself to see if it is sucking. If it is, the fault must be a blockage or air leak in the fuel pipe between the pump and the tank. A pipe blockage may be cleared by blowing through it (using a rubber hose). But an air leak can sometimes be more difficult to find: all pipe joints should be checked and tightened.

If the fuel pump is not working, it too can be blown through, but only towards the carburettor. This may clear any dirt that is stopping the valves from seating.

With electric pumps, it is always possible that one of the electrical connections has come loose. An electric pump will not work unless it is properly earthed, usually by a wire from the pump to the chassis or bodywork. Check that rust has not interrupted the earth connection.

If no fault can be found, an electric pump can sometimes be started by rapping it sharply on the body with the knuckles. If this is successful, clean and examine the pump's contact points. Depending on their condition (whether or not they can be successfully cleaned), it may be necessary to replace the complete pump unit. It can be exchanged at a dealer's.

If the first test shows that fuel is getting to the carburettor, the fault is in the carburettor itself, in which case the checks shown on this page should be carried out.

An engine which fires and dies indicates that the choke is probably not operating freely. When it fires and runs lumpily, even when warmed up, the choke may be stuck in the 'on' position. Check that the carburettor needle valve is not blocked; if it is, the engine will not get enough fuel; it may get none. A punctured float will cause the carburettor to flood, and too much petrol will reach the engine. The same situation can be caused by a fibre, or something similar, preventing the needle valve from seating.

Checks on the carburettor when the fuel supply is normal

1 With most carburettors, the whole top has to be removed to expose the float chamber. Note the position for re-assembly. On SUs, the chamber is separate

2 The float is very light and easily damaged. Remove it carefully. It is usually held by a tiny hinge pin, which must be gently pulled out to release it

3 The needle valve is then exposed and this should be unscrewed, noting any washers fitted beneath it. Use only the correct spanner, to avoid rounding the nut

4 Dirt accumulates either at the top of the valve, causing starvation, or inside, where it blocks the needle's seating, causing flooding. Clean by blowing. If worn, replace

Bi-metal spring On some fixed-jet carburettors, the choke is controlled automatically by a bi-metal spring on the spindle. If this sticks closed, tap the choke flap lightly

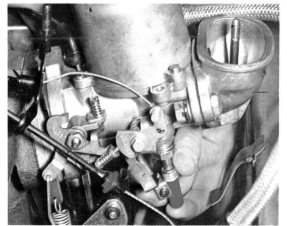

Linkages With variable-jet carburettors, ensure that operating the choke knob actually moves the jet post underneath the carburettor. The linkages may be jammed

Choke flap Ensure that the choke flap fitted in the top of fixed-jet carburettors is closing correctly when the choke knob is pulled, and opening fully when it is returned

Ignition/fault finding

USE THE LETTERED diagram on this page as a guide and carry out the tests in the sequence given. The first two tests can also be carried out when there is no fault suspected in the system, to give the home mechanic an idea of what normal sparking looks like. It would be worth while, before attempting any fault finding on the ignition system, to read the section on how the system works (see p. 66).

Hold a plug lead (A) close to a good earth point. Switch on the ignition and turn the engine. A regular spark between the lead and the earth proves that the system is working.

If there is no spark, remove the distributor cap and hold a screwdriver against a good earth, close to the centre brush or stud (B) in the cap. If there is a spark, this means the fault will lie in the rotor arm or distributor cap. Check for dampness, dirt, cracks or tracking.

If there is still no spark, turn the engine (see p. 230) and ensure that the contact points are actually opening and closing. Stop the engine with the points open. Attach a lead from a test light or circuit-testing screwdriver to a good earth and to the moving contact point (C). If the bulb lights, the points are dirty. Clean or replace them.

When the bulb fails to light, there is a fault in the low-tension (LT) system. Put the test light on the low-tension output terminal (D). If the bulb lights, there is a disconnection between D and C.

Test at E: if the bulb lights, the fault is between E and C; if it does not, the fault is between D and E.

Should the bulb not light when the test is made at D, remove the terminal connection and test again. If the bulb now lights, there is a short-circuit between the removed wire and the open contact points, all of which should be insulated from earth. The 'short' (often a loose wire or screw) will be found by close inspection.

Test at F if the bulb does not light when the wire is disconnected from D. A bulb that lights on this test indicates that there is a disconnection inside the coil. Fit a new coil. If the bulb still does not light, the supply from the ignition switch is faulty. Since the ignition circuit is rarely fitted with a fuse that could have blown (and provided the warning lights and instruments are working), the most likely cause is a loose wire or connection at the ignition switch. If the warning lights are not working, the switch unit may be faulty or not receiving current from the battery.

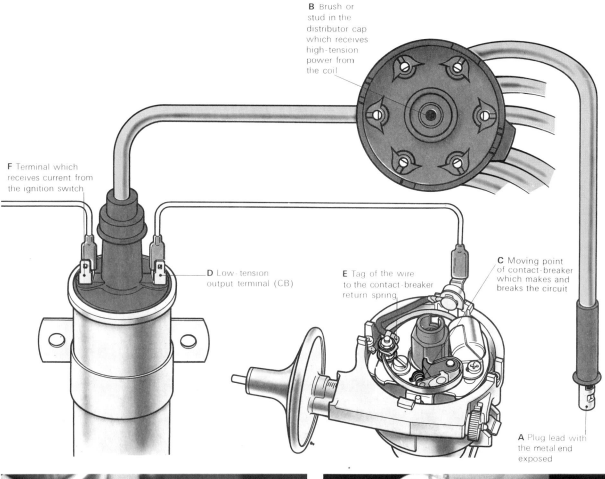

B Brush or stud in the distributor cap which receives high-tension power from the coil

F Terminal which receives current from the ignition switch

D Low-tension output terminal (CB)

E Tag of the wire to the contact-breaker return spring

C Moving point of contact-breaker which makes and breaks the circuit

A Plug lead with the metal end exposed

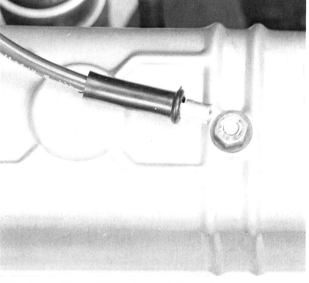

1 The first ignition test (A) is to check if there is a spark from a plug lead. Hold the lead by its insulation about $\frac{1}{16}$–$\frac{1}{8}$ in. from a good earth point. Remove the plug cap from the lead if necessary. Turn the engine with the ignition switched on

2 To test coil output (B), place a screwdriver against a good earth, with the blade close to the centre brush or stud in the distributor cap. If a spark does not jump the gap when the engine is turned and the ignition coil is dry, there is no output from the coil

3 With the contact points open and the ignition on, place a test-light lead on the moving contact point (C) and connect the other lead to a good earth. If the bulb lights, the low-tension circuit from the ignition switch through the coil to the contact point is not faulty. But if the points are dirty: it will be necessary to clean or replace them

4 The ignition coil (left) has two low-tension terminals. It may sometimes be difficult to determine which is the output terminal to the distributor contact-breaker points (D) on cars where the coil is further from the distributor. Identify this terminal by comparing the colour coding of the wiring at the distributor and at the coil

5 The fifth fault-finding test (E) may appear more difficult on some distributors. But in almost every type there is a wire which is connected to the spring of the moving contact point. The wire is moved by the operation of the vacuum-advance mechanism and it is here that a loose connection is most likely. Test on the wire tag

Battery maintenance

THERE ARE TWO basic tests for a car's battery—checking the specific gravity of the electrolyte, and checking that the battery is able to deliver the necessary quantity of electricity. The capacity test is best left to a specialist. As the battery discharges, its dilute sulphuric acid reacts with the lead of the plates. The condition of the electrolyte in the battery, therefore, reveals the state of charge. To carry out a test, siphon a sample of the electrolyte with a hydrometer.

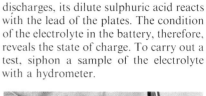

1 The float level gives the state of charge; but not if the battery has just been filled

2 Top up with distilled water until the plates are just covered. Do not overfill

1 Clean the battery terminals and smear them lightly with petroleum jelly

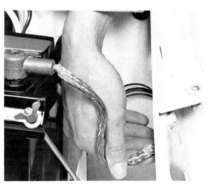

2 Clean the battery earth connection and check that it is tightly attached

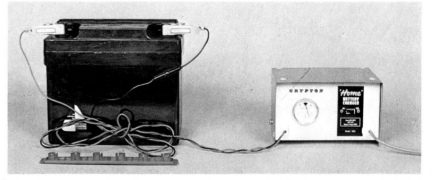

Charging Top up before charging. Do not use any naked light: gases given off during charging are explosive. Switch off the charger before disconnecting the battery

Ignition/checking the distributor

Removing and cleaning the distributor cap

THERE ARE several different makes of distributors, but the routine maintenance required is similar.

About every 3000 miles, remove the distributor cap and lubricate the centrifugal timing mechanism by injecting a few drops of thin oil into the space at the side of the cam. Keep oil off the surface of the points. On some models, there is a felt or sponge disc underneath the rotor arm. Oil this and put a drop of oil on the moving contact pivot. Clean the cam surface and apply a little grease.

Every 6000 miles, unless the distributor cap is covered with a rubber boot or cover, remove dirt and dust. Inspect the inside for signs of tracking (the mark left by high-tension arcing) and remove them with fine sandpaper.

Check that the screws retaining the base-plate are tight. The plate and screws are part of the earthing circuit.

1 Label all the leads to the spark-plugs so that they can be reconnected quickly and without any difficulty

2 Remove the leads, and wipe the insides of the plug caps at the ends of the leads with a clean, dry cloth

3 Unscrew or unplug the distributor high-tension lead from the coil. It is easily recognised and does not need a label

4 Press the centres of the distributor cap's retaining clips and pull them out and down. Then lift off the cap

5 Check that the central carbon brush (if fitted) moves freely, and clean inside the cap with a petrol-moistened rag

Lubricating the distributor

Oiling and greasing Lubricate the centrifugal timing mechanism and its weights by injecting a few drops of thin

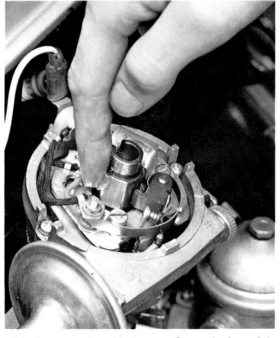

oil in the space alongside the cam. Grease the face of the cam sparingly and put a drop of oil on the moving contact

point's pivot post. Oil the felt or sponge pad (if fitted) in the centre of the cam under the rotor arm

Inspecting the distributor

1 To remove the distributor plate, undo the two screws holding it to the body of the distributor. Do not damage the earth lead or its tag. Unhook the vacuum advance, so that the distributor plate can be removed

2 Lift out the plate. This reveals the weights, which should be checked for obstructions. Both springs should be connected to their retaining-pins. Any object that has fallen in during maintenance must be removed

Vacuum lead Check the vacuum lead to the automatic timing mechanism. This is generally a thin metal pipe, although some cars have plastic tubing. This pipe can often become disconnected when the oil level is being checked

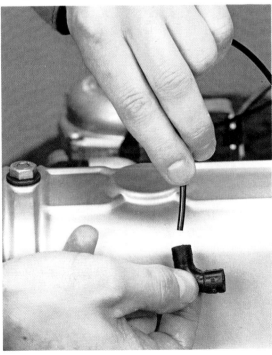

Unions Check any unions and see that the vacuum pipe is not kinked. Make sure no damage is done to the pipe when working near it. For this reason, make special checks when the rocker cover has been removed and replaced

Replacing a faulty condenser

1 Distributor condensers rarely fail. However, if there is a fault, it is quite a simple job to replace a condenser (also known as a capacitor). Undo the screw holding the earthed end to the base-plate of the distributor

2 Remove the nut and washer fixing the tag of the condenser lead to the pillar which holds the contact-breaker spring and the lead from the low-tension side of the ignition coil. Push the lead aside and remove the condenser

3 The distributor's low-tension lead tag must be located correctly when the new condenser is fitted. Note that the reassembly operation is carried out in reverse order to that for dismantling the distributor

Ignition/refitting and setting distributor contacts

Removing the distributor contacts

THE DISTRIBUTOR contact-breaker consists of two metal points—one fixed, the other sprung so that it opens and closes as the cam in the distributor revolves. The movable point is insulated, and the fixed end of the spring which carries it makes contact with an insulated terminal on the distributor case. This insulation means that the moving contact can earth only through its contact face—and so complete the circuit. If the spring itself is earthed in some way, the ignition will not work.

Inspect the distributor contacts every 6000 miles—or less if a fault is suspected.

If the points are burnt or pitted, replace them. Trying to clean the points with a file is inadvisable, except as an emergency 'get-you-home' measure.

Although there are many types and makes of contact sets available for different cars, they all work in the same way as the points shown here and the same rules for maintenance and replacement apply.

If new points burn very quickly after being fitted, check the condenser's earthing and connection. If these are both found to be good, remove and replace the condenser, which may be faulty.

1 Unclip and remove the distributor cap and lift off the rotor arm. If it is tight, lever it from below its moulding; but never try to force a screwdriver against the metal contact. It can very easily be damaged

2 Draw a simple diagram showing the position of the distributor components to act as a guide when reassembling. Use a spanner to remove the nut which secures the moving point to the base-plate

3 Remove the plastic bush, the low-tension lead and the condenser lead from their post. The fixed end of the long curved spring which carries the moving contact-breaker point will now be exposed

4 Lift the spring, together with its contact and the fibre contact-breaker shoe, clear of the pivot post. Inspect it carefully and if the point is burnt or pitted, discard the set. Do not try to file the point clean

5 The fixed contact-point and its base-plate fit over the pivot post and are held in place by a securing screw, which should be removed. Be careful not to drop any part into the lower half of the distributor

6 When removing the washers, note in which order they are assembled and store them carefully. They must be replaced on the screws or pivots from which they are taken. Keep them clean

7 Lift the fixed contact-point assembly from the pivot post, and inspect the point. If it is damaged, discard it. If either point is damaged, both must be replaced. It is not possible to fit half a contact set

8 Check the new contact set against the one removed to ensure that it is of the same type and that it is complete. Before fitting the new set, clean the distributor base-plate with a dry, clean cloth

Fitting a one-piece contact set

1 An inexpensive and readily obtainable innovation, which greatly simplifies the once intricate job of renewing contact-breaker points, is the one-piece contact set

2 After removing the old contact-breaker points, wipe clean the new contact faces to remove any grease. Remove nut on plastic bush and position new set

3 Replace the clamping screw with its washers in correct order. Reconnect the low-tension lead and the condenser lead on to the plastic bush

4 Screw the nut on to the plastic bush but not too tightly. The two lead-tags should make good electrical contact with the spring or misfiring will occur

Resetting the contact gap

WITH THE IGNITION OFF and the distributor cap and rotor arm removed, turn the engine over slowly by hand until the shoe of the moving point is on the peak of one cam. The points should now be fully open. Check the gap with a feeler gauge.

To adjust, loosen the securing screw and move the contact-breaker base-plate with a screwdriver until the points just touch a feeler inserted between them. Tighten the screw and recheck the gap.

Lightly oil the pivot post, but make sure that no oil is dropped on to the points. Smear a little light grease (of a type specified in the handbook) on to the cam. Reassemble and test-run the engine.

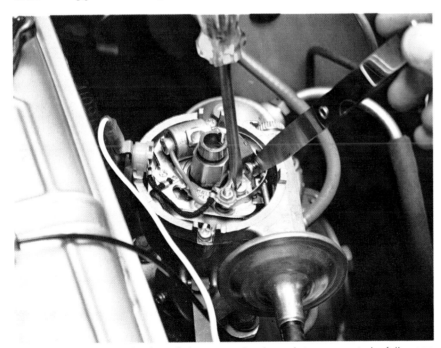

1 Turn the engine over slowly until the contact-breaker points are seen to be fully open. With the correct feeler gauge, check the gap and loosen the securing screw

2 Move the contact-breaker base-plate with a screwdriver until the points just touch the faces of the feeler gauge. Retighten the screw and recheck the gap

Ignition/checking and resetting the timing

How to mark the crankshaft pulley

THE IGNITION TIMING should be checked if the engine is found to be 'pinking' on acceleration or under a heavy load (this can also, of course, be caused by using a lower-grade petrol than the one recommended); when the engine performance is noticeably poor; or if the distributor has been moved for some reason.

In the handbook, the static timing (when the engine is not running) will be given by the manufacturer as so many degrees BTDC—before top dead centre. If the crankshaft pulley is marked as shown below, the setting is easy. But more often the top dead centre only will be marked by a line or notch.

To get the right adjustment, the degrees stipulated can be converted to length on the edge of the pulley by the following formula: pulley diameter (can be measured with a ruler) multiplied by 3·14, divided by 360, and then multiplied by the number of degrees of advance recommended. The answer (in inches) is the distance the pulley must be marked in front of the top dead centre line (clockwise).

1 Remove the distributor cap and turn the engine until the rotor arm is pointing to where the No. 1 plug lead should be, with the points just about to open. Turn the fine adjuster right in and then undo it fully. Count the number of turns and set it halfway

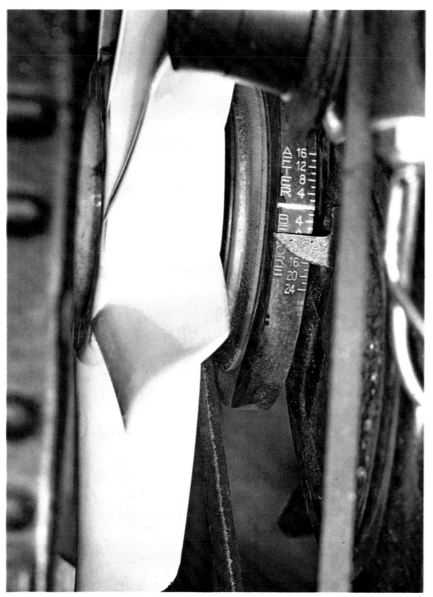

2 Identify the timing marks on the crankshaft and engine body. Chalk rubbed on the pulley will make the marking easier to read. Where the maker has not given degree markings as well as top dead centre, the owner will have to calculate the timing mark

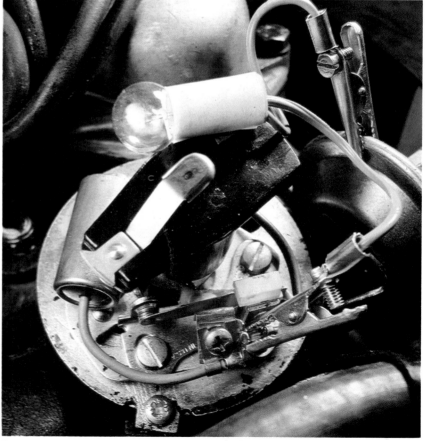

3 To check the exact moment the contact-breaker opens (it cannot be done accurately by eye), connect a test bulb between the distributor low-tension terminal and earth. With the ignition switched on, the bulb will light the moment the contact points open

How to set static timing and adjust the distributor

ONCE THE CRANKSHAFT pulley is marked according to the maker's recommended advance instructions, the setting can be started. First ensure that the contact-breaker points are clean and correctly set.

On the engine body there is a pointer, or some other marking (which will normally be identified in the handbook), which must be lined up with the right advance mark on the crankshaft pulley. When these two points are in line at the same time as the distributor points are just opening (with the rotor arm pointing to No. 1 plug lead), the timing is correct.

Remove the distributor cap and turn the engine until the rotor arm faces towards the No. 1 plug lead, with the contact-breaker points just about to open.

Turning the engine To achieve the smallest possible amount of engine movement, place the car on level ground, turn the wheels to full lock, engage top gear, let the handbrake off, and use the wheel sticking out to push the car forward and so turn the engine. This method will not work on cars with automatic transmission.

Fit a test light to the distributor low-tension terminal and earth, and switch on the ignition. Turn the engine a little more, until the correct timing marks on the crankshaft pulley and engine body are in line. Loosen the clamp holding the body of the distributor and, if the test bulb is alight, turn the distributor in the direction of the rotor arm's rotation until it goes out. Then move it slowly against the rotor arm's rotation until the light just comes on. Reclamp the distributor body.

To check, turn the engine one revolution in the direction of rotation, and make sure that as the light comes on, the crankshaft and engine-timing marks are in line.

Any small adjustment can now be made with the fine control on the distributor, repeating the tests as necessary.

Replacing the distributor If the distributor has been removed, the timing cannot be adjusted until it has been replaced properly. The restrictions imposed by the vacuum advance mechanism, and in some cases by the plug leads, mean that on many cars it has to be replaced with a fair degree of accuracy in the first instance.

Bring the timing marks together, holding the distributor in roughly the right position. Turn the rotor arm until it is pointing towards the No. 1 plug lead, and insert the distributor into the engine. It may be necessary to turn the engine one revolution (360°) to allow the distributor to engage correctly.

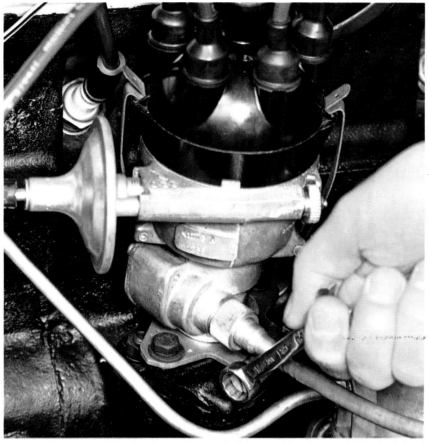

Large adjustment To make a large adjustment, turn the body of the distributor. This moves the contact-breaker points in relation to the cam. Almost every distributor is held by a clamp at the bottom where it joins the engine. Slacken this clamp

Fine adjustment Move the distributor base-plate to make any fine adjustments to the engine timing by turning the fine setting adjusting screw in either direction. It is marked A for advance, R for retard. This also moves the points in relation to the cam

Using a strobe light

IGNITION TIMING can be adjusted using a strobe light, which flashes intermittently and illuminates the timing mark. This enables the timing to be checked accurately at idling speed. When missing or poor performance occur at high speeds, the strobe light can also be used to check the ignition advance mechanism.

1 The strobe light must be triggered by the No. 1 plug lead. Attach it in accordance with the strobe manufacturer's instructions

2 When the engine is running, the flickering strobe light allows adjustments to be seen as they are made

Ignition/spark-plugs

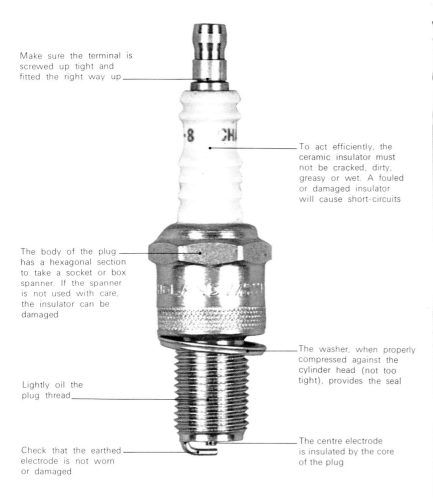

Make sure the terminal is screwed up tight and fitted the right way up

To act efficiently, the ceramic insulator must not be cracked, dirty, greasy or wet. A fouled or damaged insulator will cause short-circuits

The body of the plug has a hexagonal section to take a socket or box spanner. If the spanner is not used with care, the insulator can be damaged

The washer, when properly compressed against the cylinder head (not too tight), provides the seal

Lightly oil the plug thread

The centre electrode is insulated by the core of the plug

Check that the earthed electrode is not worn or damaged

Cleaning the spark-plugs

1 To prevent dirt entering the engine, where it will cause damage, clean around the base of the plug with a soft brush

2 Using a socket or box spanner, pushed fully home, unscrew and remove the plug. Avoid damaging the insulator

3 Clean oily plugs in white spirit and have them abrasive-blasted by a garage. Wire-brushing of plugs is not recommended

4 Before resetting the gap, first bend the earthed electrode outwards with the proper tool. Do not apply too much pressure

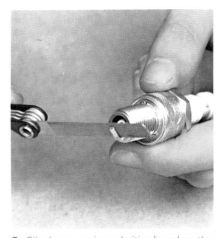

5 File down any irregularities found on the sparking surfaces of the centre and earthed electrodes until they are flat and clean

6 Gently bend back the earthed electrode until the manufacturer's specified gap, measured with a feeler gauge, is obtained

MOST SPARK-PLUGS have a recommended service life of 10,000 miles; but it is advisable to remove, clean and refit them every 3000 miles—probably more often if the engine is in poor condition.

The modern spark-plug is normally of one-piece construction. Rough handling when removing or resetting it is likely to break the ceramic insulator.

To remove the plugs, first detach the high-tension leads and mark them so that they can be replaced in the right order. Do not mark the leads by notching them—this damages the insulation. If the plug has been properly fitted, unscrewing it should not require any great effort. Use only a box or socket spanner. Ensure that the spanner is fully pushed home, but make certain that it is not tilted to one side, as this may break the ceramic insulator.

When the plug has been thoroughly cleaned and its gap reset, lightly lubricate the thread with oil before replacing it in its cylinder-block housing.

Screw in the plug by hand as far as possible, completing the job with a socket or box spanner, again bearing in mind that sideways movement on the spanner is to be avoided.

Never over-tighten spark-plugs; it can make them extremely difficult to remove again—particularly those with tapered seats and no gasket. In light alloy engines, over-tightening may damage the threads, calling for an expensive repair.

When replacing plugs, ensure that the new ones are of the recommended heat range for the engine. This is particularly important when plugs of a different make have to be fitted. The wrong plugs, especially on a high-speed trip, can cause extensive damage.

Diagnosing plug faults

Sound plug The insulator tip is clean and light brown. There is no excess oil or carbon and the electrodes are not worn

Oiled plug Oil may indicate worn piston rings or sticking valves. Try a 'hotter' plug—but seek expert advice first

Sooty plug A sign of an over-rich mixture, caused either by incorrect carburation or by excessive use of the choke

Spotty insulator Pre-ignition or a weak mixture has overheated the plug. Check that it is of the correct heat range

Eroded electrodes Continuous over-heating has severely eroded the electrodes. Always replace any plug in this condition

Loose plug Severe overheating has damaged the plug threads. Fit new plugs and clean the cylinder-head threads

Deposit fouling (1) Caused by neglect. The plugs should be inspected and cleaned every 3000 miles to avoid fouling

Deposit fouling (2) Powdery deposits—although they are not harmful—should be cleaned off before they accumulate

Deposit fouling (3) The powdery deposits melt and glaze with continuous use. This can often result in the engine misfiring

Deposit fouling (4) A further development of the glazed, powdery condition. A plug in this condition will need changing

Deposit fouling (5) The final stage of fouling. The deposits have fused into an irremovable mass. Replace the plugs

Worn plug Replace the entire set if they have given nearly 10,000 miles of service, and any single plug in this condition

Cooling system/general maintenance

THE WATER LEVEL in a non-sealed cooling system should be checked at least once a week. If the system is sealed, follow the instructions in the handbook.

Inspect the radiator at least twice a year. Its air passages must be cleared of leaves, dead flies and paper, which collect and restrict the flow of air through it.

On cars with transverse engines, the air flow through the radiator is often in the reverse direction. Oil from an engine leak, therefore, when mixed with dust from the road, can block the radiator core. Clean the radiator core thoroughly with an oil solvent and water. Do not brush or scrape. It may be necessary to remove the radiator from the car for this work.

Water normally travels through the radiator from top to bottom. Dirt will therefore hang in one direction. To remove this dirt, it is best to flush the radiator in reverse—from the bottom hose inlet. But when doing this, if the radiator is not removed, remember to cover the engine first. A heater can be cleaned by disconnecting both its pipes from the engine and flushing.

The makers of cars where the engine is of a light-alloy metal often advise that an anti-corrosive additive should be used in the cooling system.

It is advantageous to keep antifreeze in the system all the year round, as it contains additives which protect against corrosion.

Only specialist repair will make good a damaged radiator, although small leaks can be cured temporarily by adding to the cooling system a radiator sealing compound, stocked by most accessory shops.

Removing a radiator

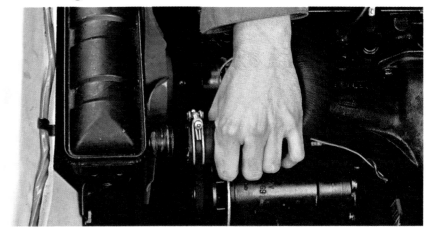

1 If a blocked radiator cannot be cleared by reverse flushing, remove it from the car and flush it upside-down. Start by draining the radiator and disconnecting all hoses

Changing a radiator hose

Removal Drain the cooling system to a level below that of the two pipes connected by the hose. Unscrew the clips and carefully ease the hose off its stub

2 Remove the nuts and bolts securing the radiator to the car body. Make sure that any pipes or cables attached to the radiator are unclipped and put aside

Replacement A new hose should overlap the end of each connecting pipe by at least 1 in. If the hose is too short or if it is kinked, the flow of water may be restricted

3 When lifting out the radiator, be careful not to dent or damage it on the fan

4 The spring-loaded pressure and vacuum valves in the radiator cap should move freely

Replacing a thermostat

1 The thermostat can be located in a cast housing where the top radiator hose connects to the engine. It restricts the water flow until the engine has warmed up

2 To remove the thermostat, drain the cooling system and unbolt the thermostat housing. The connecting hose to the radiator may also have to be removed

3 Lift out the thermostat and heat it in water, and check its operating temperature with a thermometer. Replace it if necessary. Fit a new gasket and tighten the bolts evenly

Replacing the temperature sensor unit

Usual location The temperature sensor is usually fitted in the cylinder head near and below the thermostat (centre of picture). If necessary it can be removed with a spanner

Bleeding the heater system

Air-lock If the heater does not work after the cooling system has been refilled, there is probably an air-lock in the heater radiator. Water passes through the heater from the cylinder-head connection, returning to the radiator side of the water pump. First identify the return-pipe, then remove the radiator cap and loosen the hose clip. Start the engine and remove the hose from its stub (as shown). Hold the hose until water flows from it evenly, using the other hand to stop water escaping from the stub. Push the hose back on to the stub, tighten the hose clip and, finally, top up the radiator. Do not attempt to do this when the water is hot; and keep both hands well away from the fan

Cooling system/inspection and replacement

Adjusting and replacing the fan belt

THE CORRECT operation of the cooling system depends on the fan belt, which also drives the water pump. If the belt is loose, oily or damaged, the pump's impeller may not circulate the water as quickly as necessary and the engine could overheat.

The fan belt also drives the generator. If the belt is loose, the generator will not be able to charge the battery at its normal rate and the battery will eventually go flat.

If the engine is seen to be losing water, inspect the water pump. If there is a clear leak on its underside, it is likely that the pump's seal—which is inside the pump—has itself developed a leak. On modern water pumps, the seal cannot normally be replaced by the home mechanic. Nor will a sealing compound in the radiator cure the fault. Remove the pump and exchange it for a new or reconditioned unit.

2 To replace the fan belt, slacken the generator bolts. Push the generator as close as possible to the engine. Remove the existing belt—over the generator pulley first. Fit the new belt, turning the engine slowly by hand to guide it on the pulley

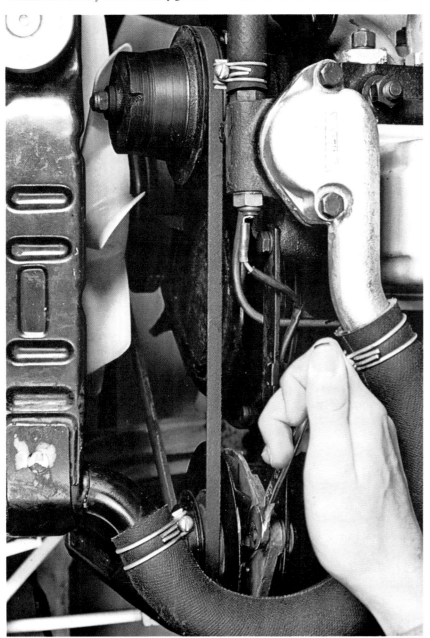

1 To adjust the fan-belt tension, slacken the three generator mounting and adjusting bolts. Move the generator away from the engine until there is about $\frac{3}{4}$ in. of play at the centre of the longest side of the belt. Retighten the bolts while holding the generator

3 With the new belt in position, adjust its tension to $\frac{3}{4}$ in. of play at the centre of its longest side, and retighten the generator bolts. A new belt may stretch and wear considerably during the first 100 miles. Check it and adjust the tension if necessary

Replacing the water pump

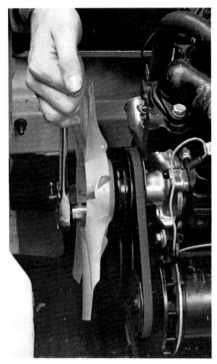

1 Drain the cooling system and remove the radiator. Undo the bolts (there are usually four) that secure the fan and the pump pulley to the water pump

2 Remove the fan. On many cars it will be made of metal. Inspect for cracks and replace it if necessary. Avoid damaging a plastic fan during dismantling or reassembly

3 Slacken the generator and push it towards the engine. Remove the fan belt and the pump pulley. The fan belt may have to be eased off before the pulley can be removed

4 Slacken the heater-hose clip and pull the hose off its stub. Check it for wear, leakage and damage and replace if necessary. Replace the by-pass hose, if one is fitted

5 Unscrew the water-pump bolts with a socket and bar. The bolts are usually different lengths. Note which goes where

6 Lift the pump away from the cylinder block. Fit the replacement and a new gasket in the reverse order from dismantling

7 Before exchanging the pump at a dealer's, unscrew the existing heater-hose connections. They will have to be fitted to the new pump. If the old pump is to be repaired by a specialist, take off the gasket and make sure a new one is available for reassembly

Lubrication/changing engine and gearbox oils

New oil for the engine

OIL SHOULD BE CHANGED at the manufacturer's recommended mileage intervals, but if necessary at certain time intervals instead (see p. 180). Make sure that a new oil-filter element is fitted every second oil change; a filter cannot be cleaned.

To change the engine oil, first ensure that the car is on level ground. It is not advisable to raise the front end on a ramp, for the oil sump is designed to drain when the car is level. If it is tipped, some—but not all—of the oil will come out.

A handy container to collect the oil, so that it does not run over the garage floor, is a one-gallon oil can, laid on its side with its top screwed on and a hole cut in the top side. This will go under most engine sumps and will hold all the oil drained off—from all but the biggest cars.

When removing the drain-plug from the sump, always use the correct-sized spanner, preferably a socket or ring. If the plug is damaged by a wrong-sized spanner, it can be extremely difficult to remove. On some plugs, there is a magnet fitted to attract small particles of metal in the engine oil. These magnets are brittle and can easily be broken by rough handling.

Before draining, run the engine to normal temperature so that the oil thins a little and comes out more easily.

When an oil filter is being removed, oil will overflow as the oil seal is broken. This is a dirty job, and the home mechanic is advised to have his sleeves rolled up.

Tap the filter to break the seal before the retaining screw is completely released. As the filter is spring-loaded, it may come off without warning unless the seal is broken first. Several rubber seals are often supplied with the replacement filter element. Compare with the one removed and ensure that a new seal of the correct size is fitted into the groove in the filter housing. The most useful tool for removing the old ring is a hat-pin or dart point.

Filters that are screwed completely into the engine may be difficult to remove. Place a large hose-clip (or a number of them joined together) around the body of the filter and tighten. Hook a loop of wire over the screw of the hose-clip. Place a piece of wood in the other end of the loop and lever the wood gently against the side of the filter—so loosening the filter unit. Do not use this method to retighten it.

Draining the sump

1 Before removing the drain-plug on the sump, make sure that a suitable container is available to catch the oil as it drains off, and that the oil can be disposed of later

2 The oil will drain out more easily if the engine oil-filler cap has been removed and if the engine has been run to normal temperature before draining is begun

Changing the oil filter

1 Two kinds of oil filter: an element filter that is inserted in a bowl (left), and a cartridge filter complete in itself

2 When a filter bowl is fitted, unscrew its retaining bolt. Break the seal and release the spring pressure before removing the bolt

3 Remove the old filter element, and clean the bowl with paraffin. Store the spring and washer where they will not be lost

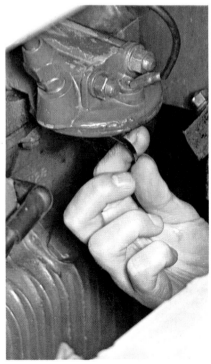

4 Remove the old gasket, compare it with the range provided in the filter kit, and choose a new one of the correct size

Refilling the sump

1 While the engine is draining, remove the rocker cover and wipe out any sludge. Replace the cover, using a new gasket to ensure that oil does not leak when refilling

2 Replace the sump drain-plug and refill the engine with the correct grade of oil. Start the engine, ensuring that the oil-pressure warning light on the fascia soon goes out

3 Keep the engine running and inspect the oil filter for leaks, which could eventually result in extensive engine damage. Stop the engine. Check and top up the level, which will have dropped a little during the test running as the oil filter is filled

New oil for the gearbox

GEARBOX OIL eventually becomes contaminated by metal particles and should be changed as recommended by the manufacturer. Make sure that the car is level before attempting to top up, or it will be difficult to find the true level of the oil.

If in doubt, check in the handbook to identify the oil-level plug and remove it. This allows air to enter the gearbox and speeds the flow of oil being drained. If the car has an overdrive, although the gearbox level plug will often serve both, the overdrive is likely to have its own drain-plug.

After draining the gearbox (and overdrive), replace the drain-plug. Be sure, especially when there is an overdrive, that the recommended oil is used.

Fill through the level plug until it starts to overflow. Allow all excess oil to escape before replacing the plug.

Clinical cleanliness is vital when topping up or changing automatic transmission oil, because if small grit particles are allowed to get into the oil they can easily damage the delicate mechanism.

Because automatic transmission has a torque converter instead of a clutch (see p. 94), the engine, in many cases, must be idling, usually with a low forward gear engaged and the handbrake on (check in handbook), when the gearbox oil level is checked. Checking under any other conditions will give a misleading impression. Do not overfill an automatic gearbox.

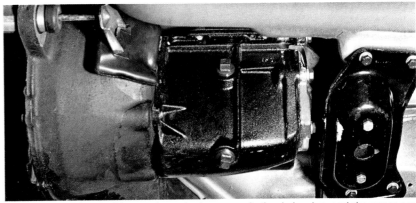

1 A gearbox is fitted with two plugs: the lower one is the drain-plug; and the upper one (usually situated on the side of the gearbox) is the oil-level plug

2 Before attempting to drain the gearbox, remove the oil-level plug so that air can enter and help the oil to drain out more quickly

3 Remove the gearbox drain-plug. Where the car has an overdrive fitted, remove the unit's separate drain-plug also

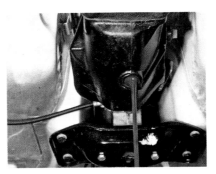

4 Draining is much easier if the car has been run for a short time immediately before, to allow the oil to warm and become thinner

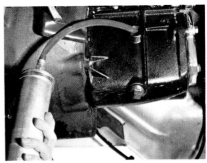

5 Replace the drain-plug and fill the gearbox through the level-plug hole. Replace the plug when the excess oil has run off

Transmission/routine servicing

Checking the components

THE TRANSMISSION system consists of all those mechanical parts of the car that help to carry the power from the engine to the road wheels: the clutch, gearbox, propeller (or drive shaft), rear axle and the differential assembly. When the car is rear-engined or has front-wheel drive, the transmission system is, of course, very much more compact, but the principles are the same.

Clutch In most cars there is little maintenance that can be done to the clutch assembly, but check whether the clutch is adjustable. Look underneath the car, where the clutch lever leaves the bell housing. It is connected by a rod, either to a hydraulic cylinder or to a cable. If the rod is threaded, with a large and a small nut, the clutch free-play can be adjusted. Follow the maker's instructions (usually in the handbook) for the amount of free movement allowed. Clutch cables are adjusted in the same way.

Over-adjustment, or a hydraulic failure, could make it impossible to change gear. While someone presses the clutch pedal, check the movement at the end of the clutch-release bearing arm under the car. The end will normally move just over an inch. If this does not happen, check the free-play. If correct, there is air in the hydraulic system or, with a cable-operated clutch, the cable is ineffective. Most hydraulic clutches can be bled as shown, but check the workshop manual as some clutches, the Rover 2000 for instance, must be bled a different way.

Gearbox The manual gearbox needs little attention except for oil-changing. Where the gearbox is automatic, however, make sure that only the correct type of oil is used. Using a type not recommended by the transmission manufacturer or allowing dirt to enter the gearbox can damage the automatic transmission system extensively.

The way in which the oil is checked varies from one automatic gearbox to another. But generally start the engine and, with the handbrake on, engage either a low forward gear or reverse gear. Check the oil level with the

dipstick and top up if necessary. It is dangerous to overfill automatic boxes: the oil will thresh, creating high temperatures, and it can reach flashpoint.

Propeller shaft On a car with a conventional transmission layout, this shaft connects the gearbox to the rear axle. Take care not to bend or knock the shaft.

Check every 6000 miles that the four bolts holding the propeller shaft to the rear axle are tight. Where the universal joints are fitted with grease nipples, grease every 3000 miles. Most, however, are sealed for life by the manufacturer and they will require no maintenance. If when the propeller shaft is held and twisted at each side of the universal joints, there is free movement, the universal joint is worn, and a replacement is necessary.

Drive shaft Front-wheel-drive or rear-engined cars have drive shafts instead of a propeller shaft. Inspect the rubber gaiter, or boot, covering the universal joint to ensure that it is not torn or split. Check by shaking the shaft that there is no wear. On rear-engined cars, check every 3000 miles that the bolts holding the universal joint to the axle are tight. On some front-wheel-drive BMC models, the inboard drive-shaft universal joint is made of metal and rubber, held by U-bolts and nuts. Inspect these for tightness and serviceability every 6000 miles. If they loosen, they can hit and fracture the gearbox casing.

Rear axle and differential assembly The final-drive assembly turns the power from the engine through a right angle to drive the road wheels. A differential unit in the final drive allows one rear wheel to travel faster and further than the other when the car takes a bend or corner.

Maintenance is limited to checking the oil level and topping up when necessary. Check every 3000 miles. It is not possible to drain some modern rear axles. But ensure when topping up the oil level that the axle is not overfilled. Too much oil can result in a blown seal and oil-contaminated rear brakes.

Topping up the clutch reservoir

When topping up the hydraulic fluid in the clutch reservoir, hold the can as close as possible to the reservoir to prevent air entering the fluid. Replace the cap securely

Bleeding the clutch

1 To bleed the hydraulic system of air, first locate the clutch slave cylinder, which is usually bolted on to the side of the clutch housing at sump height

2 Take off the dust cover, so that a rubber pipe can be fixed to the bleeder nipple. With the other end of the pipe immersed in a jar containing brake fluid, undo the nipple

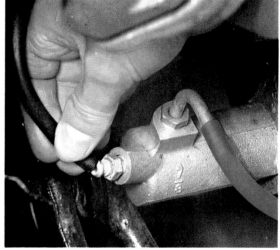

3 Pump the clutch pedal until the air is forced out. Tighten the nipple, take off the pipe and replace the cover. Check the clutch action. Constantly top up the reservoir with fluid

Topping up the rear axle

KEEP THE LEVEL topped up with the correct grade of transmission oil and, if the axle can be drained, change the oil at recommended intervals. If there is an oil leak, have a new gasket or seal fitted at a garage. The axle unit cannot be adjusted. If there is excessive noise, a proprietary anti-friction additive may quieten it; but noise usually indicates low oil level, a fault or wear.

The rear-axle level plug is normally halfway up one side or the back of the differential housing. Use the correct-sized spanner to avoid rounding the plug-head. Use an oil gun or polythene bottle with a spout to top up the level. It is now possible to buy the appropriate axle oil in such containers. Replace the plug only when the excess oil has been allowed to drip out. Never overfill the rear axle with oil, or use any oil other than the type recommended in the handbook.

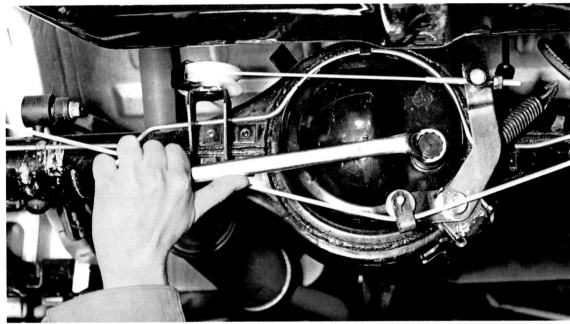

1 Remove the rear-axle level plug, which will be on one side or at the back of the differential housing. If oil runs out, the level is correct and no topping up is needed. If no oil runs out, the axle requires topping up. Make sure that only the type of oil recommended by the manufacturer—a heavy grade often used also in the steering box—is used

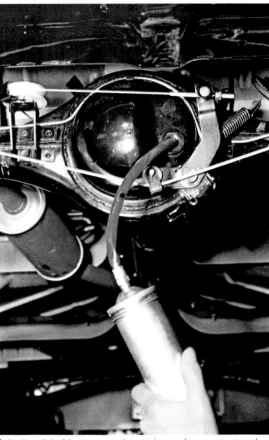

2 It is advisable to use the syringe shown or a polythene bottle with a spout to top up the rear axle. Allow the excess to drain before replacing the drain-plug

Tightening the universal-joint bolts

THE ONLY routine maintenance required on the propeller shaft is to tighten the bolts holding it to the rear axle. They will either be of the self-locking type or have spring-washers. If the nuts or bolts are found to be worn, fit new ones. This is sound practice, in any case, each time the propeller shaft has been disconnected. Check the universal joint for wear by holding the propeller shaft at each side of the universal joint and twisting in opposite directions. If there is movement, the universal joint is worn and should be replaced by a garage.

If the propeller shaft is to be removed, make a note of the marks on the flanges to ensure that the shaft will be replaced correctly. If it is not, it may be out of balance, and the car could vibrate at high speeds.

Modern universal joints are pre-lubricated and sealed for life by the maker, but on some older cars a grease nipple is provided. In such cases, apply grease every 3000 miles, or the joint will run dry and wear rapidly.

Inspect the universal joints of front-wheel-drive cars every 3000 miles. The checks made are the same as for a propeller shaft. Make sure that the bolts connecting the axle and the drive shaft are tight.

Short-handled spanner Check the tightness of the propeller-shaft retaining bolts every 3000 miles. Check also the tightness of the nuts holding the differential unit to the axle. Use a short-handled spanner to avoid overtightening, and screw the nuts evenly and alternately across the casing (top, bottom, then one side and then the other)

Brakes/checking and adjusting

REGULAR MAINTENANCE of the brakes is essential—legally and for the safety of everyone travelling in the car. Neglect will not only create possible danger: it will nullify the insurance cover in an accident caused by failed brakes.

Whatever kind of brake is fitted to the car, it will have some kind of friction surface which slows the car by coming into contact with a drum or disc attached to the road wheel. If the brake is not self-adjusting, the owner must ensure that the friction surface has the shortest possible distance to travel before it makes contact with the drum or disc. But it must not be able to touch or rub against it when the brake is not in use. Any adjustment, therefore, must be done only when the pedal or hand-brake lever is in the off position.

The car's main braking system—operated by the pedal—is now usually hydraulic (see p. 213). But every car is required to have either an alternative, entirely separate system, or at least a completely different, mechanical means of operating the brakes. Some cars have two or more hydraulic systems, but they must still have a mechanical handbrake.

Although the handbrake—which is operated through a series of rods and cables—is intended basically to hold the car when parked, it must also be able to stop it if the hydraulic system fails. While it is possible to adjust the handbrake separately (as shown on this page), any normal adjustment to the car's main rear brakes may also affect the handbrake setting.

Drums Most cars are fitted with drum brakes—which have semicircular shoes that act against the inside of a drum rotating with the wheel. They are usually adjusted by turning a nut on the outside of the back-plate. In some makes, adjustment is by a screwdriver through a slot in the wheel or back-plate. Check in the car handbook before starting any work on the brakes.

Discs Many modern cars now have disc brakes, at least on the front wheels. These brakes have two friction pads held on either side of a metal disc that rotates with the wheel. They are normally self-adjusting. But the pads should be checked regularly for thickness every 5000 miles. If they are not replaced when they are worn out, the disc itself will become damaged.

Every 1000 miles or every month Check the fluid level in the master-cylinder reservoir or separate reservoir. If fluid is needed, check that there is no leak in the system. If there is, have it repaired immediately at a garage.

Every 5000 miles Replace brake-shoe linings if they are worn close to the rivet head, or less than $\frac{1}{16}$ in. thick on bonded linings. Replace disc pads less than $\frac{1}{8}$ in. thick—or $\frac{1}{16}$ in. on swinging-caliper brakes. Adjust the hand-brake and check for frayed cables.

Every 10,000 miles Inspect all flexible hoses for wear. All brake pipes should be cleaned thoroughly. Inspect them closely for leaks, chafing or corrosion. If there is any doubt about their serviceability, change them.

Every 24,000 miles or 18 months Drain the fluid from the system and refill with clean fluid.

Every 40,000 miles or three years The rubber elements connected with the wheel cylinders, the master cylinder and any regulating valves should be replaced at a garage. Check the servo unit if one is fitted.

How to adjust drum brakes

Square peg Adjust a drum brake by turning the square peg on the back-plate with a brake-adjusting spanner. With the brake off, turn the peg until the shoe touches the drum, then slacken it until the wheel rotates freely

Screwdriver Some drum brakes are adjusted with a screwdriver instead of peg and spanner. The wheel can be left on the car, but it is advisable in all work on the brake mechanisms to jack up the car securely, with the brakes off

How to adjust the handbrake cable

1 The handbrake cable can be adjusted by turning a nut on a transverse rod at the rear axle—but only after the shoes have been properly set. The cable length and angle should be adjusted according to the maker's specifications

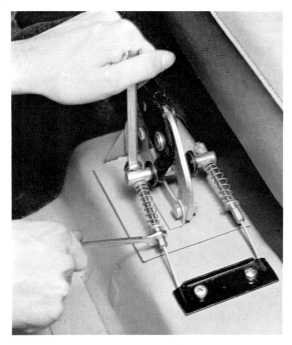

2 On some cars, the handbrake cable is adjusted by nuts at the handbrake lever. As braking systems vary from car to car, it is essential always to check instructions in the car handbook before starting any adjustment

Bleeding the system

BOTH DRUM and disc brakes are operated by some kind of hydraulic system—where a fluid (usually a special light oil mixture) transmits the pressure applied at the brake pedal to each of the brakes. To work efficiently, the hydraulic system must be completely free of air and dirt. After any of the brakes has been replaced, repaired or adjusted, the hydraulic system should always be checked and 'bled' if necessary.

Two people are required: one to sit in the car pumping the brake pedal, the other to bleed each brake in turn. As the pedal is operated, the hydraulic fluid is forced out through the opened bleeder nipple at each wheel in turn.

First clean the cap of the master-cylinder reservoir in the engine compartment. It is important that no particles of oil or grit should be allowed to drop into the reservoir when the cap is removed, for if the fluid does become contaminated, the system's rubber seals may be damaged: if so, the brakes may fail.

Topping up With the cap cleaned and removed, top up the reservoir with the correct type of brake fluid (check in the car handbook which kind should be used). Throughout the bleeding operation, take care that the level of the fluid in the reservoir is not allowed to drop below the half-full mark. If it does drop below this, the whole job may have to be started again.

Only one brake should be bled at a time, starting with the furthest from the master cylinder and finishing with the nearest. Locate the bleeder nipple—either on the disc-brake caliper, or on the back-plate of the drum brake—and make sure that it is thoroughly cleaned. Attach a length of plastic or rubber pipe to the nipple.

Correct spanner Put the free end of the pipe in a jar containing a little brake fluid, making sure that the end of the pipe is completely immersed all the time. Open the nipple with one complete turn of the spanner. It is most important when undertaking this job to use the correct size of spanner. If the nipple is not properly retightened after bleeding, fluid will escape, air will be let into the system and the brakes will eventually fail.

Press the brake pedal to the floor and let it return. Pause, and repeat the action until the hydraulic fluid being pumped out of the nipple into the jar is seen to be completely free of air bubbles. Then, with the pedal fully depressed, tighten the nipple and remove the pipe.

The master cylinder and the main brake pipe to the rear of the car will be bled with the furthest wheel brake. At this time, most of the air will be removed from the system. The master-cylinder reservoir should be checked and topped up if necessary every three or four pumps of the brake pedal. If the first brake is bled correctly, very little difficulty will be experienced with the other three.

Points to note The hydraulic fluid, when contaminated by water or mineral oil, will damage the rubber and metal parts of the braking system. Never fill from a container or funnel that has had petrol; mineral oil, paraffin or water in it. Keep a container only for hydraulic fluid.

Fluid which is bled from the system should never be used again, as it may be contaminated.

The air hole in the reservoir cap must be kept clear so that, as the fluid is drawn into the system, a vacuum is not created in the reservoir.

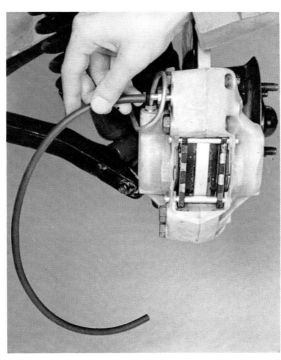

1 The bleeder nipple—which on drum brakes is on the back-plate, or on the caliper of disc brakes—must be free of all grease and dirt before the rubber or plastic tubing is attached. Make sure the correct spanner is available

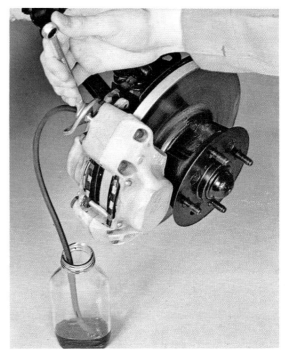

2 The free end of the pipe must be completely immersed throughout the bleeding operation, in a jar containing a little hydraulic fluid. If air is allowed to be drawn back into the system, the work will have to start again

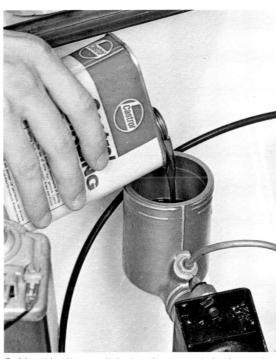

3 After bleeding each brake, the reservoir in the engine compartment should be topped up with the correct fluid (see the car handbook). Great care must be taken not to contaminate the fluid with oil, dirt or water

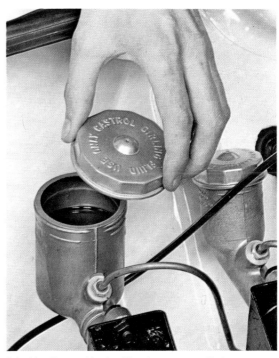

4 In bleeding and in checking the master-cylinder reservoir, always make sure that the cap is completely clean before removing or replacing it. Make sure that its small air hole is clear before screwing the cap back firmly

Brakes/replacing drum brake linings

THE FRICTION with which the brakes stop the car also causes the drum brake linings to wear. They should be checked every 3000 miles. At first the wear on the linings can be taken up by adjusting the screw on the brake back-plate. But when the linings are at least two-thirds worn, they should be replaced. If the linings are allowed to wear excessively, braking will quickly deteriorate. The drums will soon be scored and they will have to be replaced.

Never try to rivet new linings to the old brake shoes; this is a specialist's job. Brake shoes are easily obtainable and they should always be replaced on both wheels on the same axle. If only one is replaced, braking may be unstable and the car may pull to one side.

Before renewing the brake shoes, thoroughly check the tyres and the complete braking system for efficient operation. A bald tyre opposite one with a good tread will give unbalanced braking; so will two tyres inflated at different pressures and running on the same axle.

Ensure that the U-bolts securing the rear axle to the springs are tight. A loose-fitting U-bolt will let the axle roll and the brakes will seem to 'grab' on and off. Inevitably, worn wheel bearings and steering joints will cause the vehicle to pull to one side during braking.

When overhauling the brakes make sure that any replacements which may be needed—such as return springs and wheel-cylinder seals—are available. But the owner should not tackle seal replacements himself unless he is experienced: seek garage assistance. A tin of brake fluid, rubber tubing to bleed the brakes, wooden chocks or bricks and a sound jack will be needed.

1 Jack up the car and remove the wheel. When working on the front wheels, apply the handbrake; with the rear wheels, release the handbrake and chock the front of the car. Slacken off the adjuster screw on the back-plate

2 Undo the brake-drum fixing screws and remove the drum. If it sticks, tap it gently with a soft-headed hammer. Some brake drums are integral with the wheel bearing and may have to be removed with a hub-puller

3 Check the new shoes against the old for correct size and type. Clean the back-plate, the adjuster mechanism and, on rear wheels, the handbrake linkage. Replace the brake drum if it is scored inside by the rivets or worn linings

4 With pliers, grip the edge of each spring washer. Turn it through 90° until the flange on the pin will pass through the slot in the washer and remove it. Hold the pin behind the back-plate to stop it falling out

5 Remove the shoe steady-spring and withdraw its pin through the back-plate. When working on the back wheel, remove the split pin linking the brake shoe and handbrake mechanism. On removal, check all parts for wear

6 Lever off the brake shoes one at a time with a heavy screwdriver or special 'shoe-horn'; try not to damage the rubber dust cover on the wheel cylinder. Draw a diagram of the brake parts to help with reassembly

7 Lever each end of the shoes out of the abutment slots which locate them. As the pressure is released, the pull-off springs will slacken and they can be removed and checked for wear. Do not press the brake pedal with the drum off

8 With the shoes and their pull-off springs removed, wind some wire round the wheel cylinder to secure the piston. Clean out the abutment slots with a screwdriver and lubricate them lightly with high-melting-point grease

9 Connect the new shoes and pull-off springs on the ground, replacing any damaged, rusted or kinked springs. Make sure that the springs are properly positioned on the shoes and place one end of each shoe into its abutment slot

10 Remove the wire from the wheel cylinder and lever the shoes back on with a screwdriver. With rear brakes, reconnect the shoe and handbrake mechanism. Replace retaining pins, springs and washers in reverse order to removal

11 Replace the drum. Fully tighten the adjusting screw, with the ring end of a combination spanner, then unscrew it until the drum revolves. Fit the wheel, tighten the wheel nuts, press the brake pedal to centre the shoes

Brakes/replacing disc-brake pads

THE DISC BRAKE consists of a steel or cast-iron disc, which is attached to and rotates with the wheel hub, and which is straddled by a casting (the caliper) with a friction pad on each side. When the brake pedal is pressed, the pads are moved hydraulically in from each side to grip the steel disc and slow the wheel.

The whole area of the disc is directly cooled by the airstream created by the car's movement—even during braking. Unlike the drum system, discs are not subject to fading at high speeds because of this.

Unlike the drum brake, too, the disc requires no routine maintenance or adjustment. But although the two friction pads have a long life, it is advisable to inspect them once a month. Renew them if they are seen to be worn almost to the steel backing. Failure to do this will eventually result in uneven braking, and the disc itself will become scored and have to be replaced—an expensive and unnecessary repair.

The pads are easily replaced. Make sure that the replacement pads are of the correct size and grade; and have available, in case they are worn, replacement securing pins and anti-squeal shims (if they are fitted). Solid pins may be re-used, but to be safe it is always advisable to replace a split pin.

Hard 'competition' friction pads—which are widely advertised—may give marginally better braking at high speeds. But they will also require very much heavier pedal pressure and make braking much more abrupt. While they are certainly advisable and useful for competition motoring, they should not be fitted for normal running.

1 Jack up the car and remove the wheel to gain access to the brake assembly. When pads are being changed on the front wheels, have the handbrake on; with the rear wheels, chock the front ones securely and release the handbrake

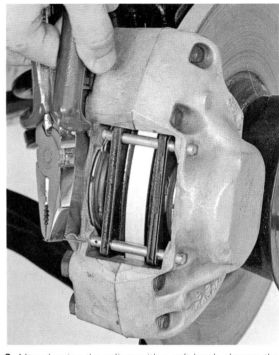

2 After cleaning the caliper with a soft brush, depress the pad retaining-springs, if they are fitted, and with a pair of pliers pull out the clip on the retaining-pins. It may be necessary to twist back and forwards gently to free the clip

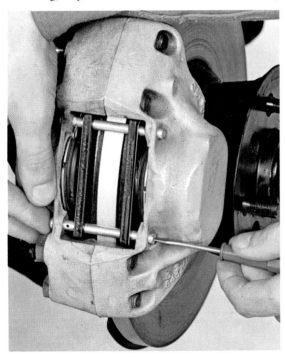

3 Pull out the retaining-pins with the pliers. If they cannot be removed in this way, it is possible to push the headless end of each pin through with a small screwdriver. On the other hand, never use extreme force

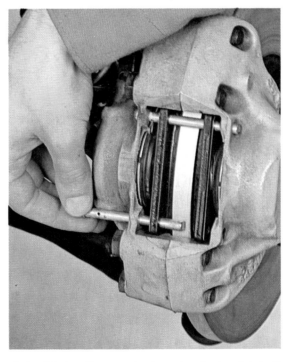

4 A solid pin will not need to be replaced unless it is badly worn. But split retaining-pins are now used on many brake assemblies and, to be completely safe, they should never be refitted. Have replacements available for reassembly

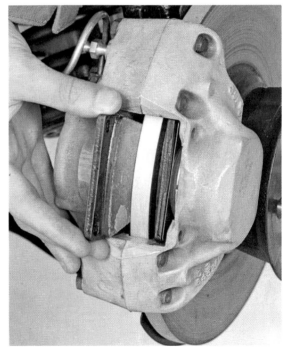

5 Lift the worn disc pads out of their recesses in the caliper. A slight twisting movement may free them and make the removal easier. Make sure that the brake pedal is not depressed when the pads have been taken out

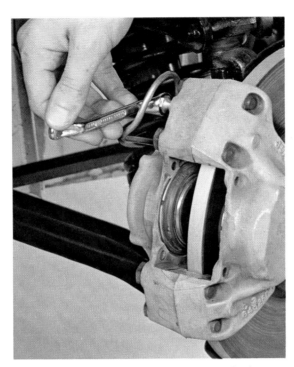

6 With the disc pads and anti-squeal shims removed, clean any rust or dirt from the pistons, which can now be seen. If there are any fluid leaks, refit the old shoes and take the car to a garage to have the seals replaced

7 Before pushing back the pistons to make way for the new, thicker pads, loosen the bleeder nipple and keep a finger over it to prevent air entering the hydraulic system. Fluid displaced by the piston can now escape

8 With the finger still on the nipple, push back the pistons with the correct tool, or a smooth piece of wood. Note that if the bleeder has not been loosened, one piston will be pushed out when the other is moved in

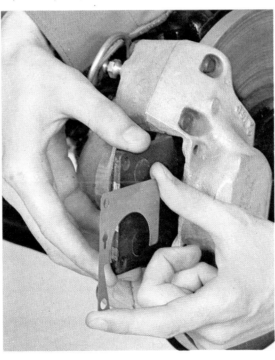

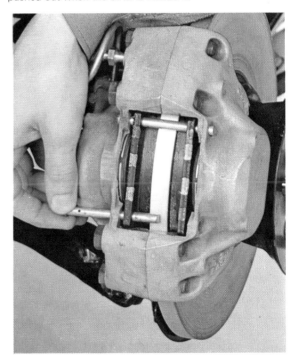

9 Having closed the bleeder nipple, check the old pads against the new ones for size and type. Identify which are the friction faces, so that they and not the backing plates face the disc when they are fitted

10 Insert the new disc pads, with the anti-squeal shims (if fitted) behind them, into the caliper recesses. Arrows marked on shims must face direction of wheel rotation. Push home the shims to line up with the retaining-pin holes

11 Replace the retaining-pins and fit the clips. Check that the bleeder nipple is tight. Pump the brake pedal to relocate the pads and check that the level of the fluid in the master cylinder is satisfactory. Top up if necessary

Wheels and tyres/general pointers

THE CAR'S ABILITY to accelerate and brake efficiently, to hold the road, and to steer depends on the tyres. All the power of the car passes through an area of rubber no bigger per tyre than a size 9 shoe.

Wheel misalignment, steering faults, bad brakes, weak suspension dampers, lack of wheel and tyre balance, and the condition of the hub bearings can all affect the roadworthiness and life of the tyres. But one of the most important single factors is correct air pressure in the tyres.

Balanced pressure (the same for both wheels on the same axle, following the maker's instructions for any difference between front and back tyres) is not only a legal requirement; it ensures that the car is at its most stable.

Using the basic 24 psi (lb. per sq. in.) as a starting point, the pressure of cross-ply tyres should be increased by about 4 psi for a maximum load or for towing, and by about 6 psi for sustained high speed. Radial-ply tyres need only about half these increases.

Tyre pressures increase in the first few miles of driving, because the air in the tyres is heated and expands. In cross-plies, the rise is about 2–4 psi after 2 miles, 4–6 psi after 10 miles in average traffic, and 10–12 psi after 10 motorway miles. It may be as much as 16 psi ($1 \cdot 12$ kg/cm²) on European motorways in summer heat. With radials the increase will be less. Do not let air out of the tyres under these conditions. Such increases are normal and the tyre manufacturer has allowed for them.

The basic types of tyre are cross-ply (bias-belted tyres should be treated as cross-plies) and radial-ply (see p. 122). Never fit radials to the front wheels only. It is illegal to have different types of tyre on the same axle. But if both types are being used on the car, front and back, a spare of each kind should be carried, since the law on tyres applies to the spare as soon as it is fitted.

Most modern tyres are tubeless. The tyre itself is sealed at the inner rim and has an unstretched rubber sealing inside the casing to minimise the effects of small punctures. A tubeless tyre is less liable to burst than one with a tube.

Small holes can be temporarily plugged. But small sharp objects must be removed before they cause irreparable damage to the interior and carcass structure. All punctured tyres should be removed from the wheel to check for internal damage, and should be repaired by hot or cold-cure vulcanising—a specialist job.

Do not try to mend even small cuts in the walls, and never try to fit an innertube to a tubeless tyre. The size may be wrong, and it can cause dangerously hot pockets of air between the tube and the tyre.

Never fit oversize or undersize tyres; and take great care when buying remoulds (even a reputable manufacturer cannot know the state of the carcass structure). No matter how good the tread seems, remoulds are not intended for continuous high-speed driving. Recut tyres —worn, but with a 'tread' cut into the remaining rubber— are not only illegal; they are dangerous.

It is false economy to periodically change the wheels round to even out tyre wear. Because of modern suspension systems, as the tyres wear those at the front take on a different shape to those at the rear. By changing the wheels round there is a period of rapid wear as the tyres take on the new shape.

Tyre inflation and inspection

Correct pressure The difference between a correctly inflated radial and cross-ply tyre. The radial tyre (left) gives a greater contact area between the tyre and road than the cross-ply tyre (right)

Stones Remove stones and grit from the tread at least once a month. Use a slim, blunt screwdriver and take care not to damage the tyre. At the same time, check the walls for damage and remove any oil or grease from the rubber

Pressure check Check the pressure once a week and certainly before a long, high-speed, maximum-load run. Always check when tyres are cool, using the same gauge each time if possible. Inflate them to the maker's instructions

Tread depth The legal minimum is 1 mm. Place the depth gauge so that the feeler pushes into the tread. The legal depth regulations apply to the entire circumference of the tyre and across at least three-quarters of the tread

Valve core If a leak is suspected, it is advisable to replace the valve core. When a new tubeless tyre is fitted, always fit a new snap-in valve. Screw the valve-caps finger-tight after inflating or checking the tyres

Wheel balance Regular checking and adjustment of the wheel balance (including the spare) should be done by specialists with the proper equipment. Balance is achieved by clipping lead weights on to the wheel rim.

Using a jack

IF THE CAR is to be jacked up, first make sure that the handbrake is on and place some chocks under one of the wheels that are to stay on the ground. Besides preventing the car from running away, the handbrake will—when a rear wheel is being changed—hold the wheel steady while the nuts are being unscrewed with the spanner.

Take off the hub cover and slightly loosen the nuts before raising the car. Check in the handbook that the jack is being used at the proper point on the car and ensure that it is steady. A small plank of wood can be placed under the jack if the ground is soft or uneven.

When the car is lifted, remove all the nuts and replace the wheel. On some older makes, it will be necessary to check that the brake-adjusting holes on the wheel are in line with the brake drums. Screw the nuts finger-tight, let down the car, and finish tightening.

Side-lift jack Lower the extending arm of the jack until it can be fitted into the appropriate body point under the sill. To raise the car, always use the tool kit's jack spanner

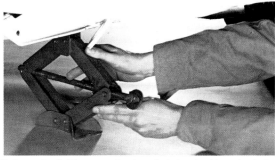

Scissor jack The operating handle is hooked into the hole at the 'scissor' hinge. To raise the car, simply turn the handle in a clockwise direction

Changing a wheel

1 The car tool kit will normally include a lever to remove the hub cover. If this is not available, use a long screwdriver or a flat-ended piece of metal (not a file). Prise off the cover, taking care not to let it fall on the road.

2 Slacken all the wheel nuts with a wheel brace before jacking up the car. Tight nuts will be loosened far more easily while the road wheel is still on the ground than when it is raised and is therefore free to rotate

3 Place chocks under one of the wheels on the side not being raised, and ensure that the handbrake is on. Even when the car is on an apparently level stretch, it could slip off the jack and injure the owner or run away

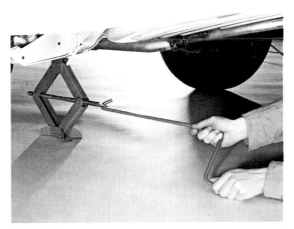

4 Make sure that the jack is standing on firm ground and that it is properly engaged at the correct point on the car. If the ground is soft, it is advisable to place a stout plank underneath the jack

5 Jack up the car, undo the nuts and remove the wheel. Put on the new wheel, steadying it with one hand. If the wheel is heavy and there is difficulty in fitting it, use a lever between the bottom of the wheel and the road

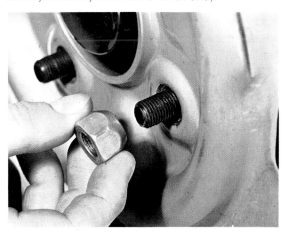

6 Fit the nuts (with the bevelled side towards the wheel), starting at the top and working diagonally across until they are finger-tight. Let the car down and, when the weight is on the wheel, finish tightening with the wheel brace

Tyres/faults and their causes

Cause and effect

TYRES can be damaged or excessively worn by mechanical faults, bad driving or inadequate maintenance. Whatever the reason, they can be a danger to the driver, passengers and anyone else on the road.

It is important, therefore, to inspect the tyres regularly —whenever the pressure is checked—to ensure that there are no dangerous cuts or wear.

It is important also to establish what caused a tyre fault. The condition of a tyre can be a valuable clue to tracking down a mechanical defect, or a pointer to bad driving habits. If unnoticed, more serious faults can develop.

Speed High-speed driving may overheat and soften the rubber of tyres not designed for high-speed operation. This will sometimes result in 'chunking', when pieces of tread are flung off the tyre carcass at speed. Bear in mind when choosing tyres the kind of job they will have to do. If the car is to be driven mainly at high speed, make sure that the tyres are suitable, and under no circumstances fit remoulds.

Stops and starts Fierce acceleration and braking remove the tread rapidly. Heavy braking may cause flat spots.

Road surfaces Unfortunately, road surfaces that give the wheels an excellent grip may also cause rapid tyre wear. But this is also true of many roads that tend to appear smooth-surfaced: they too can be quite abrasive.

Toe-in and toe-out Where two wheels on the same axle are, at hub height, significantly closer at the front than the back (or vice versa) when the car is running, the tyre is scrubbed along the road, causing feathered edges. Repairs to wheels require expensive checking equipment and must therefore be left to a garage. They should not be attempted by the owner.

Camber The camber angle of a wheel determines the angle at which the tyre meets the road. If the suspension is damaged by some slight collision—for example, striking a kerb—the camber angle may be altered sufficiently to wear one edge of the tyre tread excessively.

Castor Castor is the steering's tendency to return to its natural straight-ahead position after cornering. If there is not enough castor, the wheel will weave and the tread wear will be spotty. Too much causes flutter and irregular wear. If the front-wheel castor is uneven, the car will tend to pull to one side and the tyre will wear unevenly across its tread.

Lack of balance Tyres running out of true or badly balanced, brake-drum ovality, or high spots on the discs can all cause extra wear at one spot on the tread. Badly adjusted brakes tend to cause extra wear in several places. Irregular and rapid wear can also be caused by distorted wheels, worn wheel-bearings, suspension or steering joints, and ineffective dampers.

Oil and fluid Most oils, greases and petrol damage tyre rubber if they are not removed.

Inflation Incorrect air pressure is one of the most common faults, yet one of the easiest to find and correct. Reducing air pressure does not increase roadholding on wet, snowy or icy roads: it makes the tyre less able to clear snow and water. Too much air reduces road contact and causes wear in the middle of the tread. There are times, however, when pressures should be increased (see p. 218).

Flat tyre Running over an obstruction with a flat tyre bursts or fractures the wall of the tyre

Carcass failure This type of carcass failure is the result of prolonged running on a flat tyre

Wall wear The tyre wall may wear down to the fabric if the tyre is constantly run against kerbs

Wall scuffing The inside tyre wall becomes scuffed if it comes into contact with steering knuckle joints

Internal fracture 'Kerbing', striking the kerb momentarily at speed, fractures the inner wall of a tyre

Water damage Severe bubbling between the plies inside the tyre caused by a barely visible external fracture

Dangerous tread wear

1 An over-inflated tyre will wear excessively in the middle: this one is illegal and should be replaced immediately
2 Constant and excessive running on over-inflated tyres will eventually remove the centre-tread down to the fabric

3 A constantly under-inflated tyre will bulge at the shoulders and wear rapidly at the edges. Check pressures weekly
4 'Chunking' happens when a patch of tread has loosened and is torn off the tyre by centrifugal force at high speed

5 An incorrect camber angle causes unusual wear at one edge: check both sides of the tyre for irregular tread wear
6 A flat spot can be caused by heavy braking which makes the wheels lock and scrubs the tyres along the road surface

7 Feathering is caused by bad wheel alignment—excessive toe-in or toe-out of the wheels
8 Bad plugging of tubeless tyres, possibly using more than one plug, will distort the tread, resulting in carcass failure

9 Uneven wear of the tread is due to bad wheel balance or a fault in the suspension, steering gear or bearings
10 An illegal and totally unsafe tyre, with the tread worn not only below the legal 1 mm., but almost disappearing

11 Remove a nail from the tyre as soon as possible and repair the damage at once. Even a tubeless tyre will lose air
12 A nail penetrating a tyre will often cause irreparable internal carcass damage away from the punctured area

Suspension/cleaning, checking and lubrication

Types of suspension

THE SUSPENSION SYSTEM cushions the car body and its passengers from the shocks and bumps of normal running. Ideally, the body should remain level while the wheels, on their suspensions, move up and down.

There are many variations in suspension design; different systems may include leaf springs, coil springs, torsion bars or rubber cone springs. The British Leyland Hydrolastic suspension system has rubber cones linked at the front and rear on each side and filled with a water and alcohol mixture. It is a system which does not need dampers to prevent the suspension from continuing to bounce uncontrollably after a bump.

Most cars have different types of suspension at the front and the rear. Many need no maintenance apart from any lubrication that may be recommended in the handbook; but they should be kept clean. Check the suspension every 10,000 miles for wear and damage.

Leaf springs At the rear, many cars have leaf springs—a set of steel leaves of different lengths, clamped together in the centre, where they are connected to the axle, and mounted to the body at each end. The number of leaves used in each spring varies from one design to another.

On modern cars, the leaf-spring mountings are usually rubber bushed and require no lubrication. But on some older models, the springs may have metal bushes and drilled shackle pins, provided with grease nipples. These should be greased every 3000 miles.

The only maintenance usually needed on a coil-spring or torsion-bar system is lubrication, if any of the moving parts have nipples. Rubber cone springs need no maintenance. Check the Hydrolastic type for leaks, however, if the body is seen to droop or settle down on the suspension, reducing ground clearance. Measure the distance from the wheel centre up to the edge of the wing, to make sure that the height is as recommended by the manufacturer (in the workshop manual).

Checking for wear Whatever the suspension, check all ball-joints, trunnions, arms and links for wear. On older cars, check the king-pins (this is part of the DoE inspection). Joints can be checked when the front of the car is jacked up. While someone works the footbrake, try to rock the front wheel, top and bottom. Any excess play (where there should be free play, the maker's tolerances will be given in the workshop manual) indicates wear in one or more of the joints. Repairs of this kind are difficult for the home mechanic and garage help is usually needed.

Modern cars have telescopic hydraulic dampers. These should be inspected for leaks, and replaced if they are faulty. Some telescopic dampers limit the axle's downward movement, so to replace them it is often necessary to keep the weight of the vehicle supported on the axle or suspension unit. On a few cars, non-telescopic dampers can be topped up through a filler plug. Check the fluid level every 10,000 miles, and make sure that only the correct shock-absorber oil is used for topping up. It may be necessary, before replacing the level plug after filling, to bounce the suspension up and down for a short time to bleed any air still in the damper unit.

Any adjustments to the camber and castor angle should be left to a garage: special equipment is needed to measure the amount of correction required.

Front suspension

Suspension joints To check for wear in the suspension joints (swivel joints or king-pins), jack up the front of the car to secure it. While someone works the footbrake (to eliminate wheel-bearing play), try to rock the wheel

Tolerances Any excess play (check the workshop manual for tolerances provided for by the manufacturer) indicates wear in part of the suspension. Inspect all ball joints, trunnions and mountings while someone rocks the wheel

Grease nipples Clean the grease nipples (do not confuse them with the brake bleeder nipples). Lubricate the bearings through the nipples with a grease gun; if this is difficult, rock the bearings to and fro while greasing

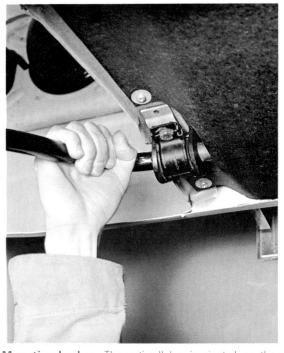

Mounting-bushes The anti-roll bar is pivoted on the chassis or sub-frame, with its ends connected to the front suspension. Check that rubber mounting-bushes at both ends and at the chassis connection are not worn or missing

Rear suspension

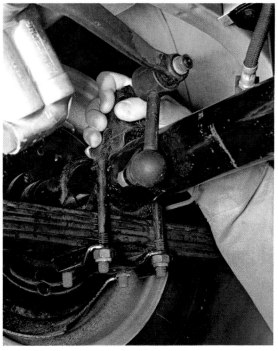

Leaf springs Most cars have leaf springs on their rear suspensions. Clean these with a wire brush and check that none of the individual leaves is broken. Inspect rubber mounting-bushes for wear, but do not try to lubricate them

U-bolts Check that U-bolts, which connect the centre of the leaf springs to the axle casing, are tight. There should be no play at all. If leaf clamps are fitted to the springs, they should also be inspected and tightened if necessary

Bump-stop There is usually a bump-stop mounted between the chassis and the axle (see handbook), and on some models there is a check-strap to limit the axle's downward movement. They should be replaced if damaged

Damper unit If a lever-type hydraulic damper requires frequent topping up, check for oil leaks where the shaft which carries the operating arm leaves the damper body. Such oil leaks cannot be repaired: replace the damper unit

Independent suspension Some cars have independent suspension at the rear. Check all arms and linkages. On old models, check that there is no corrosion at the tie-rod connecting points (at the left of the picture)

Hydrolastic suspension If hydraulic fluid is escaping, the Hydrolastic suspension may settle down too far. With the car empty, check the distance from the centre of the wheel up to the edge of the wing (see workshop manual)

Steering/servicing the two main types

The steering box

THE STEERING BOX, as opposed to the rack and pinion, is a compact unit bolted to the chassis or body and connected by an arm—known as the drop-arm—to the car's steering linkage. On cars fitted with independent suspension, there is usually also (on the opposite side of the car to the steering box) an idler box, which ensures that suspension movements do not affect the steering.

Because the steering box has a number of bearings and moving parts, it has to be well lubricated to avoid wear, which would eventually cause excessive and extremely dangerous play in the car's steering.

On the opposite side to where the drop-arm shaft leaves the steering box, there is usually a square-headed or slotted adjusting bolt, held by a lock-nut. This allows adjustment to the free play, but it is generally better to leave such adjustments to a skilled mechanic. A steering box that has been in use for some time will have worn more in the part of the gearing used for straight-ahead driving than in that used for cornering. If the free play is readjusted exactly for the straight-ahead position, it may make cornering extremely stiff. A mechanic will be able to make suitable allowances for this.

In the steering system, there are a number of connected shafts and links to control the wheel movements. One or more universal joints may be used. These joints, and the clamping nuts and bolts joining the shafts to them, should be closely inspected every 6000 miles for looseness, wear or damage. Pay particular attention if the universal joint has a flexible coupling of rubber or fabric. Consult a garage if there is any doubt about the roadworthiness of the universal joints.

The steering box is so designed that very little wheel shock is transmitted to the steering wheel. But the steering box itself is subjected to this road shock; and if it is allowed to work loose from its mountings, the chassis or body will eventually become damaged. This entails an expensive repair. Check for tightness regularly.

In cars which have power-assisted steering, the steering box itself may be lubricated in the normal way. But sometimes the box and the power-assistance unit need to be topped up with a special oil. It is therefore advisable to check the manufacturer's recommendations before attempting any maintenance.

Topping up the steering box

1 The steering box is on the driver's side of the car. It may be operated by the steering wheel through a universal joint

2 Identify (from the handbook) and remove the oil-level plug. Do not confuse it with the free-play adjuster near by

3 Top up with the recommended grade of oil. Replace the oil-level plug when the box is completely filled

4 Ensure that the box is held tightly to the body or chassis of the car. Check the retaining bolts every 6000 miles

Topping up the steering idler

1 In cars with independent suspension, a steering idler is often fitted on the side of the car opposite the steering box

2 Check in the handbook whether the idler box can be lubricated. It may have a grease nipple or an oil-level plug

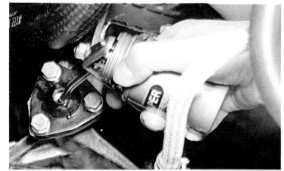

3 Wipe the grease nipple (if fitted) or remove the oil-level plug. Grease or top up as necessary

Rack and pinion

THE RACK-AND-PINION STEERING mechanism contains a long rack connected at each end by a rod to the front road wheels. It is moved by the shaft from the steering wheel through a small pinion. This arrangement is used in many different makes of car, and all systems are basically similar. There is, however, the difference that some are pre-packed with grease and rarely require any further lubrication; some need lubrication with a grease gun at the nipple provided; and others are oil-filled and have to be inspected regularly—say at 6000-mile intervals—for leaks. If any leaks should be discovered, have them repaired before adding fresh oil.

The rack and pinion, unlike the conventional steering box, is often mounted to allow some flexibility by having a rubber protector between it and its retaining U-bolts. The bolts, however, must be tight.

If the front of a car with rack-and-pinion steering is jacked up so that the front wheels are free to rotate, they should be turned with the steering wheel only. If the road wheel is moved out of straight by hand, the gearing of the rack and pinion will turn the steering wheel quite fast; the steering wheel in effect becomes a flywheel, which tends to run on even when the sideways movement of the road wheel is stopped. The result is that the steering pinion shaft could be damaged.

The rack and pinion is often driven through a universal joint and, like the conventional steering box, this joint should be checked every 6000 miles for damage or looseness. On most rack-and-pinion layouts, the end of the shaft from the steering wheel and a split collar on the pinion shaft are splined (grooved). The steering-wheel shaft fits into the split collar and is held by the splines. A pinch-bolt is tightened to keep the assembly secure. If the pinch-bolt is allowed to work loose, the splines, which are very fine, will wear; eventually the connection between the shaft and collar will be lost, and the road wheels will not react to movements of the steering wheel. Check the tightness of the pinch-bolt every 6000 miles.

Checking the retaining bolts

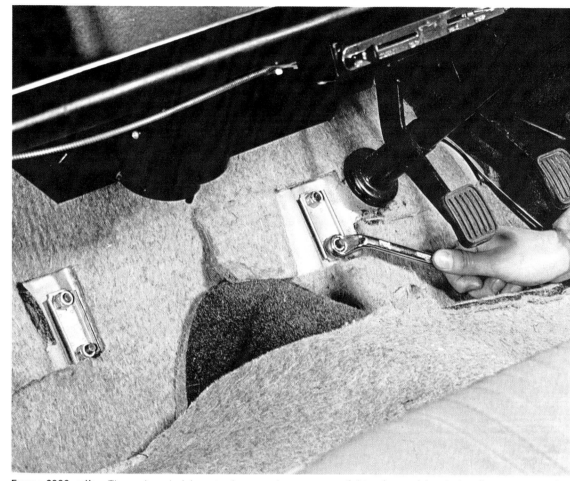

Every 6000 miles The rack-and-pinion steering gear is bolted across the body or chassis of the car. Check and if necessary tighten its retaining bolts. On some cars the carpets must be removed to gain access to the bolts

Topping up the rack tube

1 On each end of the rack housing, there is a rubber gaiter. Inspect this for damage and oil leaks every 6000 miles

2 If an oil-lubricated rack and pinion has been leaking, loosen the hose-clip on the gaiter at the driver's side

3 Push the oil-filler nozzle into the gaiter, and pump in not more than $\frac{1}{3}$ pint of the maker's recommended oil

Electrics/checking the fuses and the power supply

Essential safeguards

A CAR BATTERY, incorrectly connected, can make the wiring red-hot. The result can be a fire—or, at least, extensive damage to the wiring system. Take precautions, therefore, before attempting any repair or maintenance on or near electrical parts of the car.

Remove any rings, bracelets or a watch. Accidental shorting can cause serious burns to the hands or arms. Disconnect the earth lead from the battery.

When testing a circuit after making a repair, use a fused lead to connect the disconnected terminal to the battery. If a mistake has been made, the fuse will be blown but the circuit being tested will remain intact. A fused lead will be sufficient to carry the current for all circuits in the car, except the starter circuit.

Alternators Damage can be caused to AC generators (alternators), or to any transistorised accessory, if the battery, the battery charger or jump leads are connected to the wrong terminals. Note which is which. Connecting or disconnecting the battery when the engine is running can also damage these components.

In all electrical work, consult an expert if there is the least doubt about the safety or adequacy of a repair.

Fuses The job of the fuses is to protect the car's electrical circuits. If for some reason a circuit becomes overloaded, the fuse will blow; but when this happens the wiring and the component it serves will be protected from damage.

Many car electrical systems have only two fuses, although some have many more. In the two-fuse system, one protects some of the circuits which are live only when the ignition is switched on; the other protects some of the circuits which are connected directly to the battery, and which are therefore live all the time the battery is connected.

The rating of each fuse is normally specified on it. Always ensure that a blown fuse is replaced with one of the correct rating. If the replacement fuse also fails as soon as it is fitted, check the component and wiring for a short-circuit.

A circuit may fail, although the fuse has not blown, if the fuse becomes dirty or corroded, or if it is shaken loose by the vibration of the car. Cleaning or tightening the holder will usually cure these faults.

There is no safe substitute for a fuse. The use of silver paper wrapped round a match or blown fuse, for instance, can result in extensive damage if there is a fault in a circuit or component.

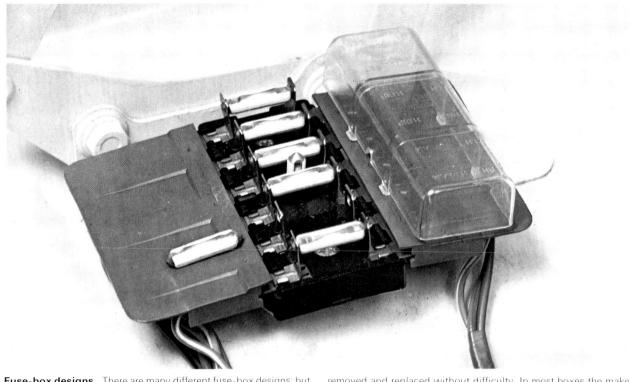

Fuse-box designs There are many different fuse-box designs; but in principle they are all similar. In every case, the fuses can be removed and replaced without difficulty. In most boxes the makers provide a slot in which spare fuses can be kept safely

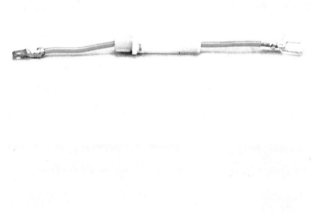

Line fuse A type of line fuse (shown connected and disconnected) used in wiring to protect one circuit. The wires are soldered in

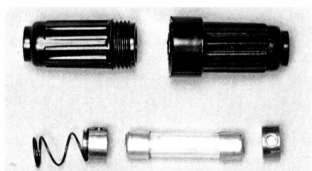

Unsoldered In some line fuses, the wires need not be soldered. They are held by simple clamp screws at each end of the fuse

Using a circuit-tester to trace faults

WHEN AN ELECTRICAL FAULT is not simply the failure of a component—a bulb or a unit, perhaps—check the circuit which serves it. Switch on and insert one lead from a circuit-tester to the power-supply cable or terminal and the other to a good earth point on the chassis. Check back at each joint and connection in the wiring until the test bulb lights or until the switch itself is reached. By checking each joint, any faulty piece of cable can be isolated (when the bulb lights). When another piece of wire is substituted, the damaged wire, if it cannot be removed, must be disconnected and insulated at both ends.

To test a switch, connect its input and output terminals. If the component or unit now works, the switch is faulty and should be replaced.

Check that the earth-return of a unit is not faulty by connecting the test bulb to the unit's earth and a power supply. If the bulb lights, the earth is adequate. This test is not suitable for the starter circuit.

If no fault can be found in any of these tests, it is likely that it is the unit itself that is faulty. It may be possible in some cases to have it repaired by a specialist; but more usually it will have to be exchanged.

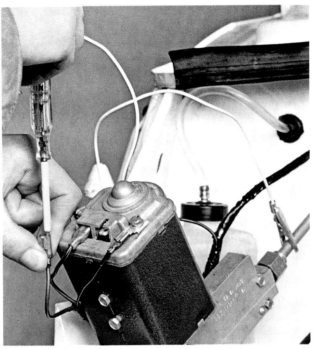

1 If a unit is receiving power, the test bulb should light when the circuit-tester is attached to a good earth point and to the unit's own power supply wire or connection

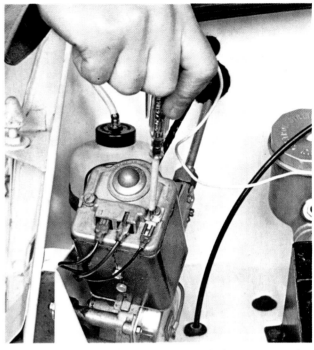

2 To check the earth of a component, attach the tester to another power supply and the earth point on the unit. The bulb will light if the earth connection is adequate

Checking control boxes

Current voltage regulator   The bulb should light if the tester is connected to the control box B terminal and to its E terminal. If it does not light, renew the earth

Voltage control box   On this type of box, connect the tester to A or A1 terminal and to E. The bulb will light if the earth is good. A bad earth can cause charging faults

Electrics/wiring and faulty components

Types of wires and their function

THE CAR'S ELECTRICAL SYSTEM contains several different types of wires. Each is used for a different job and if any wires have to be renewed, or if a new accessory is to be fitted, ensure that only the correct grade of wire is used. The wrong type may not be able to carry the necessary current, and it will overheat.

If there is an electrical fault, look for chafed wire near the connectors, or for cracked insulation which may have led to shorting. If a wire has to pass through a metal panel or bulkhead, make sure that a rubber grommet is fitted in the hole to prevent chafing.

The ignition high-tension system uses a wire with extra-heavy insulation, to prevent the 30,000 or so volts it conveys to the spark-plugs from shorting to earth, so causing the engine to stop or misfire.

The insulation of other wiring used in the car's electrical system is colour-coded, to aid identification. The wire used in accessories, for example, is often predominantly green, and the different accessories will be distinguished by different coloured stripes on the green wiring—for instance, the stop-lights are often served by green wire with a purple stripe. This varies from make to make, but the car-wiring diagram in the handbook will give the correct colour codes.

Low-current-carrying wire Interior lights, flashers and rear and sidelights use 14/0·30 (14 strands of 0·30mm²). It can also be used for ignition anti-theft devices, clocks or small lights and any of the car's small accessories

Intermediate grade Headlamps, windscreen-wiper motors, heater fans and overdrive controls are served by 28/0·30 (28 strands of 0·30mm²). It could also be used when fitting spotlights, foglamps or reversing lamps

Main charging and current-carrying wire The generator, battery and control box are connected with 44/0·30 (44 strands of 0·30mm²). It is used also for extras such as cigar lighters and electric cooling fans

High-tension (HT) lead Some ignition system leads have a copper centre like normal wire but with extra-heavy insulation; others (shown) have a carbon-impregnated fibre centre, which suppresses radio interference

Starter/battery connecting cable A very heavy gauge cable is needed to carry the high current required for the starter motor (equivalent to 100 headlamp bulbs). It must not be replaced by any other type of cable

Earthing strap This is an essential part of the earth return between the starter motor and the battery. It has to pass the high starting current and should be connected securely between the chassis or body and the engine

Joining wires and connecting them to terminals

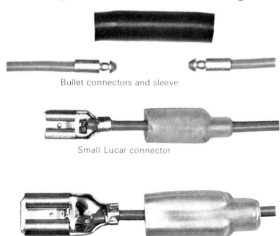

Bullet connectors and sleeve

Small Lucar connector

Large Lucar connector

WHEN TWO PIECES of car wiring have to be joined together, do not simply twist the strands together and cover with insulating tape. This is at best a temporary measure. Joins should always be made with two bullet-type connectors and a rubber sleeve. Remove $\frac{1}{8}-\frac{3}{16}$ in. of insulation from the end of each wire; slide a bullet connector as far as possible on to the ends, so that the insulation enters the bullet; then, ideally, solder at the nose of the bullet where the wires have been pushed through. Cut off any excess wire. If solder is not available, wrap the excess wire back over the bullet. The sleeve may have to be loosened slightly before the bullets can be pushed in.

When fitting accessories, Lucar-type connectors may have to be used. The large one is used for heavy current connections, generator output, control box and so on. The smaller type is used for almost every other sort of connection. Remember to push the insulator on to the wire before fitting the connector.

When making a connection to a terminal, always use a terminal tag and, if possible, solder.

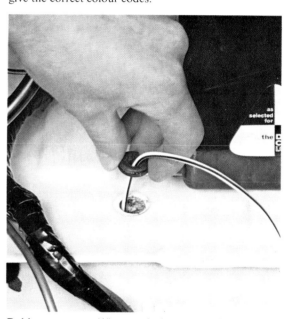

Rubber grommet Where a wire has to pass through metal, fit a rubber grommet. If the wire is not protected, its insulation can be damaged by the car's normal vibration

Earth strap Check that the earth strap from the engine or gearbox is fixed to the chassis or body. A loose strap will give the same indications as a flat battery when starting

Tracing faults in components

Flashing indicator unit Situated either in the engine compartment or under the instrument panel, the flashing indicator unit will be box-shaped or cylindrical. It is sealed and, if tests show that it is faulty, must be replaced

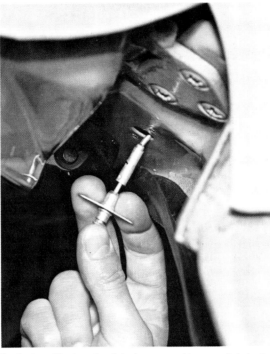

Switches The interior light is operated by a switch in the door jamb. If it does not light as the door opens, check that the switch is clean and that it is making a good earth connection. Clean if necessary. Check the switch at the light

Warning light The oil-pressure warning light is operated by a switch (shown removed) which is screwed into the engine above the sump gasket. If the light comes on during normal running, check the system

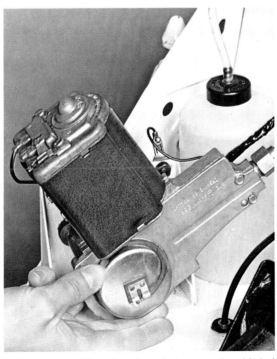

Wiper motor To adjust the windscreen-wiper blades' 'park' position, slacken the wiper-motor cover nuts. Switch on the ignition, but not the wipers. Twist the round cap in the centre to move the blades. Retighten and check

Common electrical faults

THE MOST COMMON electrical fault in a car is bulb failure. Replacement should be straightforward. Bulbs with more than one filament have a bayonet fitting whose pins can be inserted only in the correct position in the bulb-holder. On some headlamps, however, there is a separate connector block behind the bulb or sealed-beam unit. Fit the new one in the same way as the bulb or unit removed.

Brake-light failure may be due to failed bulbs, a blown fuse, bad wiring or a bad earth. Check all the possibilities. If the fault is not found, the switch itself may have failed. Some cars have a mechanical switch near to and operated by the brake pedal. On others, there will be a hydraulic switch in the braking system between the master cylinder and the wheel-cylinder units (often found in the engine compartment near the brake master cylinder). When replacing a hydraulic switch, air should not enter, provided that the brake reservoir cap is removed, and that the new switch is screwed in as soon as the old one is taken out. So the system should not need to be bled.

The switch which operates the oil warning light on the fascia is usually screwed into the side of the cylinder block or the oil-filter casing. If the light does not come on when the ignition is switched on, check that the bulb has not blown. But if the light comes on while the car is running normally, either there is a fault in the system or the oil pressure in the engine is dangerously low.

A quick check Having checked the oil level, pull the lead connector off the switch at the cylinder block. If the light stays on, it indicates that there is a short-circuit somewhere in the system. But if the light goes out, either the oil pressure is very low or the switch is faulty. The only quick check is to replace the switch.

Do not attempt to dismantle the windscreen-wiper motor. Normally, the only adjustment that can be made is to raise or lower the stopping position of the blades on the windscreen. Wet the windscreen, slacken the motor-cover screws, and with the ignition on and wiper motor off, move round the cap in the centre. The blades will be moved up or down on the windscreen. When the correct position is reached, tighten the cover and switch on the wipers to make sure that they stop in the correct position. If not, repeat the adjustment.

Earth-return circuit The interior lights in the car are operated either by switches in the door jambs or by an auxiliary switch at the light itself. In most cases, the switch closes the earth-return circuit when operated. If there is a fault, first examine and, if necessary, renew the bulb. If the bulb does not need to be replaced, check that the earth connections to the door-switches are good.

The flashing indicator unit is sealed and it cannot be repaired. There are, however, a number of tests that should be made before the unit is discarded; for the fault may be in the circuit it serves, not in the unit itself.

If the indicator warning light flashes once, then stops, check exterior bulbs and wiring. If the flashers work, but not the indicator, check the fascia bulb or its wiring.

If no flashers work, check the fuse in the circuit. Check the flasher unit by disconnecting its three wires. Connect the two from the B and L terminals. With the ignition on, switch on the indicator. If both bulbs on the side operated light, the unit is faulty. Replace it.

Electrics/solenoid and starter motor

Starter-switch remote control

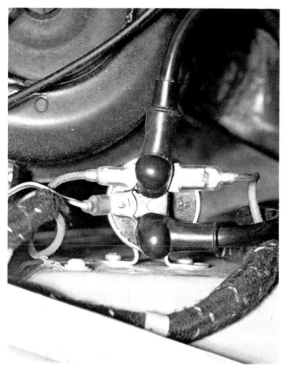

Two types of solenoid On the left, the older type and on the right, the modern one. The first can be operated by

Solenoid check If the starter motor cannot be turned, check the solenoid. Remove starter-switch connection; join the solenoid's battery lead with a short jump lead to the starter-switch terminal. The solenoid should now work

pressing a button at the far end. The other is operated by the button between the two wire connections

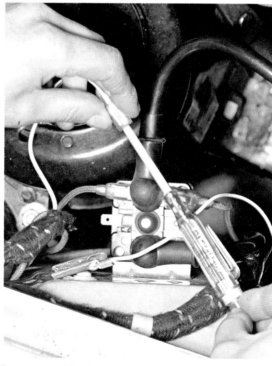

Current check To check that current is reaching the solenoid, connect one end of a test light to a good earth and the other to the starter-switch connecting wire. When the starter switch is operated, the bulb should light

When the engine will not start

THE ENGINE is started by means of a powerful electric motor which turns the flywheel. For the few seconds it works, the starter motor passes an extremely high current, up to 360 amp. (the equivalent of 100 headlight bulbs), and for this reason, connections to it are made with heavy cable. All internal connections are soldered, and the motor is controlled by a heavy-duty switch. On most cars, this starter switch is triggered by a relay or solenoid which is operated when the driver presses or turns the starter button or switch inside the car.

The solenoid is usually mounted between the motor and battery. To locate it, trace back the heavy cable carrying the current to the motor. It may have a push button to let the driver operate the starter from outside the car (but make sure that it is operated only when the car is out of gear). Other types of solenoid are completely sealed and cannot be operated from outside. These are always fitted to cars with automatic transmission, so that the car cannot be accidentally started while it is in gear.

Starter-motor failure Electrical failures in the starter motor are rare. Any trouble is more likely to be mechanical. When the motor turns, a toothed wheel, or pinion, travels along the shaft and engages with the flywheel. This mechanism is known as the Bendix gear, after its first manufacturer. Once it is engaged, it should turn the flywheel and so start the engine. A common fault, however, is for the pinion to jam in mesh with the flywheel.

Remove the cover (if there is one) from the squared end of the starter-motor shaft. Turn the shaft clockwise with a spanner until it frees the pinion. It may be possible to free the pinion without tools. Switch off the engine, engage top gear, release the handbrake and gently rock the car. Use this method only as a last resort.

Do not try to strip the starter motor: it is better to have this done at a garage. However, the motor can be removed from the car and inspected for dirt or damage. Make sure when gently unscrewing the nut which holds the power lead that the whole connecting bolt does not turn. If it does, it will probably damage the field winding connections inside, with the result that the starter-motor unit will have to be replaced.

Jammed pinion To free a jammed pinion, turn the square end of the starter-motor armature in a clockwise direction. The end is sometimes covered by a metal cap which will have to be removed before the shaft can be turned

Removing and cleaning the starter motor

1 To remove the starter motor, disconnect the power-supply lead. Undo the bolts (there are usually two) holding the motor to the engine flywheel housing

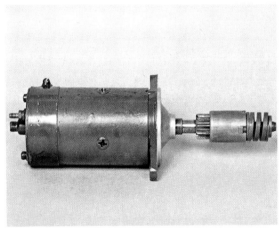

2 Having removed the starter motor, check that it is undamaged; for instance, the teeth may be badly worn. Where damage is evident, fit an exchange unit

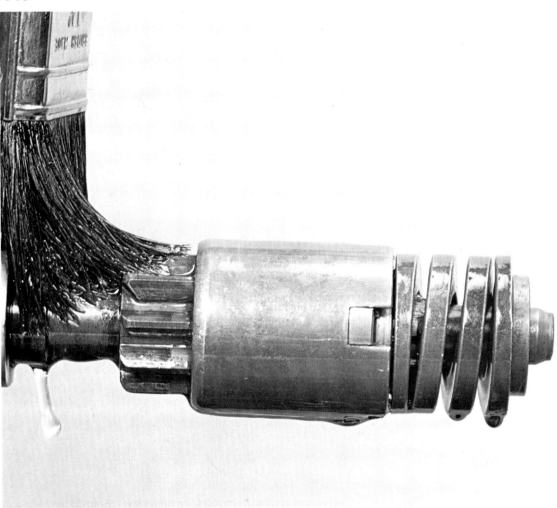

3 The Bendix gear may fail to engage with the flywheel although the starter motor turns. The gear moves along the starter-motor shaft into mesh, and if the shaft is dirty, the gear will stick. Brush the Bendix with petrol, but do not let petrol enter the motor. Operate the Bendix by hand until it is free. Do not use oil, grease or paraffin

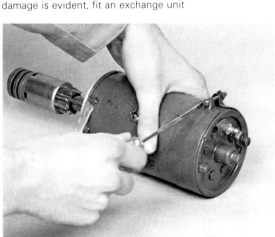

Commutator To gain access to the starter-motor commutator, first remove the band round the motor. It is held in place by a clamping bolt which should only be slackened

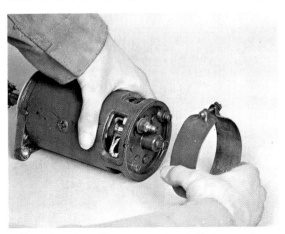

Worn brushes Remove the band. If the brushes are excessively worn, heavy-duty soldering equipment will be required to fit new ones. Seek garage assistance

Freeing brushes If the brushes are sticking, they and their guides can be cleaned with a petrol-moistened cloth. Inspect the commutator at the same time for damage

Electrics/the generator

Checking and servicing

OLDER CARS have a DC (direct current) dynamo, but most modern models have instead an alternator (see p. 145). Both are driven by the engine fan belt, and it is important to ensure that the belt is kept at the correct tension—allowing about ¾ in. play in the middle of its longest side (see p. 206).

With an alternator, this is the only maintenance that can be safely attempted by the home mechanic. There are, however, a number of servicing points on the more conventional dynamo.

At the opposite end to the fan-belt pulley, on the dynamo, there is a lubrication point for the bush inside the end-plate. A light engine or machine oil should be used every 3000 miles. There is also a bearing at the fan-pulley end, but it is pre-packed by the manufacturer and needs no attention during its normal life.

Dynamo fault If the ignition light is on while the car is running, but the fan belt is undamaged and at the correct tension, check that the dynamo is working. Remove the two wires from the dynamo end-

plate, start the engine and let it tick over. Connect one of the circuit test-light's wires to both end-plate terminals *at the same time*; attach the other wire to a good earth. The test bulb should glow at tick-over speed. Very gentle acceleration, ideally using the idling adjuster on the carburettor (see p. 188), should brighten the bulb (but note that even a little too much rpm will blow the bulb). If the test bulb does not light at all, there is a fault in the dynamo.

Remove the dynamo from the car and

inspect it through the end-plate access holes. If solder is spattered inside, there is no repair possible and both the dynamo and its control box will have to be replaced with exchange units.

Otherwise, remove the end-plate, clean the guides and renew the brushes.

Clean the commutator. If it is badly scored, the new brushes will not make good contact. In such circumstances, an exchange unit is advisable.

Check that the end-plate bush is not so worn that there is excessive play.

Removing the dynamo from the car

1 The dynamo is mounted near the front of the engine with three fixing bolts. The two on the same axis allow it to pivot, the other bolt allows its position to be adjusted

2 When removing the connectors (one large, one small) from the rear of the dynamo, do not pull them off by the wires. Hold the connector and ease it gently off the tag

3 Remove the adjusting bolt, swing the dynamo towards the engine and remove the fan belt. Remove the two remaining bolts and take the dynamo from the car

Removing the end-plate

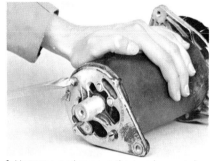

1 Unscrew and remove the two long retaining bolts. If the head of one is factory-sealed, do not remove it during the car's warranty

2 If the end-plate is tightly fixed, it may be loosened by tapping it lightly with a piece of wood. Remove the end-plate and place it on a dry, clean surface

Cleaning the commutator

1 Pull the armature assembly out of the body. In some types of dynamo a distance washer is fitted at the end of the commutator. Remove it, and make sure it is not lost

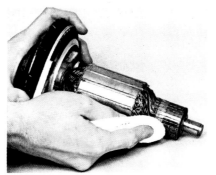

2 Clean the commutator with a cloth that has been lightly moistened with petrol

3 Use a pin to clean the grooves between the segments of the commutator

Changing the brushes

IF THE COMMUTATOR and end-plate bush are both in good order, it is advisable—whether they are badly worn or not (and only comparison with a new set will show this)—to fit new brushes.

Replace only one brush at a time. Unscrew its terminal tag and pull the brush and its connecting wire from the guide. Clean the guide with a stiff brush and wipe it with a petrol-moistened rag.

Check the brush spring for any apparent crack or weakness. If there is any doubt about its effectiveness, fit a new one.

Thread the wire of the replacement through the guide, and insert the brush. Make sure that it slides freely, but check that the correct size has been obtained and that there is no undue play. Tighten the terminal screw. Replace the second brush in the same way.

The end-plate can be refitted only if the brushes are free to move back in their guides to clear the commutator. Lift the end of the spring pressing on each brush and hook it over the outside of the guide. Push back the brushes.

Replace the armature assembly in the dynamo casing; make sure the locating rivet fits into the slot on the casing. Gently fit the end-plate over the assembled commutator, making sure that the brushes are well clear. There is also a locating rivet on the end-plate.

Replace the two long retaining bolts and tighten them. Push a screwdriver through the end-plate access holes to unhook the two brush springs so that they again press on their brushes, keeping them in contact with the commutator.

When refitting the dynamo, do not overtighten the bolts. If the end-plate is forced inwards too much, it may break.

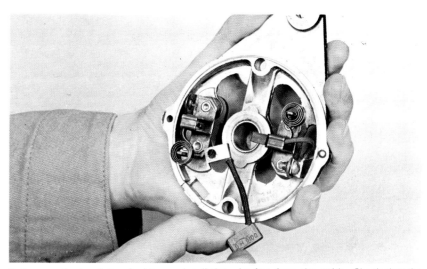

1 Remove the brush terminal tag and pull the wire free from the guide. Check that the brush springs are not broken and that there is no apparent weakness

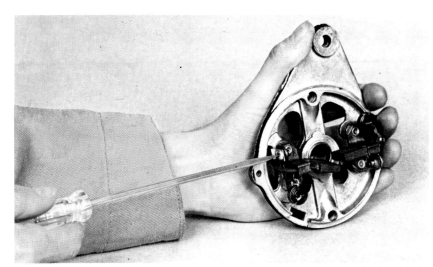

2 Clean the guides and thread the brush's connecting wire through. Insert the brush in its guide and, if it fits without sticking, tighten the terminal screw

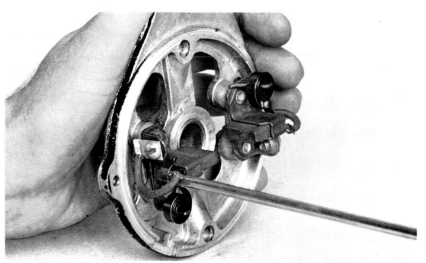

3 The brushes must clear the commutator when the end-plate is replaced. Lift both springs and hook them over the guides. Replace later from outside with a screwdriver

Bodywork/outside the car

Taking care of the car

REGULAR BODY MAINTENANCE is simple yet essential. There is, of course, the obvious financial incentive: because the mechanical parts will often outlast the car body—and indeed often be more easily and cheaply replaced—the resale value of a used car is sometimes completely dependent upon its appearance and the condition of the bodywork.

But there is a more serious factor to be considered—safety. The body of the modern car is more than a pretty shell to protect the passengers from the weather; it makes a considerable contribution to the car's overall strength. Damage, whether as a result of a collision or because the bodywork has been allowed to rust, can be extremely serious.

Body repairs Although the owner can himself successfully and safely repair quite badly damaged bodywork sections, he should confine his efforts only to those parts that are 'unstressed'—that is, that make no contribution to the car's strength. In this category come the bonnet, boot lid and doors. The strengthening sections, which vary from one type of car to another, should be taken to a specialist for all but the most superficial scratches or dents. They may have to be replaced completely with properly stressed parts.

When accident or rust damage can be safely repaired at home, however, the owner now has a range of products available to help him—from anti-rust preparations to finishing paints matching almost every modern car. It should be possible, therefore, when tackling the several repair jobs described in this section, to achieve a finish indistinguishable from the manufacturer's original. But it is important to follow all the instructions at each stage. Patience is needed, for undue haste will produce a less satisfactory repair.

Maintenance Prevention is better than repair. Regular maintenance, which will keep the car body safe and in good trim, is simple and inexpensive. Rattles and squeaks, which may at first be simply annoying, should be traced and put right as soon as possible, or more serious faults may develop. The most often neglected part of the car—the underside—should be inspected and cleaned regularly to protect it from the effects of road spray. The upholstery and carpets can be kept in good condition with cleaning agents and upholstery paints. Above all, the most obvious part—the paintwork and chrome trimming—should be washed at least once a fortnight, and more often if necessary.

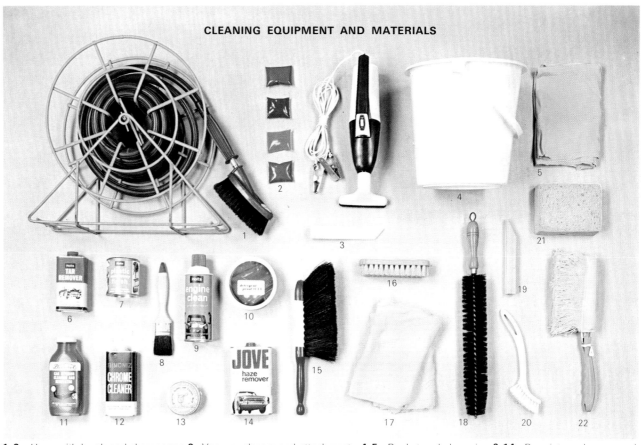

CLEANING EQUIPMENT AND MATERIALS

1-2 Hose with brush and shampoos. **3** Vacuum cleaner and attachment. **4-5** Bucket and chamois. **6-14** Proprietary cleaners and upholstery paint and brush. **15-22** Brushes, and polishing cloths, with wedge to scrape mud off wheel arches

Radiator grille Work the flexible brush or sponge between each slat. If necessary, loosen the mounting bolts and push any badges or fog and spot-lamps out of the way

Headlamps Dirty glass greatly reduces the power of the headlamps. In bad weather they should be cleaned every day. Use a proprietary cleaner for stubborn marks

Behind bumpers Remove bumpers occasionally to wash them and the bodywork behind. Smear on wax polish and leave it unrubbed to protect against corrosion

Washing and polishing

DO NOT ALLOW dirt to build up. Clean the paintwork about once a week, but never with a dry cloth; soak it with clean, cold water. Do not aim a hose straight at windows, locks or grilles. Their weather-sealing is not designed for such fierce and prolonged attacks.

After soaking, sponge the car with clean, cold water, possibly with a little washing-up liquid, car shampoo or paraffin added. But keep shampoo away from the wind-screen, and make sure that the washing-up liquid does not contain bleach.

Wash the car from the roof down, to allow stubborn dirt at the bottom to soak. Remove tar spots with white spirit and rinse with clean water.

Occasionally remove bumpers and spot-lights, to clean behind them. Do not use ordinary metal polish on chrome.

Use a clean chamois leather for the windows, and make sure that no wax polish or domestic window cleaner is used on either the windscreen or the rear window.

The car can be polished once or twice a year to remove traffic scum. Check that the polish is suitable for the paintwork, as modern metallic finishes can be dulled by wax polish. A proprietary anti-haze cleaner may remove the wax film before any further polishing is done. New cars should never be polished until the paint has been allowed to harden for about two months. This rule will also apply to cars which have been resprayed.

CLEANING SEQUENCE FOR THE OUTSIDE OF THE CAR

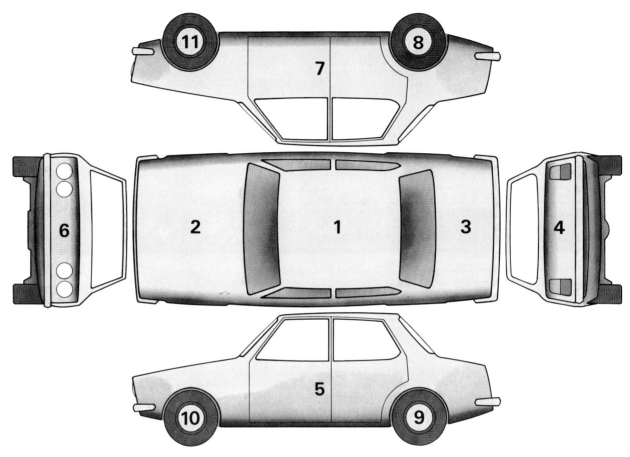

Rain channels Make sure that the rain channels are not clogged. Fill any holes immediately they are found. Wash and dry the channels carefully

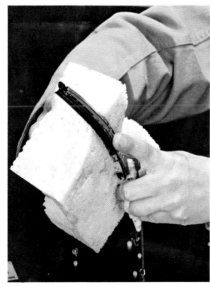

Wiper blades Use a different sponge or cloth for the wiper blades. Clean them with undiluted windscreen washer liquid. Do not use polish or any kind of grease

Quarter-lights Use a firm brush to clean the trim and sealing of the quarter-lights. Inspect inside to make sure that there are no leaks. Reseal if necessary

Wheel hubs If stubborn dirt cannot be removed with the flexible brush, use a stiff brush and paraffin and water. Remove the hub cap occasionally to clean underneath it

Bodywork/inside the car

Cleaning and inspecting the interior

THE INSIDE of the car should be cleaned regularly, and once a year be given an extra-thorough 'spring clean'. Neglect may result in discoloured upholstery, rotted carpets and general shabbiness.

One advantage of thoroughly cleaning the interior of the car is that when the seats and carpets have been removed, it is possible to check more easily for leaks in the bodywork or floor, and for mechanical faults.

Empty the ashtrays and clean the obvious rubbish from the floor, shelves, glove compartment and so on. Remove the rubber mats, carpets and underlay. They are fixed in different ways in different cars: make sure they are removed properly, to avoid damage. If the fixing studs or strips seem likely to break when they are removed, have replacements available for refitting.

Brush or shake, then beat the carpets. If necessary shampoo them, and hang them to dry. Brush and scrub rubber mats with warm water and detergent. Remove grit and dirt from the floor pan.

Floor pan Examine the floor pan carefully, and if possible put the car on a ramp so that the underside can be hosed. Any leaks at the welded seams or bung holes will then be visible. Renew the rubber bung stoppers if necessary. If there is a small leak in a welded seam, paint on a sealing compound. If the leak is large, it may affect the strength of the body. Seek garage advice.

Check the rubber gaiters on handbrake and gear levers for perishing or damage. Make sure that the gearbox cover is fixed securely.

The carpet and underfelt help to deaden road noise. If they become badly worn they will be less effective. Replace them if necessary. Torn carpets, particularly near the pedals, can be dangerous if the driver's foot becomes trapped. Mend or replace them.

Make sure when the carpets are refitted that the one at the driver's pedals is properly fixed down. It should not be able to fall back over the pedals.

The seats, although probably the least mechanical part of a car, have adjusting mechanisms and stops which prevent them from being flung forward when the car brakes sharply. Check that they are securely fixed to the floor of the car, well oiled and not worn.

Remove the seat squabs—the back and frame—and clean with a small stiff brush. Pay particular attention to the crevices and seams, where dirt collects.

Seat belts, now required by law on most cars, should be free-running, and their anchorages, usually on the floor and door frame, must be securely fixed. If the car has just been bought second-hand, make sure that the seat belts conform to the recommendations of the British Standards Institute—the only belts accepted by the Department of the Environment.

Upholstery Several proprietary cleaners are available for upholstery, trim and roof linings. Make sure that a suitable one is used for each material. Dilute for normal cleaning, but use 'neat' solution for stubborn stains. Never use a detergent or any cleaner containing bleach. Avoid using too much water, for the interior should be able to dry quickly if condensation is to be prevented.

Wipe leather with a damp cloth, or sponge it with soapy, tepid water and dry with a soft cloth. If the leather is badly stained, work the soapy water into thick suds, wipe off with a damp cloth, and rub dry. Wash plastic in warm soapy water, or wipe it with a damp cloth. Scrub lightly with a soft brush and mild detergent or cleaning fluid to restore the colour.

Water should be used sparingly on trim panels, for the board behind them is liable to twist or warp when soaked.

Wipe roof linings as lightly as possible. The older cloth linings should be vacuumed or brushed lightly, then wiped with a soft rag moistened in cleaning fluid.

Upholstery or roof lining which has been torn can be patched and if necessary repainted with special upholstery paint. But follow the maker's instructions and make sure that the paint is suitable for the materials being repaired.

Glass and paint Clean water and a chamois leather is usually all that is required but household window cleaners can be used on all the interior glass except the windscreen and rear windows. For them, use a little methylated spirit diluted in warm water—but take special care that no excess is dropped on the paintwork or interior trim: it will stain and lift paint. Brightwork or chrome—for example instrument panels—can be wiped with a damp cloth, as can plastic door handles or switches.

Wash the paintwork with a rag or sponge and clean water. Dry with a soft chamois leather.

When the trim and the fittings are clean, vacuum the inside either with an ordinary nozzle-type domestic cleaner, or a portable that works from the car battery.

Inspect the weather stripping all round the glass and if there is a leak at any point, stick it down securely or, if necessary, replace the rubber (see p. 258).

Locks, handles, window runners, even instruments, can all cause annoying rattles. Check them all for tightness.

Doors and hinges Check that all the hinges—on the doors and the glove compartment—are in good order. Do not allow fabric or metal check straps on the doors to become worn, for a free-swinging door can be extremely dangerous in traffic. Inspect the hanging straps fitted for back-seat passengers in some cars.

Rusted drain holes in doors can be redrilled, but do not use an electric drill, for water may be suddenly released and cause a short circuit.

The courtesy light inside the car is usually operated by opening the door. Make sure that the push switch is clean. If it is not working properly, check for a blown bulb or frayed wiring behind the switch, which is usually easily removed. Replace if necessary.

Check that the steering-column retaining screws are secure. If necessary, tighten with a torque spanner set to the maker's recommended pressure (see handbook).

The ventilation ducts and airflow channels must be kept clear. If the grilles can be removed, clean them thoroughly and make sure nothing is stuck in the ducts.

Inspect the rear-view mirror and make sure that it is securely fixed. Tighten if necessary.

The inside of the boot is most often forgotten. It should be cleaned and vacuumed as often as the car interior, and should be checked for weather leaks. Inspect the drain hole and check the condition of the spare wheel. See that all the car's tools are being carried, and ensure that the wires to the rear lights (if visible) are not damaged.

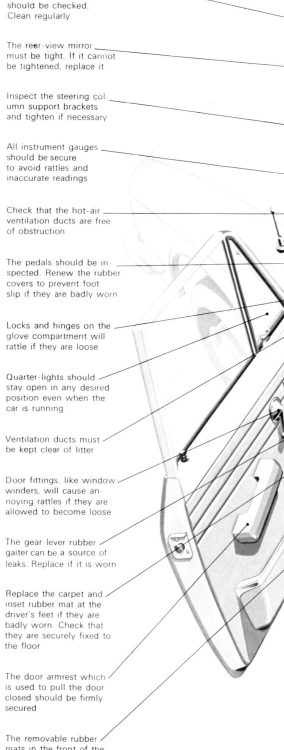

The interior light, which works from a push switch on the door-jamb, should be checked. Clean regularly

The rear-view mirror must be tight. If it cannot be tightened, replace it

Inspect the steering column support brackets and tighten if necessary

All instrument gauges should be secure to avoid rattles and inaccurate readings

Check that the hot-air ventilation ducts are free of obstruction

The pedals should be inspected. Renew the rubber covers to prevent foot slip if they are badly worn

Locks and hinges on the glove compartment will rattle if they are loose

Quarter-lights should stay open in any desired position even when the car is running

Ventilation ducts must be kept clear of litter

Door fittings, like window winders, will cause annoying rattles if they are allowed to become loose

The gear-lever rubber gaiter can be a source of leaks. Replace if it is worn

Replace the carpet and inset rubber mat at the driver's feet if they are badly worn. Check that they are securely fixed to the floor

The door armrest which is used to pull the door closed should be firmly secured

The removable rubber mats in the front of the car should be replaced if they become worn

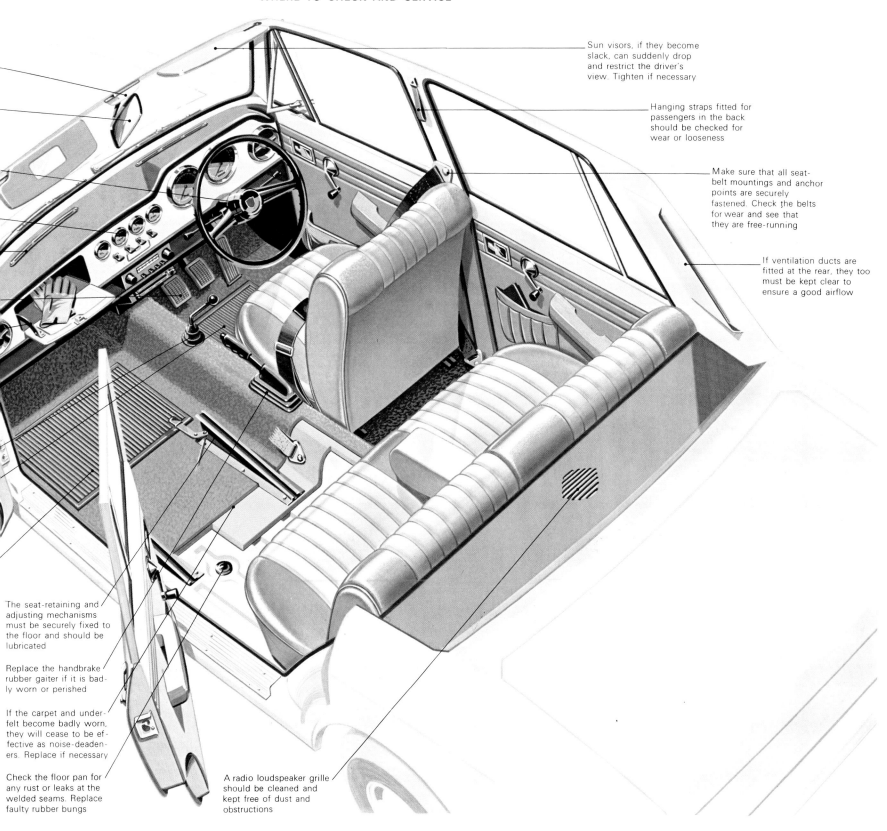

Sun visors, if they become slack, can suddenly drop and restrict the driver's view. Tighten if necessary

Hanging straps fitted for passengers in the back should be checked for wear or looseness

Make sure that all seat-belt mountings and anchor points are securely fastened. Check the belts for wear and see that they are free-running

If ventilation ducts are fitted at the rear, they too must be kept clear to ensure a good airflow

The seat-retaining and adjusting mechanisms must be securely fixed to the floor and should be lubricated

Replace the handbrake rubber gaiter if it is badly worn or perished

If the carpet and under-felt become badly worn, they will cease to be effective as noise-deadeners. Replace if necessary

Check the floor pan for any rust or leaks at the welded seams. Replace faulty rubber bungs

A radio loudspeaker grille should be cleaned and kept free of dust and obstructions

Bodywork/cleaning and repairing the inside of the car

Where to inspect and clean

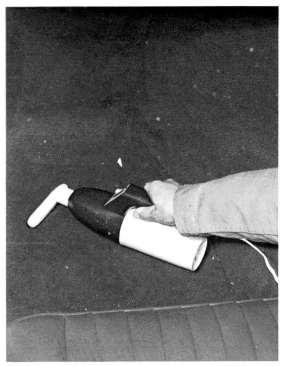

Carpet Vacuum the carpet, using either an ordinary domestic cleaner with nozzle attachments (a pointed one is useful for corners) or a portable, powered by the battery

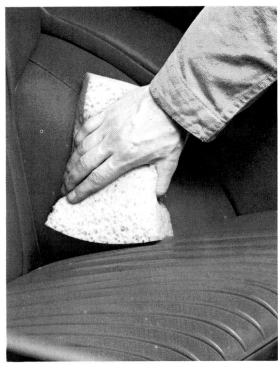

Upholstery Clean the upholstery with a proprietary cleaner suitable for the material. Most cleaners can be applied undiluted to move stubborn stains

Wood Wipe the fascia with a damp cloth, but it is advisable to avoid using too much water. The board underneath will warp if it is soaked

Pedals When cleaning the inside of the car, take the opportunity to check and lubricate the pedals. Inspect the return-springs and replace them if they have lost their tension

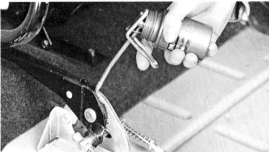

Handbrake Remove the gaiter and carpets from around the handbrake lever. Inspect the linkage and lubricate the moving parts if necessary

Steering column Check that the steering-column retaining bolts are tight and that its angled fixing plate is securely bolted to the bulkhead. There should be no play at all

Seats Inspect and lubricate the seat tip-up hinges and adjusting mechanisms. Make sure that the seat mounting bolts through the floor pan are secure

Removing and replacing the carpet

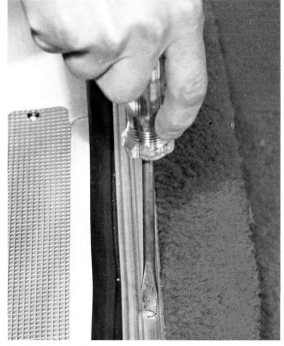

Strip fixing Occasionally remove the carpet to inspect the floor. It may be held by a long metal strip. Use a little penetrating oil if the screws have become rusted in

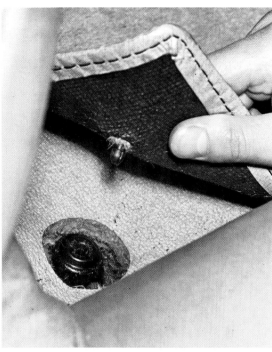

Stud fixing An alternative method of fixing is by a press stud fitted to the carpet. It is held in a matching socket on the body or floor. Older studs may break when removed

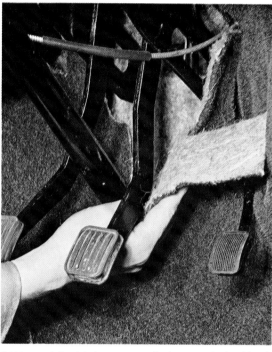

At the pedals It is important to fit the carpet in the driver's footwell so that it cannot fall back and foul the pedals. In an emergency, torn carpet could trap the driver's foot

Repairing torn trim

1 Do not mend a tear in the upholstery by sticking the edges down to the foam rubber underneath. In most cases the foam will be destroyed by the adhesive

2 Cut a patch—larger than the tear—from underneath one of the seats. (Buy matching material for large repairs.) Apply adhesive and put the patch in the hole, glue uppermost

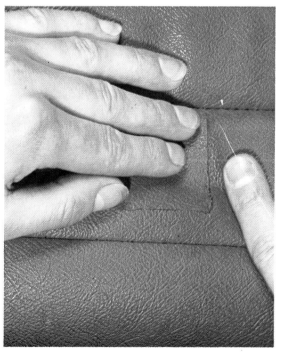

3 Press down the torn edges, and try to get them as close together as possible. Any small gap or colour difference can be touched in with a suitable upholstery paint

Bodywork/cleaning the underside

Checking and sealing against rust

THE CORROSIVE MUD underneath a car should be removed periodically, and always before and after winter. Caked mud soaks up spray which, when impregnated with salt from the roads in winter, makes it doubly corrosive.

After removing the carpets, jack the car as high as possible and support it securely on ramps, axle stands, or single blocks of wood. Remove the wheels. It is advisable to wear old clothes and some kind of headgear for the job.

Scrape as much of the loose dirt as possible from the underside with a blunted chisel, a wallpaper scraper or a piece of wood. Pay special attention to the wheel arches and crevices behind metal straps. Then hose down the entire underside.

Leaks While the car is drying, check inside for leaks at the welded seams, rubber grommets and gaiters. Use a sealing compound for any small seam leaks and replace gaiters or grommets.

When the underside is dry, inspect it inch by inch. Look for oil leaks at the master cylinder, sump, gearbox and back axle. Test the tightness of every nut and bolt. Clean and lubricate all linkages: wipe dirt off handbrake cables with a greasy rag and replace frayed cables. Clean all the hydraulic pipes and examine all hoses for damage—especially at clips or joints.

Brush off any rust, down to the bare metal, and treat with an anti-rust preparation. Make sure that the maker's instructions are followed, and apply primer.

Underbody sealing Underbody sealer will usually have been applied by the manufacturer or garage, but it can be restored or applied fresh by the owner. It is a thick substance which, when it hardens, protects the underbody metal from spray and flying stones; it also helps to deaden road noise. To ensure that it sticks firmly, and to prevent rusting underneath, never apply sealing compound to bare metal; and do not allow it to harden on the propeller shaft, suspension, steering or brakes. Paraffin will clean off stray blobs.

If the underbody is already sealed, check that the coating is still sound. Remove any flakes of loose sealer and clean down to the bare metal with a wire brush. Spray or brush on a proprietary rust neutraliser. This may have to be washed off carefully right away, for some types prevent the primer and sealing compound from sticking. Apply the primer and let it dry. Brush on the sealing compound and work it into crevices. Give a double coating to the wheel arches.

POINTS TO INSPECT AND CHECK UNDERNEATH THE CAR

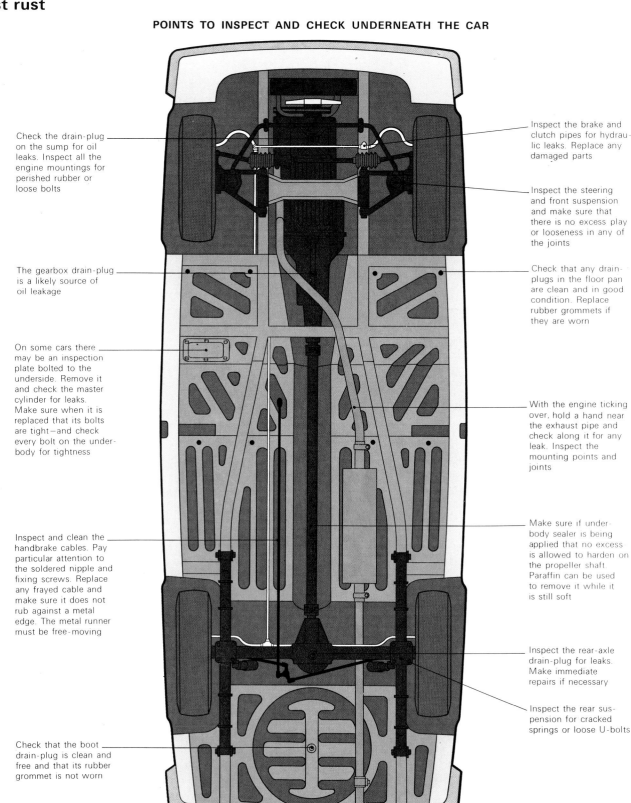

Check the drain-plug on the sump for oil leaks. Inspect all the engine mountings for perished rubber or loose bolts

The gearbox drain-plug is a likely source of oil leakage

On some cars there may be an inspection plate bolted to the underside. Remove it and check the master cylinder for leaks. Make sure when it is replaced that its bolts are tight—and check every bolt on the underbody for tightness

Inspect and clean the handbrake cables. Pay particular attention to the soldered nipple and fixing screws. Replace any frayed cable and make sure it does not rub against a metal edge. The metal runner must be free-moving

Check that the boot drain-plug is clean and free and that its rubber grommet is not worn

Inspect the brake and clutch pipes for hydraulic leaks. Replace any damaged parts

Inspect the steering and front suspension and make sure that there is no excess play or looseness in any of the joints

Check that any drain-plugs in the floor pan are clean and in good condition. Replace rubber grommets if they are worn

With the engine ticking over, hold a hand near the exhaust pipe and check along it for any leak. Inspect the mounting points and joints

Make sure if underbody sealer is being applied that no excess is allowed to harden on the propeller shaft. Paraffin can be used to remove it while it is still soft

Inspect the rear-axle drain-plug for leaks. Make immediate repairs if necessary

Inspect the rear suspension for cracked springs or loose U-bolts

Inspection points that are often forgotten

Radiator Hose the radiator 'honeycomb'. If it is badly clogged, push dirt out gently with a thin stick. Great care is needed

Electric wires Replace any frayed or cracked wire. Make sure that the grommets, where wires pass through metal, are sound

Flexible hoses Make sure that all flexible hoses are in good condition. Check especially for cracking near clips or joints

Wheel arches Scrape off as much dirt as possible, then hose or brush clean. Check any grooves or crevices for hidden grit

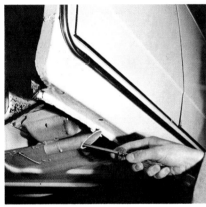

Jacking points Make sure that the jacking points are free of dirt and securely fixed. Treat with an anti-rust preparation

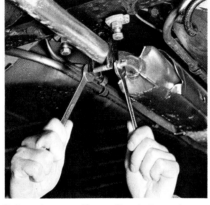

Exhaust mountings Check the exhaust system, with the engine running, for any undue vibration. The mountings must be tight

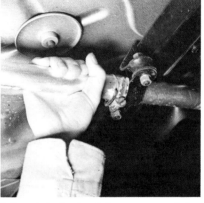

Exhaust leaks Exert firm pressure at the joints to ensure that seals are effective. With the engine ticking over, feel for exhaust leaks

Underbody sealing Make sure that underside sealing compound is sound. Remove any flaking patches with a scraper

Treating rust and sealing the underbody

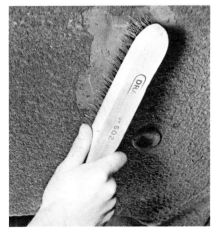

1 When the loose sealing compound has been scraped off, clean down to the bare metal with a stiff wire brush

2 Treat the bare metal with an anti-rust preparation, then follow the manufacturer's instructions. Wash it off if necessary

3 Sealing compound must never be applied to bare metal. Paint on a coat of suitable primer and allow it to dry

4 Apply the underbody sealing compound thickly: work it into crevices but make sure that none is left on any moving part

Bodywork/damage found when cleaning

Minor paint repairs

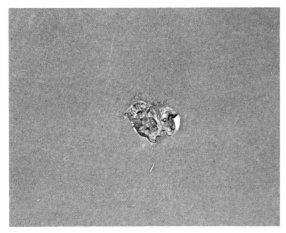

1 Small chips on the paintwork are often found during cleaning. If these are tackled at once, repair is simple; but if they are left for some time, rust will start to eat underneath

2 Carefully scrape away the edges of the good paint and make sure that there is no rust on the bare spot. If there is a more extensive repair is necessary (see pp. 244–51)

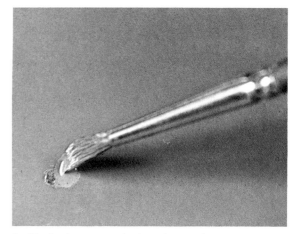

3 Obtain the correct shade and type of paint and lightly touch in the damaged spot with a fine brush. If this is done properly, it should be indistinguishable from the original

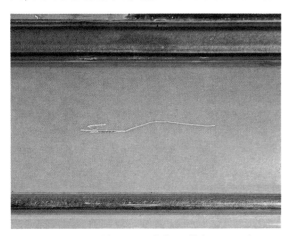

1 A scratch caused by a very light collision or, perhaps, a knife, can also be repainted. But here, too, the work must be done before the bare metal has a chance to rust

2 Rub along the scratch with a proprietary silicone solvent to remove completely any polish or grease. Wash with plenty of clean water and leather dry

3 Touch in lightly with the exactly matched paint. A full range to suit most mass-produced cars is available, but care is still necessary when matching. Use a small, fine brush

1 One of the most common areas for paint damage is the door edge. Because rust starts as soon as metal is exposed to moist air, minor damage may quickly become more serious

2 Because of the small area involved, it will still be possible to touch in with a brush, but the rust must first be removed. Treat the metal (see pp. 243–4) and apply a coat of primer

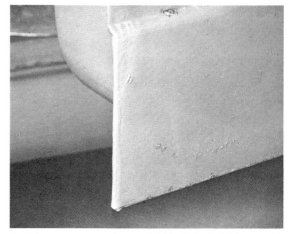

3 Take care not to paint too thickly; if the finish is unsatisfactory, the only remedy will be to rub down, possibly to the bare metal again, and repeat the entire repair work

Preparing for panel repairs

Equipment and materials

SERIOUS DAMAGE caused by extensive corrosion or a major accident is a garage job. But there are many bodywork repairs which can be done at home. A selection of the materials available is illustrated below. Some items the do-it-yourself owner will already have—an electric drill with a sanding attachment, a wallpaper scraper, paint brushes and a stiff wire brush.

It is now possible for the owner to fix loose trim with a small handyman's rivet gun—and this tool can be used for other simple riveting jobs as well.

Special cans of sealing compound for repairing weather seals on the doors and windows are obtainable, with a 'grease-gun' nozzle which allows the sealer to be applied accurately and in the correct amount.

Whenever the original paintwork is removed, the bare metal should be treated with an anti-rust preparation. Primer paint is needed before a finishing coat can be applied. For most mass-produced cars, there is a full range of finishing paint available to give a finish which should be indistinguishable from the original.

For the very small scratch or dent, rubbing compound may be sufficient. Rub down the paint around the dent or scratch with a cloth and a little compound. Treat the bare metal with a rust neutraliser, following the maker's instructions. Make sure that the metal is dry before applying the primer coat. When the primer has dried, spray on the finishing paint. Several coats may be required even with such light damage. To get a smooth finish, it is important to let each coat dry completely and rub it down with soaked wet-and-dry paper before applying the next. Do not polish the paintwork for at least six weeks, to allow the new coat to harden completely. Make sure that any polish used is suitable for the paint (see p. 235).

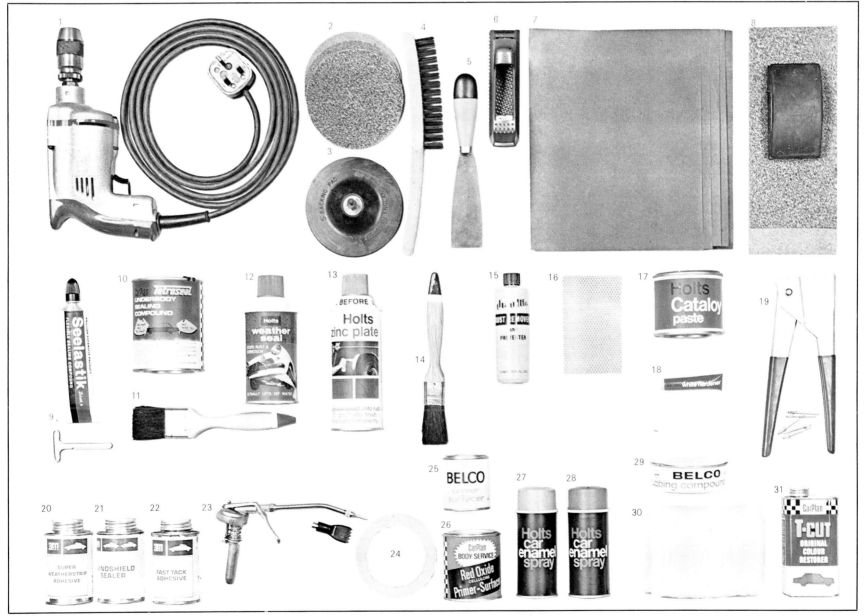

1–4 To remove rust and original paintwork, an electric drill with sanding attachments, and a stiff wire brush. **5** Flexible scraper which can also be used to apply filler. **6–8** Cheese-grater plane and abrasive paper. **9–12** Sealing compounds and brush. **13–15** Anti-rust preparations and brush. **16** Perforated zinc. **17–18** Resin and catalyst. **19** Rivet gun. **20–23** Sealers and adhesives with nozzle fitting. **24** Masking tape. **25–28** Primer and finishing paints. **29–31** Proprietary car cleaning materials available at most service stations

Bodywork/repairing a small dent or crease

Treating the damaged area

IF THE BODYWORK is scratched or dented —especially if bare metal is exposed— cover it with paint as soon as possible, to prevent rust from forming. Primer is best, but any suitable paint (see p. 250) will do as a temporary measure until the area can be properly treated.

A very light scratch or small dent can be repaired simply with a proprietary rubbing compound. But if the dent or crease is more serious, it may have to be pressed or beaten out, with a soft-headed hammer, before it is suitable for filling.

If the panel cannot be pressed out from behind, fix one or more self-tapping screws in the dent and pull it out very gently with a pair of pliers.

When the dent is pushed out, remove all the paint and any rust with a coarse sanding disc on an electric drill. Sand off all the paint from and around the damaged area until the metal is clean and bright.

Wear goggles, if possible, to protect the eyes from grit and sparks.

To minimise any later rusting, the metal can at this stage be treated with a special zinc-rich primer; but there are now available filler compounds which include an anti-rust agent.

The proprietary fillers commonly available come in two parts: a resin, and a hardener or catalyst. Follow the maker's instructions when mixing the two, and mix only enough for the immediate job in hand. If too much is prepared at once, it will harden and become unusable before it can be applied. Do not try to use filler in a damp atmosphere.

To apply the filler, use a piece of flexible hardboard or plastic. The filler should be applied in layers, until the surface comes just above the bare metal. Extend it beyond the area of actual damage, but keep it off the paintwork.

1 A superficial scratch can be treated with a simple rubbing compound but dents must be pushed out before repair

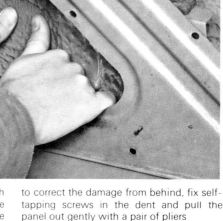

2 If a panel is accessible from behind, push very gently against the dent until the contour is restored. Where it is not possible to correct the damage from behind, fix self-tapping screws in the dent and pull the panel out gently with a pair of pliers

3 Use an electric drill with a coarse sanding disc, or orbital sander, to remove all the paint and any rust from the repair area

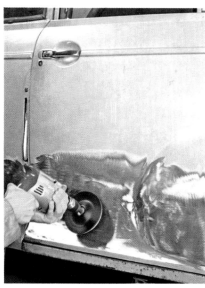

4 Work the sanding disc carefully into any crease or dent. Remove the paint beyond the damaged area until the metal is bare

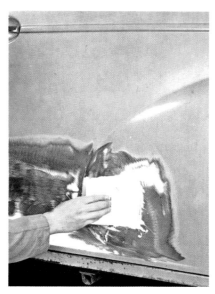

5 Mix the two-part filler (following the maker's instructions) and apply it with a hardboard or plastic strip

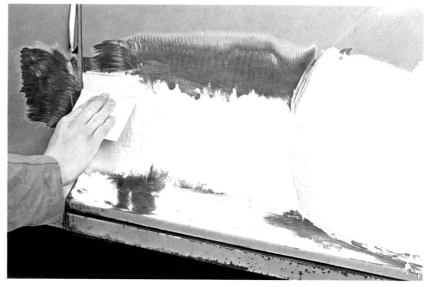

6 Put the filler on in layers, until it stands just above the level of the bare metal. Extend it an inch or two beyond the damaged area, but not on to the paintwork. Follow the panel shape and work quickly while the filler is still soft and manageable

Achieving a professional finish

WHEN THE FILLER has hardened, rub off the surplus with a sanding block and coarse paper; an electric sander or drill attachment is not advisable at this stage. A cloth mask over the nose and mouth is useful protection against the dust produced by rubbing down.

The first sanding will probably reveal small holes in the filler, or areas incompletely filled. Mix another small batch of filler and apply a thin layer where required. When this has hardened, rub it down again—first with coarse paper and then with a finer grade. For the really fine work of shaping the filler surface to match the panel contours, discard the rubbing block and use the paper by itself.

Rub down the entire area with fine wet-or-dry paper until the surface is perfectly smooth. Use plenty of water to keep the paper soaked, and feel with the fingers for any slight imperfections—especially at the edges where the filler blends with the bare metal. Wash the work thoroughly and allow it to dry.

Before painting the repaired area, mask any adjoining paintwork or trim with self-adhesive tape.

Make sure that the correct primer has been chosen for the type of finishing paint that is to be used (see p. 250). Allow the primer coat to dry completely and rub it down with very fine wet-and-dry paper. Again use plenty of water. Wash and dry the finished work.

Check the primer. If the surface is satisfactory, the finish paint can be applied. But if the primer surface is rough or blemished, rub down and apply a new coat. More than one coat can be applied, but each coat must be allowed to dry completely and should then be rubbed down lightly with soaked wet-or-dry paper before the next is applied.

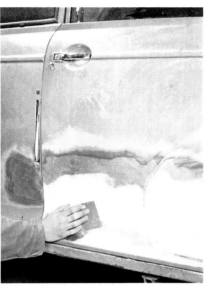

7 When the filler hardens, rub it down with a coarse sandpaper and block. Make sure its edges taper to meet the metal

8 For shaped parts of the panel, discard the block and use the paper alone, to ensure that the contour is followed

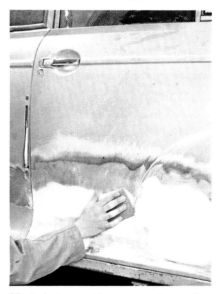

9 If the first rubbing-down reveals pinholes or blemishes, mix fresh filler and apply a little where required. Let it dry

10 Rub down with a coarse, then a fine paper, until the filler area is fairly smooth, blending into the bare metal

11 Rub down with well-soaked wet-or-dry paper. Cover the whole area. Wash thoroughly and allow the panel to dry

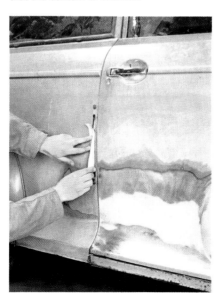

12 Before applying the primer coat, mask the adjoining panels or trim with adhesive tape. Use newspaper for large areas

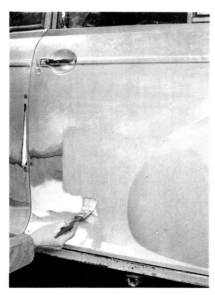

13 Check that the primer is correct for the type of finishing paint to be used. Brush or spray it on and allow it to dry completely

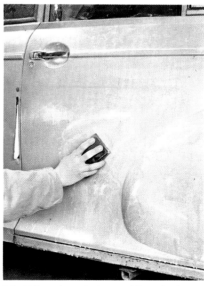

14 When dry, rub down with soaked wet-or-dry paper. Wash carefully. More primer can be applied, but rub down after each coat

Bodywork/repairing rust damage

Rubbing down

1 Steel panels rust from the inside out. By the time the rust breaks through the paint surface, in the form of blisters, drastic action may be needed

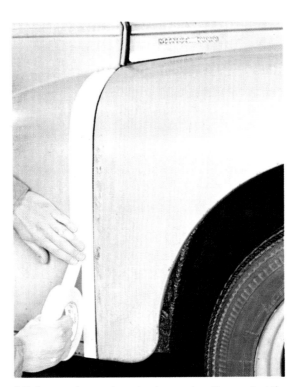

2 Before starting work on the damaged section, protect the adjoining areas of bodywork with self-adhesive masking tape or, if the area is large, with newspaper and tape

3 Use an electric drill and coarse (120 grit) sanding-disc to cut back the rust and paint to the bare metal. Clean a section some 8–10 in. beyond the area of visible rust

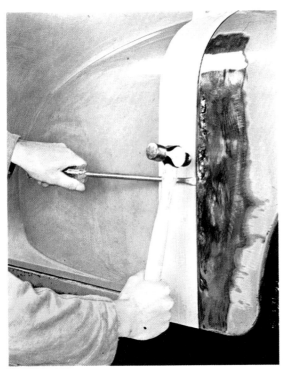

4 Hammer in the rusted area, using a screwdriver, say, as a guide to avoid damaging the adjoining good metal. The corroded metal will break away, leaving a key for the filler

5 Use a proprietary zinc-rich priming filler as a precaution against further rusting. Press the filler in firmly, so that it makes a good bond with the sound metal remaining

6 Do not lay the filler on too thickly. Build up the surface gradually with thin layers and make sure that it is moulded to roughly the original shape of the damaged panel

Shaping the repair

7 When the filler surface stands just a little above the original metalwork, check that the whole area has been covered. Smooth the surface and allow it to dry thoroughly

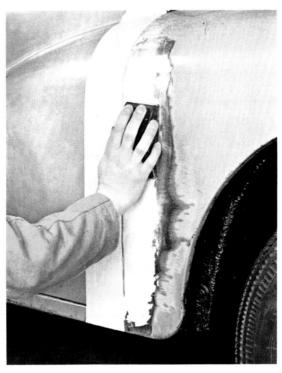

8 When it is dry, rub down with a coarse (80 grit) sandpaper on a rubbing block. The first sanding should bring the new surface almost level with the surrounding area

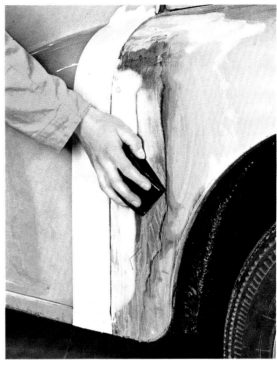

9 For final shaping use a fine (320 grit) wet-or-dry paper. Keep it soaked, and rub until the surface is smooth and level. Wash the whole area with clean, lukewarm water

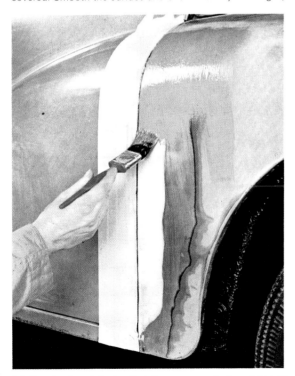

10 Check when it is dry that there are no dust particles or scum. Brush on primer paint, making sure that it is of the correct type for the finishing paint to be used later

11 Apply the primer some 2–3 in. beyond the repaired area, so that some of the original paint finish is covered. Let it dry completely, then inspect it for any blemishes

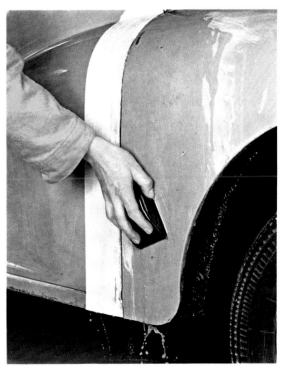

12 Rub it down with a fine (400 grit) wet-or-dry paper. Use plenty of water, and make sure that the edge of the primer area is 'feathered' into the original paintwork

Bodywork/panel-beating repairs

Removing fittings and beating out

1 Even a light collision can dent or distort a large area of bodywork. If a structural part of the body is damaged, assistance is needed; otherwise repairs can be done at home

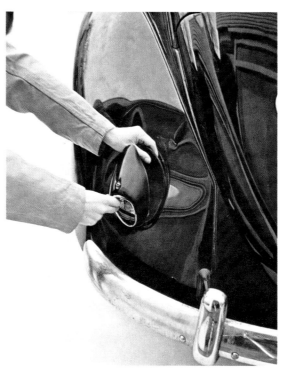

2 Remove fittings (a wheel, for example) where necessary, to allow access to the back of the damaged panel. Take off any damaged unit—it will probably have to be replaced

3 To beat out a panel, use a soft-headed hammer—or tool designed for the job. Support the front of the damaged area with the hand or a firm block of rubber

4 Do not beat the panel out too far, for it can become so stretched that repair is impossible without expert 'shrinking' Do not hit any adjacent part of the bodywork

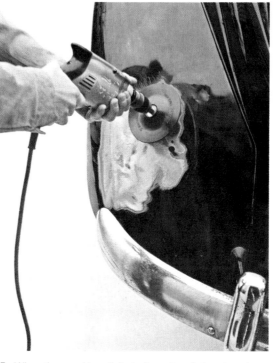

5 When the panel is satisfactorily restored almost to shape, remove the paint with an electric drill and a coarse sanding disc. Work the drill into any remaining creases

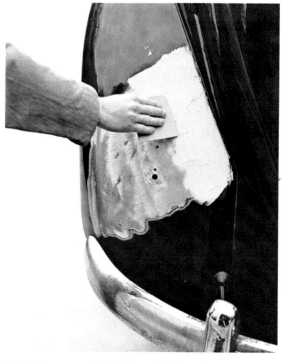

6 Mix just enough filler (see p. 244), and apply it with a plastic or hardboard 'trowel' to the whole of the cleaned area. Apply several layers thinly, not one thick layer

Filling, finishing and painting

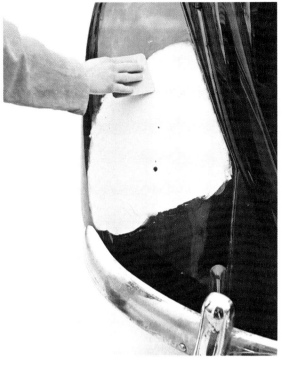

7 Work the filler quickly, for it begins to set almost immediately. Try to keep the shape of the panel. The final surface should be a little above the adjacent paintwork

8 Before rubbing down the hardened filler, mask off the adjacent bodywork panel, to avoid damaging its paintwork. Scratches on the damaged panel can be painted in

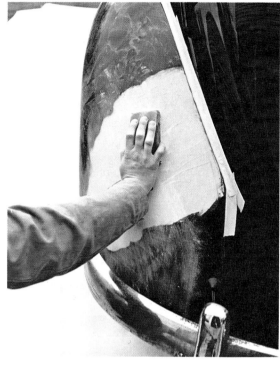

9 Rub down with soaked 120-grit wet-or-dry paper. Check that the surface is becoming smooth, and use plenty of water. If there are any blemishes, apply fresh filler

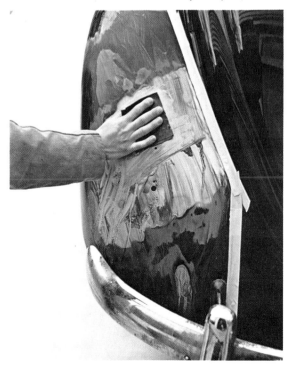

10 Keep rubbing with progressively finer papers until almost all the filler is removed, leaving only the still slightly creased parts built up. Wash thoroughly and allow to dry

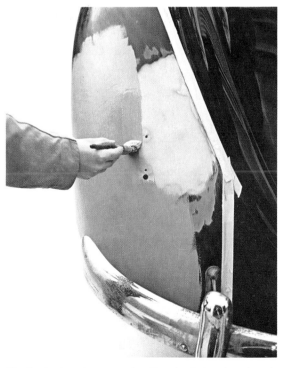

11 Apply the primer coat; but first check that the primer is suitable. If it is not, the finishing paint quality will be unsatisfactory and the job may have to be started again

12 Allow the primer to dry, and rub it down with soaked fine wet-or-dry paper. If there are holes, put on another coat. The quality of this surface determines the finish

Bodywork/finishing a repair

Aerosol-spray painting

1 Make sure that the aerosol finishing paint chosen is the exact colour match for the rest of the paintwork and that it is suitable for both primer and original paint

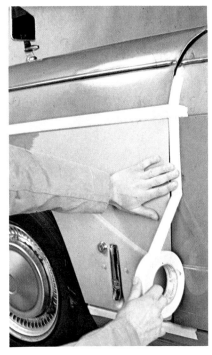

2 Mask the edges of adjoining panels with adhesive tape. When there is no edge adjacent, fix the tape several inches beyond the area to be painted, to allow overlap

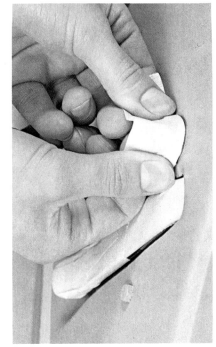

3 Cover any trim or brightwork attached to the panel which is to be sprayed. Trim the tape to fit exactly, so that it does not touch the primer and spoil the finished paintwork

4 Cover the adjoining bodywork with newspapers or large poster sheets. Use several layers and stick them securely to the masking tape already fixed

7 If the paint has been applied properly, the coat will not be too thick. Allow it to dry completely and rub it down with very fine, soaked 400-grit wet-or-dry paper

8 Wash the respray area and let it dry. Spray on further coats (rubbing down between each), until the new paint matches the colour and quality of the original

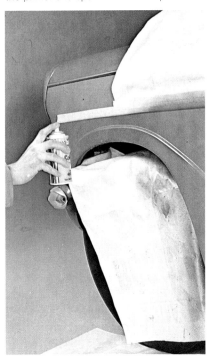

9 Make sure that the new paint overlaps the original by a few inches. This allows the finish to be 'feathered', so that there is no dividing line between the old and new paint

10 When the last coat is completely dry, rub the surface with a cloth pad and a proprietary rubbing compound. Make sure that the maker's instructions are followed

Rectifying faults

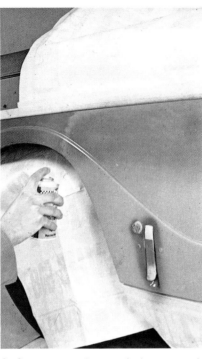

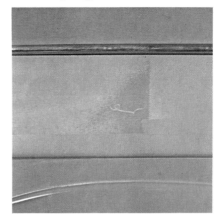

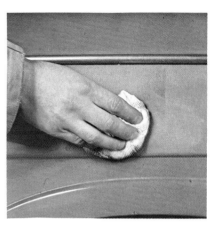

5 Follow the paint maker's instructions carefully. Start by spraying behind any fittings on the panel. If this is done later, the surrounding bodywork finish will be spoilt

6 Spray across the area in long, smooth strokes. Release the aerosol button at the end of each stroke. Move the can down slightly and spray back the other way

Unwanted paint Inspect the surrounding area, especially along the outer edges of the tape, to make sure that no paint has been allowed to stray (it may be more difficult to find spots when the adjoining section is the same colour). If the paint is still wet, remove it with white spirit. If it has hardened, use a fine rubbing compound

Creasing If a spray finish is used on an unsuitable base or top coat, it may crease. This happens when cellulose and enamel paints are mixed. The only remedy is to remove all the affected paint down to the bare metal, clean the area and repeat the entire operation. Check with the paint dealer that the paint to be used is suitable

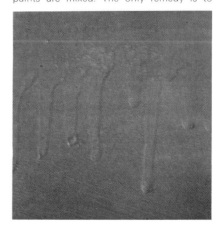

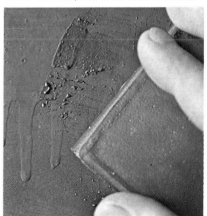

11 Wipe off the compound with a clean, soft cloth and check that there are no faults or blemishes in the paint. If there are, rub down and respray the area if necessary

12 Remove all the masking tape and paper. Do not apply any polish for six weeks; but wash the paintwork weekly with clean, lukewarm water and dry with a leather

Running It is important to apply the finishing coats thinly. If too much paint is sprayed on at once, it will run before it can dry. Smooth the surface with a rubbing compound. It is possible that a further thin spray coat will then be required, to get a good finish. Allow it to dry, then rub down and wash and dry in the normal way

Bodywork/doors, locks, hinges and windows

Checks on bodywork fittings

WORK ON THE DOORS, whether to dismantle a lock or remove or replace a window, is one of the most painstaking and complicated jobs that can be undertaken on the car. This is not because the mechanisms are themselves difficult, but because there is a restricted working space. When the door furniture and trim are removed, it will be seen that most doors have two or possibly three small holes through which access is obtained to all the working parts of the locks and windows.

Although they all work on the same principle, it is advisable, before dismantling a lock or window mechanism, to compare it with the drawings and pictures on this and the next two pages; and, if possible, obtain a copy of the workshop manual for the car.

Some windows, for example, cannot be removed with-

out first removing the window runners; others do not require this. Some door locks can be dismantled without disturbing the window mechanism; others are more difficult, and the window runner has to be removed.

Find out as much as possible about the type used on your car before attempting any repair. It may help to draw a simple diagram before the parts are dismantled.

Wherever possible, try to restrict the work being done to the bare essentials. Do not remove a window or the winding mechanism to gain access to a lock unless this is absolutely essential; it will only make the job unnecessarily complicated.

The three jobs shown on the two following pages—removing a lock, removing a window and removing the window-winding mechanism—can be carried out

separately or together. It will not usually be necessary to remove the lock or the window simply to take out the winding mechanism. But since this varies from car to car, it is advisable to check before starting.

Have the proper replacement parts available. For example, have new window runners ready when working on an older car; the runners may be rusted and may break when they are unscrewed and taken out.

The hinges on doors, boot-lids and bonnets are simple, especially on modern cars, where no adjustment is possible. Where the door or lid is not fitting properly, adjustment has to be made at the striker plate on the door jamb. The only way is to loosen it, refit and retighten it, and then try closing the door or lid. This may have to be done several times until the correct position is found.

CHECKING AND ADJUSTMENT POINTS

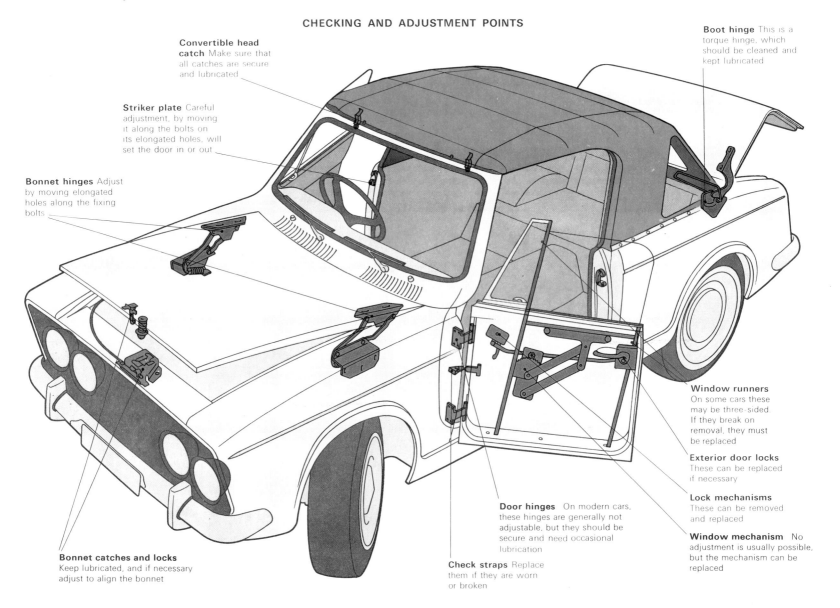

Convertible head catch Make sure that all catches are secure and lubricated

Striker plate Careful adjustment, by moving it along the bolts on its elongated holes, will set the door in or out

Bonnet hinges Adjust by moving elongated holes along the fixing bolts

Bonnet catches and locks Keep lubricated, and if necessary adjust to align the bonnet

Check straps Replace them if they are worn or broken

Door hinges On modern cars, these hinges are generally not adjustable, but they should be secure and need occasional lubrication

Boot hinge This is a torque hinge, which should be cleaned and kept lubricated

Window runners On some cars these may be three-sided. If they break on removal, they must be replaced

Exterior door locks These can be replaced if necessary

Lock mechanisms These can be removed and replaced

Window mechanism No adjustment is usually possible, but the mechanism can be replaced

Removing door trim

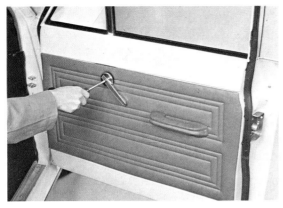

1 Remove the armrest (if fitted) and interior handles. Some may be screwed; others are held by a pin through the stalk behind the handle's escutcheon plate. Press in the door trim and push out the retaining-pin with a small screwdriver

2 Use a screwdriver under each retaining clip in turn to lever away the interior panel trim from the door or, if it is a screw fitting, unscrew it. Take care not to distort or break the fibre panel when pulling it off

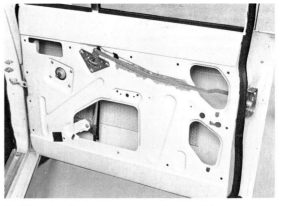

3 When the trim has been removed, take off the transparent weatherproof sheeting. The working parts can now be seen: at the top, the lock's remote control; on the left, the winding mechanism; at the bottom, the window runner

Replacing a lock

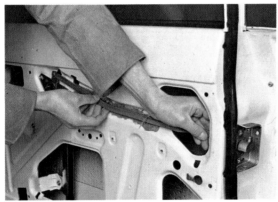

1 The method of removing a lock can vary from car to car; if possible read the workshop manual. Generally, however, the first step is to disconnect the spring clip holding the remote-control arm to the lock mechanism inside the door

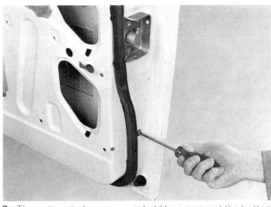

2 The outer window runner is held by a screw at the bottom of the door. Undo it if necessary, but check that it is really necessary; on some cars it may be possible to repair the lock without disturbing the window fittings

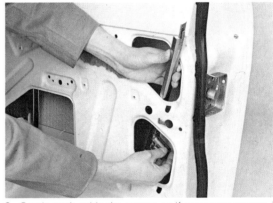

3 Gently push aside the runner, or if necessary remove it completely through the access hole in the door pressing. It is likely that the runner will have become rusted: take care not to break it. The lock itself can now be removed

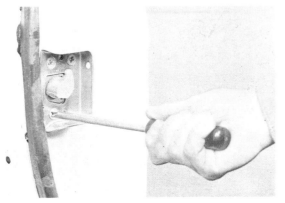

4 The lock is held inside the door by screws through the outside striker plate. Undo them a little at a time and, as they loosen, hold the lock inside with the other hand so that it does not fall out of reach at the bottom of the door

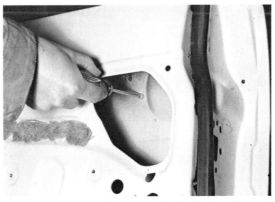

5 When the lock has been removed, the door handle on the outside of the panel can be taken out. Undo the retaining screws which hold it inside the door panel. Take care also with these that they are not allowed to fall down inside the door

6 If a new lock is to be fitted, it may be necessary to adjust the door-handle plunger. Compare it with the one just removed from the car and adjust it to the same extent. Fit it to the door and make any fine adjustment with it in place

Bodywork/windows, locks and hinges

Removing a window glass

1 Check the exact procedure recommended in the handbook before starting to remove a window glass. The order of dismantling may vary slightly from car to car. Generally, however, the window must first be wound right down

2 Identify the components. The window channel can be seen through the central access hole in the bottom of the door. On the car shown here, the window regulator assembly is held by two sets of screws seen on the left

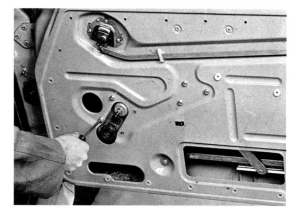

3 Unscrew the regulator assembly—four screws on the extreme left and three to the right and a little higher. The exact layout may be different on your car from that shown. Take care that no part falls to the bottom of the door

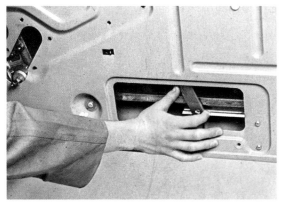

4 When the regulator is completely free, it will dangle inside the door. It is now possible to slide the regulator arm out of the window-glass holder. If the window is to be removed, take out the stop that limits its downward movement

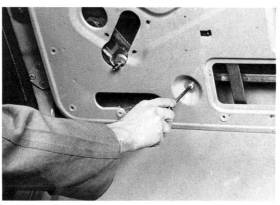

5 The inside window runner will probably have to be slackened if the window is to be removed. This may not be necessary if only the winding mechanism is being taken out. The runner's retaining screw is near the bottom of the door

6 Care is needed when the runner is pushed aside. When it is out of the way, lift the glass through the top of the door panel. It may have to be turned sideways on some cars. Fit new glass in the channel and replace it in reverse order

Removing a winder mechanism

1 If only the winding mechanism is being removed, the window runner may not need to be unscrewed. Undo the regulator and remove its arm from the glass channel. Lift the glass to the top of the door and wedge it in place

2 The window-winding linkage can now be taken out through the most convenient access hole in the door. Remember that the refitting operation is in reverse order to removal, and use the same access hole

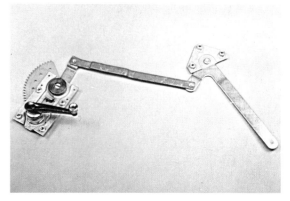

3 It is not usually possible to repair a winding mechanism. When a new one is to be fitted, check that it is of the correct size and type and smear it thoroughly with grease before putting it into the door. Make sure it does not become dirty

Adjusting locks and catches

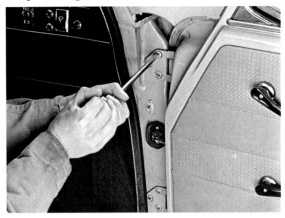

Door hinge On most modern cars it is not possible to adjust the hang of the door at the hinge. But the hinges should be regularly checked for tightness. Inspect for wear the strap or check-link which stops the door opening too far

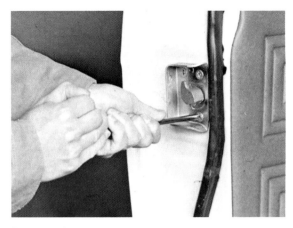

Catchpawl Before attempting to adjust the door's locking action, make sure that the catchpawl—shown here on another car—is secure. If it is not, the door may rattle and adjustments to the striker plate will not be accurate

Striker plate Door-lock striker plates—although they may vary in appearance—can all be adjusted on the door pillar. By unscrewing them slightly and moving them in or out, up or down, it is possible to alter the alignment of the door

Bonnet striker plate Lubricate the bonnet-lock striker plate regularly. The bonnet's closing position can be adjusted slightly by loosening the striker-plate screws and moving it gently. Retighten when the position is correct

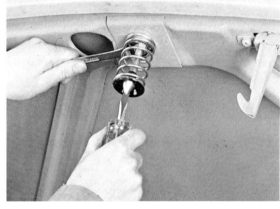

Bonnet lock The locking bolt usually has a screwdriver slot in the end. When the striker plate is correctly adjusted, the bolt can be screwed in or out to give a more secure locking action. Make sure that the lock-nut is tight

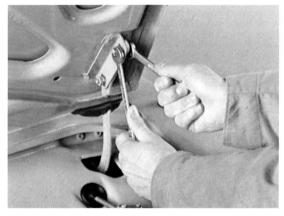

Bonnet hinge Adjustment can be made to the setting of the bonnet hinge. If the plate to which the hinge is screwed is also bolted to the body, additional adjustment at that point may be possible. Make sure the hinge is secure

Boot lock If the boot is not closing properly, adjust the position of the striker plate or U-shaped rod by loosening the nuts and moving it slightly. Tighten the retaining nuts securely when the correct closing position is reached

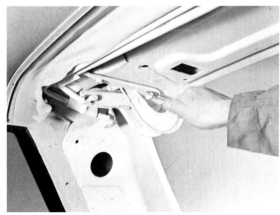

Boot hinge The hinge on the boot lid must be kept greased; but take care that no excess is allowed to drip into the boot. If the boot is fitted with a torque hinge, make sure that its torsion-bar anchorage is secure

Estate-car tailgate To correct the alignment and closing action of an estate-car tailgate, adjust the hinge retaining bolts and the lock striker plate. Unscrew a little at a time, move, retighten, and test the position each time

Bodywork/headlamps

Fitting a replacement unit

1 To replace a headlamp or adjust the aim of its beam, first undo the screw or screws retaining the headlamp trim

2 Remove the trim carefully, and check that the rubber seal behind it is in good condition. Replace if it is perished

3 Undo the three or more retaining screws around the headlamp unit. Do not loosen the beam-adjusting screws

4 When the retaining screws are removed, it should be possible to pull out the lamp unit without difficulty

5 The wiring to a sealed-beam unit is a one-piece assembly. A bulb has a bayonet fitting holder. Disconnect

6 When fitting a unit, line it up by the locating tab. Refit in the reverse order to dismantling

Main and dipped beams

THE MINIMUM requirements for a car's lighting system are that there should be two headlights, two side-lights (in some cars these are incorporated in the headlights), two red rear lights, a rear number-plate light and two red rear reflectors—all in working order.

The lights need to be checked and maintained both to enable the driver to see where he is going, and to ensure that other road users can see the car and judge its size.

The light output of a bulb decreases as the glass envelope above the filament becomes coated with a thin, light-absorbing layer of tungsten. The lamps should be inspected regularly and replaced if they are badly darkened. This is a problem that does not affect quartz-halogen bulbs or sealed-beam units (see pp. 146–7).

Dipping The lights must not dazzle oncoming drivers, and for this reason they are required to have a dipping device that shortens the range and throws the light down —on British roads, to the left. This is usually achieved by having two filaments in one bulb or unit. If only one beam works, the second filament has broken and the bulb or unit must be replaced. In the case of rectangular lamps, the right and left-hand units may be different; make sure that the correct replacement is obtained. If both dipped or main lights fail, check the dipswitch and its wiring.

For European driving, the car's headlights must dip to the right. Where bulbs are fitted, it is an easy matter to replace them temporarily. But with sealed-beam units it is easier and less expensive to fit covers (tinted amber for France) that bend the light and give the effect of right-hand dipping, although they are still working normally. It may not be possible to obtain these refraction covers for some of the more modern rectangular headlamps, in which case the entire sealed unit should be replaced before the car is driven on European roads.

Alignment The headlamps should be set to give the driver the best possible vision over the longest range, particularly at speed. If they are angled too high, much of the light does not hit the road and is lost, so that illumination comes from 'scatter' only. In addition, the dipped beam will be too high and may cause discomfort or dangerous dazzle to oncoming drivers.

If the headlamps are set too low, they will appear very bright in front of the car, but their range will be greatly reduced, particularly when dipped. The best position can be found only by adjusting the two setting screws at the headlamp unit. The screw at the top adjusts for height of the beam; the screw at the side moves it sideways.

If a new lamp is fitted, ensure that it will not dazzle oncoming drivers, particularly when it is dipped. It should be set precisely with a beam setter at a garage. But it is possible to align the lights roughly against a wall. Although the garage mechanic will align the lights on dipped beam on some cars, the do-it-yourself owner should use the main beam, because its light pattern is much more clearly defined.

On four-headlamp cars, where there are two lamps whose only job is to supply the dipped beam, it is not possible for the owner to align a replacement dip lamp precisely. He can, however, use the one not changed and the two main-beam lamps as a guide to make a temporary rough adjustment until the car can be taken to a garage.

Checking the alignment

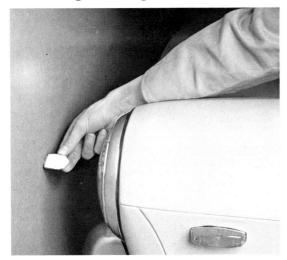

1 Choose a level piece of ground and line the car as closely as possible against a wall. Make two marks on the wall corresponding to the centre of each headlamp

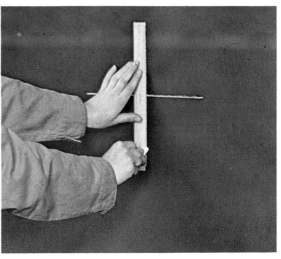

2 Check that the car is carrying its normal load and reverse it 25 ft in an absolutely straight line from the wall. Draw two crosses through the centre markings on the wall

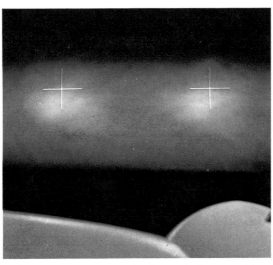

3 Switch on the headlights (main beam). The two brightest areas of light should come just under the crosses' horizontal lines and as near to centre as possible

4 Any adjustments needed are made at the setting screws at the top and side of the headlamp. Work on one lamp at a time, with the other covered

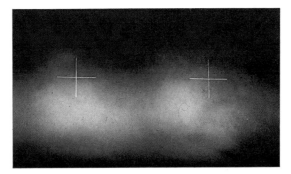

Do-it-yourself Adjust rectangular headlamps on main beam. The light pattern, less clearly defined than that of a round lamp, should be below the centre of the horizontal lines

Garage A garage will adjust rectangular headlamps on dipped beam, because their light pattern cuts off sharply, and if they are badly set they will dazzle oncoming drivers

Bodywork/trim, weather-seals and windscreen wipers

Replacing trim

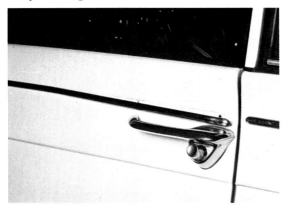

1 Refitting loose trim is a simple job, provided a rivet gun and clips of the correct type and size are available. The entire section of loose or damaged trim must be removed

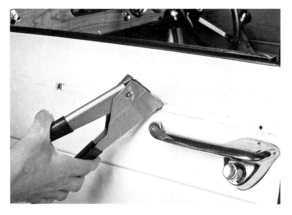

2 Drill out the existing trim clips, hold the gun flat against the bodywork with the protruding end of the clip in the drilled hole, and fire the gun

3 Hook the bottom of the trim over the clips and, while pushing upwards and inwards with one hand, force the top of the trim over the top of the clips with the other

Resealing rubber mouldings

1 If the windscreen seal is leaking, find the faulty section. Gently prise the rubber away from the glass, dry it thoroughly and apply sealing compound

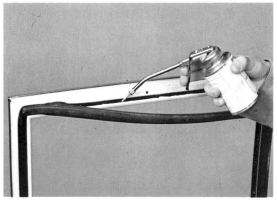

2 If the door mouldings have to be resealed, remove as long a section as possible, but take care not to damage the rubber. Apply adhesive and leave door closed until it is dry

3 The boot seal is another source of leaks. Find the faulty section and reseal. If the rubber has become badly damaged, remove it entirely and fit a replacement piece

Renewing wipers

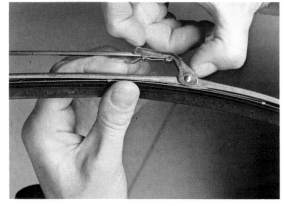

1 When a worn windscreen-wiper blade is to be replaced, make sure that one of the correct size and type is obtained. Remove the old one by freeing the clip in the centre

2 To remove a damaged wiper arm, force back the spring clip hidden underneath its fitting, using a small screwdriver. Ease off the arm. Replace and reset

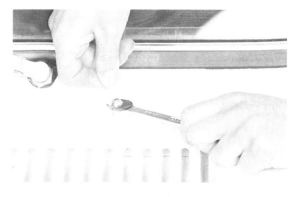

3 To raise or lower the washer jet, insert a pin in the hole and move the ball. To move it sideways, gently twist the washer body with a spanner

Convertibles

Servicing and repairing

Head catches The hood is attached to the top of the wind-screen with toggle clamps. Check that they—and the matching parts on the car—are all securely fixed

Convertible hood The transparent rear-window section is the part most likely to crack or scratch, so reducing visibility. Take care when stowing it

Cleaning Do not use polish or detergent, only soap and water. Because some hoods have a thin rubber sheet between two layers of canvas, never use chemicals

Tonneau cover The tonneau cover is most likely to tear at the press studs, where it is fixed to the bodywork. If this happens, it should be repaired by a specialist

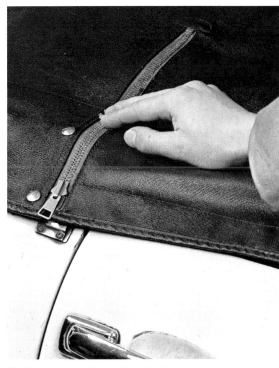

Zip fastenings To avoid strain, the tonneau cover should not be zipped closed until all the press studs are fixed. Wax the zip regularly to prevent corrosion

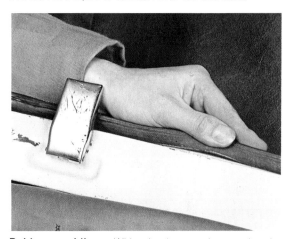

Rubber mouldings With a hard top, make sure that the rubber mouldings are in good condition. If metal is allowed to rub on metal, the paintwork will become chafed

Sliding roof On cars with a sunshine roof, keep the slides lubricated and ensure that there are no leak points. Weather-seals should be replaced by an expert if necessary

Bodywork/exhaust systems

DIFFERENT TYPES OF EXHAUST SYSTEMS

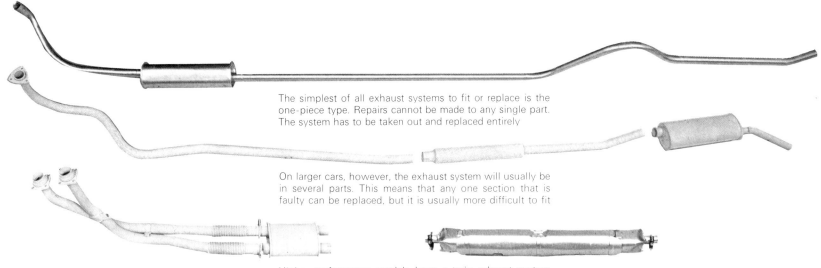

The simplest of all exhaust systems to fit or replace is the one-piece type. Repairs cannot be made to any single part. The system has to be taken out and replaced entirely

On larger cars, however, the exhaust system will usually be in several parts. This means that any one section that is faulty can be replaced, but it is usually more difficult to fit

Higher-performance models have a twin-exhaust system (left). A heat deflector (right) gives the car underside extra protection against the exhaust heat

Inspecting for leaks and fitting a new exhaust system

A FAULTY EXHAUST SYSTEM, allowing carbon monoxide fumes into the car, can kill. Check the system regularly (every time the underside is cleaned, for example) to make sure that all the joints are sound and that the structure is in good condition and securely mounted.

Unfortunately, not all exhaust leaks are accompanied by the loud 'blowing' which indicates a large hole. Many pin-point holes—just as dangerous—may appear in a worn exhaust system, and these are especially difficult to trace.

Do not examine only the underside of an exhaust system; very often the first signs of trouble appear on top of the silencer box or pipework—especially if the car is used mainly for short journeys, when the engine never gets hot enough to clear all the condensation. It is this condensation, and the acids in the cooled exhaust gases, which attack the metal and accelerate corrosion.

To trace leaks, get someone to feed upper-cylinder lubricant into the carburettor with the engine running and watch for signs of blue smoke blowing from any suspect part of the exhaust system. With very small holes, however, the exhaust gases may not be visible: for this reason manual inspection is also necessary. Keep the engine running but take care: the exhaust system gets hot quite quickly. It should be enough to run the hand along near the pipe, without touching it at all.

When renewing any part of the system, first check whether it is a one-piece system or if it can be replaced in individual sections. Make sure that any replacement is routed accurately. It is advisable to renew all hanging straps, to ensure that the system is secure. Do not finally tighten any brackets or clips until the whole unit has been assembled; and when tightening, work from the manifold end to the back of the car. Make sure that every joint is completely sealed against gas leaks.

Clamp attachment The exhaust pipe can be held at the manifold junction by a clamp. With the pipe pressed firmly against the manifold outlet, screw the clamp tight

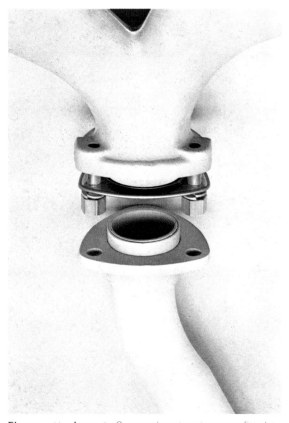

Flange attachment Some exhaust systems are fitted to the manifold by a flange attachment. When fitting, always use brass nuts, clean the mating faces and fit a new gasket

Replacing a damaged silencer

1 The main difficulty in removing an old or damaged silencer is rusted joints. To avoid damaging the connecting pipes to the silencer, it is advisable to soak all the joints in penetrating oil for a time before starting work. Very light hammering around the joint may help. To remove the silencer box, twist it gently backwards and forwards

2 If a hammer has been used, make sure that pipes are still round, and clean their ends so that the replacement silencer slides on freely. Use a clip that clamps evenly all round

Exhaust fittings

Metal strips The exhaust pipe may be held under the body by metal strips flexibly mounted on rubber-bonded blocks. Replace the mountings if the bonding breaks

Rubber ring At some points the pipe may be held by a rubber ring, which is hooked to a projection on the underbody and to a similar piece in the exhaust system itself

Rubber and webbing The strap hanger is a combination of rubber and webbing. The eyes through which the anchor bolts fit may stretch or split, or the webbing may fail

Bodywork/fitting a sound insulation kit 1

ONE OF THE CHARACTERISTICS most noticeable when driving in a quality car is its quietness; good insulation against engine and road noise makes even a short trip less tiring than it would be in a noisy car. Insulation also has the important side-effect of helping keep the interior warm.

Sound-insulation kits are readily available for almost every mass-production car. But when ordering a kit, give full details of the car—make, model and year—to ensure that the correct fit is obtained. A kit for one model may not fit another even if the manufacturer is the same: the car's bodywork sections may be slightly different.

Before the insulation can be fitted, it will be necessary to remove all the seats, carpet and felt from the interior. Leave the seat belts in position: the kit will be designed to go round them.

The insulation material needs to be stuck to the body only in places where it is vertical (the wheel arches), and where it could drop off (the underside of the bonnet or the boot). Insulation stuck to the bonnet should be regularly checked to ensure that it cannot interfere with engine operation. On the floor pan and boot floor, the material is held in position by the fittings and carpet.

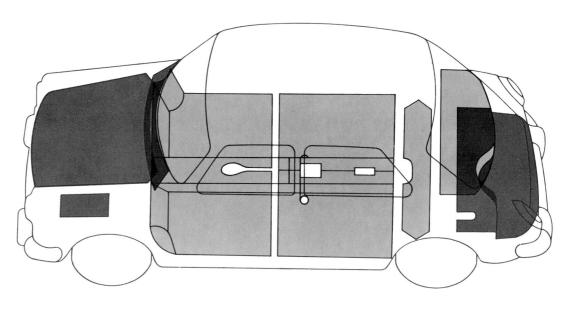

WHERE THE FELT IS FITTED

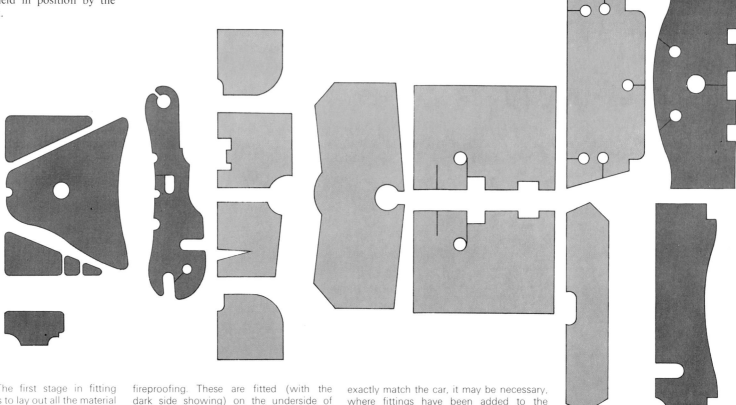

Identification The first stage in fitting sound insulation is to lay out all the material and identify each part. The sections shown in dark grey are all treated on one side for fireproofing. These are fitted (with the dark side showing) on the underside of the engine compartment bonnet and on the floor of the boot. Although the kit will exactly match the car, it may be necessary, where fittings have been added to the interior since manufacture, to cut new holes or slits to accommodate them

Wheel arch sections

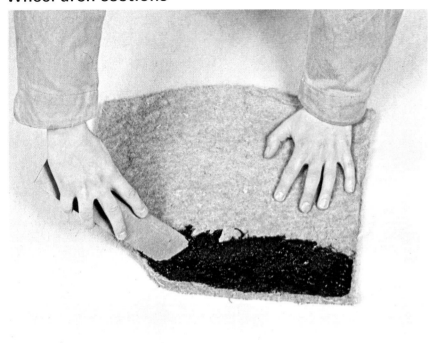

1 When the seats, carpet and any underfelt have been removed from the floor pan, pull off the carpeting stuck to the vertical side of the wheel arches. Clean the metal thoroughly with petrol. Put a fairly liberal coating of the correct adhesive on one side of the insulating felt and set it aside to become tacky for five or ten minutes

2 Stick the insulating felt carefully in position and press it firmly against the metal. It may help to use a small roller, tin or jam jar to roll the felt well down. If there is any new fitting (such as a map pocket) on the inside of the panel, use a razor or very sharp knife to cut the felt around it. Repeat the operation on the other side of the car

3 Apply adhesive to the felt in position, making sure that this is done only after it is securely stuck to metal. Make sure that the underside of the carpet which was pulled off at the start of the operation is clean, and apply adhesive to it. Avoid spilling adhesive on the pile of the carpet; but if the carpet is marked, try cleaning it with petrol

4 The carpet and felt should be left to become slightly tacky for about five minutes. Stick the carpet firmly in position on top of the insulating felt. Again use the roller or jar to remove any air pockets. If it was necessary at the beginning to remove any trim or metal strips which were holding the carpet in place, they can now be replaced

Bodywork/fitting a sound insulation kit 2

Passenger compartment

APART FROM the wheel-arch sections, none of the insulating felt in the passenger compartment needs to be stuck to either the metal or the carpet.

Take particular care when fitting the felt on the floor below the pedals at the driver's feet, and make sure that there are holes for seat-belt anchorages.

Lay the felt, fitting it exactly around any raised parts, and refit the carpets.

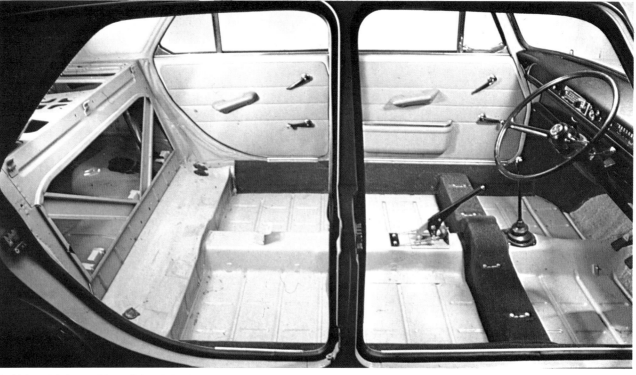

5 The felt must not restrict the operation of pedals. Check that there is enough clearance. Remove an organ-type accelerator and screw it back after the felt is fitted

6 Although it is possible to fit insulation in stages, without removing everything from the car at once, it is better to clear the entire interior. This allows checks to be made for leaks before any felt is laid down. Hose the underside and look for water inside. Seal any leaks and replace damaged rubber gaiters and plugs if necessary. If felt is fitted to a leaking floor pan, it will eventually become soggy, rotting the carpets and rusting the metal. Check all the seat mounting bolts and seat-belt anchorages for tightness

7 The sections of felt for the interior can now be fitted. In the model shown, there are five pieces, but the number may vary considerably according to the car design. Make sure that the pieces fit correctly in the car. There may already be holes for the seat-belt anchorages: if not, cut slots with a sharp blade and thread the belts through them

8 The carpet should be laid over the under-felt. Take the opportunity to replace or, if possible, repair any pieces that have become worn or torn (especially at the driver's feet). Since the carpet itself acts as an additional sound-deadener, it may be advisable to replace any very thin pieces, to get the best results from the newly fitted insulation

Engine compartment

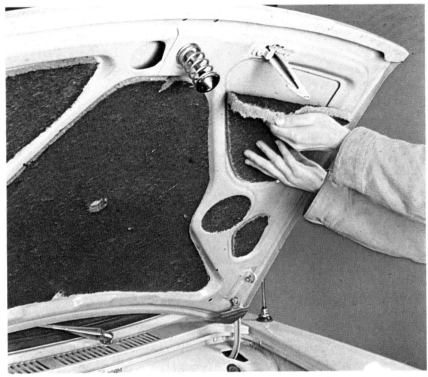

9 Clean the underside of the bonnet with a petrol-soaked rag. When it is dry, apply the adhesive. Select the pieces of felt which fit each bonnet segment and coat them on the plain side (not on the fireproof, treated skin) with adhesive. When they and the bonnet are both tacky, press the pieces firmly into place. Check that the edges are securely stuck

10 The felt which fits against the engine compartment bulkhead need not be stuck down: it is held in place by the various fittings. It will probably be necessary to disconnect any petrol or heater pipes to allow felt to be put in place. Ensure that the fireproofed black side is showing on the outside when the felt is in position

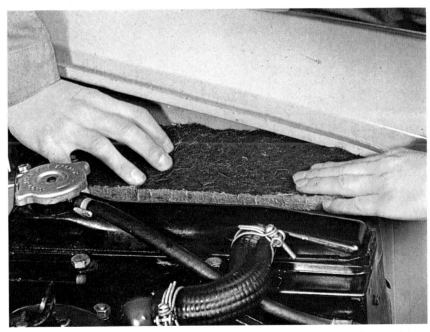

Boot interior

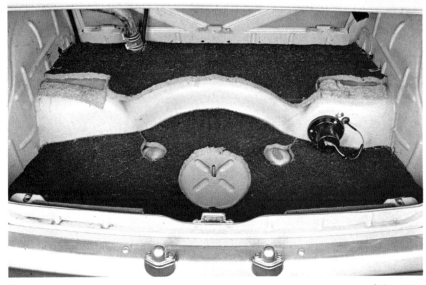

11 On some cars—here, for example, on a car with a transverse engine—there may be additional sections of felt for, say, the radiator cowling. Under no circumstances should untreated felt be used for any of these engine compartment parts, since they require fireproofing. It could quickly become oil-impregnated and be a fire risk

12 Remove all the fittings—spare wheel, tools and so on—from the boot. There will be two or more felt sections to fit the floor and wheel housing—fireproofed, as for the engine compartment, because of the proximity to the petrol pump and tank. These sections should be laid in place: adhesive is not required. The boot lid is not insulated

265

Regulations and inspection

AS SOON as a car is three years old (see p. 332), it must be given the first of what will become yearly examinations at a testing station approved by the Department of Transport.

The car's structure, brakes, steering, lights, direction indicators, exhaust system, tyres, windscreen washers and wipers, seat belts, their anchorages and the horn must comply with legal require-

ments. If they do, a certificate is issued that covers the car for one year—although this certificate is no guarantee that the car is legally roadworthy except at the time of examination.

If any one component is failed, a notification of refusal is issued to the owner, and it is then illegal for him to use or license the car, except to drive it home.

The only times a certificate is not

required for a car over three years old are when it is being driven to or from the official testing station or repair garage, or when being towed away to be broken up.

The examiner, a garage employee authorised by the Department, is required to state precisely why a test certificate was refused.

Requirements The mechanical parts of the braking, suspension and steering

systems should be effective. Visual checks, without dismantling any part of the vehicle, should satisfy the examiner that there is no malfunction, wear or corrosion that could adversely affect any part of the three systems.

With but a few exceptions, the test on a car's brakes can no longer be made on the road: it must be made on a roller machine installed in the testing garage. The brakes

Steering box The examiner uses a stout screwdriver or bar to test for firmness of the steering-box mountings. There should be no free play in the steering box. He will examine all steering linkages for damage and wear, making sure that there is no excessive rust or corroded metal in the area which could weaken the steering gear

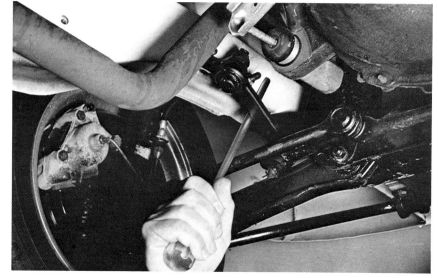

Idler arm On the passenger side of the car, the examiner will make a similar check on the steering-idler drop-arm and linkages. There must be no excessive play at the shaft or bushes. Damage to these and to the steering box is possible, especially if proper repairs have not been made after the car has been involved in an accident

Steering linkage The examiner checks for wear in the steering ball-joints. There should be no excessive stiffness. The steering rods and linkages should not be damaged in any way. All steering nuts and their retaining pins must be correctly fitted and secured. The attachment points and surrounding areas must be sound

Front suspension If a suspension strut is also part of the steering, the examiner will check for undue play or looseness, wear, cracking of rubber elements and rust. With a wishbone, there are more inspection points—connecting links, bolts and bushes. They should not be excessively worn, deteriorated or damaged

are tested separately and in pairs, which checks their efficiency as well as their balance in operation.

The lights should be in working order and be visible from 200 yds away. They must be properly aligned and they must be capable of being properly dipped on both headlamps or, in the case of a four-lamp arrangement, one headlamp on each side must be able to provide adequate dipped-beam forward illumination with four lamps. Where extinguishing the main beam is driver-controlled, it is not legal to travel on side lamps only.

Cars registered after 1964 must have seat belts, and the tyres must comply with regulations on tread, inflation, damage and mixing (see p. 125). Lumps, bulges, exposure of ply or cords, improper puncture repair, separation of recap rubber from the rest of the tyre may all result in failure. So, too, will any visible, even minor, cracking and corrosion of light alloy wheels.

The silencer and exhaust systems must be in good order and properly attached, and windscreen washers and wipers, direction indicators and stop lights must function properly. The chassis and bodywork should not be corroded or damaged to any extent that could possibly adversely affect the steering, suspension or braking systems or cause injury to another user of the road.

The examiner can refuse to test a car for any of four reasons: if it is excessively dirty; if it has insufficient petrol to allow him to drive it; if it has an insecure load (possibly on a roof rack); or if the registration papers are not available.

Top suspension mounting The area under the bonnet where the MacPherson suspension strut is mounted is a potential rust point. Because rusting here could seriously weaken the entire steering and suspension system, the examiner will fail the car if excessive corrosion is found. The retaining bolts on the strut must be secure

Track control arm Attached to the car chassis or body is the track control arm (lower suspension link). Its mounting must be secure and there should be no severe rust. The link arm itself must be securely fixed to its mounting, but it must be able to swivel smoothly on its retaining bolt with the car's movement on the road

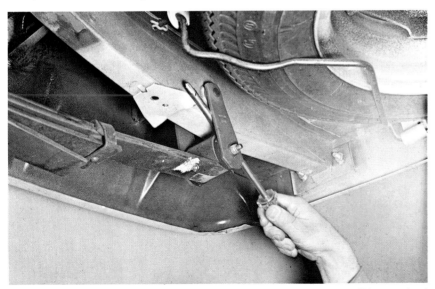

Rear suspension hanger On cars with leaf suspension springs there must be no wear in the retaining bushes of the mounting hangers. On models with independent suspension, the coil spring will be examined for wear or breakage. Loose suspension could allow excessive axle movement which might affect the brakes and steering

Rear suspension U-bolts The examiner will make sure that rear suspension U-bolts are tight, free of wear and undamaged—in as far as they are likely to affect braking and steering. Where leaf springs are fitted, he will check that there is no serious fault. The tester also examines the inside walls of the tyres for wear or damage

267

Brakes and wheels

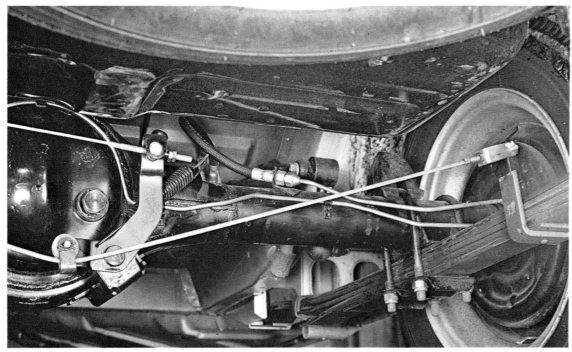

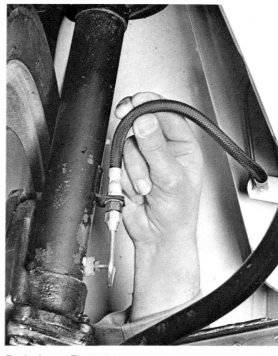

Rear-brake linkages   There must be no corrosion on any part of the underside that would have an adverse effect on the car's braking. All linkages, connecting rods, brake cables and hoses will be checked for damage, chafing, fraying, hydraulic leaks or wear. All securing and retaining pins must be in good condition. The underside must be clean to allow inspection. If it is too dirty, he is permitted by law to refuse to carry out the test

Brake hoses   The brake hoses must be in good order. A car with chafing, bulges or splits here will fail the test. The unions must be secure. The examiner will make sure that no part of the brake system is damaged or ineffective

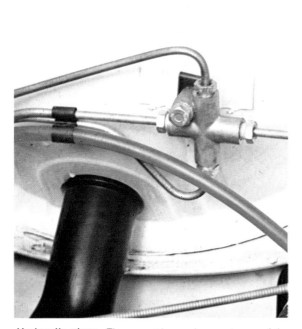

Hydraulic pipes   There must be no damage to any of the hydraulic pipes, including those in the engine compartment. Cars with hydraulic fluid leaks, or severe corrosion or loose unions in the hydraulic pipes, will fail the test

Wheel bearings   When the underside has been checked, the examiner will test all the road wheels for free play, to see that the bearings are properly adjusted and that the swivel pins and suspension bushes are in good order

Tyres   The tread must be at least 1 mm in depth, and the radial/cross-ply regulations must be observed (see p. 125). No cut must penetrate the body cords, nor be more than 25 mm long. Damaged tyres and wheels will fail

...or car roadworthiness

Lights, steering, seats and belts

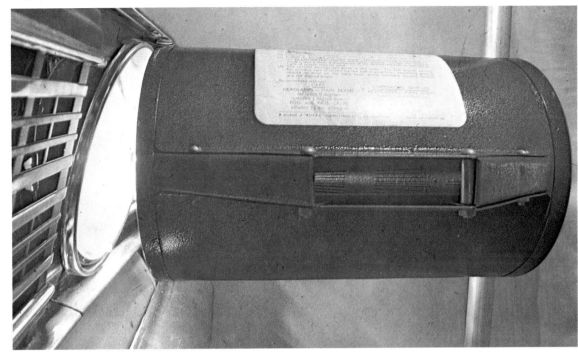

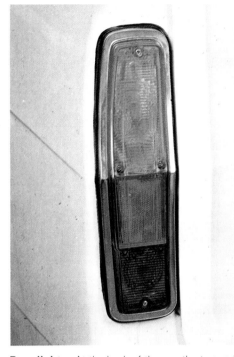

Headlamp alignment Garages approved by the Department of Transport use a headlamp beam-testing device, which allows the examiner to see that the beam will not inconvenience or annoy oncoming traffic or other road-users (see p. 267). If the headlamps fail the alignment test, only that part of the examination has to be repeated—provided that the headlamp alignment is correctly adjusted at the same garage within 14 days of the original test

Rear lights At the back of the car, the two red reflectors must be intact and both rear lights should be in working order. Indicator flashers and brake lights must also be in working order and are subject to test

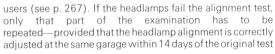

Steering The steering wheel should not be broken and the column must not be loose. By turning the steering wheel, and looking at the road wheels, the examiner checks that there is no excessive play before the wheels are moved

Seat mountings By pushing against the steering wheel and brake pedal, the examiner can check that the seat mountings are adequate to cope with emergency braking. Corrosion or loose mountings can fail the car

Seat belts The examiner will check that belts are correctly and securely fitted. All load-bearing parts of the car within 30 mm of the anchorage points must be sound. Belts must be of approved specification

Department of Transport test for car roadworthiness

Testing the brakes

MOST CARS being tested for road worthiness must now have their brakes tested on a roller brake tester in a garage.

Some cannot be tested on rollers: those with permanent four-wheel drive, with belt-driven transmission, or with a servo system that operates only when the vehicle is moving. Such exceptions can still be tested on the road, when the brake efficiency is measured by a decelerometer.

There is no statutory provision for a road test when a roller test is carried out.
Brake imbalance A decelerometer can measure the overall efficiency of a braking system, but it is not suitable to make checks on separate wheels. The roller tester can determine any imbalance between brakes on the same axle as well as make a separate check of the front and rear axles.

There are two basic types of roller brake tester that have been approved for the statutory test: high speed and low speed. The low speed is the more common.

Before testing the brakes on a roller tester, the tyres are examined to ensure that they are inflated to the correct pressure, that they are undamaged, and that there are no stones embedded in the treads.

With the front wheels centralised on the tester, the sets of rollers are run separately to test each wheel, then run together to test for imbalance between the two. If the handbrake operates on the front wheels, the procedure is repeated to test its operation.

The vehicle is then run forward until the rear wheels are on the rollers. Similar tests are applied to the rear brakes and, if appropriate, the handbrake.
Efficiency Vehicles without a split (dual) braking system must have a minimum footbrake efficiency of 50 per cent and a handbrake one of 25 per cent. Where a car has a split braking system, the footbrake requirement is still a minimum of 50 per cent but the efficiency for the handbrake is only 16 per cent. (The footbrake efficiency on new cars is generally not less than 80 per cent.)

Although much of the Department of Transport test consists of precise mechanical checks, the examiner does have some discretion. Two equally experienced mechanics may disagree, for example, whether wear or play is excessive. What the owner must remember is that, though his car may have passed the test, it is not necessarily legally roadworthy or safe even a few hours after the test has been carried out. Regular maintenance and servicing, either at a garage or at home, should ensure that the car is not allowed to become mechanically unroadworthy.

Checking the brakes on a road test

Decelerometer A floor-mounted decelerometer may be used. As the car's brakes are applied, the scale moves (in the same way that passengers move forwards as the car slows). The final reading (when the car stops) gives the percentage efficiency of the brakes

Footbrake pedal In the garage mechanical inspection, road test or on a brake dynamometer, the examiner checks that the footbrake pedal is working. There must be no excessive play at the pedal, yet there has to be the recommended free movement before the brakes are operated. The pedal must not be spongy or travel slowly down to the floor—indicating a hydraulic fault.

Handbrake lever The handbrake must be able to stay engaged: the examiner will check that its ratchet gear is working properly. He will also ensure that the brake holds the car on a hill. The handbrake lever must be securely mounted to the floor; any rust or damaged metal round its securing bolts, inoperative linkages, frayed cables or excessive handbrake travel could fail the car

ACCESSORIES AND IMPROVEMENTS

Most cars, whether new or old, can be improved by the addition of a few accessories. Many of these will enhance the appearance and comfort of a car. But most accessories, such as extra mirrors, lights, instruments, safety belts and harnesses have a practical value—they can make a car safer and easier to drive. There are also security devices to frustrate the car thief, and accessories for winter driving, touring and towing. These and other accessories, together with their fitting instructions, are described in the pages which follow

CONTENTS

Accessories

Adapting a conventional ignition system

EACH time the contact-breaker points of a conventional ignition system 'break', they use some 4–5 amps of battery current.

Even at moderate speeds they open and close about 200 times per second and, each time they do so, they arc and burn. Within a few thousand miles, high-tension voltage drops causing poor starting and rough idling; the timing becomes inaccurate, fuel consumption gradually increases.

Electronic ignition systems which have no contact-breakers overcome all these problems. No longer are they available only on expensive models, for recent developments have ensured that even the do-it-yourself owner can convert his ordinary production car. The benefits of this type of equipment, which usually costs £35 are significant.

Because the systems have no moving parts, there is virtually no ignition maintenance. There are no contact-breaker points to renew, and spark-plugs last for up to 50,000 miles.

Because there is no arcing at the contact-breaker points full sparking power is produced at the tip of each plug—which means that the plug gaps can even be opened up slightly, so producing better burning in the combustion chambers. As much as 95% of the fuel/air mixture is burnt, compared with 75% on a conventional ignition system. This, in turn, provides an increase in power output and improves fuel economy—sometimes by as much as 10 per cent.

The system illustrated on this page consists of an ignition unit, a solid-state 'triggerhead' which replaces the contact-breaker points, timing disc and the fitting kit for the particular car to which the system is to be fitted.

For a limited range of cars—mainly British-made—it is now possible to buy a complete replacement distributor.

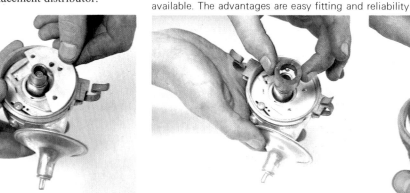

Complete replacement distributor kit For certain ranges of mass-production cars, a complete replacement distributor to convert the vehicles to electronic ignition is now available. The advantages are easy fitting and reliability

1 Remove the distributor cap and disconnect the plug leads. Remove the contact-breaker points and condenser unit from the distributor base-plate

2 Locate the electronic ignition adaptor plate in place of the contact-breakers. Secure with the original screws or with the screws supplied in the fitting kit

3 Fit the timing disc, if supplied with the kit, over the distributor cam. Make sure that it is a tight fit and that it cannot easily move on the cam

4 Locate the ignition triggerhead on the adaptor plate, using screws and washers supplied with the kit. Select a grommet to fit the hole in the distributor body

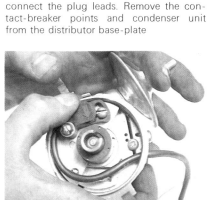   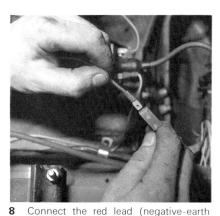

5 Crank the engine slowly clockwise until the cam peak, or timing disc pin, faces the timing arrow on the triggerhead. Adjust gap between triggerhead and cam

6 Mount the ignition unit on an earthed metal part of the body on the opposite side of the car from the exhaust system—in a position cooled by the air stream

7 Connect the green lead from the ignition unit to the negative side of the coil and the yellow lead to positive side of coil. Discard the original low tension lead from coil

8 Connect the red lead (negative-earth cars) or the black lead (positive-earth cars) to the original ignition switch lead that has been removed from the coil

Accessories/anti-dazzle mirror

Increasing the range of vision

ALL NEW saloon cars are fitted with one rear-view mirror—the minimum required by law. This is usually an interior mirror, fitted to the roof above the windscreen. But even the best interior mirror will leave blind spots, particularly in those areas masked by the rear-window pillars, so most drivers prefer to have more than one mirror.

Ordinary supplementary mirrors can be fitted on the wings, the doors or the door pillar near the driver. But there are also some for particular purposes, such as larger rear-view mirrors which can be clipped over existing mirrors, and periscopes and mirrors mounted on extra-long arms, for use when towing caravans or boats.

Types of mirrors There are three main types of mirrors—flat glass, convex glass and anti-dazzle. Flat glass mirrors give a true reflection of all objects in their range. Convex glass mirrors have a far wider range than the flat type, but they reduce and distort the image. Flat and convex mirrors can be made with tinted glass to reduce headlight glare from following cars.

The anti-dazzle mirror is more complex and more effective than the tinted-glass type. It functions as an ordinary mirror in daylight, but can be adjusted to cut the glare of following headlights at night.

Mirror fittings Mirrors can be bought with rigid arms or spring-loaded arms which allow the mirror to move if it is knocked, automatically returning it to its proper alignment without damage or the need for readjustment. Another type of wing mirror has a bullet-shaped mounting to reduce wind resistance.

Interior mirrors are usually fitted on arms for attachment to the roof or dashboard. They can also be fixed directly to the windscreen with suction pads, or fitted over existing mirrors with clips.

Modern mirrors incorporate a number of safety features, including shatter-resistant glass, plastic casings and plastic retaining rings to hold the glass in place if it is broken. Some interior mirrors also have mountings which collapse if anyone is thrown against them.

Anti-dazzle mirrors The anti-dazzle mirror illustrated (right) consists of a reflector hinged along its top edge and mounted behind a piece of plain glass. With the glass flat against the reflector, it is an ordinary mirror for day use. For night use the reflector is tilted away from the glass, which then acts as a mirror with a greatly reduced power of reflection.

The tilting can be done either by hand or automatically, under the control of a light-sensitive cell which reacts to the headlight glare of following cars.

Wing mirrors To position a wing mirror correctly, it is best if the job is done by two people—one in the driving seat, the other moving the mirror along the wing until the ideal position is found. If the job has to be done single-handed, the position for the base of the mirror can be found by moving a piece of putty from the windscreen along the centre-line of the wing, until it can be seen from the driving seat.

The outer edge of the mirror should overhang the car by $\frac{1}{2}$–$1\frac{1}{2}$ in., just off the centre-line of the wing. The mirror should then be adjusted so that the driver can just see the side of the car. This helps to locate the position of the car relative to other road-users.

Fitting a rear-view anti-dazzle mirror

1 Hold the mirror in one hand and use the other to unscrew the retaining nut from the ball-joint socket on the mirror's back-plate. Disengage the existing mirror socket from ball

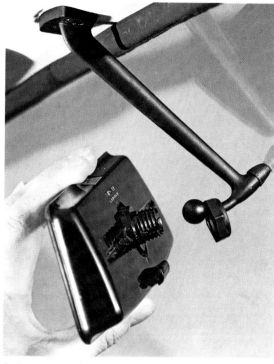

2 Put the retaining nut over the mirror arm. Fit the ball-joint socket over the ball and tighten the nut so that the anti-dazzle mirror can pivot but is held firmly in any position

3 The anti-dazzle mirror angled for use in the ordinary or 'undipped' position for daytime driving. Used in this way, it functions as a normal rear-view mirror

4 The anti-dazzle mirror in 'dipped' position for night driving. The mirror is dipped by applying pressure to its lower edge which pushes the reflector out of line with the facing glass

Accessories/wing and door mirrors

Fitting a wing mirror

Spring-loaded wing mirror The fittings include a rubber washer, steel washer and retaining nut. The plastic cover on the bottom of the retaining nut protects the spring from dirt

1 Decide the best position for the mirror, making sure that there are no obstructions on the underside of the wing. Mark out and centre-punch position for drilling pilot hole

2 Drill a pilot hole through the wing with a $\frac{1}{8}$ in. bit. Keep the drill at right angles to the surface of the wing to prevent it slipping and scoring the paintwork

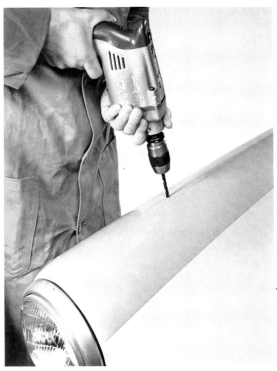

3 Enlarge the pilot hole with a larger bit to take the tank-cutter. Hook the lead to the power tool over your shoulder to keep it out of the way during drilling

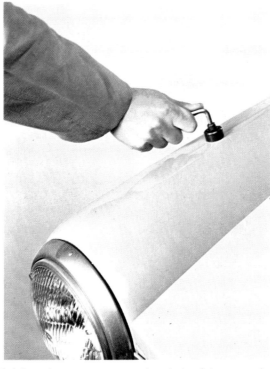

4 Adjust the tank-cutter to make a hole of the exact size needed to receive the shank of the mirror. After smoothing off the edges seal them with touch-up paint

5 Put a rubber washer over the shank of the mirror and insert the shank. Fit a steel washer on the underside, followed by a retaining nut, and tighten with a box spanner

Fitting an electrically controlled door mirror

1 Carefully remove the existing door mirror if one has been fitted. On many older cars, even where there is no mirror, fixing holes have been provided during production. Remove the covering plate

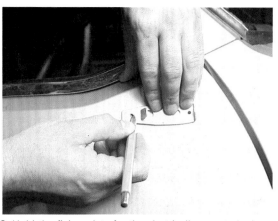

2 Hold the fixing plate for the electrically operated mirror against the door so that the holes line up—as closely matched as possible. It may be necessary to extend the existing hole in the door skin to match the fixing plate

3 Use a centre punch and hammer to dent the metal slightly where the new hole or the extension of the old hole is to be drilled. Remove the fixing plate and drill carefully through the outer skin of the door at the position marked

4 Use any kind of paint to touch up the bare edges of the new hole in the door. Reposition the fixing plate and its backing gasket and screw tightly into position with the screws provided in the fitting kit

5 Take the new door mirror and carefully feed its wires through the hole in the centre of the fixing plate. Wind the door window up and down several times to check that the wire has not fouled the mechanism

6 An ideal earthing point is the speaker of a car stereo system. Remove the trim from the door, follow the instructions in the fitting kit and wire up the mirror behind the speaker or to a piece of bare metal

7 Feed the wiring from the mirror through the door pillar, following existing wiring harness. Remove the cowling of the steering column and carefully drill a hole where you intend to fit the operating switch

8 Follow the wiring diagram in the car service hand-book and the instructions that accompany the door mirror. Wire the switch into a convenient, fused circuit in the car's electrical system. Fit the switch and replace the cowling

9 Operate the switch until the mirror is in the best position to give a clear rearward view. If it later is necessary to move the mirror count the number of audible clicks. To reposition it, count back the same number of clicks

Accessories/safety equipment

Reducing risks

SEAT BELTS could more than halve a motorist's chances of being killed or seriously injured on the road—so it makes good sense to wear them, even in countries where their use is not yet compulsory. Cars that were registered after December 31, 1964, are required by law to have front-seat belts, so on the majority of recent cars the anchorage points are built in.

To ensure adequate levels of strength and quality, approval by the British Standards Institution is a legal necessity for seat belts sold in this country, and the choice of makes and designs is now wide.

Most front-seat belts are now of the 'inertia reel' type. The belt runs out from a reel so that the wearer can move easily, but under any heavy braking or cornering (or, of course, on impact) a device in the reel automatically locks it.

In some designs any sudden movement by the wearer will cause the belt to lock; in others the locking device comes into action only when the vehicle is decelerating or cornering sharply; yet other types of inertia reel have a combination of both systems.

Because these belts are stowed when not in use, they keep clean and do not get in the way of people getting into and out of the car.

Though conventional belts provide excellent restraint for adults and older children, they are unsuitable for smaller children. Toddlers are difficult to restrain efficiently in a car, but properly installed 'safety chairs', or juvenile harnesses for older children, will help.

Headrests on the front seats can prevent neck injury in a collision from behind—provided their base fitting extends well down the seat—though they may impair vision to the rear during reversing. The best headrest is the type which is incorporated into the seat.

Accidents can be caused by animals not being restrained properly in a car; a big and lively dog free to move about is a potential source of distraction to the driver. Several accessory firms make easily fitted gates, of steel mesh or telescopic bars, to keep dogs safely within the luggage area of estate cars.

Fitting a seat belt

THE FRONT-SEAT BELTS of a new car will normally be fitted by the dealer (or by the maker of the vehicle if delivery is by road), since a car cannot legally be driven without them. However, the owner of a car with built-in anchorage points may at some time want to replace a worn or damaged belt, or to fit one of a different type, and the task is not normally a difficult one. Instructions for fitting are always provided with replacement seat belts, and they are usually both detailed and well illustrated.

If there are any complications, it is always better to consult the manufacturer.

Fitting belts to an older car without attachment points involves drilling holes in the door pillars and in the floor or central tunnel. The belt-makers can supply kits with parts to suit most popular cars, and it is essential that the instructions should be followed closely.

With those cars for which no prepared kit exists, consult a belt manufacturer before attempting the job, because of the danger that could result from drilling holes in the wrong places to anchor the belts.

1 The distance collar must be on the upper anchorage bolt under the bracket when the bolt is tightened, or the bracket will not move freely to align the belt

2 For a static belt, the bottom anchorage bracket simply bolts on, but an inertia reel (as shown) must be correctly set up on tightening, or the belt will not run freely

3 The short end of the belt, carrying the connector, is bolted to the third anchorage point, on the side of the central tunnel, remote from the seat concerned

Wearing a seat belt

1 To fasten most belts, push the tongue into the connector. On static belts, adjust by pulling the free end of the short strap. The long strap adjusts also

2 When the belt is correctly adjusted, the buckle is low down on the hip; if it is higher, on the stomach, it could cause injury to the wearer in an accident

3 Release methods vary from one make to another, but normally involve either pushing a button or tongue; instructions are usually printed on the connector

Fitting a child's safety chair and harness

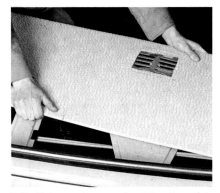

1 To fit top anchorages for either the safety seat or harness, the first stage is to remove the rear seat, backrest and parcel shelf

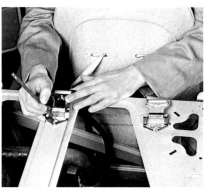

2 Hold the safety seat in position, with anchorage brackets fitted to the straps, and mark out the positions of fixing holes

3 Centre-punch the marks and drill holes. Using these holes as guides, drill pilot holes through the shelf from underneath

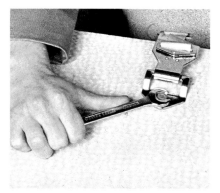

4 Drill full-sized holes through the shelf from above, then bolt on the brackets, tightening nuts firmly with a spanner

5 Bottom anchorages should be further apart than top ones; drill the bolt holes near the bottom of the rear-seat backrest panel

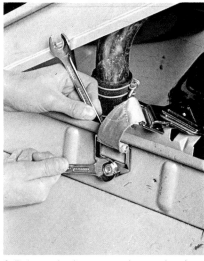

6 Bolt on the bottom anchorage brackets. Some cars will need short straps on the brackets, to clear the backrest

7 Tighten the mounting straps, making the top ones as short as possible. Adjust the harness to keep the buckle low on the body

8 When fitting the child's harness, adjust the mounting and securing straps in the same way as for the safety chair

Carrycot restraint

Keeping a dog under restraint

Do not rely on conventional back-seat belts to secure a carrycot. There are several types of special restraint systems available

Dog gate To be effective, a dog gate must have bars that are fairly close together, and that extend the full width of the car, to prevent the animal getting through. Also essential is adjustability, so that the gate can be securely mounted in any car

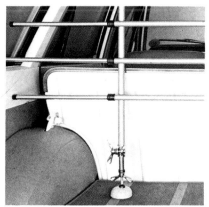

Adjustability Telescopic bars, and coarse-and-fine adjustment enable the uprights on this gate to jam between floor and roof

Accessories/Fog rearguard lamps

Fog rearguard lamps are designed to provide a rearward-facing high intensity beam of red light. In conditions of restricted visibility, for example, in fog or falling snow, a driver can see the light from a vehicle ahead long before he sees the vehicle itself or its normal rear lights.

The Department of Environment has made four recommendations about fitting these rear fog lamps:

1 They should be fitted in pairs, symmetrically, on the rear of the vehicle, but not next to the stop-lamps.

2 The individual bulb rating should not exceed 21 watts.

3 The lamps should be wired so that they can be used only while the side/tail lamps are switched on.

4 The operating switch should incorporate a 'tell-tale' or warning light. Alternatively, there should be a separate warning light, to remind the driver that the rearguard lamps are on.

Ideally, the lamps themselves should be bolted to the bumper or the valance just below it. Use at least 14/.025 mm. cable and run it either under the floor carpet or through a side box member, if possible following the same route as the existing wiring harness. Use rubber grommets in any holes you have to drill through the bodywork to allow the cables to pass through. This eliminates chafing and possible short-circuiting. Make sure that the lamp units themselves are correctly earthed.

WIRING AND CONNECTIONS

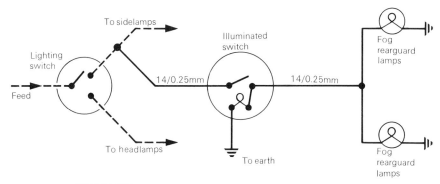

- - - - - Original cables
————— New cables

1 First decide where to fit the operating switch on the fascia. Take the supply to the operating switch from the side-lamp circuit. Connect the cable to the output side of the side-lamp switch, so that the supply is available to the new rearguard lamps only when the side/tail lamps are on. This ensures that they cannot be used separately. Install an in-line fuse holder, with a 10 amp. fuse, and connect this cable to the input side of the fog rearguard switch

2 Fit the feed cable, from the output side of the fog rearguard switch, through the car—either under the carpets or by following the wiring harness—into the rear luggage compartment. The cable termination should end with a double in-line connector, so that the supply can be distributed between the two rearguard lamp units. Make sure the cable is taped to existing harness so that it is secure

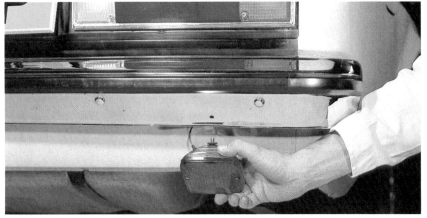

3 Decide the best place to mount the two lamp units, either in the rear bumper or the valance. Drill two holes on each side and bolt each lamp firmly in place, preferably just below the rear lamp cluster. Ensure a good metal-to-metal contact to obtain a satisfactory earth return. Feed the cables through the lower boot valance and connect them to the two lamp units. Join the cables internally to the double in-line connector

4 When the lamps have been fitted and the wiring completed, make sure any hanging cables under the fascia panel are secure, taping them if necessary to the existing wiring harness. Switch on the side/tail-lights and make sure they are working. Operate the rearguard lamp switch and check that the fog rearguard lamps are operating correctly and check that the switch warning light is working

Fitting a reversing light

A REVERSING LIGHT can either be automatic, so that it lights whenever reverse gear is selected, or it can be operated by a switch on the fascia. This switch must, by law, have a warning light on it to remind the driver that it is still on. Other regulations control such factors as wattage and the angle of the beam (see p. 330).

A reversing light is designed to give a wide area of light, but a limited range. It should be positioned on the car where it is not likely to be broken.

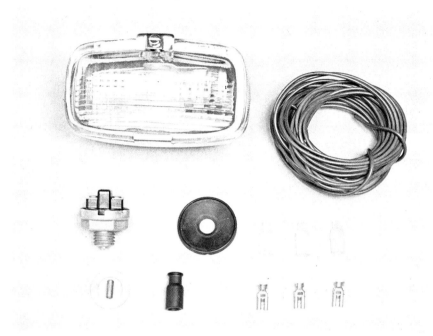

Automatic reversing light The kit is complete with wire, terminals and operating switch. Switch screws into gearbox casing and is automatically operated by reverse gear

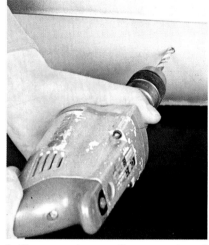

1 Disconnect battery. Centre-punch and drill pilot hole in offside of lower panel

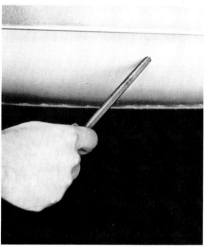

2 Enlarge the hole to take the retaining bolt fixed to the back of the lamp

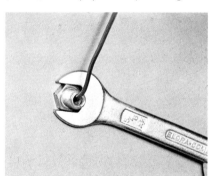

3 Feed the lead through the hole and insert the retaining bolt. Secure the nut behind

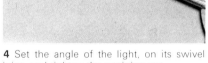

4 Set the angle of the light, on its swivel joint, and tighten the retaining nut

5 Remove plug in the switch housing on the upper side of the gearbox casing

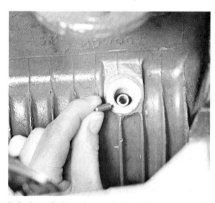

6 Before fitting the switch, refer to manual: the distance piece may not be needed

7 Thread the wire from the light unit, through the boot, under the carpets and into the engine compartment. Secure it to the loom clips and connect to the gearbox terminal

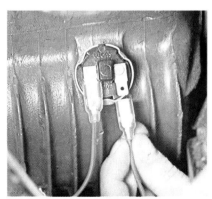

8 Connect wire from light to a terminal on switch. Connect the second wire to switch

9 Route the second switch wire to a fused power supply or ignition auxiliary terminal

Security devices/bonnet and brake locks

Discouraging the car thief

A DETERMINED THIEF can steal almost any vehicle, however well protected, but few will risk the difficulties and delay of stealing a 'thief-proofed' car. Even the simplest security device is usually sufficient to discourage the casual thief from 'joy riding', or stealing any contents.

There are three main types of anti-thief devices—immobilisers, alarms and vibration alarms. Immobilisers (see p. 282) which are compulsory on all new cars prevent the car being driven away. They can be operated by disconnecting the ignition system or battery or by locking the gear lever, steering wheel, clutch or footbrake. Some ignition immobilisers have an audible alarm warning. Another type of immobiliser cuts out the fuel supply and the ignition. A lockable top with a pipe connection at each side is fitted into the fuel pipe between the tank and carburettor; it is also wired to the coil. Once the device is locked, fuel cannot flow and the ignition system is cut out. Alarm systems (see p. 284) warn that someone is trying to enter the car. They depend upon switches similar to those for the interior light, located in the door pillars and the boot and bonnet guttering. Anyone attempting to enter the car while the system is turned on causes a switch to be earthed; this sounds the horn, or other alarm, and will sometimes flash the headlights.

Vibration alarms (see p. 282) warn that someone is tampering with the car. They have an electrical make-and-break mechanism activated by pendulum contact. Any undue movement of the car operates the pendulum and sounds the alarm until it is switched off.

Alarms and vibrators are controlled by an exterior key or switch; most incorporate an additional ignition immobiliser. Both are generally more expensive than simple immobilisers, but they prevent a thief removing contents from the car as well as from stealing the car itself.

In addition to the three anti-thief devices, a lockable petrol cap and a bonnet lock or a remote-control bonnet-release mechanism will also guard against petty thieves. Fitting charges can be as high as the cost of anti-thief devices themselves. A home mechanic can fit most of them, except for certain steering locks, provided that the device chosen is suitable for his particular make of car.

There are several points to remember when installing these devices. Some electrically operated immobilisers have an exterior switch which should not be mounted where it can easily be seen. The same rule applies to an alarm switch fitted outside the car.

Mount a key-switch on the side of the car, but not low down at the front or back where it could become corroded by road spray. Conceal alarm or vibrator-system wiring inside the car if possible, by running the wires through the bodywork where it is double-skinned; this will prevent them from being cut.

It is essential that any security device fitted is not readily accessible from outside the car.

Fitting a bonnet-release catch

FOR A CAR with an external bonnet release, a simple protection against petty thieves is a mechanism allowing the catch to be operated only from inside the vehicle.

Before fitting the kit, disconnect the car's battery to prevent any possibility of a short-circuit when working among the wires behind the fascia panel or when feeding the cable around the engine compartment. For ease of operation, mount the release handle below the right-hand end of the fascia or parcel shelf. On some cars the holes for the handle mounting bracket, and those for the cables through the bulkhead and front panel, are already drilled and sealed with rubber plugs; the hole for the spring-retaining and abutment clip may be cut already.

On cars where it is necessary to drill through the bulkhead, check that there are no fittings behind which might be damaged by drilling.

Before cutting the rectangular hole for the spring-retaining clip, assemble the new catch mechanism and lightly bolt it into position. Mark the position of the clip underneath the grille surround and drill a small pilot hole.

1 Pull back the trim below the right-hand end of the fascia shelf. Drill two holes (on some cars these may already be drilled) for the mounting bracket

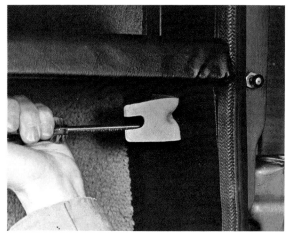

2 Replace trim, pierce for screws and securely fix the bracket with self tapping screws. Drill a hole through engine bulkhead in line with the bracket and fit grommet

3 Thread the operating cable through the hole from inside the car. Fit the bonnet-release handle to the mounting bracket and secure it with the nut provided

4 Undo the radiator-grille securing screws (or drill out the pop rivets) and remove the grille. Drill through the front panel, just to the offside of the radiator (on some cars this hole is already drilled and plugged). Slide the cable-securing cleats on to the cable, and then route them round the engine compartment and out through the hole

Fitting the remote control

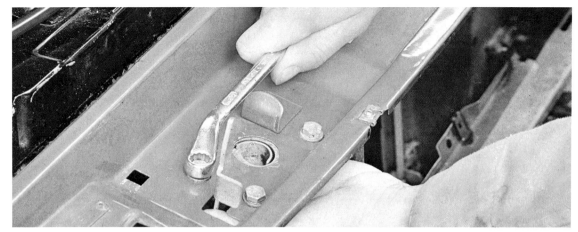

5 Unbolt and remove the existing bonnet-release mechanism. Disconnect and discard the nylon bearings and the external release lever, which is sprung out of the upper panel. On some cars, as here, the rectangular hole for the spring-retaining and abutment clip is already cut; it can be seen in the lower left of the illustration

6 Slip the spring-retaining clip over the end of the cable. The inner wire is secured in the trunnion (grip nipple), which is then fitted to the sprung arm of the catch mechanism. If there is no rectangular hole, cut one in the top of the grille surround, ensuring that it is correctly positioned to receive the clip. Use a small drill and triangular file

7 Refit the catch mechanism, securing it with the bolts. Locate the spring-retaining clip in the rectangular hole and twist it into position with a screwdriver

8 Check the operation of the mechanism and adjust the cable length as necessary. Secure the cable round the side of the engine compartment. Replace the radiator grille

Handbrake lock

A COMBINATION LOCK is available which will immobilise a floor-mounted handbrake lever by locking the release button. The lock is secured permanently to the handbrake by a shear-head bolt that snaps off when the head is fully tightened. To fit the lock, slide it over the lever as far as it will go without depressing the button. Insert the plastic packing strips provided so that the lock fits snugly. Tighten the bolt, test the operation of lock and handbrake, then fully tighten the bolt to snap off the head.

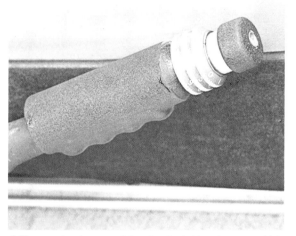

1 The mechanism consists of a lockable plunger, which operates the release button, mounted on a metal tube. It is fixed on the brake lever by a shear-head bolt

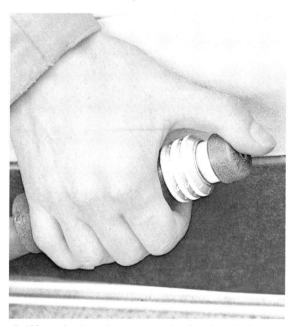

2 When leaving the car, apply the handbrake and 'scramble' the lock—with the plunger in the 'out' position—to immobilise the lever release button

Security devices/vibrator alarm

Fitting an alarm system

VIBRATORS are highly sensitive anti-thief devices which work by using a pendulum make-and-break contact mechanism. With the system switched on, anyone tampering with the car will rock the pendulum, which will complete an electrical circuit and sound the car's horn.

The key switch should be mounted in a convenient position on the outside of the car, but the back of the switch should be inaccessible when the car is locked. A common position is on the offside rear wing, just behind the door.

Mount the alarm unit as nearly upright as possible and in such a way that the pendulum swings across the car, not along it.

If the car's horn can be sounded with the ignition switched off, earth one end of a piece of wire—say to the front bumper—and, with the other end, touch each horn terminal in turn. Connect the wire from terminal 1 on the alarm to the terminal which sounds the horn.

If the horn will not sound with the ignition switched off, the same instructions apply, but disconnect the wire to the horn's 'quiet' terminal (or both wires on twin horns) and insulate its end. Route a wire from the vacant terminal (or terminals, for twin horns) to that marked 'A1' or 'B' on the car's voltage regulator (see p. 145).

Some cars have continuously earthed horns. In this circuit the horn button is between the battery and the horn—the horn being earthed.

Make the test by taking a wire from the battery instead of from earth; the blue wire bridging terminals 3 and 5 on the alarm should be moved to bridge terminals 2 and 5. Otherwise the procedure is the same.

To avoid drilling the bulkhead, it is usually possible to find the appropriate wires from the horn behind it, where they can be joined to the wires from the alarm.

If cable holes have to be drilled through the bulkhead, take care to avoid existing wiring or fittings and use rubber grommets.

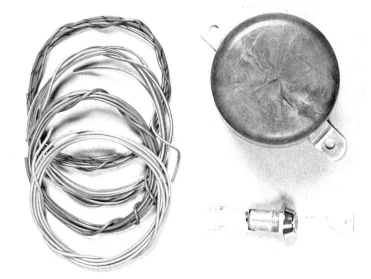

Vibrator alarm kit The alarm is easy to fit and consists of the alarm unit itself (containing pendulum, contacts, relay, thermo-switch and external junction box), the key switch with connectors and the appropriate lengths of colour-coded wire

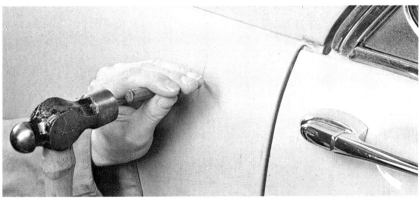

1 Select a convenient position on the car's exterior to mount the key switch. The back of the switch should not be easily accessible from outside the car, otherwise a thief would be able to interfere with it. Mark the position with a centre-punch

2 Use a small-diameter drill to make a pilot hole at the marked position, and then a larger one (up to a maximum of $\frac{3}{4}$ in., to cut down the amount of filing necessary). Take care to avoid any wiring or interior trim when drilling this hole

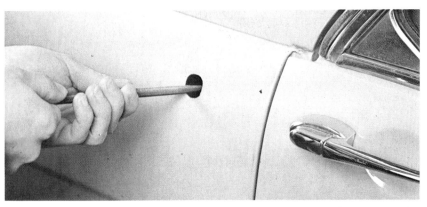

3 Using a round file, enlarge the diameter of the hole (if necessary) to match the barrel of the key switch. Remove any rough edges so that the switch fits snugly. Before filing, apply masking tape to the surrounding paintwork to protect it (see p. 250)

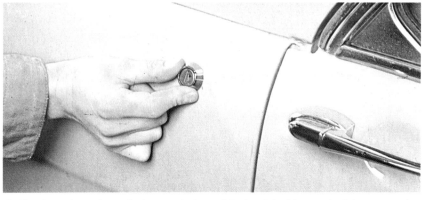

4 Touch up the paintwork; then push the key switch into the hole and secure it on the inside of the car with the nut provided. Attach plain blue and plain green wires to terminals at the back of the key switch, with cable connectors

Wiring the alarm

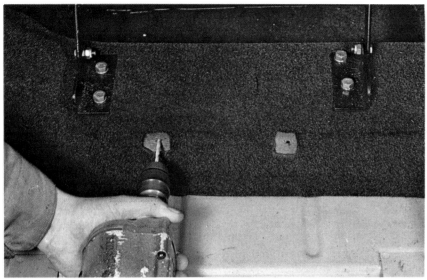

5 Select a suitable position for the alarm unit so that the pendulum swings across the car. Fit the alarm on the bulkhead or, as here, under the driver's seat or in any position where it cannot be seen from outside. Drill mounting holes for the fixing brackets

6 Route the blue and green cables behind the trim, from the key switch to the lower terminals 5 and 6 on the alarm. Connect the blue-and-black wire to the lower terminal 1, and the red-and-yellow wire to the upper terminal 5

7 Secure the alarm to the car with self-tapping screws. Route the blue-and-black and the red-and-yellow wires to the fascia, behind the trim or panelling, but not under the floor carpet where they might be damaged, causing a short-circuit

8 Check the horn system, as explained on the opposite page, and note the colour coding of the wire on the horn's 'noise' terminal; also note the colour coding of the cable that is connected to terminal 'A1' or 'B' on the car's junction box

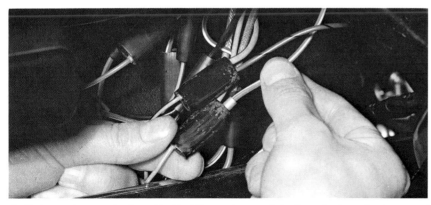

9 If these wires can be found behind the fascia, use double connectors, as illustrated, to join the blue-and-black wire from the alarm unit to the wire from the horn, and the red-and-yellow cable to the one from the junction box

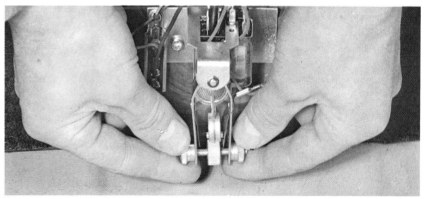

10 If these wires cannot be found, drill through the bulkhead and route the wires from the alarm directly to the horn and the junction box. Test the system. Sensitivity can be adjusted by turning the knurled brass nuts on each side of the pendulum

Winter driving/fog lamps and tyre chains

Equipment for safer driving

WINTER, with its fog, snow, ice and long hours of darkness, puts heavy demands on both car and driver. Apart from ensuring that the car is in sound mechanical condition, several extras can make winter driving safer and more comfortable.

These include studded tyres which give better grip on icy roads; tyre chains which improve grip on soft snow; mud-flaps which reduce the amount of dirt thrown on to the rear window; windscreen washers; rear-window de-misters; and fog lamps to improve visibility.

Fog lamps

Twin fog lamps must, by law, be positioned symmetrically on each side of the car, not more than 3½ ft above road level. They can be used as a substitute for headlamps only in bad visibility (see p. 330).

Fitting a pair of fog lamps

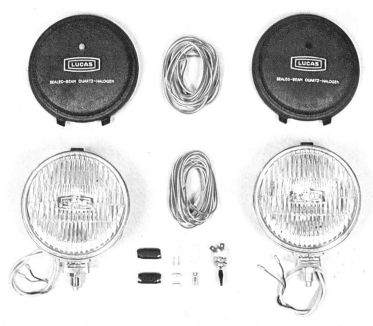

1 Mark positions for lamps, on the apron behind the front bumper, with a centre punch

2 Drill holes for the fog-lamp retaining bolts in the marked positions

3 Bolt fog lamps in position, making sure that retaining nuts are tight. Pass leads from each lamp through grille. Leads consist of a red-and-yellow wire (power) and a black wire (earth)

Twin fog lamps and their components The kit contains lens covers; wire leads; two four-way connectors; a wiring clip; terminal tags; a push-on wire connector; and a switch

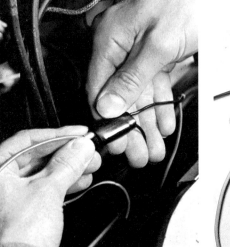

4 Plug earth wires from lamps (and separate green wire) into a four-way connector

5 Connect green wire to earth (bare metal). Here, the battery earth terminal is used

6 Plug power wire (red and yellow) from each lamp into the other four-way connector

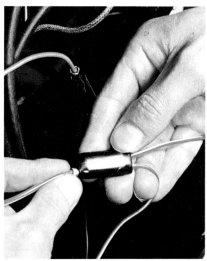

7 Plug long wire (also red and yellow) into same connector. Route to switch point

Wiring the switch

8 Drill a hole for the switch in the fascia, within easy reach of the driver

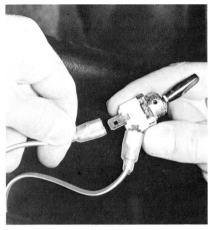

9 Connect power wire from lamps to the switch. Fit second wire to other terminal

10 Push switch head through fascia hole and fix in position with retaining nut

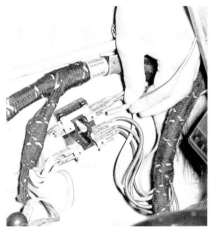

11 Connect second wire from switch to power side of 'accessory' terminal in fusebox

Mud-flaps protect a car from flying stones

A SET of mud-flaps fitted to the front wings of a car—particularly a sports car which has a curved underbody—will prevent damage from flying stones to the sills and underbody. Clean flaps regularly, or trapped mud may cause corrosion.

Fitted to the rear of a car, mud-flaps will reduce the amount of road dirt thrown on to the rear window, and prevent stones hitting following cars.

Fit mud-flaps so that they hang clear of the road surface, even when the car is fully loaded. The flaps can have red glass reflectors or reflective paint on them.

Some makes of mud-flaps can be fitted to any car, but others are designed for a particular model.

1 Jack up car, remove back wheels and drill holes in wheel arches to fix mud-flap stays

2 Screw mud-flap stay in position with self-tapping screws. Apply paint or underseal

3 Mud-flap in position. The ground clearance should allow for a fully loaded car

Chains improve grip on soft snow

TYRE CHAINS make driving easier on soft or packed snow, but they are not so effective on icy roads.

Buy the correct type of chain for a particular tyre, as it is dangerous to fit chains designed for cross-ply tyres to radial-ply tyres. Emergency grips—short chains which are clipped across the tread —are for getting out of a ditch.

Do not use them for driving on the road as they may damage the tyres and the grips will break after a few miles.

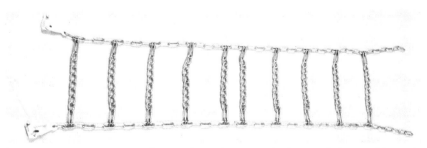

Tyre chain Long chains are for securing unit to tyre; short cross chains provide a grip on the road. Chains should not be used for driving on dry roads

Chain in position Surplus links at the coupling point allow for adjustment

Studded tyres

Studs for better grip Studded tyres give almost as good a grip as chains in snow and ice, and they can be used at much higher speeds. But they wear rapidly on dry roads, so use them only when necessary and preferably on all four wheels

Winter driving/de-misters

Installing a rear screen heater

Good all-round visibility is essential at all times and in all kinds of driving conditions. Before starting any journey, make sure that all the mirrors – including those on the wings or on the doors – are clean and properly adjusted.

Ensure, too, that the side windows of the car are clean, that the windscreen-washing reservoir has enough washing solution for the journey and that the wiper and washer mechanisms are in order.

Above all, check that the view through the car's rear screen is completely clear and unobstructed. Do not use the 'parcel shelf' for storing parcels, and make sure that the screen is at all times kept clean both inside and out.

If the car does not already have one, a useful accessory that can be fitted by the

do-it-yourself motorist is the type of rear-screen heater illustrated on these pages. It consists basically of thin wire elements that are stuck to the rear screen, and the whole heating device is wired into the car's electrical circuit.

Note that, if the car screen is less than 25 cm. (10 in.) deep, the lower part of the heater can be cut off to fit. It is always advisable to complete all the wiring before fitting the heater unit to the screen. This enables the heater to be switched on for a time and so makes the removal of the backing sheet easier, and it helps the elements to stick to the screen.

Make sure while wiring, that the battery has been disconnected. Warm the interior of the car before fitting the elements by switching on the heater and fan.

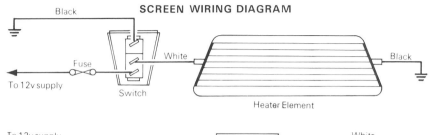

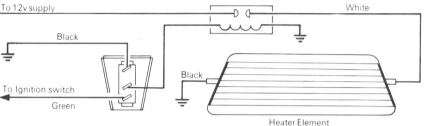

SCREEN WIRING DIAGRAM

1 Wipe the outside of the rear window dry. Tape the heater in position (black line outwards) approximately 5 cm. (2 in.) below the top of the screen. Check from the driving seat for rear viewing and outline the position of the heater with a felt-tip pen or coloured adhesive tape

2 The illuminated switch should be fitted under the instrument panel. Use a No. 30 bit to drill a 3.3 mm. hole. Connect the short black lead to a suitable earth point. Connect the length of green cable to the output side of the ignition switch

3 If the ignition circuit itself is heavily loaded, connect the green wire to a fused ignition-controlled circuit. Connect the white cable to the switch and feed it and the black cable under the carpets to the back shelf

4 Clean the inside of the rear window. Remove any wax polish and ensure the screen is absolutely free from condensation. If necessary warm the glass with a hair dryer, or warm the engine and switch on the car's fan heater

5 Place the heater element on a flat surface — black line uppermost — and carefully peel away the protective backing sheet. Do not attempt to cut the element or white backing sheet. If cutting is necessary, do so only when the element is in position

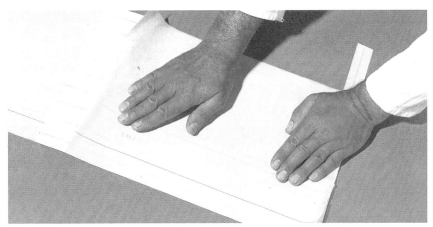

6 Fold the backing sheet in half crosswise, tear it into two pieces and refix it to the element so that you leave a 2 in. gap in the centre. This method ensures that the element can be stuck on securely and evenly

7 Hold the heater (black line towards the screen) so that it lines up with the marks. Press the exposed centre strip on to the glass. Peel off one half of the protective sheet, pressing the heater firmly into place. Repeat this operation with the other half

8 Remove the side strips and press down the lead-out wires. Connect the cables to the element terminals, reconnect the battery and switch on the heater. Leave for at least ten minutes, and while warming up smooth out the element. When hot, remove backing strip

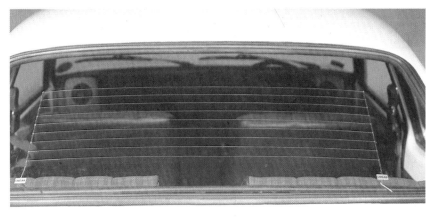

9 After the backing sheet has been removed, switch off. As the heater cools, run your thumb along the element strips to ensure that they adhere well. Do not wash or wipe the rear window for two or three days to allow the adhesive to set

Touring and towing/fitting a tow bar

Towing equipment

MODERN CARS require little extra equipment fitted to them for normal touring, and can be modified cheaply and easily to tow a caravan or other trailer, including one designed to carry a boat.

The first essential for towing work is a towing bracket which has been specifically designed for the car concerned. The bracket should be strong enough to withstand the considerable strains imposed by stopping, starting, cornering and hill climbing. It can be dangerous to use a home-made or incorrect towing bracket. A car used for towing must also be fitted with a multi-pin electric socket outlet to connect the car's indicators, rear lights and stop-lights to those of the trailer.

As most trailers obstruct vision to the rear, it is worth fitting an extra mirror. Those made for the purpose range from periscopes to clip-on mirrors with extra-long arms that can easily be removed when they are not required. Adequate rear vision is required by law (see p. 331).

Clip-on extension mirror

A CARAVAN, or boat, often obscures rear vision even if wing mirrors are fitted. A simple solution is to clip an extension mirror over the existing wing mirror.

Extensions are attached to the wing mirrors by means of an adjustable spring-loaded clamp. For security, the clamp should be adjusted before the extension is fitted, to ensure that the spring exerts its maximum pressure. Adjust the mirror so that the reflection includes the sides of both car and trailer when they are in line.

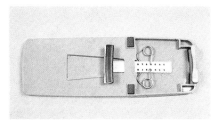

Extension mirror The plastic back has a clamp consisting of a fixed portion and an adjustable one on a spring-loaded slide

1 Adjust spring position so that sliding portion of clamp can be pulled clear of the wing mirror's outer edge during fitting

2 After attaching extension mirror, check that it is secure and then adjust angle as necessary to give the best field of vision

Fitting a towing periscope

IF A TRAILER is wide but is not very high or —as with some caravans—can be seen through from end to end, the best answer to the rear-vision problem is a periscope mounted on the car roof.

To determine the best position for the periscope, hitch up the trailer, then stand in front of the car and look back along the roof on the driver's side, noting the point from which the road behind is most clearly seen. In the case of a caravan with a window at each end, open the curtains first.

Before fitting the periscope, clean the top of the car roof around the chosen position and wipe the suction pads, allowing both to dry thoroughly.

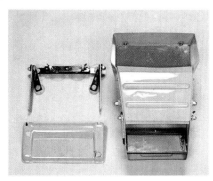

The complete kit It consists of the periscope and mounting bracket, with two rubber suction pads and a protective cover

1 Place the bracket assembly on the roof, near the front edge. Loosen the wing nuts and press each suction pad down in turn

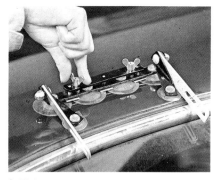

2 Tighten the wing nuts. The position of the pads should be checked from time to time whenever the periscope is in use

3 Attach the periscope to the bracket by means of the domed nuts. Adjustable rods hold it steady against the screen frame

4 Final stage is to slide on the cover. The lower front knob of the periscope body enables the mirror angle to be adjusted

Long-arm towing mirror

EXTRA-LARGE caravans and other wide loads may necessitate using an extra mirror, projecting from the driver's door.

This type is adjustable for height and angle, and is tensioned by the rubber strap to minimise the effects of vibration.

Long-arm mirror This consists of a telescopic tubular arm with a rubber-protected base, a metal stay and a rubber tension strap

Fitting the mirror Clip end of stay over the window aperture and hook strap to bottom of door. Adjust tubular arm as required

Fitting a towing bracket

TO AVOID DAMAGE to a car used for towing it is essential to fit a towing bracket that is specifically designed for the car.

Several specialist firms make towing brackets and can usually provide one suitable for most popular cars.

Towing-bracket kits vary from maker to maker, and from car to car, so the fitting instructions supplied with the bracket should be studied carefully, and followed.

The use of an inspection pit will make the job easier, and drills up to ¾ in. may be required. The following fitting sequence is typical of the work involved.

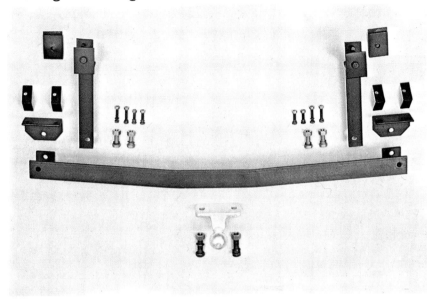

Towing-bracket kit This kit, suitable for a family saloon, contains the main transverse bar, two supporting stays, various brackets, nuts and bolts and sometimes a ball hitch

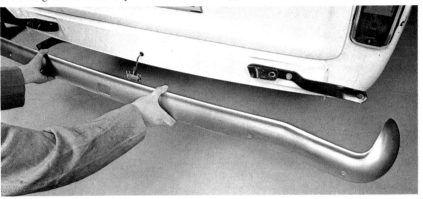

1 Disconnect the rear bumper-mounted number-plate lamp (if one is fitted) and then detach the bumper by undoing the bolts holding it to its carrier brackets

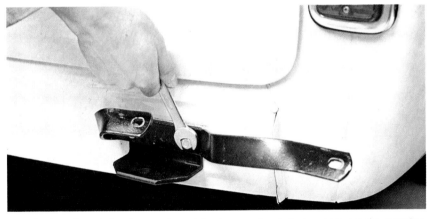

2 Fit the broad angle-brackets on top of the bumper brackets, by removing the securing bolts or nuts, adding the angle-brackets and refitting the bolts or nuts

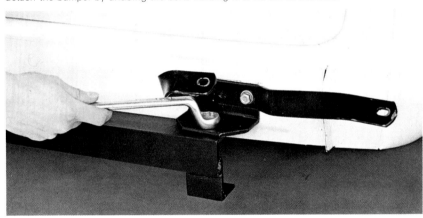

3 Attach the main towing bar to the two angle-brackets by means of the large nuts and bolts provided. Use a ring spanner and ensure that the nuts are firmly tightened

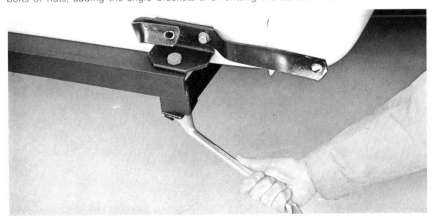

4 Bolt the stays to the underside of the main bar; drill through the boot floor or a frame member, as shown in the instructions, to take the bolts for the ends of the stays

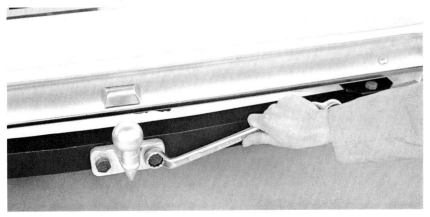

5 The towing ball is often supplied with the trailer; bolt it to the middle of the main bar— the holes are already drilled—and remount the bumper on its brackets

Touring and towing/roof rack and luggage containers

Driving abroad

ANY CAR being taken abroad must conform to the motoring regulations of the countries to be visited.

Since most countries drive on the right-hand side of the road, and British headlights dip to the left, it is safer to fit lens converters or beam deflectors—whether you are obliged to or not. Some European countries do not insist on this conversion. Beam deflectors clip over the front of the headlight lens and refract the beam to the right. Fitting them is a five-minute job with a screwdriver. Lens converters are even more easily fitted.

Touring often means carrying a lot of luggage, and for this a roof rack can be invaluable. But it should be used only when all other luggage space in the car is full; an excessive load on the roof will make a car top-heavy and affect its stability and handling.

Before buying a roof rack, check that it is suitable for your model of car, and secure the luggage firmly—preferably in a canvas bag held in place by strong elastic straps.

Fitting beam deflectors or lens converters

To fit a beam deflector, remove the headlamp trim and position the disc right way up

Clip the deflector securely and replace the trim. Refit the retaining screw or screws

Cut the converter strips to fit the lenses of your car and simply stick them in position

Fitting a roof rack

1 Fit rack on roof with angle brackets in gutters. Adjust telescopic side and cross-struts until rack is centred on the roof. Tighten the clamping screws on side and cross-struts

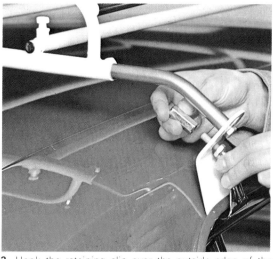

2 Hook the retaining clip over the outside edge of the gutter, passing bolt through top of bracket. Fit long nut to bolt and repeat the operation on the remaining supports

3 Adjust the locking nut—which is on the shank of the bolt—until the clip and bracket have a firm grip on the gutter. Repeat the operation on the remaining supports

Positioning the rack

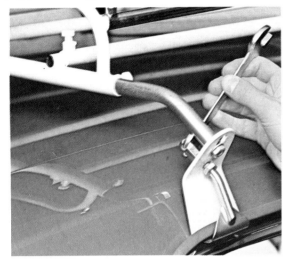

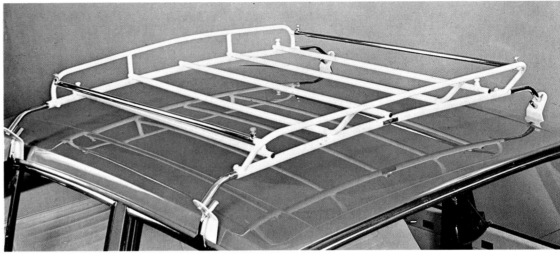

4 Tighten the long nut on the retaining-clip bolt. Repeat the operation on the remainder of the supports, and adjust them if necessary until the rack is centred and secure

5 Check the locking nuts on all the supports and the clamping screws on the adjustable side and cross-struts. Before loading the rack for the first time, drive the car for a

short distance (a mile or so) and then check all nuts and screws again—tightening them if necessary. This kind of rack can easily be dismantled and stored when not required

Loading a roof rack

Canvas luggage bag This type of waterproof bag has zip fasteners on two sides and will keep luggage firmly in place. Bags of this kind are made to suit different sizes of roof rack

Loading the rack Lay bag on rack, with one zip to the side and one to the rear, and pack as evenly as possible. Fasten zips and secure the bag with rubber luggage grips

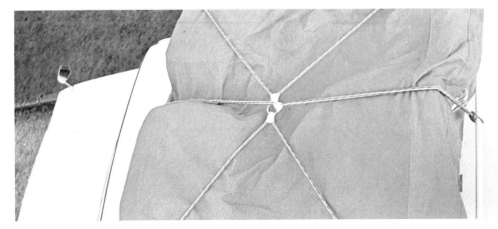

Rubber luggage grips in position These consist of six or eight fabric-covered bands, linked to a central ring. Each band has a metal hook at the outer end which clips over the

framework of the rack. The grips are easy to fit—provided they are handled firmly—and leave sufficient room for occasional access to the luggage during a journey

Car compass

Interference-free compass This car compass is mounted on the fascia directly in front of the driver. It can be adjusted by means of two screws and, once set, it automatically counteracts magnetic interference from the car.

What to carry in the car

A kit of spares and extra equipment is invaluable for any car used for touring. For travel in Britain the kit should contain the following:

First Aid box	Temporary plastic windscreen
First Aid manual	Spare set of keys
Gallon of petrol	Spare fan belt
Petrol funnel	Tow rope
List of car agents	Breakdown triangle

For continental touring carry in addition to the above:

Pint of brake fluid	Condenser
Tyre-pressure gauge	Radiator hoses
Set of contact breakers	Distributor rotor arm
Set of spark-plugs	Radiator sealant
Spare bulbs and fuses	Valve cores

Emergency equipment

Simple extras to cope with breakdowns

MODERN motoring conditions, and especially the hazards of motorway driving, have resulted in many accessories becoming more necessities than extras. Simple equipment carried in the boot, such as a torch, a tow rope and a pair of booster cables, can avoid a long delay at the roadside after a breakdown. A fire extinguisher and warning triangle can give added safety in an emergency.

Booster cables These enable a car to be started when the battery is flat, by linking it to another car's battery. Both batteries must be of the same voltage. Take extra care if either car is fitted with an alternator instead of a dynamo. If the leads are connected to the wrong terminals the alternator will be damaged. Jumper leads (see p. 19) should never be used for this purpose; they have a light-gauge wire which can overheat.

Emergency lights For a breakdown at night, particularly on a busy, unlit road, some motorists have a torch with a red warning light.

The type shown also has a white light on the side which can be used while correcting a defect or changing a wheel. But it is advisable to carry a second light so that the warning light can be used independently when work is being carried out under the bonnet.

It is not only difficult but dangerous to work on a car by the light of a match.

Lead lamp Two torches or a lead lamp which can be clipped to the car battery or plugged into a socket—provided in the fascia panel—can make repair work easier under the car or under the bonnet.

Accident warning A first essential in an accident or breakdown is to leave the road safe for others and give them an advance warning of your presence.

Warning triangles are not yet compulsory in this country—they are in several European countries—but they are a valuable aid to personal safety and can help other drivers to avoid an accident.

Car fires The most likely causes of fire in a car are fuel leakage in the engine compartment or short-circuiting, which sometimes occurs in electric cables—particularly the starter-motor cable, which is not protected by a fuse.

A fire extinguisher, mounted inside the car where it is readily accessible, could prevent a small fire getting out of hand and causing a great deal of damage.

Water should not be used on a fire caused by petrol or electrical equipment. For this sort of fire use only foam-filled or dry powder extinguishers.

Tow ropes These are useful for removing a car from a busy road after a breakdown, for getting a car out of a ditch, or for tow-starting.

Tow ropes are made of manilla or nylon rope, steel wire or nylon straps, and usually have clips or shackles at each end for attaching them to a vehicle.

When attaching a tow rope choose a safe anchorage, such as a chassis member, if there is no towing bracket; never attach the rope to bumpers since these are often incapable of withstanding towing stresses.

Warning Before towing a car which has automatic transmission, check the handbook. Damage can be caused to some automatic transmissions if the car is towed.

Emergency windscreen kit Several manufacturers now sell emergency kits to provide shelter and good visibility. Knock all the remaining windscreen fragments outwards and fit the plastic sheeting according to the maker's instructions

Booster cables To start a car using another car battery first switch off all electrical equipment and ensure that both cars are in neutral gear. Link the positive terminals of each battery with the red-handled clips, and the negative terminals with the black clips. If the car with the flat battery does not start after two or three attempts, do not persist—this may exhaust the second battery. If the car starts, remove each clip quickly to avoid arcing. Do not allow the clips to touch any metal part of the car.

Using an advance-warning triangle

MOST continental European countries now require motorists to carry in the car an advance-warning triangle which can be used at the scene of a breakdown or accident. Although the use of a triangle is not obligatory in Britain, it is undoubtedly helpful at the scene where the road has been partly blocked.

Obtaining an approved type

Most countries have established their own standards for the kind of triangle that is acceptable, but it is advisable to obtain the type that has been specifically approved under European Economic Community regulations. You are then assured that its use will be accepted in every country in Europe, whereas other types may not be accepted in certain countries—particularly France.

When you are buying a triangle make sure that it carries the European Ⓔ symbol.

The regulations governing the use of triangles vary from country to country.

Country		
AUSTRIA	Compulsory all cars	On road behind vehicle, 1 m. (3 ft 3 in.) from kerb and visible from 200 m. (219 yds).
BELGIUM	Compulsory all cars	30 m. (33 yds) behind vehicle on ordinary roads, 100 m. (109 yds) on a motorway.
FRANCE	Compulsory all cars	Placed on road 30 m. (33 yds) behind vehicle and visible from 100 m. (109 yds).
GERMANY	Compulsory all cars	On ordinary roads 100 m. (109 yds) behind vehicle and 200 m. (219 yds) on a motorway.
GREECE	Compulsory all cars	On road 50 m. (55 yds) behind vehicle. Required only outside built-up areas.
ITALY	Compulsory all cars	On road 50 m. (55 yds) behind vehicle and visible from 100 m. (110 yds).
LUXEMBOURG	Compulsory all cars	Placed on road approximately 30 m. (33 yds) behind vehicle.
NETHERLANDS	Compulsory all cars	Used at night if a vehicle's lights fail, or by day if visibility is poor.
NORWAY	Obligatory only for cars registered in Norway	Though not necessary, it is advisable for visiting motorists to carry an approved triangle.
PORTUGAL	Compulsory all cars	On road 30 m. (33 yds) behind vehicle and visible from a distance of 100 m. (109 yds).
SPAIN	Compulsory for passenger vehicles with more than nine seats	Two triangles—one back, one front—placed 30 m. (33 yds) behind and in front, with 100 m. (109 yds) visibility.
SWITZERLAND	Compulsory all cars	Placed at the edge of the road at least 50 m. (55 yds) behind vehicle.

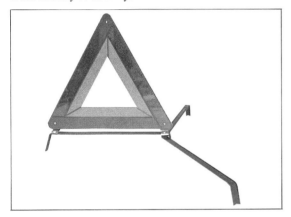

Portable and effective The luminous-faced European triangle can be folded and packed away in a special carrying case provided with it. The surface has reflectivity of at least 10,000 candelas

On ordinary roads On British roads which are not officially of motorway standard, place the triangle not less than 50 m. (55 yds) behind the broken-down vehicle or accident. If the car is near a corner, place the triangle before the bend

On British motorways If possible, drive the car on to the hard shoulder and make sure that the triangle is at least 150 m. (165 yds) behind it. The triangle will stand in winds of up to 50 km/h (30 mph)

Seeing in an emergency

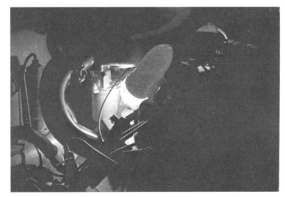

Lead lamp This lamp, which is useful for emergency repair work after dark, is small and compact and can be stored in the glove compartment. It is linked to the battery terminals by crocodile clips. A magnet on the side of the lamp allows it to be attached to most parts of the engine compartment. It can also be used for working under a car

Ready for a breakdown

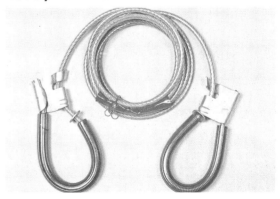

Tow rope This has a plastic-covered steel wire, 5 yds long. Fix the rope only to a substantial structural part of a vehicle—not to the bodywork or bumpers

Accessories/auxiliary instruments

Fitting a supplementary instrument panel

MOST PRODUCTION CARS leave the factory equipped with only three basic instruments —a combined speedometer/mileage recorder, a fuel gauge and a water-temperature gauge. Most, too, have warning lights to indicate a lack of oil pressure and to alert the driver when the generator is not charging the battery.

Warning lights usually respond only to major changes. This means that often the light merely shows something has gone wrong, not that something is going wrong.

But instruments such as an oil-pressure gauge, and an ammeter which measures the rate of charge and discharge of the battery, can give early warning of trouble under the bonnet. Their dials give an immediate indication of any change, allowing the driver to spot slight deviations from the normal, so that he can trace the fault and put it right in good time to prevent serious damage.

Often only minor maintenance is needed, but even this can help to keep the car's performance at its best, and so avoid major mechanical trouble.

The motorist who wants still more information from the instrument panel about the condition of his car has a wide choice of extra instruments. They include:

An oil-temperature gauge. This can give warning that the engine is overheating. An abnormal temperature rise indicated on the gauge is a danger signal.

A vacuum gauge. This is connected to the inlet manifold and can indicate causes of high consumption and erratic running.

A voltmeter shows the state of the battery charge when the ignition is on.

A tachometer shows how fast the engine is revving, and gives the maximum performance available in each gear.

A brake performance meter will show braking and acceleration figures.

An altimeter will show height above sea level by air pressure variation.

A compass can be useful when driving in a strange part of the country.

A 'speed' pilot is an instrument which correlates an odometer (see p. 150) and a time clock to give a continuous indication of average speed, but it is not easy to fit and calibrate.

An oil-level indicator, which is operated by a push-button on the instrument panel, can be fitted to the sump.

1 Select and mark position for the instrument panel, such as underside of fascia

2 Drill fixing holes for the panel, ensuring that rear of the fascia is unobstructed

3 Fix the panel's metal frame in position using the nuts, bolts and washers provided

4 Position plastic facing and secure instruments in holes with brackets provided

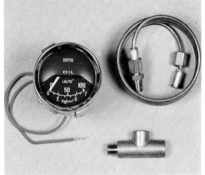

Supplementary instrument panel Metal frame has a plastic facing (top)

Oil-pressure gauge Pipeline (right), T-piece link, gauge and red (lighting) wire

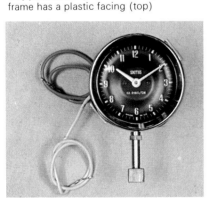

Electric car clock The red wire supplies the lighting, and the yellow wire the power

Ammeter Red wire supplies lighting, and black wire provides link to regulator box

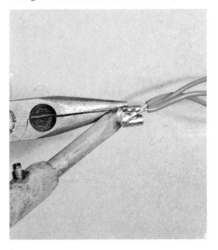

5 Solder red lighting supply wires from all three instruments to common connector

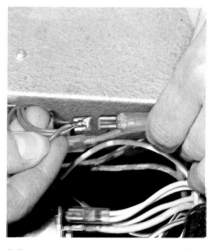

6 Take common connector and link into existing instrument lighting circuit

Oil-pressure gauge

ACCURATE registration of variations in oil pressure can provide clues to many actual and potential engine troubles which would not be revealed by a warning light.

Low pressure could indicate insufficient oil in the sump, worn bearings or a blockage in the lubrication system

High pressure can be caused by a faulty pressure-release valve, or by thick, cold oil circulating through the engine, in which case high engine revs should be avoided until the oil has heated up and can circulate more freely.

In fitting an oil-pressure gauge it is worth retaining the oil warning light which can catch the driver's attention should the pressure drop when he may have missed a change on the gauge.

1 Locate the oil-pressure warning light switch on the engine, and remove it

2 Screw T-piece into the engine casing in place of the warning light switch

3 Connect the oil-pressure warning light switch to one branch of the T-piece

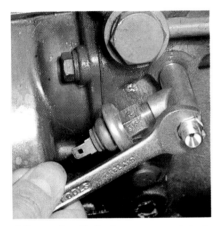

4 Screw the oil pipeline connector into the remaining T-piece connection

5 Fit the pipeline into connector using the end of pipe with the coned union

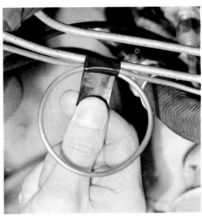

6 Coil pipeline to take up engine vibration. Connect other end of pipe to gauge

Electric clock

Clock It is essential to buy a clock that matches the car's polarity. Connect the clock supply wire to a live circuit which is independent of the ignition switch

Ammeter

ANOTHER useful instrument which is usually replaced by a warning light is an ammeter. This reveals the condition of the battery and the car's charging system.

By giving a negative reading when the engine is running above idling speed, the ammeter will indicate either an electrical fault or an excessive load on the system. The sequence shown (right) is for a car with a dynamo. For one with an alternator, connect the ammeter to the solenoid.

There are two points to watch when fitting an ammeter: always disconnect the main battery lead until installation is complete; and secondly, check the installation when the work is finished by switching on the headlights. This should produce a negative reading: if it shows positive, disconnect the battery and reverse the wires on the ammeter terminals. Use only the correct grade of wire (see p. 228).

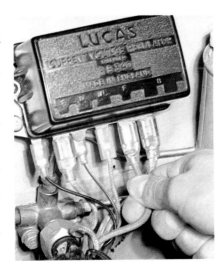

1 Disconnect the main power feed cable from the voltage regulator box

2 Connect one black wire from ammeter to power feed terminal on the regulator

3 Solder the other black wire to the wire removed from the control box

In-car entertainment/fitting and tuning a receiver

Choosing a set

FEW BRITISH, or Continental, cars have a radio fitted as a standard. Most, however, have a space in the fascia panel to enable the owner to fit equipment of his own choice.

In-car entertainment equipment is available in many packages. The basic building blocks are a AM radio—long, medium and short wave; FM radio—mono or stereo; cassette tape player—mono or stereo; and cartridge tape players—mono, stereo or quadraphonic. Some equipment combines certain of these features in a single unit. For example, a combined radio/cassette player or a combined radio/cartridge player. All require 12 volt D.C. current and all can be wired into the car's electrical system.

Prices covering the range from a simple radio with a single speaker and an aerial to a sophisticated high-quality combined stereo unit vary.

Many imported are now available but before buying one, make sure that the dealer has adequate servicing facilities. It is often difficult to get repairs carried out on some of the cheaper sets, and suitable spares may not always be available.

Installation kits to suit a particular model of car are also obtainable. Always ensure before buying that the equipment can be fitted to your car. They vary in depth from 4 in. to $7\frac{1}{2}$ in. and not all vehicle manufacturers leave enough space in the fascia for the deeper models. Single speakers can usually go in the space made available by the car manufacturers. Twin speakers can be door-mounted or positioned on the rear parcel shelf.

The radio manufacturer's leaflet and the instructions with the installation kit will give the order in which fitting should be carried out.

Most cars carry a label or mark near the battery stating whether they are negative or positive earthed. Some sets are self-adjusting and select the correct polarity automatically. But the polarity of most has to be changed from positive to negative and vice versa by a switch on the back of the receiver unit. On these sets, check that the polarity is correct.

Always fit a 5 amp line fuse (see p. 226) in the power lead from the set and connect the lead to the accessory terminal of the fusebox or to the ignition switch. This ensures that the set is switched off when the ignition key is removed. Consult the car handbook for the exact position of these terminals.

Many garages now employ skilled audio fitters who do only installation work. Prices vary considerably; always ask for an estimate for the work first.

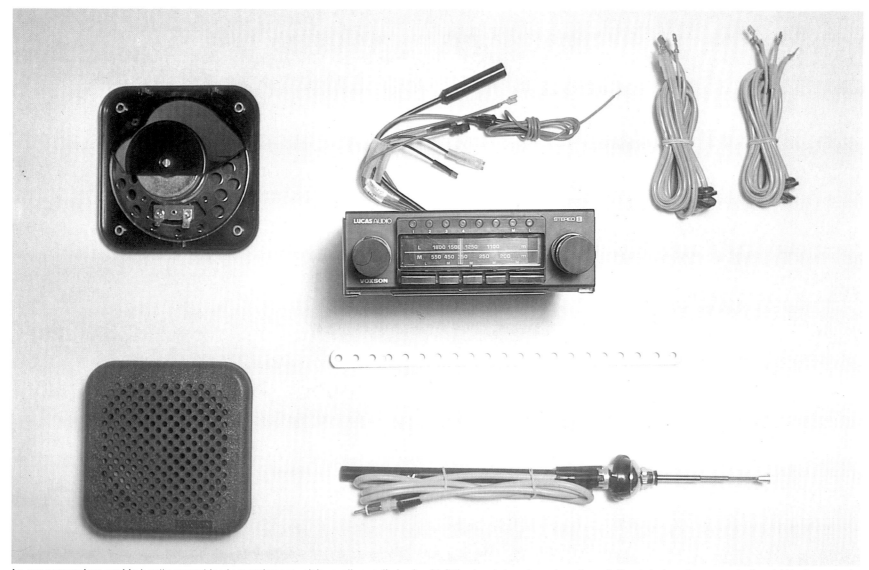

In-car entertainment kit A radio or combined entertainment unit is usually supplied only with fitting brackets and speakers: the aerial has to be bought separately. Special kits for particular car models, however, include all necessary parts. Suppressors for the car's electrical equipment (see p. 300) are sometimes supplied with a fitting kit. If not, buy them separately.

Fitting the speakers

SPEAKERS IN the fascia, on the rear parcel shelf, in the doors or above window level give the best results. A horizontal position, under the shelf or beneath the seats, gives a muffled quality.

All stereo receivers are supplied with two speakers, for door or rear-shelf mounting. To obtain better sound distribution and performance it is possible, even on mono sets, to fit a second speaker.

Single speaker

When mounting a single speaker, be sure that the speaker cone does not contact any part of the bodywork and that the speaker chassis is firmly fitted but is not in direct contact with the metal mounting panel. An insulated cork gasket is supplied with the speaker to eliminate vibrations set up when the speaker is working. Stereo speakers come ready mounted and insulated, either in pods designed to sit on the rear parcel shelf or as self-contained units complete with fascia grille for mounting in the doors.

Two stereo speakers

If two speakers are being installed with a mono set, their wires can be connected together into the output of the radio or taken through a 'balance control'. This will enable the volume from each speaker to be varied to suit listening conditions. The connections to the speaker must be secure.

Never switch on the set unless the speaker is connected, otherwise the output transistors may be damaged.

1 Twin speaker installation kits have paper templates to enable you to cut-out the door trim panel to the correct size. Cut out the templates

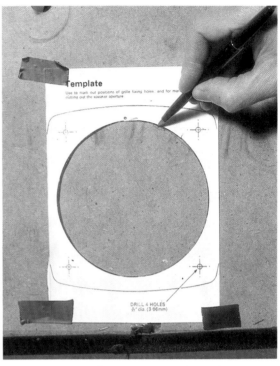

2 Carefully prise off and remove the door trim; place the template in position on the inner door skin. Mark and cut-out the opening

3 Drill and mark the four holes for the speaker-mounting screws. Fit the four spire clips over the holes. Make sure they grip firmly

4 Mark and drill the holes in the door frame and pillar through which the speaker cables must pass. Fit rubber grommets and feed the cables through into the doors

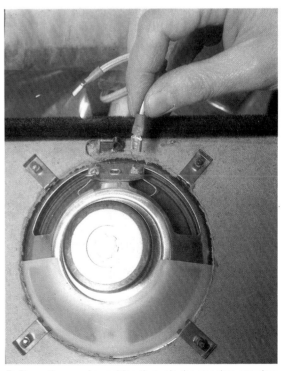

5 Draw the speaker cables through the speaker opening of the inner door skin. Connect the cables to the speaker terminals making sure they are pushed well on

Fitting an aerial

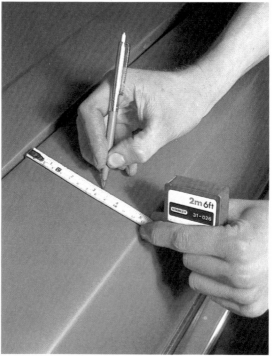

1 Carefully measure and mark the aerial's position on the car bodywork. An installation kit for the car will give the measurements and recommended position

2 Scribe and centre-punch the correct position and stick masking tape around it to ensure that the drill bit does not slip. Drill a pilot hole, then enlarge it

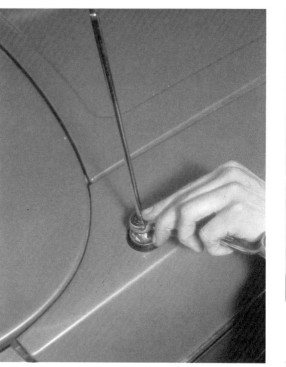

3 Smooth the edges with a file and pass the aerial through the hole. Fit the washers in their correct order, raise the aerial and tighten the securing nut

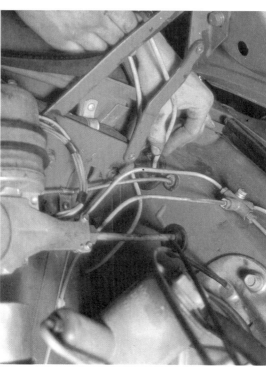

4 Drill a hole in the inside wing, fit a grommet and pass the aerial lead through. Pass the lead through a grommet in the bulkhead to the inside of the car

Fitting the receiver

1 Remove the ash tray. Undo the four screws securing the trim panel and remove it. Make sure the aerial lead is at the back of the panel

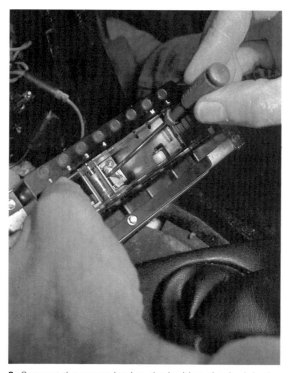

2 Connect the power lead to the ignition circuit. Join the speaker leads to the set. Raise the aerial, switch on and trim the set

Wavebands

BROADCASTING of domestic radio programmes in Britain was originally limited to only the Long and Medium wavebands.

But the crowded conditions of the Medium waveband—especially at night—helped to bring about the introduction of VHF (Very High Frequency) transmissions, which the majority of car radios are now able to receive in addition to the Long and Medium wavebands.

VHF gives a high-quality reception and is free of interference from other stations, but the range of transmission is limited. Because of this, VHF requires a number of stations—each broadcasting on a different wavelength—to cover a large area; and when travelling across country the radio needs re-tuning fairly frequently. It is intended that eventually all the local commercial radio stations will have a common frequency so that the motorist can move from area to area listening to one station after another without having constantly to change frequency. That stage has not yet been reached.

Weather reports and police and traffic information, broadcast on VHF by local and national BBC radio stations, can be of considerable value to the motorist.

Trimming the receiver

MOST CAR RADIOS have an aerial trimmer, which matches the input of the aerial to the circuits in the radio set, and can be adjusted by a screw to give the best reception.

On some modern sets this screw is behind the tuning knob and is reached with a small screwdriver after the knob has been removed. In this case the trimming can be done when the set has been installed. If, however, the adjustment is made through a hole in the body, at the side or rear of the set, trimming will have to be carried out before the fixing is completed.

To trim the aerial, switch on the set and turn the tuning knob to a weak station—in the 200-metre region on the end of the band, with the aerial fully extended, turn the aerial trimming screw until the best possible reception is received on that station. The best possible reception will then be obtained on all other wavebands.

Requirements of the law

A CAR AERIAL must not be fitted in such a way that it constitutes a danger to other road users, and cars must be fitted with suppressors to prevent ignition interference affecting nearby TV and radio reception.

It is permissible to listen to taxi, police and other private messages but illegal to act on, record or pass on any information heard.

Anyone playing a radio, tape or disc loudly in a stationary car could be regarded as a nuisance and prosecuted. Some councils have by-laws prohibiting radios being played in public places, and this includes a car radio if it can be heard outside the car. A car transmitter cannot be operated in a car without a Ministry of Posts and Telecommunications licence, and the issue of these is strictly controlled; but a receiving licence is no longer required for a car radio.

3 Slide the receiver into position. Some sets have slide support brackets, others a single rear support. Make sure the receiver unit is centrally located

4 Tighten up the support brackets and, if one is supplied, fit the front retaining plate in position. Refit the walnut fascia plate. Replace the four fascia retaining screws

5 Fit the receiver face-plate in position. This fits over the control knobs in front of the fascia panel, providing a finished appearance to the installation

6 Replace the nuts that secure the face of the receiver. Do not over-tighten these nuts or they will damage the surface of the receiver face-plate

Radio/reducing interference

Improving reception

ALL CARS built after July 1, 1953 have suppressors built into them as a legal requirement, to prevent interference to nearby television reception. But these suppressors do not prevent many of the types of interference picked up by the car's radio.

This interference is caused by pulses radiated at certain frequencies in the radio band. These can be picked up by the car aerial or the wiring of the receiver, and emerge as a crackling noise at the speaker.

The wiring of the car will also pick up interference pulses caused by the ignition, electric petrol pumps, windscreen-wiper motors, dynamo and even an electric clock.

The dynamo and the ignition system are the main causes of interference, and fitting suppressors to them will often cure it.

Static electricity A further form of interference can be caused by static electricity building up on tyres, wheels or brakes. When this discharges across the wheel bearings or brake components, sharp crackles are heard at the speaker. This can be cured by an expert.

Normally, the metal panels and bodywork of a car act as a screen between the ignition system and the aerial. But with the increasing use of plastic materials in body construction, suppression becomes more difficult. Glass-fibre bodies may require additional screening besides the standard suppression equipment.

This is achieved by covering the underside of the bonnet and engine compartment with metal foil (or an electro-conductive graphite paint) earthed to the metal chassis. Alternatively, metal screening plates bolted to the engine may be fitted over the plugs, plug leads and coil to suppress radio interference.

An interference-free radio in a car with a glass-fibre body is difficult to achieve; but experience gained by professional radio-fitting firms enables them to do the work with reasonable success.

In cases where interference persists despite the installation of several suppressors, consult the manufacturer of the set for professional advice.

Suppressing the coil and the dynamo

1 A common mounting for a coil suppressor is on the fixing bolt. Remove the nut and clean the contact area beneath it thoroughly to make a good earth connection

2 If the coil is mounted on the dynamo (as shown here) both suppressors can be earthed at the same point. Use a flat washer over the elongated slot of the suppressors

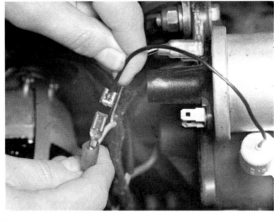

3 Most modern suppressors are equipped with a terminal tag suited to the standard Lucar connector. Fit this tightly over the connector attached to the coil power supply lead

4 Before remaking the connection, slip the protective sleeve back over the terminal tag. Fit the dynamo suppressor tag to the larger terminal on the back of the dynamo

Fuel-pump suppressors

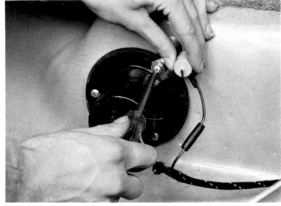

1 Electric petrol pumps can often cause radio interference. To cure it, connect a suppressor to the live lead and earth it to the pump or car body

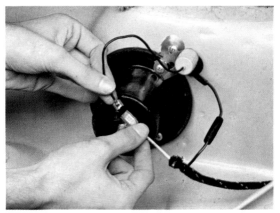

2 Remove the lead which supplies power to the petrol pump and fit the suppressor lead to it. Refit the lead to the pump. Connections should be clean and in good condition

Suppressing an HT lead

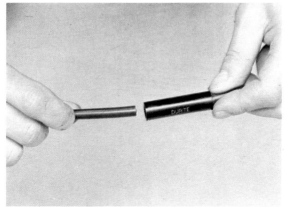

High-tension leads On cars not fitted with suppressed high-tension leads or caps, insert individual line suppressors in each HT lead as close to the spark plug as possible

THE COST OF MOTORING

When the horse was Man's principal means of transport, everyone who could afford one knew something about horse-trading. There was no question of buying a child's pony or a Suffolk Punch without a careful examination of its condition and a shrewd assessment of what it would cost to keep. The principles of buying a car and the principles of horse-trading are almost the same, and the car-buyer who applies them will get the same satisfaction as his great-grandfather did when he bought a well-bred hack, sound in wind and limb

CONTENTS

The cost of motoring/buying a used car

What you are buying—and what you should look at

EACH YEAR, more than 2½ million people in Britain buy used cars—twice as many as buy new cars. For most, it is their introduction to the pleasures of motoring; for others it is a sharp lesson in some of its pitfalls. Which one of these it is depends largely on the extent of the buyer's knowledge and common sense.

Firstly, what is being bought in a used car is the life left in that car. A three-year-old car should be regarded not as a new car with three years' wear, but as a car that is likely to be on the scrap heap in three to six years' time.

Secondly, there are few bargains in used cars. Dealers, and even private sellers, know what their stock is worth. If a car is offered at substantially below the ruling market rate, there is probably something wrong with it.

Thirdly, the cost of running a used car is greater than that of running a new car. Standing charges (see p. 314) may be slightly less because less capital is tied up in the car, but this saving will be very much less than the extra cost of servicing, repairs or replacement parts.

Depreciation

Depreciation is often considered to be the difference between the value of a car after a period and the price originally paid for it. But this definition can be unrealistic when new car prices are increasing markedly.

In any financial assessment, the present cost of the item is most important; thus depreciation can also be calculated as the difference between what the owner would be paid for the car on trade-in and the cost of buying a similar new car at that time. This is a very different proposition.

You may, for example, be able to sell your car a year after you buy it for the same price that you paid, but if a new replacement car costs 15 per cent more, the effect on your bank balance is as if your car was worth 15 per cent less. That is in addition to 'loss of interest on capital' (see p. 314).

So you cannot escape the cost of depreciation by buying a new car even though its 'value' may remain more stable. Rising new car prices are reflected in higher second-hand prices, but the actual percentage rate of capital cost is still likely to be less on a used car than on a new one.

But remember the special cases: a 'prestige' car—for example, a Jaguar or Daimler—may depreciate to an affordable second-hand price, but the new parts needed to repair and maintain it will not follow suit!

Crash damage Look along each side of the car for poor repair work. Centre the steering wheel. If there is any suspicion that the wheels are out of alignment, ask a dealer to check thoroughly.

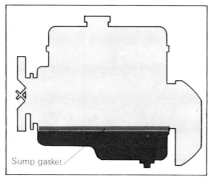

Oil leaks Insist on a 15-minute test drive, then stand the car on a clean surface. Severe oil drops indicate that a costly repair may be needed; but the cost of curing minute oil leaks far exceeds the cost of the oil lost. Slight traces are normal, but watch for excess oil which may be hidden under accumulated dirt

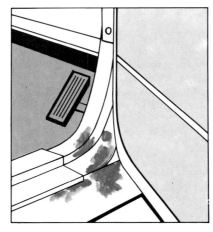

Rust Examine the sides and bottoms of the doors, the body sills below the doors, and the front and rear wing joints and surface areas for rust. Some superficial rust, particularly on chrome, can be expected in older cars, but extensive rusting is costly to repair

Suspension dampers Press down hard on each wing of the car and let go—it should go up and down again and then return to the static position. Continuous bouncing indicates faulty suspension dampers

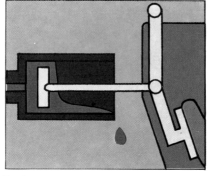

Brakes Try the brake pedal to see how far it travels before it operates the brakes. Excessive travel indicates that the brakes need adjustment. The brake pedal should feel firm when it is pressed down to put the brakes full on, but the actual condition of the system cannot be assessed without dismantling

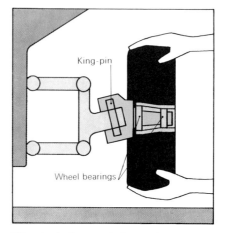

Wheels Jack up each front wheel in turn. Grasp it at the top and bottom and move it firmly backwards and forwards. More than $\frac{1}{16}$ in. movement may indicate worn bearings, king-pins or swivel-pins. Spin each wheel and look for abnormal tyre wear

Clutch Make sure that it engages smoothly and does not grab. If, on a test drive, engine revolutions rise without a corresponding increase in the car's speed, the clutch is slipping

Tyres Each tyre must have not less than 1 mm. of tread around the full circumference and across three-quarters of the breadth. Watch for incorrect mixtures of cross-ply and radial tyres. Uneven wear is a sign of mechanical defects or harsh use

Cooling system Check for leaks, preferably when the engine is cold, by looking for any sign of dirty red or blue-green anti-freeze stains. Check the condition of the hoses and suspect any that are extremely hard or soft

Switches and accessories Make sure that the indicators, windscreen wipers, dip-switch, interior light, heater, horn, windscreen washer and all other accessories are in good working order

Mileage recorder (odometer) Most cars cover about 10,000 miles a year. On this basis, and the age of a car, an estimate can be made of how much a car has been used

Bonnet safety catch Make sure it is operating properly—a faulty catch may cause the bonnet to fly open while you are driving, obscuring your view and possibly causing a serious accident

Lights Check reflector chrome for any indications of rust or flaking

Chrome Inspect chrome for pitting. Rusted chrome can be brightened with one of the patent chrome cleaners, but this does not restore the original plating

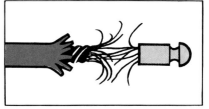

Wiring Look out for cracked, corroded or frayed wires, which can cause electrical failures. Loose or neglected wiring may rub on other parts and wear through

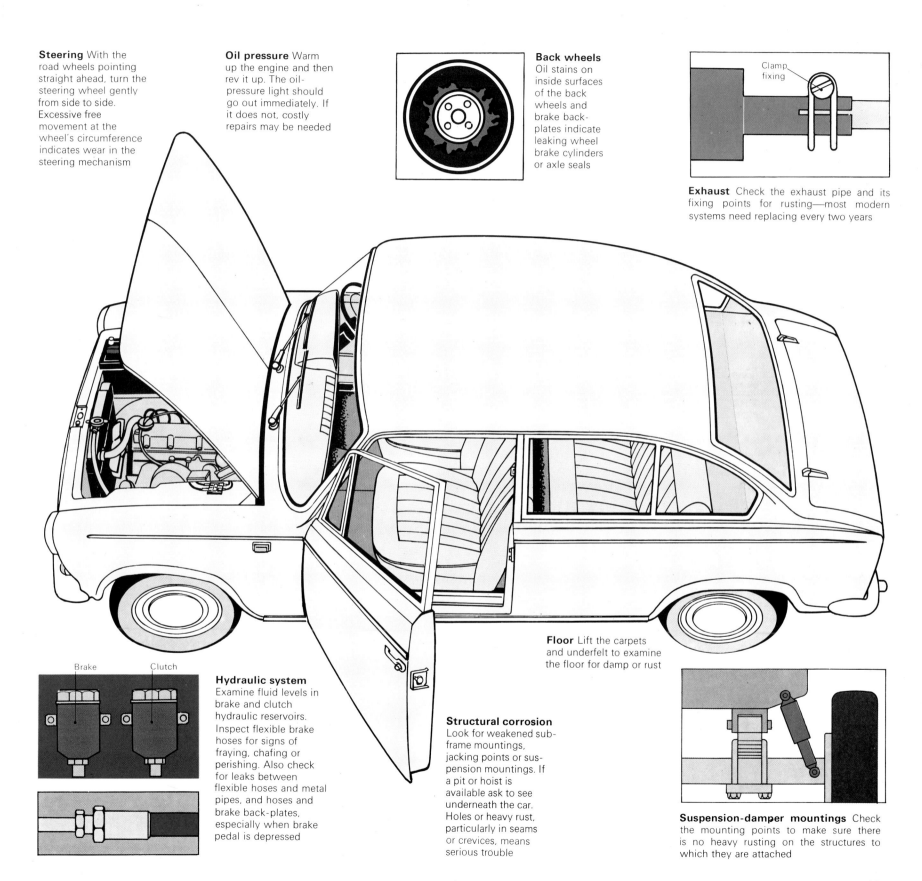

Steering With the road wheels pointing straight ahead, turn the steering wheel gently from side to side. Excessive free movement at the wheel's circumference indicates wear in the steering mechanism

Oil pressure Warm up the engine and then rev it up. The oil-pressure light should go out immediately. If it does not, costly repairs may be needed

Back wheels Oil stains on inside surfaces of the back wheels and brake back-plates indicate leaking wheel brake cylinders or axle seals

Clamp fixing

Exhaust Check the exhaust pipe and its fixing points for rusting—most modern systems need replacing every two years

Brake   Clutch

Hydraulic system Examine fluid levels in brake and clutch hydraulic reservoirs. Inspect flexible brake hoses for signs of fraying, chafing or perishing. Also check for leaks between flexible hoses and metal pipes, and hoses and brake back-plates, especially when brake pedal is depressed

Structural corrosion Look for weakened sub-frame mountings, jacking points or suspension mountings. If a pit or hoist is available ask to see underneath the car. Holes or heavy rust, particularly in seams or crevices, means serious trouble

Floor Lift the carpets and underfelt to examine the floor for damp or rust

Suspension-damper mountings Check the mounting points to make sure there is no heavy rusting on the structures to which they are attached

The cost of motoring/finding the right used car

When and where to buy

MANY USED CARS have far more internal and external accessories—fog lamps, spot-lights, radios, cigarette lighters and so on—than they had when they were new. Accessories that are decorative rather than functional may indicate that a previous owner was more interested in outward show than reliability.

Provided the accessories are useful, and work, they are worth having; but the important thing is to make sure that the car itself is sound. Be wary of sellers who try to inflate the price of a car because it is festooned with nick-nacks. The advertised or displayed price of a used private car should include VAT. On a commercial vehicle it may be shown separately, but it must be clear.

When to buy

Many new-car buyers want to part-exchange their existing vehicle in the spring, before the start of the motoring season. For that reason there is usually a good choice of used cars available. But because other motorists wait until August—so that they can get a car with the coming year's registration letter—and because few dealers want to maintain a large stock of cars over the winter, from autumn to Christmas is generally the cheapest time to buy a used car.

Where to buy

There are six sources from which second-hand cars can be purchased: franchised dealers; used-car firms; private car own-ers, and retail dealers; garages and auctions.

Franchised dealers

An increasing number of used cars are sold by franchised dealers.

Most franchised dealers have the facilities that enable them to inspect the used cars they buy and to undertake the necessary repairs; but this is not necessarily so of firms specialising primarily in used-car sales and certainly does not apply to private sellers. Dealers often have fleet cars for sale—cars formerly owned by a company or by a hire-car firm. These vehicles will almost inevitably have covered a considerable number of miles.

Hire cars will generally have been driven by a number of drivers, but may have been very well maintained. Company cars have usually been driven by one person and may be the better buy. Before buying any fleet car take the precaution of having a witness and ask the seller whether it has been a one-driver car.

Used-car firms

It is a criminal offence for anyone to try to sell a car which is unroadworthy or to falsify his description of a car he wants to sell. But this gives little protection to the buyer, unless he takes action through the courts. Get a written guarantee.

Roadworthiness in fact cannot be taken as a guarantee that the car will survive any more than a short test drive. Even if a test certificate has just been issued (under the scheme controlled by the Department of Transport), the buyer may not assume that the car is now in good condition.

A buyer should also be aware of his own legal responsibilities. If he buys a car which is found to be unroadworthy—for example, if it has jagged bodywork which could injure other road users—he must correct the faults before using it.

Private sellers and retail dealers

Buying privately means placing a high degree of trust in the integrity of someone you have never met before and may never meet again. If the buyer is subsequently dissatisfied, and the seller refuses to do anything about it, then the buyer must have recourse to the law, where the chances of recovering any costs incurred are limited.

The man who buys from an established dealer can seek satisfaction from a company with a reputation at stake. Private sellers do not usually offer easy financial terms or warranties. Small dealers sometimes also trade as private persons.

Garages

Those garages that have joined the AA graded garage scheme (see p. 326) have adopted a code of practice that normally includes guaranteeing cars less than three years old or with less than 30,000 miles' use for three months or 3000 miles, whichever comes first. AA graded garages are identified by one, two or three spanner symbols displayed in their forecourts. Some of them offer cars that have been inspected by AA engineers.

Auctions

Car auctions began soon after the First World War, but only began to attract widespread interest after the Second World War. There are now dozens each week throughout the country and as many as 1200 cars may be sold in a day. Each transaction takes about a minute-and-a-half and most buyers are in the trade.

Inevitably, some of these cars have been taken in part-exchange by dealers, and are below the minimum standard that they are prepared to handle. The dealers, considering it uneconomic or undesirable to spend money refurbishing the cars, pass them on to the auctions.

Sellers either sign a form describing the car's mechanical condition or have the car tested by a resident mechanic. If it is not as described, a buyer must return it promptly and may, subject to certain conditions, get his money back. Major auction firms refund the purchase price if a stolen car or a car under a hire-purchase agreement is sold.

Cars cannot usually be test-driven at auctions, no warranty is offered, and it is not wise to bid unless you have mechanical knowledge. Attending a few auctions before bidding will give a clear idea of cars and prices.

Estate cars and convertibles

THE FIRST thing to find out about a used estate car is whether it has carried heavy loads for most of the time—or whether it has been only a family car. A good indication is the price: a vehicle which has been used commercially should be priced accordingly, and it may be sold on the second-hand market for at least £100 less than a similar family model.

Dents in the tailgate and indentations or heavy scratches round the lower edges of the tailgate's rubber weather-sealing indicate that heavy loads may have been carried in the car. The same deduction can be made if the fold-down rear seat is fractured at the sides.

Scratches, stretch marks or tears in the roof lining are another indication that unusual loads have been carried. Estate cars are designed to take such loads, but they place extra strain on the engine, clutch, suspension dampers, suspension and brakes and cause extra wear. For that reason the car which has been used for family outings only is usually better.

Convertibles

All the special points to look for in a convertible concern the hood. First, look for cracks in the hood fabric where the metal supports hold it. Then check all the body studs, which are used for clipping the hood down, to make sure they function.

Never take it for granted that the hood will fit the studs—try it before buying. At the same time examine the hood round the studs for wear and tear.

Check carefully, when the hood is raised, for signs of rust and water stains. Make sure that the rear window is not opaque. On the road, listen for squeaks or odd noises from the roof. If the hood needs replacing, ask the seller to make allowance for this. A hood costs £30 upwards, depending on the size of the car, and is liable to VAT. A new hood can be obtained from the car's manufacturer or from a specialist trimmer.

Automatic cars

Two identical cars, one with manual gears and the other with automatic transmission, may fetch exactly the same price in the used-car showroom because automatics depreciate more quickly. But the automatic could be the better buy.

In the course of covering 80,000 miles, the average manually geared family saloon will require one reconditioned engine, about three clutches, three sets of tyres, two or three sets of steering joints, three or four sets of brake linings, a replacement radiator and possibly a replacement gearbox and back axle.

The car with automatic transmission will need neither the clutches nor the gearbox. More important, automatic transmission helps to ensure that a driver treats the car's engine properly.

Petrol consumption on automatic transmission may be as much as 10 per cent higher than on a comparable car with manual gears, but this can be partially compensated for by good driving (see pp. 353–84).

Foreign cars

The larger or more uncommon foreign cars tend to depreciate more rapidly than comparable British cars, and spare parts can be expensive and difficult to obtain. It is advisable, therefore, to buy from an accredited dealer in your own district.

Test the windscreen wipers. Even on the export versions of some foreign cars, they are still set for the left-hand-drive market and fail to clear the screen completely for a driver sitting on the right.

Wise buying and selling

Costs and guarantees

BECAUSE OF fluctuations in supply and demand, used-car prices can vary considerably throughout Britain for similar models in similar condition.

Never accept a dealer's asking price as one from which he will not budge. Detailed inspection of the car may well reveal flaws that can be used as bargaining points. Beware of high prices in spring, when some dealers work on the principle that there is no harm in asking a higher price than a car is worth, because someone may turn up prepared to pay it.

As a general principle, set aside 10–15 per cent of the amount you can afford to pay for a used car three to five years old. If you have bought wisely, that amount should be enough to get the car into a reasonable condition; but the cost of refurbishing and repairs can be heavy, even if a detailed inspection has revealed what needs to be done. And remember that a bad car can never be made into a good car.

Guarantees with used cars

Franchised dealers and reputable garages —including those in the AA's grading scheme—give written warranties under which defects may be put right. Neverthe-less, four points are worth watching when assessing a used-car guarantee:

1 Some so-called guarantees actually guarantee nothing. They merely undertake to 'consider' claims, and to repair defects at the dealer's discretion.

2 Most guarantees are for three months or 3000 miles, whichever expires first. Anything less is of limited worth.

3 Some dealers go no further than agreeing to supply new parts. A guarantee which covers labour as well is better.

4 Many guarantees stipulate that defects will be repaired only at the selling dealer's premises. They make the customer responsible for the cost of getting the car to the dealer.

The motorist who is buying from a dealer some way from his home, or who expects to move during the guarantee period, should try to get the dealer to nominate in advance another garage at which any work can be done.

An agreement along these lines should be made in writing—a letter from the dealer is adequate—*before* the customer agrees to buy the car. Otherwise, suggest a reduction in the price in consideration of your waiving the warranty. If you are in doubt about the terms, consult a solicitor.

Preparations for selling

A USED CAR may be sold or offered in part exchange for another car for several reasons: because its owner wants a bigger, better or different vehicle; because it is becoming uneconomical to run; or because the owner needs cash.

There is a large second-hand car market, and top prices are paid only for cars that are in short supply or in exceptional condition, both mechanically and bodily.

When to sell

If cash is required immediately, or a bargain must be snapped up, a seller cannot wait for the best time of the year for selling, which is normally spring. With the approach of better weather, people who in winter were not interested in owning a car often decide to buy one.

The Motor Show in October often gives a fillip to the used car trade. Concentrated publicity about cars and car buying for a month or so before the show revives the interest of motorists wanting both new and used cars.

Any relaxation, or even rumours of a relaxation, of credit restrictions is another cue to the seller. The threat of a tough Budget has in the past been sufficient to send car buyers flocking to the showrooms. But large or expensive cars can prove hard to sell all the year round.

How to sell

The way in which the car is sold depends largely on whether another car (either new or used) is going to be bought. Better prices are usually obtained when part exchanging for a new car.

A dealer taking a car in part exchange for either a new or used car may appear to be offering a good price for the car he is asked to accept; but he will take that price into account when the selling price of the car being bought is fixed.

The most significant figure in such a situation is the difference between the two prices—the amount of money that has to be found to complete the deal.

In any case, a dealer will want to make a profit on reselling your car and will expect to cover the expense of any work that may have to be done to prepare it for sale. For that reason the seller may sometimes be better off financially if he can find a private buyer.

Auctions

If a car cannot be sold in any other way, it can be put in an auction, with a reserve price. Auctions are advertised in local newspapers and motoring magazines.

Sellers sign a form describing the vehicle's mechanical condition in general terms. An entry fee of up to £5 may be charged, and the auctioneer's commission will be 5–10 per cent with a minimum of £10. Some firms have a reducing rate and a maximum. Sellers can set a reserve price below which the car will not be sold, but it must be borne in mind that most cars are bought by the trade at a relatively low figure.

Garages

A number of garages and used-car dealers are often loath to buy used cars if no part exchange is involved. Their reasons are that they do not want too much money tied up in stock, they lack space, the particular model is difficult for them to sell or the car is too old.

Always obtain quotations from as many garages as possible; their offers can vary substantially.

A dealer already holding a large stock of the type of car you want to sell will not pay as much as another who knows he will easily be able to find a customer for your car. As a rule, agents for imported cars will offer higher prices for second-hand foreign cars.

Private sale

Advertisements can be placed in shop windows, newspapers and motoring magazines. If the car is parked in a busy street, it may be worth while putting a 'For Sale' notice in one of its windows. Advertisements must be truthful: even a private individual can be prosecuted for false descriptions if he makes a habit of selling cars.

Preparing the car

The better the car is prepared for sale, the better the price it will fetch. One of the best selling points is cleanness. This means attending not only to the outside of the car, but to the inside and the engine compartment and boot as well. Rubber mats, carpets and underfelt should be removed, and the floor should be cleaned, dried and if necessary repainted. Upholstery should be cleaned and the interior tidied up.

Attend to small rusty or damaged areas and if minor repairs are needed have them done: the better the car's condition, the more impressed potential buyers will be.

Documentation

If a car is on ground to which the public has access it must be properly taxed and insured, and must conform to regulations on brakes, lights, tyres, steering and so on. Cars over three years of age must have a DoT certificate.

It may not be worth trying to recover any outstanding portion of the Road Fund Licence. Even if there is almost a full year's tax to run, recovering it means that the car must be taken off the road so that a prospective buyer cannot test drive it unless he taxes it himself. But the unexpired tax should enhance the price.

Selling price

Advertisements in newspapers and motoring magazines give a guide to prices being asked for cars. So does visiting three or four dealers and checking the prices at which they are selling models identical to your car and in similar condition.

Safeguards

Cash sales are straightforward, but a seller accepting a cheque from a private purchaser should not hand over the car until the cheque has been cleared. If the buyer does not agree to this, the seller can refuse to sell. Alternatively, ask the buyer for a bank draft.

Finally, the buyer should sign a receipt stating that he accepts the car as seen, tried and approved.

A private seller can rarely be held liable for any defects which occur after a car has been sold, but he must not mislead a potential buyer. If he does and persuades someone to buy, he may be sued in the civil courts under the Misrepresentation Act 1967, or, if in trade, be liable to prosecution under the Trade Descriptions Act.

Nor must he sell a vehicle that is to be used on a public highway if he knows it is in a dangerous condition. He can be prosecuted and sued.

If the car being sold is subject to a hire-purchase agreement, the finance company's permission to sell it must be obtained by the vendor.

It is important for the buyer to inform the licensing authorities immediately he takes possession of the car.

The cost of motoring/inspecting a used car

Checks that save time and trouble

THE BEST WAY to assess the condition of a used car is to have it inspected by one of the motoring organisations. The AA inspection, for which a fee is charged, includes a road test, and an AA engineer assesses specified parts of the car on a scale ranging from 'satisfactory' to 'dangerous'. It is as comprehensive as possible without dismantling.

There is, however, no point in calling for an AA inspection until a car has been found that seems sound and suitable.

The Vehicle Registration Document (which has replaced the 'log book') should contain the engine and chassis numbers and the number of 'keepers' the car has had since the date specified in the document. The vehicle and engine numbers should be checked against those on the car (some cars have a single number). Beware if there is any discrepancy or if the numbers stamped on the car's engine and chassis seem to have been tampered with—the car may have been stolen.

One possible safeguard against buying a car which is subject to a hire purchase agreement is to ask the person who is selling it for a *written* statement that the car is free of such an agreement.

Cars more than three years old must have Department of Transport test certificates. Remember that the test is limited and is not a guarantee that the car is fit for thousands of trouble-free miles.

Having established that the car is properly documented, the next task is to make a careful inspection of its interior and exterior condition.

A sagging driving seat may indicate that the car has been used commercially, whereas equal wear on all seats suggests that it has been used by a family. Worn carpets and pedal rubbers will normally be matched by a high reading on the mileage recorder.

The following checks can be made by a motorist who has no specialised mechanical knowledge.

Mileage recorder
The average mileage for a car used in Britain is 11,000 miles a year, so the mileage recorder, read in conjunction with the log book, usually gives a good indication of how the car has been used. But bear in mind that a car that has done four 2-mile journeys a day may well have suffered more than one that has done five 100-mile journeys a week.

Some dealers replace the car speedometer before selling, and although this is not usually an offence under the Trade Descriptions Act, it is at least a warning to the buyer to think again before buying: if possible, check with the last-named owner of the car to get an estimate of what the mileage might be.

Switches and accessories
Check that indicators, windscreen wipers, dip-switch, interior light, heater, windscreen washer, horn and any other accessories are in good working order.

Lights
Make sure they all work, and that the reflector chrome is not rusty or flaking.

Suspension dampers
Press down hard on each wing of the car in turn and let go. The wing should rise beyond its original position and then sink down again to where it started. If it continues to bounce, emits a clonking noise or shows oil leaks from the dampers, be prepared to have to get replacements.

Carpets
Lift the carpets and underfelt and examine the floor for rust. Beware the car with wet underfelt.

Door catches and hinges
Check that all doors close properly without any up-or-down movement and that they can be locked. Test all the window winders for easy operation.

Crash damage
Look along each side of the car's body for any ripples caused by an impact. Properly repaired damage need not be a barrier to purchase, but it is advisable to know the full circumstances and extent of any damage that has been mended.

Chrome
Look carefully at the chromed parts. Pitting or blistering of the surface cannot be removed permanently without replating—an expensive process.

Bonnet safety-catch
Check that it is operating properly—a faulty catch may cause the bonnet to fly open while the car is in motion. This could be extremely dangerous in the case of a rear-hinged bonnet.

Engine
If the unit, when warm, ticks over evenly, accelerates smoothly, does not generate undue or specific noises and does not emit blue or black smoke from the exhaust when idling or accelerating, it is probably in reasonable condition.

Battery
See that the battery is clean. If the sides and top show signs of swelling, the battery will soon have to be replaced.

Wiring
Look for cracked, taped or frayed wires which may cause short-circuits or fires.

Exhaust system
Check for rust, but bear in mind that many exhaust systems last approximately only two years.

Cooling system
Leaks may be indicated by dirty red or blue-green antifreeze stains, and the best time to check is when the engine is cold. Check the hoses for external damage, and remember that an extremely hard or soft hose is suspect.

Oil pressure
Switch on the ignition and start the engine running. The oil-pressure light should go out almost immediately.

Hydraulic system
Make sure that the brake and clutch hydraulic reservoirs are topped up and that the systems show no sign of leaking. Inspect the flexible brake hoses for signs of wear, perishing or chafing. Check for leaks between hoses and metal pipes, and check between the hoses and brake backplates.

Front wheels
Jack up each front wheel in turn. Grasp the top and bottom of the wheel and move it firmly backwards and forwards. More than $\frac{1}{16}$ in. of movement indicates wear in the bearings, king-pins or swivel-pins. Revolve each wheel while it is jacked up to check that the wheel bearings are quiet, the brakes are free and the wheels are not buckled. Inspect the tyres for damage.

Tyres
See that each tyre has at least the 1 mm. of tread required by law round the full circumference and throughout three-quarters of its breadth. Remember that 2 mm. is a safer minimum. Check the sides for cuts or tears and see that cross-ply and radial tyres are not incorrectly mixed. Look for unusual or uneven wear that could indicate track misalignment.

Steering
Put the car on a level surface with the wheels pointing straight ahead. Turn the steering wheel gently from side to side. Undue free movement at the rim of the steering wheel, before the road wheels begin to turn, indicates wear in the steering mechanism.

Brakes
The brake pedal should be firm when it is depressed, but the actual condition cannot be assessed without dismantling.

Test drive
There is no reason to accept in a used car a lack of comfort that would not be acceptable in a new car (see p. 308). Driving comfort depends on relationships between the driving seat, steering wheel, pedals and switches that remain constant no matter how old a car is. Other factors affecting comfort are a car's smoothness, handling and visibility. Use the test drive not only to check the car's mechanical condition, but also to make sure that you feel at home behind the wheel.

Check before test driving a used car that the dealer has it insured and, if it is more than three years old, that it has a current DoT certificate. If the car is not insured for you to drive, do not do so. Insist, however, that you are taken for a drive in it.

Make sure that the clutch operates smoothly and progressively (the pedal will normally travel about an inch before the clutch begins to operate).

If the engine revolutions rise without a corresponding rise in speed (when the car has a manual gearbox), the clutch is slipping and requires attention.

Apply the brakes fairly sharply at about 30 mph to check that the car stops in a straight line. If it does not, or if the brakes judder, repairs may be needed. Investigate unusual symptoms.

Test each gear on the over-run and see if the car jumps out of gear. If it does, get an estimate from an independent source of what the costs are likely to be.

Check that the speedometer and mileage recorder are working—the speedometer must be accurate to within 10 per cent at more than 10 mph.

At the end of the test drive, park the car on clean ground and see if oil drips from the engine or gearbox.

Bodywork and rust

Detecting damage and corrosion

A NOTICEABLE patchiness in the bodywork colour is an indication of respraying, which in turn is sometimes a sign of crash damage. Plastic filler, used to repair damage, can be located with a pocket magnet—the magnet will not pull on a deeply filled surface. Corrosion is a common fault, so examine edges and bottoms of doors, the body sills below the doors and the joints, and surface areas of the front and rear wings for rust. Some superficial rust, particularly on chrome, can be expected in older cars, but extensive rusting is costly to repair. Rust often starts from the inside and works out—small paint bubbles may indicate imminent trouble. Go underneath the car and look for evidence of major repairs, such as weld lines. Look for kinks in the chassis-box section and frame.

WHERE RUST AND CORROSION BEGIN TO ATTACK A CAR

Bumper and valances
Vulnerable to chipping by stones and loose gravel

Wings
Dirt and water trapped underneath may cause severe corrosion, which appears as blisters on surface paintwork

Exhaust system
Corrosion is increased by short journeys and frequent stops. Holes can develop and result in dangerous fume leakages

Box sections, floor panels
Corrosion from water penetration of faulty sealing causes structural weaknesses—indicated by wet carpets

Body side sills, jacking points
Internal corrosion is caused by poor drainage and insufficient protective primer. Corrosion of jacking points can become dangerous

Braking system
Watch for signs of corrosion on brake pipes, seized or corroded handbrake cables and linkage

Springs, suspension mountings
Rusting leaf springs are rarely a danger point, but corrosion on mounting points can be

Sealing will give the underneath of a car a certain amount of protection against water and corrosion, but many parts will still need regular attention

Decorative trim
Moisture can be trapped under bright trim—a starting point for corrosion

Wing mirrors, radio aerials
Corrosion around mounting holes will spread

Headlamps
Rusting around lamp rims can arise from inadequate sealing and water traps

Roof guttering
Inadequate drainage and exposed body-panel edges will result in corrosion

Door Inadequate drainage can build up water traps and result in corrosion at bottoms of door panels

Upper wings
Dirt and water trapped high in wheel arches will corrode wings

Water trapped by inadequate drainage will lead to corrosion on the doors and sides. Small brown blisters on wings are a sign of corrosion underneath

Stop and tail-lights Corrosion is likely to start under perished sealing strips

Rear under-body panels, boot underside
Liable to damage from stone chippings and road spray

Edges of boot lid Trapped water starts corrosion around boot-lid edges

Rear bumper and valances
Vulnerable to chipping by stones and liable to trap dirt and mud. Exhaust fumes may cause severe corrosion of chrome

Poor finishing or sealing of boot lids can cause rusting of both the lid edges and the floor of the boot. Deterioration of lamp sealing rubbers leads to corrosion around fittings

The cost of motoring/buying a new car

Basic costs and final outlay

MOST PEOPLE buying a car have to make a compromise between the type of car they want and one they can afford.

The most convenient time to buy a new car is usually as soon as you have sold the old one. But the best time to buy is not necessarily the best time to sell: the demand for used cars is always heaviest in the late spring.

The range of models produced by the larger manufacturers is much increased by the number of body/engine/trim permutations available. There may be as many as two dozen variations of one popular small car—with a confusion of letters, numbers and names—and a wide price range. This may give exactly what you want, but it also increases the difficulty of deciding exactly what your needs are.

As soon as they become available, most popular cars are given a thorough 750–1000-mile evaluation test by the AA's own test drivers, and reports of the tests are available to AA members on demand.

Price is the chief consideration for most car buyers. Special Car Tax, 10 per cent of the wholesale value, will normally be included in the price quoted, but Value Added Tax (VAT) will be shown separately and will add another 8 per cent. VAT will also be payable on any accessory fitted by the dealer, and on any work carried out by him. It must also be borne in mind that it can cost more than £100 to put the car on the road. This includes:

Tax Either £50 a year or £18·35 for a four-monthly period.

Insurance This depends on the type of car, type of insurance required and the driver's record (see Insurance, p. 320).

Number plates These cost between £5 and £8 a pair. For a further fee, it is usually possible to transfer the registration number from one car to another belonging to the same person.

Main distributors, and local authorities that issue registration numbers, apply to the Department of Transport for allocations of new numbers. These are issued in blocks of 60, and sometimes a customer is given a choice from one of those blocks.

Since January 1963, registration numbers have ended with a single letter, denoting the year the vehicle was first registered. In 1967 the date of the annual letter change was moved from January 1 to August 1.

Cars bearing the E registration letter were therefore first licensed between January and August 1967; cars with the

P registration came on to the road between August 1, 1975 and July 31, 1976.

Safety belts Belts are required by law to be fitted to front seats. On some cars, belts are fitted at the factory and the cost included in the purchase price. On others they must be bought and fitted as extras.

There are two types of belts, static and automatic. Automatic belts wind themselves on to spools which lock if the car suddenly changes speed or direction. They tend to remain cleaner since they do not get in the way, require minimal adjustment for different wearers, and are more comfortable. They are more expensive than static belts, but allow the wearer more freedom of movement and adjust themselves to the correct tension when worn. Seat belts cost from about £12 to £35 a pair. Fitting can cost £6 or £8 more. If you want automatic belts these must be specified when ordering a new car.

Delivery Most manufacturers charge for transporting cars from factory to dealer.

Besides these unavoidable charges, a buyer may want to equip his car with accessories. He will probably be asked if he also wants the car rustproofing.

Full rustproofing is well worth its cost (£90–£150, according to the model of car and the system to be employed), as it enhances the re-sale value of the car if it is to be disposed of after two or three years. Rustproofing should be done as soon after the car leaves the assembly lines as possible.

Running costs are just as important as the purchase price of the car and should be taken into account (see p. 314).

Where to buy

It is in your interest to buy from a dealer who is an accredited agent of the manufacturer. Car makers appoint main dealers or distributors who supply cars on a wholesale basis to retail dealers in the locality. Both main and retail dealers are said to hold a manufacturer's franchise.

Franchise holders have obligations to the manufacturer which protect the customer's interests. Appointed dealers, for instance, should have up-to-date demonstration models and stock a fixed number of vehicles for sale. Even if a particular model is not in stock, a distributor should be able to deliver one more quickly than a dealer who does not hold the franchise.

Inspecting the car

A good salesman will see that a prospective buyer is acquainted with all a car's

selling points. Make sure that all the points illustrated on these pages are covered.

Insist on testing any car you are thinking of buying. There are no obligations attached to a trial run. Before moving off, ensure that it is easy for you and your passengers to get in and out and that inside the car there is adequate head, leg and elbow room in the front and back.

Use the test drive to check the noise level, as well as the acceleration, the lightness of the controls and the smoothness of the ride. The car's virtues should not overshadow minor annoyances like a feeble heater or badly placed light switch.

Test drive

Insist on a test drive and pay special attention to the following features:

Handling If the car is to be used extensively in town, it should be easy to park and have light controls, a good turning circle and an uncluttered view out of the windows in every direction.

Silence and smoothness These are important because noise and vibration contribute to fatigue. Silence is particularly important if a car is to be used for long journeys. Broadly speaking, the bigger the engine, the more relaxing the car will be to drive. It may be possible to fit overdrive; and although this will reduce the noise and vibration when cruising on motorways, the cost is likely to be greater than the overall saving on fuel.

Performance Many cars are available with alternative engine sizes or engine modifications. Thus there may be a specially tuned 'economy' version or a larger-engined 'performance' car, with corresponding price differentials and trim options. Remember that the insurance group (see pp 320–1) will depend on the exact model chosen, and that can make a considerable difference to your annual premium.

It pays to be realistic when deciding which of the engine options will be most suitable once you have chosen the basic car. A small engine, particularly if tuned for economy, may be disappointing if you are used to a more lively car; economy and reliability will suffer if you try to make it exceed its intended limitations. The faster versions, however, will certainly use more fuel if the performance is used, and will probably be rather less flexible or tolerant of inadequate servicing.

All new cars offered for sale in show-rooms must indicate their fuel consump-

tion figures. In addition, the comparative figures for other models must be available if the customer wants to see them.

Trim styles Whereas the choice a few years ago was simply between the standard and the de-luxe version, marketing techniques now favour model packages which are designed to give our basic car several rather different styles. The 'top-end' of the range is usually very much more expensive, quieter and more luxurious, but the comparatively large outlay may not bring proportional benefits. After all, if a car is basically good, the extra fittings may not be entirely necessary; if it is basically poor, they are unlikely to make it more than acceptable.

Because the comparatively high rate of tax that is levied on a new car applies also to extras that you may not want, there is much to be said for buying a more moderate version and adding fittings.

Space Buyers must decide how they want to use the space in their car—whether they need two, three, four or even five doors, a roomy back seat or a big boot. They must also decide how much interior storage space they require.

Closing the deal

The salesman will probably take the initiative. He has various methods for doing this, such as the 'fear' technique—a warning that if the customer does not buy immediately there will be a long wait for delivery. Or he may be more subtle and inquire what colour the customer wants. It is wise not to commit yourself until you are sure you have found the right car.

Once a customer has agreed to buy, he will be asked to sign an order form, but even this is not as straightforward as it may appear (see Guarantees, p. 311). If extra equipment is to be fitted, the dealer should have a written note of it. Some order forms have a space for this.

If there is a delay in delivery, the customer will be asked for a deposit. Should an order be cancelled without good reason, he stands to lose the deposit and could also be sued by the dealer to recover any loss.

Running in

A driver is no longer required to do a steady 30 mph for the first 500 miles of a car's life; and one big manufacturer of family cars makes no recommendations at all about running-in. Luxury cars are normally delivered already run-in. Other manufacturers advise drivers not to exceed certain speeds in each gear.

Points to check in seeking a new car that suits you

THE ULTIMATE TEST of whether a car suits you is whether you find it easy to drive. This is not only a question of how the car handles, important though that is; driving ease must also take into account the view from the car (absence of blind spots, the ease with which body extremities can be located, and even the area swept by the windscreen wipers), the fittings, the ventilation and heating system, the space inside the car and the noise level.

The ideal car would, like the ideal suit, be tailor-made; as this is impossible, seek a car in which the manufacturer has anticipated your requirements.

Controls Steering, clutch, brakes and gears should be light and easy to operate. The steering wheel should transmit the feel of the road without transmitting any shock when the front wheels hit a bump

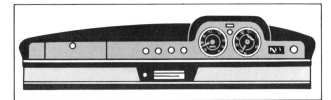

Switches On the test drive, ensure that all switches can be reached easily when a seat belt is worn and properly adjusted

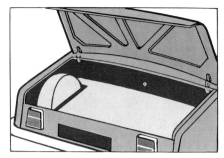

Boot Check the boot for size and for the accessibility of the spare wheel

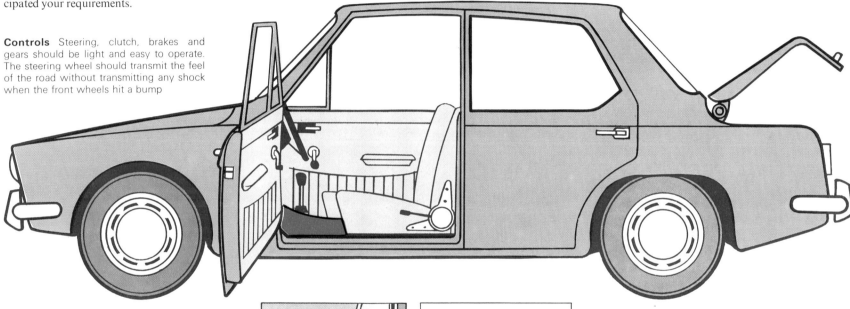

Bonnet Lift the bonnet to determine the accessibility of parts that are to be checked during routine maintenance

Suspension Make sure that good road-holding has not been achieved by making the ride very hard or, if you want a comfortable car, that its suspension is not so soft that the car wallows on corners

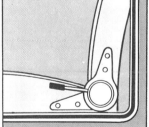

Seats An uncomfortable driving seat is dangerous because discomfort tires a driver and distracts his attention. Be certain that the seat can be adjusted and gives sufficient support. Check rear leg room

Safety Find out how the car has been designed to behave in a crash. Ideally, the steering column and the front and back of the car should collapse progressively on impact. The column should not be forced back towards the driver. Steering wheels should be padded or dished. Locks should be burstproof, and rear doors should have childproof locks. There should be no hard interior projections and the fascia at least should be padded. Front seats that tip should have catches to anchor them

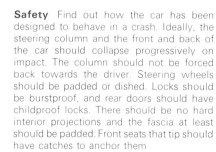

Noise Noise contributes to fatigue. There are three main sources: engine, wind and road. On the test drive, listen to each specifically

Ventilation Stuffy cars lead to driver fatigue; cold cars are uncomfortable. Heating and ventilation systems should keep the air fresh and warm, and the windows free of condensation

Interior storage Look at the space available, with your needs in mind. Places for valuables such as cameras are particularly useful, especially if they can be locked

The cost of motoring/buying a new car 2

Who pays for pre-delivery work?

DEALERS CAN charge what they like for new cars, but manufacturers do not like their agents giving big discounts because it may mean they have to skimp on after-sale service. So if you are offered a very substantial discount on a particular car, beware—it may be a model that does not fit the used car pattern.

Main dealers buy new cars from the manufacturer at a discount of about 18 per cent. They may obtain a slightly greater discount on the vehicles they buy to supply to retailers, so that the retailer, too, can buy at a 17–18 per cent discount. The main dealer would expect to take a cut of about 4 per cent for himself.

Part of the dealer's discount has to be spent on preparing the car for sale—removing the protective wax coating put on before it leaves the factory, cleaning and polishing the car and giving it a pre-delivery inspection. This inspection is designed to remedy the minor faults that have slipped through the manufacturer's quality controls.

The dealer also meets the cost of the first service, which is normally carried out after the first 500/1000 miles.

Dealers are entitled to charge the customer for some of the pre-delivery work they have done, such as fitting accessories, although some garages will absorb these small labour charges as well.

Minor adjustments, such as wheel alignment, even if not covered by the manufacturer's warranty, should be checked.

A dealer who did not sell the car in the first place would almost certainly charge for any adjustments necessary. The customer also has to pay for oils changed in the first service.

Customers are fortunate if they can take immediate delivery of their new cars. Usually there is a waiting list, especially for popular new models. Labour disputes in the car industry frequently disrupt delivery schedules.

If the price of a car goes up while the customer is awaiting delivery, the buyer may have to pay the higher price, even if the car bought was in stock before the increase. Special Car Tax, for example, is often paid by the dealer when he receives the car from the manufacturer, but in some cases it may not be paid until the car is actually sold. If therefore there is an increase in tax, the dealer may decide to pass it on to the buyer.

Convertibles

There is now no mass-produced British family car which has a folding roof. In the more expensive sector of the market it is still possible to buy a convertible, but generally it is necessary to buy a standard saloon and have it converted by a specialist coachbuilding firm. Some sports cars have folding tops as optional extras.

Before buying a convertible, check that the hood fits correctly and that there are no draughts or water-leaks. Be sure that the hood can be raised and lowered quickly, and that there is adequate visibility through the rear window.

It would be unwise to buy a convertible without a garage to keep it in. Hoods deteriorate more quickly than the rest of the car even without being exposed unnecessarily to the weather and they are easy prey for vandals.

Estate cars

These are much roomier than ordinary cars and among small cars can account for up to 15 per cent of the sales, although larger saloons outsell their sister estate cars by ten to one. Estate cars have rear doors opening on to a flat luggage platform which can be considerably extended by folding the rear seat flat.

Some cars combine the features of both saloons and estate cars. They do not have as much load space as a true estate car, but have more room than a conventional saloon and a rear door to load through. Estate cars cost about 10 per cent more than equivalent two-door saloons. Generally they are not as well soundproofed and give a harder ride than saloon cars.

Foreign cars

In recent years, foreign cars in the British market have climbed from 5 per cent to more than 50 per cent, despite inflation of many models by import duty. In 1976, for example, the general duty—on, say, Japanese cars—was 11 per cent.

Since July, 1977, cars from EEC coun-tries have carried no import duty. Nor is there any duty on Swedish cars: Sweden, a fellow member of the European Free Trade Area, negotiated free trading agreements with the EEC. Duty on the cars from Commonwealth countries is two-thirds the general rate.

Duty is also payable on spare parts for foreign cars: usually, therefore, these are considerably dearer than parts for equivalent British cars. This makes some of the imported cars more expensive to repair and maintain than comparable British models.

Some foreign cars may depreciate faster in value than British cars.

Automatic transmission

Automatic transmission can cost from £200 extra. It is chosen by about 10 per cent of buyers. Some acceleration must be sacrificed, especially in small cars. Cars with automatic transmission depreciate in value more than other cars.

Colour

There is considerable evidence that light-coloured cars are safer than drab ones. Yellow, white or red cars stand out better than cars in other colours against ordinary backgrounds.

If a dealer uses your insistence on a particular colour as an excuse to delay delivery, shop around. There is little or no excuse for failure to supply a car in any of the maker's standard colours.

Choosing the best way to borrow the money

ANYONE who wishes to have a car now and pay for it later will want to be sure that he is getting the best terms.

Some people may be fortunate enough to get a private loan, either through a bank or through a finance house. For others, the choice is likely to be between hire purchase and credit sale. Under both, the motorist pays a deposit and a number of instalments. The total sum paid may be about the same, but the consequences can be very different. (Many of these differences will disappear when the Consumer Credit Act 1974 is fully effective.)

Since both methods involve borrowing money, the first concern of the borrower will be to find out the interest rate.

This is not always easy. Though the lender is by law obliged to give clear information about the cash price, the number of instalments, the amount of each instalment, and the total sum to be paid, he need not reveal the interest rate. (Under Consumer Credit Act the true cost of credit must be disclosed.)

A true rate is calculated periodically on the outstanding loan. When repayments are weekly or monthly, the rate will generally be a little below double the flat rate. So a flat rate of 5 per cent a year becomes a true rate of more than 9 per cent a year when repayments are made monthly over two years. Under the Consumer Credit Act 1974, the Finance Company and dealer will be bound to state the true rate of total charge for credit in the agreement.

The outstanding differences between credit sale and hire purchase are connected with ownership.

Under hire purchase, the car remains the property of the lender until all payments have been made, and the customer must not sell without permission.

Under credit sale, the car belongs to the purchaser as soon as he signs the agreement, and he can, subject to the terms of the agreement, sell it whenever he likes. Such a course of action will normally terminate the credit-sale agreement and the purchaser becomes liable for immediate repayment of the balance outstanding under the agreement.

There are also differences if the motorist fails to keep up with his payments.

Under hire purchase, the lender can take back the car, though if the total cost inclusive of deposit and interest is less than £2000 and more than one-third of that total has been paid, he must first obtain a court order.

Under credit sale, the lender cannot get the car back. He can, however, take the customer to court for failure to pay the debt. The court can make such an order as it sees fit for repayment of the debt and the debtor's goods including the vehicle could be seized in order to meet the amount due.

The same issue of ownership arises if the motorist wishes to give up the car.

Under hire purchase, he can take it back to the lender at any time. But he must pay any overdue instalments, and the lender is entitled to demand that the total payments be brought up to at least half the amount due on the whole transaction. If the motorist feels that the car has not depreciated to half its original value, he can allow the matter to go to court, and the court may decide that he should be ordered to pay less, but he may be ordered to pay the other side's costs. A motorist who returns a car bought under a hire-purchase agreement can be liable for damage other than fair wear and tear.

Under credit sale, the purchaser can dispose of the car in any way he chooses and at any time though he must, of course, pay off the loan.

New-car guarantees

How to deal with defects

THE BUYER of a new car is sometimes disappointed to discover a number of imperfections when he first puts the vehicle through its paces. Usually they are minor teething-troubles; but if he is unlucky, he may find more serious defects.

The average family saloon is made up of over 13,000 parts, many of them complex. Even though the car is checked before delivery by the manufacturer or dealer, expensive adjustments may sometimes be needed after the car has been put into regular service. Car manufacturers arrange to attend to many of these adjustments free of charge by issuing the customer with a warranty (or guarantee), which is valid for up to a year, and even longer in some cases, after the car has been purchased. In some instances, it is now possible to obtain an extension to the normal warranty by payment of an additional sum, e.g., the AA's Motorsure.

The warranty system is a way of dealing smoothly with many routine repairs, but there are drawbacks. A defect will not always be eligible for repair under warranty, even though it was caused by defective design or faulty workmanship.

The manufacturer may, for instance, reject a claim if time or mileage limits detailed in the warranty have been exceeded, or if the servicing or use of the car has not been as specified.

Again, a small defect in the car, if not attended to promptly, may cause further damage—a badly fitted oil filter may lead eventually to the engine seizing up. If he is unlucky, the owner may be able to claim under the warranty only the cost of refitting the filter properly. He may have to meet the cost of a new engine out of his own pocket.

But drawbacks like these are not inescapable. The warranty system is only one way of dealing with the repair of defects.

A possible alternative method is to make a claim against the dealer.

Benefits of the warranty system

IF THE BUYER signs one of the standard dealers' order forms, he is usually promised the benefits of a warranty provided directly by the manufacturer of the vehicle, or through the dealer.

New-car warranties provide a means of dealing with some troubles which appear in cars only after they leave the factory.

Advantages
Increasing competition has led to more variety in new-car warranties. Leyland Cars offer Supercover, basically giving warranty for 12 months with unlimited mileage and the benefits of AA membership, including the Relay recovery service. Ford, Vauxhall and Chrysler offer unlimited-mileage cover for 12 months, with slightly varying conditions. It is always worth while checking the up-to-date warranty conditions before purchase.

Most defects inside the warranty period are repaired under the terms of the warranty. With a new car you can generally expect a pre-delivery check by the dealer and a free 500-mile service.

Work under warranty can usually be carried out by any authorised dealer in the United Kingdom, and often overseas, provided arrangements are made. Warranty claims can usually be made by the original purchaser, by someone who receives the car as a present, or by someone who buys it from the current owner during the warranty period.

Disadvantages
Generally, a limit is put on claims under a manufacturer's warranty—usually a year, but sometimes 12,000 miles when that occurs earlier.

Warranty claims may be rejected if the car has not been serviced regularly—even though the lack of servicing may have no close connection with a defect.

The warranty may not cover damage caused to other parts of the car by a defect.

Nor will the manufacturer or the dealer pay under warranty for the hire of another car while a defect is being repaired.

The customer has no right under the warranty to return even a seriously defective car and get his money back.

How to qualify
Simply sign the order form (the dealer often promises, in the small print, to help the buyer to obtain the benefits of the warranty).

Watch out particularly for time limits on claims under warranty. They may have to be made within, say, seven days of the trouble appearing if they are to qualify for free repair under the manufacturer's scheme.

How the law protects the buyer

ALTERNATIVELY, and in addition to the warranty, the buyer may well have a remedy against the dealer, as seller of the vehicle, under the provisions of the Sale of Goods Act 1893 as amended by the Supply of Goods (Implied Terms) Act 1973. The scope for such a claim was previously much narrower, principally because the seller was often able to escape liability entirely, simply by excluding this as a term of the agreement for sale.

Consumer sales
This is no longer possible under the radical change in the law concerning consumer sales (i.e. by traders to private individuals) under the Act of 1973 which holds that any such clause shall be void.

The result of this is that a buyer's possible rights under the Sale of Goods Act (as now amended) are left intact, whether or not he signs any document in the course of the sale which purports to exclude liability by the seller.

In the main, these are the implied conditions laid down by the Sale of Goods Act (as amended) to the effect that the goods must be 'reasonably fit' for their purpose (a question of degree in each case) and of 'merchantable quality'

Reasonably fit
If, for instance, a motor car is so defective at the outset that it constantly breaks down, then patently it is not likely to be regarded by the courts as 'reasonably fit' for its purpose.

On the other hand, whether a vehicle is of 'merchantable quality' would not easily be determinable and could ultimately be a matter for the courts, which would have regard to the standard that might reasonably be expected from such goods allowing for price and circumstances of purchase generally.

Bargaining equality
Therefore each case will unavoidably depend upon its own particular facts. It would be unwise to assume that a remedy automatically arises in law concerning every bad bargain that is made in purchasing a car, but there is no doubt that the new laws have brought the consumer an equality of bargaining power that he did not have before.

Since the remedies under the Act referred to are available *in addition* to the benefits offered by a manufacturer's warranty, the buyer can safely accept the manufacturer's guarantee.

Negligence
Until February, 1978, when the Unfair Contract Terms Act came fully into operation, a manufacturer was able to exclude, through the terms of his warranty, his common-law liability for negligence. This is no longer possible: the Act renders void any exclusion clause whereby the seller or supplier seeks to exclude liability for death or personal injury that might occur as a result of his negligence or breach of contract.

Breach of contract
Thus, a breach of one of the implied conditions referred to could well give a right to cancel the contract and recover the purchase price or a claim for damages (e.g. the cost of necessary reinstatement and possible consequential losses arising directly out of the seller's breach).

No such remedies would arise against the manufacturer, whose liability would be limited to the actual undertakings given in the written guarantee. These, moreover, may be no more than a gratuitous promise —unenforceable at law—dependent upon the exact wording of the guarantee. Certainly, there would be no question of rescinding the contract against the manufacturer if only because there is no contract of purchase between the buyer and the manufacturer.

The cost of motoring/new-car guarantees

Buying by credit

THERE ARE certain advantages in buying by hire purchase rather than with cash. The most valuable is the protection afforded by the Consumer Credit Act, 1974, which applies to transactions involving sums of credit between £30 and £5000.

Under that act, a finance company advancing money for a purchase can be held jointly liable for misrepresentations made by the dealer during negotiations and for any breach of contract by that dealer. This gives double protection to the buyer, who may be able to claim against the finance company or the supplier, or both jointly.

Should a hire purchaser wish to make a claim and find that the dealer has gone out of business, he may be able to claim against the finance company. In similar circumstances, a cash purchaser could be left with no means of redress.

Against this, the credit buyer must pay substantially more than the cash buyer who, unlike the credit buyer, is not restricted from lending or disposing of his vehicle or taking it abroad without the permission of a finance company.

Defaults in payments could lose the credit buyer the car and all monies paid, and leave him liable for damages should the finance company obtain a repossession order.

Should the car be lost by fire or theft, the credit buyer must still repay the balance due to the finance company; and that could prove to be greater than the current market value recovered through insurance.

The practical side of getting defects put right

THE BEST WAY to deal with a fault in a new car is to take the vehicle back to the dealer who sold it. Where this is not possible, check that repairs will be carried out free by another authorised dealer, provided you produce your voucher book.

If no authorised dealer is at hand when the car breaks down, the owner usually has to pay for the repair at a local garage. The cost will not be refunded under warranty, so if the job is big enough it may be cheaper to pay for the car to be towed to a garage which does warranty repairs.

Members of the AA Relay scheme may be able to have their car towed to a garage of their choice free of charge.

Claims under the Sale of Goods Act (as amended) can be made only against the dealer who sold the car. So if the repair has to be done elsewhere, ask that any defective parts are handed to the vehicle owner, and get a receipt giving full details of the repairs done. These can be shown to the original dealer when a claim is made.

Examine a car under warranty a reasonable time—say a month—before the warranty expires. Watch out for water or oil leaks and for any strange noise the car makes. Then bring any defects to the dealer's attention *in writing*. This will leave no room for argument about whether they were reported in time. If a major fault develops immediately after the warranty expires, consult the dealer to see if the cost of repairs can be shared with the manufacturer. The AA's technical service may be able to help in any negotiations.

You may in any case be able to claim against the seller under the Supply of Goods (Implied Terms) Act 1973 if you can show that the vehicle was of unmerchantable quality or that it was not fit for its purpose at the time of purchase.

Repairs

If repairs to a new car prove unsatisfactory, raise the matter first with the sales or service manager of that garage. If this fails, write to the managing director. You may also have a claim against the original selling garage—if it was different. Members of the Automobile Association should also give full details of a complaint to the nearest AA office.

In cases where the dealer does not help, a complaint can be made to the customer-relations department of the manufacturer concerned.

Letters to the manufacturer should give: the model of the car; its chassis and engine number, which will be found in the service voucher book (some manufacturers simply quote a single vehicle number); the car's mileage; the date it was bought; the name of the dealer who sold it and, if different, the name of the dealer handling the repair; and a concise account of the complaint.

Manufacturers will take no responsibility for unsatisfactory repairs carried out by dealers who are not their agents and over whom they have no control.

Your rights when buying a car

WHEN YOU BUY a new or second-hand car from a dealer, your rights are now protected by the Supply of Goods (Implied Terms) Act 1973. No longer can a dealer disclaim responsibility for the condition of the car by putting an exclusion clause in the small print of his contract or guarantee.

The customer's rights
The law protects you in four ways when you buy from someone who is in the business of selling cars.

You are entitled to know whether or not the dealer has the right to sell; that he does not make misleading statements in his description of the car; that the car is of merchantable quality; and that it is fit for the purpose for which it is being sold.

The right to sell
Under the Supply of Goods (Implied Terms) Act 1973, the buyer has the right to expect the seller to be genuine. But that simply means that he has a claim against the seller if he later finds that the car was not his to sell. If it is reclaimed by its rightful owner and the seller cannot be found, the buyer loses his money.

Under the Hire Purchase Act 1964, however, a private purchaser who buys in good faith and who has no knowledge of any outstanding hire-purchase claim against the car may keep it, even if it is later found to be still the subject of a hire-purchase agreement.

Description
Even when you have had a chance to look at a car before buying, you should be able to rely on the dealer's description of it.

If you think that his description was not factually correct, you may have a claim under the Misrepresentation Act 1967. In any case, report the matter to the local consumer protection officer (at the town hall) to find out whether an offence has been committed under the Trade Descriptions Act. Make the report even if you have bought the car 'privately', for that private transaction may in fact be a hidden trade sale.

If an offence is established, the seller may be more ready to settle a compensation claim by the buyer.

Merchantable quality
This is a legal term that simply means the car must be as fit for its purpose as it is reasonable to expect, bearing in mind the age and mileage of the car, and the price paid for it.

Fitness for purpose
If you have told the dealer that you require the car for a special purpose, such as towing a heavy caravan, you are entitled to rely on his advice. Should it turn out that the car is not suitable for towing, or for any other purpose claimed on its behalf, the dealer may be in breach of contract.

In case any dispute should arise, it is advisable to put any special requirements in writing and to get the dealer's written assurance that the car is fit for the purpose you have stipulated.

Limitations of rights
You have no right to a refund of money, or any other redress, to put right defects that were pointed out to you.

Private sales
If, during negotiations for purchase, a private seller makes a representation about the condition of the vehicle that you can prove false, in England or Wales you can bring a claim against him for damages under the Misrepresentation Act 1967. However, if you buy from such a person, you do not have the protection of the Trade Descriptions Act unless it can be shown he is 'engaged' in selling cars. Do not be deterred from reporting the facts to the consumer protection officer even though later he may say he cannot take any action.

The onus is on the buyer to examine the car for faults. Always bear in mind that you have less legal protection in a private purchase: in particular, you do not have the protection of the Supply of Goods (Implied Terms) Act.

Cost of motoring/basic costs

Approaching car ownership realistically

AT FIRST GLANCE, the cost of running a car seems insignificant compared with the advantages of having personal transport. People buying cars tot up out-of-pocket expenses for petrol and oil, add insurance and road tax, and are deluded into thinking that motoring is well within their normal financial limits.

It takes only a short time on the road to appreciate that the costs so thoughtfully anticipated are less than half the total expenses of owning and running a car. The cost of running a middle-aged family car for 10,000 miles in a year can easily be equal to mortgage repayments on an average suburban house.

Cars are usually chosen for their looks, performance and comfort. If the costs of keeping them on the road are to be kept as low as possible, they should also be chosen for their fuel consumption, ease of maintenance, insurance value, price of spare parts, and ability to hold their value against other cars when they come to be sold or traded in. Cutting the costs of motoring begins with your choice in the dealer's showroom.

Schedule of costs

Each year the AA publishes the 'Schedule of Estimated Running Costs', a pamphlet which is free to members. Its calculations are referred to by all the major companies and most ministries, including the Treasury, when they assess mileage allowances. It also provides essential information for prospective car buyers.

The schedule illustrates how visible and invisible standing charges have to be taken into account when a car owner calculates his own motoring budget. Many people pay for their motoring by the gallon and persuade themselves that other costs do not exist. They never fully appreciate how their pence—and pounds—are used up. Subsequent economy measures that they decide upon are unlikely to make a significant dent in overall costs.

Breakdown of costs

Standing charges have to be paid whether the car does 50 miles a year or 50,000. Some, like road tax and the owner's driving licence fee, are fixed regardless of the size of car. Others, like depreciation and insurance, are variable. Taking an average of all the variables, the AA schedule shows that for the motorist driving 10,000 miles a year, standing charges comprise about 60 per cent of his total costs.

When only 5000 miles are covered in a year, standing charges do not change, but they represent a higher proportion per mile of the total costs.

Running costs are the simple sums of how much it costs to drive a car on the road. The main expense is petrol, which can be slightly reduced by careful driving and regular maintenance.

To drive only 10 miles, the owner of a 1000–1500 c.c. car pays 3.34p for tyre wear, 5.66p for servicing, about 1.7p for oil, and more than 20p for repairs.

Only when a motorist's budget is put down on paper and properly tabulated on a cost-per-mile basis can the costs of items be compared to show the real value of potential economies.

Radial tyres, for example, cost about 10 per cent more than cross-plies but can reduce petrol consumption and will last longer. Over a life of, say, 20,000 miles, this small saving in consumption can more than recoup the extra cost of radials.

As the 'political' costs of motoring rise, with the Chancellor of the Exchequer able to increase motoring costs overnight, motorists should understand their budgets so that, if costs go up in one direction, savings can be made in another.

In addition to standing charges and running costs, all the incidental costs of motoring should be taken into account: parking fees, DoT test, fines, polishes and even the time the owner spends attending to his car. Motorists who go abroad often should also think of the size of their cars: a 15 ft car could cost two and a half times more to take from Dover to Calais by ferry than an 11 ft car.

Every expense should be logged in a special notebook kept in the glove box for that purpose, so that after a year's motoring every sum spent on the car can be added up and turned into a pence-per-mile figure (see Budget, p. 314).

Return on capital

The AA schedule also makes a point of the loss of income on capital invested in a car. Instead of spending £3000 on a new car, the money could be safely invested to give an annual income of not less than £240 income tax paid.

Although the loss of this earning is 'invisible', it ought to be allowed for when budgeting motoring costs. The AA conservatively allows 8 per cent, tax paid. For easy arithmetic, allow £8 a year for every £100 of the car's cost price.

Depreciation

TO ASSESS THE annual cost of running a car, an allowance must be made for depreciation—to cover the difference between what you are paid when you sell it and the cost of a new one of similar type (or one as good as the car was when you first bought it, if it was second-hand).

Depreciation is the cost of standing still, with the type of car that you have. If you change from running an older car to a new one, your capital costs will increase; conversely, changing to a smaller car should reduce capital costs. But that aspect is quite separate from depreciation.

When new-car prices were stable, it was reasonable to take depreciation as the difference between the price paid for a new car and its value after a number of years.

But if the price of a comparable new car has meanwhile increased substantially, the sum allowed on that basis will not be enough. Because the depreciation allowance has to cover the difference between the trade-in price of the used car and its replacement, so it must take increasing new-car prices into account.

Although it may at first appear anomalous, when a manufacturer increases his prices he may increase the value of your used car, but he also causes it to depreciate more. For the long-term effect, taking into account what you will eventually have to pay for a replacement, is to increase your motoring costs. The alternative would be to buy a less-expensive replacement car, but that is a means of avoiding expense rather than of avoiding depreciation.

Another aspect is the loss of capital. It is comparatively easy to work out and allow for the loss of interest on the capital you have spent on a car (see above), but inflation reduces the *real* value of that capital. On balance, however, the increase in new-car prices will approximate the rate of inflation, so you may not be very much worse off putting your money into a new car than if you kept it in a 'safe' investment.

In times of rapidly increasing prices, a good small car may hold its original price over the first year. This can also apply to the more sought-after large cars such as Rolls-Royce, but will not hold for the less-popular large foreign cars.

To some extent, the depreciation depends on the size of the car. After one year, the sum to be found to buy a replacement may be around 30 per cent of the new price for a small car or 40 per cent for a large one. To calculate the real cost to the owner however, the rate of inflation during that year can be subtracted. Compare two people with, say, £3000. One buys a car which sells a year later for £2600, when its replacement is £3300. So, he has to find £700. But the other person who invested his £3000 will have lost an amount due to inflation, reflected in the new-car prices. He might be £300 worse off in terms of real capital, so the man who bought the car is only £400 worse off than he would have been if he had invested his money.

The cost of motoring/budgeting for a car

Running costs

PETROL costs depend on the grade of petrol, the size of the car's engine, and the way the car is driven. A lot of harsh, stop-start driving, particularly in towns, will increase petrol consumption and reduce miles per gallon by as many as five.

A fair assessment of a particular car's petrol consumption is easily obtained by filling the petrol tank to the brim on two consecutive occasions and noting the mileage reading each time.

Divide the amount of petrol required to fill the tank for the second time into the number of miles covered. If, for instance, $6\frac{1}{2}$ gallons are required to fill the tank after covering 208 miles, the car is doing 32 miles per gallon.

It pays to do this simple sum frequently, as a check on the running efficiency of the car. If consumption suddenly goes up, the engine may need attention (see p. 180).

Oil

Oil consumption can vary widely between identical cars. Manufacturers would not be surprised to be told that a car was using about a pint of oil every 300 miles. Another car, of the same make and model, might need topping up only every 800 miles.

It can be false economy to use very cheap oils, because they may not be adequate for the engine's requirements or may not contain the necessary additives and will have to be changed more often.

Consumption of oil will increase if the sump is habitually overfilled, or if the engine's moving parts are badly worn.

Tyres

Tyres should last 12,000–20,000 miles, though careful driving may extend their lives. Incorrect inflation, bumping the kerb and fierce acceleration will shorten their lives. Rapid and uneven wear on tyres may suggest mechanical defects (see pp. 220–1). The false economy of running on a set of tyres until they no longer meet the requirements laid down by law hardly needs to be emphasised.

Servicing

Servicing costs, including oil changes and antifreeze in the autumn, depend on the type and size of car and the garage that does the work.

Generally, servicing costs can be reckoned to average between £5.50 and £6 per 1000 miles for most family cars. These figures are based on average labour charges throughout the country. It is important to stick rigidly to the manufacturer's recommendations on servicing, especially if only a small mileage is covered. Many of the servicing jobs should be done on a time rather than a mileage basis.

Most manufacturers now base servicing on a time basis as well as mileage.

Servicing is important, not only because it keeps the car running but because it gives a chance to inspect the car and take steps to prevent trouble before it occurs.

If a car is driven only at weekends and is serviced at 3000 mile intervals, it may be months before a small leak in the hydraulic brake system is detected; by then it could be too late because the brakes will have failed and possibly caused an accident.

It is wise to reckon that the car does 1000 miles a month, and to service it at three-monthly or 3000 mile intervals, whichever is the sooner.

Over 80,000 miles, the servicing a car required can vary from 40 to 100 hours, according to how complicated it is.

Repairs

Costs for annual repairs vary widely from one make and type of car to another. According to the AA schedule, owners should estimate about £200 a year for cars up to 1000 c.c., £250 for a 2000 c.c. model, £375 for a 3000 c.c., and about £500 for the 3000–4500 c.c. range.

There is still a wide difference in the prices of parts as well as in the times it takes to fit them.

The recommended time for relining the brakes of popular medium-sized saloons, for instance, ranges from about $1\frac{1}{2}$ to 4 hours. Some clutches take only about $2\frac{1}{4}$ hours to replace; others can take as much as 11 hours. With labour costs given an upward boost by VAT, these factors ought to be taken into consideration when choosing a car. Apart from odds and ends, repair costs of a car still under warranty should not usually have to be taken into account. When the warranty expires, costs will escalate year by year until the stage is reached where repair costs exceed the cost of depreciation.

The individual owner must then study the cost of motoring in the light of his budget and decide whether it is more economical to keep the car or exchange it.

Parking

Motorists who are forced to park their cars on city streets, or to commute to a city by car, should bear in mind the need to allow for all-day parking charges.

Insurance, licences and garaging

WITH SO MANY insurance companies quoting widely differing rates, and offering their various plans for reducing them, the cost of motoring insurance is almost as individual as a fingerprint.

Disregarding the various discounts and rebates that can be earned (see pp. 320–1), the basic cost of comprehensive insurance usually comes to about 15 per cent of the cost of running the car.

The cost can depend as much on the individual driver as on the car he owns.

Driving licence

The full driving licence, valid for the life of the driver, costs £5.

Car licence

In 1977 road tax was increased from £40 to £50 a year. It can be paid in three four-monthly instalments totalling £55.05. The extra amount (£5.05) entailed in instal-ment payments costs the motorist who drives 10,000 miles a year approximately 5p extra for every 100 miles.

Garaging

In a city like London, a rented garage can add £10 a week to motoring costs. In the country, extra rates levied on a motorist's own garage can be almost negligible.

If a car is not kept in a garage but left standing in the open air in all weathers, deterioration of bodywork may be more rapid and will add to the depreciation.

AA subscription

For £12.50 a year, AA members acquire a large number of benefits that cut the cost of motoring.

For an additional £9 the association provides a Relay service that guarantees to get a member's car and passengers home after a breakdown.

Typical budget

A family saloon with a 1300 c.c. engine bought for £2150, plus seat belts, number plates, delivery, etc., may be worth £1920 one year later. Its replacement would then cost £2569, an extra cost of £619 or 25 per cent. If the rate of inflation in that period is, say, 10 per cent, the real cost would be some 15 per cent. This would reduce in later years.

The figures below indicate what costs can be expected in, say, the third year at an annual mileage of 10,000. Covering a smaller or greater distance does not proportionally change the overall cost per mile, since the standing charges remain the same.

RUNNING COSTS	£	
Petrol 288 gallons (34.71 mpg @ 95p)	273.60	Running cost total £589.35 over 10,000 miles is equivalent to 5.893p per mile
Oil (top-up and changes)	17.10	
Tyres (cost averaged over their probable safe life)	35.90	
Servicing At 5000 and 10,000 miles	48.00	**STANDING CHARGES**
Anti-freeze, hydraulic fluid, etc.	5.00	

STANDING CHARGES	£
Vehicle Excise licence	50.00
Insurance (full premium)	155.00
Depreciation	392.59
Interest on capital	251.26
Garage (proportion of house rates) **and parking**	104.00
AA subscription	12.50
Total standing charges	965.35

Repairs	£
Spark-plugs	2.40
Battery	28.10
Top overhaul	49.50
Exhaust renewal	27.50
Points	2.00
Lamp unit, bulbs	5.25
Steering repairs	48.30
Brake overhaul	40.00
Oil filters	4.20
Air filter	2.50
Running cost	589.35

= 9.65p per mile over 10,000 miles (19.30p per mile over 5000 miles, 4.82p per mile over 20,000 miles)

STANDING COST + RUNNING COST = 15.54p per mile

Insurance/basic principles

Taking the financial risk out of motoring

THE LAW—and common sense—dictate that every motorist must be insured. However careful a driver is normally, he can still have a momentary lapse and cause an accident. Without insurance he could be faced with bills running into thousands of pounds, to be paid off at a few pounds a week for the rest of his life.

So the question for anyone taking out a policy, is not 'Shall I insure?' but 'How much insurance do I need?' and 'How can I get value for my money?'

Motor insurance has become a highly complicated business, but the basic principles are simple: the motorist pays the insurers a sum of money (called a premium); the insurers agree in return to pay out in certain circumstances (for instance, if he has a road accident). The motorist and the insurers are the First and Second Parties to this agreement, and anyone else who may become involved is called the Third Party. If more than one other person is involved in an accident for which an insurance claim is to be made, they are all known as Third Parties.

The motorist gets cover to drive a car by applying to someone who sells insurance—for example, an insurance broker who can usually advise on many different policies and insurance companies, or an individual insurer. Whichever course is taken, the motorist must complete a form (called the proposal form) with details of himself and the car to be insured.

When this has been examined, the insurers say whether they will accept the risk, and if so the annual premium required and the scope of the cover it will provide.

As soon as you have made the first payment, you receive a document called a temporary cover note, which certifies that you have the minimum insurance required by law and sets out brief details of the cover provided. It is illegal to drive without having received such a document.

When the insurers send out the policy, it is accompanied by a 'permanent' certificate of insurance, valid for the first period of insurance under the policy (usually one year). The certificate states who may drive the car, and the purpose for which the car may be used. These details should be checked, for a motorist who allows someone who is not covered by the certificate to drive, or uses his car for an unpermitted purpose, may break the law and invalidate his insurance.

If the certificate of insurance is lost, the motorist must inform his insurers immediately. If he changes his car, he may have to return the certificate and obtain one which relates to the new car, though most insurers now issue an open certificate, worded to apply to any car owned by the policy-holder. In these cases, it is still necessary to inform the insurers of the change of car, so that the premium may be adjusted. Failure to notify a change usually means that the new car has only the minimum cover required by law.

Should the insurance be cancelled—either by you or by the insurers—you must, by law, return the certificate to the insurers or one of their agents.

There are several situations which could mean financial loss to the motorist. How many of these are covered by insurance depends on which of the four main types of policy he chooses: Road Traffic Act; Third Party Only; Third Party, Fire and Theft; or Comprehensive.

Road Traffic Act policy

If, through negligent driving, you injure or kill anyone, you may become liable in law to pay compensation to them or their dependants. Under this policy the insurers will pay anyone who can establish a legal claim against you and will meet the cost of emergency medical treatment to the injured persons.

This is the minimum insurance required by law under the Road Traffic Act 1972. Anyone who drives without it may be banned from driving and fined or imprisoned for up to three months. The only people who do not need this insurance are those wealthy enough to make a special deposit of £15,000 with the High Court.

Third Party Only policy

This includes, in addition to the basic cover required by law, claims for damage to other people's property. There are other benefits, listed in the table on pp. 316–17.

Third Party, Fire and Theft policy

This extends the Third Party policy to give compensation if the policy-holder's car is damaged or destroyed by fire, or stolen. The motorist who takes out this policy is asked to state the current value of his car, but the amount he will receive if his car is lost through fire or theft will be the market value at the time of loss, which is usually less.

If the insured car is comparatively new, a few insurers will agree to a clause in the policy under which they will pay an 'agreed value' fixed at the start of the insurance year if the car is stolen or damaged beyond repair during that year.

Comprehensive policy

Essentially, this policy, bought by most policy-holders, includes compensation for damage to the policy-holder's own car, as well as the benefits of the Third Party, Fire and Theft policy. There are, in addition, a number of other benefits (typical ones are given in the table on pp. 316–17), but these differ from insurer to insurer and even from policy to policy offered by the same insurer.

Some insurers today offer two varieties of comprehensive policy, under different names, one giving more benefits than the other. The better policy may be either more expensive or issued only to mature drivers with good claim-free records.

Note that insurers are not allowed to offer policies which would compensate against any punishment imposed by a court. So they cannot issue a policy which would cover payment of motoring or parking fines.

Neither will any policy cover the motorist against depreciation; wear and tear; mechanical or electrical breakdowns, failures or breakages; tyre damage caused by braking, punctures, cuts or bursts (other damage which results from breakdowns or tyre damage usually *can* be covered); or damage resulting from riot or civil commotion outside Great Britain (Northern Ireland and the Republic of Ireland are, for example, not covered by the normal motor insurance policy).

ALL ABOUT INSURANCE COVER IN THREE ESSENTIAL DOCUMENTS

Cover note The newly insured motorist usually receives a cover note to tide him over until his certificate of insurance is prepared. It is evidence that he has the insurance required by law. The cover note is valid for a short period and must be renewed if the certificate has not been received

Certificate of insurance Legal proof that the motorist is insured is provided by the certificate of insurance. It details who can drive, and for what purpose. It must be shown on demand to any policeman (or produced at a police station within five days). It is also needed when renewing a vehicle excise licence. If the certificate has not yet been received, a valid cover note (but not the policy) will be satisfactory in both these cases. The certificate should be kept in a safe place and taken on holiday, but not left in the car—it might help a thief to convince the police that he is the rightful owner of the car

Policy The only document containing the full terms of the motorist's contract with his insurance company is his insurance policy. Its clauses set out in detail what is covered and what is excluded. Endorsements, which are often added at the end of the policy, should be carefully noted. They are alterations in the cover given by the basic policy. For instance, they may reduce the cover or make the policy-holder liable to pay the first £25 of a claim

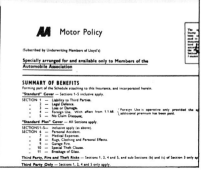

Insurance/four types of policy, and what they cover

Reason for financial loss		Road Traffic Act	Third Party only	Third Party, Fire and Theft
YOU AND YOUR HUSBAND/WIFE	Emergency medical expenses	You pay	You pay	You pay
	Compensation for injury or death (Personal Accident Cover)	No insurance cover	No insurance cover	No insurance cover
YOUR CAR	Stolen, or damaged by fire	You pay	You pay	Insurer pays for repair, or pays market value (*not* declared value) if car is a write-off*.
	Damaged by other cause	You pay	You pay	You pay
	Off the road—cost of hiring temporary replacement	You pay	You pay	You pay
	Defective—cost of replacing parts	You pay (unless you can recover under manufacturer's guarantee or from vendor)	You pay (unless you can recover under manufacturer's guarantee or from vendor)	You pay (unless you can recover under manufacturer's guarantee or from vendor)
YOUR GARAGE	Damaged by fire	You pay	You pay	You pay
YOUR PROPERTY IN YOUR CAR	Damaged or stolen	You pay	You pay	You pay
YOUR LEGAL BILLS		You pay	Insurer pays: (a) solicitor's fees for representing you at an inquest (b) cost of legal defence (limited to, say, £1000) against a charge of manslaughter or causing death by dangerous driving (not included in all policies) (c) legal costs (incurred with company's consent) in resisting claims by third parties	Insurer pays: (a) solicitor's fees for representing you at an inquest (b) cost of legal defence (limited to, say, £1000) against a charge of manslaughter or causing death by dangerous driving (not included in all policies) (c) legal costs (incurred with company's consent) in resisting claims by third parties
YOUR PASSENGERS	Compensation for injury or death (accident your fault)	Insurer pays	Insurer pays	Insurer pays
YOUR PASSENGERS' PROPERTY IN YOUR CAR	Damaged (accident your fault)	You pay	Insurer pays	Insurer pays
	Stolen	No insurance cover	No insurance cover	No insurance cover
OTHER PEOPLE	Emergency medical treatment	Insurer pays	Insurer pays	Insurer pays
	Compensation for injury or death under Road Traffic Act caused by your car (accident your fault)	Insurer pays	Insurer pays	Insurer pays
	Compensation for injury or death caused by your caravan or trailer (accident your fault)	Insurer pays if caravan was being towed at time of accident	Insurer pays if caravan was being towed at time of accident	Insurer pays if caravan was being towed at time of accident
	Compensation for injury or death caused negligently by your passengers while getting in or out of the insured car	You or your passenger (or both) pay	Insurer pays	Insurer pays
OTHER PEOPLE'S PROPERTY	Damaged by your car (accident your fault)	You pay	Insurer pays	Insurer pays
	Damaged by your caravan or trailer (accident your fault)	You pay	Insurer will pay if caravan was attached to towing vehicle at time of accident	Insurer will pay if caravan was attached to towing vehicle at time of accident
	Damaged negligently by your passengers while getting in or out of the insured car	You or your passenger (or both) pay	Insurer pays	Insurer pays
YOUR EMPLOYER	Claims against your employer when car is used on business (accident your fault)	Your employer pays (if he is liable)	Insurer will pay if policy covers business use and the employer is liable	Insurer will pay if policy covers business use and the employer is liable

Comprehensive | Extras

Comprehensive	Extras
Insurer pays for treatment up to a maximum (say £50)	
Insurer pays lump sum (usually £1000) for death of driver only *or* driver and husband/wife (age limit usually 70); smaller sums for loss of limb or sight	Insurer provides weekly payments while husband or wife is temporarily totally disabled
Insurer pays for repair, or pays market value (*not* declared value) if car is damaged beyond repair*	
Insurer pays for repair if car is damaged: (a) in an accident (b) in a riot in Great Britain (*not* in Northern Ireland) (c) maliciously (by vandals, for example) (d) by frost, provided that precautions have been taken (e) *as a result of* breakdowns or burst tyres, provided the car has been properly maintained (but not for repairing the breakdowns, or replacing the burst tyres) Insurer also pays cost of transporting damaged car to and from garage; pays market value (*not* declared value) if car is damaged beyond repair*, but does *not* pay for depreciation or wear and tear	Insurer pays total cost of repairing broken windows or windscreen
You pay	Some insurers pay towards hiring car while yours is out of action
You pay (unless you can recover under manufacturer's guarantee or from vendor)	
Insurer pays (up to, say, £150)	
Insurer pays for repairs, or pays market value for goods written off, up to a maximum of, say, £50, which may include passengers' property (trade goods, money or securities not covered)	Insurer pays higher compensation
Insurer pays: (a) solicitor's fees for representing you at an inquest (b) cost of legal defence (limited to, say, £1000) against a charge of manslaughter or causing death by dangerous driving (not included in all policies) (c) legal costs (incurred with company's consent) in resisting claims by third parties	
Insurer pays	Insurer pays fixed personal accident benefits
Insurer pays for repairs, or pays the market value for write-off. If accident not your fault, will be limited to maximum of, say, £50 for owner's and passengers' property (trade goods, money or securities not covered)	
Insurer pays	
Insurer pays	
Insurer pays if caravan was being towed at time of accident	
Insurer pays	
Insurer pays	
Insurer will pay if caravan was attached to towing vehicle at time of accident	
Insurer pays	
Insurer will pay if policy covers business use and the employer is liable	

How to use the table

▢ Covered by insurance

The table shows who pays for repair or compensation. If there is no insurance cover, you pay (unless someone else is partly or wholly to blame, and you can recover some or all of the cost from them). The table relates to the private motorist only (special conditions apply if you are an employer).

Typical benefits are shown. Some policies (such as the AA's special policies) give more and better benefits. Others, particularly some Comprehensives, offer less. So check your policy.

*A small number of insurers offer policies which pay an 'agreed value' fixed at the start of each insurance year.

Extra cover in detail

EXTRA PROVISIONS can often be added to basic insurance policies for an additional premium. Alternatively, they can be provided by a separate policy.

Some of these provisions are already included in certain Comprehensive policies; others may be provided by only a small number of insurers.

Replacement of new car
Some policies, including most of those arranged by the AA, automatically include a provision for cars less than 12 months old. If they are lost or damaged beyond 50–60 per cent of their value, the insurers provide a replacement car of the same make or model (subject to availability).

Personal injuries
The policy can usually be extended to give a weekly payment either for the policy-holder alone or for policy-holder and wife/husband while temporarily totally disabled after an accident.

Windscreen
The cost of repairing a broken windscreen or windows is included under a Comprehensive policy, but a claim may affect the no-claims discount, or the policy-holder may not be able to claim at all if he has to pay the first £15 or £25. Many policies pay the full cost up to £25 without loss of discount: alternatively the motorist can take out a separate policy.

Car hire
Even under a Comprehensive policy most insurers will not pay for the hire of another car while the policy-holder's own is being repaired, though he may be able to recover the cost from another driver (or the other driver's insurer) if it can be proved that the other driver was to blame.

A motorist who is wholly or partly to blame for the damage, or whose car is damaged without another vehicle being involved, will have to pay all or part of the cost himself. Alternatively, he may be able to obtain separate Loss of Use insurance (at Lloyd's) which will pay a fixed daily sum up to £5 towards car hire up to a maximum of, perhaps, 31 days a year.

Personal property
The Comprehensive policy limit for claims (usually £50) can often be increased, but a separate All Risks policy—covering loss in and out of the car—is usually better value for money.

Injury to passengers
Insurance cover for all passengers is compulsory, and there is no limit to claims for death or injury. Compensation, however, does depend on legal liability; one party or the other has to prove blame, before passengers who have been injured can claim against the policy.

By paying an additional premium it is possible to provide cover for passengers independently of the legal requirements. Under such a scheme, a kind of personal accident policy covers any passenger injured or killed—no matter who was to blame for the accident. The benefits are paid automatically without deciding who caused the accident.

Caravans
The policy-holder is covered under Third Party or Comprehensive policies for injuries to other people or damage to their property by the caravan while it is attached to the towing vehicle.

For an additional premium, the policy will cover claims for damage caused by the caravan while it is not attached to a vehicle, and for repairs to the caravan itself.

It is usually better value, however, to take out a separate caravan policy, which should give much wider cover to the caravan and can also include its contents.

One such scheme is the AA's own caravan policy, which members can take out for a small premium. This provides cover for loss or damage to the caravan, its contents and fittings, third party liability up to £250,000, and use on the Continent, without extra charge, for up to 30 days in any one insurance year.

Camping Equipment
Members can also obtain cover for their camping equipment and trailer through the AA's camping policy. This provides cover for the whole year, whether the equipment is in use or in store at home in the United Kingdom, and is extended, for those permanently resident here, for use in Europe without any period limitation. This policy can also be extended to cover luggage and money whilst on holiday.

It is always advisable in any insurance transaction to take advice from more than one source. Insurance brokers, who earn commission from insurers with whom they place business, can usually give information about many kinds of policy. Other sources include bank managers, motoring associations, or district offices of individual insurance companies.

Insurance/choosing a policy

How to make the most of professional advice

ANYONE taking out motor insurance for the first time, or thinking of changing to a different insurer, should start making inquiries several weeks ahead. It takes time to find a policy which gives the required cover *and* is good value for money; and people who leave things until the day before they need the policy frequently lose money or end up with a type of insurance they do not want.

The first thing to decide is what, ideally, the policy should cover, bearing in mind that to settle for less insurance than you really need can often be false economy. As the cost of motoring rises, the temptation grows to save money on insurance premiums by choosing a type of policy which gives less cover and is therefore cheaper. This, in effect, is gambling on not being involved in an accident—and it is a gamble which it could be disastrous for any car-owner to lose.

The motorist who, for the sake of a lower premium, changes his Comprehensive policy for a Third Party, Fire and Theft one forfeits accidental damage cover for his own car. If the vehicle should be wrecked in an accident which is his own (or no one's) fault, he will have to find the entire price of a new car—or give up motoring altogether.

It is far better, if finance proves an obstacle to adequate insurance, to borrow the price of the premium, or accept limitations on the insurance cover which will not bring such serious consequences in the event of an accident. (Both methods of reducing the immediate cost of insurance are dealt with fully on p. 320.)

Not all motorists, however, have a free choice of policy. People buying cars under hire purchase agreements, for example, will usually find that they have to be insured under a Comprehensive policy.

Again, motorists who are very young, have bad accident records or drive unusual or powerful cars, may have to settle for less than a full Comprehensive policy. This is because insurers may refuse them this type of cover, or accept them only at very high rates.

Next, the motorist has to decide where to obtain his insurance. Policies are issued by companies and by underwriters of the Corporation of Lloyd's. They can be obtained in a number of ways: direct from a company or one of its home service agents; through a part-time agent such as a garage, bank manager, accountant or solicitor; through a motoring organisation; or through a broker.

THE PROPOSAL FORM WITH A SNAG

DECLARATION

I declare that:

1. I have never been convicted of any offence in connection with any motor vehicle owned or used by myself, and no such prosecution is pending

2. I do not suffer, to the best of my knowledge and belief, from any physical defect

3. I have not been involved in any accident or suffered any loss in the last three years in connection with any motor vehicle owned or used by myself

4. I agree that the above items (1–3) apply to anyone who to my knowledge will drive the motor car insured under this policy

5. I agree that this declaration and proposal shall be the basis of the contract between myself and the insurance company. I further agree that where any part of this proposal is completed by any other person that person shall be my agent, and not the agent of the company

Signed . . . . Date . . . .

Every serious accident brings worry and inconvenience. For a minority of motorists it also brings the alarming discovery that their insurance is invalid. This can happen if the policy-holder fails to complete the proposal form accurately when he first takes out his insurance. The danger of returning an incorrect proposal form is probably greatest when the form contains a long declaration in small type. So make sure before signing that every word of the declaration is true for *you*. Have you driven for the last three years without a single accident? Have you never been convicted of any motoring offence? Does the same apply to all your other drivers? If any part of the declaration is not true in your case, cross it out, attach full details to the form and keep a copy. Only in this way can you be sure that your insurance will apply when you need it most

---

Companies and agents

Some people find it convenient to take out a policy direct with an insurance company, or with one of its home service agents.

Certainly anyone who has a well-established policy arranged in this way is best advised not to change simply for the sake of a slightly cheaper premium; the goodwill built up with the company (assuming few claims have been made) will be of much more value to the policy-holder in the event of a major claim than the few pence saved by changing. It is worth considering a change, though, if another company offers wider cover, larger benefits or special terms.

There are, however, disadvantages in taking out a new policy direct with a company or through one of its employees. For one thing, they will obviously offer the policies of only one company.

Some motorists try to get round this by seeking quotations from several companies and comparing them. But to be sure of what they are getting for their money, they will also need to see specimen policies, which some companies are reluctant to supply. The very least that should be obtained is a detailed summary of the policy cover. Even then, it takes experience in reading complicated legal documents to be able to understand the real effect of insurance policies in law.

Anyone who succeeds in getting this far will still not know without expert advice how each company deals with claims. This, to professionals in the insurance business, is often the real test of a policy. Some companies are quicker than others in authorising repairs and subsequent payment. Again, though all insurance companies must obviously meet their legal obligations, some have a reputation for being more 'generous' than others.

One company considering a claim might be prepared to overlook the fact that the policy-holder had innocently left some information off his proposal form. Another company might take advantage of this mistake and refuse to pay.

The motorist who decides to take out a policy direct with a company will want to be sure that the company is well run and financially sound. As a good guide, he should choose one of those which are members of the British Insurance Association (a list can be obtained from the association, at Aldermary House, Queen Street, London, EC4).

Part-time agents

Many garages, bank managers, solicitors and accountants are part-time agents for insurance companies, and earn commission for any business they introduce. The choice of insurers offered is usually small.

Not many part-time agents are likely to have specialised knowledge of insurance or the insurance market, so they will probably not be able to help in obtaining cover in unusual circumstances.

Many agents, particularly small ones, may be unable to assist the policy-holder who is having difficulty either in making a claim or in negotiating a particularly difficult claim with his insurance company.

Motoring organisations

Helping members with their insurance is one of the services provided by motoring organisations.

By recommending existing policies, for example, a motoring organisation provides valuable guidance to members who are anxious to find an insurer who is financially reliable and fair, prompt and efficient in its treatment of claims.

The AA goes further by negotiating special terms for its members. Policies are placed with an old-established group of companies, the Guardian Royal Exchange, with Cornhill Insurance Co., and with underwriters at Lloyd's.

An advantage of these policies is that, if any difference over a claim arises between a member and the insurers, the member is offered free and impartial arbitration by a special committee of the AA.

In addition, the AA employs a large staff of qualified insurance men to help members in arranging insurance and in making claims.

Other forms of insurance are also available at advantageous terms.

Insurance brokers

Brokers are individuals or companies who obtain insurance at the best possible terms for the individual by their professional knowledge of the market. Almost all of their services to clients are free, because they receive commissions from insurance companies and underwriters.

A first-class insurance broker can take most of the hard work and worry out of getting insured. He should be able to choose from among the policies of a large number of companies the ones most likely to meet the individual's needs. He should know from experience which companies are prompt in dealing with claims, and which seem over-anxious to find reasons why they should not pay.

A broker should be particularly useful if, because of a driver's type of car, his age, his driving record or any other reason, he has difficulty in getting insured.

It is important, however, to get a good broker. At present anyone can set himself up as an insurance broker, with the result that there are people offering their services to the public as brokers who are inexperienced or financially unsound, or who represent too few companies to be able to offer an adequate selection.

It is advisable, therefore, to deal only with brokers who are members of brokers' associations. The principal associations, which will supply lists of members, are:

Lloyd's Insurance Brokers' Association, 3–4 Lime Street, London, EC3M 7HA.

The Corporation of Insurance Brokers, 15 St Helen's Place, London, EC3A 6DS.

The Association of Insurance Brokers, Craven House, 121 Kingsway, London, WC2B 6PD.

Making a proposal

Wherever a driver goes for insurance, he will have to fill in a proposal form—giving details about himself, his driving record and his car—and it will have to be examined by the insurer before he is quoted an exact premium. There is no need to pay any money at this stage.

Some agents will give a quotation on the basis of verbal answers to a few questions, and will even accept money and issue a cover note. But this acceptance is only provisional, and the driver may eventually be offered harsher terms or less cover.

Worse still, if he wishes to decline these new terms and apply to another insurer, the driver may find that only a small proportion of the money he has already paid is refunded.

The explanation is that the period for which the insurance has been in force (through the cover note) is charged at a more expensive temporary rate. This is why it is so important to make inquiries about insurance before it is needed, and not to leave oneself in need of cover.

Even if a driver wants a quotation only to compare it with several others he is obtaining, he may still have to complete the proposal form. When he gets the quotation he can always turn it down.

When filling in the proposal form, it is important to take the greatest care to give full and accurate information. On no account sign the form and leave it to be filled in by the person selling the insurance.

In law, the driver is expected to show the utmost good faith in all his dealings with the insurers, and they may be within their rights in refusing to pay a claim if he does not.

This principle of 'utmost good faith' which governs all insurance—it is often referred to by the Latin words *uberrima fides*—means that a driver is obliged to inform the insurers of all the material facts affecting the risk, and to keep them informed.

The driver should take care to mention, when he is filling in the proposal form, whether the engine of his car has been supercharged; to declare as fully as possible the people who will be driving; and to state whether the car will be used for business or driving to and from work.

It is a good idea for every driver to keep a copy of his proposal form, so that he can check periodically that the information on it is still complete and absolutely accurate. If it is not, the insurer should be informed at once.

If, for example, a driver answers truthfully on his proposal form that he has no 'disability or infirmity', but suffers a heart attack a few months later, he should inform the insurer before he starts driving again. If he fails to do so, and subsequently has an accident, the insurer may be entitled to refuse the claim.

It is particularly important not to renew a policy without checking that there have been no changes, for each time a policy-holder renews he declares, in law, that all the details on his original proposal form are still entirely true.

Pitfalls that can jeopardise a policy

EVEN a well-insured driver can break the law or have a claim rejected if he fails to comply with the conditions of his policy.

If his car is poorly maintained, or has poor brakes or tyres, the insurer may be legally entitled to refuse to pay, even though poor maintenance was not the direct cause of the accident.

Similarly, all reasonable precautions must be taken to prevent fire and theft.

Borrowing

A driver who borrows a car should check whether he is covered by the owner's insurance, and if so what benefits he enjoys.

If he is not covered, he should check that his own insurance extends to a borrowed car. If so, it will normally provide cover only against claims by third parties for injury or damage to their property.

Alternatively, he can try to have the borrowed car covered by all the benefits of his own policy if he makes special arrangements with the insurer in advance.

Particular care should be taken when borrowing a car from a garage to ensure that it is fully insured. This will usually have to be provided under the borrower's policy, and he should make sure that he possesses a valid cover note before the car is driven.

Lending

Anyone who lends his car should check that the borrower has a current licence. If the licence is provisional, he should make sure that the borrower will be accompanied by a driver with a full licence.

Failure to observe these conditions will make the insurance invalid, and the lender will have to pay for damage to his own car.

The policy-holder who lends his car should make sure that it is still covered by his own insurance. If the cover is Owner Only, he should not lend the car without having the policy changed; if the cover is restricted to Named Drivers, he should lend only to those named on the certificate of insurance.

A driver may wish to lend his car in an emergency to someone not covered by his own insurance. This is legal, provided that the borrower's insurance will take over. But the borrower's policy will not cover damage to the car.

Private policies do not usually cover the loan of cars to business colleagues for use on business.

Before his children start driving, a driver should get the insurance company to confirm that they will be covered.

Hiring

Car hire firms usually arrange the insurance on the cars they hire out, but this may not include full cover for the car unless these are requested.

If you already have insurance, you may find it cheaper to have your own policy extended to cover the hire car.

People in some professions find it difficult to hire cars. Nevertheless, occupation should be correctly declared, or the insurance will be invalid.

A driver who extends the agreed period of his hire should check that the insurance does not run out.

Use

The policy-holder should use his car only for the purposes stated on the insurance certificate. Using a car on business when it is covered only for private domestic purposes invalidates the insurance.

Few private policies cover occasional use on business by the policy-holder's wife.

Anyone who plans to take part in rallies, competitions or trials, should check that his insurance will cover these. Some policies require special arrangements to be made. Remember that even a social club treasure-trail competition may be classified as rallying: check with your insurer before participating.

Tell the insurer

Information withheld from the insurer can invalidate a policy. So give a full account: if the car is garaged in the country, but used mainly in town; if particulars on the proposal form change; if you change your car; whenever you have an accident (whether you claim or not); if young or inexperienced drivers are to use the car; if you change your occupation; if you are convicted of a motoring offence; if you suffer a serious deterioration in health or sustain a physical disability.

It is important, above all, to be absolutely honest when you complete the proposal form. A mistake, however innocently made, may later invalidate the insurance cover.

Read the policy

Always read your policy carefully as soon as it is received. If there is any doubt about any part of it or if you think that it does not give the cover you anticipated, get in touch with your insurance broker or with the insurer. Note the expiry date and make sure that the next premium is paid in time (see p. 325).

Insurance/a guide to payments

Safe ways of cutting the cost

THE AMOUNT a motorist has to pay for his car insurance depends on how likely the insurer thinks he is to make a claim, and therefore to cost them money. This, in turn, depends on the chances of his being involved in an accident.

Until the insurer has examined a motorist's proposal form, no one can say with certainty whether he will be accepted, and if so what premium he will be charged. This is because the insurer is, in effect, making an informed guess about the risk the motorist presents, and there is no general agreement about how risk should be calculated.

Some insurers say that the previous driving record is the only sound basis upon which to judge (and decline to insure inexperienced motorists, as a result).

Most insurers, however, base their premium on some or all of eight factors:
1. The motorist's age, and the age of other people likely to drive the car.
2. His driving record.
3. His job.
4. The length of his driving experience in this country.
5. What the car is used for (i.e. business or pleasure).
6. Where it is garaged.
7. Its make and model.
8. Its age and value.

The premium produced by this method sometimes proves more than the motorist wishes to pay, or more than he wishes to pay in a single lump sum. If so, there are two possibilities: he can pay in instalments; and he can restrict the insurance cover in return for a lower premium.

Paying by instalments

For an extra charge, some insurers will allow premiums to be paid every three or six months, or even every month. Before accepting one of these schemes, check what happens if you forget to make a payment, or if a clerical error delays payment under a banker's order.

In some schemes the cover is reduced to the bare legal minimum as soon as a payment is overdue. This is usually the case if payment is made by credit card.

One method is the instalment scheme provided by the AA for insurance premiums that are in excess of £25. All you need to obtain credit under this scheme is a current bank account. The cost is minimal, with a service charge of 3 per cent on the total premium. You pay a deposit of 20 per cent, then four equal monthly instalments (inclusive of service charge).

The motorist can often lower the cost of his insurance by agreeing to restrict or reduce the cover it provides. The price reduction is expressed as a percentage discount off what would have been the full premium. Most insurers allow these discounts, but the percentage they will deduct varies considerably.

Owner-only driving

If the policy-holder agrees that the insurance should be restricted to himself alone, he will be eligible for a discount of between 10 and 20 per cent.

Though it may be financially attractive, this arrangement could reduce the usefulness of the car in an emergency. There would be no cover under the policy if it were necessary for someone else to take over the driving—although the emergency driver might have a policy in his own name which would provide him with Third Party cover. Neither policy, however, would then cover damage to the car.

Anyone who decides to accept this restriction should first check with the insurer that the policy will continue to apply when the car is being driven by a garage mechanic for testing or repair.

Sometimes a similar but usually smaller discount may be allowed if cover is restricted to the policy-holder and husband/wife.

Accidental damage excess

Premiums will usually be reduced if the motorist agrees to pay the first part (say £25 or £50) of any claim for accidental damage to his own car. The discount varies with the amount of the excess—10 per cent is common for a £15 excess.

All-sections excess

A number of insurers give a larger discount if the motorist pays for the first part of *any* claim under the policy—not just for damage to his own car. A £25 excess might earn a discount of 15 per cent.

If you agree to one or other of these excesses, it may mean that no claim at all is made after an accident in which only a small amount of damage is done. Nevertheless, failure to tell the insurer what has happened (even when no claim is to be made) could invalidate the policy.

No-claim discount

The best way to reduce premiums, under most policies, is to ensure that you never have to make a claim—take care of your car, drive carefully and take all possible precautions to avoid fire or theft.

Most insurers reward such care with premiums which are progressively reduced as the claim-free period grows. The insurers give a discount, known as a no-claim discount.

The amount of the discount varies from company to company. Motorists insured under the AA/Guardian Royal Exchange scheme have their premium reduced by a fifth after the first claim-free year. The discount (which is taken off the current premium each time) can rise to 60 per cent after six years:

Claim-free years	Percentage discount	£100 premium reduces to
1	20	£80
2	30	£70
3	40	£60
4	50	£50
5	60	£40

A driver who changes to a new insurer is usually allowed to transfer his no-claim discount.

A claim does not usually cancel the whole of the discount; with most insurers the policy-holder drops back two or three steps on the discount scale. Thus, the driver with four years of claim-free motoring who makes a claim under the AA/GRE scheme, will have his next premium increased so that it is only 20 per cent off the original premium, instead of 60 per cent off.

If some years have passed since you took out your policy, you might be able to have removed any loading originally imposed because of your age.

If you were originally charged a higher premium because of a bad driving record, and you have gone a few years without making a claim, ask the insurers to consider lowering your premium. Should they decline to do so, you can try for better terms with another insurer.

CALCULATING THE PREMIUM—EIGHT POINTS WHICH AN INSURER

A motorist's premium depends on how likely the insurer thinks he is to make a claim. How can this risk be assessed? The insurers' experience of meeting claims suggests that eight factors are significant:

Car use Premiums are usually cheapest for domestic and pleasure use; more expensive if you drive to work; dearer still for business

Age How it affects the accident rate

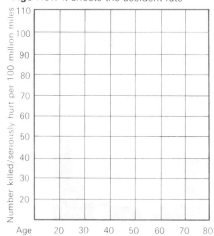

The most accident-prone drivers are those in their teens, as the graph of serious injuries per 100 million miles shows. Safest drivers are middle-aged

Job People in certain occupations may have more accidents; or they may carry passengers who are expensive to compensate. An injured actress claims more for loss of earnings than a typist

BEST TERMS	POSSIBLY ADVERSE TERMS
Accountants	Commercial travellers
Bank officials	Journalists
Civil Servants	Servicemen
Barristers	
Fire Brigade	WORST TERMS
officers	Publicans
Local Govern-	Turf accountants
ment officials	Professional sportsmen
Opticians	Entertainers
Policemen	Nightclub workers
Solicitors	Hawkers
Clerics	Scrap-metal merchants
Teachers	Foreign servicemen

UK driving experience Most insurers take separate account of a motorist's driving experience in Britain and abroad.

Driving record A driver with a long accident-free record pays less than one who has made claims.

Make and model Sports cars are usually regarded as heavy risks. Spare parts for foreign cars may cost more to obtain. The cheapest to insure are standard production British saloons.

Value Premiums are usually higher when the car is worth more than £2000.

How to keep a no-claim discount

IF YOU have a good driving record, you will naturally be anxious to preserve your no-claim discount. There are several ways in which this can be done, even if you are involved in minor accidents.

Accident no one's fault

If you are driving carefully and have an accident in which no other person is involved—perhaps you skid on a patch of muddy road—you will naturally conclude that the accident was no one's fault. If you claim the cost of repairing your car, you will nevertheless have your no-claim discount reduced.

The explanation is that it is a *no-claim* discount, not a *no-blame* discount. In general the insurer works on the principle that if he loses money through having to pay a claim, the mororist will have his no-claim discount reduced. Before he claims, the motorist should consider whether he might not be better off paying for the repair himself.

Suppose the motorist pays a basic premium of £150, but is on the maximum discount rate. Given the scale on the page opposite, his premium will be £60. The repairs will come to, say, £50. The financial comparison is therefore as detailed below:

	If he makes a claim	If he pays for repairs himself
Cost of repairs	nil	£50
Premium next year	£105	£60
Premium year after	£90	£60
Premium year after	£75	£60
Total	£270	£230

In this case the motorist would be £40 better off by paying to repair the damage himself. (The calculation assumes that premium prices remain stable for two years. It is not necessary to consider costs further than three years ahead as the maximum discount rate applies in the fourth year, whether the claim is made or not.)

If the motorist has agreed to pay the first £25 or £50 for accident damage, the calculation would be made in basically the same way, and here again it could be of advantage to pay, rather than claim, even for more expensive repairs.

Assuming, for the motorist above, a £25 excess and damage costing £75, the comparison would become:

	If he makes a claim	If he pays for repairs himself
Cost of repairs	£25	£75
Premium next year	£105	£60
Premium year after	£90	£60
Premium year after	£75	£60
Total	£295	£255

In this case the motorist would be £40 better off by paying for the repairs.

Whether or not a claim is made, it is important to notify the insurer that the accident has happened. The driver who fails to do so is breaking a policy condition, and risks having the policy invalidated when a claim arises.

If you are not making a claim, give the insurer details of the accident in writing and add that you are not claiming at this stage. This last qualification leaves you free to claim later if circumstances change—if, for example, the garage discovers that the repairs will cost not £25, but £125.

Accident another driver's fault

If an accident is *clearly* the fault of another driver, you should be able to make a claim without fear of losing your no-claim discount.

This is because, though it will pay out money to meet your claim, the insurer should, in theory, be able to recover the full sum from the other driver, or more often from his insurer.

In this case the motorist would be £40 better off by paying to repair the damage himself. (The calculation assumes that premium prices remain stable for two years. It is not necessary to consider costs further than three years ahead as the maximum discount rate applies in the fourth year, whether the claim is made or not.)

If you have agreed to pay the first £25 or £40 of a claim, this is not recovered by the insurer. You can, however, take steps to recover it yourself, from the other driver or his insurer. A broker, though he is not strictly obliged to, will sometimes help by writing a letter for you; but you may find you have to seek help from your motoring organisation or a solicitor.

Knock-for-knock agreements

Most insurers operate knock-for-knock agreements, under which they agree among themselves that when two insured vehicles are damaged in a collision, each insurer will pay the cost of repairs to the car he insures, provided they are both comprehensively insured, *regardless of whose fault the accident really was.* A motorist can thus lose his discount after an accident for which he was not to blame. He may not even find out until much later.

The aim is to remove the need for costly litigation and get the cars back on the road as quickly as possible. Because it cuts costs, it may help to reduce the general level of premiums and from the insurers' point of view, what they lose on the swings they probably gain on the roundabouts.

But from your point of view, it means that no binding decision need be reached about blame for the accident. If it was clearly not your fault, and the insurer is convinced that he would have recovered the money paid out but for the knock-for-knock agreement, your discount should remain intact.

If, on the other hand, it is not obvious who was at fault, or if both drivers were partly to blame, the motorist may suffer a loss of discount. The insurer is entitled to reduce the discount whenever a claim is made; so the motorist who loses his discount in these circumstances can do little but try to persuade the insurer to change his mind.

Accident your fault

The question of whether or not to claim if an accident is your fault will, again, depend on a comparison of the cost of the repairs and the likely loss of discount. But here there is a further complication if you also damage someone else's property, or cause an injury.

Where only a small amount of damage has been done to other people's property, it may still prove cheaper to settle with them privately, without a claim being made against the other person's insurance policy (or your own).

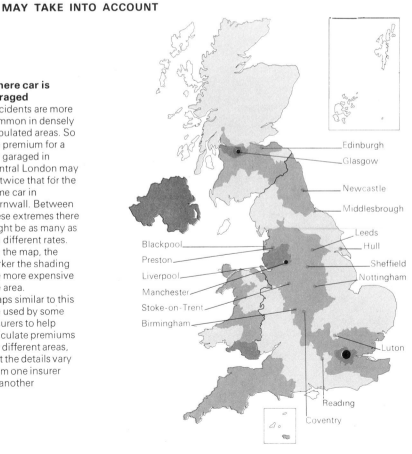

MAY TAKE INTO ACCOUNT

Where car is garaged

Accidents are more common in densely populated areas. So the premium for a car garaged in Central London may be twice that for the same car in Cornwall. Between these extremes there might be as many as ten different rates. On the map, the darker the shading the more expensive the area.

Maps similar to this are used by some insurers to help calculate premiums for different areas, but the details vary from one insurer to another

Edinburgh
Glasgow
Newcastle
Middlesbrough
Leeds
Blackpool
Hull
Preston
Sheffield
Liverpool
Nottingham
Manchester
Stoke-on-Trent
Birmingham
Luton
Reading
Coventry

Insurance/making a claim

What to do if involved in an accident

FEW PEOPLE remain completely unshaken by an accident, even a small one. Yet the best advice is to keep cool and concentrate on the essentials: get help for anyone who is injured; call the police if the accident is serious; and collect as much information as possible to help your insurance claim.

Informing the police

Not every accident need be reported to the police, but there are certain circumstances in which the law obliges a motorist to stop at the scene of an accident:

1. If anyone, apart from himself, has been injured.
2. If any vehicle, apart from his own, has been damaged.
3. If certain animals—horses, cattle, asses, mules, sheep, pigs, dogs or goats —have been injured or killed.
4. If there is damage to any property on or near the road.

The motorist must give his name, address and vehicle registration number (and the owner's name and address if he is not the owner) to anyone who has reasonable grounds for wanting them.

When someone has been injured, the motorist must also produce his insurance certificate to anyone who has reasonable grounds. If he cannot, he must report to the police within 24 hours and produce the certificate at a police station no later than five days after the accident.

Only when names and addresses are not exchanged after such an accident must the motorist report it to the police—within 24 hours. It is, however, advisable to report an accident when serious damage has been caused. It may help in a later insurance claim if police evidence can be produced. On the other hand, the motorist risks prosecution if the police think he has broken any Road Traffic Acts provisions.

The golden rule

In dealings with the police and other drivers, remember the golden rule—never admit liability, even when the accident seems clearly your fault. This is a condition of every motor policy. The blame for an accident is something that, ultimately, only a court can decide. The policyholder who admits liability is pre-judging the issue, and his insurers may refuse to handle the claim if he does so.

Similarly, the policy-holder should not answer letters, claims or legal papers, but should pass them straight to his insurers. He should tell them at once of any impending police prosecution, inquest or (if he is in Scotland) fatal inquiry.

Perhaps the most difficult thing an insurer has to advise people involved in accidents is that they should collect information on the spot, no matter how distressed they may feel.

A blameless motorist who suffers loss in an accident may later have the greatest difficulty in proving that another driver was at fault if he has no names of witnesses and no accurate sketch of the position of vehicles.

So try to make a note of the exact position of the vehicles *at the time*. If you have a camera handy, take photographs.

Whenever the police are not called, try to find independent witnesses (that is, people not in your own car). Although nobody usually wants to become involved in this kind of case, a witness has a duty to help the cause of justice.

In general it is sufficient to get the names and addresses of witnesses, so that they can be contacted later.

If you have the presence of mind to take down a statement on the spot, and get the witness to sign it, you will avoid the danger that he might forget the details, or change his mind about what happened. Tell the insurer as soon as possible of any accident, loss or damage.

If you already have a claim form, it will save time to complete it and send it off as soon as possible. If your policy was arranged through a broker, he will pass on the details to the insurer, and will help you to make a claim.

Repairing the damage

Arrangements can be made straight away for a local garage to tow away the car from the scene of the accident. It is wise not to give the garage instructions to go ahead with the repairs until the insurers have been advised.

If possible, give the insurers a rough estimate of the cost of repairs when you report the accident; a detailed estimate will be needed later. Many insurers will allow the owner to authorise repairs up to a specified figure, provided that a written estimate is obtained from the garage and that the garage keeps the damaged parts for inspection later.

Insurers are anxious to keep costs down, so some will arrange for an engineer-assessor to inspect the damage if it is estimated at more than £35 or so. They will agree a repair cost with the garage before work is started.

A few insurers specify which garage will carry out repairs, or they may suggest one or two which they know have facilities to do the job and with which they have agreed a basis of working.

It is usually better to let the insurers give repair instructions, because they will get the bill, check it and pay it.

The insurers will probably not settle a repair bill until a note has been signed by the owner to say that the repairs are satisfactory. This note may be signed, perhaps

---

HOW TO FILL IN A CLAIM FORM—WORDS AND ROUGH SKETCHES WHICH TELL THE INSURERS ALL

A motorist making an accident report to his insurers will be expected to provide a sketch showing—as here—the course being taken by all vehicles concerned in the accident with their final positions and approximate measurements, and the position of witnesses, pedestrian crossings, beacons or other road signs.

This sketch should be accompanied by an account of how the accident happened, mentioning as many of the following details as are relevant:

Width of the road
Class of road—main or secondary
Whether the car was on its correct side
  (a) immediately before the accident
  (b) at the moment of impact
Whether the driver of the insured car gave ample and proper warning of approach and/or signals
Speed of the insured car
  (a) immediately before the accident
  (b) at the moment of impact
Whether the insured car had no lights on, sidelights only, or sidelights and headlights
Whether the driver of the other vehicle gave proper warning and signals
Estimated speed of the other vehicle
  (a) immediately before the accident
  (b) at the moment of impact
Whether the scene of the accident is controlled by traffic lights or road signs

The Claim Form will also ask specific questions about:
Date, time and place of the accident
Address to which car was taken for repair
Names and addresses of passengers travelling in the car at the time of the accident
Whether they were injured
Whether they were taken to hospital
Apparent nature of their injuries
Names and addresses of witnesses, other than anybody in the vehicle involved
Name or number of policeman who took particulars of the incident
Address of police station at which the incident was reported
Names and addresses of drivers of other vehicles or of pedestrians involved
Description of damaged property
Registration number of other vehicle
Names and addresses of owners of other vehicles or property damaged
Name of company insuring other vehicles or property, and certificate number
Details of damage to other vehicles or property
Names and addresses of passengers in other vehicles involved
Names and addresses of cyclists, pedestrians or others who were injured
Whether they were taken to hospital
Apparent nature of injuries

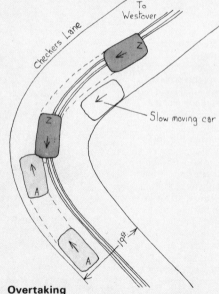

Overtaking

❝I was driving along Checkers Lane towards Westover at about 30 mph in my vehicle Reg. No. A——, and at the point where the road makes a right-hand bend a vehicle, Reg. No. Z——, driven by Mr P. Jones, coming from the opposite direction, overtook a slow-moving car, crossed the double white continuous lines and collided with my vehicle❞

after extensive repairs, before the car owner has a chance to try out the car; if a fault is later found, a reasonable repairer will put it right. In cases of difficulty, or if the repairs were made far from home, the insurers should be consulted. They should help, even if it entails having the fault fixed by another garage.

Reporting the accident
If the damage is minor, it may not be worth making a claim, in view of the possible loss of no-claim discount. There is a stronger case for not claiming if the repairs are likely to cost only a little more than the amount of the excess (see How to keep a no-claim discount, p. 321).

Even if you are not claiming, it is a condition of the policy that any accident must be reported to the insurers.

Telling the insurers is a wise safety precaution anyway. A claim could turn out to be more expensive than was at first thought, or a third-party claim could arise which was unforeseeable at the time. In these cases, the insurers would be entitled to refuse to deal with the claim if not told about the accident in the first place.

The insurers should be given details of the accident with a note explaining that it is not intended to claim at the moment. This leaves the way open for a claim to be made later if circumstances change. Merely reporting an accident will not prejudice the no-claim bonus. This should not be affected unless you make a claim or another motorist claims after an accident in which you were at fault.

Additional repairs resulting from wear and tear or a previous minor knock are often carried out at the same time as damage repairs, but you cannot claim for them. The insurers may ask for a contribution towards damage repairs because of the 'betterment' which will result.

This request is likely to be made if the whole car has to be resprayed due to an accident involving part of it; and if a damaged tyre is replaced the owner must expect to pay for the amount of wear before the accident.

An important point about making a claim is that the claim form must be completed accurately. It will save time and difficulty to have one or two forms in hand before a claim needs to be made. If you carry one in the car, it can be filled in while the accident is fresh in your mind.

However unnecessary questions may seem, settlement of the claim will be reached more quickly if all questions are answered fully and accurately.

The Motor Insurers' Bureau
Although a minimum of motor insurance is compulsory, cars are still driven without it. To compensate people who are injured on the road in these circumstances (and also when insurers are unable to meet their financial obligations), the insurance industry operates and finances the Motor Insurers' Bureau.

The object of the Bureau is to provide the victims of road accidents with compensation in cases where, although insurance was compulsory, there was none in operation. Whenever, in one of these cases, damages and costs awarded by a court are not paid in full within a week, the Bureau foots the bill.

When the Bureau settles a claim, it has a right to recover as much as possible from the person responsible for the accident. So, far from being shielded by the Bureau, a careless motorist who allows his insurance to become invalid can still find himself having to pay for the damage.

Anyone injured by a hit-and-run motorist has no one against whom he can claim. He may, however, apply to the Bureau for compensation. It will consider the case and may make an award. An injured party who is dissatisfied with the Bureau's judgment on an accident may appeal to an independent arbitrator whose decision will be binding.

THEY WANT TO KNOW ABOUT THE ACCIDENT

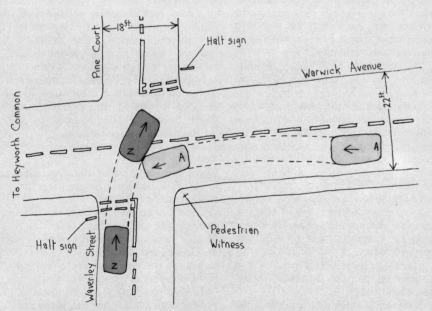

Crossroads
❝I was driving at about 35 mph along Warwick Avenue (unclassified highway) in my vehicle Reg No. A——, towards Heyworth Common. When I was about 100 yds from the crossroads I saw a vehicle coming from Waverley Street on my nearside. Although I was on the major road, I reduced speed to about 20 mph. But Mr Peters, driving vehicle Reg. No. Z——, shot across towards Pine Court and, despite my braking hard and taking all possible avoiding action, a collision took place. Pedestrian witness was at corner of Waverley Street and Warwick Avenue.❞

Turning right
❝I was travelling along Market Street in my vehicle Reg. No. A——, in the direction of Brailey, at about 15–20 mph when suddenly, without warning or signal of any kind, the vehicle in front of mine, Reg. No. Z——, driven by Mr Owens, made a right-hand turn into Gaythorne Garage. Though I braked at once, I could not avoid a collision. Independent witnesses who informed me they would be prepared to give statements were the garage employee and the driver immediately behind❞

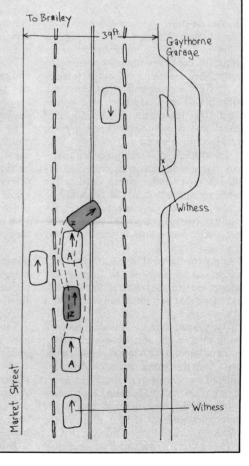

Insurance/going abroad

How to get full cover for a holiday

FEW GENERAL POLICIES give full cover while the car is out of the country. This has to be paid for separately.

If you expect to motor abroad at all, find out how much the extra insurance would cost before arranging your main insurance. It may be worth paying a slightly higher annual premium on the main policy if the extension covering motoring abroad will be cheaper.

The extra cover should be arranged as an extension to the main policy because it is more costly to get cover separately for only a short period abroad. An insurer in the country to be visited may give cover, but the premium will be high since it is calculated on the expensive 'short-period' rate; and cover may differ greatly from what British insurers offer.

A motorist needs insurance while abroad not only to give him financial protection in case of injury to third parties or damage to the car, but also because many countries insist that drivers should have full third-party insurance; and in some countries the requirements are far more stringent than in Britain.

The Green Card

Every United Kingdom motor insurance policy now gives the minimum cover required to comply with laws relating to compulsory insurance of motor vehicles in all EEC and several other European countries. The production of a Green Card (the International Certificate of Insurance) is no longer necessary for travel within this area.

Nevertheless, it is recommended that a motorist should obtain extension of his full UK cover and a Green Card before travelling abroad: it is still necessary to produce the card before entering certain countries (see map opposite), and it will be acceptable to most authorities in the event of an accident.

Apply for the card at least three weeks before leaving and tell the insurers the dates of the trip, the countries to be visited, and those that may have to be crossed in an emergency.

The Green Card is not acceptable in many remote and less developed countries, and some British insurers may refuse to provide the necessary cover. A broker will find the best insurer, but cover is likely to be expensive. It may even be necessary to arrange the insurance on arrival in the country concerned. If in doubt, ask the London tourist office of the country.

The cost of insuring a car while abroad varies. A few insurers still charge £2 for a two-week holiday, but most now require between £3 and £6 for that period.

Along with the Green Card, the insurer may supply a list of local offices and agencies which will help the motorist in case of trouble. Any accident in which someone is hurt or property is damaged should be reported *without delay* to the nearest insurance bureau whose address is on the Green Card.

Going to Spain

A trip to Spain needs special insurance protection. The police are allowed to impound the car and/or detain the driver after an accident unless a deposit is paid to cover liabilities for damages or fines. For a £1.50 premium, most insurers will provide a £500 bail bond.

But if the motorist is fined, he will have to refund the amount to the insurers, as it is considered 'against the public interest' for people to be insured against fines.

The need for extra protection

Insurance for the Continent may not always give exactly the same protection as that given in Britain, particularly if someone other than the regular driver is going to drive.

When arranging the extension of cover, find out exactly what it will be. If important types of cover are to be dropped, it may be possible to have them restored by paying more.

By extending his regular insurance, the motorist going on holiday abroad is usually able to enjoy the same security as he does in this country. But there are several other risks—not covered under normal comprehensive insurance—which can jeopardise a foreign holiday.

A breakdown or an accident at such a time can involve far more than the expense of garage repairs or replacements. For instance, if the repairs cannot be completed immediately, there may be the cost of an unscheduled stay for the whole family at a roadside hotel, or the family's rail fares or car-hire bill.

Some of the extra costs of holiday mishaps can be covered by extra insurance under a travel policy.

Package deals

Alternatively, there are package-deal plans provided by motoring organisations and travel agents to protect holiday-makers who get into difficulties.

Among the most comprehensive of these 'trouble-shooter' plans is the AA's 5-Star Travel Service, which provides a wide range of benefits if the member's car breaks down, or is damaged or stolen abroad, or if the motorist himself becomes medically unfit to drive.

The first part of the scheme, known as Vehicle Security, provides for the recovery of cars which cannot be repaired economically abroad. The AA makes all the arrangements for transporting the car home and pays all the expenses, apart from cross-Channel freight fares.

In cases where the motorist is declared to be medically unfit to drive, a chauffeur may be provided to bring the car and passengers home.

In addition, Vehicle Security provides for towing damaged cars to a garage, transporting spare parts from Britain, and replacing shattered windscreens. Credit vouchers are given to cover legal, hiring or return travel expenses after an accident or motoring offence.

Under this plan, the AA also gives protection against the substantial customs charges which may be levied if the car is either stolen or completely destroyed by fire or accident while abroad. These charges are imposed by the country in which the car is lost or damaged, on the grounds that the vehicle has not been taken out of that country as required by import/export regulations.

The second part of the service, Touring Security, provides some reimbursement for hiring a car to continue the journey, rail or air fares for the whole party to return home; and payment for extra hotel bills that may arise after fire, theft, accident or breakdown for more than eight hours, and for the driver becoming medically unfit to drive and there being no other qualified driver in the party.

The third part, Personal Security, provides compensation for loss of baggage, camping equipment, tickets, travellers' cheques, passports, credit cards and personal money.

There are also several benefits if a member of the party suffers an injury, becomes ill or dies.

If this leads to the tour being cancelled or cut short, accommodation and transport deposits will be refunded.

In cases of illness or death *during* the holiday, extra benefits include medical expenses, fares and hotel bills to enable a friend or relative to stay with a sick person; a payment of £2000 in the event of death or permanent disablement in an accident;

and even the cost of conveying the body of a member of the party to his home for burial or cremation.

Journeys by sea and air

Normally, when an insurance policy is extended for continental motoring, cover will automatically be provided for a sea crossing of 65 hours or less by any 'recognised' route between countries where the green card is valid—including hovercraft ferries. A longer crossing, or one by an unusual or 'unrecognised' route, will need an extra premium. If a claim is made, it will affect the no-claim discount.

For a voyage where there is an appreciable risk of minor damage (if, say, a drive-on/drive-off ferry is not used), it may be worth arranging separate cargo insurance for the car.

Several insurance policies do not cover a car going by air, but air-ferry operators generally make themselves responsible if loss or damage occurs while the car is in their care. This should be checked when making the booking; separate insurance should be taken out if compensation is not payable by the air ferry.

Unusual risks

War risks, such as the ship hitting a mine, can also be insured against. It is possible, too, to insure against what are called 'general average charges'—levies which may be imposed on all owners of cargo if drastic steps have to be taken for the common good of the ship and her cargo. For instance, if two or three cars have to be pushed overboard, the cost must be shared by all those with cargo aboard.

Caravans

Check the caravan policy. If it is restricted to use of the caravan in Britain, the policy will have to be extended.

The motor insurers, who may not be the same as those covering the caravan, should be asked to include a description of it on the Green Card. This guarantees that the caravan's insurance conforms to the legal requirements of the countries to be visited.

Third-party liability for the caravan, while it is attached to the car, is covered by the car's insurers—not the caravan's.

For a small extra fee, motorists travelling with the AA's 5-Star Travel Service can extend the benefits of Vehicle Security to cover their caravans

There is also an AA Camping Service which provides, among other benefits, third party insurance cover of up to £250,000.

Countries which accept the green card

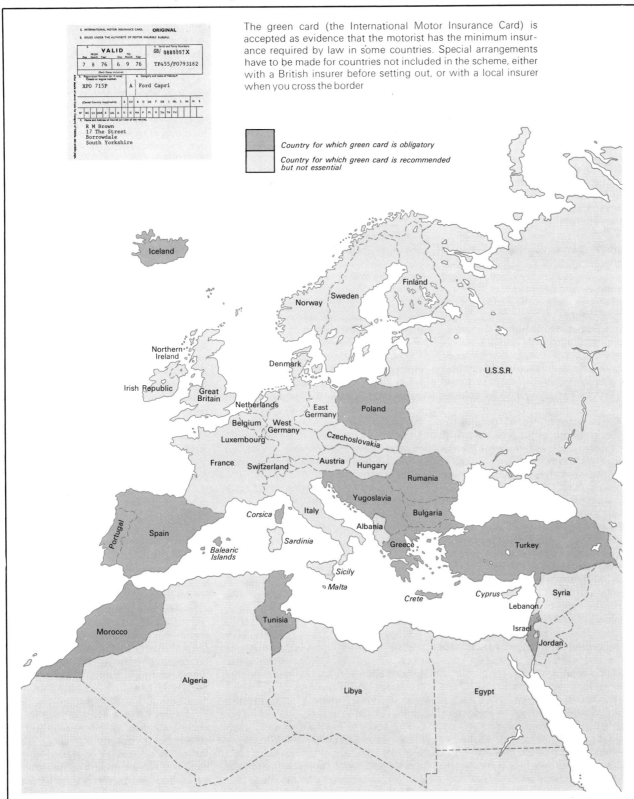

The green card (the International Motor Insurance Card) is accepted as evidence that the motorist has the minimum insurance required by law in some countries. Special arrangements have to be made for countries not included in the scheme, either with a British insurer before setting out, or with a local insurer when you cross the border

Country for which green card is obligatory

Country for which green card is recommended but not essential

Renewals

MOST MOTOR INSURANCE POLICIES are annual contracts which have to be renewed, usually by paying a fresh premium, every 12 months. It is a motorist's responsibility to make certain that he is insured at all times, and though it is customary for the broker or insurer to send a renewal notice, never rely on this.

Instead, make a diary note of the policy renewal date and contact the broker or insurer if the renewal notice is not sent two weeks before the policy expires. If you are going away, ask for details of the renewal premium early.

Always insist on receiving the insurer's own printed renewal notice. Many brokers and agents send out their own forms, keeping the insurer's notice on their files. This deprives the policy-holder of evidence of the 15-day temporary Road Traffic Act cover, and of any no-claim discount he has earned.

If the renewal terms are satisfactory, pay the new premium at once, so that the renewal receipt and certificate of insurance for the following year are issued before the date of renewal.

If any change has taken place during the year in the particulars on the proposal form, and the insurer has not yet been informed, he should be told without fail when the policy is renewed. He should be informed, for instance, if the policy-holder has changed his occupation, or if he has suffered a deterioration in health or been convicted of a motoring offence since filling in the form.

Extensions

The renewal notice usually includes what appears to be an extension of the policy, but it is unwise to rely on this. The most it may cover is the minimum insurance required by law—cover against claims for injury from third parties. So the man with a Comprehensive policy who fails to pay his premium before the renewal date will suddenly be deprived of protection for himself and his car.

Even this insurance will not apply unless the motorist can prove that he had no intention of taking out insurance elsewhere (which could be difficult if he had been trying to obtain a cheaper quotation), *and* that he intended to renew the policy (which could be difficult if he had been trying to sell the car).

So if you intend to change your insurer, or to sell your car and give up motoring for a time, on no account rely on the renewal notice extension for cover.

How to get the best from a garage

Making sure the job is done well—at the right price

THE MOTORIST choosing a garage to service and repair his car looks for prompt attention, good workmanship and a reasonable price. If he is wise, he will also foresee that disputes can occasionally arise, so that a garage which belongs to a scheme for settling disputes is better than one which does not.

How does a motorist find out whether a garage does a good job for a fair price? Obviously the recommendations of friends are valuable, especially if they have been going to the garage for some time.

But not all garages are equally suited to deal with each type of car. The complexity of modern motor vehicles makes it essential that major repairs should be carried out with specialised tools and equipment, by trained mechanics experienced in dealing with your make of car. In practice, this means using a garage which is the manufacturer's authorised franchise-holder.

These garages are the specialists. They should have a comprehensive stock of essential spare parts and a staff of mechanics with the relevant experience. In addition, they will be kept informed by bulletins from the manufacturer about modifications and defects affecting the models they sell and service.

Motoring organisations experienced in dealing with complaints about garages have found that the greatest single cause of dispute is repair work carried out by garages which are not the appropriate franchise-holders (for instance, the replacement of the clutch or the hydrolastic suspension unit of a BMC Mini by a garage which is not a BMC franchise-holder).

Garages and their facilities vary considerably—from the filling station type, mainly interested in selling petrol, oil and possibly a few accessories, to the large garage which deals with insurance, car hire, new and used car sales and major body repairs. It is unreasonable to expect the same kind of service from both these types of garage.

A detailed guide to the size, facilities and equipment of garages is provided by the spanner gradings of the Automobile Association's Garage Plan. Under this scheme, garages are allowed to display a one, two or three-spanner sign, according to the range of services they are equipped to provide to the public.

A garage displaying any one of the spanner signs has been inspected and found to be well equipped and staffed by trained mechanics, and has agreed to be bound by the AA's Code of Practice covering such sensitive points as estimates, guarantees and delays over repairs.

In addition, the AA breakdown truck sign indicates garages with a breakdown service, offering mechanical and electrical first aid up to midnight, or beyond.

A good way of ensuring reliable service is to become a regular customer. The motorist who goes to the same garage for his petrol, spares and routine work is valued.

What will it cost?

Garage charges for repair work are made up of two elements: the retail cost of any parts supplied plus VAT, and the cost of labour, charged at an hourly rate, plus VAT.

Labour charges vary from one part of the country to another, but there is usually little or no difference between rates charged by franchise and non-franchise garages in the same area, or by garages with one, two or three-spanner gradings.

Experience shows that most customers' ideas of what a repair will cost are wide of the mark. To avoid unpleasant surprises, always ask for an estimate before authorising a garage to go ahead. If the price quoted is more than £30, ask to have the estimate in writing.

The garage may say that it is not possible to give a reliable estimate without first dismantling parts and investigating the cause of the trouble.

In this case it should give an estimate of the cost of this exploratory work, and a second estimate of what the repair itself is likely to cost.

If either estimate appears to be unreasonably high, there may be another franchise-holder near by whom you can ask to estimate for the same job. But beware of giving the job to a non-franchise garage, even if it quotes a substantially lower price—this could easily turn out to be a false economy.

If the work is eventually done by a second garage, expect to pay a fair charge to the first garage for investigating the cause of a breakdown.

An estimate which appears to be too high can also be checked with your motoring organisation. If a repair is going to be costly and you are unsure whether you can afford it, ask for an estimate giving the upper and lower limits of the cost.

Many disputes over bills are caused by the variation between estimates and bills. Usually this variation arises because the garage has found additional repair work urgently needing attention, and has gone ahead without consulting the car owner.

A good garage will not proceed with these extra jobs without authority. But to be on the safe side, the motorist can set a cash limit on repairs when leaving the car, and ask the garage manager to get in touch with him before this limit is exceeded. He should also give a telephone number where he can be reached during the day. He will then be liable to pay only for the work he has authorised.

When ordering repairs to dents and other body damage, ask for a written estimate, divided into these two categories:
1. Removal and refitting of any parts.
2. The cost of any new panels or parts.

An estimate in this form can be easily and fairly assessed.

How long will it take?

It is always wise to ask a garage how long it will take to do the work. If you need the car at a particular time on a particular day, make sure that the garage can do the job in time before they start work.

If a replacement of parts or a body repair is involved, it may take several days before the car will be ready; and a good garage will not make rash promises about completing work. If it does take longer than anticipated, the delay may be due to something happening which genuinely could not have been foreseen—such as an industrial dispute holding up the delivery of spare parts.

A motorist has little redress if his car is not ready at the time promised, even though the delay causes inconvenience or financial loss. In practice, all he can do is take his custom elsewhere in future.

What the garage does

Servicing Manufacturers usually recommend servicing at intervals of 3000 or 5000 miles or, if this comes sooner, every three months.

When booking a service, give details of any additional work required, so that time can be allotted for it. It is not reasonable to book a small service and then ask, after the garage has arranged its day's working schedule, for a number of major items to be done at the same time.

The items of work necessary at each service have been compiled from many years of experience and research, and include additional checks to make sure that the car complies with the law.

With regular servicing, faults which might otherwise develop into serious and dangerous defects can usually be detected before they have gone too far.

Motorists planning holidays abroad should book a major service in good time to have it completed before they go.

Repairs When something goes wrong, always give the symptoms, not what you believe to be the cause. Rely on the garage man's experience to decide this. If you tell him to do a particular repair, he will probably do it—and you will have no comeback if this fails to correct the fault.

Many repairs can be planned in advance. When a car is serviced, the garage will be able to see the signs of wear. A general falling-off in efficiency or a partial failure causing a minor breakdown are other indications that repairs are becoming necessary.

This is the time to fix a convenient date for the repairs to be carried out. With prior notice, the garage can make sure that any spare parts needed will be available.

Repairs of this kind, made necessary by normal wear, include tuning the engine, fitting new suspension elements, re-lining the brakes, overhauling the clutch and fitting new tyres.

Ideally, dents and body damage should be dealt with by garages with their own bodywork department. Where this is not possible, the garage will usually send the work out to a specialist firm.

Breakdowns The motorist in difficulties should give all the details of the breakdown symptoms, as this will help the garage man to decide what equipment to send to the spot.

A wide range of breakdown services is provided by the motoring organisations to members who are in difficulties. Generally, they will send one of their patrols to a roadside breakdown.

It may subsequently prove necessary for the car to be taken to a garage for repairs to be done; and under the terms of the AA's free breakdown service, a car can be collected only by the nearest AA appointed garage, regardless of whether or not it is the local franchise-holder for that model of car.

This can cause difficulties when major repairs are needed, or when a car is subject to a maker's warranty. While the car is covered by warranty, always have any repairs needed carried out by a franchised garage. Never try to persuade a garage to do work for which it may not be qualified.

Alternatively, the motorist himself can ask that the work be done by a franchise-holder once the cause of the breakdown has been diagnosed.

When a car is transferred in this way, the first garage will rightly expect to be paid for any work done in tracing the fault. The AA does not pay for any repairs carried out at a garage, or the cost of having the car towed to another garage.

Note that if the breakdown occurs on a motorway, the regulations do not permit a garage or a motoring organisation patrol to carry out major repairs at the roadside.

Motorists who need help on the motorway must use one of the emergency telephones provided. They will be connected directly with the local police control centre which will arrange breakdown assistance.

Breakdowns on motorways are subject to high minimum charges, because of the long distances involved. If you are a member of a motoring organisation, do not forget to tell the police control centre and ask for the organisation's free breakdown assistance.

When a breakdown vehicle arrives, make sure it is the one which has been called for you.

AA service covers towing a member's car to the nearest garage or to a motorway service area. If it proves necessary to take it from there to another garage for repair, this will be at the member's expense.

Trouble with your garage

Disputes between garages and their customers are far too common for the good of either—the AA alone deals with thousands a year. If you do have the misfortune to become involved, you can make it as painless as possible by following the correct procedure.

First, take up the complaint with the garage manager. Nothing is gained by bringing in a third party until the motorist has put his case directly to the people who are involved.

If the complaint is about the repair itself and is a fair one, there is a good chance that the garage will look into it.

If complaining to the garage manager fails to produce results, motorists can ask their motoring organisation to help them.

The AA, for example, advises its members to ask the association's help in such a dispute, and not to take further action themselves without advice.

If the garage has an AA spanner or breakdown grading, it will have agreed to co-operate with the AA in attempting to

resolve amicably any dispute with an Association member. In such cases, the AA's own team of expert engineers will frequently succeed in sorting out the problem. Disputes with garages which do not belong to the AA Garage Plan may not be so easy to settle; but in most complaints referred to them by members, the AA is able to promote a settlement acceptable to both parties.

The motorist who does not belong to a motoring organisation can still enlist help in a dispute with a garage.

One channel is the trade itself. If the garage is a franchise-holder, the motorist can complain to the manufacturer, who may be prepared to look into the case.

If the garage belongs to the Motor Agents' Association, which is a trade body, the motorist can refer the case to the MAA Investigation and Advisory Service, at 201 Great Portland Street, W1N 6AB. A similar scheme is operated in Scotland by the Scottish Motor Trade Association at 3 Palmerston Place, Edinburgh, EH120PQ.

The MAA only considers disputes which are referred within three months of the incident which led to the complaint.

The service is in two parts. First the association's staff will attempt to produce a settlement.

If conciliation fails, they will then try to persuade the two sides to take their case to arbitration. This means that both garage and customer agree to accept the decision of an independent outside arbitrator as final and forfeit their right to sue in the courts. If either party does not want arbitration, it cannot proceed.

The MAA pays the fees of the arbitrator and his expert assessors. The motorist pays a deposit, which will be returned to him if he wins his case.

The parties themselves are not present at the hearing. The arbitrator considers written evidence from each side, consults his assessors, and gives his verdict.

In any dispute with a garage, the ultimate recourse is to legal action. In some instances a letter from the motorist's solicitor may persuade a garage to compromise. In others it may be necessary to go through the expensive and time-consuming business of going to court.

Solicitors usually advise against this unless the claim is for a large sum of money. Indeed it has been calculated that most people going to court with a claim for less than £30 actually end up out of pocket —even if they win their case and have costs awarded in their favour.

The AA's system of grading garages . . .

 1 Spanner

These are smaller garages with adequate facilities for customers. At least half the staff are trained and qualified. They are able to adjust and replace all major mechanical components for a particular range of vehicles and have a limited range of tools, parts and accessories

 2 Spanners

These are medium-sized garages, with comfortable customer reception areas and parking facilities. At least two-thirds of the staff are trained and qualified. They are able to carry out all routine service and repair tasks as well as specialised tuning and brake testing

 3 Spanners

These are large garages, with comfortable customer waiting areas and parking space. Almost all the adult staff are trained and qualified. They are able to carry out inspection, servicing, diagnosis and repair with the minimum need for advance booking. They have equipment to detect obscure electrical and mechanical faults, and they can also produce the highest standard of bodywork repairs

 Breakdown truck

These are garages which can recover damaged or broken-down cars and provide reliable mechanical and electrical first aid, until at least midnight. They carry a range of spares for most makes of car and have good communications with AA emergency services. Because motorists may have to wait while their cars are being attended to, they usually have waiting-room facilities

---

. . . and the Code of Practice they follow

1. If the cost of repair is likely to exceed £30, the garage should supply, on request, a written estimate for the work required and the parts needed. This normally includes:

(a) extent of dismantling and exploratory work required before a proper final estimate can be prepared;

(b) lower and upper limit of the cost of repairs.

These estimates should be submitted before the work is started. The AA member then has the right to instruct the garage within 48 hours not to proceed—in which case he is liable to a fair charge for any costs incurred by them.

2. The garage has the right to refuse to take on a particular repair job, especially if it could be complex, or if the vehicle is one for which the garage does not hold a franchise. However, once repair work has been started, it must be carried through speedily to a satisfactory conclusion.

3. The garage must guarantee the effectiveness of the repaired or renewed parts or components under normal operating conditions for not less than three months. The member must be warned if, due to the age or condition of his vehicle, there is a risk that the repair may not be wholly satisfactory; if, in the circumstances, further work

does become necessary, the member will be liable for the cost of labour.

4. When selling a secondhand car less than three years old or with less than 30,000 miles on the mileometer, the garage should normally give an adequate and clear warranty, understood and accepted by the member.

This should indemnify the purchaser against the cost of rectifying faulty workmanship, or defective materials, parts and components (other than as a result of wear and tear), for a period of three months or 3000 miles, whichever expires earlier.

The warranty would not be transferable to another owner and would apply only where the vehicle is operated under normal conditions and maintained according to the manufacturer's published Service and Replacement Schedules.

5. The garage agrees to co-operate with the AA in speedily resolving disputes between the garage and AA members.

If, after three months of negotiation, all reasonable attempts at settling the dispute have failed, the case may be submitted to an arbitration panel for a final and conclusive decision, legally binding on all parties. Such disputes must be notified to the AA within three months of the date of the incident.

ABC of car law

SOME POINTS THE POLICE MAY CHECK

Seat belts — Mirror
Windscreen wipers and washers
Speedometer
Steering gear
Rear lights and stop-lights
Number plate
Reflectors
Windows
Mirrors
Direction indicator
Side-lamp
Springs
Headlamps
Silencer
Horn
Vehicle excise licence
Number plate
Handbrake
Brakes
Wings
Tyres
Headlamps
Side-lamp
Direction indicator

Liability and penalties

THE CONSTRUCTION and maintenance of a car and its accessories are controlled by law. This control extends to the wattage of the headlamp bulbs and the place on the windscreen where the vehicle excise licence must be displayed.

Anyone using a car which does not meet the requirements of the law can be prosecuted. Trivial offences are often dealt with by a police caution, either on the spot or by letter; but the penalty for more serious offences is usually a fine, plus an endorsement or even disqualification.

That most feared of punishments, disqualification from driving, can be imposed, for example, on anyone using a car in Britain if it is a danger or a potential danger by its condition (including its parts or accessories, its load, the number of passengers carried) or because of the unsuitability of the purpose for which it is being used. Such a driver can also be disqualified if the Construction and Use Regulations covering brakes, steering gear, tyres or weight are broken.

The motorist cannot escape liability by showing that he did not know of the defects, but he can avoid disqualification and endorsement if he proves that he did not know and had no reasonable cause to suspect that the offence would be committed.

In Northern Ireland a Resident Magistrate can disqualify for any breach of Construction and Use Regulations.

Responsibility for defects in construction or maintenance is put on the person who *uses* the car or *permits its use* or *causes it to be used.*

These terms have legal definitions which go beyond the obvious ones. If you are driving your employer's car on business, both you and your employer are using it.

If your son borrows your car, he is using it, but you are permitting its use.

The person who causes a car to be used is anybody who gives someone an express or positive order to use it. If a company manager tells a driver to take out a certain car, the driver will be the user of the car and the manager will be causing its use. If the car is being used on business, the company will also be the user.

Because the car is a potentially dangerous piece of machinery, the law has imposed certain obligations on anyone offering one for sale or selling one.

It is an offence to sell or supply, or even offer to sell or supply, a car or trailer, including a caravan, that is not roadworthy. The penalty for such offence is a fine of up to £200.

This means that a dealer must not display for sale a car or trailer that is unroadworthy. He has a defence, however, if he can prove that he had reasonable cause to believe that the car or trailer would not be used until its faults had been put right.

The fact that the seller has committed this offence does not mean that the buyer can automatically get his money back.

There are similar provisions relating to the sale and fitting of unsuitable parts.

After a car has been bought, responsibility for its condition rests with the user or person who permits or causes its use.

The following summary of some of the main regulations concerning the construction and use of cars was correct at the time of going to press.

KEY TO PENALTIES

A key letter or figure indicates the penalty, or combination of penalties, which a court can apply to any breach of the regulations in England, Scotland or Wales.

Fine **£50** The figure gives the maximum fine which a motorist committing the offence can be ordered to pay.

E A conviction will, in the absence of special reasons, be endorsed on the offender's driving licence. Under the 'totting-up' procedure, the third endorsement within three years (before the offence that gives rise to that endorsement) brings automatic disqualification for at least six months, unless there are mitigating circumstances (which take into account the circumstances of the offence and the motorist). Then the court may disqualify for a shorter period or not at all.

d Anyone convicted of this offence *may* be disqualified from driving for a period to be decided by the court (though this is not automatic).

In Northern Ireland the penalty for offences listed in the ABC of car law is a fine of up to £400 for those relating to brakes, steering gear and tyres and up to £100 for others. In addition, the offender's licence can be endorsed and he can be disqualified from driving. There is no 'totting-up' procedure.

Car law/A-L

Alterations to a vehicle

It is an offence to alter a car or trailer so that it fails to comply with the construction (including lighting) regulations.

Fine £200

Brakes

A car must have either one braking system with two means of operation or two braking systems each having a separate means of operation. Most cars have two systems—a mechanical one operated by a handbrake, and a hydraulic system operated by a footbrake.

The braking system must be so made that if there is a failure of any part (except a fixed member or a brake-shoe anchor pin) through which the braking force is transmitted, the driver can still apply brakes to at least half the number of wheels (two wheels on a three-wheeler) to stop within a reasonable distance. This means, for example, that if the brakes are hydraulic and the system springs a leak, the driver must still be able to apply brakes to two wheels. This will usually be done by the handbrake.

Many cars have a fail-safe (dual) braking system in which the footbrake operation still performs on part of the braking system even if one hydraulic circuit has failed.

Braking systems must meet prescribed efficiency levels—usually determined by an instrument called a decelerometer, or by a roller brake tester.

Special rules apply to motor cars first registered before 1915. Cars first used on or after April 1, 1938, must not have a braking system that is rendered ineffective by the non-rotation of the engine.

Cars first used before 1968 need a parking braking system that can always effectually prevent at least two wheels (one on a three-wheeler) from turning while the car is not being driven or is left unattended. Those first used after that date must have a parking braking system independent of the main braking system and which can be kept on by direct mechanical action, without any hydraulic, electric or pneumatic device. When so operated it must be capable of holding the vehicle on a gradient of 1 in 6·25, without the assistance of stored energy.

Every part of every braking system and of its means of operation must be in working order and be properly adjusted. This covers such faults as worn brake pad and brake-shoe linings, over-stretched

and frayed cables, worn linkages, hydraulic fluid falling below the proper level and excessive wear of the parking-brake ratchet.

Special provisions apply to cars for which EEC technical certificates have been issued.

d E Fine £100

Caravans see *Trailers*

Direction indicators see *Lighting*

Dual-purpose vehicles

A vehicle that is constructed or adapted to carry both passengers and goods (or burden of any description) is a dual-purpose vehicle if (a) its unladen weight does not exceed 2040 kg. and (b) it has four-wheel-drive (such as Land Rovers, Range Rovers and Jeeps) or complies with four specifications:

1. It has a permanently fixed rigid roof, with or without a sliding panel.
2. There is at least one permanently fitted row of sprung or cushioned seats with upholstered backrests for at least two passengers, set across the vehicle behind the driver's seat.
3. There are side windows behind the driver's seat with a total area of at least 1850 sq. cm. on each side, and a rear window or windows of not less than 700 sq. cm.
4. The distance between the rearmost part of the steering wheel and the

rearmost backrest is, when the seats are ready for use, at least one-third of the distance between the rearmost part of the steering wheel and the rearmost part of the floor.

A dual-purpose vehicle not exceeding two tons unladen weight and not adapted to carry more than seven passengers plus the driver is subject to the same speed limits as an ordinary car.

A dual-purpose vehicle is taxed at the goods-vehicle rate of excise duty if it is used to carry goods or burden for hire or reward, or in connection with a trade or business.

Dual-purpose vehicles do not require an operator's licence.

CAR TAX Vans are not liable to Car Tax, but the tax is payable if a van is converted into a vehicle which attracts Car Tax, for example, where side windows are fitted in a van to the rear of the driver's seat. The amount of tax to be paid is calculated at 10 per cent of the current wholesale value of the vehicle.

A motorist who intends to convert his vehicle should inform Customs and Excise, his insurers and the licensing authority before ordering parts and undertaking conversion work.

Estate cars see *Dual-purpose vehicles*

Headlamps see *Lighting*

Horn

Every car must be fitted with an instru-

ment capable of giving audible and sufficient warning of its approach or position. The sound emitted by such an instrument on a car first used after July 1973 must be continuous and uniform and not strident. Only certain cars (such as those used for fire brigade, ambulance or police purposes) may have a gong, bell, siren or two-tone horn.

It is generally illegal to sound a horn when a car is stationary, or to sound a horn between 11.30 p.m. and 7 a.m. when a car is travelling on roads subject to a 30 mph speed limit.

Fine £100

Licence, vehicle excise

Any other permit or licence

Excise licence

This licence must be shown on the car at all times it is used or kept on a public road. The licence must be in a holder to protect it from the weather, and is best placed on the nearside lower corner of the windscreen, so that all particulars are clearly visible by daylight from the near side of the road. The licence should not be fixed behind the rear-view mirror.

Anything else on the windscreen, such as a resident's parking permit, can be in any position, provided that it does not obscure the driver's view of the road and traffic ahead.

Fine £20

Lighting

The law about lighting is based on the principle that a vehicle should show white lights at the front and red lamps at the rear, and that the spacing of the lights should indicate the vehicle's width.

There are exceptions: for example, headlamps may be yellow, and white lights are allowed at the rear for one or two reversing lights and to illuminate the number plate.

Even during the day, a car must be equipped with such lighting equipment and reflectors as will enable it to be driven at night without contravening the lighting laws.

In poor day-time visibility, a car that is

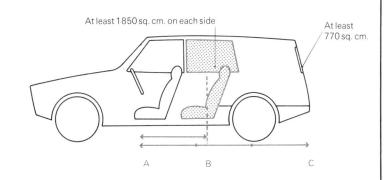

ONE WAY OF CONVERTING A VAN TO A DUAL-PURPOSE VEHICLE

At least 1850 sq. cm. on each side

At least 770 sq. cm.

A   B   C

A van must have a rigid roof (with or without a sliding panel). Windows must be made or enlarged, and seats installed so that the distance from A (the rearmost part of the steering wheel) to B is at least one-third of that from A to C

moving must keep its side, rear and headlamps (or equivalent) lit.

During the hours of darkness—from half an hour after sunset to half an hour before sunrise—cars must carry:

1. Two front side lamps, showing a white light visible from a reasonable distance.
2. Two rear lamps, showing a red light visible from a reasonable distance.
3. Two headlamps or groups of headlamps (except for three-wheeled cars and some others).

POSITION OF LIGHTS

Obligatory side and headlamps Max. 400mm

Side-lights with frosted glass and not more than 7 watts
Maximum 1700mm

Obligatory headlamps
Max. 1200mm
Min. 500mm

Front The minimum distance between the headlamps is measured from their inner lit areas. The maximum height above the ground for headlamps is measured from the highest part of the illuminated area. Side light measurements, from the ground and edge of the car, are taken to the highest and outermost parts of the illuminated area.

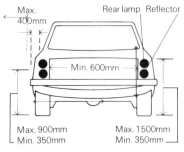

Max. 400mm

Rear lamp   Reflector

Min. 600mm

Max. 900mm
Min. 350mm

Max. 1500mm
Min. 350mm

Rear The minimum distance between the reflectors is measured from their inner reflecting areas. The maximum permitted distance between lamps/reflectors and the outermost side of the car or its equipment is measured to the nearest part of the lit/reflecting area. The height for rear lamps and reflectors is measured from the ground to the top and bottom of the lit/reflecting areas.

4. Two rear-facing red reflectors.
5. A lamp capable of illuminating the rear number plate.
6. Two stop lamps—if the car was first used on or after January 1, 1971.
7. Direction indicators optically separated from other lamps if the car was first used after September 1, 1965.

All equipment must be clean and in working order.

Fine £100

DIRECTION INDICATORS Direction indicators on all vehicles with certain exceptions are compulsory. Regulations govern their design and positions.

Cars first used before September 1, 1965, may have either electrically operated semaphore arms or flashing-light indicators.

Cars first used on or after that date must have flashing all-amber indicators optically separated from other lamps.

On pre-September 1965 cars, indicators showing to the front and rear must be amber. If showing only to the front they may be amber or white. If showing only to the rear, they may be amber or red.

A flashing-lamp indicator must wink at between 60 and 120 flashes per minute.

The maximum height for direction indicators is 7 ft 6 in. above ground level. The minimum height on pre-1965 cars is 1 ft 5 in. above ground level; on post-1965 cars, the minimum is 1 ft 3 in.

All indicators on the same side of a car must be worked by the same switch, and a car must have a readily visible or audible warning device to show that the compulsory indicators are working if the car is not fitted with at least one indicator on each side which makes the driver aware that it is in operation.

Drivers have been successfully prosecuted for careless driving because they failed to cancel their indicator signals.

Direction indicators fitted to cars first used on or after January 1, 1974, must be marked with an 'E' approval mark and a specified number. Each rear-direction indicator on such cars may be of either the single or dual-intensity type. If they are dual-intensity, they must meet specified wiring conditions.

When a car is stationary, hazard warning lights may be operated to warn other road users by simultaneously illuminating direction indicators.

Fine £100

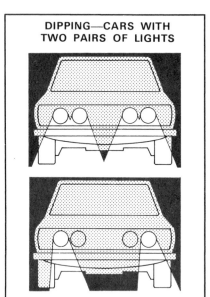

DIPPING—CARS WITH TWO PAIRS OF LIGHTS

Cars with two equal groups of headlamps must have them so arranged that when the outermost lamps are dipped the main beams shown by the other headlamps are extinguished

HEADLAMPS A car must generally have (a) two matched headlamps that can show together either main beams or dipped beams (dipped beams only for cars incapable of exceeding 25 mph) or (b) two or more matched pairs of headlamps so arranged that, when the outermost lamps are dipped, the main beams shown by the others go out.

Each beam should come from at least one filament of not less than 30 watts. Every headlamp that emits a dipped beam must be so positioned on one side of the car that no part of its lit area is less than 600 mm. from any part of the lit area of any lamp on the other side (350 mm. in the case of a car first used before October 1, 1969). On cars first used on or after January 1, 1972, the outermost part of the lit area must not be more than 400 mm. from the outermost part of the car on the side on which the lamp is placed.

The highest part of a lit area must be not more than 1200 mm. from the ground; and, except in the case of a lamp used only at night in fog or falling snow, or in daytime during poor visibility, the lower part may not be less than 500 mm.

In each matched pair, headlamps must be at the same height, have the same shape and area, give same coloured beams, and go on and off together.

A dipped beam means a beam light deflected down, or down and to the left, so as not to dazzle others—technically, anyone more than 7.7 m. away whose eyes are not less than 1.1 m. from the ground.

Headlamps must be kept switched on when a car is in motion on a road: (a) during the hours of darkness, except when the road has street lights lit, not more than 200 yds apart ('a built-up area'); and (b) in daytime poor visibility. ('Poor visibility' means when conditions seriously reduce the driver's ability to see other vehicles or persons on the road, or when other road users have difficulty seeing the vehicle). For cars with four or more wheels, the poor-visibility regulation means that at least a matched pair of obligatory headlamps must be kept lit.

At night in fog or falling snow, or in daytime poor visibility, cars that have two 'permitted' lamps may keep them both lit instead. 'Permitted' lamps are two fog lamps or one fog lamp and one headlamp (in addition to the obligatory headlamp) in symmetrically prescribed positions on each side of the car, with their centres at the same height above the ground.

Front lamps that are used only at night in conditions of fog or falling snow or in daytime poor visibility, may have their centres less than 500 mm. from the ground, but if they exceed 7 watts they must be permanently deflected downwards and/or to the near side.

A single front fog/spot lamp is permitted in any built-up area. Outside such an area, it must be used only with lit obligatory headlamps.

Headlamps must be switched off when a car is stationary, except in traffic stops.

Fine £100

PARKING LIGHTS Cars standing or parked at night must generally show two white lights to the front, two red lights and reflectors to the rear, and the rear number plate must be illuminated. However, a car to which a trailer is not attached may be left without lights provided that the road is subject to a 30 mph speed limit or less and the vehicle is either lawfully in an authorised parking place, or is more than 15 yds from a road junction with its nearside close and parallel to the edge of the carriageway. (In a one-way street, it may have its offside close and parallel to the right-hand edge of the carriageway.)

Fine £100

REAR LAMPS A car must have two matched rear-facing lamps each showing a red light visible from a reasonable distance. The lamps must be fitted on each side of the centre line of the car; they must be not more than 16 in. (24 in. in certain exceptional cases) from the outermost side of the car or its equipment, and not more than 30 in. from the rearmost part of the car.

The maximum height from the ground of the top of the lit area of the rear lamps must be the same, and not exceed 3 ft 6 in. The minimum height from the ground of the bottom of such area must be at least 15 in. (although there is no minimum in certain cases). On cars made after July 1973 the lamps must be marked with an 'E' approval mark and a specified symbol (a BS marking is needed on cars registered between April 1959 and the end of 1973).

Fine £100

REFLECTORS Every car needs two rear-facing reflectors, one on each side of the centre line of the car. The reflecting areas must be at least 21 in. apart (600 mm. in some cases), and the nearest part of the reflecting areas must be not more than 30 in. from the rearmost point of the car.

The height of the top of the reflecting area of each reflector must be the same and its height above ground level must not exceed 3 ft 6 in. (900 mm. in some cases). The bottom must be not less than 15 in. (350 mm. in some cases) above ground.

The reflecting area must be vertical and face squarely to the rear. If an unlit rear lamp fulfils a reflector's requirements, the lamp is treated as a reflector, whether lit or not. Reflectors must have an 'E' approval mark incorporating a specified number, or a BS marking.

Fine £100

REVERSING LAMPS Up to two reversing lamps are permitted, but they are not obligatory. A reversing lamp may be switched on only by (a) selecting reverse gear or (b) using a switch which, except for cars first used before July 1, 1954, serves no other purpose. In that case, subject to the same qualification, the car must be equipped with a device readily visible to the driver to indicate that the lamp is on.

Neither lamp shall exceed 24 watts, and each can show only a white light to the rear for the purpose of reversing. It must not dazzle other road-users—technically,

anyone more than 7.7 m. away with his eyes 1.1 m. from the ground.

Fine £100

REAR FOGLAMPS All cars made after September 1979 and first used after March 1980 must have either a single rear fog lamp marked with an 'E' approval mark or two rear fog lamps similarly marked; and the car must be fitted with a device to indicate to the driver whether or not the fog lamp is illuminated.

A single rear fog lamp must be on the offside of the vehicle, and two rear fog lamps must be fitted symmetrically.

In all cases, the surface illuminated by rear fog lamps must be not less than 250 mm. nor more than 1 m. from the ground; and rear fog lamps must be so designed that they can be lit only when the car's headlamps, front fog lamps or side lamps are also lit.

After September 1979, a rear fog lamp may not be fitted less than 100 mm. away from a stop lamp and may not be fitted so that it can be illuminated by operation of the car's brakes.

Rear fog lamps may be used only in poor visibility when the car is in motion or during an enforced stoppage.

SIDE LAMPS A car must have two front-facing white lights visible from a reasonable distance. These must be on opposite sides of the car at the same height. The highest part of the lit area of each lamp, if fitted with frosted glass and a bulb of less than 7 watts, must be not more than 1700 mm. from the ground and not more than 400 mm. from the outermost side of the car or its equipment.

On cars first used on or after January 1, 1972, the lamps must have an 'E' approval mark and a specified symbol; on other cars, the bulbs and sealed-beam lamps must be indelibly marked with their wattage.

If frosted glass is not fitted or if the bulb is more than 7 watts, the lamps are classed as headlamps and, for example, must be capable of being dipped.

Fine £100

STOP LAMPS Every car first used on or after January 1, 1971, must have at the back two red stop lamps of not less than 15 or more than 36 watts. These must be symmetrically positioned at the same

height on each side of the vehicle, and be so placed that the lit areas are at least 600 mm. apart, and at least 400 mm. but not more than 1500 mm. (2100 mm. in some exceptional cases) above the ground. They must be wired so that if the bulb in one lamp fails the other still operates. Every lamp must be operated when the brakes are applied and it must show a steady red light visible to the rear.

Cars first used before January 1, 1971, must have at least one red stop lamp. A duplicate may be fitted to such cars.

A stop lamp fitted to a car first manufactured after July 1973 must have an 'E' approval mark and may be of single or dual-intensity. If it is of the latter type, it must conform to wiring regulations.

Loading
The number of passengers carried in or on a car or trailer, and the weight, distribution, packing and adjustment of its load must always be such that no danger is likely to be caused to anyone in or on the vehicle or on the road.

The load carried by a car or trailer must also be so secured, and be in such a position, that neither danger nor nuisance is likely to be caused to any person or property by any movement of the load or part of it.

d E Fine £100

Maintenance and use
A car, a trailer and all parts and accessories must be in such condition that no danger is likely to be caused to anyone.

Further, a car or trailer must never be used for any purpose for which it is so unsuitable as to be likely to cause danger or nuisance to anyone.

d E Fine £100

Mascots
Mascots are illegal on cars registered on or after October 1, 1937, if they have any projections likely to cause injury to anyone with whom the car collides.

Fine £100

Mirrors
All cars must be fitted with a rear-view mirror, which may be either inside or outside. But if it is a vehicle which has been adapted to carry more than seven passengers—not including the driver—or a

dual-purpose vehicle, or a goods vehicle, it must have at least two mirrors; one must be externally on the offside; the second may be inside the vehicle, or externally on the nearside.

These mirrors must assist the driver, if he wishes, to become aware of traffic to the rear and on both sides rearwards.

If the car was registered on or after April 1, 1969, the inside mirror must have protective edges.

Cars manufactured after November, 1977, and first used after May, 1978, must have an interior rear view mirror as well as an exterior one on the off-side. They must meet certain positioning and technical specifications. When drawing a trailer, the exterior mirror must assist the driver to become aware of traffic to the rear of the trailer.

Fine £100

Number plates
A car's registration number must be shown at the front and rear, either on a flat, rectangular plate or on a rectangular, flat and unbroken area on the surface of the car. The letters and figures must be white, silver or light grey on a black background; or, on reflective plates, black on a white background at the front and black on a yellow background at the rear. All cars first registered after 1972 must have reflective plates.

Every letter and figure of the rear registration mark must be lit at night, unless the car is left where lights are not needed. It is an offence if the mark is not easily distinguishable; but it is a defence to prove that reasonable steps had been taken to prevent the mark from being obscured.

A car can be driven on a public road without a registration number if it is on its way to be registered.

First offence Fine £20

Later offence Fine £50

Parking lamps see *Lighting*

Rear lamps see *Lighting*

Reflectors see *Lighting*

Reversing lamps see *Lighting*

Seat belts
With few exceptions, cars registered after December 31, 1964, must have seat belts

for the driver and for one front-seat passenger. These belts must comply with the standard laid down by the British Standards Institution and meet additional requirements concerning use and stowage.

If there are seats for more than one passenger in the front, the seat belt must be provided for the passenger farthest from the driver.

Seat belts are not required in cars made before June 30, 1964.

Fine £100

Side lamps see *Lighting*

Silencers
Every car must be fitted with a silencer, which must be efficient and must not be altered to increase noise.

It is an offence to use or cause or permit to be used, a car that creates any excessive noise. It is illegal for cars, when used on roads, to emit a noise in excess of prescribed sound levels.

Fine £100

Smoke
It is an offence to use a car which, through the emission of smoke, vapour or sparks, causes, or is likely to cause, damage to property or injury to anyone on, or reasonably expected to be on, a road or ground to which the public has right of access.

Modern cars must meet smoke-emission standards.

Fine £100

Speedometers
Every car first used after September 30, 1937, must have a speedometer indicating its speed within a 10 per cent margin of accuracy when the car is driven at more than 10 mph. (A revolution counter alone is not sufficient.)

The speedometer should be kept free from any obstruction which might prevent its being easily read by the driver.

If a speedometer is defective, it is a defence to the charge to prove that any defect occurred during the journey, or that steps had already been taken to have the defect put right.

Fine £100

Springs
Every car first used after December 31,

1931, must have efficient springs between each wheel and the frame. This regulation does not apply to a broken-down car which is being towed.

Fine £100

Steering gear
Steering gear must be maintained in good working order and be properly adjusted at all times.

Modern cars must have a protective steering mechanism meeting international standards.

d E Fine £100

Stop lamps see *Lighting*

Television sets
If a television set is installed in a car, the driver must not be able to see the screen, or even a reflection of it. The controls, other than the sound/volume and main switch, must not be within the driver's reach. The set must not distract the driver of another vehicle.

Fine £100

Tests
A car becomes due for a Government-controlled examination on the third anniversary of its first registration in Britain, and this is also the case with a car not less than three years old which has been used on roads (whether in Britain or elsewhere) before being so registered (disregarding use before retail disposal).

It is an offence to use or cause or permit such cars to be used without a test certificate issued during the past 12 months. However, there are exceptions to this requirement. No certificate is needed, for example: if the car is going, by appointment, to or from a test; or, where a test certificate is refused on a test, if it is going to or from a place where, by appointment, the defects because of which the test certificate was refused are to be put right (although the motorist can be prosecuted should the police find the vehicle defective in law, and the car must be covered by insurance); or, if a car which has failed its test is being towed to where it is to be broken up.

The examination, originally called the MoT Test, is now controlled by the Department of Transport.

The test, which must be repeated annually, covers 12 main items: brakes,

steering, tyres, lighting equipment, stop lamps, reflectors, indicators, seat belts (when required by law), exhaust, wind-screen clearing, audible warning instrument, and the general condition as it may affect the brakes and steering.

A vehicle can be tested up to a month before its test certificate is due for renewal, in which case the new certificate will run from the expiry date of the old one.

The test is carried out at approved testing stations (normally commercial garages) by an authorised examiner who issues either a test certificate (valid for one year) or a notification of refusal, which specifies the defect or defects.

Anyone dissatisfied with the test can appeal within 14 days to the Department of Transport, who will re-test the car and may refund all or part of the appeal fee if it is found that the motorist has a valid complaint.

Fine £100

ROADSIDE TESTS An authorised examiner can make a roadside test on a car to check its brakes, silencers, steering gear, tyres, lighting equipment and reflectors.

Only a policeman in uniform can stop a car for such a test.

The driver may elect for the test to be deferred unless a policeman believes that a test is necessary after an accident has occurred or that the vehicle is too defective to be driven.

A uniformed policeman or authorised examiner may also test a car or trailer at any premises where it happens to be, subject to consent of the owner of the premises. The consent of the vehicle owner is also needed unless notice of the proposed test is given to him at least 48 hours before, or sent by recorded delivery at least 72 hours before. No such consent or notice is required in the case of a test and inspection made within 48 hours of the vehicle's involvement in a reportable accident.

Trailers
A trailer is defined in law as 'a vehicle drawn by a motor vehicle'. A towed caravan is classed as a trailer, and as such is subject to a number of restrictions. For example, it is illegal to carry passengers in a caravan which has less than four wheels or is a four-wheeled trailer with two close-coupled wheels on each side.

When it is being towed, a trailer must have an attendant in addition to the

driver—either in the towing vehicle or in the trailer—unless (a) it has not more than two wheels; (b) it has four wheels with two close-coupled wheels on each side; or (c) it has only both automatic overrun and parking brakes.

The maximum overall width permitted for a trailer is generally 2.3 m. The overall length may not exceed 7 m.; but if the trailer has four wheels with a wheel base not less than three-fifths its overall length, and is drawn by a car weighing at least 2030 kg., the maximum length permissible is 12 m.

Fine £100

BRAKES A trailer weighing more than 102 kg. unladen must have an efficient braking system, whose requirements vary according to the date of manufacture.

Unless its brakes automatically come into operation on the overrun, a trailer manufactured after 1967 must have a braking system so made that when the trailer is being drawn: (a) the brakes of that system can be applied to all its wheels by the car driver operating those car brakes that are designed to be most efficient (usually the footbrake); and (b) if any part (other than a fixed member or a brake-shoe anchor pin) of the car's braking system (excluding the means of operation of a split braking system) fails or, with exceptions, if any part of the trailer's braking system fails, brakes can still be applied to at least two wheels of the trailer (one in the case of a two-wheeled trailer).

Even if the trailer has overrun brakes, the braking system must be so constructed that when the trailer is stationary: (a) the brakes of that system can also be applied to at least two of its wheels and released by a person standing on the ground by a means of operation fitted to the trailer; (b) the braking force of that system can be maintained by direct mechanical action alone; and (c) such braking force can hold the trailer stationary on a gradient of at least 1 in 6·25 without assistance.

Automatic overrun brakes are permitted on trailers with a total laden weight not exceeding 3560 kg. (3500 kg. for trailers manufactured after February 26, 1977).

The braking system of trailers manufactured on or after April 1, 1938, must be so made that it is not rendered ineffective by switching off the car engine.

Where a car is drawing a trailer, the driver must be able readily to operate the brakes of the car and the trailer, unless some other person is in a position and competent to apply the trailer brakes. These requirements do not apply to a trailer legally fitted with automatic over-run brakes or where the trailer is a broken-down vehicle which cannot be steered by its own steering gear.

When the trailer is detached from its drawing car, at least one of its wheels must be prevented from turning by the setting of the brake or the use of a chain.

The trailer brakes must be properly adjusted and maintained.

d E Fine £100

TRAILER CLOSETS It is illegal to permit the contents of any closet, urinal, lavatory basin or sink fitted to a trailer, or any tank into which such equipment drains, to be discharged or to leak on to a road.

Fine £100

DIRECTION INDICATORS Most trailers made since July 1955, must have direction indicators. Those trailers drawn by cars registered after September 1, 1965, should have flashing amber indicators optically separated from other lamps.

The principal exceptions are where the trailer is such that, loaded or not, the car's direction indicators are visible at 6 m. (about 20 ft) from behind the rear of the trailer if the vehicle has broken down.

Fine £100

TRAILER LAMPS Two red lamps, two red reflectors (triangular) and an illuminated number plate are needed at the rear.

If the sides of the trailer or any part of its load extend more than 12 in. beyond the outermost point of the side lamps of the towing car, front side lamps must also be carried on the trailer. They must be within 12 in. of the outside edges, to indicate the width of the trailer or its load. If the front of the trailer is more than 5 ft from the car drawing it, the car must also show rear lights and the trailer front side lamp.

Every trailer manufactured after 1970 must be fitted with two red stop lamps (one if trailer was made before 1971).

Fine £100

TRAILER REGISTRATION MARKS A trailer must carry at its rear the same registration mark as the towing car.

First offence Fine £20

Later offence Fine £50

TRAILER TYRES The general regulations as to the condition and maintenance of car tyres apply to trailer tyres. A trailer drawn by a car must have pneumatic tyres (not re-cuts—unless the trailer weighs not more than 1020 kg. unladen or, in the case of a caravan, 2040 kg. unladen).

d E Fine £100

TRAILER WINGS The rear wheels of a trailer—if a two-wheeled trailer, both its wheels—must have wings, unless adequate protection is given by the body. This regulation does not apply to caravans.

Fine £100

Tyres

All cars must have pneumatic tyres, but on cars weighing less than 1020 kg. and cars first used before January 3, 1933, the tyres can be soft or elastic.

A car must not be used with a tyre which is unsuitable either in itself or in combination with the other tyres. An illegal combination would be to mix cross-ply with radial-ply on the same axle, or to have cross-ply at the rear of the car and radial-ply at the front (see p. 125).

A tyre must be properly inflated and should not have any break in the fabric or any cut down to the body cords which is more than 25 mm. long or 10 per cent of the section width, whichever is the greater.

It must not have a lump or bulge caused by separation or partial failure of its structure, or have any part of the ply or cord structure exposed. The tread pattern must be at least 1 mm. deep for at least three-quarters of the tread's width all round the tyre.

It is now lawful to use a car or trailer with a damaged tyre if that tyre has been so constructed as to make it safe in certain damaged conditions (see p. 123).

All tyres must be fit for the use to which the car is being put, and free from any defect which might damage the road or which might endanger anyone in the car or using the road.

d E Fine £100

Veteran cars

The law is a little less strict with the owners of veteran cars. If a certificate has been issued by the London Science Museum indicating that the car was designed before January 1, 1905, and built before December 31, 1905, certain of the construction regulations do not apply.

These include the need for wings and a speedometer; the ban on a gong bell, siren or two-tone horn; and the detailed requirements about brakes (although the car must have an efficient braking system, including a parking brake).

Even veteran cars, however, must be roadworthy and must not be in a condition where they could be a danger to other road-users, including pedestrians. They have to be tested annually under the scheme controlled by the Department of Transport and they must be registered and taxed.

They are not required to have in-

dicators, but if they are to be used after darkness, they must have front side lamps, rear lamps and reflectors.

Windows

The windscreen and outside windows of a car or dual-purpose vehicle first used after January 31, 1959, must be made of safety glass. On other vehicles only the windscreen and front windows must be of safety glass. All glass must be maintained so that the driver's vision is not in any way obscured.

Fine £100

Windscreen wipers and washers

Most cars must be fitted with one or more efficient automatic windscreen wipers. The wipers, in conjunction with screen washers, must be capable of cleaning the screen to give the driver an adequate view of the road in front and to the nearside and offside.

Fine £100

Wings

Every car must have wings to catch mud or water thrown up by the wheels, unless adequate protection is provided by the body of the car.

Fine £100

Zebra crossings

Special rules cover the crossing itself and the 'controlled areas' indicated by a give-way line across the carriageway and zig-zag marks.

A driver must give precedence to a pedestrian who is on an uncontrolled crossing. He is prohibited from stopping his car on a zebra crossing, unless prevented by circumstances beyond his control or to avoid an accident, in a 'controlled area' except for these reasons and certain other specified ones, such as giving way to pedestrians.

In 'controlled areas', drivers proceeding towards an uncontrolled crossing must not overtake any vehicle moving in the same direction or one that has stopped to give way to a pedestrian.

If the crossing is dissected by a street refuge or a central reservation, each side of the refuge or reservation is treated as a separate crossing.

E Fine £100

LIGHTS NEEDED ON A TRAILER

Front side lamp on each side

Red lamp on each side

Illuminated number plate

Red reflector on each side

Trailers must carry front side lamps if the outermost edge of the trailer (A) is more than 12 in. beyond the outermost point of the towing car's side lamps (B), or if the front of the trailer is more than 5 ft from the towing car

Law/essential documents of motoring

How to obtain or renew the registration papers and licenses

ANYONE WHO owns or drives a car must be able to produce certain documents if requested by a policeman. They may be produced either on the spot or within five days at a police station specified by the motorist at the time production is required.

If someone fails to produce his driving licence on the spot the five-day exemption operates only if he himself subsequently produces the licence at the police station.

The registration papers

Every car kept or used on any public road must be registered and the appropriate vehicle excise licence duty paid in respect of it. This is done by applying for a vehicle excise licence.

The registration papers are issued with the first licence; and the car is given a registration number. Before the papers are issued, the owner can be required to produce his car for inspection.

It is illegal to deface or mutilate the registration papers, to alter or obliterate any entry or, except on changing ownership, to make any entry in them.

The owner must return the registration papers to the relevant registration authority if he changes his address and if alterations are made to the car which render the details in the papers incorrect, such as altering the colour, changing the weight or seating capacity.

The papers must be surrendered to the appropriate authority when the car is destroyed or permanently exported.

The penalty for failing to disclose an alteration affecting the rate of excise duty (such as putting a heavier body on a dual-purpose vehicle) is a fine of up to £50 or five times the difference in duty rates, whichever is the greater. The penalty for failing to fulfil any other requirement is a fine of up to £20.

If registration papers are lost, destroyed, mutilated or defaced, duplicates can be obtained for £2. If they become illegible or the colour has altered for any reason other than the holder's neglect, duplicates are free.

A computer system of registration and licensing is now in force for the majority of vehicles.

There are presently two types of registration papers—the old log book for cars covered by the non-computer system, and registration documents for those on the computer.

A registration document is a print-out form which gives the name and address of the registered keeper and particulars of the vehicle, as on the log book. It does not give the names of previous registered keepers because a new document is produced and the old one destroyed whenever a change is recorded; such details are obtainable by the current owner of the car free of charge from the Driver and Vehicle Licensing Centre, Swansea.

On a change of ownership, the seller must give the registration papers to the new owner. If the car still has a log book, the old owner must send the licensing authority the new owner's name and address, together with the number of the car and its make and class. The new owner, if he intends to use or keep the car on the road, must write his name and address in the log book and send it to the local vehicle licensing office.

In the case of the new registration papers, both the former and the new owner should complete the relevant section and send it to the licensing centre at Swansea.

Excise licence

Application to register or licence a new vehicle must be made to one of the Department of Transport's 81 local vehicle licensing offices. The local office issues the licence and returns the insurance certificate and any other supporting documents, but it forwards the application form to the Swansea centre where details of the car are recorded. The centre issues the registration document.

When cars are to be re-licensed and taken on to the computer, the centre sends a brief application form (V11) to the registered keeper about a fortnight before the licence is due to expire. This should be used if all the details on the registration document are still correct. The completed V11 must be either; (a) posted with the necessary enclosures to Swansea or (b) taken—not posted—with the enclosures, to a post office authorised to issue vehicle licences (not more than 14 days after the expiry of the old licence); or (c) taken or posted with the enclosures, to any local licensing office.

If any changes have taken place, the V11 should be destroyed. Application must be made on form V10, obtainable from a post office authorised to issue vehicle licences or a licensing office. The completed V10 should be either posted to Swansea or taken to any local office.

Eventually all vehicles will be handled by the computer system, but until a vehicle has been taken on to the system, it is dealt with by the appropriate local licensing office.

Licences for vehicles that still have the old-style log book can no longer be renewed at a post office.

The application must be made within 14 days before and 14 days after the expiry of the old licence, and any change of ownership or address since the licence was issued must have been notified to the council and recorded in the log book. Re-licensing in this way is by personal application only.

To obtain an excise licence, you must produce: the completed licence application form; the car's registration papers; a current test certificate where appropriate: a valid certificate of insurance (not the policy itself): and the expiring licence (if you apply at a post office).

LAYING A CAR UP Motorists who want to save paying duty for a few months—by not using their car in the winter—do not need an excise licence as long as the car is kept in a garage or a private drive and not taken on to any public road.

If the licence has one or more complete calendar months to run, it can be surrendered and a refund obtained. This will be an amount equal to one-twelfth of the annual rate of duty for each remaining complete month. Where the car has a log book the completed refund application form should be taken or sent, with the vehicle licence disc attached. to the local vehicle licensing office.

Where the car has a registration document, the completed refund, application form should be sent by post, with the vehicle licence disc attached, to Swansea or be handed in—not posted—to the local vehicle licensing office.

The refund payable is determined by the date of surrender of the licence and not the date on which the vehicle ceased to be used or kept on the public road. To obtain a refund in respect of any given month the licence must either; (a) be posted before midnight on the last day of the preceding month; or (b) be handed in on or before the last day of the preceding month.

A motorist without a garage or private drive, however, cannot leave his car on a public road unlicensed, even though it is never driven. Any car which is kept or used on a public road must be licensed and insured. To use or keep an unlicensed car on a road is an offence punishable by a fine of up to £50 or five times the duty due, whichever is the greater. In addition,

the court often makes an order for payment of the back-duty.

Driving licence

Anyone who drives a car on a public road must have a current driving licence. There are two types—full and provisional.

You may apply for a full driving licence if, during the last ten years, you have (i) held a British full licence, or (ii) passed the British Driving Test, or (iii) held a full licence issued in Northern Ireland, the Channel Islands or the Isle of Man. Otherwise you may only apply for a provisional licence.

All applications for a first driving licence, or one following a period of disqualification, and applications to renew a new-style licence issued originally by the Swansea centre must be made direct to Swansea. Applications to renew an old (red cover) licence must still be made to the local vehicle licensing office—which issues a receipt instead of a licence and sends the application to the Swansea centre which issues the actual licence. The receipt is proof that an application has been made.

A person may usually drive although he has not received his licence, provided that a valid application for the grant or renewal of the licence has been received by the licensing authority.

If you have been disqualified from driving, you may apply to the court that imposed disqualification to have it removed—if the disqualification is for less than four years, after two years; if the disqualification is for 4-10 years, after half the period of disqualification; and after five years in any other case.

Where a conviction has been endorsed on a driving licence, the Department of Transport will issue a licence free of that endorsement four years after the conviction (11 years in certain drink/drug driving convictions).

Driving without a licence is punishable with a fine of up to £100 and disqualification. The offender's eventual licence may be endorsed. The penalty for driving whilst disqualified is, on summary conviction, three months' imprisonment or a fine of up to £400 or both and, for conviction on indictment, 12 months' imprisonment or a fine or both. In each case disqualification may be ordered, and licence endorsement is obligatory.

For most other breaches of the driving-licence regulations, the penalty is a fine of up to £100.

FITNESS TO DRIVE

Drivers are coming to appreciate that there is an important relationship between an overall standard of good health and the safe, efficient control of their cars. Fatigue, pain, stress, vision defects, discomfort, degeneration, seemingly innocuous everyday drugs—the informed motorist will recognise that all can affect driving performance, and will check his physical condition before taking the wheel

CONTENTS

Medical/fitness to drive

Road safety and health

DRIVING a car can make certain physical and mental demands on the driver. The motorist must, for his own and other road-users' safety, make sure that he is as fit for the road as his vehicle is.

Happily, no one needs to have the physique of an athlete to handle a family car efficiently; but a minimum standard of well-being in mind and body is essential. Few motorists would be at ease taking an ailing car on a 150-mile journey. Many, however, think nothing of driving the same distance when in less than peak physical condition themselves.

Fatigued, uncomfortable, emotionally upset, suffering from a headache or a heavy cold, dosed with pills and medicines—motorists take to the road seemingly unaware that even minor ailments can lead to misjudgment, loss of concentration and erratic performance, which will possibly end in tragedy.

The motorist who enjoys a general standard of good health, yet considers that unfitness to drive involves only serious illness like epilepsy, diabetes and disabling heart disease, drives with a false sense of security. Experience indicates that collapse at the wheel due to killer diseases is rare. The threat to road safety from minor complaints is far more real—and involves every motorist at one time or another.

Basically, all the law requires, as far as fitness is concerned, is that the motorist fills in the application form for a driving licence honestly.

The onus is therefore on the motorist throughout his driving career to assess his fitness as conscientiously as he would the roadworthiness of his vehicle.

If he has any reason to question his ability to drive safely due to a change in health, he *must* consult his doctor. The lives of others could be at stake.

By law a driver must:
Read in daylight (with glasses if worn) a vehicle registration number with symbols $3\frac{1}{2}$ in. high from a distance of 75 ft (or $3\frac{1}{8}$ in. high from 67 ft). One-eyed drivers must inform the licensing authority of their defect. A driver must also declare the following disorders and disabilities: epilepsy; liability to sudden giddiness or fainting; specified mental disorders or defects; loss of hand or foot; defects in movement, control or muscular power of an arm or leg; deafness and dumbness; any other disease or disability liable to make him a dangerous driver.

POTENTIAL DANGERS FOR THE MOTORIST

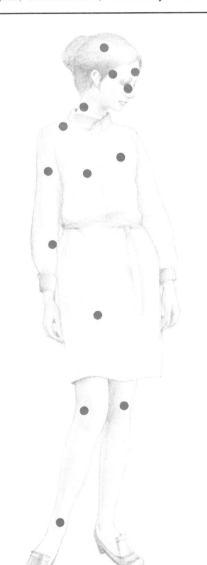

Fatiguing, distracting aches and pains in the arms, thighs, back, shoulders, neck, knees and ankles—triggered by inadequate car seats and poor posture (see pp. 338–41)

Illusions and hallucinations, lapses of attention, slowed reaction and decision-making times, impaired muscular co-ordination and loss of concentration—the by-products of fatigue (see pp. 342–3)

Irritation, headaches, aggressive behaviour, erratic blood pressure and pulse rates—due to the emotional stresses and strains of difficult driving conditions (see p. 342)

Shallow breathing for long periods while in the driving position (see p. 339)

Progressive deterioration of eyesight: chances of inferior depth-perception, focusing defects, 'tunnel' vision, loss of visual field and reduced night vision (see p. 344)

Headaches, dizziness, sometimes outright collapse—due to carbon monoxide poisoning from an idling engine in an enclosed area, or a leaking exhaust system (see p. 345)

In women, judgment often affected by menstruation

Blurred vision, lethargy, palpitations, confusion, emotional instability—some of the side-effects that threaten the motorist who drives while under the influence of everyday, seemingly innocuous drugs (see pp. 346–7)

The effects of age: impaired memory and hearing, slowed reaction and decision-making times, increasing errors of judgment, risk of heart attacks and degenerative diseases

Driving and age

ALTHOUGH the processes of ageing are inescapable and bring decreased ability to perform skilled or complicated tasks, age can compensate in the provision of temperamental balance and experience.

The motorist's life may be broken down into six broad age groups.

17–21 years
The young driver is inexperienced and most prone to accidents. Through over-confidence and ignorance he will take risks, thinking 'It can't happen to me'. Physical fitness cannot compensate for reckless-ness. Aggressive behaviour is common.

21–25 years
A greater sense of responsibility, more experience and better judgment lead to safer driving. Sports cars—sometimes rashly driven—have their greatest appeal. Women drivers are less aggressive, but their judgment may be affected before the menstrual period.

25–40 years
This is the age group in which most people settle down and start a family. This leads to more responsible road behaviour, with much less risk-taking. Degenerative

diseases, such as heart complaints, are rare, and there is little risk of a sudden illness while at the wheel.

40–55 years
The family man may buy a sports car at this stage in his life. Weight increases, and so do the chances of a heart attack. Eyesight may deteriorate. However, experience makes up for these defects and the middle-aged man is probably the safest driver on the road.

55–65 years
Eighty per cent of drivers have vision defects by the age of 60. Short-term memory may also be impaired and re-action times slowed considerably. Heart attacks become even more likely. Pro-gressive hearing loss, although not dangerous in itself, becomes more of a handicap when coupled with failing sight.

65 years and older
Drivers past retiring age are faced with degenerative diseases and slower reac-tions. Over 70, the motorist should seek medical advice annually as to his fitness to drive. Driving at night, on motorways or in large cities should be avoided.

Driving and illness

A HISTORY of heart disease is in itself no barrier to driving. As a general rule, heart attacks give sufficient warning for the driver to pull up at the side of the road. No one should drive within three months of having suffered from an attack of coronary thrombosis.

Diabetes
In a mild case of diabetes, controlled by diet alone, there is no risk to driving. In more serious cases, however, the driver must ensure that his condition is well con-trolled, that he can recognise the symptoms of *hypoglycaemia*, and that he always carries emergency supplies of sugar (at least 12 lumps) or glucose in the car.

If a diabetic is taken ill on the road, he must leave the driving seat and remove the ignition key. Failure to do so entails risk of prosecution for being in charge of a car while under the influence of a drug (insulin).

Epilepsy
An epileptic can be issued with a driving licence only on production of proof, such as a certificate issued by his doctor, that he has suffered no attack for at least three years.

Deafness
In law, deafness is no barrier to driving. The deaf motorist is obviously at a disadvantage, but on the road—as in many other situations—knows best how to compensate for the lack of hearing.

Vertigo
Anyone who suffers from giddiness or balance defects should seek medical advice before attempting to drive.

Loss of co-ordination
Motorists who experience muscular weak-ness, Parkinson's disease, brain disorders affecting movement or loss of sensation in hands or feet, should not drive unless declared fit to do so by a doctor.

Migraine
Warning symptoms, such as double vision or nausea, must not be ignored by the motorist. They are the signal to stop driving until the attack has passed.

Mental disorders
Licensing authorities are empowered to grant mental sufferers driving licences provided they are satisfied there is no danger to the public.

Driving and disablement

DISABLED PEOPLE over the age of 16 who are eligible for a Mobility Allowance, because they are unable, or virtually unable, to walk, can apply to have an invalid three-wheeler instead of the weekly allowance.

This is supplied, in approved cases, by the Department of Health and Social Security, or the Scottish Home and Health Department, and is maintained and in-sured against third-party risks by the Department concerned. An annual allow-ance of £10 is paid to help offset the cost of VAT on petrol, and the vehicle is replaced when necessary without charge except where the need for a replacement is caused by the driver's negligence.

Not an option
Four-wheeler cars are not supplied as an option to the cash allowance, but they are issued as replacements to those supplied with one under a previous scheme so long as the driver remains eligible. A mainten-ance allowance is paid to people supplied with cars.

When the Department supplies a vehicle, it pays for driving lessons. Owners of con-

verted private vehicles must pay for such lessons themselves, but discounts are available to some, including members of the AA. Driving lessons for the disabled are obtainable in any part of the country through local branches of the British School of Motoring.

Driving tests, conducted by Depart-ment of Transport examiners, usually last about an hour.

Drivers of invalid three-wheelers are tested by examiners on foot.

Special parking concessions are avail-able for disabled drivers under the Orange Badge scheme (details are available from the local council's Social Services depart-ment).

Useful addresses
The Disabled Drivers' Association, Ashwellthorpe, Norwich NR16 1EX (branches all over Britain).
The Disabled Drivers' Motor Club, 9 Park Parade, Acton, London W3 9BD.
The British School of Motoring Disability Training Centre (head office), 269 Kensington High Street, London W8 6NA.

Invalid three-wheelers

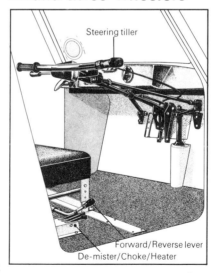

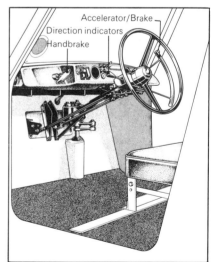

The invalid three-wheeler has a glass-fibre body and is designed to allow the driver to take his folding wheel-chair with him. Auto-matic transmission relieves the driver of having to cope with a manually operated clutch.

Most models have a steering tiller that is operated in the same way as the steering on a bicycle: the driver pulls the left-hand end towards him to steer left, the right-hand end to steer right. A twist grip on the tiller operates the throttle, and depression of the tiller operates the hydraulic brakes on all three wheels.

A few models have a steering wheel, which is operated in the same way as a conventional one, and a lever behind that wheel to operate the throttle and brakes.

Medical/driving in comfort

SITTING PROPERLY in the driving seat is not simply a matter of sitting comfortably. The motorist who settles unthinkingly into his seat may be relaxed initially, but will find that aches and pains develop as the journey lengthens.

Slouching, sitting too close to the steering wheel, cramping the legs, failing to support the small of the back—all give rise to dangerous, distracting discomfort and lead to the early onset of fatigue.

The correctly seated motorist has the best possible view of the road ahead, has the car's controls within easy reach and is able to drive the vehicle with the minimum effort and the maximum efficiency for long periods.

Steering, for example, is not at all taxing if the driver's body is firmly supported and his arms and hands placed to exert maximum leverage on the rim of the steering wheel. Continued operation of the pedals will not prove tiring if the angle of the foot to the shin is correct.

After years of neglect, the design of car seats and the relationship of the driver to the hand and foot controls are at last being given attention by manufacturers.

But, even so, few seats have a means of varying the amount of lumbar support provided by the backrest, and it is unusual to find a car in which the position and angle of the steering wheel can be altered to suit the individual.

However, as shown on the next three pages, car seating with the minimum of built-in adjustment can often be modified to provide an improved driving position. Having identified the cause of discomfort and pain, the home mechanic can usually rectify it.

Seat runners can sometimes be reversed to give the seat greater rearward travel. Packing and wedges beneath the runners can tilt the seat as necessary. Cushions, proprietary backrests, extensions to gear levers and fascia switches can all help to make driving easier.

THE IDEAL DRIVING POSITION

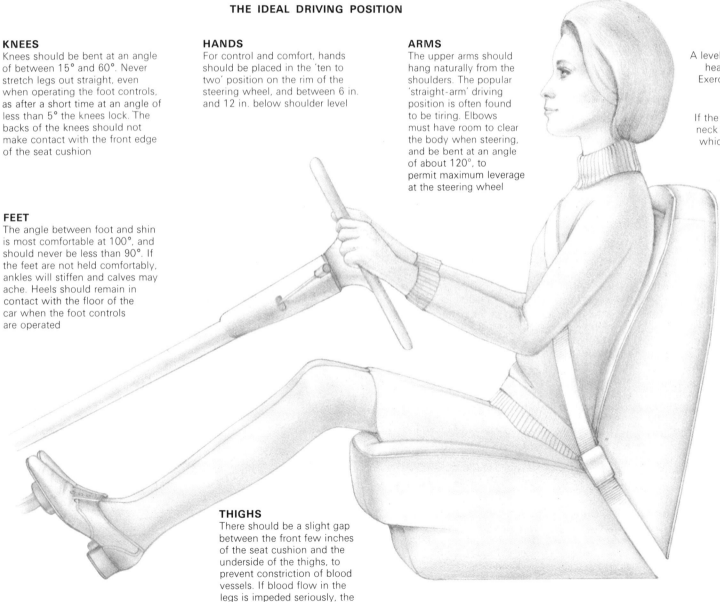

KNEES
Knees should be bent at an angle of between 15° and 60°. Never stretch legs out straight, even when operating the foot controls, as after a short time at an angle of less than 5° the knees lock. The backs of the knees should not make contact with the front edge of the seat cushion

FEET
The angle between foot and shin is most comfortable at 100°, and should never be less than 90°. If the feet are not held comfortably, ankles will stiffen and calves may ache. Heels should remain in contact with the floor of the car when the foot controls are operated

HANDS
For control and comfort, hands should be placed in the 'ten to two' position on the rim of the steering wheel, and between 6 in. and 12 in. below shoulder level

THIGHS
There should be a slight gap between the front few inches of the seat cushion and the underside of the thighs, to prevent constriction of blood vessels. If blood flow in the legs is impeded seriously, the feet will swell and the legs will become painful

ARMS
The upper arms should hang naturally from the shoulders. The popular 'straight-arm' driving position is often found to be tiring. Elbows must have room to clear the body when steering, and be bent at an angle of about 120°, to permit maximum leverage at the steering wheel

HEAD
A level gaze is important. Hold the head high and tuck in the chin. Exercise neck muscles frequently

NECK
If the head is carried properly, the neck will find its correct position, which is leaning slightly forward about 15° from the vertical

SHOULDERS
The seat's backrest should not be too short; but too snug a fit round the shoulders may limit freedom of movement

UPPER BACK
Recline the back at an angle between 15° and 30° from the vertical. Beyond 30° there is a risk of having to carry the head too far forward, causing pain in shoulders, neck and possibly arms

LOWER BACK
The small of the back should be slightly hollowed. Good driving seats provide support to encourage this. A rounded back strains ligaments in the lumbar region. Eventually permanent damage may be caused to the vertebrae and a slipped disc may result. Settle into the seat so that the small of the back is thrust snugly against the backrest. The backrest should slope at an angle of about 5° from the vertical

Study the illustration opposite. Ask yourself if your driving position permits a level gaze through the windscreen and if the angles of your elbows, knees and ankles are correct. Question the amount of lumbar support your seat gives you.

Do not resign yourself to the seating position the manufacturer has given you if it does not suit you. There is almost always something that can be done to improve it.

Once you have experimented and found the ideal position, set the interior rearview mirror carefully. If on subsequent journeys the mirror appears to be wrongly adjusted, you will know that you are sitting sloppily and not taking advantage of the improvements you have made. A correctly adjusted seat belt will locate and hold you in the ideal position.

Exercises

Inevitably, some parts of the body are neglected even when the driver is sitting correctly and comfortably. Simple exercises, performed when the car is stationary, can tone up unused muscles.

To prevent the neck muscles becoming stiff, rotate the head in each direction, describing a circle with the tip of the nose, and turn the head from side to side.

Two minutes of deep breathing in every hour at the wheel will bring oxygen into the lower parts of the lungs.

Do not give yourself unnecessary discomfort: never maintain an excessive grip on the steering wheel, clench your teeth, hunch your shoulders or screw up your eyes. None of these unconscious driving habits improves performance. Relax—try to enjoy motoring.

Pain in back, neck, shoulders and abdomen Many drivers adopt a hunched position close to the steering wheel

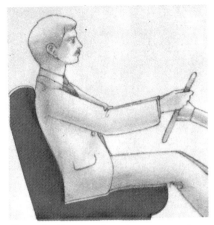

Remedy Try to adjust the seat to give a relaxed driving position, allowing the seat to support you; or fit a backrest

Pain in the knees A seat that lacks sufficient rearward adjustment may force the driver to sit with knees bent too far

Remedy Try tilting the seat backwards to increase the trunk angle by putting a wedge beneath the seat runners; or reverse them

Stomach pains Drivers of some cars must lift their feet off the floor when braking or declutching, straining their stomach muscles

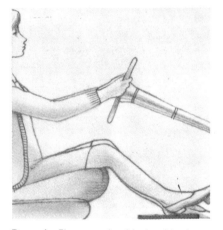

Remedy Fit a wooden block with chamfered edges beneath the carpet in front of the pedals, making sure that it cannot slip

Pain in the neck and shoulders In cars with low rooflines, the driver has sometimes to lean forward to read road signs

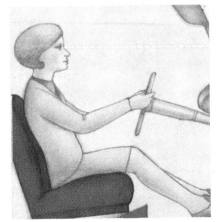

Remedy Adjust the seat angle so that a normal driving position will permit good visibility; or fit wedges beneath the runners

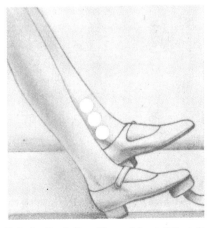

Pain in the left ankle and foot If the left foot has nowhere to rest, both the unsupported foot and ankle will ache

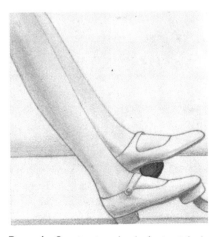

Remedy Construct a simple footrest from angle-iron, and clamp it to the side of the transmission tunnel or to the floor

Medical/avoiding aches and pains

Strain, discomfort, bruising Passengers who have to brace themselves against road shocks are quickly fatigued and often hurt

Remedy Insist that passengers always wear seat belts. Correctly adjusted belts will hold them comfortably—and may save their lives

Thigh, leg and back pain Some driving seats are poorly designed: the cushion is too short, supporting the legs inadequately

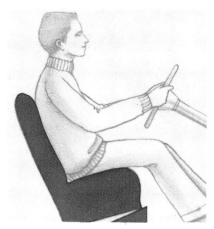

Remedy Fit yourself as deeply into the seat as possible, tilting it back if necessary. If this fails, fit a new seat

Leg pain Some steering wheels are so large that drivers have to adopt an uncomfortable splayed-knees position to control the car

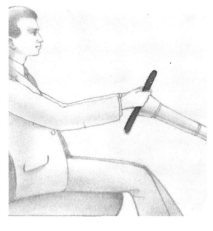

Remedy Try lowering the driving seat. Alternatively, consider fitting a smaller steering wheel, such as a sports wheel

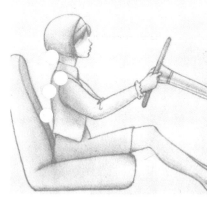

Neck, shoulder and back pain Low seats cause discomfort if the driver has to strain upwards to see over the steering wheel

Remedy If the seat springs have sagged, replace them or tie a cushion on to the seat to give firm, level support

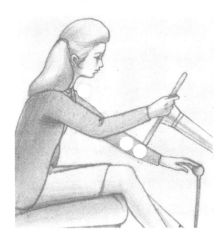

Numbness and tiredness in the left arm The gear lever may sometimes be just beyond comfortable reach, producing strain

Remedy Accessory manufacturers have recognised the problem. There are several types of proprietary gear-lever extensions

Aching neck Tall people are prone to slouch forward in the driving seat, then look upwards through the windscreen

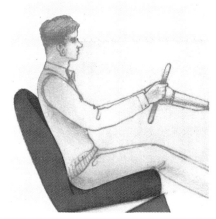

Remedy Raise the front of the seat to tilt the driver into a more natural and comfortable sitting position

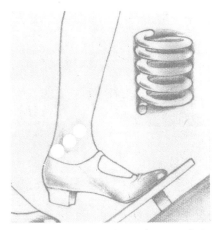

Ankle strain Excessive resistance of the return spring of the clutch, brake or accelerator pedal is frequently overlooked

Remedy Fit a lighter spring—ensuring, of course, that it is strong enough to return the pedal when foot pressure is eased

Shoulder and neck pain Thickly padded 'glamour rolls' on seat backs thrust the shoulders forward uncomfortably

Remedy Maintain a level line of vision by flattening the roll. The simplest way is to clamp it between boards for a while

General discomfort and fatigue A seat-belt buckle worn high up will dig into the wearer and cause injury in an accident

Remedy A correctly adjusted seat belt, with the buckle low down on the hip, increases comfort by locating the wearer in the seat

Stiffness in neck and shoulder muscles Even a correct driving posture may produce some stiffness during a long journey

Remedy A headrest, used during traffic hold-ups, will ease the muscles. It may also help to guard against 'whiplash' injuries

Thigh pain, possible cramp In an older car, sagging seat springs may let the thighs rest on the seat's thinly covered metal frame

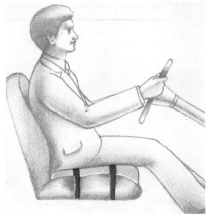

Remedy If possible, replace the seat springs. If not, tie a cushion on to the seat to provide firm, level support for the thighs

Neuralgia caused by draughts Drivers, who open the window wide when perspiring, are liable to pains in the face and neck

Remedy See if opening more than one window stops the draught, or fit a draught-deflector to the driving window

Medical/avoiding fatigue

Threats to concentration

DRIVING is a skill that demands a high degree of concentration. When fatigue sets in, concentration and performance decline. For a while these effects can be masked, but eventually lapses of attention occur, judgment falters, performance becomes erratic and reaction times slow up. Drivers may even find themselves suffering from illusions and hallucinations.

Tests on lorry drivers have shown that, at the end of a long journey, the steadiness of the hands and muscular co-ordination are impaired.

Other medical studies have demonstrated that the tired driver works harder than normal but achieves a poorer level of performance. He tends to over-manipulate the steering wheel, maintaining course by a series of constant corrections.

These signs and symptoms of fatigue in some ways mimic the effects of alcohol. The tired driver can fairly be described as 'drunk with fatigue'. In either state, he is more prone to accidents.

Start off fresh

Have a good night's sleep before a journey. Vigilance and ability to maintain a high level of concentration fall off rapidly with the onset of tiredness. At this point the driver begins to make simple but potentially dangerous errors of judgment.

Plan your journey: build rest periods into your time-table. Allow at least ten minutes' relaxation for each hour behind the wheel. Get out of the car—stretch your legs and breathe in some fresh air.

Do not start a journey hungry. Muscular efficiency reaches its peak an hour after a satisfying meal—when the blood-sugar level is at its maximum—and then begins to deteriorate. However, it is unwise to begin a journey immediately after a large meal, as this can have a soporific effect. Taking snacks frequently during a long drive maintains a steady blood-sugar level and guards against fatigue.

Sharing a long journey with a friend can make it seem shorter. Sharing the driving reduces fatigue even further.

Be alive to the dangers of alcohol and drugs (see pp. 346–7). Even in small quantities, they can lead to drowsiness.

Ventilation

Stuffiness inside the car leads to lethargy and loss of concentration. Even in the coldest weather, air must circulate freely. Adjust the heater output and fresh-air supply to get an agreeable temperature and efficient ventilation without draughts.

A disadvantage of the modern car's heating/ventilation system is that it upsets the composition of the 'fresh' air.

Physical strain

Driving a well-maintained and efficiently operating car is not particularly exacting physically. In normal conditions it requires less energy than a simple weekend task like polishing the car. The motorist can do little about road conditions that increase strain (driving in traffic is twice as tiring as driving on the open road), but

he can ensure that his car is working smoothly and that no component is difficult to operate.

Irritating noises and vibrations within the car contribute to fatigue. Exhaust systems can work loose and rattle, and should be checked frequently. Regular engine servicing reduces both noise and vibration. Wheel-balancing cures vibration at the steering wheel. An additional layer of felt under the floor carpet helps to muffle unwelcome mechanical sounds.

Inactivity

While it is important to sit comfortably and relaxed in the driving seat (see pp. 338–41), total inactivity can lead to lethargy and drowsiness. Movement is necessary to maintain warmth and circulation throughout the body. The driver who makes a point of exercising during a long trip, and takes rest breaks, stays alert.

Tension is a common cause of fatigue. The impatient motorist who tries to beat the clock becomes excessively irritated by traffic delays, wastes energy on aggressive behaviour and invites tension-headaches and tiredness.

Monotony contributes towards fatigue. Road-planners, learning from earlier mistakes, are now building gentle curves into otherwise featureless stretches of motorway; but boredom can still afflict the motorist. Companionship, small talk and listening to the radio are perhaps the best cures. For the lone driver, acknowledging the problem is halfway to beating it.

TRAFFIC-JAM EXERCISES

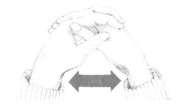

Clasp the hands, then try to separate them without breaking the grip

Press the knees together with the hands. Still pressing, try to separate the knees

Draw a deep breath, hold it and pull your stomach in for 10 seconds. Then relax

Stress of traffic jams

EMOTIONAL STRAIN inevitably produces fatigue. The graphs opposite reveal the invisible effects of a traffic jam on a driver in a hurry—a 34-year-old man sitting for 16 minutes in a 1·35-mile main-road hold-up.

Blood pressure and heart or pulse rate (black lines) can be seen to fluctuate sharply as events influence his behaviour and attitudes, although some fluctuations are to be expected even in normal conditions (sepia lines). Stop-start motoring in the traffic-jam queue raises his blood pressure by 30 per cent and quickens his pulse rate by as much as 50 per cent.

The fluctuations can prove more exhausting than high-speed motoring and are most significant towards the end of the hold-up, when the driver can see a clear road ahead but is still trapped behind a long line of other vehicles.

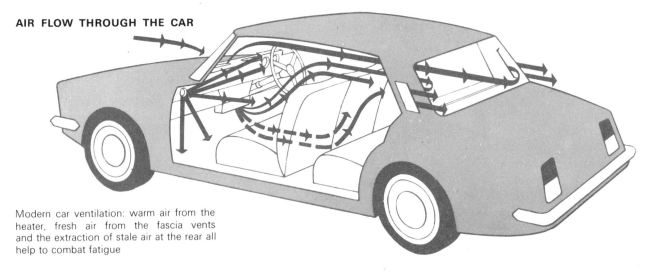

Modern car ventilation: warm air from the heater, fresh air from the fascia vents and the extraction of stale air at the rear all help to combat fatigue

The road to exhaustion

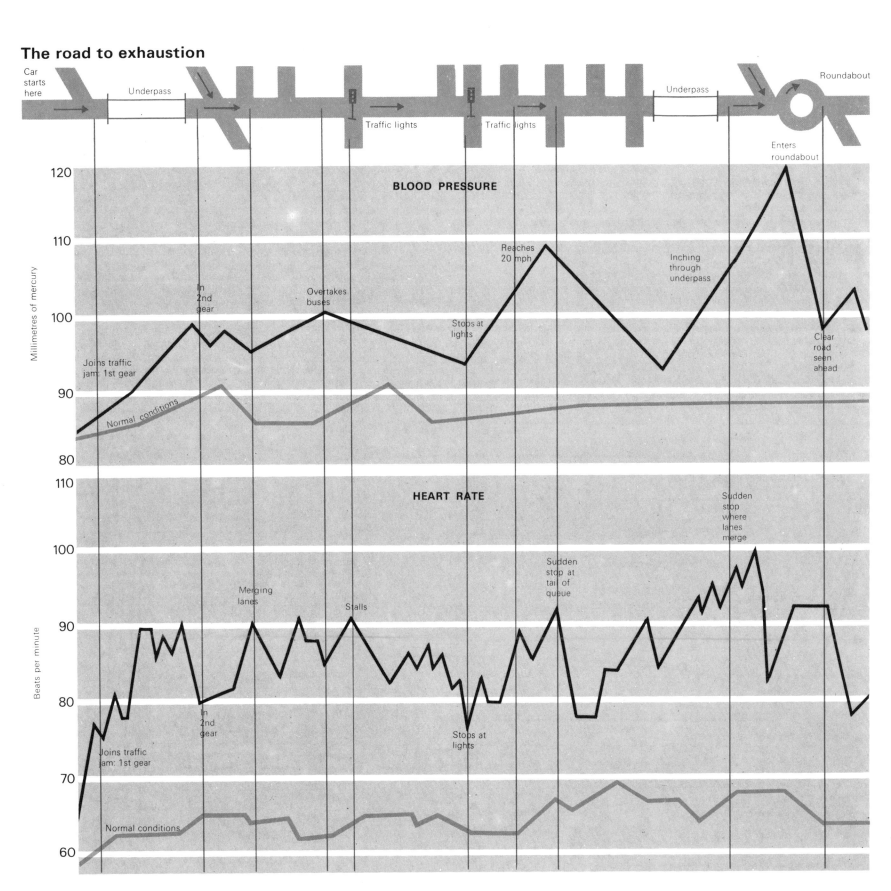

Medical/vision and car sickness

Seeing what lies ahead

EIGHTY PER CENT of the information received, and needed, by the driver comes through his eyes. But surprisingly, the legal requirement on eyesight standards is not high: it is the ability to read a clean number plate at 25 yds in good daylight, wearing corrective lenses (spectacles or contact lenses) if they are needed.

Clearly this is no guarantee that a driver's eyesight is adequate. In a West London survey, one in seven drivers tested found difficulty in judging distance due to 'inferior depth perception'. Even people who have good distance vision may suffer from focusing defects or from 'tunnel' vision, which means that they can see only what is happening straight ahead.

Loss of visual field—which can be experienced by those with normal eyesight when driving at speed—is a feature of certain eye complaints. Its existence is not always appreciated, because what is not seen by one eye is very often seen by the other. However, as the condition worsens, objects outside the affected driver's narrowing field of vision remain unseen. To be quite safe, the motorist should make sure that he has his eyes tested every two or three years.

'Colour blindness' The inability to distinguish between certain colours, which is commonly known as 'colour blindness', is more common among men than women. Few people are totally colour blind. The most common defect, affecting about $2\frac{1}{2}$ million Britons, is red-green blindness.

Many people do not realise that they are colour blind, and wonder why they keep making the same mistake for no apparent reason. Drivers who are aware of the defect rarely have real difficulty in interpreting traffic signals correctly.

Spectacles In Britain, the law does not insist that drivers with defective vision must wear spectacles. In some other countries, drivers who need spectacles have their licences marked accordingly.

If a driver needs spectacles, either to correct a visual defect or to prevent eye strain, he should wear them when on the road. This is particularly necessary in fading light or at night, when eye-strain or out-of-focus effects become both troublesome and dangerous. Take care when selecting spectacle frames that the rims and side pieces are not unduly thick, otherwise the field of vision will be reduced. The blinkering effect is even more marked with some types of sunglasses, particularly those for women. However, none of the spectacles supplied under the National Health Service is likely to introduce unnecessary blind areas.

Bifocal spectacles have their disadvantages for the driver. In a car, the dashboard is often too far away to be seen clearly through the lower reading segment. Many motorists prefer to drive with normal, single-sight distance spectacles.

Sunglasses Many drivers find it helpful to wear tinted lenses on bright days. Eventually there may be an international standard for sunglasses for drivers. For the moment, the best protection is to buy sunglasses from an optician.

Cheaper sunglasses with plastic lenses are much more prone to scratching than those with glass, and this in itself constitutes a hazard. A scratched lens will scatter light and give 'veiling glare', which reduces clear vision. If, on brilliant days, the car's sun visor is used, keeping the lenses of the sunglasses in shadow, the glare effect largely disappears.

Sunglasses with polarised lenses have the advantage of cutting down light reflected from horizontal surfaces, such as the road or the car's bonnet, but they will tend to show the streaky pattern in toughened glass windscreens.

The spectacle-wearer can obtain prescription lenses in a variety of tints, some of which automatically change their density according to light conditions.

Night driving At dusk or night, colour largely disappears, depth perception blurs and range of vision decreases with speed; the normal daylight vision of 10–15 per cent of drivers declines so sharply at night that they are a positive traffic hazard.

Some motorists with normal sight during daylight tend to become short-sighted at night. In the dark, eyes are drawn to the lightest areas; there is a danger that dark

TRAINING THE EYES FOR WIDE-ANGLE VISION

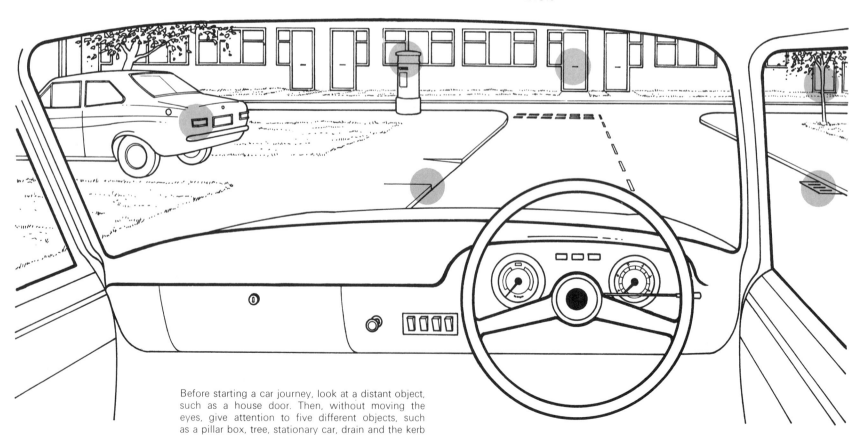

Before starting a car journey, look at a distant object, such as a house door. Then, without moving the eyes, give attention to five different objects, such as a pillar box, tree, stationary car, drain and the kerb

objects close at hand may be overlooked. It takes anything up to half an hour for a driver with good eyesight to become fully adjusted to night conditions. Night vision can be improved simply by sitting in the car for a few minutes before setting off—perhaps using this time to carry out a cockpit drill (see p. 354).

After driving for some while in the dark, a visit to a brightly lit garage or café can badly upset the adjustment the eyes have made to night-driving conditions. It can take several minutes for the eyes to re-adjust when driving is recommended. It sometimes helps to wear sunglasses when away from the car.

Not only those with weak sight or minor eye diseases are troubled by dazzle from oncoming headlights. Some people whose eyesight is otherwise normal are particularly susceptible to dazzle and may take several seconds to recover.

Never wear sunglasses of any type in the car at night. Along with amber 'night-driving spectacles', they are more likely to handicap vision than enhance it.

EXERCISES BEFORE SETTING OFF

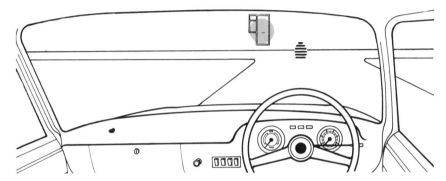

To stimulate changes of focus Make a thumbprint on the windscreen, focus the eyes on it, then focus on an object ahead, such as a front door. Repeat the exercise six times

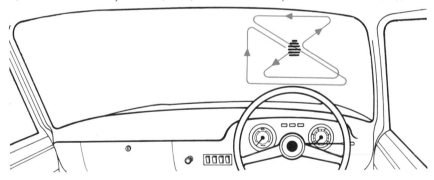

To loosen eye muscles Use thumbprint as centre and move eyes in Z-pattern twice

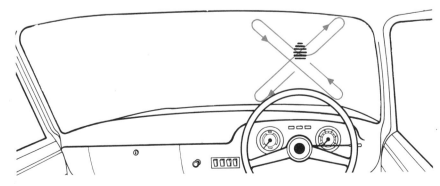

Using same thumbprint for intersection, move eyes in X-pattern twice

Poisonous car fumes

CARBON MONOXIDE, a highly poisonous gas with no colour, taste or smell to warn of its presence, is one of the by-products of the internal combustion engine, and is released when petrol is burnt.

In a confined space it can be lethal, and even when present in the atmosphere in concentrations of only 100 parts per million can have an adverse effect on mental performance if breathed in for several hours.

Victims of carbon monoxide poisoning exhibit symptoms ranging from headache and dizziness to difficulty in breathing and outright collapse.

The motorist is placed at risk by fumes from his own and other drivers' vehicles. Engines idling in confined spaces can give off localised exhaust concentrations containing 50,000 parts per million of carbon monoxide. This can build up rapidly into a lethal concentration. For this reason, engines should never be allowed to idle for long periods in a garage, tunnel or underground car park.

Traffic jams constitute another hazard. Switch off the ignition during a long hold-up; do not add to the build-up of carbon monoxide. Avoid sucking fumes from surrounding vehicles into the car through the heater's booster fan.

Carbon monoxide cannot be completely eliminated from a car's exhaust fumes, but it can be reduced by keeping spark-plugs clean and the carburettor properly adjusted to ensure efficient combustion, and by not leaving the choke out longer than necessary after a cold start.

The exhaust system itself may leak carbon monoxide fumes into the car and should be inspected regularly. The average life of an exhaust pipe is only 18 months.

Cars that are used only for short journeys are more liable to develop exhaust leaks, since the engine is not run long enough to heat and disperse the moisture that collects inside the exhaust pipe. Rust develops and weakens the system.

Eliminate holes and cracks between the engine and the passenger compartment, to prevent fumes seeping in.

Estate cars should not be driven with the rear loading door open, nor saloon cars with the boot open, since exhaust fumes will inevitably be drawn into the vehicle. If the door or boot cannot be closed, have at least one window open.

Fresh air is the best safeguard against carbon monoxide poisoning and, in many cases, the most effective cure for it (see First Aid, pp. 348–9).

Car sickness

CHILDREN between the ages of five and 15 are most susceptible to car sickness: excitement and energetic movement can lead to upset stomachs. Babies suffer less; the elderly rarely experience travel sickness. Among younger adults the risk is highest for women during menstruation.

The car driver, fully occupied and firmly located in his seat, is the least prone to travel sickness. He can prevent discomfort among his passengers by thoughtful preparation and by smooth driving.

Children should be kept busy, but discourage them from reading or writing and restrict 'spotting' games to those that keep the eyes ahead: watching for objects flashing past the sides of the car can cause eye strain, giddiness and nausea.

Some travel-sickness preparations should be used with caution (see pp. 346–7). Ask a doctor about them, especially in the case of children and expectant mothers.

The family dog can suffer even more from car sickness than human beings (see p. 352). Travel-sickness pills for animals are obtainable from pet shops.

PREVENTING CAR SICKNESS

Get a good night's sleep

Seek advice about travel pills

Prepare car: remove dangling ornaments — Avoid rich food and alcohol

Fasten safety belts — Play car radio occasionally

Start journey without delays or last-minute panics — Take light refreshments—meat sandwiches, fruit and water

Maintain good ventilation — Do not keep asking person if he feels ill

Raise children high enough to see out of front windows easily — Watch for sickness symptoms—yawning, cold, sweating, pallor, shivering, loss of interest

Stop car frequently (say, every hour)

Drive smoothly, corner slowly, and brake gently

In case of sickness: stop car, let person walk a little and have a sip of water, then put him in front seat

Medical/the danger to driving in everyday drugs

Why caution is needed

UNDER THE Road Traffic Act 1962, driving under the influence of drink or drugs is one of six offences for which a driver is disqualified for at least a year.

Since 1967 the motorist has been in no doubt about the law's demands where drink is concerned: the new Road Safety Act, which introduced breathalyser tests, defined his responsibility. Any driver found to have a blood/alcohol level of more than 80 milligrammes of alcohol per 100 millilitres of blood (urine/alcohol level exceeding 107 mg/100 ml) faces prosecution, a heavy fine and the loss of his licence.

For drugs the law's requirements are far less explicit. Few of the 2 million British motorists taking everyday medicines and pills would consider they were breaking the law. But within medical and pharmaceutical circles it is common knowledge that nearly all drugs—not just powerful narcotics—represent a potential threat to driving ability. Cough syrups, anti-rheumatic preparations, insulin for diabetics, pills for erratic blood pressure—all these and more contain ingredients that can affect a driver.

The most obvious risks are contained in two broad groups: those drugs that stimulate the central nervous system and those that depress it.

The effects differ with the type of drug, the dosage, physical and mental condition, and even body weight. Age comes into it, too: elderly people tend to react more to drugs than younger men and women.

Drugs impair driving in three ways: by direct effects, by side-effects, or by aggravating the effects of alcohol or other drugs. Occasionally, too, patients over-react to normal doses, or the action of the drug is reversed (in some cases stimulants have produced depression and tranquillisers have brought on aggression).

There are, unfortunately, no easy guidelines to which drugs are safe to take if you are going to drive. Doctors freely admit that not enough is known about the drugs they prescribe, and some chemists go as far as to claim that no preparation currently available will place its consumer outside the reach of the law. Side-effects, particularly in combination with alcohol or other drugs, range in intensity from mild dizziness to outright collapse and there is no guarantee that the victim will be able to judge his own fitness to drive.

Such is the potential risk of taking any drug and then driving that the only safe course for the motorist is to seek advice from his family doctor or from a chemist.

Central nervous system depressants

Group	Type	Mainly for
SEDATIVES/HYPNOTICS	BARBITURATES	The distinction between hypnotics and sedatives is mainly one of dose. Sedatives induce tranquillity and therefore decrease anxiety and restlessness; hypnotic doses directly induce sleep of varying duration. Barbiturates are chiefly given for insomnia, mild emotional upset, anxiety, tension, excitable conditions and irritability. They can also be used to control epilepsy
	NON-BARBITURATES	
TRANQUILLISERS	MAJOR	Here again the distinction is one of dose. Although the major tranquillisers are principally associated with psychiatric hospital practice, they are also widely prescribed in general practice, usually for anxiety, tension or agitation
	MINOR	Common nervous disorders complicated by anxiety or tension of a mild to moderate degree
ANTI-ALLERGICS	ANTIHISTAMINES	Allergic conditions generally, e.g. hay fever and skin allergies. Also for travel sickness, nasal congestion and conjunctivitis

Central nervous system stimulants

Group	Type	Mainly for
STIMULANTS AND APPETITE SUPPRESSANTS	AMPHETAMINES AND RELATED COMPOUNDS	General depressive states, fatigue and obesity
ANTI-DEPRESSANTS	MONOAMINE OXIDASE INHIBITORS	Depression and anxiety states
	THYMOLEPTICS	

Possible side-effects include	Action with alcohol/other drugs	Comments
Sleepiness, lassitude, vertigo, mental confusion and slurred speech. Effects are particularly noticeable in the elderly. Clinical symptoms of barbiturate intoxication are similar to those of alcohol: difficulty in thinking, emotional instability, euphoria, poor judgment and lack of muscular co-ordination (leading to falls, injuries, etc.)	The action of both sedatives and hypnotics is exaggerated by alcohol and antihistamines. A German study revealed that when drivers combined sedatives with alcohol, their accident rate went up by 77 per cent. With barbiturates the mixture is sometimes fatal. One-third of a lethal dose of barbiturate can kill if alcohol is taken at the same time	Barbiturates in general use can be classified in three ways, distinguished by the speed and duration of their action. The quickest-acting types are also expelled from the body quickest, but the effects of barbiturates have been noticed for as long as 72 hours. Sedatives and hypnotics generally, particularly the longer-acting ones, should not be taken in the early hours if the patient intends driving the same day
Drowsiness, fatigue, nausea, loss of control over voluntary movements, hangover, mental confusion and slurred speech		
Lack of muscular co-ordination, mental sluggishness, slowed reflexes, Parkinsonism (muscular rigidity) and sometimes even coma and convulsions. May cause drowsiness in initial stages of treatment	Effects of many tranquillisers can be dramatically increased with alcohol	Such is the danger of driving while under the influence of major tranquillisers that medical advice should always be sought
Drowsiness, lethargy, blurred vision, slurred speech, sensitivity to glare, mental confusion and, occasionally, a feeling of inebriation. High doses may lead to faintness and indifference to one's surroundings		In a 90-day experimental period in America, 68 drivers taking normal doses of a well-known minor tranquilliser were involved in ten minor and six major road accidents
Sedation, ranging from drowsiness to deep sleep, is very common. Also lassitude, muscular weakness, loss of co-ordination, inability to concentrate, dizziness, headache, blurred vision, ringing in the ears and irritability	Antihistamines heighten the effects of alcohol and barbiturates	Available over the counter, antihistamines must carry the warning— Caution. This may cause drowsiness. If affected, do not drive or operate machinery.' There is, however, still no compulsory warning of their danger in combination with alcohol
While the drug remains active, the following common side-effects are seen: impaired judgment, increased impulsiveness, over-confidence, euphoria and disorientation. Equally important from the point of view of driving are the hangover effects. These include: headaches, dizziness, nausea, irritability, palpitations, agitation, confusion, apprehension, depression, fatigue, lack of mental and muscular co-ordination, and even hallucinations	Under certain circumstances, alcohol and other drugs may heighten the effects of amphetamines and related compounds	Although amphetamines may be useful in postponing fatigue and increasing alertness, there are built-in dangers in delaying the onset of normal exhaustion. The longer it is delayed, the worse the hangover effects are likely to be. Another inherent danger with pep pills is the tendency to increase dosage to boost the feeling of euphoria. These drugs have been found to have been taken by drivers in a large number of fatal traffic accidents
Palpitations, sweating, blurred vision, defects of colour vision, agitation, increased excitement, diminished self-control, and anxiety	Particularly dangerous in combination with alcohol, many other drugs and with some foods like cheese, yeast extracts and broad beans	Frequently prescribed for long-term treatments, anti-depressants can mistakenly be thought to represent less of a risk than other drugs
Drowsiness, tremor, fatigue, palpitations, convulsions, blurred vision, agitation and sensitivity to glare	Effects can be exaggerated under certain circumstances	

Medical/First Aid until expert help arrives

Emergency treatment

NOT ALL accidents involving motor vehicles occur on the open road: the handyman is at risk in his own garage. Basic First Aid knowledge and two well-stocked First Aid kits—one in the garage and one for the car—equip the motorist to deal with most emergencies while awaiting expert help. However, always remember that well-meant but clumsy treatment may actually cause damage.

Coping with an accident

Do not panic

Protect the victim from further injury

Check that he is breathing

Stop any bleeding

If injuries look serious, do not move him more than is essential for safety

Call skilled aid as quickly as possible, passing on vital information calmly

Protect the casualty from cold and do what you can to reassure him

Do not give him anything to eat or drink

1 Maintaining respiration

ANYONE who is unconscious is always in danger of suffocation. It is vital to ensure that normal breathing is maintained.

First, make sure that the victim's air passages are clear: loosen restrictive clothing round the neck, remove false teeth or any other obstructions from the mouth, and tilt the head backwards until the chin juts out. This will make the tongue lie flat in the mouth. Then turn the victim so that he is lying in a position halfway on to his face—the 'coma' position (below). This position prevents the tongue falling back and restricting the passage of air to the lungs, and allows blood and vomit to drain out of the mouth. It may in itself restore quiet, easy breathing and consciousness. If the victim cannot be moved into the 'coma' position, clear the air passages and tilt his head back. Again, this may restore breathing and consciousness.

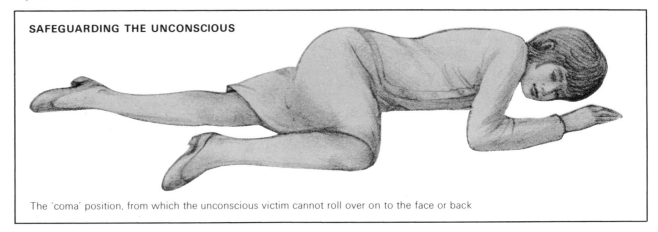

SAFEGUARDING THE UNCONSCIOUS

The 'coma' position, from which the unconscious victim cannot roll over on to the face or back

2 The kiss of life

IF THE VICTIM does not begin to breathe freely, artificial respiration is essential. To give the kiss of life:

1 Remove any obstruction, such as false teeth, from the victim's mouth. Tilt his head back with the heel of one hand on the forehead. With the thumb and forefinger of the same hand, pinch the nostrils together.
2 With the other hand, push the jaw upwards so that the chin juts out.
3 Take a deep breath. Seal your lips round the victim's mouth and blow steadily, watching for chest movements. If treating an infant, do not pinch the nose, but cover both nose and mouth with your mouth.

4 When the victim's chest has risen, remove your mouth and wait for it to fall before continuing. Repeat the kiss of life until normal breathing is restored.

An alternative method is to breathe into the victim's nose, holding his lips closed to prevent air loss through the mouth.

When the victim has begun to breathe, place him in the 'coma' position, with the upper knee drawn well up and the under arm placed behind him.

This position allows fluid to drain from the mouth easily should he vomit, and his tongue will not fall to the back of his throat and choke him.

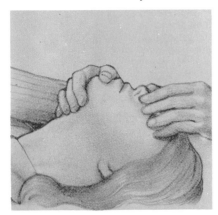

Preparing to give the kiss of life Tilt the head back and close the nostrils with one hand. Push the jaw upwards with the other

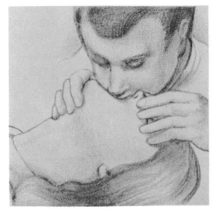

Seal your lips firmly round the victim's mouth, take a deep breath and blow steadily into the lungs

3 Restarting the heart

IF THERE is no response to the kiss of life, the heart may have stopped beating.

Check for pulse and heartbeat. Even if neither appears to be present, and the pupils of both eyes are widely dilated, the victim may still not be beyond help. Rapid action is essential. To try to restart the heart, first make sure that the victim's air passages are clear. Next, lay him flat on his back. Place the heel of one hand on the lower half of the breastbone, and cover it with the heel of the other hand.

Press downwards to a depth of approximately 1½ in., holding palms and fingers upwards, away from the victim's rib cage. This will compress the heart against the spine and cause blood to flow through the arteries. (If the patient is a child, the pressure should be much lighter and applied with the fingertips.)

Press downwards fifteen times at the rate of once a second.

Do not attempt this treatment if you suspect the patient may have a chest injury.

If this method is tried and brings no result, try alternate stimulation of the lungs and heart. Inflate the patient's lungs, using the kiss of life technique, continuing if necessary until the ambulance arrives.

When heart and lung action is restored, place the patient on his side in the 'coma' position, as vomiting may occur.

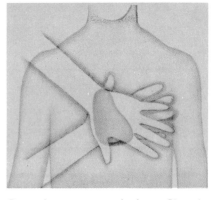

Preparing to restart the heart Place the heel of one hand on lower half of breastbone and cover it with the heel of other hand

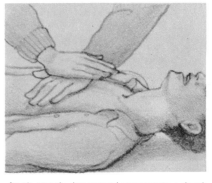

Apply steady downward pressure to a depth of about 1½ in., keeping the palms and the fingers up off the chest

Controlling bleeding

LOSS OF BLOOD is always alarming, both to casualties and would-be helpers. Most wounds look worse than they really are; unless blood is spurting from a main artery, there is little possibility of blood loss leading rapidly to death.

However, the more bleeding there is the greater the degree of shock suffered by the casualty. For this reason, try to staunch the flow immediately.

Severe bleeding

Act swiftly. Do not waste time looking for dressings. Make the casualty sit or lie down and, unless fractures are suspected, raise the bleeding part so that it is 'uphill' from the heart.

Tourniquets applied by the inexperienced do more harm than good. As soon as possible, cover the wound with some form of dressing—in an emergency, a handkerchief or scarf may serve—and bandage firmly. Do not remove dressings soiled by blood; simply add another dressing and bandage again, firmly.

In all cases of severe bleeding, prompt skilled medical aid is vital.

Cuts and abrasions

Most ordinary bleeding soon stops of its own accord. Remove any foreign bodies that can be picked out easily. Wash the wound carefully with soap and water, rinse, dry and cover with a dressing. Change soiled dressings, taking care if they are stuck to the wound.

Internal bleeding

Get medical assistance as fast as possible. Keep the victim still and quiet, preferably lying down. Loosen tight clothing and protect him from the cold—but do not overheat with too much covering. Above all, never attempt to give food or drink.

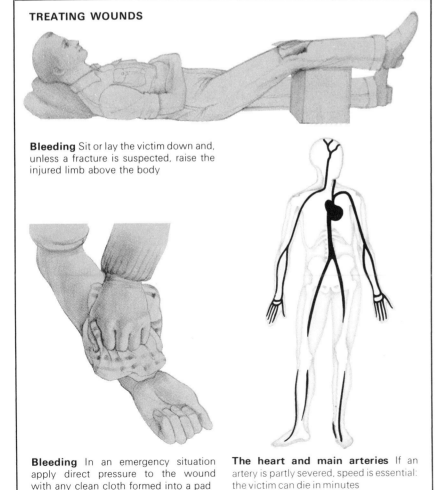

TREATING WOUNDS

Bleeding Sit or lay the victim down and, unless a fracture is suspected, raise the injured limb above the body

Bleeding In an emergency situation apply direct pressure to the wound with any clean cloth formed into a pad

The heart and main arteries If an artery is partly severed, speed is essential: the victim can die in minutes

Protecting possible fractures

ALL FORMS of bone and joint injuries—fractures, dislocations and sprains—can be made worse by inexpert handling.

Bones that protrude through flesh are obvious fractures. But painful, swollen and mis-shapen limbs may also be fractured, and may have caused internal injuries and bleeding. No attempt should be made to move an accident victim with a suspected fracture unless he is in immediate danger by not being moved.

With this kind of injury, it is important not to try to straighten a twisted limb. It is much better to reassure the victim, steadying and supporting the broken limb, than to attempt to use splints. Splints applied by laymen can be harmful and may not always be necessary.

Treat dislocations as fractures; do not attempt to correct the deformation.

Sprained joints should be rested and bandaged firmly to limit swelling. A sling may give support and comfort to a sprained arm joint. It is not necessary to remove the victim's shoe if he has a sprained ankle.

In all doubtful cases treat sprains as fractures—they may be. Call a doctor.

Relieving shock

ALL ACCIDENT VICTIMS suffer from some degree of shock. Prompt First Aid attention will help to control it.

If there is no need to use the 'coma' position, lay the casualty down with his head turned to one side and his legs (unless fractured) raised above the level of his head. Keep him still, quiet and warm.

Loosen tight clothing round his neck and chest. If he loses consciousness, place him on his side in the 'coma' position.

A severely shocked person urgently needs hospital attention.

Treating eye injuries

RUBBING an eye to remove dirt or grit could damage the surface of the eyeball.

It is sometimes possible to remove a foreign object by using the corner of a clean, moist handkerchief, or by making the patient blink under water.

If this fails, sit the patient down, ask him to look up and gently pull the lower eyelid down and out, to reveal the dirt or grit. If it is concealed beneath the upper lid, pull this out and over the lower lid, while the patient looks down.

Corrosives

Lay the victim down, with his head turned so that the affected eye is nearer the ground. Protect the unharmed eye with a dressing and immediately flood the damaged eye with clean water.

This and immediate hospital attention may prevent serious damage.

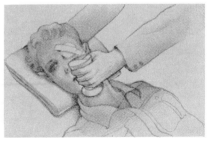

Acids Cover the unharmed eye and repeatedly flood the other with clean water

Soothing burns

SEVERE BURNS or scalds can be dealt with only by a hospital. Lay the victim down and keep him calm until help arrives.

Clothing soaked in boiling water or chemicals should be removed carefully. Clothing that has caught fire but has cooled need not be removed.

Immersion in cool, clean water, and a dry dressing, can ease pain in less severe cases. Calamine lotion soothes minor burns. Remove rings, watches, shoes and anything else of a constricting nature where there is a risk of swelling.

Carbon monoxide poisoning

EXHAUST GASES can be lethal if inhaled in a confined space such as a garage (see p. 345). Motorists exposed to this hazard suffer headaches, dizziness and laboured breathing, and eventually collapse.

Take a deep breath of clean air at the last moment before entering a poisonous atmosphere. Drag the victim out into fresh air, or open all doors and windows after switching off the car's engine.

If the victim is unconscious but still breathing, it is sufficient to put him in the 'coma' position and watch him until expert help arrives. If he is conscious, recovery will be quite rapid. If he is not breathing, give the kiss of life.

Medical/First Aid kits

Emergency essentials

A QUARTER of all British motorists claim to keep some sort of First Aid kit in their cars. Many of the kits contain either too much or too little.

The car kit below contains simple but essential items, enabling even a motorist who is unskilled in First Aid to cope with emergencies until expert help arrives.

In the garage and home workshop, accidents can range from cuts and scratches from a sharp metal edge to serious injuries resulting from, say, the collapse of a jack. Therefore the First Aid kit for the home, opposite, needs to be more comprehensive than that carried in the car.

Airtight plastic containers are better than metal boxes. They keep the contents in good condition and cannot cause annoying rattles. It is wise to label each item for rapid identification, and to make sure that every member of the family knows exactly where each kit is stored.

A KIT FOR THE CAR

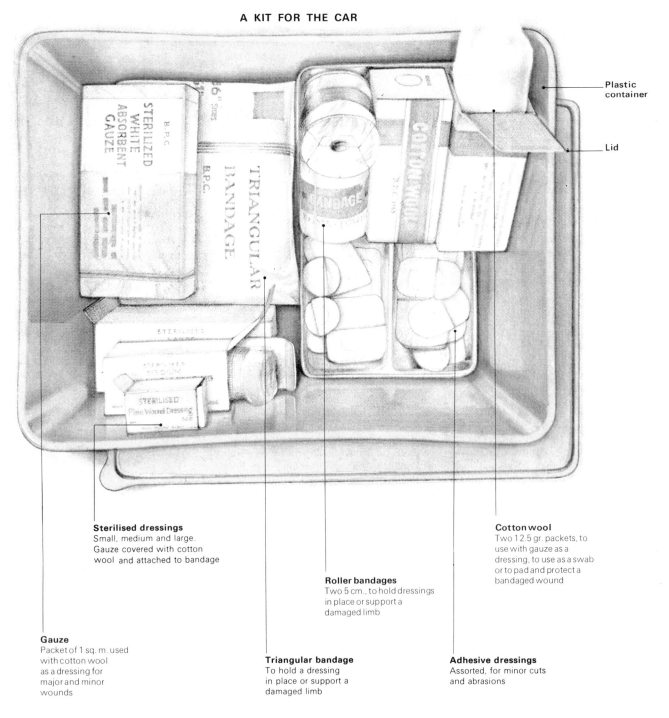

Plastic container

Lid

Small plastic bowl
For washing cuts, wounds

Graduated polythene medicine glass
For water and sal volatile

Cotton wool
Two 12.5 gr. packets, to use with gauze as a dressing, to use as a swab or to pad and protect a bandaged wound

Sterilised dressings
Small, medium and large (two packets of each). Gauze covered with cotton wool and attached to bandage

Roller bandages
2.5 cm, 5 cm (two), 6.25 cm (two) and 7.5 cm., to hold dressings in place or support a damaged limb

Magnifying glass
To help locate wood and metal splinters

Tweezers
To remove loose splinters

Polythene bags
Two, to protect remaining contents of opened packets

Wire closures
To seal polythene bags

Glucose sweets
Emergency supply for diabetics suffering from excess insulin

Triangular bandages
Four, to hold dressings in place or support damaged limbs

Sterilised dressings
Small, medium and large. Gauze covered with cotton wool and attached to bandage

Roller bandages
Two 5 cm., to hold dressings in place or support a damaged limb

Cotton wool
Two 12.5 gr. packets, to use with gauze as a dressing, to use as a swab or to pad and protect a bandaged wound

Gauze
Packet of 1 sq. m. used with cotton wool as a dressing for major and minor wounds

Triangular bandage
To hold a dressing in place or support a damaged limb

Adhesive dressings
Assorted, for minor cuts and abrasions

A KIT FOR THE GARAGE AND THE HOME

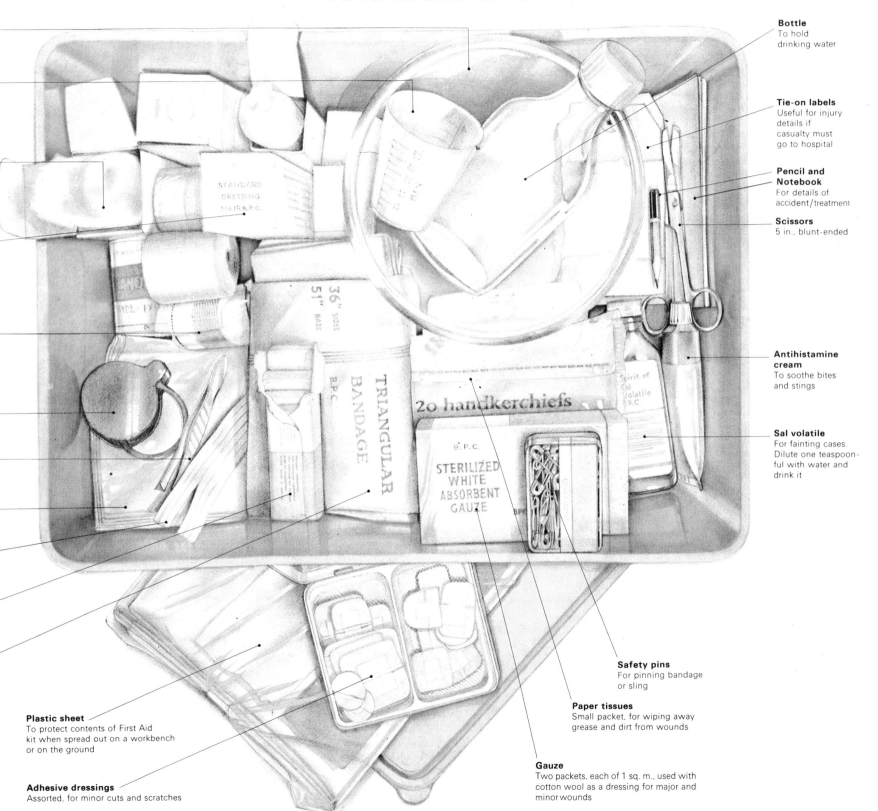

Bottle
To hold drinking water

Tie-on labels
Useful for injury details if casualty must go to hospital

Pencil and Notebook
For details of accident/treatment

Scissors
5 in., blunt-ended

Antihistamine cream
To soothe bites and stings

Sal volatile
For fainting cases. Dilute one teaspoonful with water and drink it

Safety pins
For pinning bandage or sling

Paper tissues
Small packet, for wiping away grease and dirt from wounds

Gauze
Two packets, each of 1 sq. m., used with cotton wool as a dressing for major and minor wounds

Plastic sheet
To protect contents of First Aid kit when spread out on a workbench or on the ground

Adhesive dressings
Assorted, for minor cuts and scratches

Medical/animals and the car

Travelling with pets

THERE ARE 20 million domestic animals in Britain. Treated with care and consideration, most can be safe, happy travellers.

Pets in transit need plenty of fresh air—but not draughts—and, except on short journeys, an adequate supply of water and food. Excesses of heat or cold, and sudden loud noises or flashing lights, distress them.

Injuries inside the car often occur when the driver has to make an emergency stop or corner sharply. Drive gently. Remember that animals have no warning of changing road situations. They are unable to brace themselves for the unexpected.

If an animal must be left on its own in a parked car, ensure adequate ventilation. Leave a side window open, or fit a proprietary ventilator that will permit all windows to be shut against thieves. In hot weather, always park the car in the shade. Never carry an animal in the boot.

Provide dogs and cats with a collar disc bearing your name, address and telephone number. Cats' collars should have an elastic insert to prevent strangulation.

Dogs

Of all pets, dogs can make the best travellers. They are adaptable and intelligent, eager to obey orders, and can be encouraged to regard the interior of the family car as an extension of home.

If a dog travels in the car from the time it is a puppy, it is unlikely to suffer from car sickness. Its first journeys should be associated with something it enjoys, like a walk in the woods or a swim.

It is dangerous to drive a car with a dog moving about freely inside. But, equally, it can be impractical to put a large animal into a container: its anxiety may make the journey intolerable for everyone.

Safety harnesses for dogs are available, but have met with limited commercial success. In estate cars, a grille behind the rear seat can seal off the animal in the rear luggage compartment. In ordinary saloons, however, large dogs are best left unrestrained. If well trained, they will settle down on the floor, preferably in one of the footwells behind the front seats.

Dogs that suffer from car sickness should be given sedatives or tranquillisers prescribed by a veterinary surgeon, who will advise on the correct time for dosage. (Never give animals drugs which are intended for human consumption.) Dogs may also prefer to travel in an adequately proportioned, ventilated container.

The most efficient is a wire-mesh basket, which will allow the animal to see and be seen and which can be cleaned easily. Line the bottom of the basket with newspaper—never fabric, which can easily suffocate a small or young animal.

Discourage dogs from putting their heads out of windows. When the car is stationary, they may distract other drivers or snap at passers-by. When the car is moving, dust and dirt can cause eye irritation. There is also the chance that, seeing or smelling something of interest, they may try to leap from the car.

Stop the car regularly to exercise the animal, taking precautions to ensure that, in its excitement, it does not rush into the road and cause an accident or chase farm stock. If possible, turn off the main road. Always keep the dog on a lead.

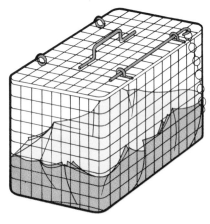

Wire-mesh baskets measuring 12 by 12 by 18 in. are sold by pet shops

Grilles fitted to estate cars leave dogs free to move about (see Accessories, p. 277)

Cats and other small pets

Cats, mice, hamsters and other small creatures are happiest travelling in a well-proportioned container, with a supply of fresh air and ample food and drink.

Birds

Since birds are easily frightened, transport them in their own cages whenever possible, partly covering the cage with a cloth. Unless the ride is exceptionally bumpy, a bird will retain a hold on its perch and be unaffected by the motion of the vehicle.

Amphibians

Newts and toads travel happily on wet sponges in plastic bags punched with air holes. Exotic creatures may need special conditions. Always seek expert advice before taking them in the car.

Fish

Do not transport fish in an aquarium. The motion of the car sets up a violent splashing that makes them sick and dizzy and throws them against the glass, causing bruising that can prove fatal. Carry fish in a plastic bag three-quarters full of water from the aquarium, and open the top of the bag every thirty minutes to renew the oxygen. Place the bag in a cardboard or wooden box for rigid support. Use a small net to transfer the fish to and from the plastic bag; never use your hands.

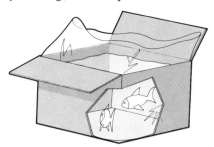

Carry fish in a plastic bag filled with aquarium water and placed in a box

Injuries

IF AN ANIMAL is severely injured, avoid moving it more than is absolutely necessary, other than to ensure its safety and that of road-users. Call a veterinary surgeon, the RSPCA or the PDSA.

Keep the animal warm and give First Aid cautiously. Even the most placid, faithful pet may bite when in pain. Wear gloves to guard against bites and scratches. Throw a coat over a dog's head to calm it, and muzzle it with a soft cloth.

Bleeding Saturate a swab with clean water and squeeze it over the wound to cleanse it. A weak solution of antiseptic or a solution of one teaspoonful of salt in a pint of water may be used instead of water.

Prolonged bleeding Apply a pressure bandage and keep the animal warm.

Bandaging Avoid tourniquets. In inexpert hands, they can do more harm than good. A piece of lint held in place with a bandage is best until skilled help arrives.

Burns and scalds Apply strong, cold tea.

Nose bleeding Do not pack the nostrils. Hold cold packs to the face.

Choking This is difficult to treat. If skilled help is not available, a small pair of pliers—or the fingers if there is no danger of being bitten—can be used to remove objects from the throat.

Fractures Do not treat. Keep the animal still and quiet until help comes.

Action after accidents All car accidents involving injury to dogs, horses, sheep, goats, pigs and oxen must be reported to the police and, if they can be traced, to the owners of the animals.

BETTER DRIVING

Nearly anyone of sound mind and body can learn to drive a car—but to drive it safely and well, with consideration and skill, is an art which only really begins when the driving test is over. Experience alone is not enough; unless the right techniques are learnt, mistakes are repeated and become habit. This section is aimed not at teaching you how to drive, but at showing how to drive better

CONTENTS

Better driving/moving off

The driving method

DRIVING A CAR is such a personal, pleasurable and generally emotional experience, and so apparently simple to do, that almost every motorist is convinced he drives superbly.

Yet the perfect driver—the man who always drives smoothly, safely and methodically—does not exist. Every driver is only on the way to perfection, no matter how many years of driving experience are behind him.

Smooth driving means a relaxed and gentle relationship between a driver and his vehicle, whether road and traffic conditions are good or bad.

Safe driving calls for total awareness of what other road-users are doing, and the ability to communicate with them. The methods given on this page and the following 30 pages are simply ways of putting the many functions of driving into logical order so that they can be safely carried out before a hazard is reached.

A hazard is anything that calls for a change of direction, speed or gear. Usually, if a driver has only to lift his foot off the accelerator for it, it is a hazard.

If everyone drove methodically, using the same method and adopting the same mental attitude to the experience, there would be fewer misunderstandings and therefore fewer accidents.

Many mishaps are caused more by a driver's failure to communicate—to make clear his intentions to other drivers—than by his physical driving of the car.

Moving off

CAR ENGINES stall when they are asked to do too much work for the power they are producing. A driver's hearing plays an important part in keeping the right balance between load and power.

When a car is being moved from a standstill—one of the hardest pieces of work its engine is called on to do—the engine note will indicate if the engine is being stressed: it will sound like a wind-up gramophone running down. Drivers can also 'feel' the engine revolutions through the steering wheel and pedal controls. At the point of stalling, the clutch will judder and the steering wheel vibrate.

Starting on an upward slope calls for a faster-running engine to compensate for the greater load.

The engine note will drop more quickly as the clutch is released. To stop the car running backwards, release the handbrake slowly and progressively as the car begins to strain forward.

Cockpit drill for the driver setting out

A DRIVER'S COMFORT and physical alertness are as important for safety as is the efficiency of the car.

Before moving off, carry out a routine cockpit drill in the order shown in the illustration.
1. Check that the handbrake is on.
2. Check that the gear lever is in neutral.
3. Check that all doors are firmly closed.
4. Adjust the driving seat so that all the controls can be operated without discomfort or the need to stretch.
5. Fix your seat belt, taking care the buckle is properly placed (see pp. 338–41).
6. Adjust the driving mirror.
7. Limber up for the task ahead: flex the wrist and fingers, pedal with the feet half-a-dozen times to stimulate circulation, and briefly focus your eyes alternately on long and short-range objects.
8. Look in the mirrors.
9. Look over your right shoulder before moving off and signal.

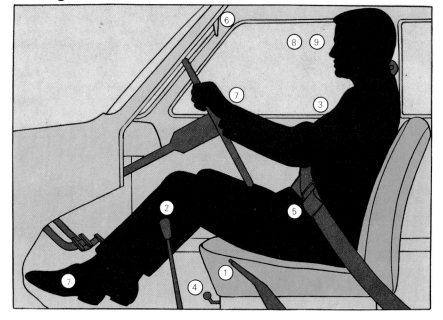

Clutch control on starting

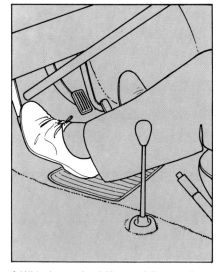

1 With the engine idling and the gear lever in neutral, depress the clutch pedal. The engine will run more freely

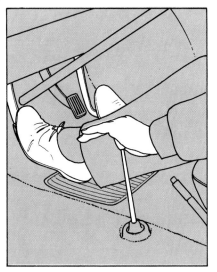

2 Engage first gear and depress the accelerator gently, slightly increasing the engine revs to prevent it stalling under load

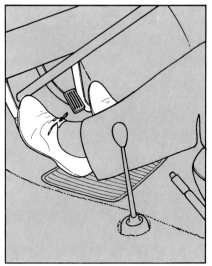

3 Release the clutch pedal slowly until you hear the engine note begin to drop, indicating that the clutch is starting to engage

4 Ease off the handbrake gradually while depressing the accelerator and releasing the clutch. Do not let the car roll back

Gear changing

Changing gear

CHANGING GEAR smoothly and economically demands one basic driving virtue—gentleness. Apart from hearing a different note from the engine, a passenger should never know when the car has changed gear, even on the most tortuous route. There should be no jerks, no excessive revs, no labouring of the engine.

A common fault when changing up—and sometimes when changing down—is delay in releasing the clutch pedal when the gear lever has been moved into the next position. This results in a jerky gear change which can be harmful to the transmission and unpleasant for passengers.

When changing gear, cup the hand and 'palm' the lever, turning the hand in the direction of the lever's travel. The wrist should be loose and flexible.

After changing gear, bring the hand back to the steering wheel, even if another gear-shift is imminent.

First gear

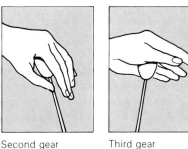
Second gear

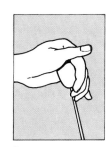
Third gear

Fourth gear

Double de-clutching

ALL MODERN CARS have synchromesh (see pp. 90–1), but on some models it is not available on first gear. To change down smoothly into first gear may call for double de-clutching, especially on wet roads, as it reduces the risk of skidding.

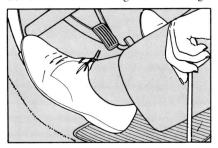
1 Take your foot off the accelerator, depress the clutch and move the gear lever to neutral

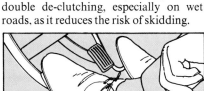
2 Release the clutch pedal and press the accelerator pedal to 'rev' the engine

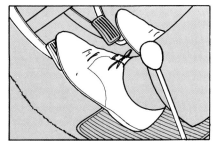
3 Release the accelerator, depress the clutch and change into the lower gear

4 Let the clutch pedal up and, simultaneously, increase pressure on the accelerator

Heeling and toeing

THIS IS A technique used by rally drivers to condense braking and gear changing into one operation. It requires skill and is definitely not for the novice. Do not try to teach yourself: take expert tuition and practice off the public roads.

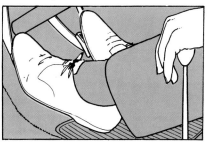
1 Brake with ball of right foot, depress clutch and move gear lever to neutral

2 Let the clutch up and, still braking, press the accelerator with heel of right foot

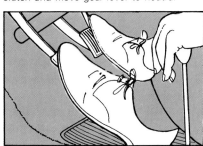
3 If heel cannot be used, use side of foot in rocking movement to brake and accelerate

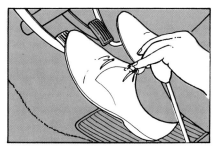
4 Release accelerator, depress clutch, select gear and let the clutch pedal up

Driving automatics

AUTOMATIC TRANSMISSION is like a single-minded brain that will change gear for you as road speed varies but will take no heed of hazards, or of the need for a lower gear for better handling.

To overcome this, automatic boxes have a low or lock-up position that gives the driver partial control of the gearbox.

On steep hills the car's speed may be such that the automatic transmission is just at the point where it is about to change up. If it does change and lacks the power to pull the car up the hill, it will promptly change down again. The use of lock-up prevents the change-up and gives a better-balanced ride; downhill, braking and setting the control on lock-up will change down and give positive engine braking.

Once selected, lock-up will allow only downward gear changes. If the car is in third gear, it will drop to second; if the speed then falls to about 3 mph, first gear will automatically be selected and locked until the lever is returned to D (Drive).

While the car is in 'Drive', a light pressure on the accelerator will give quiet, easy gear changes. A firmer pressure will result in the gears being held for a little longer. By pressing the pedal down hard the accelerator reaches kick-down, which causes an immediate change into second gear and holds it there until the accelerator is eased.

Be careful when using kick-down to overtake; when pressure on the accelerator is eased only fractionally, the car will change into top gear and move ahead under almost full acceleration. This could mean that the car is moving into a small gap at a speed that is too high. Instead, use lock-up or try to judge the rate of acceleration and then smoothly release the pedal completely, picking up just the amount of throttle needed to complete the manoeuvre safely and smoothly.

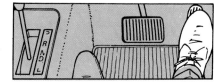
Automatic transmission Use the right foot only for both pedal controls

Better driving/braking and stopping

The braking method

A CAR has three braking systems—the accelerator, the gears and the brakes themselves. A controlled, well-anticipated and unhurried act of slowing down or stopping will involve the use of all three.

With proper observation of the road and traffic ahead (see pp. 358–9), a driver can see the need for a reduction in speed long before he has to apply the brakes. The accelerator becomes a brake as soon as the foot is lifted from it; a period of deceleration should, ideally, always precede use of the footbrake.

Acceleration and braking cost money, in consumption of petrol and wear of tyres and brake linings. Accelerating until the last possible moment, followed by harsh and violent braking, is simply wasting money twice over.

When approaching a hazard, first decelerate, then apply the footbrake, and finally change to a lower gear. The sooner you begin braking, when the need is obviously going to arise, the more time you will have to think as the hazard, with all its implications, draws nearer.

Braking should be progressive and smooth. As the footbrake is applied, the weight of the car is transferred on to the front wheels, increasing the risk of a four-wheel skid in bad weather.

Over the last yard or two before stopping, pressure on the brake pedal should be almost negligible. Holding the brake on hard makes the car stop with an ugly jolt: passengers are thrown forward and then sharply back.

Try to brake only when the car is travelling in a straight line, because it is then at its most stable. If you have to brake on a bend, do so as lightly and smoothly as practicable.

Do not brake when the car is skidding, as you will not regain control if you do (see Skidding, pp. 378–9).

Before descending steep hills, change down a gear—or two, if the slope is very steep—to help hold the car back and relieve some of the strain on the brakes. This allows maximum use of deceleration and gears to prevent the brakes becoming overheated and less efficient.

When road surfaces are bad, try to brake firmly on the good patches and ease off when the grip is poor.

When you use the choke, on cold, frosty mornings, remember that it gives faster running and the pull of the engine can be too much for the brakes to overcome. If you must stop suddenly in these conditions, depress the clutch quickly.

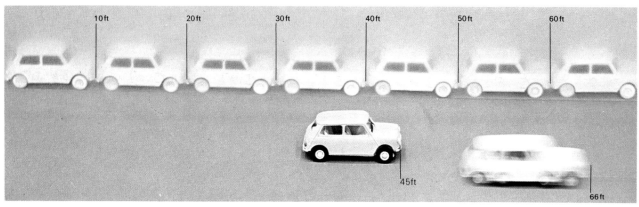

Changing gear Brake first, then change gear. The driver of the yellow car, travelling at 30 mph, brakes normally and stops in 45 ft.

The driver of the white car changes gear, then brakes. If he changes down in 1½ sec., he covers 66 ft before he even starts braking

Driving down steep hills Control the car with a combination of brakes and gears—and change down before the descent begins. The yellow car is using an intermediate gear and braking spasmodically. The white car is descending in top gear and braking continuously. In this car, continuous friction is causing brake-lining temperatures to soar. This leads to 'brake-fade', and the car's

stopping power is reduced. Not only are the brakes absorbing all the energy of the car's momentum, but the descent is more rapid, allowing less time for them to cool. In the yellow car, engine braking means that the energy is being dissipated by means of the cooling system; the fan speed is fairly high, even though road speed is low. The brakes, when used only in bursts, remain cool and efficient

A typical saloon car can descend a gradient of 1 in 16 (top) in third gear, or 1 in 12 (centre) in second gear, at 30 mph without using

the brakes. Brakes and engine will probably do equal work on a 1 in 6 gradient (bottom) if a car is in second gear

Power-assisted brakes

WITH servo-assisted brakes, the force applied by the driver's foot is supplemented by power produced by the engine (see p. 114). This reduces the amount of pressure needed on the brake pedal, so when first driving a car with servo-assisted brakes, try them carefully soon after moving off, to see how the car reacts to the pressure of your foot on the pedal.

If the engine stops or the servo system fails, power-assisted brakes will still work, but they will be less effective. The greater foot pressure you then have to apply will at first lead you to think that the whole braking system has failed.

To learn the car's braking characteristics if the power system should fail, try stopping it in a safe place away from traffic and with the ignition switched off. Operate the pedal several times to use up the reserve vacuum provided by the engine and you will realise how much more foot pressure is needed to apply the brakes without power assistance.

Braking automatics

LEARN to accelerate and brake with the right foot only. You may drive cars with manually operated gears from time to time and mistakenly stab the brake in an automatic car with your left foot because you have become used to de-clutching. The result will be a violent and unexpected stop that could cause an accident.

The handbrake

DO NOT apply the handbrake until you have completely stopped, as passengers will be jolted and the car may skid with locked rear wheels, especially on a loose or wet surface.

Pulling the handbrake up on the ratchet with a loud clicking noise is unnecessary and will cause needless wear.

Even if you think you are on level ground when stopping, do not release the footbrake until the handbrake is on.

Testing the brakes

WHEN the car has been standing for some time, such as overnight, test the brakes before moving off to make sure that the operating fluid has not leaked away. If the pedal travels more than halfway to the floor (see p. 212), drive cautiously and test again at low speed before you reach the first hazard. Check too that the brakes are not pulling to one side.

Stopping in time

A CAR's stopping ability depends on its driver's reaction time (on average, half a second); on the pressure he applies to the brakes; on the car's own braking characteristics; on the condition of the tyres; and on the surface of the road—whether it is wet or dry, firm or loose.

Recommended following distances (see Overtaking, pp. 370–1) are closer than actual braking distances: crowded roads make ideal spacing impracticable and the car in front will always, short of colliding with a solid and stationary object, have its own braking distance. In theory, that doubles the distance needed by the car behind. However, driving too closely behind another vehicle, especially on motorways, is a common British failing and the cause of many accidents.

Stopping distance is reaction (or thinking) distance plus braking distance (which is dependent on speed). The reaction distance is the minimum safe distance at which you should follow another car.

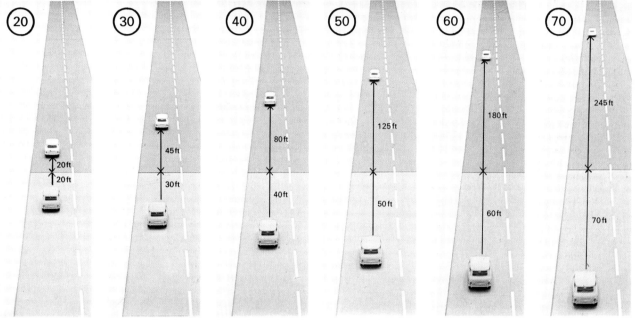

Good conditions Average stopping distances in good weather. Distance travelled in reaction time is that between car and dark grey tarmac

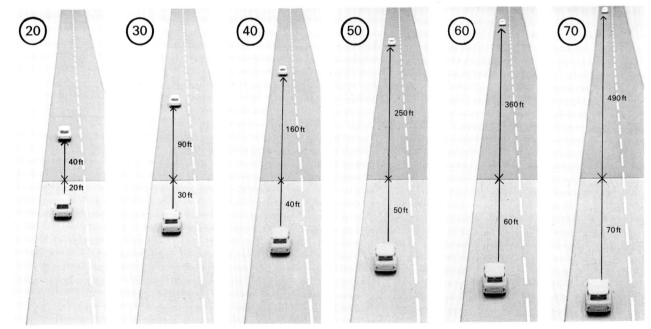

Bad conditions In bad weather, reaction time remains the same but braking distances are *at least* doubled. The stopping distances will be greater than those illustrated if the condition of the tyres, brakes or the road surface itself is poor

Better driving/road observation

Cultivating awareness

DRIVING WELL demands total involvement of most of the senses. It is not enough to gain physical mastery over the mechanical functions of the car without cultivating full, *thinking* awareness of the environment in which it is being used.

A driver must take in the whole scene around him, evaluate it, then decide how it should affect his actions. He must see, then interpret, then anticipate, then act.

Perfect road observation needs, therefore, concentration, reaction, anticipation, accurate interpretation of the smallest detail and even, on occasions, intuition. The driver has to consider not only what he can see, but also what he cannot see. Use the rear-view mirrors often—and always before changing direction or speed.
The view ahead The driver's view from the car must be clear and unobstructed. Even a perfectly clean windscreen filters out about 15 per cent of the light available; a dirty windscreen can obstruct more than half of the light available outside the car.

Dust can build up on a windscreen so gradually that the deterioration in visibility is hardly noticed. In bad weather, windscreen wipers and washers should be used often—the danger comes not so much from reduction in the amount of light available as from the blotchy nature of dirt and spray, which often obscures whole areas of vision.

Smoking in the car also causes a film to form on the driving mirror and the inside surfaces of the windows.

The more the driver can see what is going on around him, the more clues he will pick up about likely hazards.

Resist the temptation to look at a passenger when speaking to him. Instead, continually scan the road ahead and to the side as well as the driving mirrors, rather like a radar beam sweeping the horizon.
Reading the road Loss of the view ahead through any cause, such as from buildings, hedges or trees, is as much a hazard as any crossroads, obstruction or other vehicle. Therefore the car should be positioned to obtain the best possible view without endangering other traffic.

The contours of an open road can sometimes be judged by the line of a hedge or telegraph poles. But hedges and poles sometimes cross fields: take them as a general guide, but wait until you can see clearly before committing yourself.

Watch the condition of road surfaces, especially on narrow country lanes. Mud, loose gravel and pot-holes or gullies can easily cause you to lose control.

Take advantage of gaps between buildings for advance road information

If a car glimpsed through a narrow gap is travelling slowly, this may indicate that it is trailing other traffic which is screened from the driver's view by buildings or other obstructions

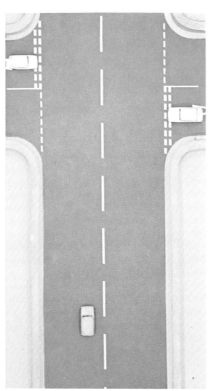

Hedges and trees can obscure the view into side turnings and entrances

If it is safe to do so, move nearer the centre line for maximum angle of vision and a better warning of cars joining the main road. If there is other traffic, keep left

Interpreting the signs

OBSERVATION alone is not enough: the driver needs the eyes of a detective—looking for clues, *interpreting* them, then deciding what they portend.

Sometimes the seasons of the year can suggest the likelihood of hazards to be met. In spring there can be sheep on the roads, looking for lost lambs. In summer, beware of new drivers, hikers, insecure loads on roof racks, holiday coaches, trailers and caravans. Signs of a village fête can mean slow traffic, jay-walkers, pets and excited children.

In autumn, high winds can cause fallen branches on the road, or drifts of leaves; blackberry hedges may mean blackberry pickers. In winter, large numbers of sea or marsh birds circling inland can suggest flooding nearby. On unfenced roads, beware of wandering animals.

If one vehicle emerges from a side turning, assume that there may be others behind it

Road-building materials often warn of men and machinery round the next corner

In rural areas, cow pats on the road indicate that cattle may be a hazard ahead

Near hospitals, expect ambulances—and drivers who may be preoccupied or distressed

Skid marks on the road mean someone has braked hurriedly. A bad bend may be ahead

Watch for fresh hedge or grass cuttings on the verge. There may be men still at work

Drive cautiously past farms offering produce for sale. Cars may be parked badly

Rocks are usually dislodged by water. In winter, this may mean ice on the road

Better driving/parking

The method

FEW MANOEUVRES cause more difficulty than parking in a small space. It calls for skilful positioning as well as delicate, precise handling of the clutch, accelerator and steering wheel. Yet if the few basic rules are understood, parking becomes a simple and straightforward operation.

To park successfully in a limited gap parallel to the kerb, you need a space at least one and a half times the length of the car, if reversing in, and at least twice the car's length if heading in. Parking in a smaller space creates problems for drivers of cars in front and behind. It is preferable to reverse into a space: a car swings in more easily this way, and it is useful to have driven past the gap to assess its size.

Try to park 4 in. from the kerb. Avoid mounting or scuffing the pavement with the wheels, as this can damage the outside wall of the tyre, the rim of the wheel or even the steering mechanism.

Always look in the mirror and signal your intentions before parking.

Stop the engine and apply the handbrake before you leave the car; it is illegal —and dangerous—to leave a car unattended with the engine idling.

Parking forward

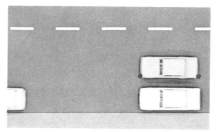

1 Go slowly past the car parked just before the gap, driving about 3 ft out from it

2 At no more than walking pace, turn left into the centre of the gap

3 As you near the kerb, turn the steering wheel in the opposite direction, so that the front wheels are moving in a line parallel to the pavement and close to the kerb

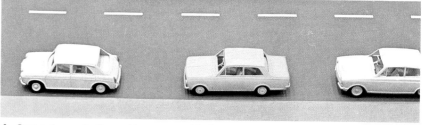

4 Centre the car in the parking space with the wheels parallel to the kerb. Leave enough room for the vehicles behind and in front to get out without excessive manoeuvring

Parking uphill

When a car is travelling uphill, it will slow down rapidly the moment deceleration begins, so judgment of speed, distance, deceleration and braking are critical if you are to stop at the exact spot you require. Just before the car stops, turn the front wheels to the *right*, so that if the car does roll backwards, the nearside front wheel will be checked by the kerb. If there is no kerb, turn the wheels to the left: at least then, if the car does roll backwards, it will move out of the way of moving traffic. Always, when parking uphill, leave the car in *first* gear with the handbrake on

5 If you find you are too far from the kerb, move forward on slight right lock

6 Reverse on left lock until the rear of the car is close to the kerb

Parking downhill

7 Move right back on reverse, straightening the wheels so they are parallel to the kerb

8 Centre the car in the gap, leaving room for other parked vehicles to get out

Braking needs to be heavier when coming to a stop downhill, and a longer braking distance should be allowed. A lower gear will help to hold the car back by engine braking, but the gear change must be completed before beginning the descent. A slow gear change on the slope itself will mean that the clutch will be disengaged for a long time and the car will gain instead of reduce speed. Turn the front wheels to the nearside, whether or not there is a kerb. Set the handbrake and leave the car in *reverse* gear

Reversing into a parking space

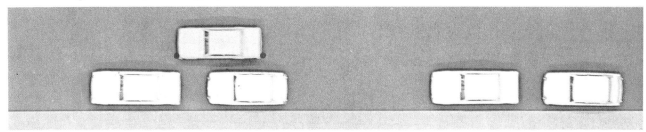

1 Stop about 2½–3 ft from the first parked car past the gap, with the rear of your car at least 3 ft in front of the rear of the parked vehicle (with most average-sized saloons you will find yourself sitting abreast of the other car's front wheel)

2 Move back, steering left, with the clutch engaged slightly to give crawling speed

3 Aim the car's nearside rear corner for the centre of the gap. Back the car at a 45 degree angle to the kerb. Begin steering right as the front of the car clears the rear of the one ahead

4 As the car drops into the space, increase the right lock but do not increase speed. Remember to watch for any overtaking traffic on the road

5 Continue reversing until the car is parallel to the kerb, and is close to it. Then straighten the front wheels. Take care not to bump the car behind

6 Centre the car in the gap, leaving room for other vehicles parked in front and behind to get out. Be careful of passing traffic when opening the offside door

Angle parking

MOST ANGLED parking bays are designed to face away from the direction of travel so that cars can only be backed in. However, head-in bays do exist. When leaving a head-in bay, use extreme caution: move very slowly, look over your shoulder, and dab the footbrake frequently so that oncoming traffic can see your brake lights. If you have a passenger, ask him to guide you out into the traffic lane.

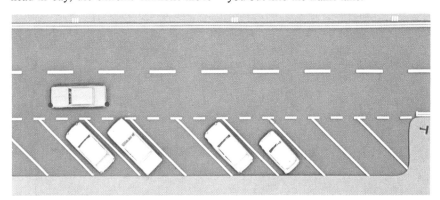

Reversing into angled bays **1** Use mirror, signal left and drive slowly past vacant bay. Stop with left end of rear bumper opposite centre of bay just beyond the one you wish to use

2 Back slowly, steering left as far as is needed to line the car up for entering the centre of the space. Ease in very slowly and stop with the rear of the car just short of the kerb

Better driving/reversing

The method

THE CAR can easily handle jerkily when reversing as it responds sensitively to even a little steering. The slower the speed, the smoother will be the reversing.

When turning and reversing simultaneously, remember that the front of the car will swing out wide, and beware of overtaking drivers who may come too close.

Do not rely on mirrors alone. Look over whichever shoulder gives the best view. Steer one-handed—with the right hand when reversing left, and *vice versa*—grasping the wheel near the top and steadying it with the other hand if necessary.

Make sure the area behind the car is clear before reversing. If the car is parked, approach the driver's door from the rear to see if there are any obstructions.

A reversing light is not only useful at night, but it can also serve as a warning to other drivers of an intention to reverse—in daylight as well as at night.

Never reverse from a side road into a main road. There are no exceptions.

Reversing right into a minor road

THIS is much riskier than reversing left and should be avoided if possible.

First cross to the offside of the road, facing oncoming traffic, then reverse on the right-hand side of the side road; then move across to the left. Only one thing makes the turn easier—you can see the kerb by looking over your right shoulder.

1 After choosing the turning for the manoeuvre, look in the mirror and signal right

2 Approach with the offside wheels just inside the centre line. See that the road is clear

3 Move across and stop about 2 ft from the kerb on the far side of the junction

4 Turn to look out of the driver's window and rear window, and move slowly backwards

5 As the rear wheel meets the corner, steer to the right and follow the kerb line round

6 While turning, watch for traffic on the main road from which you have come

7 When past the corner, continue to look both forward and to the rear, and make sure the car is running parallel to the kerb line

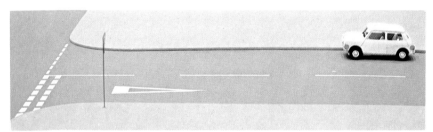

8 Continue down the right-hand side of the turning for at least five car lengths

9 Check the rear-view mirror, signal left and move to the left-hand side of the road

Reversing left

CHOOSE a side road off a straight stretch so that you and other drivers have a good view for some distance. As you pass the turning before beginning the manoeuvre, go slowly and check that it is clear of parked cars and pedestrians.

1 Look in the mirror and slow down. When passing the turning, signal as for a stop

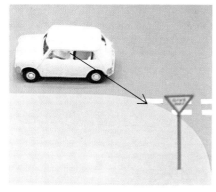

2 Stop about 2 ft from the kerb. Try to retain even a limited view into the side road

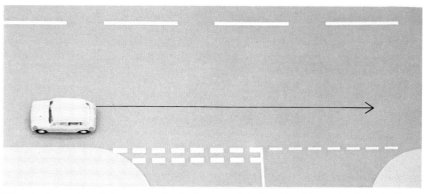

3 Turn in the seat so that you see clearly over your left shoulder. Move slowly back. Keep the car straight until the corner of the kerb appears in the rear nearside window

4 Steer left. See that the road behind is still clear and the car is not too near the kerb

5 As the front of the car draws abreast of the corner, straighten it to run parallel to the kerb

6 Check that the road behind you is clear. Go back five car lengths, so that there is room to take the proper position for turning right (see p. 364)

Making a 3-point turn

TO TURN the car in the least number of movements, remember that the faster you go the less effective the steering will be.

Steering while the car is stationary will only strain the steering gear, especially when radial tyres are fitted, so the car must be moving when you change direction. Aim to have a slow-moving car and fast-moving steering.

1 Stop on the left on a straight stretch of road where there is good visibility in both directions

2 Check the mirrors, then move forward slowly in first gear. Apply full right lock as soon as the car is moving

3 When descending the camber, steer fully left and stop just before reaching the kerb without actually touching it

4 Select reverse gear, then transfer from the footbrake to the handbrake. See that the road is clear, and move slowly back. The car is still on left lock. Control the car with clutch and footbrake as it crosses the crown of the road on to the opposite camber

5 When the car begins to descend the opposite camber steer right and stop just short of the kerb. If the camber is steep and the kerb high, stop far enough from the road edge to avoid scraping the underside of the car on the pavement

6 Select first gear, hold the car on the handbrake and, checking that the road is still clear, move forward to the left side of the road and drive off normally. No signals are made; the manoeuvre should not be attempted if there is other traffic

Better driving/turning

The method

ONE IN FIVE of all accidents involves a vehicle that has been negotiating a turn—and turning right is three times more dangerous than turning left. Turning requires every skill the driver possesses: observation, anticipation, judgment and complete control over speed, gears and brakes. Many accidents arise from a combination of late positioning and signalling. It is vital that other road-users should be clear about your intentions, and should not be forced to avoid you hurriedly.

The steering wheel

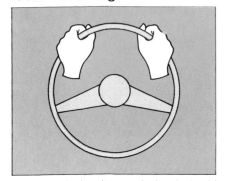

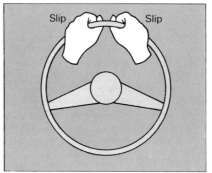

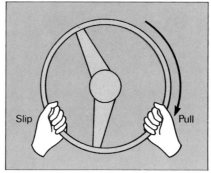

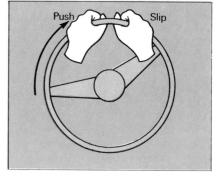

Before beginning the turn, the hands should be at the normal 'ten to two' driving position, and not lower than 'quarter to three'. Slide

both hands up to the top of the wheel. For a right turn, pull down with the right hand, allowing the left hand to slip down the

wheel in the other direction. When the right hand is down to the 'twenty or twenty-five past' position, push up with the left

hand and slip the right hand up the wheel again. At all times, try to keep both hands at a similar height on the wheel

Turning right

THERE ARE two manoeuvres in turning right: moving from the nearside of the road to a position just inside the centre-line, and the turn itself. Avoid leaving preparation for the turn until the last moment and blurring the two movements into one, as following traffic may try to overtake or have no time to position itself to pass on your nearside. Position the car so it causes least inconvenience to other traffic.

In the first manoeuvre, always follow the sequence: mirror–signal–steer.

In the turn itself, reduce speed with the *brakes* and only then select the gear needed. It is not necessary to change down in sequence, because while this is being done valuable braking time is lost and you may enter the turn too fast.

It is better to change direct from top gear to second or even first gear, provided the car has been progressively braked to the appropriate speed.

Turning right into a side road

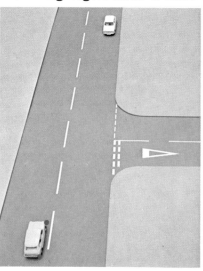

1 Check the mirrors, signal, and position the car parallel to and just inside the centre-line

2 Let oncoming traffic pass. Select the right gear for your speed. Check mirrors again

3 Turn in a gentle arc that will bring you into the left-hand side of the side road

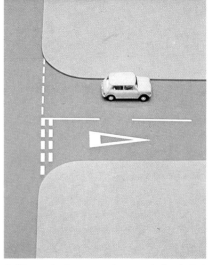

4 Glance in the rear mirror and check that the signal has cancelled

T-junctions

FOLLOW the same procedure as for turning right into side roads, but always prepare for a possible 'Stop' or 'Give Way' sign; Even at a 'Give Way' sign you may have to stop. Do not move out until you have a clear view of traffic coming from both directions. Take care when a driver coming from the right is signalling a left-turn. Do not move out until he actually begins the turn, as you could be held legally in the wrong in a collision.

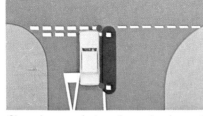

Slow down and stop, then edge forwards until you can see clearly both ways

Go slowly, as achieving good each-way vision will place the front of your car in the path of oncoming traffic. Parked vehicles will obstruct your view of the road

Turning left

NORMALLY, a left-hand turn is not an especially hazardous manoeuvre—provided that the driver's observation, signalling and positioning are correct. When merging with other traffic on a left turn, watch not only traffic coming from the right but also beware of pedestrians, parked vehicles or cyclists on the left.

Drill Turning left can be turned into a drill like the pedestrian kerb drill

1 Look right: assess oncoming traffic

2 Look left: note any obstacles

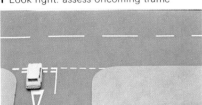

3 Look right again: await a gap in traffic

4 Look left again before moving out

Turning left into a side road

1 Check mirrors. Signal before the turn, but *after* passing other left-hand entrances

2 Position the car 3–4 ft from the kerb or from parked vehicles

3 Start the turn when your front wheels are opposite the point where the kerb begins to curve. If you turn too soon, the rear wheels may mount the kerb; if too late, the car will swing wide into the wrong side of the road. Sound the horn if a pedestrian is likely to step off the kerb in front of you

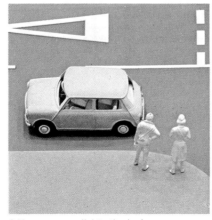

4 Keep car parallel to the kerb

Turning right at crossroads

WHEN TWO CARS which have been travelling in opposite directions both wish to turn right at a crossroads, they should pass behind each other—that is, offside to offside, as though turning round a small centre island. Both drivers then have a clear view of traffic that may be crossing their path on the main carriageways. However, watch for police control or road markings indicating that you are intended to turn nearside to nearside. Always approach the junction slowly, selecting a lower gear well in advance.

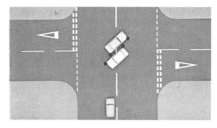

If several cars are turning right, all but the first should hold back from moving into the junction, so that oncoming right-turning traffic is not blocked

Staggered crossroads only

At some irregular, staggered junctions it may be more convenient and practical to turn nearside to nearside, but beware of oncoming traffic being obstructed from view. Go very slowly, making sure that the other driver understands the type of turn required

Turning into driveways

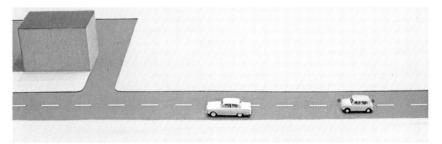

IF YOU ARE turning either left or right into a narrow entrance, especially from a stream of traffic on a de-restricted road, start signalling well in advance. Remember that following traffic may think you are going to overtake.

Make use of the rear lights by dabbing the footbrakes gently on and off as you approach the entrance, and give a clear hand signal. When turning right, it may often be safer to continue to the next junction or roundabout and approach the entrance from the other direction.

Make sure there are no pedestrians crossing the driveway who will cause you to stop in the path of oncoming traffic.

Do not reverse into main roads from narrow entrances. Come out head first so that other traffic can be clearly seen

Better driving/roundabouts

The method

A ROUNDABOUT is an alternative to a cross-roads, for no matter how you approach, you must turn left into it. Usually there are no marked lanes—though some roundabouts carry specific direction markings—so correct positioning on the approach, followed by consistent steering through the imaginary lanes of the roundabout, is important.

When approaching a roundabout, select the *left-hand* lane if you want to turn left and the *right-hand* lane if you want to turn right. Either is correct for straight ahead.

Traffic on the roundabout has priority; always give way to the right. Early in the approach, look to the right to estimate what traffic is likely to be there when you arrive. Then judge your speed of approach so that you arrive when a gap occurs. See that the gear change is completed before you enter the roundabout.

Signal for your exit off the roundabout only when you are at or just past the centre of the exit that precedes it.

Turning left

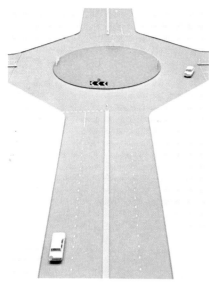

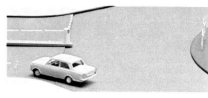

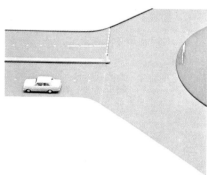

1 Position the car in the nearside lane, check the mirrors, signal left and slow down, braking and then changing to a lower gear

2 Give way to traffic already on the roundabout, still signalling left, and turn when there is an adequate gap in traffic

3 Take the left-hand lane of the exit road. Keep signalling until the turn is complete, then check that the indicator has cancelled

Turning right

1 Check mirrors and signal for moving into the right-hand lane. Slow down

2 Still signalling right, take up position in centre of lane before entering roundabout

3 Give way to traffic on the roundabout

4 Move out and across to the lane nearest the central reservation, still signalling

5 Remain close to the centre island and begin to signal left when opposite or just past the centre of the exit before the one being taken. Use rear-view mirrors

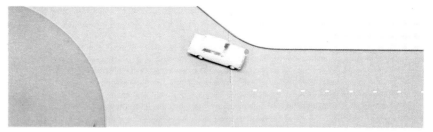

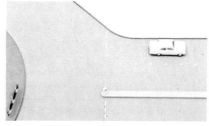

6 Continue to signal left while turning

7 Take whichever lane of the exit road causes least inconvenience to others

8 Check that the indicator has cancelled

Straight forward from left-hand lane

  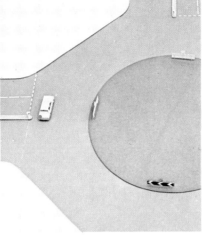 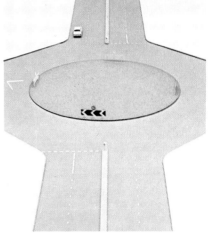

1 Use the left-hand lane for preference. Make no signal, but brake and then change down a gear on the approach

2 Give way to traffic on the roundabout then, when the way is clear, move out, keeping to the left-hand lane

3 Keep well to the left and begin the left-turn signal when at or just past the centre of the first exit. Keep to your 'lane'

4 Remain well to the left, and do not forget to cancel the signal when the car is again travelling in a straight line

Straight forward from right-hand lane

   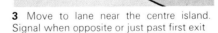 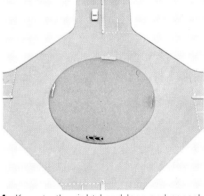

1 If the nearside lane is already occupied you may take the right-hand lane

2 Give way to traffic that is already on the roundabout before attempting your turn

3 Move to lane near the centre island. Signal when opposite or just past first exit

4 Keep to the right-hand lane and cancel signal when travelling straight

Complex roundabouts

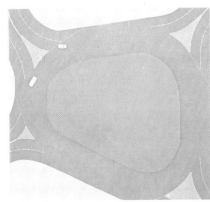 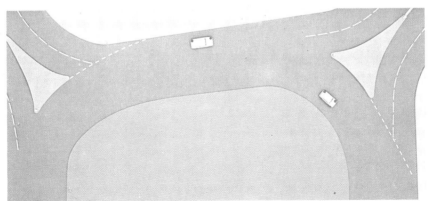 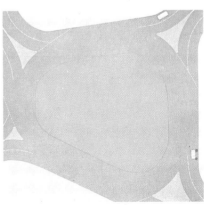

1 Choose the lane appropriate to the exit to be taken—traffic allowing—and signal

2 Take up a position that makes your intentions clear, and signal when opposite or just past the exit before the one you have chosen to take

3 At your exit select the lane that causes least inconvenience to others

Better driving/cornering

The method

A CAR is most stable when it is travelling in a straight line at a steady speed. As soon as it enters a corner it is subject to forces that act in almost direct opposition to the driver's wishes.

Centrifugal force throws the car outwards from the centre of the curve; the greater the speed and the sharper the bend, the stronger the centrifugal effect.

Changes of speed, or use of the brakes, will alter the weight distribution of the car, shifting its centre of gravity and affecting the steering response.

When a car is turning, the front wheels do not move in the direction in which they are pointing. The tyres become distorted and their contact with the road is reduced.

The car is balanced best if it is being 'driven' rather than coasting or decelerating, and is sitting evenly on its suspension under steady throttle. Proper use of the gears will give maximum road-holding without the need for sudden increases or decreases in speed.

The same rule cannot be applied to every corner and bend. Road speed, engine speed and positioning will vary according to the width of the road, the density of traffic, the severity of the bend and the view that you have into it.

Road speed should be at its lowest just before you enter a bend, so that as you progress through it the car can be kept under slight acceleration. This gives more control. Sudden acceleration should be avoided just as much as sudden deceleration. Observation on the approach to a bend—and assessment of what you see—are vital. If either is faulty, everything that follows will be faulty or hurried.

THE CAR'S BEHAVIOUR

Braking

Under firm braking, a car's weight will be thrown forward on to the 'front wheels and the back of the car will lighten. The front dips, reducing the grip of the rear wheels on the road. This makes the steering heavier

Acceleration

Firm acceleration causes the rear of a car to go down and the front to rise. This provides stability when the car is travelling in a straight line, but in the middle of a corner it can cause the front of the car to slip away

Understeer

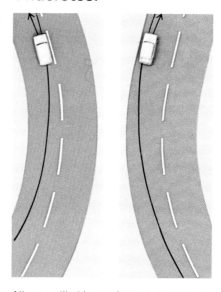

All cars will either understeer or oversteer, depending on their design, if driven too fast through a bend. Understeer results in the car's describing a more gradual curve than it should for the amount of steering applied (the arrowed lines, above, indicate the steered direction compared with the car's

Oversteer

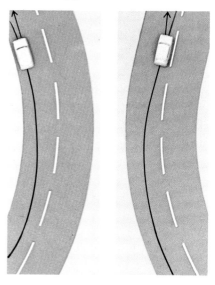

actual path). In a left-hand bend, it carries the car to the centre of the road; on a right-hand bend, to the left. Oversteer produces the opposite effect: the car describes a tighter curve than it should. Reducing speed as gradually as possible by decelerating restores normal steering performance

Centrifugal force

This is like a horizontal gravity, drawing a car to the outer rim of the curve. If the tyres lose their grip, centrifugal force will assert itself and the car will slide away to the outside of the curve

Coarse steering

Violent steering causes a sudden transfer of weight to the outside wheels so that, in addition to the fore-and-aft movement caused by acceleration and braking, the car is given a sideways lean

Positioning

THE FASTEST and most direct line through a bend is not necessarily the safest, even if it is the one that minimises the effects of centrifugal and other forces on the car.

For left-hand bends, the Department of Transport's recommended procedure is illustrated. Some experienced drivers prefer positioning the car nearer the centre line for a better view.

In towns, lane discipline is more important than perfect positioning. Exaggerated positioning at corners in towns is unnecessary anyway, because speeds are low.

If positioning the car to your own advantage causes concern or confusion to other road users, it must be wrong to do it.

Sharp left-hand bends

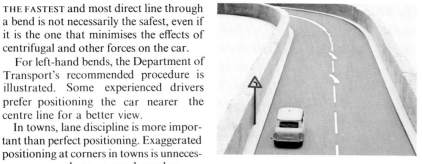

If the road is narrow and the severity of the bend unknown: **1** Position the car to the left of the carriageway. Check mirrors and slow the car by braking

2 Select a lower gear appropriate to the speed *before* the bend is reached. Sound the horn as a warning if the bend is blind—but not after 11.30 at night

3 As you leave the bend, you should be well to the left and able to stay there

Wide left-hand bends

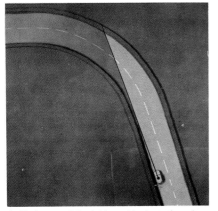

1 If the road is fairly wide but the view restricted—by a hedge, for example—be ready to slow down

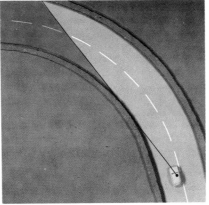

2 Position the car near the centre of the road, your side of the white line, as you go round the bend

3 Keep the car on a smooth and consistent course, keeping to your side of the central white line

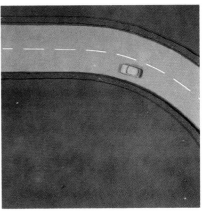

4 Take a line out of the bend that ensures you are still on the left; avoid drifting across the white line

Right-hand bends

1 Position the car well to the left, but not so close that you risk clipping the kerb

2 Choose a safe speed for the severity of the bend, then select the appropriate gear

3 Stay on the left until you can see the exit of the bend

4 Check the mirrors, then regain a straight course as soon as possible

Hairpin bends

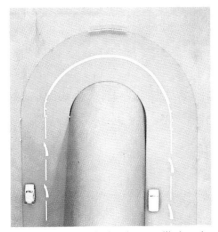

1 A hairpin bend is the sharpest likely to be met, but at first seems like any other

2 Follow the basic rule: keep well left until you can see what lies ahead

3 As you get into the bend, the road is still turning. Maintain position and speed

4 When you can see the exit, begin to take the line that will bring you back on a straight course. Accelerate only when the car is leaving the bend

Better driving/overtaking

The method

OVERTAKING a moving vehicle is nearly always voluntary: you *have* to turn left or right at times, but you seldom *have* to overtake, except to avoid needlessly slowing and disrupting other traffic. But overtaking is also one of the most difficult and most hazardous manoeuvres to master.

There are two basic rules for overtaking. One is that you must be able to see clearly and be seen by everyone else involved. The second is that other drivers must know what you intend to do—before you begin to do it.

Safe overtaking requires use of the mirrors, indicators and gears; it means a change of course and speed; it needs anticipation and judgment of speed and distance.

Acceleration is more important for safe overtaking than high speed. A car at top speed can only go slower; it has nothing in hand for correcting errors in anticipating the speed of oncoming traffic.

An 1100 c.c. family car will accelerate from 0 to 50 mph in about 16 seconds. More powerful cars can reach the same speed in 5 seconds. It will ease traffic congestion and relieve the frustration of other drivers if you let faster traffic pass. It does not matter if you are following a vehicle at 50 ft or 50 yds—your speed is the same. Nothing is gained by delaying others.

Avoid overtaking a fast-moving vehicle on a hill unless it is a long, straight, gradual gradient with a dual carriageway. Traffic coming downhill is less able to slow down or stop quickly.

Preparing to overtake

THERE IS a following distance and an overtaking distance, and you should take care not to confuse the two.

Following distance is the gap between two cars travelling in the same direction, when the driver of the second vehicle has no intention of overtaking. On a main road it should be not less than 30 ft at 30 mph. For every mile an hour over 30 mph, add 3 ft. At 40 mph, for instance, the distance would be 30 ft plus 30 ft—60 ft, or the length of two buses.

Overtaking distance is the minimum distance ahead that is needed for safe overtaking. It is governed by the view ahead and this in turn depends on the width and speed of the vehicle in front, the width of the road and the density of traffic.

Other factors setting the overtaking distance are the acceleration of the car being driven, the speed limit of the road, and the gradient, if any.

Positioning

THE POSITION in which the car is placed is just as important as the overtaking distance. Overtaking does not begin when the vehicle in front is reached. It starts once a driver can see clearly the traffic ahead on both sides of the road. Having seen that the road is clear, discount the nearside traffic and concentrate on the offside and oncoming traffic. Never overtake on the approach to: 1. A pedestrian crossing; 2. A road junction, corner or blind bend; 3. The brow of a hill or a hump-backed bridge; 4. A level crossing; 5. A narrowing stretch of road, or where you would cause another driver to swerve or slow down; 6. No-overtaking signs; 7. Where there is a double white line, or where the line nearest to you is unbroken.

Your car need be only 2 ft nearer the crown of the road than the vehicle in front. This will give a complete view ahead on the offside and oncoming drivers will be able to see you

Positioning about 2 ft beyond the offside of a slow vehicle ahead gives a clear view

The view ahead

TRAVELLING squarely behind and close to a large, solid vehicle obscures what is ahead of it. A car in such a position is also hidden from oncoming traffic.

The further back a driver places his car, the more he will see. If he is too close to the vehicle to be overtaken, he sweeps out almost 'blind' into the path of oncoming traffic; if too far back, he may miss his chance. Drivers of low-powered cars need to anticipate gaps, beginning to accelerate just before they occur.

The gear

THE RIGHT GEAR for overtaking is the one that allows the manoeuvre to be made with both hands on the steering wheel, free of any need to change gear once it has been started.

Except on long, straight, multi-carriageway roads, it is usually advisable to change down at least one gear before overtaking. The gear selected must give sufficient acceleration to take the car safely past the vehicle ahead and back on to the left side of the road. Overtaking time should be reduced to a minimum. This is best done by anticipating the manoeuvre, selecting the right gear early and then building up speed, so that the vehicle in front can be overtaken just when the observed gap in oncoming traffic makes it possible. This permits a higher overtaking speed than if the manoeuvre had begun close behind the vehicle ahead. Direction changes are also less extreme. When overtaking uphill, remember that you will need a lower gear than on a level stretch of road.

Speed and distances

OVERTAKING SAFELY needs accurate judgment of the speed of traffic ahead and coming towards you. Two cars travelling at 50 mph in opposite directions are approaching each other at 100 mph—they are drawing 147 ft closer every second. In two seconds, the gap between the two will have been closed by 294 ft, or nearly the length of a football pitch.

The assessment of speed and distances at night is even more difficult. If in doubt, do not overtake. Use signals courteously and intelligently; they are for warning other drivers of your intentions, not for ordering them to take avoiding action.

A fifth of a mile sounds ample space for overtaking. But if a car that far away is approaching at 65 mph, and you are travelling at 60 mph, you will draw abreast in 6 sec. If you were overtaking a vehicle travelling at 50 mph, all three vehicles would meet at the same point

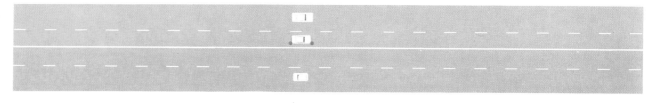

The overtaking sequence

1 Look in the mirror. Do not overtake if another car behind is likely to pass first

2 Take up the position and distance that give the best view ahead

3 Check driving mirrors and change into the gear that will give maximum acceleration

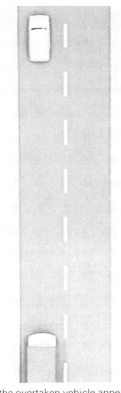

7 When the overtaken vehicle appears in the mirror, return to the nearside of the road

4 Signal, then move out smoothly. Check that there is a gap ahead to move into

5 Consider whether the driver ahead should be warned that he is being overtaken

6 Overtake with firm acceleration, keeping well out from the vehicle you are passing

Two-way roads

ON NARROW, two-way roads, avoid leaving insufficient clearance on the nearside. If it is safe to move out, there is nothing to be gained by not using all the available space. If you pass too close, the vehicle being overtaken need only wobble slightly to cause a collision that could make you spin off and overturn.

Do not overtake a line of cars on a two-way road without making sure that ahead of each car there is a gap equivalent to a safe overtaking distance. With room for only two abreast, you could otherwise be left facing oncoming traffic head on.

If, in a long line of traffic, a car ahead pulls out to overtake, do not take this as a sign that it is safe to follow. The other car may have a gap to pull into; you may not. Select the gear that will take you through the manoeuvre in the shortest time.

Three-lane roads

USE THE MIDDLE LANE for overtaking and turning right only. This lane is for traffic travelling in both directions and should be used for overtaking only when there is as much clear road ahead as you would need anywhere else.

Unless traffic is congested and slow-moving, avoid creating a three-abreast situation: it needs only a slight error in one driver's steering to cause a collision.

Never use the centre lane on or approaching bends, and beware of traffic which might be standing stationary ahead in the centre lane waiting to turn right. The centre lane near right-turn junctions may be marked with cross-hatched lines indicating that it is not for the use of through traffic; you must then stay on the left.

At dusk, it is difficult to recognise which way a car in the centre lane is travelling.

Passing on the left

1 You may pass on the left when the driver ahead has signalled his intention to turn right. Do so slowly and with great care, making sure that the other driver knows you are there

2 You may pass on the left when there are queues of slow-moving traffic

3 You may also pass on the left when travelling along a one-way street

Better driving/rain and floods

Driving in the rain

ON AVERAGE, Britain's roads are wet for one-fifth of the year—and accidents are twice as likely in the rain as on a dry day. Rain means reduced visibility, the risks of 'aquaplaning' and skidding (see below and pp. 378–9), and deterioration in the car's stopping ability.

Rain is most dangerous when it falls after a long, dry spell on to roads that have become polished and smooth: the rain blends with oil and rubber-dust deposits on the road surface to form a highly dangerous skid mixture.

Wet-weather driving demands gentle use of all the main controls—steering, clutch, brake and accelerator—and a larger allowance for errors and emergencies. Remember also when you begin a journey in rain that your shoes will be wet and liable to slip off the pedals. Scuff the soles on the rubber matting or carpeting of the car before you start the engine.

Visibility

WIPERS will often clear light rain from the windscreen with a few sweeps, then run on an almost-dry screen and leave smears of drying dirt. Use the window washers liberally and operate the wipers in short, frequent bursts. Heavy rain, on the other hand, can overload the wiper blades, allowing an almost continuous sheet of water to flow over the screen. Reduce speed even more than you would otherwise have done or, if the reduction in visibility is severe, pull into a side-turning or lay-by until the storm passes—which seldom takes more than a few minutes.

Rain can also cause windows to mist up inside the car. The windscreen is easily cleared by the de-mister, by fresh air or by the use of an impregnated cloth.

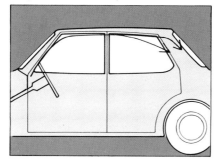

To clear the rear window, adjust the heater to blow at full power on to the windscreen, so that the heat flows under the roof and down to the rear window

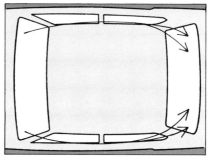

If the car has swivelling fascia vents, adjust them so that the air flow strikes the upper edge of the side windows and moves along the side windows to the rear of the car

If demisters are ineffective, open both front windows about half an inch; the air will be drawn into the car and circulated across the inside of the rear window

Aquaplaning

WHENEVER it rains, a film of water forms on the road. If a car is being driven fast, or if its tyres have lost so much tread that the water cannot be squeezed from underneath them, a wedge of water will form in front of, and under, the tyres. The car will then be sliding on the surface of the water and not driving on the road—the condition known as aquaplaning. This results in loss of steering control. On a smooth, polished road in moderate rain at 60 mph, each tyre has to displace about a gallon of water every second from beneath a contact patch no bigger than a size nine shoe. Each gripping element of the tread is on the ground for only 1/150th of a second; during this time it must displace the bulk of the water, press through the remaining thin film, and then begin to grip the road surface. Bald tyres give better grip on dry roads than treaded tyres, provided the car is travelling in a straight line. But they are unsafe because water is a lubricant on rubber—as borne out by the fact that rubber is best cut with a wet knife. (Also, punctures are more common in the rain.)

With good tyres, only moderate rain and a well-drained surface, aquaplaning should not occur below 60 mph. However, it *can* happen at speeds as low as 35 mph.

As soon as the water on the road is deeper than the tyre tread depth, the car is likely to aquaplane. When a car starts to aquaplane, the steering will feel extremely light. Slow down gently by decelerating—not by braking—until the steering feels normal again. In general, no speed can be recommended for safe driving in the rain. The slower you drive, and the better your tyres, the less likely you will be to aquaplane.

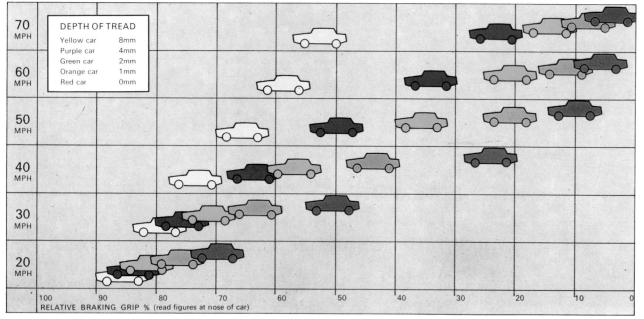

DEPTH OF TREAD

Yellow car 8mm
Purple car 4mm
Green car 2mm
Orange car 1mm
Red car 0mm

RELATIVE BRAKING GRIP % (read figures at nose of car)

On a typical motorway-type surface, water can lie to a depth of $\frac{3}{32}$ in. (2·5 mm) in a heavy rainstorm. This chart shows how relative braking grip—that is, the initial retardation which the tyres give when the brakes are applied—decreases with shallow depth tread and high speeds

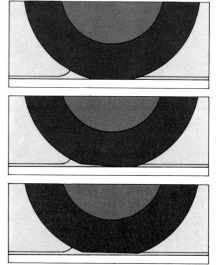

Aquaplaning This is what happens to the front wheels as speed increases in the rain and grip decreases. When tyres are water-borne, steering control is lost. Reduce speed by easing the accelerator. Do not brake until tyre grip is re-established

Flooded roads

IF YOU DRIVE into flood water at speed, the effect is almost like hitting a wall: you will first lose control, then come to a violent stop, risking injury to passengers.

Watch particularly where the road is undulating or where there is a dip under a railway bridge. These are places where water collects quickly.

At night, in the beam of a dipped headlight, you will need good road observation to notice a difference between a wet road surface and flood water. Watch the contours not only of the road but also of fences, trees, hedges and buildings at the side of the road ahead—if they appear to be unnaturally low, the road is probably flooded. Slow down at once.

Generally, if the water is deeper than the bottom of the cooling-fan blades—on average, 10–12 in., or roughly to the centre of the wheel hub cap—it is inadvisable to attempt driving through it.

If you do decide to go on, go slowly and avoid making a bow wave. Removing the fan belt lessens the risk of the engine

and electrical components becoming wet. Engage first gear and keep the engine running fast by slipping the clutch—that is, releasing the clutch just far enough to partially engage gear and giving more acceleration than usual. This keeps the exhaust gases moving fast, helping to prevent water entering the exhaust tailpipe; if this is submerged too deeply, however, not even the fast-moving gas will hold the water back and the engine will stall.

Should the engine die in deep water, it is sometimes possible to 'wind' the car out by using the starting handle, if there is one, with a gear engaged and *the ignition off*. If you remove the spark-plugs there is less compression and the task is easier. Do not let water enter the cylinders.

Immediately after passing through deep water, test the brakes. They may be saturated, and only driving very slowly and braking lightly at the same time will generate enough heat to dry them out. Be sure they are pulling evenly on all wheels before building up speed again.

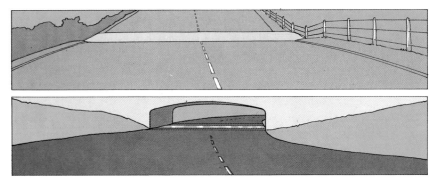

Deep water areas Be prepared to find water in dip in road (top) and under bridges (bottom)

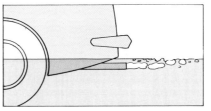

If the exhaust is under water rev the engine hard and 'slip' the clutch to keep going

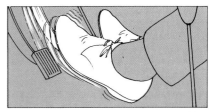

After passing through deep water, drive slowly and pump the brakes to dry them out

Escaping from a sinking car

A CAR will sometimes float on deep water for a short time—and if it does, that is the time to get out. The concentration of weight is at the engine end of the car and this end will sink first.

There are many apertures through which water will enter—holes in the floor for the handbrake cable and pedals, and holes in the dashboard and the engine bulkhead for controls and wiring.

If the car sinks quickly, it will be almost impossible to open the doors until inside and outside water pressures are nearly equal. It is vital not to panic.

1 Close all windows as quickly as possible to prevent the water entering

2 Release seat belts

3 Get the heads of children and any injured passengers above water level

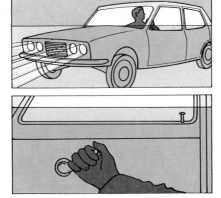

4 Turn on all lights to aid rescuers. See that doors are unlocked, but still closed, and keep hold of door handle

5 When water reaches chin level, try to open door. This may require repeated efforts

6 Form a human chain of passengers by holding on to their clothes or legs when they are leaving the car so that a door cannot close and thereby trap someone

Better driving/fog and mist

The driving method

FOG is the worst weather hazard that faces the driver, because no amount of skill can increase visibility or allow speed to be increased safely.

You must drive only within the limits of the distance you can see ahead. But that alone is not enough: precautions should be taken to lessen the risk to yourself and other road-users.

Because visibility is the most important factor involved, the windscreen should be kept clean by using the washers and wipers often. Fine globules of moisture can build up almost unnoticed, and they can easily give the misleading impression that the fog is getting thicker.

Keep to main roads as much as possible and try to travel on routes you know well, so that familiar landmarks stand out. Hesitation and doubt lead to erratic speeds and manoeuvres, which result in other traffic being unable to anticipate or interpret your intentions.

In fog you need every item of information you can gather. Sound is one important source of information—so drive with the side window partly open, even if this is uncomfortable and cold.

Try to relax, and avoid hunching forward over the wheel in trying to see more clearly. If the windscreen is clean this will not help you at all. Your gaze tends to be concentrated at the end of the bonnet and you will see more, both ahead and to the side, by sitting in the normal position.

Take the nearside kerb as your guide and do not wander, but beware of vehicles parked without lights. It is usually better to follow another car, provided you allow an adequate stopping distance.

Overtaking

The urge to overtake in fog should always be resisted. If it is essential to overtake, remember that the basic principle (see pp. 370–1) does not change in fog: you must have sufficient visibility ahead to be able to complete the manoeuvre safely within the limits of your speed and stopping distance. Even if you come to a tempting clear patch, remember that fog conditions can change so rapidly that you can arrive at a much denser area before you have completed the manoeuvre. If you must overtake, sound your horn and flash your headlights alternately from dipped to full beam. A large vehicle will tend to push the fog or mist aside (above), giving a false impression of the distance a following driver can see ahead and concealing oncoming traffic or a bend (right). To overtake in fog, you must be able to see a good clear distance ahead of the area illuminated by the dipped headlights of the vehicle you are passing

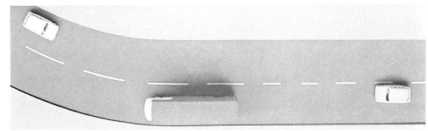

Turning right

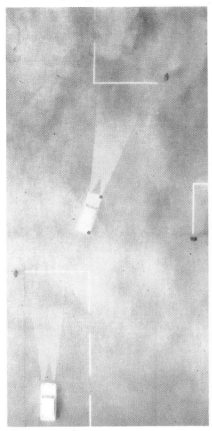

If you can, turn at a major junction, even if this means passing the side turning you actually want and doubling back later. While in the middle of a turn you are in danger from following as well as oncoming traffic, so use both horn and lights to make your presence and intentions known. Go slowly, and pause in the centre of the road before crossing, listening through the opened window for oncoming traffic

Lights—daytime

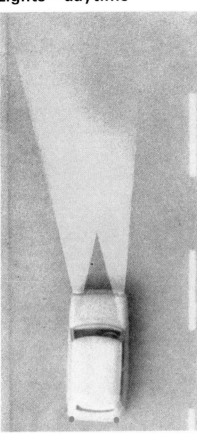

Lighting costs nothing: to drive in fog on side-lights only is false economy. It is just as important for other drivers to see you as it is for you to see them, and you cannot know their ability or their problems. Use headlights always, dipping the beam if light reflects back. Fit and use rearward-facing, high-intensity red fog lamps and use the footbrake lights to warn following drivers of hazards ahead

Lights—at night

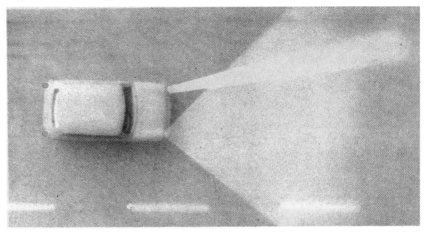

Foglights can be bought in pairs; one combination will give a powerful beam to pick out the nearside edge, and another to cast an apron of light ahead of the car. Yellow lighting will not enable you to see further ahead in fog, except possibly in light mist

The lower the beam of light, the better fog penetration will be. Full beams (top) will bounce back from a wall of fog; dipped beams (centre) will do the same on a lesser scale. Foglights (lower) will give best fog penetration

Parking

If the fog is so thick that you cannot continue your journey, park the car well off the highway where it is safe to abandon the car without lights. But leave the side-lights on if you are near the main carriageway or in any position where other cars might follow

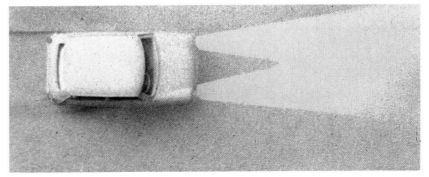

If you must park on a roadway because of a breakdown or emergency, then leave the lights *on*. Always park well to the left facing the direction of travel so that oncoming traffic can see the rear lights and reflectors. Remove the car as soon as you can

Better driving/snow and ice

Snow: the driving method

IT IS FAIRLY EASY to drive fast on snow, but almost impossible to stop quickly. Speed therefore should be strictly limited and the normal following distances should be doubled or even trebled.

Light use of the brakes and accelerator is essential to avoid turning minor slips and slides into real skids. The more a driver knows about the control of skids (see pp. 378–9) the less likely he is to have one.

When moving off, select the highest gear possible—usually second—and let the clutch out gently to avoid wheel spin. A slippery surface under even one driven wheel is sufficient to cause loss of traction by the other, due to the effect of the differential gear through which the drive is taken to the wheels (see p. 100). Some cars, usually only the more expensive models, are fitted with a limited-slip differential to overcome this.

Wheel spin can sometimes be stopped by applying the handbrake halfway and releasing it gradually as the car begins to move forwards. This will not work, however, on front-wheel-drive cars where the handbrake works on the rear wheels only.

See that the front wheels are straight when starting, and turn them only when the car is moving.

Small hills and bridges can be troublesome when traffic is heavy and slow moving. Try to avoid stopping on an uphill approach. It is better to stay at the bottom of a hill until the top can be reached in one movement. If the hill is long, try at least to keep moving. Any slow speed is better than stopping on a surface of snow.

As a general rule, select a gear one higher than usual when driving on snow. This reduces the amount of torque (turning effort) going through the wheels and so lessens the risk of wheel spin.

Usually it is safest to follow the tracks of other vehicles. When overtaking on a dual carriageway or motorway, be prepared for ridges of snow thrown up by vehicles from the other lanes.

Stopping and slowing

THE PRINCIPLES of braking and stopping (see pp. 356–7) do not change when driving on snow, except that braking should begin much sooner. First decelerate—gently. Then brake—gently, with a feather touch. Finally, change gear—again gently; and try to keep engine revs constant by accelerating slightly as you let the clutch out.

Using only the gears for reducing speed can cause the rear wheels to lock and can put the car into a skid if the change of pace is too great.

The main aim when slowing down is to keep the wheels decelerating, and this is best done by applying the brakes with a smooth on–off motion.

The wheels are prevented from locking by the last-minute release and then re-application of the brakes.

But avoid braking on corners, when the car is at its least stable.

Visibility

DRIVING through a heavy snowstorm can affect visibility as badly as fog can. Keep the warm air from the heater directed at the windscreen, and if necessary stop and clear the screen so that the full arc of vision is maintained.

In heavy snow everything, including vehicles, becomes white and difficult to see. Switch on dipped headlights or foglights as well as side-lights, according to the severity of the storm.

Deep snow

IT IS USUALLY impossible to drive a car in snow more than a foot deep, because the snow builds up in a heap in front of the number plate or bumper skirt. If a car will not reverse out of a drift, try rocking it or digging it out. Beware of the exhaust silencer being torn off in deep snow.

Tyres

KEEP TYRES at the pressure recommended by the manufacturer. They will bite into snow and give good grip provided the controls are handled lightly. Soft tyres give less grip and the tyre walls are prone to become soggy, which allows side movement of the wheel within the tyre.

Drivers who live in remote areas should consider buying chains or studded tyres (see p. 285) for use in winter.

Rope can be used temporarily instead of chains. Bind it tightly round the tyre, passing each loop through the gaps in the wheel. Remember that the rope will not last long; when it is worn it could become tangled around brakes or steering.

After driving through snow, inspect the tyres carefully for fragments of grit, which can work down with needle-like points into the tyre fabric and cause a puncture or blow-out later on.

Tyres Rope bound tightly round tyres is an effective temporary measure in snow and ice

Rocking

If the car is stationary in snow and the tyres cannot grip sufficiently to move off, impetus can sometimes be obtained by rocking the car backwards and forwards

Engage first gear and, keeping revs fairly low and slipping the clutch, try to move the car forward an inch or two. Then catch it on the rebound by moving quickly into reverse.

Repeat this until the car has mounted the snow piled in front or behind it. Be ready to keep the car moving under steady throttle once it is out of the trough

Do not allow helpers to push from the front to aid the backward roll in rocking. The car may regain its grip on the forward swing and run them down. They are safer pushing from the side, holding on to a door-post

Digging out

1 Clear away the snow for not less than 3 ft ahead of the front wheels and for the full length of the ground between the front and rear wheels

3 Try to push the car so that the driving wheels are on the packing. Engage second gear and let the clutch in very slowly to avoid wheel spin. Keep moving

2 Spread sacks, matting, bracken or twigs on the ground in front of the driving wheels and tuck the packing as far under the tyres as possible

4 Make sure all four wheels are in line before starting, even if this will mean turning quickly once the car is moving. Keep the car in second gear until the tyres get a good grip

Blizzards

IF THE CAR is stranded in deep snow, stay inside it; most fatalities in blizzards occur because drivers panic and walk for help without having sufficient protective clothing. Skilled rescue teams usually arrive within a few hours.

Try to keep moving inside the car to maintain circulation. If the engine is running and the heater working, fight off drowsiness by occasionally opening a window on the lee side. Never go to sleep while the engine is running: it can prove fatal. If you live in an area prone to blizzards, carry a blanket and a flask of hot drink. A bar of concentrated food, which will last several months, can be kept in the glovebox for emergencies.

When retrieving the car after it has been marooned, check that the radiator water has not frozen, and test the brakes.

Blizzards If trapped in the car, turn the heater off unless wind is blowing strongly from the front: poisonous exhaust fumes may otherwise be blown back into the car

Ice: the driving method

ALL THE RULES about driving on snow apply also to ice; in fact, snow itself becomes ice when it has been compressed by traffic in freezing weather.

Braking distances on ice can be ten or more times normal. Drive slowly and with extra caution, avoiding any sudden changes of speed or direction, or any braking in bends and turns.

Always steer as straight a course as possible, even in corners if the view ahead is clear and there is no possible risk of meeting oncoming traffic.

When beginning a journey in freezing weather, be alert for unusual sluggishness in the car, as the handbrake may have frozen on. Even if the handbrake lever can be fully released, the brake shoes may still be stuck to the drums: do not attempt to drive until they have thawed.

Parking

When parking outdoors in snow and ice, use a level place. In your drive, leave the handbrake off, place car in gear and chock wheels. Cover front and rear windows

Anticipating ice

PATCHES of ice are likely to form on exposed bends, in shaded areas beneath trees and bridges, on bridges themselves, and on any other elevated roads where the thin road fabric can be frozen from above and below by icy winds.

Ice patches are also a hazard in winter on gently cambered surfaces that allow only a slow run-off of water.

Every rainstorm in cold weather, especially at dusk when temperatures are falling, should be read by a driver as a warning that ice may form on the road.

Do not be misled by signs of a thaw, as a sheet of ice may lie beneath the slush and it is even more dangerous with a covering of water than usual.

Road and tyre noise diminishes markedly when the car is on ice. As soon as this happens, decelerate very gently; to change into a lower gear, use the double declutching method (see p. 355).

Better driving/skidding

How skids happen

A CAR skids when it is driven too fast for the condition of the road. The excessive speed forces the driver to brake, steer, change gear or decelerate too abruptly and hurriedly for the road-holding and road-space available. He has been going too fast for where he is, what he has to do and the surface he is driving on.

Skids happen when the grip of the tyres becomes less than the other forces acting on the car, so that the wheels start sliding instead of rolling. The forces may be either straight ahead, or to one side. In bad road conditions, road observation (see pp. 358–9) plays a large part in preventing skids. If a hazard or manoeuvre is anticipated well in advance, the car can be in the right position and moving at the appropriate speed without any need for exaggerated correction. Smooth handling of the car is essential.

On a long journey in winter, especially in darkness, open the windows occasionally so that you can feel any drop in temperature which might foreshadow frost or icy patches on the road.

Never allow speed to be dictated by an impatient driver behind; it is better to slow down or even to pull in to let him pass.

When driving in bad weather, try to relax. A tense driver will grip the wheel too tightly and lose his 'feel' for the road.

Only racing and rally drivers skid deliberately. For ordinary drivers, it is always a mistake. The cure is to correct the error that caused it—without panicking.

Avoid braking at all costs. When the car is under control again, continue under gentle acceleration. If the throttle is reapplied too soon, before the corrective steering lock has been removed, there is a danger that the car will skid in the opposite direction.

Successful control of a skid depends on the driver recognising it as soon as it begins to happen. A skid very quickly reaches the stage where not even an expert rally driver could correct it.

Types of skid

FRONT-ENGINED, rear-wheel-drive cars are prone to three types of skid (for front-wheel-drive cars, see opposite). They are:

1 Rear-wheel skid This is the most common skid, inherent in the rear-wheel-drive car. The rear wheels cease to grip, and slide sideways; the vehicle will turn around its centre of gravity until it eventually slides back to front. It happens usually when a car is taking a bend or corner too fast. But even slight road imperfections, such as surface unevenness or too steep a camber, will start a back-end swing if the rear wheels are locked by harsh braking.

Once the car has deviated about 45 degrees from its intended line of travel even an expert will have difficulty in regaining control if the car is moving fast.

2 Front-wheel skid Harsh acceleration, especially when moving into a corner or bend, can cause the front wheels to lose their grip. The car will slide forward in the previous direction of travel, driven by the rear wheels but out of control. The driver is in danger of a head-on collision with approaching traffic. No amount of corrective steering lock will bring the car back to its proper course until the wheels are gripping again.

3 Four-wheel skid This is brought about by sudden hard braking. The car loses steering and direction control; it will go straight on, its direction often being dictated by the camber of the road. The car loses speed very slowly if the surface remains smooth.

The brakes of most cars are powerful enough to lock all four wheels, even on a dry road; but usually the rear wheels lock first and the car moves into a rear-wheel skid before the driver has applied enough brake-pressure to lock the front wheels as well.

Rear-wheel skid

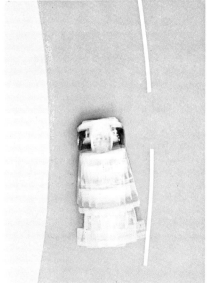

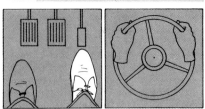

1 Without touching the brake or clutch, take the foot off the accelerator

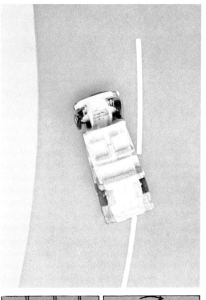

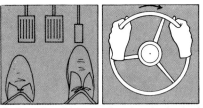

2 Steer in whichever direction the back of the car is sliding. Do not over-correct

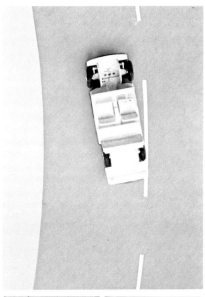

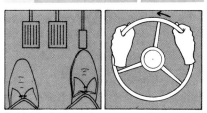

3 Hold the steering on until the skid lessens, then smoothly straighten the wheel

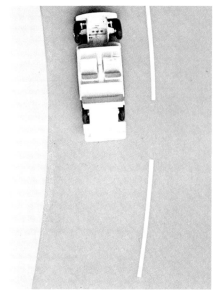

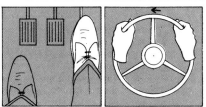

4 When the four wheels are back in line, gently reapply acceleration

Front-wheel skid

Four-wheel skid

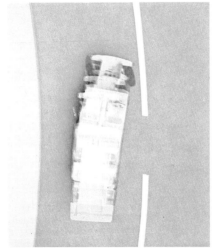

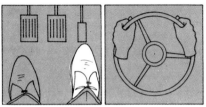

1 Release the accelerator and do not touch the brake. As speed decreases, so will the severity of the skid

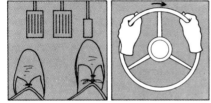

2 Straighten the front wheels so that they are lined up with the direction in which the front of the car is heading

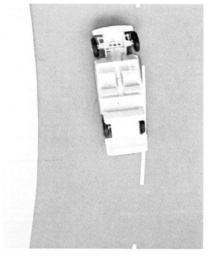

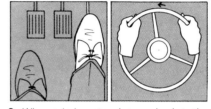

3 When grip is restored, move back to the left-hand side of the road and gently reapply acceleration

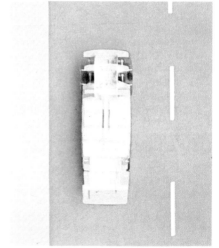

Reduce braking enough to allow the wheels to roll and regain their grip. Reapply the brakes with smooth on-off movements

Front-wheel-drive cars

FRONT-WHEEL-DRIVE cars will behave in the same way as ordinary cars in a front-wheel skid: they will skid front-first. But the methods of correcting the skid are very different. To follow the routine for rear-wheel-drive cars could send a front-wheel-drive vehicle off the road.

Generally, front-wheel-drive cars give better road-holding than conventional rear-wheel-drive vehicles and they have to be badly misused to skid at all.

If the car does skid—usually on a bend—ease off the accelerator smoothly; but if deceleration is too rapid, the wheels will reassert their grip and the front of the car will hook itself round at a much sharper angle than the bend, while the back of the car will go straight on.

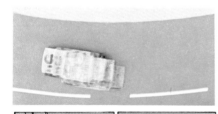

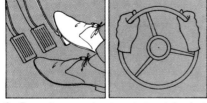

1 Ease the accelerator, but retain just enough drive to keep the car moving

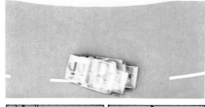

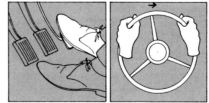

2 Keep steering into the corner, being careful not to physically oversteer

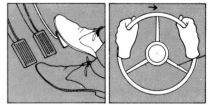

3 As the car regains its course, straighten the wheels and gently accelerate

Anticipating skids

APART FROM rain, ice and snow, which are obvious skid hazards, watch out for mud, fallen leaves, oil and grease, shingle, grit, sand and dust. All are potentially dangerous. Beware also of roads covered with a sprinkling of rain after becoming highly polished during a long dry spell.

Learning to control a skid

THE ONLY WAY to learn to recognise a skid when it begins to happen, and to find out how to correct it, is to experience one deliberately—not on the road, but on a properly constructed private skid-pan, under expert instruction. The AA will provide members with lists of skid-pans.

Locked wheels

A WHEEL is locked when it is no longer turning and the tyre has lost adhesion. All wheels will lock if the brakes are applied too hard, unless the car is fitted with an anti-lock device (see pp. 106–7). The wheels will begin to lock much sooner on a slippery road. All steering control is lost as soon as the wheels lock. The brakes should be released immediately to allow the wheels to roll so that adhesion and steering control is regained.

To avoid wheel-lock, gently pump the footbrake on and off, avoiding keeping it applied either too hard or too long.

Better driving/motorways

The method

MOTORWAYS are the safest roads in the country—but because of the higher sustained speeds they allow, and the heavy volume of traffic they often carry, they present special hazards. A motorway accident is nearly always serious.

Because speeds are so much higher, the margin for error is less: often there is none at all. The basic skills and rules of driving must be unfailingly applied, without hesitation. Motorway driving demands total concentration and total awareness. Just one second's distraction at 70 mph means that you have travelled 'blind' for more than 100 ft—the length of ten minis placed nose to tail.

There are three main causes of motorway accidents:

Excessive speed for the weather and traffic conditions.

Faulty observation or anticipation.

Driving too close behind other vehicles. (On the M4, collisions with the rear of other vehicles account for about one-quarter of all accidents—and for half of all accidents on the two-lane elevated section.)

All three faults are the result of breaking basic rules of driving. The motorway has not created these special hazards—only lessened a driver's chances of escaping a breach of the rules.

Speed Drive always within the limits of visibility and road-holding. Fog is the greatest danger. Because landmarks disappear, speed is often underestimated—so use the speedometer. A driver on the motorway becomes cocooned in a snug isolation that feels misleadingly safe. In fact he is never less safe if he allows concentration to lapse and speed to rise out of proportion to visibility. Drive at a speed that allows a safe stopping distance for the amount of road that can be seen ahead. Rain, especially after several days of dry weather, greatly reduces the grip of the tyres on the road (see p. 372), and so of course do snow and ice.

Observation Use the rear-view mirrors continually so that you know as much about the traffic situation behind as in front. When overtaking or changing lanes, remember the sequence: look–signal–act. Always double-check the view behind before changing lanes, being especially careful of traffic that may be hidden in the 'blind spot' at the rear quarters of the car.

Following distance Leave a gap of at least a yard for every mph of your speed. In wet weather or icy conditions, double or even treble the following distance.

Lanes

ALTHOUGH there are stretches of two-lane motorway, most have three lanes in each direction. The left-hand lane is used by slow-moving traffic, mainly commercial vehicles, but it should also be used by faster cars if it is clear for a sufficient distance ahead to avoid repeated pulling out to overtake. If the left-hand lane is occupied, use the middle lane.

The outside lane is for overtaking only: you should return to the appropriate lane as soon as it is safe to do so. However, do not use the outside lane to overtake vehicles in the left-hand lane: instead, remain in the middle lane. The outside lane is banned to vehicles weighing more than 3 tons or drawing trailers.

On a two-lane motorway, travel in the left-hand lane and use the outside lane for overtaking only.

Having chosen your lane, drive in the middle of it. If you drive close to the markings on either side, it is disconcerting to other traffic, as the slightest twitch in your steering or a heavy gust of wind could force you to wander into a neighbouring lane.

When overtaking, change lanes one at a time. Use the mirrors and if it is safe to alter course, signal in time for following traffic to interpret your intentions.

Avoid creating a three-abreast situation when overtaking in the outer lane.

The hard shoulder

IF THERE IS an emergency, or if you break down, stop the car on the hard shoulder to the left of the nearside lane. You should not use the hard shoulder if you can safely reach the next service area. Stop as far as you can to the left and leave the car from the passenger side: the slipstream from passing lorries can easily snatch open a part-opened door.

Allow only responsible adults to get out to help you. In dense fog, however, consider evacuating passengers up the grassy bank well out of harm's way. Children should be in the care of an adult. If there is an animal in the car, see that it is tethered or held before anyone opens a door.

Telephones are provided at intervals of 1 mile; there are marker posts every 110 yds marked with an arrow pointing towards the nearest telephone.

Do not regard the hard shoulder as a convenient lay-by. It is for emergencies only—defined broadly as any incidents which make the driver or his car unsafe.

Parking

PARKING is allowed only at a service area. It is forbidden on the carriageway, the slip roads, the hard shoulder (except in emergencies) and on the central reservation.

Warning triangles

CARRY a red warning triangle, and if you are forced to stop on the hard shoulder, place the triangle 150 yds behind the car on the edge of the hard shoulder, to warn other drivers that you are ahead.

Stop on the extreme left of the hard shoulder, well clear of the carriageway

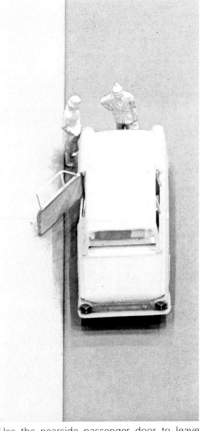

Use the nearside passenger door to leave the car. Keep children under control

A warning triangle alerts other traffic to your presence on the hard shoulder

Joining the motorway

ENTER by the left-hand lane of the slip road, looking over your right shoulder to assess the speed and density of traffic in the left-hand lane of the motorway.

Try to adjust your speed to arrive on the 'acceleration strip' running parallel to the motorway as a gap occurs. When you see a suitable gap, increase your speed to that of the traffic in the left-hand lane, check your mirrors again, signal and join the motorway.

Continue driving in the left-hand lane until you become accustomed to the speed of other vehicles on the motorway.

Leaving the motorway

WHEN you anticipate leaving the motorway, move into the left-hand lane. A direction sign will give warning of the exit.

Slow down in good time and begin signalling when you reach the 300 yd marker post, shown by three oblique stripes. Steer smoothly into the slip road leading to the exit, gradually reducing speed. Check the speedometer. High-speed driving on the motorway will have affected your ability to assess slower speeds.

If you miss the exit, continue on to the next. Never stop, make a U-turn or cross the central reservation.

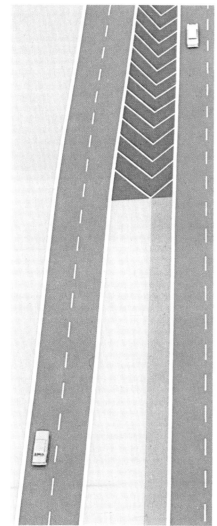

1 Keep to the left of the slip road. Begin to look for a gap in the motorway traffic

2 Adjust your speed to that of traffic in the left-hand lane, signal and move out

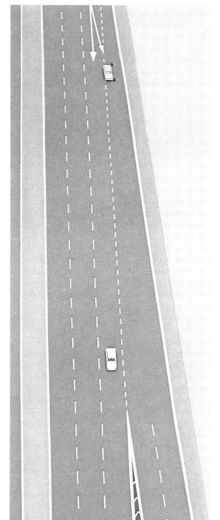

1 Slow down and leave by the left-hand lane of the slip road, signalling well in advance

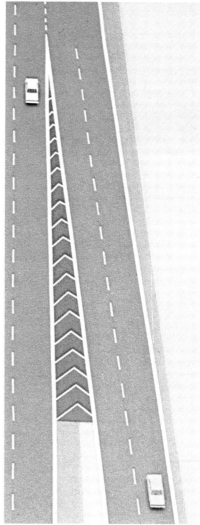

2 Keep to the left. Check the speedometer and see that the signal has cancelled

Concentration and fatigue

DRIVING long distances at a steady speed quickly induces boredom and fatigue. To combat this, make slight variations in speed, posture and eye-focus lengths, and make sure the car is well ventilated. Keep a car window open so a stream of fresh air blows into the car; and if there is a radio, vary the type of programme. Singing aloud can also help relieve tension and keep the mind alert. Make frequent stops at service areas even if you do not need refreshments or petrol.

If possible, change drivers at these rest stops, and clean the windscreen.

Drumming of the tyres and the rushing of the wind can tire a driver without his noticing it. A slight reduction in speed will often markedly reduce the noise.

Wind

WIND is an invisible hazard on most motorways. Because they are so open, there are often no swaying trees or hedges to indicate a strong wind or to give protection; your first warning may be when you emerge from a cutting or from under a bridge.

If you are driving in a crosswind from the left, you will be steering slightly left to counteract it; if, then, you overtake a large van, there is a danger that with the sudden protection it gives from the wind you will swerve left and perhaps even collide with the van. Prepare also to counteract slipstream when passing large vehicles.

Large vans and cars towing caravans are likely to weave about in a high wind, so give them a wide berth.

Better driving/emergencies

Broken windscreen

THE MOST USUAL cause of a shattered windscreen is a stone thrown up from the wheels of another vehicle or shaken from a loaded gravel lorry. When roads have been newly surfaced, there will usually be signs warning of the danger of flying stones. Reduce speed and increase the following distance behind other vehicles.

When a screen shatters it becomes opaque and almost all forward vision is lost. This is an emergency and you must slow down and get off the road quickly. Keep calm: avoid jerking the steering and braking too violently.

If your concentration on the road ahead was good up to the moment the windscreen shattered, you should be able to regulate braking pressure according to your memory of what road and traffic conditions were when the screen broke.

Punch a hole through the shattered screen and then brake. You are unlikely to be cut if you punch smartly and

briskly, keeping the forearm straight and taking care that the wrist is not bent. Some cars are provided with zone-toughened glass in a panel in front of the driver's field of vision (see Safety, p. 416). This glass breaks into larger pieces than ordinary windscreen safety glass, and does not become completely opaque.

Pull over to the side of the road as quickly as possible. The law requires you to have all-round vision, so knock out the whole of the screen. Always knock the glass *outwards* away from you.

Ideally, you should carry an emergency windscreen to fit your car, but if you must continue the journey without one, close all the windows tightly and drive until the air inside the car begins to 'flutter'. At this point air pressure is equalised inside and outside the car and you can sit in comparative calm. Do not exceed this 'flutter point'; if pressure inside the car builds up, the rear window may fly out.

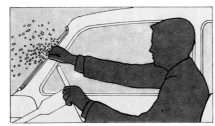

Shattered windscreen 1 Keep the wrist and forearm straight when punching hole

2 Pull over to the side of the road as quickly as possible without causing a hazard

3 Cover windscreen heating vents and bonnet before pushing out rest of glass

4 Close windows when driving without a screen and do not exceed 'flutter point'

Animals on the road

ADVICE that you should run down a cat or dog rather than make an emergency stop is wise but rather callous, and needs interpreting with humanity and common sense. A far better attitude is to hit the animal if you must, but avoid it if you can.

With good road observation and use of the mirrors you will always know how far behind other cars are and be able to assess immediately whether it is safe to take avoiding action.

Do not sound the horn or rev the engine

when approaching horses or farm stock on the road, as the animals may panic. A horse could shy and throw its rider, and cows may stampede, damaging the car and injuring themselves.

Always slow down and pass animals cautiously signalling if you are crossing the centre line or pulling in to let oncoming traffic pass.

If you meet cattle coming towards you in a narrow lane, back off and find a space to pull into. Cows have been known to

climb right over a car when they have been given no space to pass.

Unless a shepherd creates a strip of road space for passing, do not try to force the car through a flock of sheep moving in the same direction as the car, as there is great risk of killing or injuring an animal and you may be held liable for damages.

Remember that if you kill or injure certain animals (see p. 322), the law requires you to report the incident to the police within 24 hours.

Power-steering failure

IN MANY CARS the power steering system will fail if the fan belt breaks, but there can be other causes also.

The steering will become spongy and very heavy and the car will wander, responding to every irregularity in the road surface. Reduce speed immediately and, if the steering response is still inadequate, stop and summon assistance—the AA, if you are a member. Even if it is possible to continue, the car should be examined at a well-equipped garage as soon as possible.

Tyre blow-out

A BLOW-OUT need not lead to loss of control, provided you keep both hands on the steering wheel and do not panic.

If a blow-out occurs in the outside lane of a motorway and traffic is heavy, it is

better to run on to the central grass strip once the car is under control than to swerve in front of two other lanes of traffic. The main consideration is to get out of other people's way.

Rear tyre blow-out The back of the car will bump and sway, but if the steering grip is firm the car can usually be kept on a straight course. Pump the brakes with an on-off movement, throwing the weight of the car forward on to the sound tyres and relieving strain on the tyre that has blown. Do not brake any harder than is necessary

Front tyre blow-out This is more serious than a rear tyre blow-out as the steering can be severely affected. Brake lightly if you can, to avoid throwing too much weight forward, as the burst tyre will be rolling unevenly and may be torn from the rim. Keep both hands tightly on the steering wheel, counteracting any violent changes of direction

Jammed throttle

IF THE THROTTLE jams when there is plenty of road space, declutch, put the gear in neutral, switch off without removing the ignition key, and coast to the nearside of the road, braking normally.

However, if it happens in an outer lane of traffic, such as on a motorway or dual carriageway, the car must be 'driven' under control to safety.

Brake, and 'slip' the clutch, feeding just enough power through the transmission to carry the car to safety.

If the engine revs are not too high, changing down a gear will also help. The brakes will fall well below normal efficiency because the high-revving engine will be pulling against them.

When the speed of the car is down to a safe level, try raising the accelerator pedal by hooking the right toe underneath it.

Wheel falling off

If the car loses a wheel—usually because of loose wheel nuts—it becomes completely unbalanced and will tend to slew around, with the exposed brake drum (or, on some cars, the axle) gouging into the road surface and acting as a pivot. This slewing is less marked if a rear wheel is lost. Brake for an emergency stop and steer strongly against the direction in which the car is slewing

Emergency stops

WHEELS that are rapidly decelerating will come to a stop sooner than wheels that are locked (see pp. 378–9). In an emergency stop, the driver's greatest enemy is panic: stamping on the brake and keeping it fully applied may put the car into a skid and greatly reduce its stopping ability and steering control.

Even if a collision is inevitable, it is better to use the 'cadence braking' method, pumping the brakes quickly on and off and releasing them each time just as they are on the point of locking.

Steer the car in whatever direction will be likely to minimise the impact: a glancing blow is always less serious than a head-on collision.

If there are no passengers, it is safer to hit the object with the nearside of the car than with the offside.

Keep both hands on the steering wheel, leave the handbrake alone (applying it will increase the likelihood of the wheels locking) and do not de-clutch or change gear to reduce speed.

Brake failure

TOTAL FAILURE of the footbrake system is rare, but if it does happen there is often no warning or obvious deterioration in the brakes beforehand. What you do depends on the distance you have in which to stop.

If there is no real emergency, nothing is gained by violent use of the handbrake, but in an emergency apply it quickly and hard. Double de-clutching (see pp. 354–5) will help to engage low gear at speed.

On wet or icy surfaces, be prepared for a skid. There may be occasions when a skid will lead you into more trouble than if you had steering control, so you should consider releasing the handbrake again to give the tyres some grip, then steer for a safe gap—a hedge or some other soft object that will lessen the impact.

In a car with automatic transmission, decelerate and apply the handbrake. If there is a 'lock-up' position, move the lever into it as soon as speed has dropped sufficiently (get to know the maximum recommended gear speeds from the car's handbook) and try to steer out of trouble.

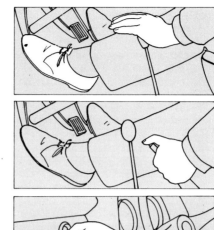
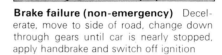

Brake failure (non-emergency) Decelerate, move to side of road, change down through gears until car is nearly stopped, apply handbrake and switch off ignition

Brake failure (emergency) Apply handbrake, change into a lower gear and, as the car slows, keep changing down. Be prepared to steer out of danger

Towing

TOWING or being towed requires a great deal of skill by both drivers—and a pre-arranged set of signals.

The tow-rope should be kept taut: any slackness will result in jerking which will break the rope or damage the cars.

The towing driver should hold up two, three or four fingers as appropriate to indicate when he is going to change gear so that the driver behind can brake gently to prevent a surging forward. Never tie the tow-rope to any part of the steering mechanism. If the towed car has power brakes, remember that they become inefficient after the first two or three applications when the engine is not running.

The maximum legal length for a tow-rope is 15 ft and if it is more than 5 ft in length it must be made visible with a white marker. The vehicle being towed should carry a temporary sign at the rear saying 'On tow'. Signals (right) should be pre-arranged

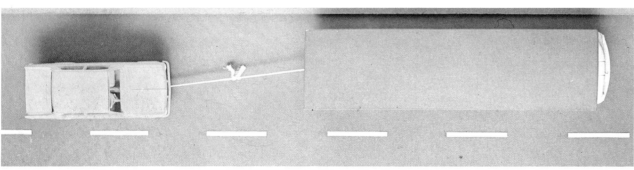

Unless there is a clear view through the towing vehicle, a driver being towed should move out slightly to retain some view ahead so that he can see hand signals and anticipate hazards. Steer with the offside a little nearer the centre of the road than the towing vehicle

Better driving/safety

Principles and aids

SAFETY on the road depends on a great deal more than a knowledge of the Highway Code. Once the mechanics and laws of driving have been learnt, alertness, concentration, observation and commonsense must also be cultivated and applied. In addition, the driver must be fit and the car must be functioning properly.

Safety can be improved by many devices, including the following:

Seat belts These are the most important safety aids of all. They halve the risk of death or serious injury in an accident.

Fit the belt so that the lap strap goes across the hips, not the abdomen. The buckle of the older type should be close behind the hip and the belt must not be slack. Adjust the shoulder strap so that it is well clear of the neck (see p. 338).

Anti-burst door locks It is only in recent years that anti-burst locks have become standard fittings, and already they have saved many lives. The chances of being killed in an accident are doubled if you are thrown from the car. Without seat belts, front-seat passengers stand a 60 per cent greater risk of being thrown out than do drivers. The risk of being thrown from cars with two doors is about 40 per cent greater than from four-door cars.

More people are thrown from open-top cars than from saloons, but the chance of being killed is statistically the same.

Baby harnesses If they are well-designed and approved (see p. 277), these can be useful. Never allow children in the front seat; even sudden deceleration can throw them forward and cause injury.

Windscreens There are several types of windscreen, with differing advantages:

1. Heat-toughened glass shatters on impact and splinters are unlikely to cause more than superficial injuries in an accident. It is easily broken by flying stones.

2. Since about 1961, however, most British cars have been fitted with zone-toughened glass, which is the same as the type described above but has a strip of extra-tough glass about 8 in. deep running across the line of vision.

When the screen breaks, the particles within the zone are large enough to give the driver some vision without being so big that they increase the dangers of superficial injuries.

3. Laminated glass has a 0·015 in. interlayer of polyvinyl butyral (commonly called vinal), which will only crack on impact instead of shattering into many small fragments. This leaves vision through the cracked glass unimpaired.

4. Because 0·015 in. glass increases the likelihood of severe head injuries, it has been replaced since 1967 by a laminated glass with a 0·03 in. interlayer. The thicker layer has no adverse effect on vision through the glass, but it minimises the chance of head penetration since the glass tends to bulge on impact. It is compulsory on all cars sold in America and Italy.

Restraining catches Front seats fitted with these catches will not tip forward in a collision. Many older cars lack them, but they can usually be fitted or made by a good garage. They are especially important when there are children in the back and there is no front-seat passenger. Even moderate braking can cause the empty, unsecured seat to tip, and the children may be thrown over it into the front.

Anti-glare mirrors These are useful for overcoming glare from the headlights of following vehicles. The smoked glass softens headlights to a gentle glow.

Night driving

DRIVING at night involves restricted vision, dazzle from the lights of other vehicles and the need to operate your own car's lighting system properly.

There are also advantages. Vehicles that would normally be out of sight are revealed by the glow of their lights. A vehicle ahead will show you the contour of a bend long before you reach it; sudden changes of course and the appearance of brake lights give advance warning of possible hazards. Learn to use the lighting available to the best advantage and with the least discomfort to others. Headlights are obligatory on all roads. The only exception is where the street lights are spaced less than 200 yds apart (see p. 330).

Unlit roads On these roads, drive on headlights, using full beam only when other drivers will not be inconvenienced. Drive at such a speed that you can stop within the distance illuminated.

Avoid dazzling the driver ahead with the reflection of your headlights in his driving mirror; keep far enough behind for your dipped beams to strike the road.

Lit roads On these roads, select the lighting that is appropriate to how much you can see and how readily you can be seen. Generally, dipped headlights are safest, but they will annoy other drivers if the road is busy and brightly lit.

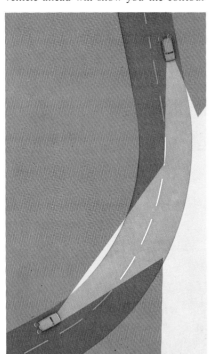

1 On normal bends, headlights give ample warning that another car is coming

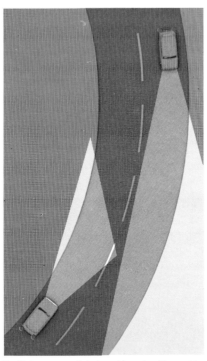

2 Drivers on a left-hand bend will need to dip lights first to avoid causing dazzle

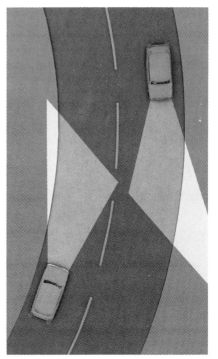

3 As they draw closer, the driver on the right-hand bend must also dip his headlights

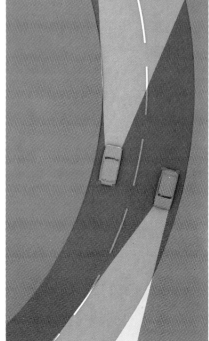

4 Neither driver should switch back to main beams until the cars have passed

GLOSSARY OF CAR TERMS

Engineers, mechanics and car enthusiasts use a language of their own when the conversation turns to cars. Terms such as aquaplaning, limited-slip differential and dashpot are often misunderstood or used wrongly. This glossary is intended to explain commonly used technical terms and motoring expressions to give you a better understanding of your car, and make it easier to discuss faults with a garage

Glossary of car terms

Abbreviations

A, amp	Ampere	cc	Cubic centimetre	i.o.e.	Inlet over exhaust	psi	Pounds per square inch
AC	Alternating current	c.b.	Contact-breaker	IRS	Independent rear suspension	rpm	Revolutions per minute
AF	American Fine	DC	Direct current	k/h	Kilometres per hour	sv	Side valve
Ah	Ampere hour	DoT	Department of Transport	LT	Low tension	SW	Switch
BDC	Bottom dead centre	emf	Electromotive force	mep	Mean effective pressure	TDC	Top dead centre
bhp	Brake horsepower	GT	Gran Turismo (or Grand Touring)	mpg	Miles per gallon	thou.	Thousandths of an inch
BSF	British Standard Fine	hp	Horsepower	mph	Miles per hour	UNC	Unified Coarse
BSW	British Standard Whitworth	HT	High tension	ohc	Overhead camshaft	UNF	Unified Fine
BTDC	Before top dead centre	IFS	Independent front suspension	ohv	Overhead valve	VI	Viscosity index

Abrasion resistance
Ability of a material—e.g. tyre rubber—to resist wear when rubbed or dragged against another surface.

Abrasive
Substance used for grinding or polishing.

Accelerator (or accelerator pedal)
Pedal that controls the power output of the engine.

Accelerator pump
Small pump—either piston or diaphragm-operated—in some types of carburettor. It is designed to enrich the petrol/air mixture momentarily when the accelerator is suddenly depressed.

Accumulator
Term for a rechargeable battery.

Ackermann principle
Basis of a steering system in which, during turns, the inner wheel is pivoted through a greater angle than the outer.

Additives
Chemicals added to petrol and oil to give them special properties—e.g. a higher anti-knock rating in a petrol.

Aerodynamics
Study of the motion of solid bodies through the air.

Air bleed
Small drilling or jet used in fixed-jet carburettors to mix some extra air with the petrol supply. A pilot air bleed emulsifies the petrol flow necessary for engine idle, and a main air bleed corrects any over-richness of the mixture at larger throttle openings.

Air-bleed screw (or nipple)
Sometimes referred to as an air-bleed plug, this is a small screw to release unwanted air from a sealed fluid system.

Air-bleed valves
Term often used to describe the 'bleed' system on a hydraulic braking or clutch assembly. It can also be applied to some car heater units that have a means of 'bleeding' air from the system.

Air-cooled engine
Engine cooled directly by air, which is blown (usually by a fan) over the finned cylinder barrels and cylinder heads.

Air filter
Unit mounted on the carburettor air intake for filtering dirt and dust from the air drawn into the engine. Sometimes called an air cleaner. Also the filter of a brake servo-unit.

Air horn
Audible means of warning that receives its power from compressed air. Also used for horn that is suction-operated by low pressure in the inlet manifold.

Air resistance
Resistance of an object to movement through the air; the amount of resistance depends on the frontal area and shape of the object, and increases with the square of the vehicle's speed.

Air suspension
Type of suspension in which compressed air forms the resilient medium instead of steel or rubber springs; air suspension systems usually incorporate self-levelling. More common on heavy commercial vehicles, buses and coaches than on cars.

Air vent
The small hole in the top of a fluid reservoir (brake or clutch) or carburettor float chamber to apply atmospheric pressure to the fluid.

Aligning torque
Tendency of a tyre to return to its straight-ahead position when deflected from it by the steering.

Alignment
State of adjustment or setting generally applied to the front wheels of a car. Also used to describe the setting of the headlamp beams.

All-indirect gearbox
Gearbox having only two shafts—input and output. In each ratio the drive therefore passes through two gears. one on each shaft, whereas in a conventional three-shaft gearbox, top gear has direct drive.

Alternating current
Electric current that continuously reverses its direction of flow.

Alternator
Engine-driven electric generator which produces an alternating current, in contrast with the dynamo which produces direct current. The main advantage is a higher output at low engine speeds.

American Fine
US system of defining screw-threads. Spanner size is based on the distance across the flats of the nut.

Ammeter
Instrument that measures the amount of electric current being supplied to, or taken from, a car's battery under normal running conditions. If the needle shows a positive reading ($+$), the battery is being charged, but if a negative ($-$) reading is registered, the battery is being drained.

Ampere
Unit of electric current produced by 1 volt acting through a resistance of 1 ohm. Commonly referred to as an amp.

Ampere hour
Unit of capacity obtained by multiplying current in amps by the hours for which it flows. A typical car battery has a capacity of 38 Ah.

Annulus
Name given to the internally toothed outer ring of an epicyclic gear.

Anodised aluminium
Material widely used for radiator grilles and other 'bright' parts of the modern car. The aluminium is treated to give it a hard corrosion-resistant skin.

Anti-burst lock
Specially designed lock that prevents the door from flying open in a crash.

Antifreeze
Chemical mixture, usually based on ethylene glycol, added to the cooling system to lower the freezing point of water, allowing it to remain liquid when the outside temperature falls below freezing point (0°C, 32°F).

Anti-knock rating
A measure of a petrol's resistance to detonation when being burnt in the cylinder of an engine.

Anti-rattle spring
Spring designed to eliminate unnecessary rattle. Used in some types of clutch and on many of the modern disc-brake systems.

Anti-roll bar
Steel torsion bar across the chassis with its end swept back or forward to either the front or rear suspension. When both wheels move together on bumps, the bar rotates bodily, but cornering roll of the body 'winds up' the bar and is resisted.

Anti-theft device
Device fitted to discourage a thief. Electric ones may isolate the ignition circuit or sound the horn if the car is tampered with. Mechanical ones lock the steering, gear lever or clutch pedal.

Aquaplaning
Condition in which a tyre loses its grip in very wet weather and 'skates' over the water on the surface of a road.

Armature
Rotating part of a generator or electric motor. It consists of coils of wire wound on a soft iron core that revolves between the poles of an electromagnet.

Atmospheric pressure
Pressure exerted by the atmosphere due to its weight—at sea level approximately 14·7 psi.

Atomisation
Breaking down of liquids into very fine particles. The carburettor atomises fuel, mixes it with air and discharges the mixture into the inlet manifold in the form of a fine mist.

Automatic advance
Method of automatically varying the ignition spark timing according to the needs of the engine.

Automatic choke
Device in the carburettor that is pre-set to provide the rich mixture needed for cold

starting, and then weaken the mixture automatically as the engine warms up.

Automatic cut-out
Electro-mechanical device for automatically opening and controlling an electrical circuit. It prevents the battery from discharging back through the dynamo when this is stationary or not running fast enough to charge the battery.

Automatic transmission
Gearbox that automatically alters the gear ratio to suit vehicle speed and road conditions, thus eliminating the need for a conventional clutch and gear lever.

Auxiliary spring
Additional rear spring, usually of rubber, fitted to each side of a car that is to be particularly heavily loaded.

Axle
Transverse beam carrying the wheels and supporting the body through the road springs.

Axle casing
Outer portion of a driving axle assembly, enclosing the final drive and the half-shafts.

Axle ratio
Ratio between the revolutions per minute (rpm) of the propeller shaft and the rpm of the driven road wheels. Reduction is achieved by the final drive gears.

Backfire
Explosion in the exhaust system, usually caused by a leak in the exhaust system, retarded ignition or too weak a mixture.

Back-flushing
Method of cleaning out the engine cooling system by pumping water in the reverse direction to the normal flow.

Back-pressure
Resistance to flow, usually applied to exhaust gases. If the exhaust pipe is too small or the silencer too restrictive, for example, enough back-pressure can occur to impair the engine's performance.

Baffle
Partition in an exhaust silencer designed to change the direction of the gases, so using up some of their noise-producing energy. Also used to describe a partition in a tank or sump.

Ball bearing
Bearing in which a rotating shaft or a rotating wheel on a fixed shaft is supported by one or more rows of steel balls revolving between inner and outer races.

Ball joint
Method of coupling two components together, end to end, so that each can pivot in any direction relative to the other.

Ball race
Inner or outer ring on which the balls of a ball bearing run.

Ball valve
Valve consisting of a ball and seat. Fluid can pass in one direction only; when it attempts to flow the other way, it is checked by the ball settling on the seat.

Band brake
Externally contracting brake commonly used to control rotation of the annulus of an epicyclic gear, as in an automatic gearbox.

Banjo connection

Method of connecting a petrol or oil pipe. It consists of an annular member with an internal groove round which the liquid flows from a feed pipe attached to it.

Banjo rear axle
Type of axle casing made in one piece with a hoop-shaped portion in the middle to house the final-drive assembly.

Base circle
Circular portion of a cam, having no lifting effect on the follower.

Bath-tub combustion chamber
Simple design of a chamber for overhead-valve engines. It has semicircular ends, parallel or near-parallel sides and a flat roof in which the valves are situated with their stems parallel.

Battery
Assembly of two or more cells for storing electricity. Necessary for starting a car, because the generator produces current only when the engine is running.

Baulk-ring synchromesh
System for ensuring quiet gear changes. The more force the driver applies to the gear lever, the quicker the synchronisation of the engaging portions of the gears.

Beads
Thickened and wire-reinforced inner edges of a tyre. They seat on the wheel rim.

Beam axle
Rigid transverse member carrying front wheels that do not have independent suspension.

Bearing
Device for supporting a rotating shaft, or a moving component, to permit movement with the minimum amount of wear and friction.

Bench seat
One-piece full-width seat, often fitted to cars with steering-column gear change.

Bendix drive See INERTIA DRIVE MECHANISM

Bevel gears
Gears of conical shape used to transmit motion through an angle, usually 90 degrees, from one shaft to another.

Big-end
Larger end of a connecting rod, mounted on the crankpin of the crankshaft.

Big-end bearing
Bearing material between the connecting rod big-end and the crankpin.

Big-end bearing cap
Lower half of the connecting rod big-end, secured by bolts or studs and nuts.

Big-end knock
Term used to describe the low metallic knock emitted by a worn big-end bearing. It is more obvious under load than when the engine is running light, but is always audible.

Bi-metallic strip
Strip made of two metals that expand at different rates, so arranged that the strip bends when subjected to a change in temperature. Commonly used as a switch in electric circuits.

Blow-back
Minor explosion in a carburettor caused by some of the still-burning gases escaping through the inlet valve and igniting the incoming charge. Sometimes referred to as popping-back or spitting-back.

Blow-by
Leakage of compressed petrol/air mixture or burnt gases from the combustion chambers past the piston rings and into the crankcase.

Blower
Slang term for supercharger.

Blown gasket
Colloquial term for a gasket that is damaged and therefore leaking.

Bonnet
Part of a car's bodywork that covers the engine compartment and can be lifted to give access to the engine.

Boot
Luggage compartment. In rear-engined cars the boot is at the front.

Bore
Internal wall of an engine cylinder, or the diameter of the cylinder; also diameter of
any hole, e.g. the hole in which a bush or bolt fits.

Bottle-screw jack
Type of lifting device so named because of its bottle-shaped base.

Bottom dead centre (BDC)
Lowest position a piston reaches in its cylinder, at the bottom of its stroke.

Box spanner
Tubular spanner that has a hole drilled to take a tommy-bar or lever.

Brake
Apparatus that stops or slows down a car by applying friction at or near the wheels, converting the energy of motion into heat. Brakes may be operated mechanically or hydraulically, and two types—drum brakes and disc brakes—are in common use on present-day cars. It is possible to have drums or discs on all four wheels, or a combination of discs on the front and drums on the rear.

Brake back-plate
Fixed portion of a drum-brake assembly carrying the brake shoes.

Brake cam
Eccentrically shaped component of a mechanically operated drum brake. When rotated by operation of the brake lever, it forces the shoes apart, into contact with the inside of the brake drum.

Brake disc
Steel or iron disc that rotates with the wheel as part of a disc-brake system. When the brake pedal is operated, the disc is squeezed between two friction pads, slowing the car.

Brake dive
Pronounced 'dipping' of the front of a car under heavy braking, caused by the transfer of weight from rear to front suspension.

Brake drums
Metal drums which turn with the car wheels as part of a drum-brake system; brake shoes are pressed against the inside of the drums to slow or stop the car.

Brake-fade
Deterioration of brake efficiency often encountered after repeated hard application of the brakes. It is caused by loss of efficiency by the friction material due to overheating and is more likely with drum brakes than with disc brakes.

Brake fluid
Special liquid used in a hydraulic braking system for transmitting effort from the pedal to the brakes.

Brake horsepower
Unit used in measuring engine power output.

Brake lights
Red warning lights at the rear of a vehicle that are automatically activated when the brake pedal is applied.

Brake linings
Friction material riveted or bonded to the brake shoes of a drum-brake assembly.

Brake master cylinder
See MASTER CYLINDER

Brake pads

Flat metal plates with friction material bonded to one side. They are mounted in the caliper unit on each side of the rotating disc of a disc-brake assembly.

Brake pedal
Foot-operated lever that applies the brakes through cables, rods or a hydraulic system.

Brake shoe
Metal component, of segmental shape, to which the brake linings are attached.

Brake shoe return springs
Coil springs stretched between the two brake shoes in each drum to return the shoes to their 'off' position when the brake is released.

Brake slave cylinder
See SLAVE CYLINDER

Braking distance
The distance in which a vehicle stops from a given speed once the brakes have been applied. This does not allow for 'thinking distance'. For example, at 30 mph a car could travel as much as 30 ft during the thinking period of an emergency and another 45 ft during the actual braking, making an overall distance of 75 ft before it comes to rest.

Braking force
Vehicle-retarding force produced between tyre and road surface when the brakes are applied.

Breather
Vent to permit entry of air into a space or to relieve internal pressure.

British Standard Fine
Type of screw thread commonly used on British cars until the general adoption of Unified or metric threads.

British Standard Whitworth
Coarse screw thread, now obsolescent.

Brushes
Carbon pads that make contact with the commutator of a dynamo or electric motor, receiving current from the armature of a dynamo or supplying current to that of an electric motor.

Bucket seat
Individual seat with good side location for driver or passenger. Derives from the seats fitted to early racing and sports cars, which had deeply curved backrests to hold the occupants in position.

Bumper
Metal bar mounted across the front or rear of a car, designed to protect bodywork in a minor collision.

Bump-steer
Tendency of a car to veer from its path on a bumpy surface; usually the result of rear-suspension geometry that causes the wheels to depart slightly from their straight-ahead alignment as they move up and down.

Bump stop
Rubber buffer mounted between the body or chassis and the wheel suspension linkage or axle, to limit the upward movement of the wheel over severe bumps.

Bush
Sleeve fitted in a bore to act as a bearing. Bushes are usually of metal, rubber or a plastic material such as nylon.

Butterfly
Short for butterfly valve, otherwise known as the throttle valve. It is a metal disc mounted on a spindle in the main air passage of the carburettor.

By-pass filter
Oil filter which receives some of the lubricant delivered by the engine's oil pump and filters it before it is circulated through the engine.

Cable
Strong, flexible wire made of strands and commonly used to operate handbrake, clutch or throttle. It can operate in the open, or can run in a flexible outer casing.

Cable brakes
Braking system actuated by cables, as opposed to rods or hydraulic fluid. Most handbrake systems are cable operated.

Cadence braking
Technique applied when braking in adverse conditions, to prevent the rear wheels from locking and skidding. It consists of intermittent braking in harmony with suspension movement.

Calibration
Correct and accurate setting of instruments—e.g. a speedometer is calibrated according to a car's gearing and the rolling radius of the tyre.

Caliper unit
Part of a disc-brake assembly; horseshoe-shaped member that straddles the rotating disc and carries the hydraulic piston assemblies and brake pads.

Cam
Eccentric projection on a shaft for moving another component as the shaft revolves—e.g. the engine camshaft that opens the inlet and exhaust valves.

Cam-and-peg steering
Type of steering box in which rotation of the steering wheel is transmitted to the linkage via a cam track and a peg follower.

Camber angle
Angle at which wheels are tilted from the vertical. With positive camber the wheels are further apart at the top, and with negative camber they are closer together at the top. A wheel with negative camber generally has greater cornering power.

Cam follower
Component that bears directly on a cam and transmits its motion to another component such as a push-rod or valve.

Camshaft
Revolving shaft incorporating cams to operate the engine valve gear. It is chain, gear or belt-driven from the crankshaft at half the crankshaft speed. The camshaft may drive the distributor and fuel pump.

Capacitor See CONDENSER

Capacity
Volume swept by all the pistons of an engine, within their bores, from the top to the bottom of their travel. Measured in litres, cubic centimetres or, mainly in the USA, in cubic inches.

Capillary tube
Small-bore tube used, for example, as part of a cooling system's thermometer, to carry a liquid signal from the coolant to the instrument.

Carbon formation
Build-up on engine parts of deposits produced by combustion of the fuel. Carbon forms on piston crowns, piston rings, combustion chambers, valves and other components, causing loss of efficiency.

Carburettor
Device in the fuel system that mixes petrol and air, atomising the petrol as it does so, in the correct proportions and delivers the mixture to the engine in the quantity demanded by the operating conditions.

Carcass
Body of a tyre, comprising the rubber-covered fabric 'plies' to which the tread, sidewall and wire rim beads are added. Sometimes called the casing.

Castellated nut
Nut with three equally spaced diametrical slots cut in the top face. A split-pin can be fitted through them, and through a hole drilled in the bolt, screw or stud, to lock the nut in position.

Casting
Component formed by pouring molten metal into a mould and allowing it to solidify. The mould may be sand, metal or ceramic. Iron and aluminium are the most common metals for vehicle castings.

Castor angle
Angle by which the steering pivots or king-pins of the front wheels lean back from the vertical so that the wheels are given a 'trailing' and self-centring effect that causes them to return to the straight-ahead position after cornering.

Cell
One of the compartments of an electric battery. In the lead/acid battery normally fitted to a car, each cell produces about 2 volts, so a 6 volt battery has three cells and a 12 volt battery has six cells.

Centre electrode
Part of a spark-plug that is situated axially in the middle of the plug and carries the high-tension current from the distributor.

Centrifugal clutch
Type of automatic clutch. Pivoted, spring-loaded weights rotating with the flywheel move outwards under centrifugal force as the engine speed increases. This movement brings friction material, attached to the outer face of the weights, into contact with a drum (the driven member), causing it to revolve also.

Centrifugal force
Outward force exerted by anything travelling in a curved path. When a car is cornering, it causes the body to roll and the occupants of the vehicle to tend to slide towards the outside of the corner.

Chain tensioner
Device for keeping a driving chain at the correct tension.

Charge
Input of electric current from the generator or outside charging source to the battery.

Childproof lock
Special door lock that can allow the door to be opened only from the outside, thus eliminating the possibility of a child inside a moving car opening the door.

Choke
A means for enriching the petrol/air mixture delivered by the carburettor by reducing the air supply or increasing the fuel supply; used for cold starting. Sometimes used also to describe the venturi—the waisted portion of the carburettor air passage which is designed to increase suction on the jets.

Choke flap or valve
Spindle-mounted disc that can be rotated inside the carburettor air intake to reduce the amount of air supplied during cold starting. Operated by means of a manual or automatic control.

Circlip
Spring locating or retaining clip; can be fitted on to a spindle (in an external groove) or in a bore (in an internal groove). Circlips are used in some pistons to locate and secure the gudgeon pin.

Clutch
Mechanical means of connecting and disconnecting the drive from the engine to the gearbox (and hence the road wheels). Most clutches are of the friction type, the gripping load being provided by a spring, or springs, or by centrifugal force.

Clutch adjustment
Means of restoring full and correct clutch-pedal travel as the clutch lining wears.

Clutch drag
Reluctance of the clutch to disengage when the clutch pedal is depressed. Usually caused by mechanical wear or incorrect adjustment.

Clutch driven plate
Metal disc to which the clutch linings are riveted or bonded; it is mounted on the input shaft to the gearbox.

Clutch fork
Fork attached to the clutch thrust bearing at one end and connected by rod, cable or hydraulic mechanism to the clutch pedal at the other.

Clutch lining
Ring or segments of friction material riveted or bonded to each side of the clutch driven plate.

Clutch master cylinder
See MASTER CYLINDER

Clutch pedal
Floor-mounted pedal operated by the driver's left foot to engage or disengage the clutch by rods, cables or hydraulically.

Clutch pressure plate
Smooth, heavy spring-loaded metal disc that clamps the clutch driven plate to the flywheel.

Clutch slave cylinder
See SLAVE CYLINDER

Clutch slip
Occurs when the pressure plate fails to grip the driven plate fully, usually because of oil contamination or excessive wear.

Clutch spring
Spring that provides part or all of the gripping load of a clutch.

Clutch thrust bearing
Encased ball bearing or carbon pad mounted in a cast housing. It is attached to the end of the clutch fork and bears on a thrust ring in the centre of the clutch pressure-plate assembly, transmitting pedal pressure to the springs.

Clutch withdrawal mechanism
The clutch disengaging system, but usually refers to the clutch fork and thrust bearing only.

Coast
To let a car run on by its own momentum, without use of the engine power. Usually the gear lever is put in the neutral position; to coast by simply disengaging the clutch causes undue wear of the clutch.

Cogged belt See TOOTHED BELT

Coil
Electrical device for converting low-voltage current supplied by the battery to the high voltage necessary to provide ignition sparks at the spark-plugs.

Coil ignition
Ignition system in which a coil is used to induce high voltage.

Coil spring
Helix of spring steel, rod or wire, which is twisted when the spring is compressed or extended.

Collapsible steering column
Steering column designed to collapse in a collision to reduce risk of injury.

Collapsible steering wheel
Steering wheel so designed that its rim and spokes will deform in a frontal crash.

Collets
Half-conical pieces of metal for securing one component to another. The collets fit into a recess in each component.

Column stalk
Slender lever attached to the steering column shroud. A form of easy-to-reach switch used for controlling horn, head-lamps, flashers, dip-beam and turn indicators. Can also be used to engage or disengage an overdrive.

Combustion
Burning of the fuel/air mixture, usually when ignited by a spark, in the combustion chamber of an engine.

Combustion chamber
Space in an internal combustion engine in which the fuel/air mixture is burnt. In the case of a piston engine it is in the cylinder head or the piston crown, or both.

Commutator
Ring of copper segments connected to the armature coils of a dynamo or electric motor. The segments, which are separated by thin insulators, convey current between the brushes and the coils.

Compression
Increasing the pressure of a gas by reducing its volume, as during the compression stroke in an engine.

Compression gauge
Workshop instrument for testing cylinder gas tightness. It is fitted into the spark-plug hole in the cylinder head, the engine is rotated, and the cylinder pressure is shown on a dial. A low reading indicates leakage past the piston rings, valve seats or cylinder-head gasket.

Compression-ignition engine
Internal combustion engine in which ignition is achieved by the heat generated by compressing air. A diesel engine works by compression-ignition; a charge of atomised fuel is injected into the very hot compressed air in the combustion chamber. See also DIESEL ENGINE.

Compression ratio
Ratio of the volume above the piston at the bottom of its stroke to the clearance volume left when the piston is at the top of its stroke. The higher the compression ratio the greater the power output. An average-sized car engine has a compression ratio between 8·5:1 and 9·5:1.

Compression ring
Type of piston ring usually fitted to the uppermost grooves of a piston and designed to form a sliding seal between piston and cylinder.

Compression stroke
The second stroke in the 4-stroke cycle, during which the piston moves upwards, compressing the fuel/air mixture ready for ignition and combustion.

Compressor
Mechanical device for providing air at a pressure higher than atmospheric pressure. Usually a piston or rotary vane or fan.

Condenser
Electrical component capable of storing an electrical charge; it forms part of the conventional coil-ignition system and is usually housed in, or close to, the distributor. The internationally accepted name for this component is capacitor.

Conduit
Tube or sleeve, usually made of plastic, enclosing electric cables to protect them from damage.

Cone clutch
Type of friction clutch made up of two conical members, one fitting inside the other. One member is usually faced with a friction material and when pressed into contact it transfers the drive from one component to the other. A cone clutch is used in overdrive units. The term is applied also to certain parts of a synchromesh mechanism.

Connecting rod
Metal component, usually of forged steel, connecting the gudgeon or piston pin of the piston to the crankpin of the crankshaft. It converts the reciprocating (up-and-down) motion of the piston into the rotary motion of the crankshaft.

Con-rod
Abbreviation for connecting rod.

Constant-mesh gears
Those gears in a gearbox that are in mesh at all times. To take the drive through a pair of constant-mesh gears, one gear is fixed to its shaft and the other connected to another shaft by a dog clutch that is slid into engagement by the gear lever.

Constant-mesh pinion
Smaller of a pair of constant-mesh gears.

Constant-vacuum carburettor See VARIABLE-CHOKE CARBURETTOR

Constant-velocity joint
Type of universal joint fitted on front-wheel-drive cars to allow snatch-free drive to the road wheels when steering.

Contact area
Area of a tyre in contact with the road surface.

Contact-breaker
Mechanically operated switch in the ignition system for rapid interruption of the low-voltage primary current to the coil; this interruption induces the high-voltage secondary current necessary for the ignition spark. Usually incorporated in the distributor and actuated by a cam on the distributor spindle.

Control box
Part of the electrical system; sealed unit containing automatic cut-out, voltage regulator and, when fitted, current control. More often referred to on the modern car as the c.v.c.—compensated voltage control—unit.

Convertible
Type of car that can be converted from closed to open by folding a collapsible fabric roof.

Cooling system
Method of disposing of the waste heat resulting from the burning of the fuel/air mixture in the engine's combustion

chambers. This is usually achieved by water circulation round the engine block and cylinder head. On air-cooled engines, air is directed round the cylinders and head by a mechanically driven fan.

Cords
The stranded textile threads or steel wires that are woven into the plies from which a tyre is constructed.

Core plug

Convex plug used to close a core hole in a cylinder-head and cylinder-block casting. It can be replaced easily if forced out by internal pressure.

Cornering force
Sideways force created by the grip of the tyres on the road when they are at an angle to the direction of travel. It is this force that enables a car to be steered.

Corrosion
Oxidation of a metal through attack by damp, acid or other chemicals. Rusting of iron and steel is the most common form.

Cotter
Securing device fitting into a slot, groove or hole; also called a cotter-pin. Collets are a form of cotter.

Coupé
Type of closed car body having a shorter (and often lower) passenger compartment than a saloon, giving a more sporting appearance, though less space for the occupants. Some have no rear-seat.

Courtesy light
Small light in the car switched on automatically when the doors are opened.

Crankcase
Iron or aluminium casting enclosing the crankshaft; it is usually in one with the cylinder block.

Crankcase ventilation valve
Valve that prevents pressure build-up in the crankcase caused by combustion gases that escape from the combustion chambers past the piston rings.

Crankpins
Offset bearing surfaces of the crankshaft; they carry the big-end bearings of the connecting rods.

Crankshaft
Shaft embodying the crankpins by means of which the reciprocating (up-and-down) motion of the pistons is converted into rotary motion through the action of the connecting rods.

Crash gearbox
A gearbox without synchronising units. Rarely fitted to modern cars.

Crocodile clip
Spring clip with serrated jaws, usually soldered to the end of an electric cable and used for making temporary electrical contact with various components. Ideal for test purposes.

Cross-ply tyre
One of the two common types of tyre casing, in which the textile cords in each ply are oblique to the circumference.

Crown wheel and pinion
Part of the final-drive assembly; a pair of bevel gears, one large (crown wheel) and one small (pinion). The propeller shaft or gearbox output shaft is connected to the pinion, and the crown wheel is connected to the transverse half-shafts through the differential.

Crush zones
Structural regions, one at each end of a modern car body, designed to collapse progressively in a crash, thus absorbing energy that would otherwise be transmitted to the occupants.

Cycle
Complete sequence of events—e.g. the 4-stroke cycle of an engine.

Cylinder
In the engine, the cylindrical opening in which the piston moves up and down. It is bounded at one end by the cylinder head and at the other end by the crankcase.

Cylinder block
Casting of iron or aluminium alloy in which the cylinders, and their water-cooling passages, or fins in air-cooled engines, are formed. Usually in one with the crankcase on water-cooled engines.

Cylinder head
Iron or aluminium-alloy casting bolted on top of the cylinder block. Normally contains the combustion chambers, valve gear and water passages or fins.

Cylinder-head gasket
Thin sealing member, usually of metal, copper/asbestos or some other composite material, interposed between the cylinder head and cylinder block. It is designed to prevent leakage of gases outwards from the cylinders and also prevents water entering the cylinders from the cooling system.

Cylinder jacket (water jacket)
Space between the cylinders and the outside walls of the cylinder block of a water-cooled engine; the water circulates through this space to cool the engine. It is often called the water jacket.

Cylinder liners
Sleeves, usually of cast iron, fitted inside the cylinder block where the piston does not run directly in the block itself. An aluminium block, for instance, has liners fitted. There are two types. Dry liners are surrounded by the metal of the block; wet liners are exposed to the cooling water.

Damper
A device in a variable-choke carburettor to ensure controlled movement of the suction piston. See also SUSPENSION DAMPER

Dashboard
Panel in front of the driver in which the instruments are mounted. Nowadays often known as the fascia.

Dashpot
Small oil-filled chamber, into which the damper fits, in the top of the piston guide-rod of a variable-choke carburettor.

Dead steering
Slang term to describe steering that has no 'feel' to it—a steering system that conveys to the driver little or no information about which way the wheels are pointing or how much grip they have.

Decarbonising
Process of removing carbon deposits from the combustion chambers, piston crowns and valves of an engine.

Decibel
Unit of measurement of the pressure or intensity of sound.

Declutch
Action of depressing the clutch pedal to disengage the drive.

de Dion suspension
Form of rear-wheel suspension in which the final drive is mounted on the vehicle chassis or body structure and the wheels are connected by a separate axle, which is guided vertically at its middle, and is also free to tilt.

Defensive driving
Art of being alert to every potentially dangerous situation.

Defroster
Facility provided by most modern car heater/ventilator systems, whereby all the available heat can be directed to the screen to melt frost or ice.

De-ionised water
Water treated to make it suitable for use in batteries; cheaper than distilled water.

Demister
Part of a heater/ventilator system; heated air is directed over the screen to clear internal condensation or misting. Rear window demisting can be achieved by a special glass incorporating a heater element or by attached anti-mist panels.

Desmodromic valve gear
Valve-gear system in which the valves are closed mechanically instead of by the usual valve-spring system.

Detergent oil
Engine oil having additives to keep the engine interior clean by holding sludge-forming matter in suspension, instead of allowing it to settle.

Detonation
Excessively rapid burning of the fuel/air mixture inside the combustion chamber, giving rise to a metallic 'knocking' noise. Most commonly caused by using petrol of too low octane rating, or by over-advanced ignition timing. Also referred to as knocking or pinking.

Diaphragm pump
Type of pump, often used in fuel systems, in which movement of a flexible diaphragm in one direction causes liquid to be drawn into the pump body through a non-return valve. Movement in the opposite direction delivers the liquid through another non-return valve.

Diaphragm spring
Type of conical spring shaped like a ring with inward-pointing radial fingers. Increasingly used in modern clutches instead of coil springs.

Diaphragm-spring clutch
Type of clutch in which the clamping or gripping load is applied by a diaphragm spring.

Diesel engine
Type of internal combustion engine that has no spark-plug and is technically a 'compression-ignition engine'. Air is drawn into the cylinder, where it is highly compressed and so becomes very hot. Fuel oil is then sprayed into the cylinder where it ignites spontaneously on meeting the hot air.

Differential gear
Form of gearing in the final drive that allows the road wheels to be driven at different speeds when the car is travelling on a curved path. On a corner the outside wheels cover a greater distance than the inside wheels, and so should rotate faster.

Dipped headlights
Headlamps with the 'meeting' beams switched on; these point slightly downwards so that oncoming drivers are not

dazzled. Where only two headlamps are fitted, dipping is usually achieved by switching to a second filament in each.

Dipstick
Graduated rod for measuring the amount of oil in the engine sump or gearbox.

Dipswitch
Electric switch, mounted on the dashboard, steering column or floor, for selecting headlamp main or dipped beams.

Direct current
Electric current flowing in one direction only, as produced by a conventional dynamo or a battery.

Direction indicators See INDICATORS

Disc
Part of a disc brake—the circular metal plate that revolves with the wheel.

Disc brakes
Braking system in which, when the pedal is pressed, friction pads carried in the caliper press against the metal disc that rotates with the wheel.

Displacer unit
Part of the Hydrolastic suspension system. Four displacer units are fitted—one for each wheel—and they contain a conical rubber spring, valves and fluid. As one unit comes under compression, fluid is displaced to the other on the same side.

Distilled water
Specially pure water used for topping up battery cells; water boiled off as steam and then condensed.

Distributor
The unit that delivers the high-voltage ignition current produced by the coil to each of the spark-plugs in turn. It contains the contact-breaker assembly, which is timed to deliver the current to the correct spark-plug at a particular point in the cycle of the engine.

Distributor cam
Specially shaped cam, with a 'lobe' for each of the cylinders, that is attached to the distributor drive shaft. The function of the cam is to move the insulated rocker arm of the contact-breaker, so making and breaking the low-tension circuit.

Distributor cap
Moulded plastic cap that fits on top of the distributor body and carries the high-tension leads from the coil and to the spark-plugs.

Distributor drive shaft
Shaft that rotates the distributor rotor arm and cam; usually driven by the camshaft at half engine speed.

Distributor rotor arm
Plastic moulding with a brass contact plate bonded to it. It is mounted above the distributor cam, making contact with the coil high-tension lead via a spring-loaded brush in the centre of the distributor cap and with each HT lead in turn.

Distributor weights
Spring-loaded weights that revolve with the distributor drive shaft. As engine speed increases the weights move outwards under centrifugal force, advancing the ignition timing.

Dog clutch
Means of transmitting drive from one component to another. Blocks, or tongues, on the circumference of one part of the dog clutch are slid into corresponding indentations on the other. Commonly used in gearboxes.

Dogs
Mating blocks or protrusions forming part of a dog clutch.

DoT test
Test of vehicles demanded by law when they reach a certain age—for cars, three years—and annually thereafter. Still often called the MoT (Ministry of Transport) test.

Double declutching
Technique used to ensure quiet gear changing on a gearbox that has no synchromesh. The clutch pedal is momentarily released after the gear lever has been moved into neutral, to allow the gear speed to be adjusted by the accelerator, before the clutch is depressed again and the desired gear selected.

Doughnut coupling
Flexible ring-shaped rubber coupling between the final drive and drive-shafts of some independent-suspension cars to transmit drive and compensate for geometry changes with wheel movement.

Downdraught carburettor
Usually a fixed-jet carburettor in which the air enters the carburettor vertically from the top.

Drag coefficient
Numerical value giving an indication of the air resistance of a moving object.

Drag-link
Rod connecting the drop-arm of the steering box with the track-rod linkage.

Drain-plug
Screwed plug fitted at the lowest point of the sump, gearbox or final-drive housing for draining the oil, and at the bottom of the radiator for draining the cooling system.

Drift
Rod or bar used to drive a pin, bolt or other object into or out of a hole or housing; a form of punch.

Drifting
Cornering technique, normally confined to racing, in which the bend is taken with all four wheels sliding to a certain extent, with the car fully under control.

Drive-shafts
Alternative term for half-shafts. Usually applied where the shaft is not enclosed in an axle casing.

Drop-arm
Operating lever mounted on the outside of the steering box.

Drophead
Colloquial term for a convertible car.

Drum brakes
Braking system in which curved metal shoes faced with friction material are forced outwards, by operation of the brake pedal, into contact with a drum attached to the wheel.

Dry-sump lubrication
Lubrication system often used on racing and other competition cars. Instead of being carried in the sump, the oil is circulated by pump pressure from and back to a separate tank. Because the tank is remote from the engine, better oil-cooling is achieved than with the conventional wet-sump system.

Dual-braking
Hydraulic-brake system divided into two separate circuits so that a failure in one does not mean a complete loss of braking ability. In one system the complete front and rear brake circuits are duplicated; in a more simple system there are separate front and rear circuits. In other systems the two circuits both go to the front brakes, with one circuit controlling one rear brake and the second circuit controlling the other.

Dual-control car
Car with controls duplicated on the passenger side, used for driving instruction.

Dust cap
Screw-on cap fitted to a tyre valve to retain air and keep out dust.

Dust excluder
A rubber or plastic sleeve or gaiter fitted over a mechanical assembly to keep out dust or mud.

Dwell meter
Workshop instrument for checking the distributor dwell period.

Dwell period
Period during which the distributor contact-breaker points remain closed; sometimes called the dwell angle.

Dynamometer
Sometimes referred to as a 'brake'. A hydraulic or electric device that absorbs and measures the torque, or turning effort, delivered by an engine under test; from the torque and rotational speed, the brake horsepower can be calculated.

Dynamic balance
State of balance of a rotary assembly—e.g. a crankshaft or wheel and tyre—when it is revolving.

Dynamo
Direct-current generator.

Earth
Connection from an electrical component to the chassis or body as part of an earth-return system completing a circuit.

Earth electrode
Earthing part of a spark-plug—usually a small tongue attached to the bottom of the spark-plug body that has to be moved towards or away from the centre electrode to achieve the correct spark-plug gap.

Earthing strip
Thick braided wire connecting the earth (usually negative on modern cars) terminal of the battery to the body of the car, so providing a return circuit for the car's electrical system.

East-west mounting
Term applied to an engine that is mounted across the vehicle, as opposed to the more conventional longitudinal mounting.

Economy jets
Special jets in a carburettor, designed to provide a weaker, and therefore more economical, mixture at cruising speed.

Electrode
One of the terminals through which electric current is fed from or into a battery. Also part of a spark-plug.

Electrolyte
Solution of sulphuric acid and distilled water in which positive and negative plates must be immersed.

Electromotive force
Force from a battery or generator that causes a flow of electricity in a circuit.

Electronic ignition
System devised originally for very high-revving engines where a conventional system could not produce enough high-voltage sparks. The contact-breaker is replaced by a form of pulse-generating unit. Electronic systems are now being introduced more widely because their improved efficiency helps reduce toxic exhaust emission.

Electronic petrol injection
System of petrol injection in which the amount of fuel delivered is controlled by an electronic device that senses the suction in the inlet manifold, engine temperature, engine rpm and throttle position.

Emery cloth
Abrasive cloth for rubbing down metal.

Emulsion block
Part of a fixed-jet carburettor; the component that contains the emulsion tube, or tubes, where the petrol and air are mixed.

Emulsion tube
Part of the fixed-jet carburettor. A tube with holes in it for additional air to be mixed with the petrol to prevent an over-rich mixture and to emulsify the petrol.

End-float
Amount of end movement of a component such as a crankshaft along the bearing axis; sometimes called end-play.

Engine braking
Deceleration caused by releasing the accelerator, and so closing the throttle. The engine is then driven by the wheels and absorbs some of the energy of the car's motion.

Epicyclic gearing
Train of gears consisting of a central gearwheel (sun wheel) in mesh with one or more pinions (planet pinions) which themselves are in mesh with a toothed ring (annulus).

Equalising link
Mechanical device that ensures an equal effort on the brake shoes of both rear wheels when the handbrake is operated.

Ethylene glycol
Basis of most antifreeze compounds; corrosion-inhibiting chemicals are added so that the ethylene glycol will not corrode the metals of the cooling system.

Exhaust gases
The gases formed by the combustion of fuel and emitted by the exhaust system. They include water vapour, carbon dioxide, carbon monoxide, oxides of nitrogen and unburnt hydrocarbons.

Exhaust manifold
Iron casting or group of pipes bolted to the engine to take exhaust gases into the exhaust system.

Exhaust silencer
Chamber in the exhaust system that lowers the energy of the exhaust gases before they reach the atmosphere and so reduces the noise they make.

Exhaust stroke
Final stroke in a 4-stroke cycle, during which the piston rises and the burnt gases escape past the open exhaust valve.

Exhaust system
System of metal pipes and silencers through which the exhaust gases flow from the engine to the atmosphere.

Exhaust turbocharger
See TURBOCHARGER

Exhaust valve
Valve in the cylinder head that opens to allow the burnt gases to escape from the cylinder during the exhaust stroke.

Expansion chamber
Small tank in a sealed cooling system; it receives from the radiator any overflow due to expansion on heating, and siphons it back into the main cooling system when necessary, so maintaining coolant in the system at a constant level. Also a chamber into which exhaust gases expand and cool.

External-combustion engine
Type of engine that burns fuel outside the working cylinders or turbine assembly—e.g. the steam engine.

Extreme-pressure lubricant
Lubricant used in mechanisms where one moving part slides and presses heavily against another—e.g. in a hypoid-bevel axle.

Fan
Air-moving propeller that can be used to draw or force air through the radiator of a liquid-cooled engine, or over the cylinders and heads of an air-cooled engine, to cool a generator or to blow heated air from the heater system into the passenger compartment of a car. Engine-cooling fans are driven either by the fan belt from a pulley on the crankshaft or by an electric motor.

Fan belt
Belt used to drive the fan, and sometimes the water pump and generator, from a pulley on the crankshaft. It is usually of V-section and has to be maintained at the correct tension to avoid slipping.

Fastback
Body in which the roof line runs in an uninterrupted sweep to the tail of the car and embodies a rear window at a considerable angle to the vertical.

Fatigue
Weakness in metals caused by repeated stress—e.g. vibration or road shock.

Feeler gauges
Set of thin hard-metal strips of different thicknesses, usually from 0·002 in. to

0·025 in., used for measuring the clearance between two components—e.g. between a valve and its rocker.

F-head
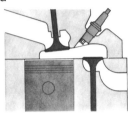

Name given to valve-gear layout in which the inlet valves are in the cylinder head and the exhaust valves in the cylinder block. It is an intermediate stage in engine design between a side-valve and an overhead-valve system.

Ferrule
Metal band round the handle of a tool, shrunk on to strengthen the handle, or the metal sheath at the end of the outer member of a control cable. Also the small copper ring fitted on a fuel pipe and compressed by the union nut to make a leakproof joint.

Fibreglass
Trade name of a brand of glass fibre, but often (incorrectly) used as meaning glass-reinforced plastic.

Field coils or windings
Wire windings on the pole pieces of an electric motor or generator; they energise the pole pieces, thus providing a magnetic field in which the armature rotates.

Field terminal
Terminal on a generator from which a lead is taken to the control unit where the magnetic field is varied according to operating conditions.

Filler cap
Lid of a petrol or oil tank, or of a radiator header tank.

Filter element
Unit that fits inside a filter bowl, or housing, providing the means for filtering fluids and gases. Most modern filter elements are made either of felt or of porous, impregnated housing, paper, folded in a special way to trap particles of foreign matter while maintaining a free flow of fluid or gas.

Final drive
Last section of the transmission system between the engine and the road wheels; usually consists of the crown wheel and pinion, and differential gears.

Finger
Cam-follower used in some overhead-camshaft engines; the finger is a lever,

interposed between the cam and valve stem as an alternative to a tappet.

Firing order
Order in which the cylinders of an engine fire, counting from front to rear. In a normal 4-cylinder engine, for example, the order is usually 1, 3, 4, 2.

First-motion shaft
Input shaft of a gearbox, driven from the clutch, normally at engine speed.

Fixed-jet carburettor
Most common type of carburettor. It has several fixed-size jets which are brought into use progressively as the throttle is gradually opened from the engine idling position to full throttle.

Flasher
Short for headlamp flasher. Electric spring-back switch usually mounted on the steering column. When operated it flashes the headlamps as a warning or signal to other drivers.

Flasher unit
Electrical unit that operates the turn indicators by an automatically controlled make-and-break circuit controlled by a bi-metallic strip or heated wire.

Flat spot (carburettor)
Hesitancy in the response of an engine at a certain throttle opening or when the accelerator is depressed.

Flat spot (tyre)
Temporary tyre-carcass distortion which is caused when a tyre that is constructed with nylon cords has been at rest in the same position for some time.

Float
Buoyant component inside a carburettor float chamber; it rises with the fuel and connects with a needle-valve to cut off the fuel delivery from the pump when the chamber is full.

Float chamber
Petrol reservoir in the carburettor. It is automatically kept full by the float and float needle. Sometimes also called the float bowl.

Float needle
Small needle in the fuel-inlet port of a carburettor. It is moved against its seating by the rising float and thus cuts off the fuel supply from the pump.

Fluid coupling
Type of automatic clutch. Power is transmitted through oil from a driving to a driven member, both having internal radial vanes. See TORQUE CONVERTER.

Fluid reservoir
Container in the engine compartment for the hydraulic fluid needed to operate a clutch or brake system.

Flushing oil
Fluid passed through an engine or other mechanism to remove sludge and impurities from the system.

Flywheel
Heavy disc bolted to the engine crankshaft; it acts as an energy reservoir and smooths out the individual power impulses of the pistons.

Flywheel markings
Grooves cut in the flywheel and its casing as a guide for determining piston position for timing valves or ignition.

Fog lamps
Auxiliary lamps mounted low on the front of a car for use in fog. They cast broad, flat beams to the nearside kerb.

Footbrake
Main braking system of a vehicle, operated by a pedal on the floor.

Four-stroke cycle
Operating system for an internal-combustion engine, in which four strokes—full up or down movements of the piston—are required to complete each working cycle. In order of operation, these strokes are inlet or suction (downward stroke), compression (upward stroke), power or expansion (downward stroke) and exhaust (upward stroke).

Four-valve head
High-performance cylinder head having two inlet and two exhaust valves per cylinder instead of the usual one of each. The resulting greater valve-opening area gives better volumetric efficiency and so enables more power to be developed.

Four-wheel drive
Transmission system in which the engine power is transmitted to all four wheels, not just two.

Free travel
Distance which a control lever or pedal must be moved before the 'play' is taken up and the control begins to take effect.

Freewheel
One-way clutch which transmits the drive only when the engine is pulling; when the accelerator is eased or released, the freewheel disengages the drive and vehicle motion is not retarded by engine braking. Current use of freewheels in cars is virtually confined to the bottom-gear systems of some automatic transmissions to ensure a smooth performance at slow, dense-traffic speeds.

Friction pads
Parts of a disc brake. They are segments of friction material that are carried in the caliper and pressed against the disc to slow the wheel.

Front panel
Forward panel of car, usually carrying headlamps and radiator grille.

Front-wheel drive
Type of transmission system in which the engine drives the front wheels. This results in a compact engine/gearbox/final-drive assembly; also, because more than half the car's weight is on the driven wheels, traction is good in slippery conditions and handling is usually very safe, with good directional stability.

Fuel
Source of energy by combustion; usually petrol in the case of a car, but it may be diesel oil.

Fuel cell
A unit in which chemical energy is converted directly to electric power; one or two of the various types currently being experimented with have been used to drive electric cars.

Fuel gauge
Dashboard instrument that indicates the amount of fuel remaining in the tank. Most gauges are electrically operated and are generally only approximate in their readings.

Fuel pump
Pump used to transfer the fuel from the tank to the carburettor. It can be mechanically operated by a cam on the camshaft, or electrically actuated.

Fuel starvation
Condition in which insufficient fuel reaches the engine. It can be due to an obstruction in the carburettor jets, the fuel filter or the pipeline from the tank—or to an almost empty fuel tank.

Fulcrum ring
Part of a diaphragm-spring clutch; the ring about which the fingers of the diaphragm spring pivot to release the clutch when the pedal is depressed.

Full-flow filter
Type of oil filter through which all the engine oil is circulated continuously, in contrast with a by-pass filter.

Full lock
When a steering wheel is fully turned in one direction or the other to give the minimum turning circle.

Fuse
Safety device that protects electrical wiring from the effects of excess current. It usually contains a thin wire that melts and interrupts the circuit when heated by a current higher than the circuit it is protecting can withstand.

Fuse block
Fuse rack in a fuse box.

Fuse box
Box that contains a group of fuses on their fuse block, to protect them from dirt and damage; it is usually attached to the engine bulkhead, but may form part of the instrument assembly.

g
Acceleration due to gravity. Acceleration of a vehicle from rest, its cornering power and its deceleration under braking are all colloquially referred to in terms of 'g'. This acceleration is approximately 32 ft per second every second, so $\frac{1}{2}$g braking would mean a deceleration of 16 ft per second in every second of braking.

Gaiter
Protective or draught-excluding shroud; usually made of leather, plastic or rubber. A common use is at the bottom of a gear lever, to seal the hole through which the lever passes.

Gasket
Sheet of jointing material placed between two metal surfaces which must be gas-tight or liquid-tight when bolted together.

Gas-turbine engine
Rotary internal combustion engine in which the gases, formed by burning the fuel, are made to rotate a vaned disc—like a multi-bladed fan—and the shaft on which it is mounted. Part or all of the power thus fed into the shaft is used to drive a compressor that delivers air to the engine.

Gearbox
The unit that overcomes the inability of most engines to produce much torque or turning effort at low running speeds. It is an assembly comprising sets of gears that serve to multiply the engine torque by various amounts with proportional reductions in output shaft speed. For example, if the gearbox output shaft is made to revolve at half engine speed, its torque will be double that of the engine.

Gear lever
Lever for changing from one set of gears in the gearbox to another.

Gear ratio
Relative speeds at which two gears, or their shafts, revolve; if the input gear rotates twice as fast as the output one (and therefore is of half the diameter), the gear ratio is 2:1.

Gears
Mechanical system to transmit torque or rotation from one shaft to another. In essence a gear is a disc with teeth round the edge; these teeth mesh with similar ones on the adjacent gear.

Gear train
A number of gears—usually more than two—used to drive one or more shafts from another.

Gear-type pump
Pump comprising a pair of meshing gears that rotate inside a closely fitting casing. The rotation carries the fluid round, between the teeth and the surface of the casing, from the inlet to the outlet of the pump.

Gear wheel
Disc with teeth cut at regular intervals round its edge, for meshing with similar teeth on another gear or component, as a means of transmitting motion or power.

Generator
Machine for producing the vehicle's supply of electricity, which it does by converting mechanical energy of rotation into electrical energy. See also ALTERNATOR and DYNAMO.

Glass-reinforced plastic
Laminated material used for the building of some car bodies and for body repairs often called GRP.

Glove compartment
Small cupboard in the dashboard, usually on the passenger's side.

Governor
A mechanical attachment that limits the speed of a particular component. A governor in an automatic transmission controls gear changing in relation to car speed.

Grand Touring (or *Gran Turismo*)
Description that should be applied only to fast, luxurious cars suitable for long-distance touring at high speeds; but the term is applied to high-performance versions of saloon cars.

Graphite grease
Heavy-duty lubricant containing colloidal graphite, for bearings where the relative movement is limited or slow.

Grease
Non-flowing lubricant used in situations where an oil would tend to run out.

Grease gun
Pump for injecting grease into the nipples of a chassis lubrication system.

Grease nipple
Small, shaped grease point with a spring-loaded non-return ball-valve in its head, designed to accept a grease gun.

Grille
Decorative grid on the front of a car. Usually bright metal, but chromium-plated or black plastic is used on some modern cars.

Grinding-in
Using an abrasive paste to lap-in the engine's valves on their seats during a top overhaul, to restore the valves' sealing ability.

Grommet
Rubber sleeve fitted to a cable or control rod where it passes through a bulkhead or other panel, to seal the hole against leakage of fumes, water or noise and to protect the cable or rod from chafing.

Gudgeon pin
Steel pin, usually hollow, used for coupling the piston to the small-end of the connecting rod. Sometimes referred to as a pistol pin.

Half-liners
Halves of a split shell bearing; each comprises a semicircular steel backing coated thinly with white metal, copper-lead or some other bearing metal.

Half-shaft
Axle shaft conveying the drive from the differential gear to one of the road wheels.

Handbrake
Lever pulled on by hand to operate usually the rear-wheeled brakes, to hold the vehicle when it is parked or to act as an emergency brake.

Handbrake quadrant
Toothed ratchet by means of which the handbrake can be held in the 'on' position.

Handling
The steering and cornering characteristics of a car, particularly when it is driven hard.

Hard top
Term used to describe a rigid roof attached to a sports-car body. It can be part of the body structure or be fitted as an alternative to a soft top or fabric roof.

Head distortion
Warping of the lower face of the cylinder head, usually caused by overheating.

Header tank
Water reservoir at the top of a radiator; it has an inlet pipe for the return of the hot water from the engine for cooling and, usually, a filler cap—which is also a pres-surising cap—for topping-up the coolant.

Headlamps
Powerful electric lamps mounted at the front of the vehicle to illuminate the road ahead at night.

Heater
System for warming the air reaching the passenger compartment by means of waste heat from the engine.

Heat exchanger
Part of a car heater system; hot water from the engine passes through one set of passages of the heat exchanger and air passes through another, being warmed in the process.

Heel-and-toe
Technique used to facilitate rapid downward gear changing while braking. The accelerator is 'blipped' with the heel or side of the foot, while the toe is operating the brake pedal at the same time as the clutch is depressed with the left foot and a change to a lower gear is made.

Helical gear
Gear in which the teeth are at an angle to the axis of the gear.

Helix (of starter motor)
Screwed sleeve on the shaft of the starter motor; it carries the starter pinion which moves along by inertia, when the motor is energised, to engage with the toothed starter ring on the flywheel.

Hemispherical chamber
Most efficient form of combustion chamber, because of its compact form and good gas-flow characteristics. It is shaped like an inverted bowl in which the valves are inclined at an angle to each other, with the spark-plug between them.

High-octane petrol
Suitable for high-compression engines.

High-tension current
High-voltage current induced in the coil by the collapse of the coil's primary circuit. The current itself is small, although the voltage is very high.

High-tension leads
Heavily insulated lead from the centre of the coil to the distributor cap, and also the leads from the distributor cap to the plugs.

High-tension pick-up
Carbon rod or brush in the distributor cap which, when the cap is in position, makes an electrical contact with the rotor arm so that the high-tension current is distributed through it to the appropriate spark-plug as the rotor arm revolves.

Highway Code
Code of recommended behaviour issued by the Department of Transport for the guidance of all road users.

Hood
Folding roof of an open sports car or convertible. A term used in the US for the bonnet.

Horizontally opposed engine
Engine with an equal number of cylinders horizontal on each side of the crankshaft.

Horsepower
Unit for defining the power output of an engine. One British horsepower equals 33,000 ft lb. of work per minute. The metric horsepower is slightly smaller.

Hotchkiss drive
Rear suspension in which semi-elliptic road springs absorb the driving torque reaction.

Hot-spot
Part of the wall of an engine's inlet manifold heated by the exhaust gases; this aids vaporisation of the petrol in the petrol/air mixture entering the engine.

Hub bearings
Bearings on which a road wheel revolves, normally of ball or taper-roller type.

Hunting
Erratic running of the engine, usually due to the carburettor supplying too weak a mixture of petrol and air.

Hydragas suspension
Interconnected suspension developed from the Hydrolastic system. Fluid is used in the same way, but the Hydrolastic's conical rubber springs are replaced by gas springs.

Hydraulic brakes
Braking system in which the pressure from the brake pedal is transmitted to the shoes or pads by means of hydraulic fluid.

Hydraulic coupling
See FLUID COUPLING

Hydraulic damper See SUSPENSION

Hydraulic fluid
Special oil used in a hydraulic system.

Hydraulic shift valve
Valve operated to effect a change of gear in an automatic gearbox.

Hydraulic system
Control system in which remote operation is obtained by the transmission of pressure from a pedal or lever by means of the hydraulic fluid. It is commonly used for clutch and brake control.

Hydrocarbon
Compound made of the elements hydrogen and carbon; petrol and most lubricating oils are hydrocarbons.

Hydrolastic suspension
System of car suspension in which a fluid works in conjunction with conical rubber springs to provide interconnection of the front and rear suspension units.

Hydrometer
Device used to measure the specific gravity of fluids—the battery's electrolyte, say, or antifreeze in the cooling system.

Hydropneumatic suspension
Suspension system in which a combination of fluid and compressed gas forms the springing elements.

Hypoid-bevel gears

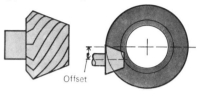

Offset

Form of spiral-cut gears commonly used for the crown wheel and pinion of the final-drive assembly. Because of the special geometry of the teeth on both components, the pinion can be set below the centre-line of the crown wheel to lower the vehicle's propeller shaft.

Idle (or idling)
Running condition of the engine when no pressure is applied to the accelerator; also known as slow running or tickover.

Idler gear
Additional gear in a train, its purpose being to reverse the direction of rotation or to connect shafts some distance apart without using a large gear wheel.

Idling-mixture screw
Adjustable means on all fixed-jet carburettors for varying the richness of the mixture supplied for idling.

Ignition
Firing of the compressed fuel/air mixture in an engine's combustion chambers; in a petrol engine it is achieved by a high-voltage electric spark, while in a compression-ignition (diesel) engine the heat of compression ignites the fuel.

Ignition advance
See IGNITION TIMING

Ignition system
System for providing ignition; it comprises battery, ignition switch, coil, contact-breaker, condenser and distributor, spark-plugs and connecting low-tension and high-tension leads.

Ignition timing
Relationship between the beginning of opening of the contact-breaker points and

the position of the piston in its cylinder. In a typical engine the points should separate when the piston is $\frac{5}{16}$ in. before top dead centre—called ignition advance. Retarded ignition occurs when the c.b. points separate after TDC.

Ignition vacuum pipe
Pipe leading from the inlet manifold to the distributor as a means of actuating the vacuum-control mechanism, which advances and retards the spark according to how hard the engine is working.

Ignition warning light
Red light on the instrument panel that comes on when the ignition key is turned to the 'on' position. It should go out when the engine has started, though it may glimmer at idling speeds. If the light comes on while the engine is running, it indicates that the generator voltage has fallen below the battery's voltage and hence the battery is not being charged.

Impeller
Rotating portion of a fluid pump; it has vanes on it to impart motion to the fluid.

Independent suspension
Suspension system in which each wheel has its own linkage to the vehicle body or chassis, and its own spring, allowing it to move without influencing another wheel. Most cars have independent front suspension: many also have independent rear suspension.

Indicators
Short for direction or turn indicators. When operated by the driver, through a switch on the steering column, the indicators flash externally, warning other road users of the driver's intentions. May also be operated simultaneously as hazard warning indicators.

Induction
One of the strokes of a 4-stroke cycle. With the exhaust valve closed and the inlet valve open, the piston descends so that fuel/air mixture enters the cylinder.

Induction manifold
See INLET MANIFOLD

Inertia drive mechanism
Part of starter motor that causes the pinion on the motor shaft to move into engagement with the starter ring gear on the flywheel when the motor is energised; also referred to as the Bendix drive.

Injection See PETROL INJECTION

Infinitely variable transmission
Transmission system in which the gear ratio is varied not in stages but steplessly between its high and low limits according to requirements. In modern examples, both mechanical and hydraulic, the

variation is effected automatically by a control unit that responds instantly to changes in speed and load.

Inlet manifold
Metal casting or group of pipes bolted to the engine for conveying the petrol/air mixture from the carburettor(s) to the inlet ports.

Inlet over exhaust
Valve-gear layout comprising overhead inlet valves and side exhaust valves.

In-line engine
Engine having all the cylinders in a single line, with their axes parallel.

Inner race
The inner ring or track of a ball or roller bearing.

Inner tube
The doughnut-shaped rubber tube fitted inside a tyre to contain the air; it has a valve for inflation purposes. Not required, of course, when the tyre is of the tubeless type.

Input shaft
Shaft that delivers power into an assembly; the gearbox first-motion shaft is an input shaft.

Instrument panel
Panel on which a vehicle's instruments or gauges are mounted.

Insulated wire or cable
Wire for carrying an electric current, protected by a non-conducting covering (the insulation). Usually the covering is plastic, because this resists oil and petrol.

Insulator
Ceramic part of a spark-plug; encases the centre electrode and is secured in the metal body.

Integral construction
Body structure that has no separate chassis; also called unitary construction.

Interconnected suspension
Suspension system in which there is a mechanical or hydraulic connection between the two wheels on each side of the car. When one wheel rises over a bump, the other is pushed downward by the interconnection, thus reducing the tendency of the body to pitch.

Internal-combustion engine
Type of engine in which the fuel is burnt internally, and the high pressure so caused is used directly to impart movement. This movement may be imparted to the pistons, as in the conventional petrol or diesel engine, or to a rotor, as in the Wankel and gas turbine engines.

Iso-octane
Test fuel that shows great resistance to knocking, used in various proportions

with heptane for assessing the anti-knock characteristics of various fuels.

Jack
Device for raising a car, usually to change a wheel or to enable stands to be put under it for repairs to be carried out.

Jacking point (or socket)
Built-in bracket underneath the car to take the pad or arm of the jack. On some smaller cars there are only two jacking points, one each side, but on larger cars there is usually one fitted close to each of the wheels.

Jet
Part of a carburettor; usually a brass component with a small hole that provides the correct flow of fuel.

Jet gland
Sealing ring on the jet of a variable-choke carburettor.

Jet lever
Small lever on variable-choke carburettors for raising and lowering the jet relative to the needle to alter mixture strength. For cold starting, which requires a richer mixture, the jet is lowered.

Journal
Part of a shaft in contact with a bearing.

Judder
On-and-off snatching action or shaking effect. Snatching can occur in clutch or brake assemblies, due to uneven wear or distortion of certain components. Shaking is usually caused by imbalance or wear and can occur in the transmission or steering.

Jump leads
Heavy-duty electric cables with crocodile clips at each end. They are used to make temporary connections from a serviceable vehicle battery to one that is run down.

Key
Small block of metal that fits into grooves cut in two components of an assembly

(e.g. a gear wheel on a shaft) and locks them together.

Kick-down switch
Floor-mounted switch operated by full depression of the accelerator pedal against the resistance of a spring. It is found on most cars with automatic transmission; its operation causes the gearbox to change down to a lower gear, thus giving maximum acceleration.

King-pin (swivel pin)
Hardened-steel pin carrying the swivel member by which a front wheel is steered. In modern independent front-suspension systems, king-pins have been replaced by ball joints.

King-pin inclination
Inward tilt given to the king-pins for light steering. The term is also used for the inclination of the imaginary line through the centres of the upper and lower ball joints of a modern independent front-suspension system.

Knife cuts
Narrow slots moulded in the ribs or blocks of a tyre tread to increase road grip, particularly in the wet; called sipes in the tyre industry.

Knocking See DETONATION

Knock-on wheel
Type of wheel that fits on to a splined hub and is usually secured by a central nut with large protruding lobes.

Labouring
Term applied to an engine pulling hard at low speed.

Laminated safety glass
Type of safety glass made of two thin sheets of glass bonded one to each side of a thin sheet of transparent plastic.

Laminated spring See LEAF SPRING

Land
Portion of the piston exterior between or above the piston-ring grooves.

Lap-strap
Type of safety harness consisting of only a single belt passing across the lower part of the body.

Layshaft
Secondary shaft of a conventional gearbox; it is usually fixed, and the group of gears (called a cluster) that runs on it is in mesh with the gears on the mainshaft. Also called second-motion shaft.

Leading shoe
Brake shoe which, because it is pivoted at its trailing end, tends to be pulled outwards by the drag of the rotating drum as drum and shoe contact each other.

Leaf spring
Suspension spring built up from a series of steel strips, or leaves; normally the top leaf is the longest and the bottom the shortest, and they are held together by clips. Each end of the longest leaf is rolled into an eye for attaching the spring to the vehicle chassis or body.

Level plug
Plug that can be unscrewed to check the level of the oil in the gearbox or final-drive assembly.

Lever-type damper
Hydraulic-suspension damper having a lever to transmit the wheel movement to a double-ended piston in an oil-filled cylinder.

Lift (of a valve)
Distance the valve moves off its seating when fully open. Valve lift is provided by the contour of the cam lobe.

Limited-slip differential
Type of differential gear fitted to some powerful cars to improve grip on slippery road surfaces or in full-throttle starts. In contrast to the normal differential, it limits the amount one wheel can slip relative to the other, so preventing all the power being fed to the slipping wheel.

Liner
Term used to describe the halves of a shell bearing for a crankshaft or connecting-rod big-end. See also CYLINDER LINERS.

Linkage
Mechanical means of connecting components that have to be moved, e.g. the brake linkage, between the brake pedal and the master cylinder.

Live rear axle
Beam-type axle containing the crown wheel and pinion, differential gears and half-shafts.

Load-sensing valve
A valve in some rear-brake hydraulic circuits to vary the maximum braking effort according to the weight on the rear wheels, thereby reducing the risk of these locking—and therefore of skidding. Developed from the pressure-limiting valve.

Lobe (of a cam)
Part of the cam above the base circle which causes movement of the follower.

Lock
Measure of the turning circle of a car; one with a 'good lock' can turn in a tight circle.

Locking washer
Split spring or serrated washer designed to bite into the surface of the component it bears against, to prevent loosening of a nut or screw which is tightened on to it.

Locknut
Nut that is tightly screwed down on top of another, to stop the lower nut from coming undone.

Low-tension current (ignition)
Current in the primary windings in the coil; its collapse, when the contact-breaker points open, induces the high-tension current in the secondary winding in the coil.

Lubricant
Substance introduced between surfaces that are in relative motion, to reduce friction; the most common types are oil and grease.

Lucar connector
System of electrical connections, made by Lucas and standard on British cars; it features a spring-loaded connector that slides over a blade-type terminal.

MacPherson suspension
Type of suspension in which the wheel is carried on a stub axle integral with the lower end of a telescopic strut. It incorporates a coil spring and a suspension damper.

Magneto
Special type of electrical generator for producing a high-voltage ignition current without a battery.

Main beam
Light produced by the main filament of a headlamp. This gives maximum illumination of the road ahead.

Main bearings
Bearings that support the crankshaft in the crankcase.

Main jet
Principal jet of a fixed-jet carburettor; it supplies petrol once the throttle is opened beyond the idle stage, but its effect may be modified by other jets.

Mainshaft See THIRD-MOTION SHAFT
Manifold See INLET MANIFOLD and EXHAUST MANIFOLD

Manual gearbox
Gearbox in which the selection of each gear is effected by the manual operation of a lever by the driver.

Master cylinder
First stage of a hydraulic clutch or brake system; operation of the pedal causes the piston in the master cylinder to move, thus developing hydraulic pressure in the pipelines and flexible tubing leading to the clutch or brakes.

Mechanical efficiency
In an engine, the ratio between the horsepower actually developed in the cylinders and that delivered by the crankshaft.

Meshing
Engagement of the teeth of gear wheels, so that one drives the other.

Metric thread
Screw thread with dimensions according to the continental system.

Micrometer
Instrument for making accurate dimensional measurements of components where precision is important.

Micrometer adjustment
See VERNIER ADJUSTMENT

Mileage recorder See ODOMETER
Mileometer
Colloquial expression for odometer.

Mirror dazzle
Reflection in the rear-view mirror of the headlights from a following vehicle.

Misfiring
Behaviour characteristic of an out-of-tune engine when one cylinder or more sometimes fails to fire, causing erratic running.

Mixture
Shortened expression meaning the petrol/air mixture supplied to the engine by the carburettor or injection system.

Molybdenum disulphide
Lubricant that has affinity for metals, adhering to rubbing surfaces even under high pressures; it is added to some oils or greases to enhance their effectiveness in arduous conditions.

Monobloc
Type of engine in which the crankcase and cylinder block are cast in one.

Monocoque
Term correctly applied to bodies of single-skin construction, without main longitudinal frame members.

Mud flaps
Flaps, usually made of rubber, mounted behind the wheels to reduce the amount of mud or water thrown up by the wheels into the path of following vehicles.

Multigrade oil
Engine lubricating oil, the viscosity of which does not vary as much with temperature as that of a normal single-grade oil; such a lubricant does not thicken up as much when cold, or thin out as much when hot.

Naturally aspirated engine
An engine that is fed with petrol/air mixture or air (diesel) under atmospheric pressure only, without the assistance of a supercharger.

Nave plate
Metal plate that clips over the central part of the wheel to hide the hub cap and wheel nuts; usually an embellishment.

Needle valve See FLOAT NEEDLE
Negative camber
Inward tilt sometimes given to the front or rear wheels of vehicles with independent suspension, to increase the cornering power of the tyres.

Negative earth
Electrical wiring system; the negative terminal of the battery is earthed to the vehicle structure.

Neutral
State of a gearbox in which no gear is engaged, so that the engine can run without turning the road wheels. In a normal manual gearbox it is necessary to go through neutral to change from one gear to another.

Nipple See GREASE NIPPLE
Non-return valve
Valve that will allow fluid to pass in one direction only. For example, there are two non-return valves in a mechanical fuel pump; one allows the fuel into the pump chamber but not back to the tank, and the other allows the fuel to pass to the carburettor, but not to return.

Notchy gear change
Slang term for a gear change in which lever movement feels obstructed or rough.

Number plates
Plates attached to the front and rear of a vehicle, carrying its registration number. This comprises white figures on a black background or, if a plate of approved reflecting material is used, black on yellow at the rear and black on white at the front.

Number-plate light
Small white light that illuminates the rear number plate.

Octane rating
Numerical expression of a petrol's resistance to detonation. The higher an engine's

compression ratio, in general, the higher-octane petrol it needs.

Odometer
Instrument for recording distance covered; usually an integral part of the speedometer. It records miles and sometimes tenths of a mile also.

Ohm
Unit of electrical resistance—the resistance offered by any conductor to the flow of electricity through it.

Oil-bath cleaner
Air cleaner that prevents impurities in the air entering the carburettor by trapping them on the surface of a bath of oil.

Oil change
The draining of the oil in an engine or transmission unit, and its replacement with new oil. Engine oil changes are usually recommended every 3,000 – 6,000 miles nowadays, but the intervals are much longer for gearboxes and final drives.

Oil-control ring
Piston ring fitted below the compression rings of a piston to scrape excess oil from the cylinder walls and return it to the sump through holes in the piston-ring groove.

Oil filler cap
Cap that seals the hole through which oil is poured into the engine sump. For ease of access, this hole is usually in the cover on top of the engine.

Oil filter
Filter, usually embodying an element of impregnated paper, fitted to an engine to prevent dirt, metal particles and other impurities from circulating in the engine's lubrication system.

Oil gallery
Passage or pipe in the crankcase, cylinder block or cylinder head through which lubricating oil is circulated to the various bearings. The main oil gallery runs along the crankcase and feeds the main bearings through oilways.

Oil-pressure gauge
Instrument showing the pressure of oil in the engine lubrication system.

Oil-pressure warning light
Coloured instrument-panel light fitted to some cars in place of an oil-pressure gauge; it lights up when the pressure in the lubrication system falls too low.

Oil pump
Pump that circulates lubricating oil from the engine's sump through the lubrication system.

Otto cycle
Named after the inventor, Dr Nikolaus Otto, it is the 4-stroke engine-operating cycle with combustion occurring at con-

stant cylinder volume (i.e. at the top of the stroke); the spark-ignition petrol engine operates on an approximation to this cycle.

Outer race
The outer ring or track of a ball or roller bearing—that which fits into the bearing housing.

Output shaft
Any shaft that transmits the turning effort produced by a component or assembly. The third-motion shaft, or main shaft of a gearbox, for instance, is the gearbox output shaft.

Overall gear ratio
Number of engine revolutions per revolution of the driving wheels; determined by multiplying the ratio in use in the gearbox by the final-drive ratio.

Overdrive
Supplementary two-speed gear unit, usually controlled electro-hydraulically, to provide extra gear ratios. The normal types are fitted immediately behind the gearbox and are arranged to operate on third and top gears of a four-speed gearbox. Engagement and disengagement is by means of a switch.

Overhead camshaft
Camshaft mounted above the cylinder head, operating overhead valves through tappets, rockers or fingers.

Overhead valves
Most common arrangement of the valve-gear in modern car engines; valves are in the cylinder head above the combustion chambers. They are operated either by push-rods and rockers or by an overhead camshaft.

Overrun
Condition when the throttle is shut and the wheels are driving the engine.

Over-square engine

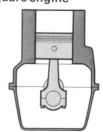

Engine in which the piston stroke is less than the diameter of the cylinder bore.

Oversteer
Handling characteristic causing the driver to lessen the amount of steering lock applied to keep on his intended course. It is inherent in some cars, notably most with the engine at the rear.

Paper element
Air or oil-filter core made of pleated, resin-impregnated paper.

Parallel connection
Method of connecting batteries by individually wiring the positive terminals together and the negative terminals together. The voltage remains that of one battery, but the current is increased.

Parking light
Small light on the side of a car, switched on as a warning when the car is parked at night; it shows a white light to the front and a red light to the rear.

Pedal pad
Rubber cover over a pedal to give a comfortable feel and to reduce the risk of the foot slipping.

Petrol
Motor spirit; a mixture of light, volatile hydrocarbons produced by the distillation of petroleum. Today's petrols are further refined by other means and have a number of additives to improve anti-knock rating and reduce deposit formation.

Petroleum
Liquid, otherwise known as crude oil, from which petrol is refined.

Petroleum jelly
Soft, greasy, non-conductive substance used to protect the battery terminals against corrosion. It is one of the many by-products of petroleum refining.

Petrol filter
Fine gauze sieve incorporated in the petrol pump to prevent any foreign matter in the petrol from reaching the carburettor. Other types of petrol filters are sometimes inserted in the fuel lines.

Petrol gauge See FUEL GAUGE

Petrol injection
Alternative to a carburettor as a means of supplying the engine's petrol requirements. An injection system squirts precisely metered quantities of fuel into the inlet ports.

Petrol pump
Pump that draws fuel from the tank and delivers it to the carburettor or injection system; it is operated mechanically, usually by an additional cam on the camshaft, or by electricity.

Pick-up
Response of the engine to pressure on the accelerator.

Pick-up truck
Small utility vehicle, usually adapted from a saloon car; it has a closed front section for the driver and one or more passengers, and an open rear portion with low, fixed sides and a tailgate.

Pilot jet
Part of a carburettor; the jet that supplies petrol when the throttle is closed or only slightly open.

Pilot light
Small bulb in the wiring circuit of an electrical component; it lights up to indicate that the component is switched on.

Pinion
Generally, the smaller of a pair of gears. Commonly used to describe the smaller of the final-drive gears (crown wheel and pinion) or the starter-motor gear that engages the flywheel to turn the engine.

Pinking See DETONATION

Piston
Bucket-shaped component that is a sliding fit inside a cylinder. In the engine, it is driven down by the expansion of burning fuel/air mixture to transmit driving effort to the crankshaft, by way of the connecting rod. Pistons are also used in hydraulic dampers and braking systems.

Piston clearance
Gap between a piston and the cylinder within which it operates, to allow for expansion of the piston when it gets hot under working conditions. If this clearance were not provided, the piston would seize in its bore and cause damage. Because the piston crown gets hotter than the skirt, the clearance is generally greater at the top of the piston than at the bottom.

Piston crown
Top area of the piston on which the pressure of expanding gases is exerted.

Piston-lifting pin
Small pin in the body of a variable-choke carburettor designed to enable the suction piston to be lifted fractionally when the carburettor is being tuned, without obstructing the air flow.

Piston pin See GUDGEON PIN

Piston rings
Thin, gapped bands of metal, usually cast-iron or steel, that fit into grooves around the piston to make seals against the cylinder wall. There are two types, compression and scraper or oil-control rings.

Piston-ring grooves
Grooves cut round the body of a piston to carry the piston rings.

Piston skirt
That part of the piston situated below the gudgeon pin.

Piston slap
Tapping sound, caused by the piston slapping against the cylinder wall with each reversal of direction. It is more noticeable when the engine is cold because, when it warms up, the piston expands more than the cylinder. It can be a sign of cylinder or piston wear.

Pitch
Distance between successive points on a component, such as the circumferential distance between two gear teeth and the distance between crests of a screw thread.

Pitching
Alternate up-and-down movement of the ends of a car—nose-up/tail-down then tail-up/nose-down—when moving on a bumpy road surface.

Pitting
Small craters found on contact points and valve seats caused by burning of the metal. Also found on gear teeth where there is excessive surface loading.

Pivot pin
Pin at a joint in a brake linkage or other mechanism, on which components pivot.

Plain bearing
Bearing in the form of a cylinder, either in one piece (a bush), two pieces (shells) or wrapped from strip material. Bearings are usually of metal but may be of plastic if the loading is light. Most engines have plain main and big-end bearings (both shells).

Planet gears
Components of an epicyclic gear system; small gear wheels situated between the sun gear and the annulus. Also refers to the intermediate gears in a differential unit.

Play
Free movement in a mechanism; it has to be taken up by initial travel before effective movement starts.

Plug lead
High-tension cable from the distributor cap to the spark-plug.

Plug spanner
Special type of spanner for tightening or loosening spark-plugs.

Plunger (gearbox)
Spring-loaded steel ball or cylinder that engages a groove in the selector rod to help hold the gear in engagement. More commonly referred to as a detent ball.

Ply
Layer of rubberised textile or steel fabric, in the form of parallel cords, in a tyre carcass; there are usually from two to six plies in a car tyre.

Pocketing
Extensive wear of a valve seat through excessive grinding-in during mainten-

ance. The depression so formed causes masking of the initial opening of the valve and hence a reduction in the engine performance.

Points
Hard-metal contacts of the ignition-system contact-breaker, inside the distributor. When they are separated by the action of a cam, the primary circuit is interrupted, so causing a breakdown of current in the coil and inducing a high-voltage current in the secondary circuit. Also used to refer to the tips of the electrodes in a spark-plug.

Polarity plug
Device in a car radio that adjusts the polarity to suit the car's electrical circuit.

Pole shoe
Part of a dynamo or electric motor; one of the pole pieces that produce a magnetic field, in which the armature revolves.

Poppet valve
Type of valve comprising a disc-shaped head from which projects a stem running in a valve guide. The head has a conical seating face on its circumference, on the same side as the stem. This is the type of valve used in virtually all 4-stroke vehicle engines. See VALVE.

Port
Passage between the combustion chamber and the inlet or exhaust manifold.

Positive camber
Term used for wheels tilted outwards at the top. See CAMBER ANGLE.

Pots
Slang term for cylinders.

Power steering
Steering system in which the driver's effort on the steering wheel is reduced by assistance from hydraulic pressure, supplied by an engine-driven pump. More correctly called power-assisted steering.

Power stroke
Third stroke of the 4-stroke cycle; the petrol/air mixture burns and the hot gases expand, driving the pistons down the cylinder to turn the crankshaft.

Pre-focus bulb
Type of headlamp bulb having an accurately positioned filament; since the bulb is also set accurately in the reflector at the manufacturing stage, no adjustment is necessary to get the best beam from the lamp.

Pre-ignition
Premature ignition of the mixture in an engine cylinder before normal ignition by the spark-plug begins. Usually caused by local overheating in one or more of the cylinders.

Pre-selector gearbox
Earlier type of gearbox of the epicyclic pattern, usually combined with a fluid coupling; the gear required was selected in advance and engaged by the operation of the equivalent of a clutch pedal.

Pressure cap
Filler cap on the radiator, designed to maintain pressure in the cooling system above that of atmospheric pressure (14·7 p.s.i. at sea level). This raises the boiling temperature of the coolant, so giving a bigger margin of cooling.

Pressure-limiting valve
Device sometimes incorporated in the hydraulic circuit of rear brakes to prevent excessive pressure being applied; this reduces the risk of locking the rear wheels, but is less effective than a load-proportioning valve.

Pressure plate
Spring-loaded metal plate that clamps the clutch driven plate to the flywheel to transmit the drive from engine to gearbox.

Primary circuit
Low-voltage part of the ignition system; includes the battery, ignition switch, contact-breaker and coil primary winding.

Primary current
Low-tension current that flows through the primary winding of a coil and which is switched on and off by the contact-breaker in the distributor.

Primary winding
Part of the ignition coil in which the low-tension current flows from the battery.

Priming lever
Small operating lever on a mechanical fuel pump. It can be actuated by hand to refill the carburettor float chamber after servicing, or to check that petrol is actually coming through should the engine fail to start.

Propeller shaft
Driving shaft connecting the gearbox to the final drive. Sometimes called the prop-shaft for short.

Pull-off spring
Strong coil spring connecting the brake shoes inside a drum-brake system to pull them together (away from the drums) when the brake is released.

Pump-braking
Technique of braking on a slippery surface by pressing and releasing the brake pedal in rapid sequence. See CADENCE BRAKING.

Push-rods
Parts of an overhead-valve operating system; rods that transmit the cam lift from the tappets to the rockers, which in turn open the engine's valves.

Quarter-light
Small, often triangular side window either at the front of each front-door window, the rear of each rear-door window or immediately behind each rear door. Some can be opened for ventilation.

Quartz-halogen bulb
Modern type of headlight bulb which, for a given wattage, produces a much brighter, whiter light than does an equivalent normal tungsten-filament type of bulb.

Quench area
Combustion chamber region that stays cool enough during combustion to control the burning locally, and to terminate combustion at the correct time.

Race (of a bearing)
Part of a ball or roller bearing; one of the tracks on which the balls or rollers run. Normally a bearing will have an inner race and an outer race, one fixed and the other rotating.

Rack and pinion
Type of steering unit in which a pinion at the bottom of the steering column engages a straight rack that moves sideways in relation to the car as the pinion is turned. The ends of the rack are connected to the steering arms by short, jointed links.

RAC rating
Early taxation formula relating the size of an engine to its estimated horsepower; it was the number of cylinders multiplied by the square of the bore in inches, divided by 2·5, the stroke being disregarded.

Radial-ply tyre
Type of tyre having a soft-walled casing with the cords of the plies approximately perpendicular to the rim of the wheel. Gives better handling and longer life.

Radiator
Device for dissipating heat from the water in a car's cooling system; consists of thin-walled passages, with large surface areas, through which the water circulates.

Radiator blind
Fabric roller-blind, or shutter, under the driver's control, mounted directly in front of or behind the grille to give a rapid warm-up in cold weather.

Radiator filler cap
Filler cap on top of the radiator header tank. See also PRESSURE CAP.

Radiator hose
Rubber/fabric pipe between the radiator and engine. The top hose feeds hot water to the radiator, and the bottom hose returns the cooled water to the engine.

Radius arm
Part of a suspension linkage; usually an arm pivoted on the body at one end and connected to another arm at an angle, giving triangulation and resistance to fore-and-aft and sideways forces.

Reach
Length of a spark-plug's threaded portion that screws into the cylinder head.

Reamer
Tool for accurately enlarging an existing hole. A reamed hole has a better finish than a drilled one.

Rear lamps
Red lamps mounted on the rear of a vehicle, near the corners; they are a legal requirement at night, and a minimum intensity is specified.

Rear-view mirror
Mirror mounted inside the car, or on a wing, to enable the driver to see behind without having to turn his head.

Rear-wheel drive
Common transmission system in which the drive from the engine is conveyed to the rear wheels only.

Rebore
Reconditioning a worn cylinder by boring it out to restore circularity and parallelism; a replacement piston of an appropriately increased diameter is required.

Rebound valve
One of the valves in a hydraulic shock absorber or damper; it controls the flow of fluid when the wheel is moving downwards—when it is returning after striking a bump or is dropping into a hole.

Reciprocating motion
Straight-line motion of an object between two positions—backwards and forwards or up and down. The pistons, connecting rods, push-rods and valve gear all exhibit reciprocating motion.

Recirculating-ball steering gear
Type of worm-and-nut steering box in which movement between the two components is conveyed through a series of steel balls that minimise friction.

Reflector
Red plastic disc or plate carried on the rear of the vehicle to reflect the lights of following vehicles as a hazard warning in the event of rear-light failure.

Relay
Electromagnetic device by which a small electric current is used to control a larger one. A starter motor, for example, is operated through a relay to avoid its heavy current having to be taken through the ignition switch. See also SOLENOID.

Reserve tank
Additional petrol supply on some cars, for use if the main one runs out; it is brought into use by operating a switch or tap.

Retarded spark
Ignition spark that occurs after TDC, usually as a result of too small a gap between the points of the contact-breaker, due to wear or incorrect ignition timing.

Retreading
A method of reconditioning a worn tyre by top-capping, recapping or remoulding.

Rev-counter
Colloquial term for a tachometer which records the rate at which the crankshaft is rotating.

Reverse pinion
Additional gear in the gearbox to reverse the direction of rotation of the output shaft and so make the car go backwards. It is brought into engagement when reverse gear is selected.

Reversing light
Rear light usually switched on automatically when reverse gear is selected, to enable a driver to see behind him when backing in the dark. It is sometimes manually controlled by a switch inside the car, in which case the law demands that an indicator light be installed in the circuit.

Revolutions per minute
Measure of rotational speed such as the rate at which a crankshaft revolves, as indicated by a tachometer.

Rheostat
Device for varying electrical resistance; in cars it is usually a variable switch that allows the instrument lighting to be dimmed or brightened at will.

Rich running
Term applied to a carburettor fault when there is too much petrol in the petrol/air mixture. The symptoms are irregular running and black exhaust smoke.

Riding the clutch
Slang term for the bad habit of driving with the left foot resting on the clutch pedal; almost always causes wear of the withdrawal bearing and clutch lining, and can lead to clutch slip.

Rigid front axle See BEAM AXLE

Rim
Outermost circular part of a wheel, carrying the tyre.

Ring spanner
Spanner with its head in the form of a ring which encircles the nut or bolt head.

Roadworthiness
Suitability of vehicle, in terms of mechanical condition, to be driven on the road.

Rocker
Double-ended lever that opens one of the inlet or exhaust valves of a normal ohv engine; it is operated by a push-rod, the lower end of which sits in a tappet which in turn is moved by the camshaft, or is operated directly by the camshaft.

Rocker cover
Cover, like an inverted trough (usually of sheet steel or cast aluminium), attached to the top of the cylinder head of an ohv engine to keep oil in and dirt out.

Rocker shaft
Stationary steel shaft mounted on pillars on top of the cylinder head of an ohv engine, to carry the rockers.

Roll
Sideways movement of a car's body on its suspension during cornering.

Roller bearing
Anti-friction bearing in which the rotating load is supported by small steel rollers, revolving between inner and outer races. The rollers are normally short cylinders, but in a needle-roller bearing they are long and thin, and in a taper-roller bearing are of part-conical shape.

Roller chain
Type of open-link driving chain having a bearing pin, a bush and a surrounding roller at each link joint. The rollers engage between the teeth of the driving and driven sprockets to give a positive drive, and their freedom to rotate minimises friction when the links engage and disengage the sprockets. Widely used for camshaft drives.

Roll-steer
Steering effect of the rear wheels as a result of cornering roll. It may result from skewing of the axle, due to different shapes adopted by the inside and outside springs, or from alteration in camber angle or toe-in with suspension movement.

Rotary engine
Any type of engine in which the movement involved in producing power is rotary, not reciprocating.

Rotary valve
Cylindrical or conical valve that rotates in the cylinder head, performing the same function as a sleeve valve or pair of poppet valves. It contains inlet and exhaust ports which align successively, as it rotates, with a port to the cylinder.

Rotor arm
See DISTRIBUTOR ROTOR ARM

Rubber solution
Rubber carried in a solvent which evaporates when exposed to air; it can be used to stick a rubber patch on an inner tube that is punctured, or as an adhesive for other jobs.

Running boards
Long steps on the sides of most earlier cars to make getting in and out easier.

Running-in
Initial period of operating a new or rebuilt car, during which time the various moving parts gradually obtain their final surface finish as they run together.

Running-in speeds
Speeds recommended by the manufacturers as a maximum during running-in. Most manufacturers recommend at least one increase in the maximum speed during the running-in period.

Running-on
Continued running by the engine after the ignition has been switched off; usually caused by hot cylinder deposits igniting the mixture drawn in.

SAE oil grades
System of classification of lubricants based on their viscosity at given temperatures. First drawn up by the Society of Automotive Engineers in America.

Safety harness See SEAT BELTS

Safety shoulder
Step in the section of a wheel rim, to prevent a tubeless tyre coming off completely following a sudden deflation.

Saloon
Closed type of car body with accommodation for at least four people.

Scraper
Metal-working tool with a hardened-steel blade for scraping bearings, etc. Also a small tool used for clearing snow or ice from a windscreen.

Scraper ring See OIL-CONTROL RING

Screen washer
Device to squirt water over the windscreen to clean it.

Screen wipers
Mechanical means of clearing excess water or dirt off the car's windscreen; they consist of rubber blades on metal arms which are usually driven by an electric motor through a linkage giving oscillatory motion.

Scuffing
Occurs when a metal component 'picks-up' on another because of lubrication failure and suffers surface damage. Also the roughening of a tyre tread because of the abrasive effect of the road surface.

Sealed-beam unit
Headlight unit with filaments, reflector and lenses forming one completely sealed assembly, like a large bulb; it is more efficient than a light with separate bulbs.

Sealed bearing
Bearing (which may be of plain, ball or roller type) sealed to prevent the entry of dirt and the escape of its life-long lubricant; it has no provision for greasing or oiling.

Seat belts
Securely mounted webbing straps for retaining car occupants in their seats, thus preventing them from being thrown forwards by the impact of a collision. A seat belt can take the form of a lap-strap, a diagonal belt, a combination of the two called a lap-and-diagonal belt, or a full shoulder harness.

Seat runners
Rails on which the front seats can be slid backwards and forwards.

Secondary circuit
High-voltage section of the ignition system; comprises the secondary winding in the coil, the distributor, rotor arm and cap, high-tension leads and spark-plugs.

Secondary current
High-voltage current that is produced in a coil's secondary winding and passed to the distributor and spark-plugs through the secondary circuit.

Secondary winding
One of the windings in the ignition coil; it comprises thousands of turns of fine wire and, when the primary current is interrupted by the contact-breaker, generates high-voltage current for the spark-plugs.

Second-motion shaft
The layshaft of a gearbox; carries the lay-gears which mesh with the gears on the main shaft.

Sediment chamber
Space below the plates of a battery designed to trap dirt in the electrolyte. Also the sediment trap in a fuel system.

Seize-up
Situation in which two moving parts weld themselves immovably together because of overheating caused by insufficient lubrication or excessively heavy loading. A seize-up will cause the mechanism concerned to slow rapidly and can cause considerable damage.

Selector fork
Part of the gearbox; fork-shaped part mounted on the selector rod for engaging one or other of two gears. When the gear lever is moved towards either of these gear positions, a control rod engages with the selector fork and moves it in the appropriate direction.

Selector mechanism
Mechanism of the gearbox, operated either by hand or automatically, that selects a desired gear.

Selector rod
Part of the gearbox; a sliding rod that carries the selector fork and is moved by the gear lever.

Selector shaft See SELECTOR ROD

Self-aligning torque See ALIGNING TORQUE

Self-levelling suspension
Type of suspension that automatically keeps the vehicle body at a constant height off the road, regardless of the load carried.

Self-locking nut
Nut containing a nylon or composition insert or mechanical locking device. When the nut is tightened on to a thread, the insert binds against the latter and prevents the nut from working loose.

Self-servo effect
Tendency of a leading brake shoe to clamp itself to the drum when brought into contact with it.

Semi-automatic transmission
Transmission system in which the clutch functions are performed automatically, but the driver still has to select the various gears manually.

Semi-elliptic spring
Normal leaf spring, the middle of which is attached to the axle and the ends to the chassis or body structure. Alternatively, such a spring can be used in an independent suspension system, in which case the middle is attached to the body and the spring is installed transversely between the wheel hub carriers.

Semi-floating axle
Type of driving axle in which the half-shafts support part of a car's body weight as well as transmitting turning effort to the wheels.

Semi-trailing arms
Layout used in many independent rear suspension systems; the wheels are carried on arms that pivot about axes converging towards the rear. The arms project rearwards and sideways from the axes.

Series connection
Connecting the positive terminal of one battery to the negative terminal of another, to give a higher voltage; the cells of a battery are themselves connected in this way. Electrical components also can be connected in series.

Servo system
Control system in which a small amount of effort is augmented to perform a large amount of work. A vacuum-servo operating system, for example, is often used for disc brakes, which normally require a heavy pedal effort.

Shackle
Link attaching one end of a leaf spring to a vehicle frame. It accommodates variation in the effective length of the spring as the road wheel moves vertically over an uneven surface. It usually comprises steel plates separated by two shouldered bolts, one passing through the spring eye and the other through a bracket on the vehicle.

Shackle pin
Shouldered bolt that connects the side plates of a shackle.

Shell bearing
Type of plain bearing used in car engines for the crankshaft and connecting rods. It comprises a removable steel-backed shell or liner, coated with metal having good wearing properties; the liner is usually made in semicircular halves and is secured by a bearing cap.

Shim
Thin metal washer used to adjust an operating clearance (such as that between an overhead camshaft and a tappet) or the meshing depth of one gear with another (e.g. crown wheel and pinion).

Shimmy
Sideways wobbling of the front wheels due to unbalanced wheels or wear in the steering system.

Short-circuit
Occurs when an electrical component is prevented from working because the positive and negative leads to it have been bridged so that current fails to reach it. The current instead follows a short circuit back to its source.

Short motor (or engine)
Reconditioned or new engine block complete with pistons, connecting rods, crankshaft, timing gears, bearings, etc.: but not including cylinder head and accessories.

Shunt coil
Part of the voltage-regulator unit of an electrical system; essentially a high-resistance coil, wired in parallel.

Siamesed ports
Ports in a cylinder head—either inlet or exhaust—that run into each other from different combustion chambers or valves.

Side-lights
Small lamps on the front of a car spaced to give some indication of its width; so called because on early cars they were mounted on the sides of the body just ahead of the windscreen. These are now subject to government Regulations.

Side-screens
Clear plastic and fabric side panels that clip to the tops of the doors of an open sports car for weather protection.

Side-valve engine
Engine in which the inlet and exhaust valves are alongside the cylinder, not in the cylinder head. The system is mechanically efficient, simple and cheap to produce, but has fallen out of favour because its compression ratio and breathing are both limited, so power output and petrol consumption are inferior to those of an overhead-valve engine.

Single-cylinder (brakes)
Braking system, usually on the back wheels only, in which there is only one hydraulic slave cylinder to expand both brake shoes in the drum; one is a leading shoe and the other a trailing shoe, and their hinge points are adjacent.

Single-piston caliper
Form of disc-brake caliper in which only one hydraulic piston is used. As the piston presses one pad on to the disc, the whole caliper pivots, bringing the static pad into operation.

Single-plate clutch
Type of clutch fitted to most cars; it has only one friction plate, which is clamped against the flywheel by the pressure plate to transmit the drive.

Skew-gear drive
Method of driving one shaft from another at an angle to it (usually 90°); skew gears are cheaper than bevel gears but suitable for light drives only because of the sliding that takes place between the gear teeth.

Slave cylinder
Cylinder at the component end of a hydraulic system (brakes or clutch) that converts hydraulic pressure back to mechanical effort.

Sleeve valve
Type of valve gear used in one or two earlier cars and in many Second World War aero-engines. A metal sleeve is interposed between the cylinder and piston, and is given an elliptical (part reciprocating, part rotary) motion by a crank driven at half engine speed. In the sleeve are ports that line up, at the appropriate stages in the operating cycle, with inlet and exhaust passages in the cylinder.

Sliding gears
Gear wheels inside a gearbox that are slid into mesh to select a certain ratio. In modern car gearboxes they are normally used only for reverse gear. See also SLIDING-PINION GEARBOX

Sliding joint
Connection at forward end of propeller shaft allowing the length of the shaft to vary, to accommodate axle movement. Splines on the two portions of the shaft allow one to slide within the other.

Sliding-pinion gearbox
Earliest and simplest type of gearbox; pairs of gear wheels are on parallel shafts, those on one shaft being fixed and those on the other being free to slide on splines. Movement of the gear lever slides one gear along the shaft into engagement with its mating gear.

Slip angle (of a tyre)
Angle between the direction of travel of the car and the direction in which a tyre is pointing. This angle produces the lateral force that enables the car to be steered.

Slipping the clutch
Driving with the clutch partially engaged, e.g. when moving off or creeping along in heavy traffic so slowly the transmission snatches if the clutch is fully engaged.

Slipstream
Airstream immediately behind a moving vehicle; originally behind a propeller-driven aircraft. Also used as a verb meaning to follow closely enough behind another vehicle to travel in its moving wake, thus reducing air resistance.

Slow-running screw See THROTTLE-STOP SCREW

Sludge
Thick black sediment formed in the sump and on other engine parts due to oxidation of the oil through attack by acids formed in the combustion process. Sludging occurs most readily in cold running conditions.

Small-end
Smaller end of the connecting rod, connected to the piston by the gudgeon pin. Sometimes called the little-end.

Snail cam

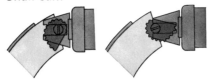

Device for brake adjustment. A snail cam is so shaped that the farther it is rotated the higher it lifts, until after nearly 360° it returns to the starting point.

Snap-in valve
Type of tyre-inflation valve fitted to a wheel carrying a tubeless tyre; it embodies a seal that fills the hole into which it is fitted, preventing leakage of air.

Snap-on connector
Type of electrical cable joint in which a metal plug, soldered to the end of a cable, is pushed into a rubber-covered connecting piece.

Socket spanner
Short, cylindrical spanner; it is very strongly made and has the same type of gripping hole as a ring spanner at one end, and a square hole at the other to take the operating handle—which can be in the form of a lever or wrench, ratchet lever or extension knuckle joint.

Socket wrench
Lever or 'tommy-bar' used with a socket spanner; usually has a turned-over, squared end that engages in the hole in the top of the socket spanner.

Solder
Alloy of tin and lead which has a low melting point and is used for jointing metals; it is generally applied with a heated soldering iron and is often used for making electrical connections. Also used by body repairers as a means of filling irregularities.

Solenoid
Electromagnetic actuating device consisting of a wire coil embracing a movable iron plunger. As the coil is energised, by passing current through it, a magnetic field is set up that draws the plunger along within the coil. A solenoid is frequently used as a heavy-duty switch, as in a starter motor.

Spade connector
Electrical wiring connection consisting of a spade-shaped metal plate soldered to a cable. A slot in the plate slides over a threaded terminal post, and the spade is secured by a nut on the terminal post.

Spark-plug
High-voltage electric device for igniting the petrol/air mixture in the cylinder.

Speedometer
Instrument that indicates the speed of a vehicle. Usually cable-operated from the output shaft of the gearbox, but some of the latest speedometers are electronic.

Spigot
Cylindrical projection from a component that fits a corresponding recess in another.

Spigot bush
Central guide-bearing in the flywheel end of the crankshaft, locating the end of the gearbox first-motion shaft that carries the clutch plate.

Spiral-bevel gear
Form of final-drive gearing used for the crown wheel and pinion; to get more than one tooth in mesh at a time, the teeth are cut at an angle to the axis instead of in line with it, as in a plain bevel gear. With such gearing the propeller shaft is at the same height off the ground as the half-shafts, so the floor level is high or a deep tunnel is needed.

Spit-back
Firing of petrol/air mixture in the inlet manifold, usually caused by over-advanced ignition timing.

Splash lubrication
Early lubrication system in which the big-end of the connecting rod dips into the oil in the sump and splashes it around to the other bearings.

Splines
Grooves along a shaft and in a component carried on it; they can allow longitudinal movement between the two, while preventing relative rotational movement.

Split cones (collets)
Halves of a divided cone that fit into grooves round the top of a valve stem to hold the spring-locating plate in position.

Split-pin
Piece of metal of semicircular section bent into the shape of a keyhole with the flat faces lying close together. It is used to lock nuts or other components on to a shaft. The shank is passed through aligning holes or slots and the ends are then splayed to hold the parts.

Spring blade
Single leaf of a laminated spring.

Spring clip
Steel clip that holds together the blades of a leaf spring. Also a small securing clip.

Spring compressor
Tool similar to a G-clamp, used for compressing the valve springs for installation or removal. Sometimes incorrectly called a valve lifter.

Spring hanger
Body-mounted bracket carrying one end of a leaf spring.

Springing See SUSPENSION

Sprocket
Toothed wheel that drives or is driven by a roller chain; most commonly used in a car for the camshaft drive where two sprockets are used, one on the crankshaft and the other on the camshaft.

Sprung weight
Weight of all parts of a car that are carried by the suspension. In general this means the total weight of the car less that of the wheels, the axle, hubs and brakes, and part of the weight of the springs and the suspension linkages.

Spur gear
Cylindrical gear wheel with the teeth cut around the outside. The teeth may be straight-cut (parallel to the axis of the gear) or helical (at an angle to the axis).

Squab
Backrest of a seat.

Square engine
Engine in which the piston stroke is equal to the diameter of the cylinder bore.

Stabiliser
Anti-roll bar.

Stalling
Sudden stoppage of the engine, usually through clumsy engagement of the clutch, or insufficient throttle when moving off.

Star pinion
Term sometimes used for an epicyclic planet pinion or an intermediate pinion in a differential gear; a two-star differential is one with two such pinions.

Stars (petrol rating)
British Standards Institution grading of petrol according to its octane rating. 5 star=100 octane or above, 4 star=97-99 octane, 3 star=94-96 octane and 2 star =90-93 octane.

Starter motor
Powerful electric motor used to rotate the engine to start it. The starter's current is taken directly from the battery.

State of tune
Current level of performance and condition of an engine.

Static electricity
Electricity generated by means other than the usual one of passing a conductor through a magnetic field. Usually caused by friction.

Static strap
Flexible strap hung from the body of the car and extending down to the road. It prevents the build-up of static electricity in or on the car when it is moving, by acting as an earth.

Stator
Member of a torque converter, sometimes called the reaction member, or the stationary part of an electric generator.

Steering arms
Levers attached to the steering swivel members and connected by linkage to the steering box; they cause the front wheels to swivel when the steering wheel is turned.

Steering box
Mechanical device at the lower end of the steering column; it transmits the rotation of the steering wheel to the steering linkage controlling the position of the front wheels.

Steering column
Metal shaft that carries the steering wheel at its upper end and is connected to the steering box at the other end.

Steering feed-back
Indication, passed back through the steering system to the driver's hands, of where the front wheels are pointing or how much grip their tyres have.

Steering geometry
Basic layout of the steering system. The interrelation of king-pin inclination, wheel alignment, camber and castor angle.

Steering lock
Locking device on the steering column for preventing the steering wheel being turned when the key has been removed. See also TURNING CIRCLE.

Steering pivot See STEERING SWIVEL

Steering play
Slackness in the steering box or linkage, causing the steering wheel to require appreciable rotation before it begins to turn the road wheels.

Steering ratio
Relationship between the angle through which the steering wheel is rotated and that through which the front wheels swivel as a result.

Steering rod
Ball-jointed rod connecting one end of the rack member of a rack-and-pinion steering system to the adjacent steering arm.

Steering swivel
Also called a steering swivel member. The part of the steering/front suspension system carrying one of the stub axles and steering arms. It is free to swivel on a king-pin or between universal joints on the outer ends of the suspension wishbones or links.

Stellite
Hard metal alloy deposited, for example, on the seating rim of an exhaust valve to resist corrosion and impact wear at high temperatures.

Sticky clutch
Clutch in which the driven plate continues to revolve with the flywheel after the clutch pedal has been fully depressed. This is usually the result of incorrect adjustment, or of oil contaminating the lining.

Stop-light indicator
Indicator light wired into the stop-light system that is automatically switched on if one or more of the brake stop-lights fail.

Straight-cut gears
Gear wheels having the teeth cut parallel to the shaft.

Straight eight/six
Engine with eight or six cylinders in line.

Stroboscope
Instrument for checking engine ignition timing while the engine is running. Also known as a strobe light.

Stroke
Distance travelled by the piston between its highest and lowest positions, measured in millimetres or inches.

Stub axle
Short, non-revolving shaft carrying a front wheel of a rear-wheel-drive car or a rear wheel of a front-wheel-drive car.

Studded tyres
Tyres with hard metal (tungsten-carbide) studs inserted in the tread pattern to improve tyre grip on ice or packed snow.

Sub-frame
Steel framework carrying one or more mechanical assemblies (engine/gearbox, suspension, etc.) and bolted to the main body-structure of a car.

Suction chamber
Part of a variable-choke carburettor. Suction in the chamber controls the position of the piston carrying the fuel-metering jet needle.

Suction wipers
Windscreen wipers that operated through suction (partial vacuum) applied to their motor from the inlet manifold.

Sump
Oil container bolted to the bottom of the crankcase; normally, lubricant is drawn from it by the oil pump and distributed to engine bearings and other moving parts.

Sump filter
Wire-mesh strainer immersed in the oil in the engine sump and connected to the oil pump to prevent sludge or foreign matter in the sump being drawn into the pump.

Supercharger
Air-pump or compressor fitted to some engines to push the petrol/air mixture into the cylinders, increasing the power output.

Suppressor
Resistor to counteract interference with radio and television reception.

Suspension
System for supporting the body of a vehicle and minimising transmission of road shocks from wheels to body.

Suspension damper
Device for controlling relative movement between the vehicle's body and suspension system, so preventing continuous bouncing on the springs. Almost all modern suspension dampers are hydraulic, the telescopic pattern being the most popular. Also called a shock absorber.

Swing-axles
Drive shafts connected to the final drive by universal joints, but rigidly connected to the wheels at their outer ends.

Swinging caliper See SINGLE-PISTON CALIPER

Swivel-pin See KING-PIN

Synchromesh
Device for facilitating gear changing on cars with manually operated gearboxes; it consists of a form of cone clutch that synchronises the speeds of two members before one can be engaged with the other.

Tab washer
Locking washer with projecting ears; one of these is bent down to engage in a hole or recess, and the other is bent up against one flat of the nut or bolt-head.

Tachometer
Instrument for indicating the rotational speed of the engine. See REV-COUNTER

Tail-pipe
Last section of the exhaust system, behind the silencer(s).

Tandem master cylinder
Part of a dual-circuit hydraulic braking system; two master cylinders combined in one unit—mounted one behind the other—and supplied by a fluid reservoir divided into two compartments.

Taper-roller bearing
Type of bearing in which the inner and outer races have angled track surfaces and the rollers are part-conical.

Tappet
Part of an engine's valve-operating mechanism; usually a short steel cylinder which bears on the cam.

Taps and dies
Tools for cutting screw-threads. A tap cuts an internal thread in a hole, while a die cuts an external thread on a rod.

Telescopic damper (or shock-absorber)
Tubular-shaped hydraulic damper; basically it comprises a piston in a cylinder, with valves to control the flow of fluid.

Telescopic steering column
Steering column designed to collapse, or telescope, in a head-on collision thereby reducing the risk of injury.

Temperature gauge
Instrument used to indicate the temperature of liquids; in a car one is used to show the temperature of the engine coolant.

Tensile strength
Strength of a material when stretched.

Thermostat
A heat-sensitive valve that opens and closes according to the temperature around it. Water-cooled engines have one in the cooling system to prevent circulation of the coolant to the radiator until the engine has warmed up.

Thermosyphon
Water-cooling system in which circulation is not assisted by a water pump, relying on the natural tendency of water to rise on heating.

Third-motion shaft
Output shaft or mainshaft of an orthodox gearbox; it carries the main gear train and is driven in all intermediate gears through the layshaft (second-motion shaft).

Three-quarter-floating axle
Type of rear axle in which only a small portion of the vehicle weight is taken by the half-shafts, the rest being carried by the casing.

Throat
The venturi or choke of a carburettor.

Throttle valve
Variable valve, usually of the butterfly type, fitted to a carburettor; its position, controlled by the accelerator pedal governs the amount of petrol/air mixture fed to the engine.

Throttle-stop screw
Screw, usually spring-loaded, that varies the closed position of the throttle valve and therefore the engine's idling speed.

Throw (crankshaft)
Distance (half the piston stroke) between axis of the crankshaft and that of the crankpin.

Thrust bearing
Any bearing that has to resist end thrust.

Thrust ring
Part of a clutch-release mechanism; carbon collar that transmits push on the clutch pedal to the pressure-plate assembly.

Tickover See IDLE

Tie-rod
Metal rod between the steering arm of each front-wheel assembly and the rest of the steering linkage, forming part of the track-rod assembly. The term is also used to describe a bar forming part of a suspension link.

Tightening torque
Specified turning effort applied with a torque wrench to a nut or bolt. Usually measured in pounds feet (lb. ft).

Timing See IGNITION TIMING and VALVE TIMING

Timing drive
Method of driving the camshaft from the crankshaft so that the inlet and exhaust-valve opening sequence is timed correctly in relation to piston position.

Timing marks
Grooves cut on the flywheel rim and its housing, or the crankshaft pulley and timing case, to indicate correct ignition timing. The term also applies to the marks on the teeth of the timing gears or sprockets to ensure that they are in the correct relative positions to give the required valve timing.

Toe-in
Setting of the front wheels so that they point slightly inwards. This is normal practice on undriven front wheels.

Toe-out
Setting of the front wheels so that they point slightly outwards; more usually found on front-wheel-drive cars where driving torque is applied to the steered wheels.

Tonneau
Waterproof fabric cover that fits over the passenger compartment of an open sports car to protect it in wet weather when the hood is down.

Toothed belt
Strong flexible belt consisting of composition rubber reinforced internally with steel or glass-fibre cords; it is used for camshaft and other drives on some engines. Teeth or projections on the inner surface engage with slots in the drive pulleys.

Top dead centre (TDC)
Position of a piston at the top of its stroke in the cylinder.

Top overhaul
Overhaul of the top end of the engine; this usually involves removal of the cylinder head, decarbonising, valve grinding-in and fitting new valve springs.

Torque
Turning effort exerted by or on a revolving part. In the case of an engine it is the mean turning effort exerted on the crankshaft by the pistons and is available for propelling the car. Maximum torque is usually produced at half to two-thirds of the speed at which the engine develops its maximum power.

Torque converter
In its simplest form, a torque converter is similar to a fluid coupling but with the addition of a single non-rotating set of vanes (the stator). It provides, within limits, a variable gear ratio and acts as an automatic clutch.

Torque reaction
Natural tendency of an engine to rotate in the opposite direction to its crankshaft when it is producing torque. Applies also to any other power source involving rotation.

Torque wrench
Spanner that measures the tightening torque applied to a nut or bolt, so that it can be correctly tightened.

Torsion bar
Steel bar used in some suspension systems instead of a spring. The bar is fixed at one end and twisted at the other by a lever attached to the suspension linkage.

Torus
Driving or driven member of a torque converter or fluid coupling.

Toughened glass
Single-sheet safety glass specially heat-treated so that, if broken, it separates into granules which do not cause injury. See also ZONE-TOUGHENED GLASS.

Track
Transverse distance between front or rear wheels, measured between the centres of the tyre contact areas on the road.

Track rod
Metal bar or system of links connecting the front wheels so that, when the steering wheel is turned, they swivel together.

Traction
Grip between the tyres of the driving wheels and the road.

Trafficators
Earlier type of turn indicators with hinged illuminated arms instead of flashing lights.

Trailing shoe
Part of some drum-brake assemblies; a brake shoe that trails behind its pivot.

Tramp
Alternate winding-up and unwinding of a Hotchkiss drive axle on its leaf springs under fierce acceleration; more likely on rough or loose surfaces which cause the wheels to lose traction and thus allow the springs to unwind.

Transmission
Mechanical system that transmits the torque from the engine to the driving wheels; it usually consists of clutch and gearbox (or automatic transmission), propeller shaft, final drive and half-shafts.

Transverse engine
Engine placed across the car, instead of lengthwise. Examples include the British Leyland, Honda and Fiat front-wheel-drive cars.

Trickle charger
Car-battery charger that will supply a small charge from domestic AC mains.

Trunnion
Member in some independent-front-suspension systems for connecting the lower wishbone with the steering swivel.

Tubeless tyre
Tyre that needs no inner tube but retains its pressure by forming an airtight seal between the tyre beads and the wheel rim.

Tungsten-halogen bulb See QUARTZ-HALOGEN BULB

Tuning
Adjustment of the engine to achieve the best performance.

Tuning for performance
Adjusting and modifying an engine to give more power than the manufacturer's standard for the engine.

Turbocharger
Type of supercharger driven by the waste energy in the exhaust gases instead of mechanically from the crankshaft.

Turnbuckle
Coupling with two screw-heads, one left-hand and the other right-hand, for adjusting tension or length of a linkage.

Turning circle
Diameter of the circle described by the outside front wheel when the steering is on full lock.

Twin-carb
Colloquial term for an engine equipped with two carburettors, providing a higher power output than the same engine with one carburettor.

Twin-choke carburettor
Fixed-choke carburettor with two chokes or throats side by side in a single body. In one type the two throttle valves open together, feeding different sections of the inlet manifold. In the other type, known as compound, the first throttle valve opens two-thirds of the way before the second throttle valve starts to open, providing the extra charge needed for quicker acceleration or higher speeds.

Two-cylinder brakes
Braking system, usually on the front wheels only, in which each brake-shoe assembly has its own hydraulic actuating cylinder, thus enabling two leading shoes to be used.

Two-leading-shoe brakes
Type of drum brake in which each shoe has its own expander and points forward from its pivot. See also LEADING SHOE.

Two-level signalling
Device to reduce the intensity of the rear turn indicators and stop-lights at night. When the side-lights are on, current-limiting resistors reduce the brightness of the rear stop-lights and indicators.

Two-plus-two (or 2+2)
Sporting type of car that has room for two adults in front but only limited seating space in the rear.

Two-stroke cycle

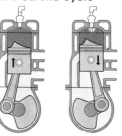

Engine operation in which every second stroke of the piston is a power stroke, instead of every fourth stroke as in a 4-stroke engine. The rising piston sucks mixture behind it into the crankcase through the inlet port, at the same time as it compresses the mixture above it. The downward stroke after ignition is the normal power stroke, but also partially compresses the new charge in the crankcase. Part-way down the power stroke, the piston uncovers exhaust ports and, almost immediately afterwards, transfer ports which allow the partly compressed charge to flow from crankcase to cylinder in the wake of the exhaust gases.

Two-stroke fuel
Mixture of petrol and oil, usually in proportions of between 20:1 and 40:1, used in 2-stroke engines with no separate lubrication system.

U-bolt
U-shaped, double-ended bolt, such as that securing a leaf spring to its axle.

Undersquare engine
Engine in which the piston stroke is greater than the diameter of the cylinder.

Understeer
Handling characteristic that tends to make the car run wide when taking a bend, causing the driver to apply more steering lock.

Unitary construction See INTEGRAL CONSTRUCTION

Universal joint
Type of joint that can swivel in any direction.

Unsprung weight
Weight of those parts of the car that are not supported by the suspension.

Vacuum control
System for varying the ignition timing according to the suction in the inlet manifold, by means of a spring-loaded flexible diaphragm.

Valve
Device for controlling the flow of gases or liquids. In a car engine, valves control the entry of the petrol/air mixture into the cylinders and the exit of the exhaust gases.

Valve clearance
Amount of free movement between the rocker, finger or tappet operating an engine valve and the end of the valve stem. It ensures that the valve closes fully when the engine is hot.

Valve guide
Cylindrical metal sleeve in which an engine valve stem moves; it is normally pressed into the cylinder head, but some manufacturers run their valves directly in a cast-iron cylinder head.

Valve head
That portion of a poppet valve that actually opens or closes a port.

Valve overlap
Period during which the inlet and exhaust valves of a cylinder are open at the same time.

Valve-seat insert
Ring of hard, corrosion- and heat-resistant metal alloy, inserted into the cylinder head to provide a more durable seating for a valve than would the metal of the head.

Valve timing
The positions, relative to TDC and BDC, at which the inlet and exhaust valves begin to open and return to their seats.

Vapour lock
Vaporising of petrol in the supply pipe from the tank, the petrol pump or the carburettor, due to overheating. It prevents normal flow of fuel and causes faulty running or complete stoppage.

Variable-choke carburettor
Type of carburettor in which varying low pressure, or suction, in the inlet manifold controls the position of a piston that governs the area of the choke through which the air passes.

Variable jet
Part of a variable-choke carburettor; a tapered needle moves in a jet to vary the area of the opening according to the engine's petrol requirements.

V-belt
Belt with a V-shape cross-section, commonly used for driving the fan, water pump and generator.

V-engine
Engine that has two banks of equal numbers of cylinders in a V-configuration.

Venturi
Reduced-section passage for air or fluid. In a carburettor, the reduced area of the venturi causes the airstream to speed-up, so reducing its pressure and sucking petrol from the jet.

Vernier adjustment
Fine adjustment method fitted to some distributors for precise setting of the ignition timing.

Viscosity
A liquid's resistance to flow—particularly that of oil. The viscosity falls as the oil gets hotter.

Viscosity index (VI)
Measure of the amount by which the viscosity of an oil varies with temperature. An oil with a high VI has a smaller variation than one with a low VI.

Volatility
Tendency of a liquid to vaporise. Petrol, for example, has a much higher volatility than water.

Voltage regulator
Electrical device for ensuring that the battery is correctly charged by the generator, according to its need.

Volumetric efficiency
The ratio between the volume (or air) actually drawn into an engine, during one induction stroke of every cylinder, and the engine's swept volume, expressed as a percentage.

Wander
Tendency of a car to depart slightly from a straight course; as in a crosswind or when the tyres come on to a raised irregularity in the road surface.

Wankel rotary engine
Type of engine without pistons; instead, it has a triangular rotor, revolving eccentrically within a chamber of a wide-necked figure-8 shape.

Water-cooled engine
Engine in which waste heat is transferred to circulating water rather than directly to air that is blown by fan over cylinders and heads.

Water jacket See CYLINDER JACKET

Water pump
Small pump in an engine's cooling system to aid water circulation; it is usually driven from the crankshaft, in tandem with the fan, by a V-belt.

Water-temperature gauge
Instrument that indicates the temperature of an engine's coolant before it returns to the radiator for cooling. In some cars it is replaced by a warning light.

Wax element
Part of most modern thermostats, controlling the opening of the water valve.

Web
Connecting portion of a crankshaft between a main journal and a crankpin, or between two adjacent crankpins.

Wedge-shape combustion chamber
Development of the bath-tub chamber giving better gas flow past the valves. The valves are parallel in the sloping roof and the spark-plug is usually positioned at the thick end of the wedge.

Wet-sump lubrication
Lubrication system in which the supply of oil is carried in a sump or oil pan underneath the crankcase.

Wheel alignment
Position, relative to one another, of a pair of wheels; front-wheel alignment is set by means of adjusters in the track-rod assemblies. See also TOE-IN and TOE-OUT.

Wheelbase
Distance between the front and rear-wheel axles of a vehicle, when the steering is set straight ahead.

Wheel-brace
Socket spanner with integral lever, issued in most tool kits, for slackening and tightening wheel nuts.

Wheel cylinder See SLAVE CYLINDER

Wheelspin
Condition in which the driving wheels fail to grip the road surface and so do not transmit the available thrust to push the car forward.

Wheel track See TRACK

Wheel wobble
Steering fault indicated by sideways flutter of the wheels and shaking of the steering wheel, usually due to wear or wheel imbalance; it may occur only at certain speeds and can often be checked by braking or accelerating.

Whitworth thread See BRITISH STANDARD WHITWORTH

Windscreen wiper See SCREEN WIPERS

Wing nut
Nut with large integral ears, to enable it to be tightened or loosened by hand.

Wiper blade
Rubber blade carried by a screen-wiper arm to sweep rain and mud off the surface of the windscreen.

Wishbones
Pivoted triangle-shaped links that connect each wheel in an independent suspension system to the car's body.

Withdrawal bearing See CLUTCH THRUST BEARING

Worm and nut
Steering box in which rotation of a screw-thread, by means of the steering column, causes movement of a nut on the thread to pivot the drop-arm.

Worm axle
Driving axle in which the gearing reduction is effected by means of a worm (a type of screw-thread on a shaft) and a meshing wheel, rather than the more usual crown wheel and pinion.

Worm-drive clip
Clip for securing water or other hoses; the tightening screw engages with a series of inclined grooves on the band of the clip. The best known is probably the proprietary Jubilee type.

Wrench
Term used in Britain for an adjustable spanner or the lever of a socket spanner. In the USA it is used to describe any type of spanner.

Wrist pin
American term for gudgeon pin.

Yoke
U-shaped saddle of a universal-joint assembly; the part that carries the bearing cups and needle-roller bearings. The term is sometimes also used to describe the fork of the clutch-withdrawal mechanism.

Zinc interleaf
Anti-friction strip between two leaves of a laminated spring.

Zinc-oxide grease
High-melting-point lubricant used for hub bearings and water pumps.

Zone-toughened glass
Type of toughened glass which has a specially treated area in front of the driver. In the event of impact, this special area of the windscreen fractures in larger fragments than the rest of the glass, thus ensuring that the driver has reasonably clear forward vision.

Index

The figures in bold type indicate a main reference to a subject; the figures in italic indicate pages dealing with fault-finding, maintenance, routine servicing and repair work; and those in ordinary type refer to pages in which some other aspect of the subject is covered, or where the subject is mentioned briefly.

Printing and binding by: IL RESTO DEL CARLINO, OFFICINE GRAFICHE, BOLOGNA, ITALY; MULLIS-MORGAN LIMITED, LONDON; VANTAGE PHOTOSETTING COMPANY LIMITED, SOUTHAMPTON.